KT-573-398

CMMI®

Second Edition

PARK LEARNING CENTRE
UNIVERSITY OF GLOUCESTERSHIRE
PO Box 220, The Park
Cheltenham GL50 2RH
Tel: 01242 714333

Carnegie Mellon
Software Engineering Institute

The SEI Series in Software Engineering represents a collaboration between the Software Engineering Institute of Carnegie Mellon University and Addison-Wesley to develop and publish a body of work on selected topics in software engineering. The common goal of the SEI and Addison-Wesley is to provide the most current software engineering information in a form that is easily usable by practitioners and students.

For more information point your browser to www.awprofessional.com/seiseries

Dennis M. Ahern, et al., *CMMI® SCAMPI Distilled.* ISBN: 0-321-22876-6

Dennis M. Ahern, et al., *CMMI® Distilled, Second Edition.* ISBN: 0-321-18613-3

Dennis M. Ahern, et al., *CMMI® Distilled: A Practical Introduction to Integrated Process Improvement, Third Edition.* ISBN: 0-321-46108-8

Christopher Alberts and Audrey Dorofee, *Managing Information Security Risks.* ISBN: 0-321-11886-3

Julia H. Allen, et al., *Software Security Engineering: A Guide for Project Managers.* ISBN: 0-321-50917-X

Len Bass, et al., *Software Architecture in Practice, Second Edition.* ISBN: 0-321-15495-9

Marilyn Bush and Donna Dunaway, *CMMI® Assessments.* ISBN: 0-321-17935-8

Carnegie Mellon University, Software Engineering Institute, *The Capability Maturity Model.* ISBN: 0-201-54664-7

Mary Beth Chrissis, et al., *CMMI®, Second Edition.* ISBN: 0-321-27967-0

Paul Clements, et al., *Documenting Software Architectures.* ISBN: 0-201-70372-6

Paul Clements, et al., *Evaluating Software Architectures.* ISBN: 0-201-70482-X

Paul Clements and Linda Northrop, *Software Product Lines.* ISBN: 0-201-70332-7

Bill Curtis, et al., *The People Capability Maturity Model®.* ISBN: 0-201-60445-0

William A. Florac and Anita D. Carleton, *Measuring the Software Process.* ISBN: 0-201-60444-2

Brian P. Gallagher, et al., *CMMI®-ACQ: Guidelines for Improving the Acquisition of Products and Services.* ISBN: 0321580354

Suzanne Garcia and Richard Turner, *CMMI® Survival Guide.* ISBN: 0-321-42277-5

Hassan Gomaa, *Software Design Methods for Concurrent and Real-Time Systems.* ISBN: 0-201-52577-1

Elaine M. Hall, *Managing Risk.* ISBN: 0-201-25592-8

Hubert F. Hofmann, et al., *CMMI® for Outsourcing.* ISBN: 0-321-47717-0

Watts S. Humphrey, *Introduction to the Personal Software Process^{SM}.* ISBN: 0-201-54809-7

Watts S. Humphrey, *Managing the Software Process.* ISBN: 0-201-18095-2

Watts S. Humphrey, *A Discipline for Software Engineering.* ISBN: 0-201-54610-8

Watts S. Humphrey, *Introduction to the Team Software Process^{SM}.* ISBN: 0-201-47719-X

Watts S. Humphrey, *Winning with Software.* ISBN: 0-201-77639-1

Watts S. Humphrey, *PSP^{SM}: A Self-Improvement Process for Software Engineers.* ISBN: 0-321-30549-3

Watts S. Humphrey, *TSP^{SM}—Leading a Development Team.* ISBN: 0-321-34962-8

Watts S. Humphrey, *TSP^{SM}—Coaching Development Teams.* ISBN: 0-201-73113-4

Robert C. Seacord, *Secure Coding in C and C++.* ISBN: 0-321-33572-4

Robert C. Seacord, *The CERT® C Secure Coding Standard.* ISBN: 0321563212

Jeannine M. Siviy, et al., *CMMI® and Six Sigma: Partners in Process Improvement.* ISBN: 0321516087

Richard D. Stutzke, *Estimating Software-Intensive Systems.* ISBN: 0-201-70312-2

Sami Zahran, *Software Process Improvement.* ISBN: 0-201-17782-X

3704333792

Generic Goals and Practices as Presented in the Continuous Representation

GG 1   Achieve Specific Goals

    GP 1.1   Perform Specific Practices

GG 2   Institutionalize a Managed Process

    GP 2.1   Establish an Organizational Policy

    GP 2.2   Plan the Process

    GP 2.3   Provide Resources

    GP 2.4   Assign Responsibility

    GP 2.5   Train People

    GP 2.6   Manage Configurations

    GP 2.7   Identify and Involve Relevant Stakeholders

    GP 2.8   Monitor and Control the Process

    GP 2.9   Objectively Evaluate Adherence

    GP 2.10 Review Status with Higher Level Management

GG 3   Institutionalize a Defined Process

    GP 3.1   Establish a Defined Process

    GP 3.2   Collect Improvement Information

GG 4   Institutionalize a Quantitatively Managed Process

    GP 4.1   Establish Quantitative Objectives for the Process

    GP 4.2   Stabilize Subprocess Performance

GG 5   Institutionalize an Optimizing Process

    GP 5.1   Ensure Continuous Process Improvement

    GP 5.2   Correct Root Causes of Problems

Continuous Representation

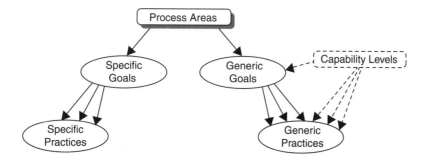

CMMI®

Guidelines for Process Integration and Product Improvement

Second Edition

Mary Beth Chrissis
Mike Konrad
Sandy Shrum

✦✦ Addison-Wesley

Upper Saddle River, NJ • Boston • Indianapolis • San Francisco
New York • Toronto • Montreal • London • Munich • Paris • Madrid
Capetown • Sydney • Tokyo • Singapore • Mexico City

Carnegie Mellon
Software Engineering Institute

The SEI Series in Software Engineering

Many of the designations used by manufacturers and sellers to distinguish their products are claimed as trademarks. Where those designations appear in this book, and the publisher was aware of a trademark claim, the designations have been printed with initial capital letters or in all capitals.

CMM, CMMI, Capability Maturity Model, Capability Maturity Modeling, Carnegie Mellon, CERT, and CERT Coordination Center are registered in the U.S. Patent and Trademark Office by Carnegie Mellon University.

ATAM; Architecture Tradeoff Analysis Method; CMM Integration; COTS Usage-Risk Evaluation; CURE; EPIC; Evolutionary Process for Integrating COTS Based Systems; Framework for Software Product Line Practice; IDEAL; Interim Profile; OAR; OCTAVE; Operationally Critical Threat, Asset, and Vulnerability Evaluation; Options Analysis for Reengineering; Personal Software Process; PLTP; Product Line Technical Probe; PSP; SCAMPI; SCAMPI Lead Appraiser; SCAMPI Lead Assessor; SCE; SEI; SEPG; Team Software Process; and TSP are service marks of Carnegie Mellon University.

Special permission to reproduce portions from CMMI for Development with IPPD, Version 1.2, © 2006 by Carnegie Mellon University, in this book is granted by the Software Engineering Institute.

The authors and publisher have taken care in the preparation of this book, but make no expressed or implied warranty of any kind and assume no responsibility for errors or omissions. No liability is assumed for incidental or consequential damages in connection with or arising out of the use of the information or programs contained herein.

The publisher offers excellent discounts on this book when ordered in quantity for bulk purchases or special sales, which may include electronic versions and/or custom covers and content particular to your business, training goals, marketing focus, and branding interests. For more information, please contact:

   U.S. Corporate and Government Sales
   (800) 382-3419
   corpsales@pearsontechgroup.com

For sales outside the United States, please contact:

   International Sales
   international@pearsoned.com

Visit us on the Web: informit.com/aw

Library of Congress Cataloging-in-Publication Data
Chrissis, Mary Beth.
   CMMI : guidelines for process integration and product improvement
/ Mary Beth Chrissis, Mike Konrad, and Sandy Shrum.—2nd ed.
      p. cm.—(The SEI series in software engineering)
   Includes bibliographical references and index.
   ISBN 0-321-27967-0 (hardcover : alk. paper)
   1. Capability maturity model (Computer software) 2. Software
engineering.   I. Konrad, Mike. II. Shrum, Sandy. III. Title.
QA76.758.C518 2006
005.1068'5—dc22

                               2006023484

Copyright © 2007 Pearson Education, Inc.

All rights reserved. Printed in the United States of America. This publication is protected by copyright, and permission must be obtained from the publisher prior to any prohibited reproduction, storage in a retrieval system, or transmission in any form or by any means, electronic, mechanical, photocopying, recording, or likewise. For information regarding permissions, write to:

   Pearson Education, Inc.
   Rights and Contracts Department
   501 Boylston Street, Suite 900
   Boston, MA 02116
   Fax: (617) 671-3447

ISBN-13: 978-0-321-27967-5
ISBN-10:   0-321-27967-0
Text printed in the United States on recycled paper at Courier in Westford, Massachusetts.
7th Printing   February 2009

CONTENTS

PERSPECTIVES

PREFACE

Capability Maturity Model Integration (CMMI) is a process improvement maturity model for the development of products and services. It consists of best practices that address development and maintenance activities that cover the product lifecycle from conception through delivery and maintenance.

This latest iteration of the model as represented herein integrates bodies of knowledge that are essential for development and maintenance, but that have been addressed separately in the past, such as software engineering, systems engineering, hardware and design engineering, the engineering "-ilities," and acquisition. The prior designations of CMMI for systems engineering and software engineering (CMMI-SE/SW) are superseded by the title "CMMI for Development" to truly reflect the comprehensive integration of these bodies of knowledge and the application of the model within the organization. CMMI for Development (CMMI-DEV) provides a comprehensive integrated solution for development and maintenance activities applied to products and services.

CMMI for Development, v1.2 is a continuation and update of CMMI v1.1 and has been facilitated by the concept of CMMI "constellations" wherein a set of core components can be augmented by additional material to provide application-specific models with highly common content. CMMI-DEV is the first of such constellations and represents the development area of interest.

Purpose

The purpose of CMMI for Development is to help organizations improve their development and maintenance processes for both products and services. This book is based on CMMI for Development, v1.2, which was produced from the CMMI Framework[1] in August 2006. The CMMI Framework supports the CMMI Product Suite by allowing multiple models, training courses, and appraisal methods to be generated that support specific areas of interest.

A constellation is a collection of CMMI components that includes a model, its training materials, and appraisal-related documents for an area of interest. Currently there are three planned constellations supported by the v1.2 model framework: development, services, and acquisition. "Additions" are used to expand constellations for specific additional content.

This book contains the CMMI for Development constellation and contains both the base CMMI-DEV as well as CMMI-DEV with the IPPD group of additions (CMMI-DEV +IPPD). If you are not using IPPD, ignore the information that is marked "IPPD Addition" and you will be using the *CMMI for Development* model.

CMMI v1.2 Contributors

Many talented people were involved in the development of the CMMI v1.2 Product Suite. Three primary groups involved in this development were the Steering Group, Product Team, and Configuration Control Board.

The Steering Group guides and approves the plans of the Product Team, provides consultation on significant CMMI project issues, and ensures involvement from a variety of interested communities.

The Product Team writes, reviews, revises, discusses, and agrees on the structure and technical content of the CMMI Product Suite, including the framework, models, training, and appraisal materials. Development activities are based on multiple inputs. These inputs include an A-Specification and guidance specific to each release provided by the Steering Group, source models, change requests received from the user community, and input received from pilots and other stakeholders [SEI 2004].

The Configuration Control Board is the official mechanism for controlling changes to the CMMI models and *Introduction to CMMI*

---

1. The CMMI Framework is the basic structure that organizes CMMI components and combines them into CMMI constellations and models.

training. As such, this group ensures integrity over the life of the product suite by reviewing all proposed changes to the baseline and approving only those changes that satisfy the identified issues and meet the criteria for the upcoming release.

Members of the groups that were involved in developing CMMI for Development v1.2 are listed in Appendix C.

Audience

The audience for this book includes anyone interested in process improvement in a development and maintenance environment. Whether you are familiar with the concept of Capability Maturity Models or whether you are seeking information to get started on your improvement efforts, this book will be useful to you.

This book also is intended for people who want to use an appraisal[2] to see where they are, those who already know what they want to improve, and those who are just getting started and want to develop a general understanding of the CMMI for Development constellation. Thus, the audience for this book includes process appraisal teams; members of process improvement groups; project managers; product or service developers and maintainers, including software and systems engineers; and project management, computer science, and engineering and business educators.

Organization of This Book

This book serves as a guide for improvement of organizational processes. It is organized into three main parts:

- Part One—About CMMI for Development
- Part Two—Generic Goals and Generic Practices and the Process Areas
- Part Three—The Appendices and Glossary

Part One, "About CMMI for Development," consists of six chapters:

- Chapter 1, "Introduction," offers a broad view of CMMI and the CMMI for Development constellation. It introduces you to the concepts of process improvement and describes the history of models used for process improvement, and different process improvement approaches.

---

2. An appraisal is an examination of one or more processes by a trained team of professionals using a reference model (e.g., CMMI) as the basis for determining strengths and weaknesses.

- Chapter 2, "Process Area Components," describes all of the components of CMMI for Development that appear in Part Two.
- Chapter 3, "Tying It All Together," assembles the model components and explains the concepts of maturity levels and capability levels.
- Chapter 4, "Relationships Among Process Areas," provides insight into the meaning and interactions of the CMMI for Development process areas.
- Chapter 5, "Using CMMI Models," describes paths to adoption and use of CMMI for process improvement and benchmarking.
- Chapter 6, "Case Study: Applying CMMI to Services at Raytheon," is an additional chapter in this book that describes the real-life experiences of an organization as it applied CMMI best practices in a services context.

Throughout Part One we added perspectives on process improvement. Each perspective provides insight into a CMMI-related topic from an expert in the field. You will notice that each piece has a style that reflects the contributor.

Part Two, "Generic Goals and Generic Practices and the Process Areas," contains all of the CMMI for Development constellation's required and expected components. It also contains related informative components, including component names, subpractices, notes, and typical work products.

Part Two contains twenty-three sections. The first section contains the generic goals and practices, including a description of how they are used and how they relate to the process areas. The remaining twenty-two sections each represent one of the CMMI for Development process areas.[3] To make these process areas easy to find, they are organized alphabetically by process area acronym and have tabs on the outside edge of the page. Each section contains descriptions of goals, best practices, and examples. To supplement model material, we, the book authors, have added tips, hints, and cross-references in the outer margins that, although not part of the model, may help explain concepts and relationships, and provide other useful information.

Part Three, "The Appendices and Glossary," consists of five information resources:

- Appendix A, "References," contains references you can use to locate documented sources of information such as reports, process improvement models, industry standards, and books that are related to CMMI for Development.

---

3. A "process area" is a cluster of related best practices in an area, which when implemented collectively, satisfy a set of goals considered important for making significant improvement in that area. We will cover this concept in detail in Chapter 2.

- Appendix B, "Acronyms," defines the acronyms used herein.
- Appendix C, "CMMI for Development Project Participants," contains lists of people and their organizations who participated in the development of CMMI for Development, v1.2.
- Appendix D, the "Glossary" defines many of the terms used in CMMI.

How to Use This Book

Whether you are new to process improvement, new to CMMI, or already familiar with CMMI, Part One can help you understand why CMMI for Development is the best model to use for improving your development and maintenance processes.

Readers New to Process Improvement

If you are new to process improvement or new to the CMM concept, we suggest that you read Chapter 1, "Introduction," first. Chapter 1 will give you an overview of process improvement and explain what CMMI is all about.

Next, skim Part Two, including generic goals and practices as well as specific goals and practices, to get a feel for the scope of the best practices contained in the model. Pay closest attention to the purpose and introductory notes at the beginning of each section.

In Part Three, look through the references in Appendix A and select additional sources you think would be beneficial to read before moving forward with using CMMI for Development. Read through the acronyms and glossary to become familiar with the language of CMMI. Then, go back and read the details of Part Two, including the tips and hints.

Readers Experienced with Process Improvement

If you are new to CMMI but have experience with other process improvement models, such as the Software CMM (v1.1) or the Systems Engineering Capability Model (i.e., EIA 731), you will immediately recognize many similarities [EIA 1998].

We recommend that you read Part One to understand how CMMI is different from other process improvement models, but you may want to read some of the sections more quickly than others. Read Part Two with an eye open for best practices you recognize from the models you have already tried. Identifying familiar material gives you a feel for what is new and what has been carried over from the model you already know. Review the tips, hints, and cross-references to see details and relationships that will help you understand CMMI better.

Next, review the glossary to understand how some terminology may differ from that used in the process improvement model you know. Many concepts will be repeated, but they may be called something different.

Readers Familiar with CMMI

If you have reviewed or used a CMMI model before, you will quickly recognize the CMMI concepts discussed and the best practices presented. The differences between v1.2 and v1.1 are explained in detail on the SEI Web site in the v1.2 release notes. These differences reflect the enhancements suggested by the users of v1.1. Focus in on the tips, hints, and cross-references in the process areas to discover new ideas, relationships, or details you may have missed before.

What's New

This book has significant improvements over the first edition. This second edition has new features we've added that you won't find in the v1.2 models available online.

What's New in Version 1.2

The following improvements were made to v1.2:

- Both representations are presented together.
- The advanced practice and common feature concepts have been removed.
- The generic goal and practice descriptions were moved to Part Two.
- Hardware amplifications were added.
- All definitions were consolidated in the glossary.
- IPPD practices were consolidated and simplified There are no longer any separate IPPD process areas.
- Supplier Agreement Management (SAM) and Integrated Supplier Management (ISM) were consolidated and Supplier Sourcing was removed.
- Generic practice (GP) elaborations were added to the level 3 GPs.
- An explanation of how process areas support the implementation of GPs was added.
- Material was added to ensure that standard processes are deployed to projects at their startup.

What's New in the Second Edition

We added several features to the second edition that you will not find in the first edition.

- We added tips, hints, and cross-references in the margins throughout the process areas to help you better understand, apply, or find more information about the content of the process areas.
- We asked experts from various backgrounds to provide their perspective on process improvement. These Perspectives are placed throughout Part One and provide you with opinions from those with rich experience in process improvement.
- We added a case study applying CMMI to services that demonstrates how CMMI can be applied in different environments given persistence and insight. This case study replaces the one in the first edition that described an early adopter's experience with CMMI.

Additional Information and Reader Feedback

You can find additional information from various other sources about CMMI, such as the background and history of the CMMI models, as well as the benefits of using CMMI models. Many of these sources are listed in Appendix A and are also published on the CMMI Web site— http://www.sei.cmu.edu/cmmi/ [SEI2].

Suggestions for improving CMMI are welcome. For information on how to provide feedback, see the CMMI Web site at http://www.sei.cmu.edu/cmmi/models/change-requests.html. If you have questions about CMMI, send an email to cmmi-comments @sei.cmu.edu.

ACKNOWLEDGMENTS

This book builds on the CMMI Framework developed by the CMMI project, which involved numerous people from different organizations throughout the world. Without the work of those involved in the CMMI project since it began in 1998, this book would not exist.

The authors would like to acknowledge the many individuals who directly contributed to this second edition of the book.

Version 1.2 was largely based on the manuscript of the first edition of this book, thanks largely to the efforts of Mike Phillips. Building on v1.1, the CMMI Model Team developed the majority of the content of this book. Our colleagues on the Model Team, Jim Armstrong, Roger Bate, Sandra Cepeda, Aaron Clouse, Mike D'Ambrosa, Craig Hollenbach, and Karen Richter, we consider to be not only respected model developers, but also good friends. To help address Japanese translation, one additional team member, So Norimatsu, was added near the end. Over the years, So has worked hard to ensure that CMMs are accessible to Japanese industry. We are also proud to consider So a colleague and friend.

As with the first edition, we want to thank Bill Peterson once again for his continued support and for his leadership of the Software Engineering Process Management Program (which includes CMMI) at the SEI. Bill is always there to guide us and look out for us to ensure that we are able to produce our best work.

We would also like to thank our colleagues and friends at the SEI, including: Barbara Baldwin, Rhonda Brown, Stacey Cope, Annette Haughey, Will Hayes, Georgeann Knorr, Keith Kost, Barbara Mattis,

Bill McSteen, Joanne O'Leary, Mary Lynn Russo, Mary Lou Russo, Linda Shooer, John Waclo, and others who help us on a daily basis with maintaining the CMMI Product Suite.

We have special thanks for the contributors to our Perspectives and Case Study. All of these authors were very willing to share their insights and experiences and met very aggressive deadlines to do so.

The Perspectives authors, Victor Basili, Roger Bate, David Card, Bill Curtis, Khaled El Emam, Watts Humphrey, Gargi Keeni, Hans Juergen Kugler, Tomoo Matsubara, Jim Moore, Lynn Penn, Bill Peterson, Mike Phillips, Bob Rassa, and Hal Wilson, are all leaders in their respective fields. We are honored that all of them agreed to contribute to our book and are proud to include their Perspectives.

The Case Study authors, Juan Ceva, Mark Pumar, John Ryskowski, and Gordon Ward, were involved in applying CMMI to Raytheon's Pasadena Operations. Their well-written report and compelling story inspired us to include an abbreviated version of it here in the book. We are delighted that they agreed to contribute their experiences to our book.

We are grateful to the reviewers of this book: Aaron Clouse, Lynn Penn, Mary Sakry, Rich Turner, and others. Their insightful comments helped us to improve the book and to better convey our ideas.

Special thanks go to Addison-Wesley Publishing Partner, Peter Gordon, for his assistance, patience, and expertise. He is much more to us than a business partner. We trust him implicitly and consider him a personal friend. We'd also like to thank Kim Boedigheimer, John Fuller, Julie Nahil, Stephane Nakib, and Beth Wickenhiser, for their help with the design and final production of this book.

From Mary Beth Chrissis

I would first and foremost like to thank everyone I work with as well as the many people that I've gotten to know over the years from working on CMMs. I have learned so much from so many people and without everyone's belief in me and sharing their knowledge and experience, my contribution to this book would not be possible. I have a very special thank you to all of the students I have had the pleasure of teaching. Every class afforded me the opportunity to learn more about CMMI and share with many of you the different ways that it can be interpreted and applied. As those who know me well, my family is an important and integral part of my life and I'd like to express my sincere gratitude to my husband, Chuck, and my children, Adam, Pam, and Kevin. Somehow they are always there to help me to juggle my career, family, and this book. For this edition, we had a more demanding schedule than usual and they were there all of the way; picking up extra tasks, encouraging me to keep working, and providing me with hugs and kisses in the morning after they knew I had a long night. I thank all four of you and I love you dearly. Lastly, there are two very important people that I need to thank, and they are Mike and Sandy. I couldn't ask for two better coauthors. We have known each other for many years now and with each day I feel that our bond and friendship continue to grow. I appreciate both of you and am so happy that I could be part of this experience with you again.

From Mike Konrad

I came to the SEI almost twenty years ago hoping to contribute to an international initiative that would fundamentally improve the way that software was built. First, the Software CMM and now CMMI has become that initiative. For this, I thank my many colleagues at the SEI, past and present. Over the years, I've been honored to work with some of the most talented individuals in systems and software engineering and some of the best management in the field. I've learned much from all of these individuals, but especially from Watts Humphrey and Bill Peterson. I also continue to learn from my two coauthors, Mary Beth and Sandy; one could not hope for better and more talented coauthors. With respect to my family, words cannot express adequately my heartfelt thanks to my wife, Patti, for twenty-five years of encouragement and patience; our children, Paul, Katie, Alison, David, and Walter, for their patience when I was too busy, but still sharing their time and insights of this world so that we learn more about it together; my parents, Walter and Renée, for their nurturing and years of sacrifice; and my sister, Corinne, for her encouragement over the years and love of philosophy and the arts. Finally, I'd like to give a special thanks to my favorite author, Bill Pronzini, creator of the Nameless Detective series, for many years of suspense, entertainment, and wonder.

From Sandy Shrum

I sometimes look at where I am today and I am amazed that I've had the opportunity to be part of writing this book. I remember back to 1998 when Mike asked me to join the newly formed CMMI project. I've learned so much since then and met a lot of great people that I now consider friends. I continue to learn from my colleagues on the project in so many ways. I'd like to thank my parents John and Eileen Maruca, for their unwavering support. I'd like to also thank my friend Susan Edwards. Until her death last year, she was a constant source of encouragement and praise. My friends Marcy Marley, Kim Baker, and Rhonda Brown provided the support I needed during those hectic times when it seemed that all I was doing was working on the book or working at the SEI. I'd like to thank Nicholas Rogers for helping me see this work with a fresh perspective and enabling me to be proud of myself and my work. Finally, I'd like to thank Mary Beth and Mike. Without them I would not be who I am today. They are both mentors and friends.

PART ONE

About CMMI for Development

CHAPTER 1

INTRODUCTION

Now, more than ever, companies want to deliver products and services better, faster, and cheaper. At the same time, in the high-technology environment of the twenty-first century, nearly all organizations have found themselves building increasingly complex products and services. Today, a single company usually does not develop all the components that compose a product or service. More commonly, some components are built in-house and some are acquired; then all the components are integrated into the final product or service. Organizations must be able to manage and control this complex development and maintenance process.

The problems these organizations address today involve enterprise-wide solutions that require an integrated approach. Effective management of organizational assets is critical to business success. In essence, these organizations are product and service developers that need a way to manage an integrated approach to their development activities as part of achieving their business objectives.

In the current marketplace, there are maturity models, standards, methodologies, and guidelines that can help an organization improve the way it does business. However, most available improvement approaches focus on a specific part of the business and do not take a systemic approach to the problems that most organizations are facing. By focusing on improving one area of a business, these models have unfortunately perpetuated the stovepipes and barriers that exist in organizations.

Capability Maturity Model Integration (CMMI) provides an opportunity to avoid or eliminate these stovepipes and barriers through integrated models that transcend disciplines. CMMI for Development consists of best practices that address development and maintenance activities applied to products and services. It addresses practices that cover the product's lifecycle from conception through delivery and maintenance. The emphasis is on the work necessary to build and maintain the total product.

About Capability Maturity Models

In its research to help organizations develop and maintain quality products and services, the Software Engineering Institute (SEI) has found several dimensions that an organization can focus on to improve its business. Figure 1.1 illustrates the three critical dimensions that organizations typically focus on: people, procedures and methods, and tools and equipment.

But what holds everything together? It is the processes used in your organization. Processes allow you to align the way you do business. They allow you to address scalability and provide a way to incorporate knowledge of how to do things better. Processes allow you to leverage your resources and to examine business trends.

This is not to say that people and technology are not important. We are living in a world where technology is changing by an order of magnitude every ten years. Similarly, people typically work for many companies throughout their careers. We live in a dynamic world. A focus on process provides the infrastructure necessary to deal with an ever-changing world, and to maximize the productivity of people and the use of technology to be more competitive.

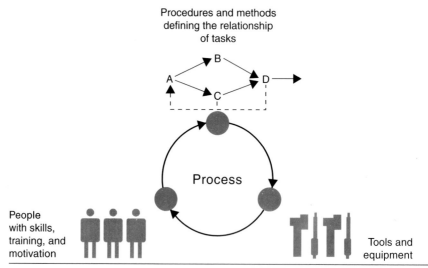

FIGURE 1.1
The Three Critical Dimensions

Manufacturing has long recognized the importance of process effectiveness and efficiency. Today, many organizations in manufacturing and service industries recognize the importance of quality processes. Process helps an organization's workforce meet business objectives by helping them work smarter, not harder, and with improved consistency. Effective processes also provide a vehicle for introducing and using new technology in a way that best meets the business objectives of the organization.

In the 1930s, Walter Shewhart began work in process improvement with his principles of statistical quality control [Shewhart 1931]. These principles were refined by W. Edwards Deming [Deming 1986], Phillip Crosby [Crosby 1979], and Joseph Juran [Juran 1988]. Watts Humphrey, Ron Radice, and others extended these principles even further and began applying them to software in their work at IBM and the SEI [Humphrey 1989]. Humphrey's book, *Managing the Software Process,* provides a description of the basic principles and concepts on which many of the capability maturity models (CMMs) are based.

The SEI has taken the process management premise, "the quality of a system or product is highly influenced by the quality of the process used to develop and maintain it," and defined CMMs that embody this premise. The belief in this premise is seen worldwide in quality movements, as evidenced by the International Organization for Standardization/International Electrotechnical Commission (ISO/IEC) body of standards.

CMMI: History and Direction

by Watts S. Humphrey

To understand the future, we must consider where we have been, how we got here, and our current direction. I will describe the genesis of CMMI, the ideas that contributed to its design, some current issues, and thoughts on what to do next.

History
Five principal ideas from a broad array of fields originally inspired the CMMI model and appraisal process. These ideas were

1. Planning, tracking, and schedule management
2. Requirements definition and configuration control

3. Process assessment
4. Quality measurement and continuous improvement
5. Evolutionary improvement

We now know that these concepts apply to software and systems development work, but it was not obvious in 1986 when CMM development started, or in 1966 when I first tried to apply some of these ideas as IBM's director of software development.

Planning, Tracking, and Schedule Management

After completing my technical studies, I got an M.B.A. in manufacturing. Professor Judson Neff asserted that the only way to manage complex operations was to manage to detailed and precise plans. In my first job, I inherited a troubled development project. We made plans and tracked schedules and the project recovered.

Later, when in charge of all of IBM's programming development, my projects were again troubled and I again had everyone make and track to detailed plans. We did not miss a commitment for several years. We quickly got schedule control of an organization of 4,000 developers in 15 laboratories and 6 countries.

Requirements Definition and Configuration Control

I soon learned two more critical lessons. First, if you don't allow any requirements changes, you could build the wrong product and waste the entire development effort. Second, if you don't rigorously control changes, you will never finish development.

Process Assessment

Later, Dr. Art Anderson, IBM's senior vice president for development and manufacturing, asked me to fix IBM's semiconductor operations. We used an assessment method he had tried in IBM Research to help people solve their own problems. In IBM's Burlington, Vermont, semiconductor operation, Art explained that IBM could buy imported chips from Japan at lower prices than Burlington's costs. Even IBM could not afford to do this. If this operation was not soon competitive, we would shut it down. By assessing their own operations, this team solved their cost problem and soon became the world's lowest-cost semiconductor producer.

Quality Measurement and Continuous Improvement

The Burlington engineers controlled their costs through yield management. By more than doubling yield, they cut costs by more than half. To do this, even the factory workers had to measure, track, and analyze every step of their work.

Evolutionary Improvement

When I was IBM's director of software quality and process, Ron Radice and I attended a Phil Crosby quality management course that used a five-level maturity model. Ron then used Crosby's maturity framework and Anderson's assessment strategy to accelerate IBM's software process improvement. A laboratory's first assessment was generally successful but the second and third ones were not. The problem was that the Crosby maturity levels were based on subjective attitude judgments rather than specific software activities.

Air Force Acquisition

When I retired from IBM, my first SEI assignment was to improve software source selection for the U.S. Air Force. We worked with Col. Jack Ferguson of the Air Force and Martin Owens and others from MITRE on a way to evaluate organizational capability. Organizations that used the best management and technical practices in their development projects seemed likely to do the best work, so we devised an 85-question questionnaire that covered

- Project planning
- Project tracking
- Schedule management
- Requirements management
- Configuration control
- Quality measurement
- Continuous process improvement

To rank the results, we grouped the 85 questions in a Crosby-like maturity framework. This became the first version of what ultimately became CMMI.

Current Challenges

The ideas behind CMMI came from many fields and benefited from many people's experiences. Three issues now lie ahead of us.

First, with increasing marketplace pressure, organizations often focus on maturity levels rather than process capability. Maturity levels cannot comprehensively measure organizational capability. They can indicate risky process areas or guide process improvement by describing a minimum set of activities necessary. We now see cases where high-maturity ratings do not indicate effective, high-maturity practices. It is not that the appraisal process is faulty or that organizations are dishonest, merely that the maturity framework does not look deeply enough into all organizational practices.

The second issue concerns adjusting the CMMI Framework and appraisal methods to address this problem. Without change, we can expect more cases where high-maturity ratings will not generally correlate with better performance. Two lessons from my earlier experiences suggest a way to address this issue.

1. To truly control complex and precise work, everyone must manage to detailed and precise plans.
2. Everyone must measure and manage quality.

To guide software developers in applying these principles to their work, the SEI developed the Personal Software Process (PSP) and the Team Software Process (TSP). When developers have used the PSP and TSP, appraisers have detected these practices with a CMMI appraisal. It therefore appears that the PSP and TSP can help foster mature developer practices. The SEI is now adapting the PSP and TSP to systems development and acquisition work.

This, however, leads to the third issue: flexibility. CMMI does not define in detail how to do development work; the focus is on what to do. However, the PSP and TSP specify how project planning, tracking, and quality management are performed. The issue concerns ways to incorporate such practices and principles into the CMMI model and method without switching the focus from what to how. The need is to encompass these proven principles and practices without constraining development organizations as the technology advances. The SEI is working on these issues as we strive to improve the effectiveness of these methods and models.

CMMs focus on improving processes in an organization. They contain the essential elements of effective processes for one or more disciplines and describe an evolutionary improvement path from ad hoc, immature processes to disciplined, mature processes with improved quality and effectiveness.

The SEI created the first CMM designed for software organizations and published it in a book, *The Capability Maturity Model: Guidelines for Improving the Software Process* [SEI 1995].

The SEI's book applied the principles introduced almost a century ago to this never-ending cycle of process improvement. The value of this process improvement approach has been confirmed over time. Organizations have experienced increased productivity and quality, improved cycle time, and more accurate and predictable schedules and budgets [Gibson 2006].

Evolution of CMMI

CMMI: From the Past and into the Future

by Mike Phillips

As we launch this update to the CMMI models, it is appropriate to view the heritage that led us to this point, and give some insight into where we believe the work is headed in the future.

The Past

Models with levels of improvement go back to the emphasis on manufacturing quality expressed by Philip Crosby. Shortly after the creation of the SEI, the U.S. Air Force asked the SEI to identify key practices that a contractor had to perform to deliver software-intensive systems reliably. By 1991, this tracking of practices, and measurement across a stepped approach for improvement like that pioneered by Crosby, had matured into the Capability Maturity Model for Software (SW-CMM).

The success of this model for one engineering discipline led to similar efforts for other elements of the product development community. Interest in such models for systems engineering process improvement led to two models produced in 1994. The first was the Systems Engineering CMM, created by the Enterprise Process Improvement Collaboration (EPIC), with SEI participation.

The second model, the Systems Engineering Capability and Assessment Method, or SECAM, was created by the International Council on Systems Engineering (INCOSE). Four years later these two models were successfully merged into Electronic Industries Alliance (EIA) Interim Standard 731 as a result of a collaborative effort of EIA, EPIC, and INCOSE. In 1996, a sister to the SW-CMM was created to cover key practices in software acquisition—the Software Acquisition Capability Maturity Model, or SA-CMM. Concerns about preserving and enhancing the capabilities of developmental engineering staff led the SEI to create the People Capability Maturity Model (P-CMM) in 1995.

That year, work was also underway at the SEI to produce an update to the SW-CMM, and to produce a model that would capture concurrent engineering practices in an Integrated Product Development CMM. The Institute's sponsor, the U.S. Department of Defense (DoD), determined that these efforts should be merged into an integrated model, to be called the model we now know as Capability Maturity Model Integration (CMMI).

The feasibility of integrating a diverse set of maturity models had been demonstrated earlier that year by the Federal Aviation Administration (FAA), which had developed an integrated capability maturity model (FAA-iCMM v1.0). Due to the widespread focus on integrated product and process development (IPPD) by the DoD and industry, it was decided that the initial focus of the CMMI effort would be integration of systems engineering, software engineering, and IPPD.

The CMMI Product Team produced two draft versions of the CMMI models before settling on the combination that became an initial release in 2000, which included versions for systems engineering, software engineering, and integrated product and process development. Due to minor changes as we released versions, these became known as v1.02 by the December 2000 release. At the same time, we released a draft version to provide initial thinking about acquisition, called v1.02d.

We then took a year to gather results from the initial release before producing a refinement of the material that we wished to stabilize for a longer period. The first of these models was released in December 2001 as v1.1. With CMMI Steering Group approval, we added a variant that included some of the acquisition practices as a Supplier Sourcing addition in April 2002. This version became the basis for the previous edition of this Addison-Wesley book.

The Present

The use of CMMI v1.1 has exceeded our expectations. As I write this in February 2006, the SEI and its Partners have trained more than 45,000 people and conducted about 1,500 appraisals to measure process improvement progress. The model has become a de facto standard for software-intensive system development, and has shown value for demonstrating process discipline against governance audits like Sarbanes-Oxley.

As we investigated what changes might be needed for a next version, the CMMI Steering Group agreed that we should reexamine the architecture of the existing version to see if it might be improved. The Architecture team agreed that with some relatively minor changes, we could make the overall framework more easily extensible into domains of interest to the community that found some parts of the existing models very useful, but other parts difficult to apply in their domains. The changes to the architecture that were approved had little impact on the development elements, but did allow some consolidation of the practices that you will see inside this book. They were, however, highly significant in allowing synergistic expansion into areas closely related to development, like services and acquisition.

The Future

We see both near-term and more distant opportunities to expand the value of the CMMI Product Suite. As I mentioned earlier, we have a near-term opportunity to expand coverage through the use of variants we are currently calling "constellations." Two that are under initial development are constellations for acquisition and for services. Each will have elements that are the same as those in this book, plus some elements of coverage that may be unique to the domain, and perhaps some elements shared with another constellation.

While these new constellations are in early development, the clear commitment of both development teams for these domains is to maximize the commonality across the constellations. This commonality will aid in reducing the amount of training or appraisal preparation required for the various areas of CMMI coverage. Commonality will also aid us in addressing other standards, such as ITIL, in a complementary fashion.

We have also heard from the community of its interest in covering other areas that deserve the focused attention of process improvement. While some may need the full treatment of a new constellation, others may be best addressed by providing interpretive guidance or expanded coverage of specific practices and goals for an area. For areas like safety, security, and design engineering, we will be investigating approaches that will build on the value of the CMMI Framework to provide support to more and more of the community.

Since 1991, CMMs have been developed for myriad disciplines. Some of the most notable include models for systems engineering, software engineering, software acquisition, workforce management and development, and integrated product and process development (IPPD).

Although these models have proven useful to many organizations in different industries, the use of multiple models has been problematic. Many organizations would like their improvement efforts to span different groups in their organizations. However, the differences among the discipline-specific models used by each group, including their architecture, content, and approach, have limited these organizations' capabilities to broaden their improvements successfully. Further, applying multiple models that are not integrated within and across an organization is costly in terms of training, appraisals, and improvement activities.

The CMM Integration project was formed to sort out the problem of using multiple CMMs. The CMMI Product Team's initial mission was to combine three source models:

1. The Capability Maturity Model for Software (SW-CMM) v2.0 draft C [SEI 1997b]
2. The Systems Engineering Capability Model (SECM) [EIA 1998][1]
3. The Integrated Product Development Capability Maturity Model (IPD-CMM) v0.98 [SEI 1997a]

The combination of these models into a single improvement framework was intended for use by organizations in their pursuit of enterprise-wide process improvement.

These three source models were selected because of their widespread adoption in the software and systems engineering communities and because of their different approaches to improving processes in an organization.

Using information from these popular and well-regarded models as source material, the CMMI Product Team created a cohesive set of integrated models that can be adopted by those currently using the source models, as well as by those new to the CMM concept. Hence, CMMI is a result of the evolution of the SW-CMM, the SECM, and the IPD-CMM.

Developing a set of integrated models involved more than simply combining existing model materials. Using processes that promote consensus, the CMMI Product Team built a framework that accommodates multiple disciplines and is flexible enough to support the different approaches of the source models [Ahern 2003].

---

1. The Systems Engineering Capability Model is also known as Electronic Industries Alliance 731 (EIA 731).

CMMI: Integration and Improvement Continue

by Bob Rassa

It is hard to believe that CMMI is almost ten years old: nearly five years in development and slightly more than five years since its first release. When the National Defense Industrial Association's (NDIA) Systems Engineering Division was just a fledgling, I, as the director of systems engineering, got together with Mark Schaeffer, of the office of the U.S. Under Secretary of Defense, and we decided that the current CMM environment was diverging. We saw that software was going in one direction and systems engineering was going in another direction, and that other discipline-specific maturity models were popping up. Because of the nature of this environment, we decided it was time to take positive action. Despite a competent software process maturity model, the U.S. DoD realized that software problems were still a large cause of program failures. Bringing stronger systems engineering into play was considered an important part of solving this problem. It was clear that the divergence of maturity models kept these two communities apart.

We consulted with Roger Bate, now the CMMI chief architect, about the feasibility of building an integrated model that could support best practices in multiple areas. After conducting in-depth analyses, Roger confirmed that this new idea could be implemented. We then decided it was time to create an integrated CMM.

The result of this decision was CMMI-SE/SW, an integrated maturity model that brought these two important disciplines together in terms of process maturity. As CMMI development ensued, we realized that most of the critical processes for these disciplines were in fact common, thus validating the concept. Shortly after the initial release of CMMI-SE/SW in November 2000, we released the IPPD environment, and then Supplier Sourcing (SS) to round out the product suite.

Even though it was designed to apply to all aspects of product or service design (including hardware design) the model retained the SE and SW designations to preserve ties to the legacy models (i.e., EIA 731 and the Software CMM). Whether this was a good decision is moot, since the results are impressive. Far more than 1,000 Class A appraisals have been reported in just four years after the release of CMMI, and as of January 2006, more than 45,000 individuals have received "Introduction to CMMI" training, and this number typically increases between 1,000 and 1,500 per month. The success in CMMI recognition and adoption by the industrial complex is undeniable.

One downside to the naming convention used for CMMI models has been the view that the principal activities within the organization to which CMMI applies are software and systems engineering, and of course, nothing can be further from the truth. To gain maximum benefit from CMMI adoption and implementation, CMMI must be applied to the entire development structure of the organization, and to that end the latest release of CMMI (v1.2) is called CMMI for Development (CMMI-DEV) to clearly signify its application to the full spectrum of product and service design.

The v1.2 architecture has also undergone a slight morphing to accommodate two additional applications of CMMI, designated CMMI for Acquisition (CMMI-ACQ) and CMMI for Services (CMMI-SVC). CMMI-ACQ is the name of a process maturity model for acquisition organizations. CMMI-SVC is the name of the model for organizations providing services. Both of these models are being developed at the request of the industrial complex and will appear shortly after CMMI-DEV v1.2 is released. These two additional "constellations," as they are called in CMMI parlance, will round out the product suite.

One additional legacy of the pre-CMMI models is retained in v1.2—namely, the concept of both staged and continuous representations—but they are taught in a common "Introduction to CMMI" course which is the only introductory course now offered.

CMMI is truly state of the art in terms of process maturity, and substantive benefits have been reported to and summarized by the designated CMMI steward, the SEI, of Carnegie Mellon University. However, to be truly effective CMMI must be applied in a conscientious manner within the organization. When we started the initial development of CMMI, it was well publicized that its purpose was to integrate the divergent maturity models. We soon realized that the real purpose that should have been communicated as the ultimate benefit of CMMI was that CMMI would integrate the design disciplines in terms of both process and performance. To achieve this ultimate benefit, care is needed to make sure that integrated processes are put into place within the organization, that such processes are implemented across the enterprise on all new programs and projects, and that such implementation is done in a thorough manner to assure that new programs start out on the right foot.

This book provides the latest guidance toward CMMI implementation. It covers all the specifics, addresses nuances of interpretation, and contains expert advice useful to both new and experienced practitioners. Hundreds of process improvement experts have contributed to CMMI development, and many of them contributed their expertise to this volume for the benefit of the industrial complex. We trust you will enjoy their work.

History of CMMs

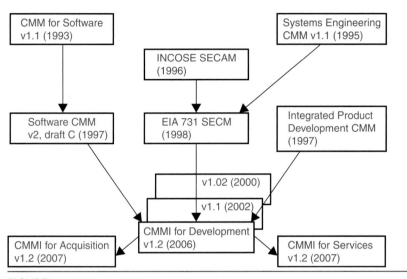

FIGURE 1.2
The History of CMMs

Since the release of CMMI v1.1, we have seen that this improvement framework can be applied to other areas of interest [SEI 2002a, SEI 2002b]. To apply to multiple areas of interest, the framework groups best practices into what we call "constellations." A constellation is a collection of CMMI components that are used to build models, training materials, and appraisal documents.

Recently, the CMMI model architecture was improved to support multiple constellations and the sharing of best practices among constellations and their member models. Work has begun on two new constellations: one for services (CMMI for Services) and the other for acquisition (CMMI for Acquisition). Although CMMI for Development incorporates the development of services, including the combination of components, consumables, and people intended to meet service requirements, it differs from the planned CMMI for Services (CMMI-SVC), which focuses on the delivery of services. The CMMI models that have been available in the community prior to 2006 are now considered part of the CMMI for Development constellation.

The Architecture of the CMMI Framework

by Roger Bate

The CMMI Product Suite has been published in two main versions: version 1.0 released in 2000, and version 1.1 released in 2002. As the product suite was used in disparate industries and organizations, it became apparent that CMMI could be applied to all kinds of product development, especially if the terminology was kept general for similar practices.

A further revelation was that the process and project management practices of the model are suitable for a wide range of activities besides development. This discovery led me to propose that we should enable the expansion of CMMI, including the extension of the scope of the CMMI Framework, by creating a new architecture for the CMMI Framework.

This new architecture would accommodate other areas of interest (e.g., services, acquisition, and development). I was musing one day about the valuable best practices that were contained in models. I began to think of them as the *stars* of process improvement. I pushed this metaphor a little further to call the collection of components that would be useful in building a model, its training materials, and appraisal documents for an area of interest a *constellation*. This was the beginning of the architecture that was eventually created.

There are two primary objectives for the CMMI Framework architecture.

1. Enable the coverage of selected areas of interest to make useful and effective processes.
2. Promote maximum commonality of goals and practices across models, training materials, and appraisal methods.

These objectives pull in opposite directions; therefore, the architecture was designed as a bit of a compromise.

The CMMI Framework will be used in CMMI v1.2 and beyond to accommodate additional content that the user community indicates is desirable. The framework contains components used to construct models and their corresponding training and appraisal materials. The framework is organized so that the models constructed will benefit from common terminology and common practices that have proven to be valuable in previous models.

The CMMI Framework is a collection of all model components, training material components, and appraisal components. These components are organized into groupings, called "constellations," which facilitate construction of approved models and preserve the legacy of existing CMM and CMMI models.

In the framework, there are constellations of components that are used to construct models in an area of interest (e.g., Acquisition, Development, and Services). Also in the framework, there is a CMMI model foundation. This foundation is a skeleton model that contains the core model components in a CMMI model structure. The content of the CMMI model foundation is apropos to all areas of interest addressed by the constellations. A CMMI model for a constellation is constructed by inserting additional model components into the CMMI model foundation.

Since the CMMI architecture is designed to encourage preserving as much common material as is reasonable in a multiple-constellation environment, the framework contains and controls all CMMI material that can be used to produce any constellation or model. However, a majority of components of the framework are expected to be shared among most of the constellations and models.

CMMI models have a defined structure. This structure is designed to provide familiar placement of model components of various constellations and versions. If you look at the structure of a process area, you'll see components including Process Area Name, Category, Maturity Level, Purpose, Introductory Notes, References, and Specific Goals. You will also find that every process area in this model (i.e., CMMI for Development) and all other CMMI models produced from the CMMI Framework have the same structure. This feature helps you to understand quickly where to look for information in any CMMI model.

One of the benefits of having a common architecture and a large portion of common content in the various models is that the effort required to write models, train users, and appraise organizations is greatly reduced. The capability to add model components to the common process areas permits the models to expand their scope of coverage to a greater variety of needs. In addition, whole new process areas may be added to provide greater coverage of different areas of interest in the constellations.

CMMI models have a great deal of well-tested content that can be used to guide the creation of high-performance processes. The CMMI architecture permits that valuable content to continue to work in different areas of interest, while allowing for innovation and agility in responding to new needs.

So, you see that CMMI is growing beyond the star practices of the three original source models, and into constellations. This expansion into the "galaxy" is possible only with a well-thought-out and designed architecture to support it. The CMMI architecture has been designed to provide such support and will grow as needed to continue into the future.

CMMI for Development

The CMMI for Development constellation consists of two models: CMMI for Development +IPPD and CMMI for Development (without IPPD). Both models share much of their material and are identical in these shared areas. However, CMMI for Development +IPPD contains additional goals and practices that cover IPPD.

Currently, only one model is published since the CMMI for Development +IPPD model contains the full complement of practices available in this constellation, and you can derive the other model from this material. If you are not using IPPD, ignore the information that is marked "IPPD Addition," and you will be using the CMMI for Development model. If the need arises or the development constellation is expanded, the architecture will allow other models to be generated and published.

CMMI for Development is the designated successor of the three source models. The SEI has retired the Software CMM and the IPD-CMM. EIA has retired the SECM. All three of these models are succeeded by CMMI for Development.

The best practices in the CMMI models have gone through an extensive review process. CMMI version 0.2 was publicly reviewed and used in pilot activities. The CMMI Product Team evaluated more than 3,000 change requests to create CMMI version 1.0. Shortly thereafter, version 1.02 was released, which incorporated several minor improvements. Version 1.1 incorporated improvements guided by feedback from early use, with more than 1,500 change requests submitted as part of the public review, and hundreds of comments as part of the change control process.

CMMI version 1.2 was developed using input from nearly 2,000 change requests submitted by CMMI users. More than 750 of those requests were directed at CMMI model content. As you can see, not only is CMMI widely adopted, but it is improved based on the feedback received from the community.

Stewardship of the CMMI Product Suite

by Bill Peterson

CMMI has become widely used in various industries around the world. CMMI's development and enhancement are sponsored by two organizations: the Office of the Under Secretary of Defense for Acquisition, Technology, and Logistics (OUSD/AT&L), and the National Defense Industrial Association (NDIA) Systems Engineering Committee (SEC). These two organizations, and others from government, industry, and the SEI, work hand in hand to ensure that CMMI continues to meet the needs of and is available for government and industry use.

The SEI serves as the steward of the CMMI Product Suite. As steward, the SEI has the responsibility to coordinate CMMI-related activities and communicate with CMMI users and the public. This role fits nicely with the SEI's mission to "advance software engineering and related disciplines to ensure the development and operation of systems with predictable and improved cost, schedule, and quality." Certainly CMMI aids organizations in meeting these goals, and the SEI's role as steward enables it to maintain quality in the product suite, promote proper application of CMMI, and communicate to those who need information about CMMI. The SEI as steward provides coordination to ensure that members are involved across government, industry, and academia.

The CMMI Steering Group is the executive team that steers the development of CMMI and makes decisions on the direction of the CMMI Product Suite. The steering group consists of members appointed from government, industry, and the SEI. This group now directs and oversees CMMI maintenance and enhancements, the introduction of new disciplines to be included in CMMI, and the chartering of new development and maintenance projects. The group also reviews plans and sponsorship support of work proposed by others.

The development and maintenance of CMMI rest with the CMMI Product Team, a multiorganizational mix of people from government, industry, and the SEI. The CMMI Product Team is composed of different project teams that develop and maintain CMMI products, such as CMMI models and "Introduction to CMMI" training, as well as the SCAMPI A appraisal method. Team members represent the various disciplines and domains covered in CMMI's best practices. Also included in the product team are a project manager and a chief architect. The project manager coordinates the work of the product teams and the chief architect coordinates with the CMMI Steering Group to chart the future expansion of CMMI models and related products.

As part of the stewardship role, the SEI coordinates a change request process to gather feedback about the CMMI Product Suite from CMMI users and the public. Any individual from anywhere in the world can submit a change request. These change requests are reviewed and designed into product improvements proposed by the Product Team, which are then reviewed and approved or rejected by the CMMI configuration control board (CCB) for inclusion into an update release of the product suite. The CCB consists of members from multiple organizations and represents different roles/segments of the CMMI user base. Change requests that would result in significant change to the CMMI Product Suite are also reviewed with the CMMI Steering Group.

All of these groups must interact in order to continually improve the CMMI Product Suite in a way that best meets the needs of CMMI users. Further, the results of the efforts of these groups must be communicated to CMMI users and the public.

The activities of the CMMI steward support and facilitate the coordination of all of these groups as well as the maintenance and evolution of the CMMI Product Suite. The steward is responsible for providing project management coordination of CMMI Product Suite maintenance and enhancements. This responsibility includes facilitating the gathering of feedback from CMMI users and the product team, distributing new and improved best practices in the field, and integrating new disciplines or additional features (as directed by the steering group).

Beside managing updates to the CMMI Product Suite, the steward has other responsibilities that occur on a regular basis and include the following:

- Providing broad access to CMMI models, the appraisal method definition, and other information on the SEI Web site
- Creating and maintaining training materials
- Conducting and managing the authorizations of CMMI instructors and lead appraisers and licensing the network of CMMI partners
- Maintaining a quality assurance program that oversees appraisal and training activities to ensure that they support results that are valid, consistent, repeatable, comparable, and of the highest integrity and credibility

- Communicating to CMMI users and the public about the CMMI Framework and Product Suite
- Supporting relevant national and international standardization activities as part of leveraging developer and user investments in CMMI
- Identifying, measuring, and reporting on successes and barriers to success as experienced by CMMI users
- Funding stewardship activities
- Ensuring that standard procedures are followed for soliciting, processing, reporting, and testing improvements to existing CMMI work products

CMMI's sponsors, steering group, product team, CCB, and steward all share a long-term vision for CMMI. These groups see CMMI continuing to be widely adopted both nationally and internationally. Because CMMI supports the business goals and objectives of organizations that use it, the groups also see CMMI as the framework of choice for process improvement across multiple disciplines in an organization. Finally, these groups envision CMMI as being supported by appraisal methods that ensure efficient and cost-effective appraisals that provide the highest quality and integrity measures of an organization's capabilities.

The role of the CMMI steward, with the assistance of all the other CMMI groups, continually improves the CMMI Product Suite so that it better meets the needs of organizations worldwide, and realizes the vision shared by all.

The Scope of CMMI for Development

CMMI for Development is a reference model that covers the development and maintenance activities applied to both products and services. Organizations from many industries, including aerospace, banking, computer hardware, software, defense, automobile manufacturing, and telecommunications, use CMMI for Development.

Models in the CMMI for Development constellation contain practices that cover project management, process management, systems engineering, hardware engineering, software engineering, and other supporting processes used in development and maintenance. The CMMI for Development +IPPD model also covers the use of integrated teams for development and maintenance activities.

The Group of IPPD Additions

In CMMI, "additions" are used to include material that may be of interest to particular users. For the CMMI for Development constellation, additional material was included to address IPPD.

The IPPD group of additions covers an IPPD approach that includes practices that help organizations achieve the timely collaboration of relevant stakeholders throughout the life of the product to satisfy customers' needs, expectations, and requirements [DoD 1996]. When using processes that support an IPPD approach, you should integrate these processes with other processes in the organization. To support those using IPPD-related processes, the CMMI for Development constellation allows organizations to optionally select the IPPD group of additions.

When you select CMMI for Development +IPPD, you are selecting the CMMI for Development model plus all the IPPD additions. When you select CMMI for Development, you are selecting the model without the IPPD additions. In the text in Part One of this book, we may use "CMMI for Development" to refer to either of these models, for the sake of brevity.

Resolving Different Approaches of CMMs

The definition of a CMM allows the community to develop models supporting different approaches to process improvement. As long as a model contains the essential elements of effective processes for one or more disciplines and describes an evolutionary improvement path from ad hoc, immature processes to disciplined, mature processes with improved quality and effectiveness, it is considered a CMM. CMMI enables you to approach process improvement and appraisals using two different representations: continuous and staged.

The continuous representation enables an organization to select a process area (or group of process areas) and improve processes related to it. This representation uses capability levels to characterize improvement relative to an individual process area.

The staged representation uses predefined sets of process areas to define an improvement path for an organization. This improvement path is characterized by maturity levels. Each maturity level provides a set of process areas that characterize different organizational behaviors.

Choosing a Representation

If you are new to process improvement and are not familiar with either the staged or the continuous representation, you cannot go wrong if you choose one representation or the other. There are many valid reasons to select either representation.

If you have been using a CMM and you are familiar with a particular representation, we suggest that you continue to use that representation because it will make the transition to CMMI easier. Once you have become completely comfortable with CMMI, you might then decide to use the other representation.

Because each representation has advantages over the other, some organizations use both representations to address particular needs at various times in their improvement programs. In the following sections, we provide the advantages and disadvantages of each representation to help you decide which representation is best for your organization.

Continuous Representation

The continuous representation offers maximum flexibility when using a CMMI model for process improvement. An organization may choose to improve the performance of a single process-related trouble spot, or it can work on several areas that are closely aligned to the organization's business objectives. The continuous representation also allows an organization to improve different processes at different rates. There are some limitations on an organization's choices because of the dependencies among some process areas.

If you know the processes that need to be improved in your organization and you understand the dependencies among the process areas described in CMMI, the continuous representation is a good choice for your organization.

Staged Representation

The staged representation offers a systematic, structured way to approach model-based process improvement one stage at a time. Achieving each stage ensures that an adequate process infrastructure has been laid as a foundation for the next stage.

Process areas are organized by maturity levels that take some of the guesswork out of process improvement. The staged representation prescribes an order for implementing process areas according to maturity levels, which define the improvement path for an organization from the initial level to the optimizing level. Achieving each maturity level ensures that an adequate improvement foundation has been laid for the next maturity level and allows for lasting, incremental improvement.

If you do not know where to start and which processes to choose to improve, the staged representation is a good choice for you. It gives you a specific set of processes to improve at each stage that has been determined through more than a decade of research and experience with process improvement.

Comparison of the Continuous and Staged Representations

Table 1.1 compares the advantages of each representation and may assist you with determining which representation is right for your organization.

Factors in Your Decision

Three categories of factors that may influence your decision when selecting a representation are business, culture, and legacy.

Business Factors

An organization with mature knowledge of its own business objectives is likely to have a strong mapping of its processes to its business objectives. Such an organization may find the continuous representation useful to appraise its processes and in determining how well the organization's processes support and meet its business objectives.

If an organization with a product-line focus decides to improve processes across the entire organization, it might be served best by the staged representation. The staged representation will help an organization select the critical processes to focus on for improvement.

TABLE 1.1 Comparative Advantages of Continuous and Staged Representations

Continuous Representation	Staged Representation
Grants explicit freedom to select the order of improvement that best meets the organization's business objectives and mitigates the organization's areas of risk	Enables organizations to have a predefined and proven improvement path
Enables increased visibility of the capability achieved in each individual process area	Focuses on a set of processes that provide an organization with a specific capability that is characterized by each maturity level
Allows improvements of different processes to be performed at different rates	Summarizes process improvement results in a simple form—a single maturity-level number
Reflects a newer approach that does not yet have the data to demonstrate its ties to return on investment	Builds on a relatively long history of use that includes case studies and data that demonstrate return on investment

The same organization may opt to improve processes by product line. In that case, it might select the continuous representation—and a different appraised rating of capability might be achieved for each product line. Both approaches are valid. The most important consideration is which business objectives you would like your process improvement program to support and how these business objectives align with the two representations.

Cultural Factors

Cultural factors to consider when selecting a representation have to do with an organization's capability to deploy a process improvement program. For instance, an organization might select the continuous representation if the corporate culture is process based and experienced in process improvement or has a specific process that needs to be improved quickly. An organization that has little experience in process improvement may choose the staged representation, which provides additional guidance on the order in which changes should occur.

Legacy

If an organization has experience with another model that has a staged representation, it may be wise to continue with the staged representation when using CMMI, especially if it has invested resources and deployed processes across the organization that are associated with a staged representation. The same is true for the continuous representation.

Why Not Both Representations?

Whether used for process improvement or appraisals, both representations are designed to offer essentially equivalent results. Nearly all of the CMMI model content is common to both representations. Therefore, an organization need not select one representation over another.

In fact, an organization may find utility in both representations. It is rare that an organization will implement either representation exactly as prescribed. Organizations that are successful in process improvement often define an improvement plan that focuses on the unique needs of that organization and therefore use the principles of both the staged and the continuous representations.

For example, organizations that select the staged representation and are at maturity level 1 often implement the maturity level 2 process areas but also the Organizational Process Focus process area, which is included at maturity level 3. Another example is an organization that chooses the continuous representation for guiding its internal process improvement effort and then chooses the staged representation to conduct an appraisal.

CMMI and Six Sigma

by Lynn Penn

Capability Maturity Model Integration (CMMI) and Six Sigma are increasingly being discussed in the same conversation. While they do not share a common heritage—one is from the software engineering world and the other is from the manufacturing world—they do share common roots in the principles of Crosby, Deming, et al. Organizations that have endeavored to apply them both typically have managed, budgeted, and resourced the two initiatives separately. This led to not only minimal integration of the initiatives, but also competition between them. Recent research, however, has shown that these initiatives can be jointly leveraged to accelerate implementation of both and accomplishment of mission.[2]

Six Sigma is a holistic approach to business improvement that includes philosophy, performance measurements, improvement frameworks, and a toolkit—all of which are intended to complement and enhance existing engineering, service, and manufacturing processes. Because of its many dimensions, Six Sigma can serve as both an enterprise governance model and a tactical improvement engine.[3]

Six Sigma originated in the manufacturing industry. It was a clear way of identifying acceptable variances around the production of material. It also could be associated with identifying the ability to measure the variance or tolerance around the use of that product or the actual performance of the product itself. Thus, Six Sigma became the quality engine for manufacturing. Although Six Sigma does not guarantee quality, it does provide

---

2. Siviy, Jeannine; Penn, M. Lynn; and Harper, Erin. Relationships Between CMMI and Six Sigma (CMU/SEI-2005-TN-005). Pittsburgh: Software Engineering Institute, Carnegie Mellon University, December 2005;
www.sei.cmu.edu/publications/documents/05.reports/05tn005/05tn005.html.

3. Bergey, J.; et al. Results of SEI Independent Research and Development Projects and Report on Emerging Technologies and Technology Trends (CMU/SEI-2004-TR-018). Pittsburgh: Software Engineering Institute, Carnegie Mellon University, October 2004.

expectations of program performance that can be equated to customer satisfaction, thus implying quality.

CMMI is the integrated approach to process and product development. Over the past several years, numerous Capability Maturity Models (CMMs) have been developed. Software engineering, systems engineering, integrated teams, risk management, and acquisition each had its own model. So industry and government collaborated to establish one model with common terminology, common appraisal methods, and common disciplines.

CMMI, although a collection of multiple models, is most closely associated with the Software and Systems Engineering models. Therefore, it has been adopted primarily by software development organizations. The model is not prescriptive, but is a collection of best practices that, when interpreted in a specific organization, imply a quality product. Like Six Sigma, there is no guarantee of quality, but there is an expectation of product quality as it relates to performance.

There is no question that these two approaches are focused on quality. They are different but not disjointed methodologies. When integrated, these two methodologies can stimulate even more benefits for the organization than if they were used alone.

Let's say an organization has adopted Six Sigma and then decides to adopt CMMI as well. Six Sigma has already established the measurement program, thus satisfying the multiple CMMI generic practices for each CMMI process area associated with measurement and improvement. Six Sigma has also laid the foundation for satisfying the Measurement and Analysis process area. The maturity of the Six Sigma program can also enhance the capability of the organization to adopt CMMI high-maturity process areas such as Quantitative Process Management and Causal Analysis and Resolution.

If an organization first adopts CMMI and then decides to adopt Six Sigma as well, a measurement program already exists. The measurements may be immature, strictly collected, and in some way analyzed, but perhaps not statistically managed. Six Sigma will lead the organization into a high-maturity measurement program. Six Sigma will also be the stimulus for process improvement since it will target variance and where improvements will best benefit the organization, its products, and its customers.

In some cases, organizations simultaneously adopt Six Sigma and CMMI. It has been demonstrated that the rate of recognizing CMMI maturity is clearly enhanced by the adoption of Six Sigma.

Likewise, by using CMMI, the organization can recognize the measurements and process effectiveness that would be of the greatest benefit to assign a tolerance. Realistic control limits or tolerances assist managers in using measurement effectively to manage the project. Without realistic tolerances on measurement, decisions can be erroneous at worst, or hampered at best. The Six Sigma methodologies coupled with CMMI processes allow the organization the capability to focus on the voice of both the customer and the process. Thus, the benefits are recognized both internally and externally. In addition to enhancing the normal rate of level recognition, benefits associated with defect reduction and defect rate detection can be enhanced significantly.

It is very difficult for any organization to spend internal dollars wisely. There is a constant battle for resources. There is also the burden of proof for return on investment. An organization has a short timeline for seeing the benefits of adopting process improvement methodologies. Therefore, an informed decision is critical for the organization. It is valid to assume that two separate process initiatives, disjointed but overlapping, will cost the organization more than two integrated process improvement initiatives. I hope that this perspective starts some organizations with a thought process toward ascertaining that integrated adoption of CMMI and Six Sigma is cost effective for organizations committed to quality. References are provided to enhance the organization's decision analysis and resolution process as it decides how to spend its resources to improve quality.

Your Approach to Process Improvement

To demonstrate how to use this model, let us look at two different scenarios. Scenario 1 is an electronic systems developer that wants to improve its product development processes using a continuous approach. Scenario 2 is a software development company that uses IPPD, has been using the Software CMM, and now wants to use CMMI. This company most recently has been rated at maturity level 3 using the Software CMM (version 1.1).

Scenario 1

In this scenario, you are using a continuous approach and therefore you select the processes that are important to your business objectives.

Since there are 22 process areas to choose from, this is usually too many to focus on when starting out. You may need to narrow your focus. For example, you may find that your competitor always releases its product before yours. You may choose to focus on improving your engineering and project management processes.

Building on this decision, you select all the Engineering process areas as a starting point: Product Integration, Requirements Development, Requirements Management, Technical Solution, Validation, and Verification. You also select Project Planning and Project Monitoring and Control.

You may at this point decide that eight process areas are still too many to focus on initially, and you decide that the requirements process is really where the problems are. Consequently, you select the Requirements Development and Requirements Management process areas to begin your improvement efforts.

Next you decide how much improvement is needed in the requirements area. Do you have any processes in place already? If you do not, your process improvement objective may be to get to capability level 1.

Do you have your requirements development and management processes in place for each project, but they are not managed processes? For example, policies, training, and tools are not implemented to support the processes. If your requirements processes are in place but there is no supporting infrastructure, your process improvement objective may be to get to capability level 2.

Do you have all your requirements development and management processes and their management in place, but each project performs these processes differently? For example, your requirements elicitation process is not performed consistently across the organization. If this is the case, your process improvement objective may be to get to capability level 3.

Do you consistently manage and perform your requirements development and management processes, but do not have an objective way to control and improve these processes? If this is the case, your process improvement objective may be to get to capability level 4.

Do you want to ensure that you are selecting the right subprocesses to improve based on quantitative objectives to maximize your business? If so, your process improvement objective may be to get to capability level 5 for selected processes. In the description of each process area, remember to look for amplifications introduced by the phrases "For Hardware Engineering," "For Systems Engineering," and "For Software Engineering." Use all information that has no specific markings, and the material in the shaded boxes labeled "Continuous Only."

As you can see from this scenario, you need to understand which processes need improvement and how much you want to mature each process. This way of proceeding reflects the fundamental principle behind the continuous representation.

Scenario 2

In the second scenario, you are a software development company using IPPD, using the Software CMM, and you want to use CMMI. You select the process areas at maturity levels 2 and 3 and choose the CMMI for Development +IPPD model.

This selection includes the following seven process areas at maturity level 2: Requirements Management, Project Planning, Project Monitoring and Control, Supplier Agreement Management, Measurement and Analysis, Process and Product Quality Assurance, and Configuration Management. It also includes the following 11 process areas at maturity level 3: Requirements Development, Technical Solution, Product Integration, Verification, Validation, Organizational Process Focus, Organizational Process Definition +IPPD, Organizational Training, Integrated Project Management +IPPD, Risk Management, and Decision Analysis and Resolution. You will also include the IPPD additions.

Since you have already been rated at maturity level 3 for the Software CMM, look at the CMMI process areas that were not in the Software CMM. These process areas include Measurement and Analysis, Requirements Development, Technical Solution, Product Integration, Verification, Validation, Risk Management, and Decision Analysis and Resolution. Determine if you have these processes in your organization even though they were not described in the Software CMM. If any processes in place correspond to these process areas and the other process areas that were in the Software CMM, perform a gap analysis against the goals and practices to make sure you addressed the intent of each CMMI process area.

Remember, in each process area you select, to look for information labeled "For Software Engineering" and "IPPD Addition." Use all information that has no specific markings, as well as the material in boxes labeled "Staged Only."

As you can see, the information provided in this book can be used in a variety of ways, depending on your improvement needs. The overall goal of CMMI is to provide a framework that can share consistent process improvement best practices and approaches, but can be flexible enough to address the rapidly changing needs of the community.

CHAPTER 2

PROCESS AREA COMPONENTS

This chapter describes the components of each process area, generic goal, and generic practice. Understanding the meaning of these components is critical to using the information in Part Two effectively. If you are unfamiliar with Part Two, you may want to skim the Generic Goals and Generic Practices section and a couple of process area sections to get a general feel for the content and layout before reading this chapter.

Required, Expected, and Informative Components

Model components are grouped into three categories—required, expected, and informative—that reflect how to interpret them.

Required Components

Required components describe what an organization must achieve to satisfy a process area. This achievement must be visibly implemented in an organization's processes. The required components in CMMI are the specific and generic goals. Goal satisfaction is used in appraisals as the basis for deciding whether a process area has been achieved and satisfied.

Expected Components

Expected components describe what an organization may implement to achieve a required component. Expected components guide those who implement improvements or perform appraisals. Expected components include the specific and generic practices.

Before goals can be considered satisfied, either the practices as described, or acceptable alternatives to them, are present in the planned and implemented processes of the organization.

Informative Components

Informative components provide details that help organizations get started in thinking about how to approach the required and expected components. Subpractices, typical work products, amplifications, generic practice elaborations, goal and practice titles, goal and practice notes, and references are examples of informative model components.

The CMMI glossary of terms is not a required, expected, or informative component of CMMI models. You should interpret the terms in the glossary in the context of the model component in which they appear.

Components Associated with Part Two

The model components associated with Part Two can be summarized to illustrate their relationships, as shown in Figure 2.1.

The following sections provide detailed descriptions of the model components.

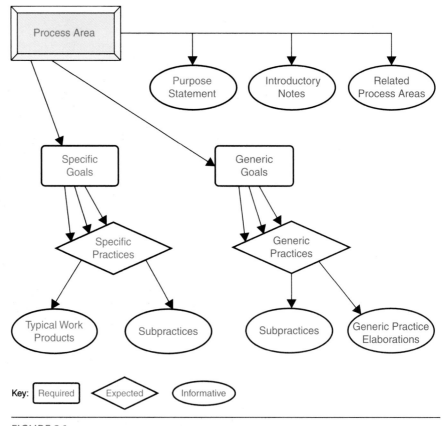

FIGURE 2.1
CMMI Model Components

Process Areas

A process area is a cluster of related practices in an area that, when implemented collectively, satisfy a set of goals considered important for making improvement in that area.

There are 22 process areas, presented here in alphabetical order by acronym:

- Causal Analysis and Resolution (CAR)
- Configuration Management (CM)
- Decision Analysis and Resolution (DAR)
- Integrated Project Management +IPPD (IPM+IPPD)[1]
- Measurement and Analysis (MA)
- Organizational Innovation and Deployment (OID)
- Organizational Process Definition +IPPD (OPD+IPPD)[1]
- Organizational Process Focus (OPF)
- Organizational Process Performance (OPP)
- Organizational Training (OT)
- Product Integration (PI)
- Project Monitoring and Control (PMC)
- Project Planning (PP)
- Process and Product Quality Assurance (PPQA)
- Quantitative Project Management (QPM)
- Requirements Development (RD)
- Requirements Management (REQM)
- Risk Management (RSKM)
- Supplier Agreement Management (SAM)
- Technical Solution (TS)
- Validation (VAL)
- Verification (VER)

Purpose Statements

The purpose statement describes the purpose of the process area and is an informative component.

For example, the purpose statement of the Organizational Process Definition process area is "The purpose of Organizational Process Definition (OPD) is to establish and maintain a usable set of organizational process assets and work environment standards."

---

1. This process area has "+IPPD" after its name because it contains a goal and practices that are specific to IPPD. The material specific to IPPD is called an IPPD addition. All process areas with IPPD goals have "+IPPD" after their name.

Introductory Notes

The introductory notes section of the process area describes the major concepts covered in the process area and is an informative component.

An example from the introductory notes of the Project Planning process area is "Planning begins with requirements that define the product and project."

Related Process Areas

The related process areas section lists references to related process areas and reflects the high-level relationships among the process areas. The related process areas section is an informative component.

An example of a reference found in the related process areas section of the Project Planning process area is "Refer to the Risk Management process area for more information about identifying and managing risks."

Specific Goals

A specific goal describes the unique characteristics that must be present to satisfy the process area. A specific goal is a required model component and is used in appraisals to help determine whether a process area is satisfied.

For example, a specific goal from the Configuration Management process area is "Integrity of baselines is established and maintained."

Only the statement of the specific goal is a required model component. The title of a specific goal (preceded by the goal number) and any notes associated with the goal are considered informative model components.

Generic Goals

Generic goals are called "generic" because the same goal statement applies to multiple process areas. A generic goal describes the characteristics that must be present to institutionalize the processes that implement a process area. A generic goal is a required model component and is used in appraisals to determine whether a process area is satisfied. (See the Generic Goals and Generic Practices section on page 151 for a more detailed description of generic goals.)

An example of a generic goal is "The process is institutionalized as a defined process."

Only the statement of the generic goal is a required model component. The title of a generic goal (preceded by the goal number) and any notes associated with the goal are considered informative model components.

Specific Goal and Practice Summaries

The specific goal and practice summary provides a high-level summary of the specific goals, which are required components, and the specific practices, which are expected components. The specific goal and practice summary is an informative component.

Specific Practices

A specific practice is the description of an activity that is considered important in achieving the associated specific goal. The specific practices describe the activities that are expected to result in achievement of the specific goals of a process area. A specific practice is an expected model component.

For example, a specific practice from the Project Monitoring and Control process area is "Monitor commitments against those identified in the project plan."

Only the statement of the specific practice is an expected model component. The title of the specific practice (preceded by the practice number) and any notes associated with the specific practice are considered informative model components.

Typical Work Products

The typical work products section lists sample output from a specific practice. These examples are called typical work products because there are often other work products that are just as effective but are not listed. A typical work product is an informative model component.

For example, a typical work product for the specific practice "Monitor the actual values of the project planning parameters against the project" in the Project Monitoring and Control process area is "Records of significant deviations."

Subpractices

A subpractice is a detailed description that provides guidance for interpreting and implementing a specific or generic practice. Subpractices may be worded as if prescriptive, but are actually an informative component meant only to provide ideas that may be useful for process improvement.

For example, a subpractice for the specific practice "Take corrective action on identified issues" in the Project Monitoring and Control process area is "Determine and document the appropriate actions needed to address the identified issues."

Generic Practices

Generic practices are called "generic" because the same practice applies to multiple process areas. A generic practice is the description of an activity that is considered important in achieving the associated generic goal. A generic practice is an expected model component.

For example, a generic practice for the generic goal "The process is institutionalized as a managed process" is "Provide adequate resources for performing the process, developing the work products, and providing the services of the process."

Only the statement of the generic practice is an expected model component. The title of a generic practice (preceded by the practice number) and any notes associated with the practice are considered informative model components.

To reduce the repetitiveness of this information and to conserve the number of pages required to present this information, only the generic practice title, statement, and elaborations appear in the process areas. (See the Generic Goals and Generic Practices section on page 151 for a complete description of the generic practices.)

Generic Practice Elaborations

A generic practice elaboration appears after a generic practice in a process area to provide guidance on how the generic practice should be applied uniquely to the process area. A generic practice elaboration is an informative model component.

For example, a generic practice elaboration after the generic practice "Establish and maintain an organizational policy for planning and performing the project planning process" in the Project Planning process area is "This policy establishes organizational expectations for estimating the planning parameters, making internal and external commitments, and developing the plan for managing the project."

Supporting Informative Components

In many places, further information is needed to describe a concept. This informative material is provided in the form of the following components:

- Notes
- Examples
- Amplifications
- References

Notes

A note is text that can accompany nearly any other model component. It may provide detail, background, or rationale. A note is an informative model component.

For example, a note that accompanies the specific practice "Implement the selected action proposals that were developed in causal analysis" in the Causal Analysis and Resolution process area is "Only changes that prove to be of value should be considered for broad implementation."

Examples

An example is a component comprising text and often a list of items, usually in a box, that can accompany nearly any other component and provides one or more examples to clarify a concept or described activity. An example is an informative model component.

The following is an example that accompanies the subpractice "Document noncompliance issues when they cannot be resolved within the project" under the specific practice "Communicate quality issues and ensure resolution of noncompliance issues with the staff and managers" in the Process and Product Quality Assurance process area.

Examples of ways to resolve noncompliance within the project include the following:

• Fixing the noncompliance
• Changing the process descriptions, standards, or procedures that were violated
• Obtaining a waiver to cover the noncompliance issue

Amplifications

An amplification is a note or example that is relevant to a particular discipline. The disciplines covered in this model are hardware engineering, systems engineering, and software engineering.

Each amplification is labeled with a heading that indicates the discipline to which it applies. For example, an amplification for software engineering is labeled "For Software Engineering." An amplification is an informative model component.

An example of an amplification is the one that accompanies the specific practice "Establish and maintain the overall project plan content" in the Project Planning process area. The amplification states "For Hardware Engineering: For hardware, the planning document is often referred to as a hardware development plan. Development activities in preparation for production may be included in the hardware development plan or defined in a separate production plan."

References

A reference is a pointer to additional or more detailed information in related process areas and can accompany nearly any other model component. A reference is an informative model component.

For example, a reference that accompanies the specific practice "Select the subprocesses that compose the project's defined process based on historical stability and capability data" in the Quantitative Project Management process area is "Refer to the Organizational Process Definition process area for more information about the organization's process asset library, which might include a process element of known and needed capability."

Numbering Scheme

Specific and generic goals are numbered sequentially. Each specific goal begins with the prefix SG (e.g., SG 1). Each generic goal begins with the prefix GG (e.g., GG 2).

Each specific practice begins with the prefix SP, followed by a number in the form $x.y$ (e.g., SP 1.1). The x is the same number as the goal to which the specific practice maps. The y is the sequence number of the specific practice under the specific goal.

An example of specific practice numbering is in the Project Planning process area. The first specific practice is numbered SP 1.1 and the second is SP 1.2.

Each generic practice begins with the prefix GP, followed by a number in the form $x.y$ (e.g., GP 1.1). The x corresponds to the number of the generic goal. The y is the sequence number of the generic practice under the generic goal. For example, the first generic practice associated with GG 2 is numbered GP 2.1 and the second is GP 2.2.

Typographical Conventions

The typographical conventions used in this model were designed to enable you to select what you need and use it effectively. We present model components in formats that allow you to find them quickly on the page.

Figures 2.2 through 2.4 are sample pages from process areas in Part Two; they show the different process area components, labeled so that you can identify them. Notice that components differ typographically so that you can easily identify each one.

Representation-Specific Content

In Part Two, you will notice that some components in the Generic Practices by Goal section of each process area are shaded and labeled "Staged Only," "Continuous Only," or "Continuous/Maturity Levels 3–5." Sometimes these labels are abbreviated, if the amount of space available makes it necessary.

Components that are not marked apply to both representations. Components marked "Staged Only" apply only if you are using the staged representation. Components marked "Continuous Only" apply only if you are using the continuous representation. (See Figure 2.4 for an example.)

Components marked "Continuous/Maturity Levels 3–5" apply if you are using the continuous representation or if you are using the staged representation and are pursuing maturity level 3, 4, or 5. However, these components do not apply if you are pursuing a maturity level 2 rating using the staged representation.

Additions

An addition can be informative material, a specific practice, a specific goal, or a process area that extends the scope of a model or emphasizes a particular aspect of its use. In this document all additions apply to IPPD. An example of an addition is the one from the Organizational Training process area that appears after specific goal 1, "Establish an Organizational Training Capability." The addition states, "Cross-functional training, leadership training, interpersonal skills training, and training in the skills needed to integrate appropriate business and technical functions is needed by integrated team members. The potentially wider range of requirements and participant backgrounds may require relevant stakeholders who were not involved in requirements development to take cross training in the disciplines involved in product design in order to commit to requirements with a full understanding of the range of requirements and their interrelationships."

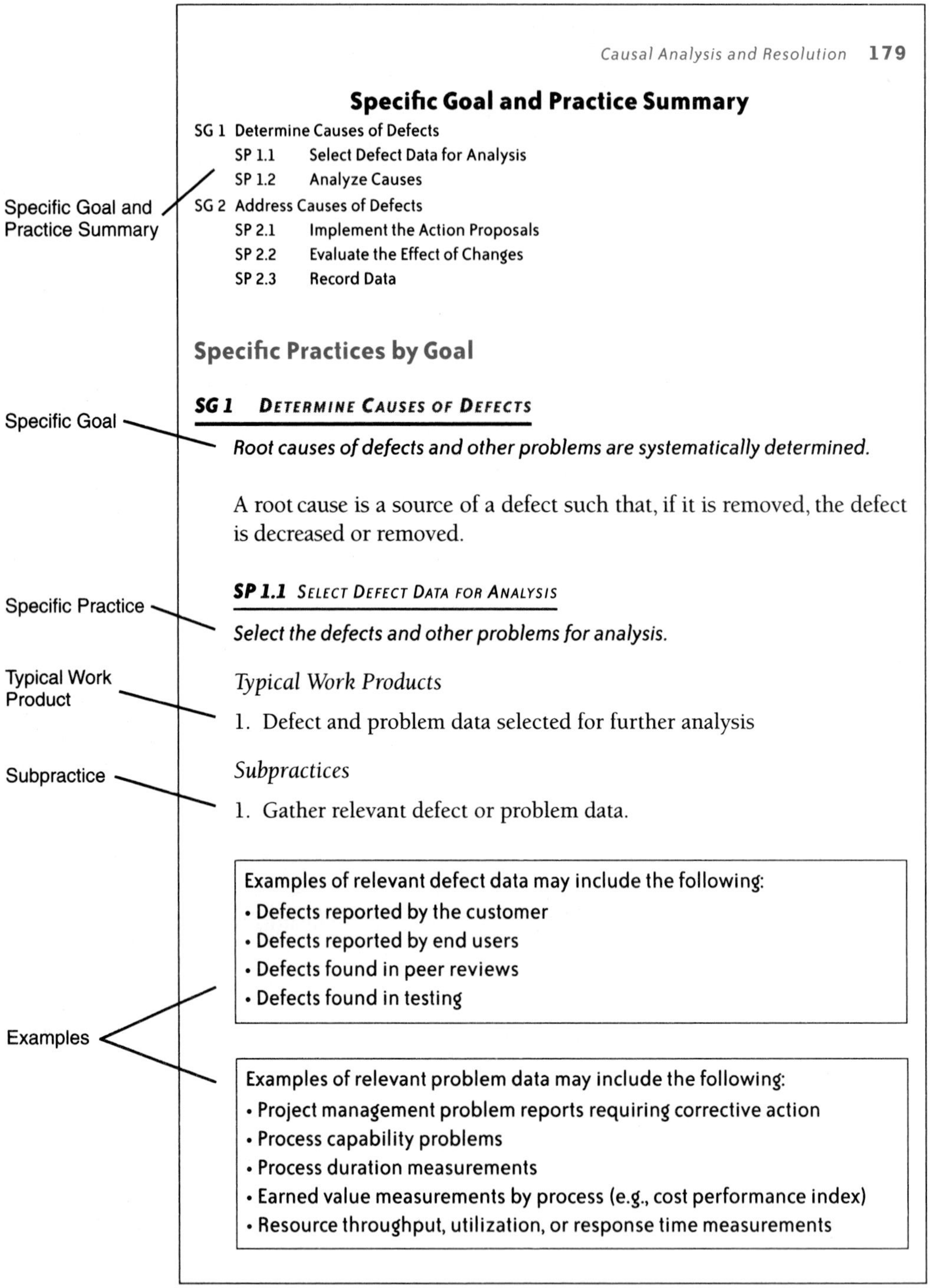

Specific Goal and Practice Summary

Specific Goal

Specific Practice

Typical Work Product

Subpractice

Examples

Specific Goal and Practice Summary

SG 1 Determine Causes of Defects
    SP 1.1   Select Defect Data for Analysis
    SP 1.2   Analyze Causes
SG 2 Address Causes of Defects
    SP 2.1   Implement the Action Proposals
    SP 2.2   Evaluate the Effect of Changes
    SP 2.3   Record Data

Specific Practices by Goal

SG 1   DETERMINE CAUSES OF DEFECTS

Root causes of defects and other problems are systematically determined.

A root cause is a source of a defect such that, if it is removed, the defect is decreased or removed.

SP 1.1   SELECT DEFECT DATA FOR ANALYSIS

Select the defects and other problems for analysis.

Typical Work Products

1. Defect and problem data selected for further analysis

Subpractices

1. Gather relevant defect or problem data.

> Examples of relevant defect data may include the following:
> - Defects reported by the customer
> - Defects reported by end users
> - Defects found in peer reviews
> - Defects found in testing

> Examples of relevant problem data may include the following:
> - Project management problem reports requiring corrective action
> - Process capability problems
> - Process duration measurements
> - Earned value measurements by process (e.g., cost performance index)
> - Resource throughput, utilization, or response time measurements

FIGURE 2.2
Sample Page from CAR

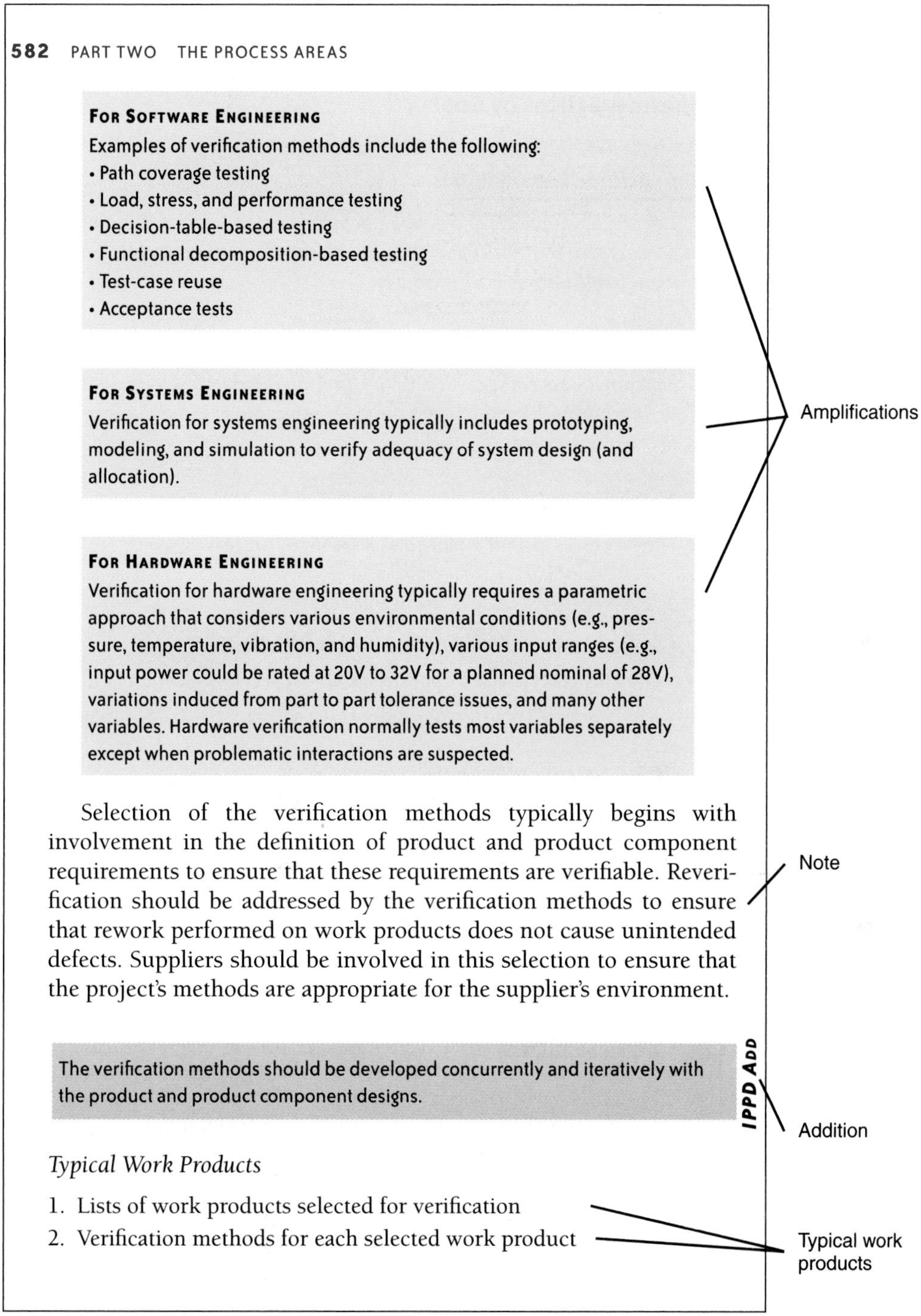

FOR SOFTWARE ENGINEERING

Examples of verification methods include the following:
- Path coverage testing
- Load, stress, and performance testing
- Decision-table-based testing
- Functional decomposition-based testing
- Test-case reuse
- Acceptance tests

FOR SYSTEMS ENGINEERING

Verification for systems engineering typically includes prototyping, modeling, and simulation to verify adequacy of system design (and allocation).

FOR HARDWARE ENGINEERING

Verification for hardware engineering typically requires a parametric approach that considers various environmental conditions (e.g., pressure, temperature, vibration, and humidity), various input ranges (e.g., input power could be rated at 20V to 32V for a planned nominal of 28V), variations induced from part to part tolerance issues, and many other variables. Hardware verification normally tests most variables separately except when problematic interactions are suspected.

Amplifications

Selection of the verification methods typically begins with involvement in the definition of product and product component requirements to ensure that these requirements are verifiable. Reverification should be addressed by the verification methods to ensure that rework performed on work products does not cause unintended defects. Suppliers should be involved in this selection to ensure that the project's methods are appropriate for the supplier's environment.

Note

The verification methods should be developed concurrently and iteratively with the product and product component designs.

IPPD ADD

Addition

Typical Work Products

1. Lists of work products selected for verification
2. Verification methods for each selected work product

Typical work products

FIGURE 2.3
Sample Page from VER

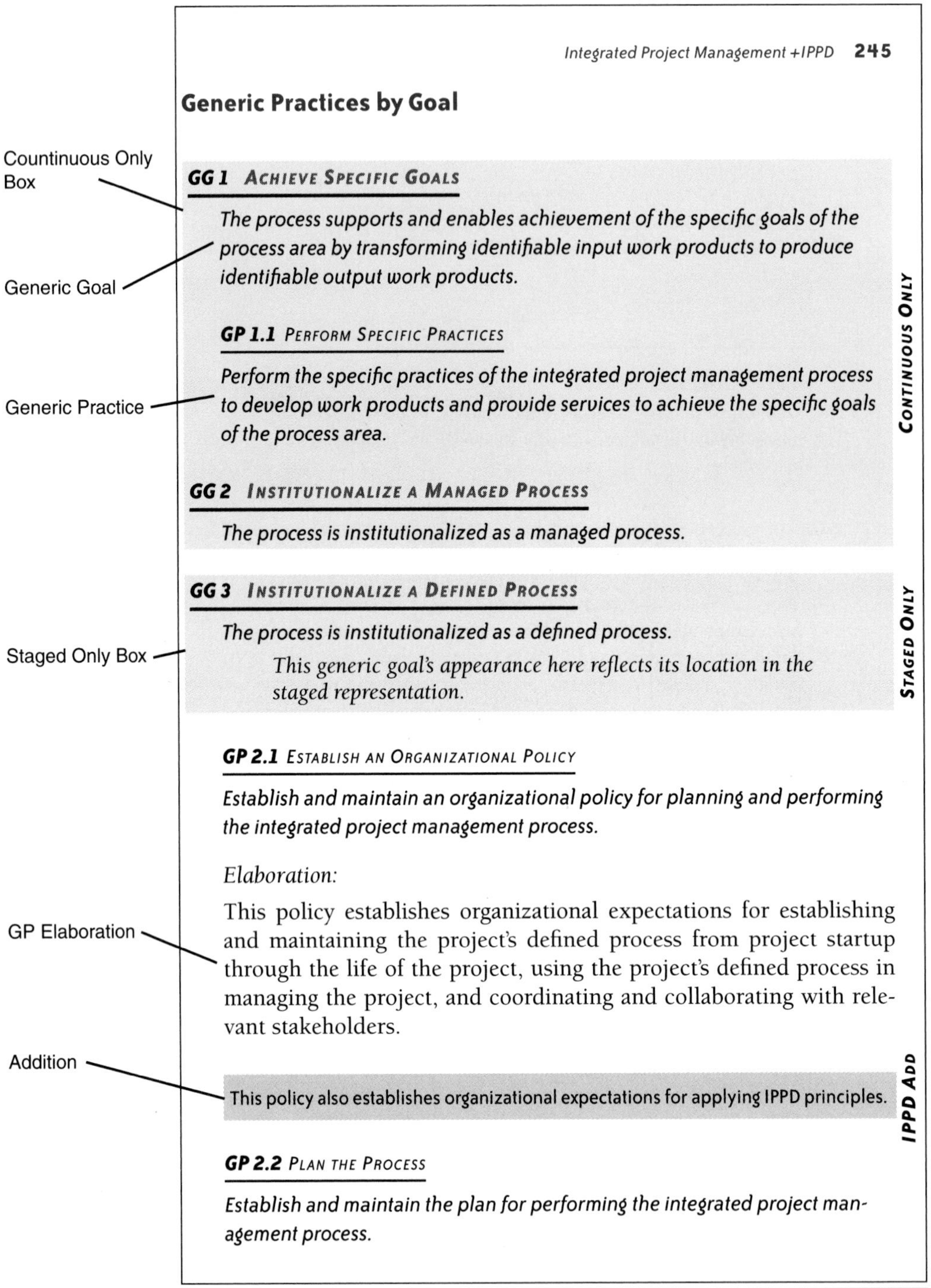
Countinuous Only Box
Generic Goal
Generic Practice
Staged Only Box
GP Elaboration
Addition
Integrated Project Management +IPPD 245
Continuous Only
Staged Only
IPPD Add

Generic Practices by Goal

GG 1 ACHIEVE SPECIFIC GOALS

The process supports and enables achievement of the specific goals of the process area by transforming identifiable input work products to produce identifiable output work products.

GP 1.1 PERFORM SPECIFIC PRACTICES

Perform the specific practices of the integrated project management process to develop work products and provide services to achieve the specific goals of the process area.

GG 2 INSTITUTIONALIZE A MANAGED PROCESS

The process is institutionalized as a managed process.

GG 3 INSTITUTIONALIZE A DEFINED PROCESS

The process is institutionalized as a defined process.

This generic goal's appearance here reflects its location in the staged representation.

GP 2.1 ESTABLISH AN ORGANIZATIONAL POLICY

Establish and maintain an organizational policy for planning and performing the integrated project management process.

Elaboration:

This policy establishes organizational expectations for establishing and maintaining the project's defined process from project startup through the life of the project, using the project's defined process in managing the project, and coordinating and collaborating with relevant stakeholders.

This policy also establishes organizational expectations for applying IPPD principles.

GP 2.2 PLAN THE PROCESS

Establish and maintain the plan for performing the integrated project management process.

FIGURE 2.4
Sample Page from IPM +IPPD

CHAPTER 3

TYING IT ALL TOGETHER

Now that you have been introduced to the components of CMMI models, you need to understand how they all fit together to meet your process improvement needs [Dymond 2004]. In this chapter, we introduce the concept of levels and show how the process areas are organized and used. To do this, we need to revisit the discussion that began in Chapter 1.

Understanding Levels

Levels are used in CMMI to describe an evolutionary path recommended for an organization that wants to improve the processes it uses to develop and maintain its products and services. Levels can also be the outcome of the rating activity of appraisals.[1] Appraisals can be performed for organizations that comprise entire (usually small) companies, or for smaller groups such as a group of projects or a division within a company.

CMMI supports two improvement paths. One path enables organizations to incrementally improve processes corresponding to an individual process area (or process areas) selected by the organization. The other path enables organizations to improve a set of related processes by incrementally addressing successive sets of process areas.

These two improvement paths are associated with the two types of levels that correspond to the two representations discussed in Chapter 1. For the continuous representation, we use the term "capability level." For the staged representation, we use the term "maturity level."

---

1. For more information about appraisals, refer to *Appraisal Requirements for CMMI and the Standard CMMI Appraisal Method for Process Improvement Method Definition Document* [SEI 2006a, SEI 2006b].

Regardless of which representation you select, the concept of levels is the same. Levels characterize improvement from an ill-defined state to a state that uses quantitative information to determine and manage improvements that are needed to meet an organization's business objectives.

To reach a particular level, an organization must satisfy all of the appropriate goals of the process area or set of process areas that are targeted for improvement, regardless of whether it is a capability or a maturity level.

Both representations also provide ways to implement process improvement to achieve business objectives. Both representations provide the same essential content and use the same model components.

Structures of the Continuous and Staged Representations

Figure 3.1 illustrates the structures of the continuous and staged representations. The differences jump out at you immediately when you look at the structure of both representations. The staged representation utilizes maturity levels, whereas the continuous representation utilizes capability levels.

What may strike you as you compare these two representations is their similarity. Both have many of the same components (e.g., process areas, specific goals, and specific practices) and these components have the same hierarchy and configuration.

What is not readily apparent from the high-level view in Figure 3.1 is that the continuous representation focuses on process area capability as measured by capability levels and the staged representation focuses on organizational maturity as measured by maturity levels. These dimensions (the capability/maturity dimensions) of CMMI are used for benchmarking and appraisal activities, as well as guiding an organization's improvement efforts.

- Capability levels, which belong to a continuous representation, apply to an organization's process improvement achievement in individual process areas. These levels are a means for incrementally improving the processes corresponding to a given process area. There are six capability levels, numbered 0 through 5.
- Maturity levels, which belong to a staged representation, apply to an organization's process improvement achievement across multiple process areas. These levels are a means of predicting the general outcomes of the next project undertaken. There are five maturity levels, numbered 1 through 5.

Continuous Representation

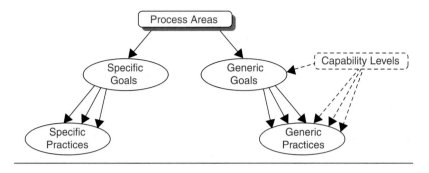

Staged Representation

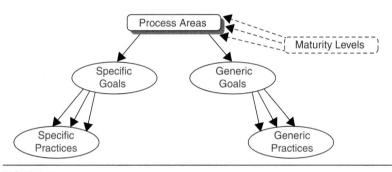

FIGURE 3.1
Structures of the Continuous and Staged Representations

Table 3.1 compares the six capability levels to the five maturity levels. Notice that the names of four of the levels are the same in both representations. The differences are that there is no maturity level 0 for the staged representation, and at level 1, the capability

TABLE 3.1 Comparison of Capability and Maturity Levels

Level	Continuous Representation Capability Levels	Staged Representation Maturity Levels
Level 0	Incomplete	N/A
Level 1	Performed	Initial
Level 2	Managed	Managed
Level 3	Defined	Defined
Level 4	Quantitatively Managed	Quantitatively Managed
Level 5	Optimizing	Optimizing

level is Performed, whereas the maturity level is Initial. Therefore, the starting point is different for the two representations.

The continuous representation is concerned with selecting both a particular process area to improve and the desired capability level for that process area. In this context, whether a process is performed or incomplete is important. Therefore, the name "incomplete" is given to the continuous representation starting point.

Because the staged representation is concerned with the overall maturity of the organization, whether individual processes are performed or incomplete is not the primary focus. Therefore, the name "initial" is given to the staged representation starting point.

Both capability levels and maturity levels provide a way to measure how well organizations can and do improve their processes. However, the associated approach to process improvement is different.

Understanding Capability Levels

To support those using the continuous representation, all CMMI models reflect capability levels in their design and content. A capability level consists of a generic goal and its related generic practices as they relate to a process area, which can improve the organization's processes associated with that process area. As you satisfy the generic goal and its generic practices at each capability level, you reap the benefits of process improvement for that process area.

The six capability levels, designated by the numbers 0 through 5, are as follows:

0. Incomplete
1. Performed
2. Managed
3. Defined
4. Quantitatively Managed
5. Optimizing

The fact that capability levels 2 through 5 use the same terms as generic goals 2 through 5 is intentional because each of these generic goals and practices reflects the meaning of the capability levels in terms of goals and practices you can implement. (See the Generic Goals and Generic Practices section on page 151 for more information about generic goals and practices.) A short description of each capability level follows.

Capability Level 0: Incomplete

An "incomplete process" is a process that either is not performed or partially performed. One or more of the specific goals of the process area are not satisfied, and no generic goals exist for this level since there is no reason to institutionalize a partially performed process.

Capability Level 1: Performed

A capability level 1 process is characterized as a "performed process." A performed process is a process that satisfies the specific goals of the process area. It supports and enables the work needed to produce work products.

Although capability level 1 results in important improvements, those improvements can be lost over time if they are not institutionalized. The application of institutionalization (the CMMI generic practices at capability levels 2 through 5) helps to ensure that improvements are maintained.

Capability Level 2: Managed

A capability level 2 process is characterized as a "managed process." A managed process is a performed (capability level 1) process that has the basic infrastructure in place to support the process. It is planned and executed in accordance with policy; employs skilled people who have adequate resources to produce controlled outputs; involves relevant stakeholders; is monitored, controlled, and reviewed; and is evaluated for adherence to its process description. The process discipline reflected by capability level 2 helps to ensure that existing practices are retained during times of stress.

Capability Level 3: Defined

A capability level 3 process is characterized as a "defined process." A defined process is a managed (capability level 2) process that is tailored from the organization's set of standard processes according to the organization's tailoring guidelines, and contributes work products, measures, and other process improvement information to the organizational process assets.

A critical distinction between capability levels 2 and 3 is the scope of standards, process descriptions, and procedures. At capability level 2, the standards, process descriptions, and procedures may be quite different in each specific instance of the process (e.g., on a particular project). At capability level 3, the standards, process descriptions, and procedures for a project are tailored from the organization's set of standard processes to suit a particular project or organizational unit and therefore are more consistent, except for the differences allowed by the tailoring guidelines.

Another critical distinction is that at capability level 3, processes are typically described more rigorously than at capability level 2. A defined process clearly states the purpose, inputs, entry criteria, activities, roles, measures, verification steps, outputs, and exit criteria. At capability level 3, processes are managed more proactively using an understanding of the interrelationships of the process activities and detailed measures of the process, its work products, and its services.

Capability Level 4: Quantitatively Managed

A capability level 4 process is characterized as a "quantitatively managed process." A quantitatively managed process is a defined (capability level 3) process that is controlled using statistical and other quantitative techniques. Quantitative objectives for quality and process performance are established and used as criteria in managing the process. Quality and process performance is understood in statistical terms and is managed throughout the life of the process.

Capability Level 5: Optimizing

A capability level 5 process is characterized as an "optimizing process." An optimizing process is a quantitatively managed (capability level 4) process that is improved based on an understanding of the common causes of variation inherent in the process. The focus of an optimizing process is on continually improving the range of process performance through both incremental and innovative improvements.

Remember that capability levels 2 through 5 use the same terms as generic goals 2 through 5, and a detailed description of these terms appears in the Generic Goals and Generic Practices section on page 151.

Advancing through Capability Levels

The capability levels of a process area are achieved through the application of generic practices or suitable alternatives to the processes associated with that process area.

Reaching capability level 1 for a process area is equivalent to saying that the processes associated with that process area are "performed processes."

Reaching capability level 2 for a process area is equivalent to saying that there is a policy that indicates you will perform the process.

There is a plan for performing it, resources are provided, responsibilities are assigned, training to perform it is provided, selected work products related to performing the process are controlled, and so on. In other words, a capability level 2 process can be planned and monitored just like any project or support activity.

Reaching capability level 3 for a process area assumes that an organizational standard process exists associated with that process area, which can be tailored to the needs of the project. The processes in the organization are now more consistently defined and applied because they are based on organizational standard processes.

Reaching capability level 4 for a process area assumes that this process area is a key business driver that the organization wants to manage using quantitative and statistical techniques. This analysis gives the organization more visibility into the performance of selected subprocesses that will make it more competitive in the marketplace.

Reaching capability level 5 for a process area assumes that you have stabilized the selected subprocesses and that you want to reduce the common causes of variation within that process. Remember that variation is a natural occurrence in any process, so although it is conceptually feasible to improve all processes, it would not be economical to improve all processes to level 5. Again, you would concentrate on those processes that would help you to meet your business objectives.

Empirical Software Engineering Principles As a Basis for Process Improvement

by Victor R. Basili, Kathleen C. Dangle, and Michele A. Shaw

Thinking empirically about software engineering changes the way you think about process improvement.

Software engineering is an engineering discipline. Like other disciplines, software engineering requires an empirical paradigm that involves observing, building models, analyzing, and experimenting so that we can learn. We need to model the products, the processes, and the cause/effect relationships between them in the context of the organization and the project set. This empirical mindset provides a basis for choosing the appropriate processes, analyzing the effects of those selections, and packaging the resulting knowledge for reuse and evolution; it drives an effective process improvement initiative.

Empirical Software Engineering Principles

Several principles are associated with Empirical Software Engineering. In this section, we discuss a few of these principles related to software process improvement.

P1. Observe your business. Organizations have different characteristics, goals, and cultures; stakeholders have different and competing needs. Well-engineered software depends on many variables and context plays a significant role in defining the goals and objectives for what can be and what must be achieved. Organizations must strive to build quantitative and qualitative models to understand the cause-and-effect relationships between software processes and products in the context where software is being developed.

How else can these organizations articulate the differences and similarities among projects in the organization so that they know the context for selecting the processes to use to achieve their goals?

P2. Measurement is fundamental. Measurement is a standard abstraction process that allows us to build models or representations of what we observe so that we can reason about relationships in context. The use of models in conjunction with experience, judgment, and intuition can guide decision making. Measurement through models provides a mechanism for a fact-based investigation so that decisions are supported with facts versus a system of pure beliefs.

P3. Process is a variable. Process needs to be selected and tailored to solve the problem at hand. Organizations must find the right process for the right situation, so they need to understand the effects of the process under differing conditions. This means a practice must be measurable so that its effects can be quantified. It also means organizations need to compile evidence of what works under what circumstances.

P4. Stakeholders must make their goals explicit. There is a wide range of stakeholders for any project (e.g., customers, end users, contract managers, practitioners, and managers). The organization itself and different stakeholders have different goals and needs. Organizations must make these goals and needs explicit through models and measures so that they can be communicated, analyzed, synthesized, evaluated, and used to select and tailor the right processes. Making them explicit allows them to be remembered or packaged so that they can be used again.

P5. Learn from experience. Organizations have the opportunity to learn from their experiences and build their core competence in software engineering. For process improvement, the focus should be on learning about processes and how they interact with the environment on each project. This learning is evolutionary and each project should make the organization smarter about how to do the next project. But this learning must be deliberate and explicit or it will not be available for the organization to leverage.

P6. Software engineering is "big science." Improving the software engineering process must be done through observation and experimentation where the actual processes are performed and products developed. There is a synergistic relationship between practice and research. Industrial, government, and academic organizations must partner to expand and evolve software competencies. There are so many facets to software engineering that it requires multiple talents and differing expertise. We need real-world laboratories that allow us to see the interactions among teams, processes, and products.

Effective organizations understand and apply these principles in their day-to-day business.

The Role of Empirical Software Engineering in CMMI

At CMMI level 5, process improvement is intended to be an empirically based activity. Each project is planned and executed using practices that are selected based on the context of the environment, the project needs, and past experiences. A level 5 organization understands the relationship between process and product and is capable of manipulating process to achieve various product characteristics. It is this capability that provides the greatest value from process improvement to the organization.

Empirical thinking shifts the process improvement mindset from "putting processes in place" to "understanding the effects of processes so that *appropriate* processes can be adopted." Different decisions are made regarding how we choose improvement initiatives (prioritize), how we implement practices, and how we manage software efforts in projects and in organizations when our explicit approach is based on principles of empirical software engineering. That mindset should be in place at the beginning of the process improvement initiative, thereby focusing the effort on the real objectives of the project, the specific product and process problems, relevant experience with methods, and so on.

Organizations that are effective at implementing process improvement understand and apply empirical software engineering principles. Additionally, practices that support these principles are evident within CMMI, particularly at level 5. CMMI prescribes that data be used to make decisions about process definition at the project level as well as process change at the organizational level. *Measurement* and *learning* are catalysts for all of the practices; that is, they provide the bases for why specific practices are selected and how practices are implemented. Software engineering practices are refined and fine-tuned as their effects are better understood.

Adopting these principles early can have a profound effect on the success of the organization as you embark down the process improvement path.

Understanding Maturity Levels

To support those using the staged representation, all CMMI models reflect maturity levels in their design and content. A maturity level consists of related specific and generic practices for a predefined set of process areas that improve the organization's overall performance. The maturity level of an organization provides a way to predict an organization's performance in a given discipline or set of disciplines. Experience has shown that organizations do their best when they focus their process improvement efforts on a manageable number of process areas at a time and that those areas require increasing sophistication as the organization improves.

A maturity level is a defined evolutionary plateau for organizational process improvement. Each maturity level matures an important subset of the organization's processes, preparing it to move to the next maturity level. The maturity levels are measured by the achievement of the specific and generic goals associated with each predefined set of process areas.

There are five maturity levels, each a layer in the foundation for ongoing process improvement, designated by the numbers 1 through 5:

1. Initial
2. Managed
3. Defined

4. Quantitatively Managed
5. Optimizing

Remember that maturity levels 2 through 5 use the same terms as capability levels 2 through 5. This was intentional because the concepts of maturity levels and capability levels are complementary. Maturity levels are used to characterize organizational improvement relative to a set of process areas, and capability levels characterize organizational improvement relative to an individual process area.

Maturity Level 1: Initial

At maturity level 1, processes are usually ad hoc and chaotic. The organization usually does not provide a stable environment to support the processes. Success in these organizations depends on the competence and heroics of the people in the organization and not on the use of proven processes. In spite of this chaos, maturity level 1 organizations often produce products and services that work; however, they frequently exceed their budgets and do not meet their schedules.

Maturity level 1 organizations are characterized by a tendency to overcommit, abandonment of processes in a time of crisis, and an inability to repeat their successes.

Maturity Level 2: Managed

At maturity level 2, the projects of the organization have ensured that processes are planned and executed in accordance with policy; the projects employ skilled people who have adequate resources to produce controlled outputs; involve relevant stakeholders; are monitored, controlled, and reviewed; and are evaluated for adherence to their process descriptions. The process discipline reflected by maturity level 2 helps to ensure that existing practices are retained during times of stress. When these practices are in place, projects are performed and managed according to their documented plans.

At maturity level 2, the status of the work products and the delivery of services are visible to management at defined points (e.g., at major milestones and at the completion of major tasks). Commitments are established among relevant stakeholders and are revised as needed. Work products are appropriately controlled. The work products and services satisfy their specified process descriptions, standards, and procedures.

Maturity Level 3: Defined

At maturity level 3, processes are well characterized and understood, and are described in standards, procedures, tools, and methods. The organization's set of standard processes, which is the basis for maturity level 3, is established and improved over time. These standard processes are used to establish consistency across the organization. Projects establish their defined processes by tailoring the organization's set of standard processes according to tailoring guidelines. (See the glossary for a definition of "organization's set of standard processes.")

A critical distinction between maturity levels 2 and 3 is the scope of standards, process descriptions, and procedures. At maturity level 2, the standards, process descriptions, and procedures may be quite different in each specific instance of the process (e.g., on a particular project). At maturity level 3, the standards, process descriptions, and procedures for a project are tailored from the organization's set of standard processes to suit a particular project or organizational unit and therefore are more consistent, except for the differences allowed by the tailoring guidelines.

Another critical distinction is that at maturity level 3, processes are typically described more rigorously than at maturity level 2. A defined process clearly states the purpose, inputs, entry criteria, activities, roles, measures, verification steps, outputs, and exit criteria. At maturity level 3, processes are managed more proactively using an understanding of the interrelationships of the process activities and detailed measures of the process, its work products, and its services.

At maturity level 3, the organization must further mature the maturity level 2 process areas. The generic practices associated with generic goal 3 that were not addressed at maturity level 2 are applied to achieve maturity level 3.

Maturity Level 4: Quantitatively Managed

At maturity level 4, the organization and projects establish quantitative objectives for quality and process performance and use them as criteria in managing processes. Quantitative objectives are based on the needs of the customer, end users, organization, and process implementers. Quality and process performance is understood in statistical terms and is managed throughout the life of the processes [SEI 2001].

For selected subprocesses, detailed measures of process performance are collected and statistically analyzed. Quality and process-performance measures are incorporated into the organization's measurement repository to support fact-based decision making [McGarry 2000]. Special causes of process variation are identified and, where appropriate, the sources of special causes are corrected to prevent future occurrences. (See the definition of "special cause of process variation" in the glossary.)

A critical distinction between maturity levels 3 and 4 is the predictability of process performance. At maturity level 4, the performance of processes is controlled using statistical and other quantitative techniques, and is quantitatively predictable. At maturity level 3, processes are typically only qualitatively predictable.

Maturity Level 5: Optimizing

At maturity level 5, an organization continually improves its processes based on a quantitative understanding of the common causes of variation inherent in processes. (See the definition of "common cause of process variation" in the glossary.)

Maturity level 5 focuses on continually improving process performance through incremental and innovative process and technological improvements. Quantitative process improvement objectives for the organization are established, continually revised to reflect changing business objectives, and used as criteria in managing process improvement. The effects of deployed process improvements are measured and evaluated against the quantitative process improvement objectives. Both the defined processes and the organization's set of standard processes are targets of measurable improvement activities.

A critical distinction between maturity levels 4 and 5 is the type of process variation addressed. At maturity level 4, the organization is concerned with addressing special causes of process variation and providing statistical predictability of the results. Although processes may produce predictable results, the results may be insufficient to achieve the established objectives. At maturity level 5, the organization is concerned with addressing common causes of process variation and changing the process (to shift the mean of the process performance or reduce the inherent process variation experienced) to improve process performance and to achieve the established quantitative process improvement objectives.

Advancing Through Maturity Levels

Organizations can achieve progressive improvements in their organizational maturity by achieving control first at the project level, and continuing to the most advanced level—organization-wide continuous process improvement—using both quantitative and qualitative data to make decisions.

Since improved organizational maturity is associated with improvement in the range of expected results that can be achieved by an organization, it is one way of predicting the general outcomes of the organization's next project. For instance, at maturity level 2, the organization has been elevated from ad hoc to disciplined, by establishing sound project management. As your organization achieves the generic and specific goals for the set of process areas in a maturity level, you are increasing your organizational maturity and reaping the benefits of process improvement. Because each maturity level forms a necessary foundation for the next level, trying to skip maturity levels is usually counterproductive.

At the same time, you must recognize that process improvement efforts should focus on the needs of the organization in the context of its business environment and that process areas at higher maturity levels may address the current needs of an organization or project. For example, organizations seeking to move from maturity level 1 to maturity level 2 are frequently encouraged to establish a process group, which is addressed by the Organizational Process Focus process area that resides at maturity level 3. Although a process group is not a necessary characteristic of a maturity level 2 organization, it can be a useful part of the organization's approach to achieving maturity level 2.

This situation is sometimes characterized as establishing a maturity level 1 process group to bootstrap the maturity level 1 organization to maturity level 2. Maturity level 1 process improvement activities may depend primarily on the insight and competence of the process group staff until an infrastructure to support more disciplined and widespread improvement is in place.

Organizations can institute specific process improvements at any time they choose, even before they are prepared to advance to the maturity level at which the specific practice is recommended. In such situations, however, organizations should understand that the success of these improvements is at risk because the foundation for their successful institutionalization has not been completed. Processes without the proper foundation may fail at the very point they are needed most—under stress.

A defined process that is characteristic of a maturity level 3 organization can be placed at great risk if maturity level 2 management practices are deficient. For example, management may commit to a poorly planned schedule or fail to control changes to baselined requirements. Similarly, many organizations prematurely collect the detailed data characteristic of maturity level 4, only to find the data uninterpretable because of inconsistencies in processes and measurement definitions.

Another example of using processes associated with higher maturity-level process areas is in the building of products. Certainly, we would expect maturity level 1 organizations to perform requirements analysis, design, integration, and verification. These activities are not described until maturity level 3, however, where they are described as the coherent, well-integrated engineering processes that complement a maturing project management capability, put in place so that the engineering improvements are not lost by an ad hoc management process.

Process Improvement in a Small Company

by Khaled El Emam

In this brief perspective, I will describe how a small company implemented maturity level 2 and 3 processes of a CMMI staged model. In this case, both the organization (30 staff members) and the organizational unit developing software (a ten-member software development group and a five-member quality assurance group) were small.

Context

TrialStat Corporation develops software used in clinical trials of drug development. A number of FDA regulations apply to both the software and the processes used to develop and maintain that software. Because the software is used to collect and store sensitive personal health information, the security of the application is critical and is usually included in the scope of regulatory audits.

Implementing an Iterative Process

Because of competitive pressures, the release cycle for the application had to be short. A decision was made to adopt an agile methodology, which promised rapid releases—a release cycle lasting three weeks or less.

At the outset, the three-week release cycle created many problems and resulted in rapid burnout of the development team. The company was at risk of losing key developers, who were unwilling to work overtime and weekends to maintain the rapid release cycle. The short cycle also required curtailing many requirements analysis activities and minimizing quality assurance of the product—both of which were unacceptable.

The development team then experimented with increasing the release interval. After a few attempts, it was decided that a three-month interval was sufficient. This interval was short enough to address the rapidly changing business needs, but long enough to avoid some of the problems encountered with the shorter interval. The longer interval resulted in a development team that was not overburdened, early and sufficient requirements analysis work, and effective quality assurance.

This process demonstrated that that there is no inconsistency between using CMMI and implementing an agile development process with short release cycles. It was, in fact, an advantage to implement process improvements within this framework.

Introducing CMMI Practices Iteratively

Because of the regulated nature of the company's business, a strong process focus (Organizational Process Definition, or OPD) was necessary from the start. Standard operating procedures documenting all of the engineering and business processes were developed at the same time as project management practices were being implemented. Regular internal audits (Process and Product Quality Assurance, or PPQA) ensured process compliance.

Because of TrialStat's small size, there was no difference between organizational and project procedures. Training capabilities were not developed in-house, but were outsourced. However, training plans and records were maintained for all staff as part of the company's regulatory requirements (Organizational Training, or OT).

The iterative development process enabled the continuous introduction of new project practices (in the Project Management, Engineering, and Support process areas), and rapid feedback on their effectiveness. Each iteration represented an opportunity to introduce new processes, a new technology, or expertise (e.g., an individual with specialized skills). After three months, it was possible to determine whether the intervention succeeded and had the desired impact. If it did, it was kept for subsequent iterations. Those that caused problems were either adjusted or eliminated.

This mode of introducing changes imposed some constraints. The interventions could not be large; the development team had to learn, master, and apply them well enough to provide feedback.

Therefore, new practices had to be introduced gradually. For example, when peer reviews were introduced, they initially focused only on requirements. Only one or two interventions could be introduced in each iteration. If there were too many interventions, the development team could not focus on delivering features.

Formal CMMI-based process appraisals were not utilized. However, audits against FDA regulations and guidelines were commonly performed by third parties and clients to ensure compliance.

Measurement and Decision Making

The collection and use of metrics for decision making (Measurement and Analysis, or MA) started from the very beginning of the project, and was subsequently expanded in a series of iterations. First, data on post-release defects was collected. This data was necessary to manage and prioritize defect correction activities and resources. Once that system was in place, the metrics related to the ability to meet schedule targets were collected.

Scope management was the next issue. Because the delivery date of each iteration was fixed, flexibility involved controlling the scope. Features scheduled for each iteration were sized for a three-month cycle. In some cases, features were split and implemented over multiple releases. The challenge was coming up with an appropriate approach to measuring the size of the requirements early. Currently, using the number of use cases to measure the size of requirements has worked well in this environment.

The measurement of size and complexity became the subsequent focus of measurement. As the system grew, it became critical to manage its size and complexity. One approach used was to refactor specific parts of the system to reduce complexity.

Lessons Learned

Surprisingly few fundamental changes were needed to apply CMMI in a regulated environment. Many of the practices required in larger settings still applied. Because the company operates in a regulated environment, executive and investor support for process improvement existed from the outset. Therefore, in a different environment, additional effort may be required to obtain such support.

The iterative approach to implementing process improvements allowed the organization to incrementally and continuously improve its practices, and provided a rapid feedback mechanism to evaluate process changes. As more metrics are collected, it will become possible to quantitatively evaluate the improvements.

Process documentation proved helpful for this small organization, making it easier to integrate new staff and ensure that they contributed sooner. Without that documentation, corporate growth would have been more painful. The people typically attracted to a small organization are not necessarily process oriented. Process documentation contributed to establishing clear ground rules for new staff and enforcing a process-oriented corporate culture.

Requirements development and requirements management processes ensured predictability. These processes were addressed early in the improvement effort and served as a foundation for other engineering processes. For a company in the early stages of market penetration, it is critical that the requirements are right for each iteration.

Measurement began, and was needed, from the start. As the organization's practices matured, the types of things that were measured changed, as did the types of decisions made based on that data.

TrialStat's experience demonstrated that CMMI can work well in a small organizational setting. Process improvement in a small setting requires a gradual and incremental approach to introducing change to ensure that the organization is not overburdened with a level of change that affects its ability to deliver its product. A pure agile approach did not seem to work well; however, with some modification and in combination with CMMI, some agile practices could be of benefit to the organization.

Process Areas

Process areas are viewed differently in the two representations. Figure 3.2 compares views of how process areas are used in the continuous representation and the staged representation.

The continuous representation enables the organization to choose the focus of its process improvement efforts by choosing those process areas, or sets of interrelated process areas, that best benefit the organization and its business objectives. Although there are some limits on what an organization can choose because of the dependencies among process areas, the organization has considerable freedom in its selection.

To support those using the continuous representation, process areas are organized into four categories: Process Management, Project Management, Engineering, and Support. These categories emphasize the relationships that exist among the process areas and are discussed in Chapter 4.

Continuous
Target Profile

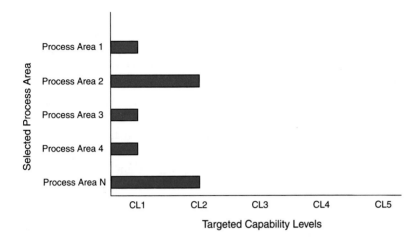

Staged
Selected Maturity Level

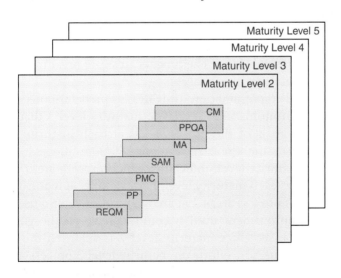

▨ = Groups of process areas chosen for process improvement to achieve maturity level 3

FIGURE 3.2
Process Areas in Continuous and Staged Representations

Once you select the process areas, you must also select how much you would like to mature the processes associated with those process areas (i.e., select the appropriate capability level). Capability levels and generic goals and practices support the improvement of processes associated with individual process areas. For example, an organization may wish to strive to reach capability level 2 in one process area and capability level 4 in another. As the organization reaches a capability level, it sets its sights on the next capability level for one of these same process areas or decides to widen its view and address a larger number of process areas.

This selection is typically described through a target profile. A target profile defines all of the process areas to be addressed and the targeted capability level for each. This profile then governs which goals and practices the organization will address in its process improvement efforts.

Most organizations will, at minimum, target capability level 1, which requires that all specific goals of the process area be achieved. However, organizations that target capability levels higher than 1 will concentrate on the institutionalization of the selected processes in the organization by implementing the associated generic goals and practices.

Conversely, you will see that the staged representation encourages you to always look at process areas in the context of the maturity level to which they belong. The process areas are organized by maturity levels to reinforce this concept.

The staged representation provides a predetermined path of improvement from maturity level 1 to maturity level 5 that involves achieving the goals of the process areas at each maturity level. To support those using the staged representation, process areas are grouped by maturity level, indicating which process areas to implement to achieve each maturity level. For example, at maturity level 2, there is a set of process areas that an organization would use to guide its process improvement until it could achieve all the goals of all these process areas. Once maturity level 2 is achieved this way, the organization focuses its efforts on maturity level 3 process areas, and so on. The generic goals that apply to each process area are also predetermined. Generic goal 2 applies to maturity level 2 and generic goal 3 applies to maturity levels 3 through 5.

Table 3.2 provides a list of all process areas and their associated categories and maturity levels. To explain how the components of the process areas are viewed in each representation, we must discuss how the representations address specific practices.

TABLE 3.2 Process Areas and Their Associated Categories and Maturity Levels

Process Area	Category	Maturity Level
Causal Analysis and Resolution	Support	5
Configuration Management	Support	2
Decision Analysis and Resolution	Support	3
Integrated Project Management +IPPD	Project Management	3
Measurement and Analysis	Support	2
Organizational Innovation and Deployment	Process Management	5
Organizational Process Definition +IPPD	Process Management	3
Organizational Process Focus	Process Management	3
Organizational Process Performance	Process Management	4
Organizational Training	Process Management	3
Product Integration	Engineering	3
Project Monitoring and Control	Project Management	2
Project Planning	Project Management	2
Process and Product Quality Assurance	Support	2
Quantitative Project Management	Project Management	4
Requirements Development	Engineering	3
Requirements Management	Engineering	2
Risk Management	Project Management	3
Supplier Agreement Management	Project Management	2
Technical Solution	Engineering	3
Validation	Engineering	3
Verification	Engineering	3

Generic Goals and Practices

Generic goals are required model components that apply to all process areas. Figure 3.3 illustrates the generic goals and practices. All of the generic goals and practices are used in the continuous representation. (See the Generic Goals and Generic Practices section on page 149 for a more detailed description of generic goals and practices.) The capability level you are targeting for your improvement effort will determine which generic goals and practices you will apply to the process area you have selected.

In the staged representation, only generic goals 2 and 3 are used, as illustrated by the generic practices highlighted in gray in Figure 3.3. When you try to reach maturity level 2, you use the

Generic Goals and Generic Practices

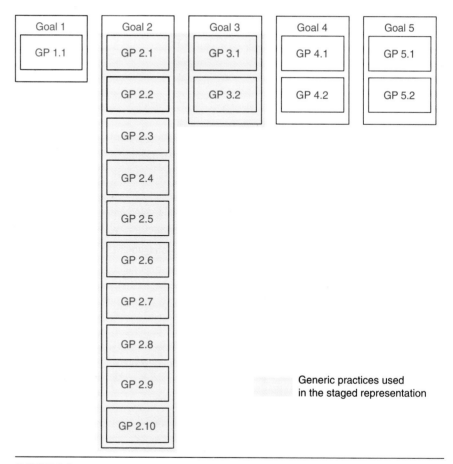

FIGURE 3.3
Generic Goals and Generic Practices

process areas at maturity level 2 as well as generic goal 2 and its generic practices.

Notice that generic goals 4 and 5 and their associated generic practices are not used. This is because not all processes will be "raised" above (i.e., matured beyond) a defined process. Only select processes and subprocesses will be quantitatively managed and optimized, and which processes and subprocesses are selected is addressed by the process areas at maturity levels 4 and 5.

When you reach maturity levels 3, 4, and 5, you use the process areas at the appropriate maturity levels as well as all of those at the lower maturity levels. In addition, generic goal 3 and its associated generic practices (which include the generic practices associated with generic goal 2) are applied to all of these process areas. This means that even though you have already achieved a maturity level 2 rating, to achieve a maturity level 3 rating you must return to the maturity level 2 process areas and apply generic goal 3 and its generic practices as well.

Representation Comparison

Table 3.3 summarizes the differences between the two representations.

TABLE 3.3 Comparing Continuous and Staged Representations

Continuous Representation	Staged Representation
The organization selects process areas and capability levels based on its process improvement objectives.	The organization selects process areas based on the maturity levels.
Improvement is measured using capability levels. Capability levels • Measure maturity of a particular process across an organization. • Range from 0 through 5.	Improvement is measured using maturity levels. Maturity levels • Measure maturity of a set of processes across an organization. • Range from 1 through 5.
Capability level profiles are used to target and track process improvement performance.	Maturity levels are used to target and track process improvement performance.
Equivalent staging allows an organization using the continuous approach to process improvement to derive a maturity level as part of an appraisal.	There is no need for an equivalence mechanism back to the continuous approach.

Equivalent Staging

Equivalent staging is a way to compare results from using the continuous representation to those of the staged representation. In essence, if you measured improvement relative to selected process areas using capability levels in the continuous representation, how would you compare that to maturity levels? Is this possible?

Up to this point, we have not discussed process appraisals in much detail. The SCAMPI method[2] is used for appraising organizations using CMMI, and one result of an appraisal is a rating [Ahern 2005]. If the continuous representation is used for an appraisal, the rating is

---

2. The SCAMPI method is described in Chapter 5.

a capability level profile. If the staged representation is used for an appraisal, the rating is a maturity level (e.g., maturity level 3) rating.

A capability level profile is a list of process areas and the corresponding capability level achieved for each. This profile enables an organization to track its capability level by process area. The profile is an achievement profile when it represents the organization's actual progress for each process area. Alternatively, the profile is a target profile when it represents the organization's planned process improvement objectives. Figure 3.4 illustrates both a target profile and an achievement profile. The gray portion of each bar represents what has been achieved. The unshaded portion represents what remains to be accomplished to meet the target profile.

An achievement profile, when compared with a target profile, enables an organization to plan and track its progress for each selected process area. Maintaining capability level profiles is advisable when using the continuous representation.

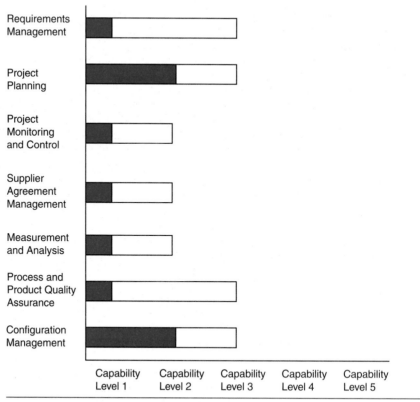

FIGURE 3.4

An Example of an Achievement Profile and a Target Profile

Target staging is a sequence of target profiles that describes the path of process improvement to be followed by the organization. When building target profiles, the organization should pay attention to the dependencies between generic practices and process areas. If a generic practice depends on a certain process area, either to carry out the generic practice or to provide a prerequisite product, the generic practice may be much less effective when the process area is not implemented.[3]

Although there are many reasons to use the continuous representation, the ratings provided by capability level profiles are limited in their ability to provide organizations with a way to generally compare themselves with other organizations. Capability level profiles could be used if each organization selected the same process areas; however, maturity levels have been used to compare organizations for years and already provide predefined sets of process areas.

Because of this situation, equivalent staging was created. Equivalent staging enables an organization using the continuous representation for an appraisal to convert a capability level profile to the associated maturity level rating.

The most effective way to depict equivalent staging is to provide a sequence of target profiles, each of which is equivalent to a maturity level rating of the staged representation. The result is a target staging that is equivalent to the maturity levels of the staged representation.

Figure 3.5 shows a summary of the target profiles that must be achieved when using the continuous representation, to be equivalent to maturity levels 2 through 5. Each shaded area in the capability level columns represents a target profile that is equivalent to a maturity level.

The following rules summarize equivalent staging.

- To achieve maturity level 2, all process areas assigned to maturity level 2 must achieve capability level 2 or higher.
- To achieve maturity level 3, all process areas assigned to maturity levels 2 and 3 must achieve capability level 3 or higher.
- To achieve maturity level 4, all process areas assigned to maturity levels 2, 3, and 4 must achieve capability level 3 or higher.
- To achieve maturity level 5, all process areas must achieve capability level 3 or higher.

---

3. See Table 7.2 on page 172 in the Generic Goals and Generic Practices section for more information about the dependencies between generic practices and process areas.

Name	Abbr	ML	CL1	CL2	CL3	CL4	CL5
Requirements Management	REQM	2					
Project Planning	PP	2					
Project Monitoring and Control	PMC	2					
Supplier Agreement Management	SAM	2	Target Profile 2				
Measurement and Analysis	MA	2					
Process and Product Quality Assurance	PPQA	2					
Configuration Management	CM	2					
Requirements Development	RD	3					
Technical Solution	TS	3					
Product Integration	PI	3					
Verification	VER	3					
Validation	VAL	3					
Organizational Process Focus	OPF	3					
Organizational Process Definition +IPPD	OPD +IPPD	3		Target Profile 3			
Organizational Training	OT	3					
Integrated Project Management +IPPD	IPM +IPPD	3					
Risk Management	RSKM	3					
Decision Analysis and Resolution	DAR	3					
Organizational Process Performance	OPP	4		Target Profile 4			
Quantitative Project Management	QPM	4					
Organizational Innovation and Deployment	OID	5		Target Profile 5			
Causal Analysis and Resolution	CAR	5					

FIGURE 3.5
Target Profiles and Equivalent Staging

These rules and the table for equivalent staging are complete; however, you may ask why target profiles 4 and 5 do not extend into the CL4 and CL5 columns. The reason is that the maturity level 4 process areas describe a selection of the subprocesses to be stabilized based, in part, on the quality and process-performance objectives of the organization and projects. Not every process area will be addressed in the selection and CMMI does not presume in advance which process areas might be addressed in the selection.

So, the achievement of capability level 4 for process areas cannot be predetermined because the choices depend on the selections made by the organization in its implementation of the maturity level 4 process areas. Thus, Figure 3.5 does not show target profile 4 extending into the CL4 column, although some process areas will have achieved capability level 4. The situation for maturity level 5 and target profile 5 is similar.

The existence of equivalent staging should not discourage users of the continuous representation from establishing target profiles that extend above capability level 3. Such a target profile would be determined in part by the selections made by the organization to meet its business objectives.

CHAPTER 4

RELATIONSHIPS AMONG PROCESS AREAS

In this chapter, we describe interactions among process areas to help you see the organization's view of process improvement and which process areas build on the implementation of other process areas. Relationships among process areas are presented in two dimensions.

The first dimension comprises the interactions of individual process areas that show how information and artifacts flow from one process area to another. Shown by the multiple figures and descriptions in this chapter, these interactions help you see a larger view of process improvement.

The second dimension comprises the interactions of groups of process areas. Shown by the classification of some process areas as Basic and others as Advanced, these classifications illustrate that the Basic process areas should be implemented before the Advanced process areas to ensure that the prerequisites are met to successfully implement the Advanced process areas.

Successful process improvement initiatives must be driven by the business objectives of the organization. For example, a common business objective is to reduce the time it takes to get a product to market. The process improvement objective derived from that might be to improve the project management processes to ensure on-time delivery; those improvements rely on best practices in the Project Planning and Project Monitoring and Control process areas.

Four Categories of CMMI Process Areas

Process areas can be grouped into four categories:

- Process Management
- Project Management

- Engineering
- Support

Although we are grouping process areas this way to discuss their interactions, process areas often interact and have an effect on one another regardless of their defined group. For example, the Decision Analysis and Resolution process area provides specific practices to address the formal evaluation that is used in the Technical Solution process area for selecting a technical solution from alternative solutions. Technical Solution is an Engineering process area and Decision Analysis and Resolution is a Support process area.

Being aware of the interactions that exist among CMMI process areas and which process areas are Basic and Advanced will help you apply CMMI in a useful and productive way. The following sections describe the interactions of process areas within the categories and only briefly describe the interactions among process areas in other categories. Interactions among process areas that belong to different categories are described in references within the Related Process Areas section of the process areas in Part Two. Refer to Chapter 2 for more information about references.

Process Management

Process Management process areas contain the cross-project activities related to defining, planning, deploying, implementing, monitoring, controlling, appraising, measuring, and improving processes.

The Process Management process areas of CMMI are as follows:

- Organizational Process Focus
- Organizational Process Definition + IPPD[1]
- Organizational Training
- Organizational Process Performance
- Organizational Innovation and Deployment

Basic Process Management Process Areas

The Basic Process Management process areas provide the organization with a capability to document and share best practices, organizational process assets, and learning across the organization.

---

1. Organizational Process Definition (OPD) has one additional goal that applies only when using CMMI with the IPPD group of additions.

Figure 4.1 provides a bird's-eye view of the interactions among the Basic Process Management process areas and with other process area categories. As illustrated in Figure 4.1, the Organizational Process Focus process area helps the organization to plan, implement, and deploy organizational process improvements based on an understanding of the current strengths and weaknesses of the organization's processes and process assets.

Candidate improvements to the organization's processes are obtained through various means. These include process improvement proposals, measurement of the processes, lessons learned in implementing the processes, and results of process appraisal and product evaluation activities.

The Organizational Process Definition process area establishes and maintains the organization's set of standard processes, work environment standards, and other assets based on the process needs and objectives of the organization. These other assets include descriptions of lifecycle models, process tailoring guidelines, and process-related documentation and data. Projects tailor the organization's set of standard processes to create their defined processes. The other assets support tailoring as well as implementation of the defined processes. Experiences and work products from performing these defined processes, including measurement data, process descriptions, process artifacts, and lessons learned, are incorporated as appropriate into the organization's set of standard processes and other assets. With the +IPPD additions, Organizational Process Definition +IPPD provides IPPD rules and guidelines to the projects.

The Organizational Training process area identifies the strategic training needs of the organization as well as the tactical training needs that are common across projects and support groups. In particular, training is developed or obtained to develop the skills required to perform the organization's set of standard processes. The main components of training include a managed training development program, documented plans, personnel with appropriate knowledge, and mechanisms for measuring the effectiveness of the training program.

Advanced Process Management Process Areas

The Advanced Process Management process areas provide the organization with an improved capability to achieve its quantitative objectives for quality and process performance.

Figure 4.2 provides a bird's-eye view of the interactions among the Advanced Process Management process areas and with other process area categories. Each of the Advanced Process Management

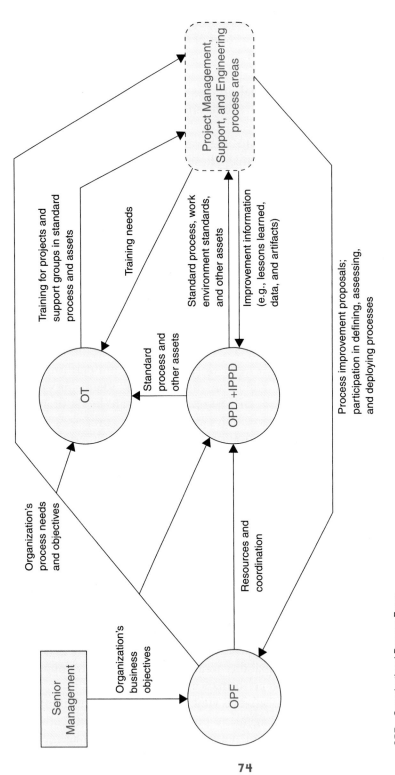

OPF = Organizational Process Focus
OT = Organizational Training
OPD +IPPD = Organizational Process Definition (with the IPPD addition)

FIGURE 4.1
Basic Process Management Process Areas

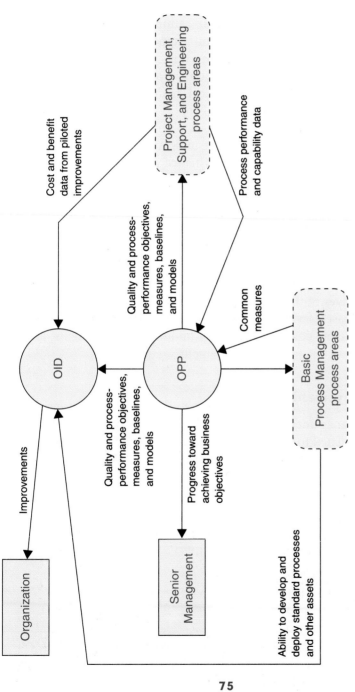

OID = Organizational Innovation and Deployment
OPP = Organizational Process Performance

FIGURE 4.2
Advanced Process Management Process Areas

process areas depends on the ability to develop and deploy processes and supporting assets. The Basic Process Management process areas provide this ability.

As illustrated in Figure 4.2, the Organizational Process Performance process area derives quantitative objectives for quality and process performance from the organization's business objectives. The organization provides projects and support groups with common measures, process-performance baselines, and process-performance models. These additional organizational assets support quantitative project management and statistical management of critical sub-processes for both projects and support groups. The organization analyzes the process-performance data collected from these defined processes to develop a quantitative understanding of product quality, service quality, and process performance of the organization's set of standard processes.

The Organizational Innovation and Deployment process area selects and deploys proposed incremental and innovative improvements that improve the organization's ability to meet its quality and process-performance objectives. The identification of promising incremental and innovative improvements should involve the participation of an empowered workforce aligned with the business values and objectives of the organization. The selection of improvements to deploy is based on a quantitative understanding of the likely benefits and predictable costs of deploying candidate improvements, and the funding available for such deployment.

Project Management

Project Management process areas cover the project management activities related to planning, monitoring, and controlling the project.

The Project Management process areas of CMMI are as follows:

- Project Planning
- Project Monitoring and Control
- Supplier Agreement Management
- Integrated Project Management + IPPD[2]
- Risk Management
- Quantitative Project Management

2. Integrated Project Management (IPM) has one goal that applies only when using CMMI with the IPPD group of additions.

Basic Project Management Process Areas

The Basic Project Management process areas address the activities related to establishing and maintaining the project plan, establishing and maintaining commitments, monitoring progress against the plan, taking corrective action, and managing supplier agreements.

Figure 4.3 provides a bird's-eye view of the interactions among the Basic Project Management process areas and with other process area categories. As illustrated in Figure 4.3, the Project Planning process area includes developing the project plan, involving stakeholders appropriately, obtaining commitment to the plan, and maintaining the plan. When using IPPD, stakeholders represent not just the technical expertise for product and process development, but also the business implications of product and process development.

Planning begins with requirements that define the product and project ("What to Build" in Figure 4.3). The project plan covers the various project management and development activities performed by the project. The project reviews other plans that affect the project from various relevant stakeholders and establish commitments with those stakeholders for their contributions to the project. For example, these plans cover configuration management, verification, and measurement and analysis.

The Project Monitoring and Control process area includes monitoring activities and taking corrective action. The project plan specifies the appropriate level of project monitoring, the frequency of progress reviews, and the measures used to monitor progress. Progress is determined primarily by comparing project status to the plan. When the actual status deviates significantly from the expected values, corrective actions are taken as appropriate. These actions may include replanning.

The Supplier Agreement Management process area addresses the need of the project to acquire those portions of work that are produced by suppliers. Sources of products that may be used to satisfy project requirements are proactively identified. The supplier is selected, and a supplier agreement is established to manage the supplier. The supplier's progress and performance are tracked by monitoring selected work products and processes, and the supplier agreement is revised as appropriate. Acceptance reviews and tests are conducted on the supplier-produced product component.

Advanced Project Management Process Areas

The Advanced Project Management process areas address activities such as establishing a defined process that is tailored from the

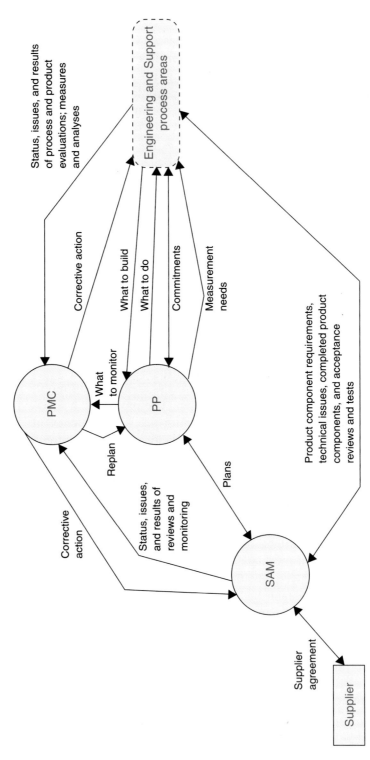

Status, issues, and results of process and product evaluations; measures and analyses

Engineering and Support process areas

Corrective action

What to build

What to do

Commitments

Measurement needs

What to monitor

PMC

Replan

PP

Corrective action

Status, issues, and results of reviews and monitoring

Plans

Product component requirements, technical issues, completed product components, and acceptance reviews and tests

SAM

Supplier agreement

Supplier

PMC = Project Monitoring and Control
PP = Project Planning
SAM = Supplier Agreement Management

FIGURE 4.3
Basic Project Management Process Areas

organization's set of standard processes, establishing the project work environment from the organization's work environment standards, coordinating and collaborating with relevant stakeholders, managing risk, forming and sustaining integrated teams for the conduct of projects, and quantitatively managing the project's defined process.

Figure 4.4 provides a bird's-eye view of the interactions among the Advanced Project Management process areas and with other process area categories. Each Advanced Project Management process area depends on the ability to plan, monitor, and control the project. The Basic Project Management process areas provide this ability.

The Integrated Project Management process area establishes and maintains the project's defined process that is tailored from the organization's set of standard processes. The project is managed using the project's defined process. The project uses and contributes to the organization's process assets. The project's work environment is established and maintained from the organization's work environment standards.

The management of the project ensures that the relevant stakeholders associated with the project coordinate their efforts in a timely manner. It does this by providing for the management of stakeholder involvement; the identification, negotiation, and tracking of critical dependencies; and the resolution of coordination issues within the project and with relevant stakeholders.

With the +IPPD additions, Integrated Project Management +IPPD establishes and maintains the shared vision of the project and an integrated team structure for the project and then establishes integrated teams to perform the work of the project, ensuring the appropriate collaboration across teams.

Although risk identification and monitoring are covered in the Project Planning and Project Monitoring and Control process areas, the Risk Management process area takes a continuing, forward-looking approach to managing risks with activities that include identification of risk parameters, risk assessments, and risk mitigation.

The Quantitative Project Management process area applies quantitative and statistical techniques to manage process performance and product quality. Quality and process-performance objectives for the project are based on the objectives established by the organization. The project's defined process comprises, in part, process elements and subprocesses whose process performance can be predicted. At a minimum, the process variation experienced by subprocesses critical to achieving the project's quality and process-performance objectives

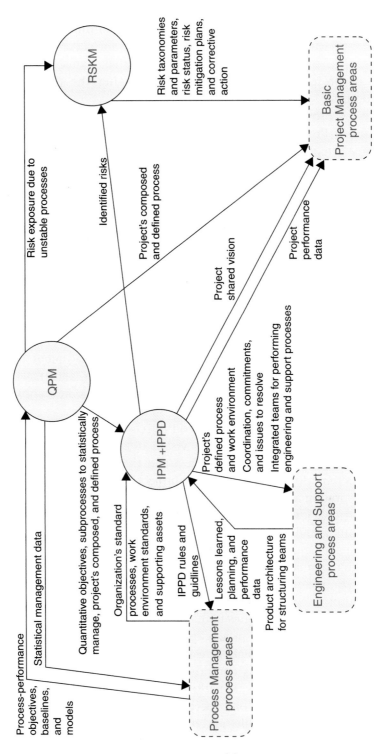

IPM = Integrated Project Management (+IPPD addition)
QPM = Quantitative Project Management
RSKM = Risk Management

FIGURE 4.4
Advanced Project Management Process Areas

is understood. Corrective action is taken when special causes of process variation are identified. (See the definition of "special cause of process variation" in the glossary.)

Engineering

Engineering process areas cover the development and maintenance activities that are shared across engineering disciplines. The Engineering process areas were written using general engineering terminology so that any technical discipline involved in the product development process (e.g., software engineering or mechanical engineering) can use them for process improvement.

The Engineering process areas also integrate the processes associated with different engineering disciplines into a single product development process, supporting a product-oriented process improvement strategy. Such a strategy targets essential business objectives rather than specific technical disciplines. This approach to processes effectively avoids the tendency toward an organizational "stovepipe" mentality.

The Engineering process areas apply to the development of any product or service in the development domain (e.g., software products, hardware products, services, or processes).

The technical foundation for IPPD is grounded in a robust systems engineering approach that encompasses development in the context of the phases of the product's life. The Engineering process areas provide this technical foundation. The implementation of IPPD is further addressed through amplifications to specific practices in the Engineering process areas that emphasize concurrent development and focus on all phases of the product's life.

The Engineering process areas of CMMI are as follows:

- Requirements Development
- Requirements Management
- Technical Solution
- Product Integration
- Verification
- Validation

Figure 4.5 provides a bird's-eye view of the interactions among the six Engineering process areas.

The Requirements Development process area identifies customer needs and translates these needs into product requirements. The set

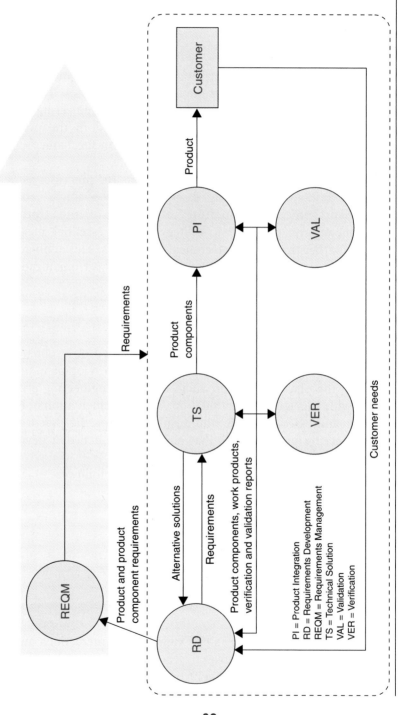

FIGURE 4.5
Engineering Process Areas

82

of product requirements is analyzed to produce a high-level conceptual solution. This set of requirements is then allocated to establish an initial set of product component requirements. Other requirements that help define the product are derived and allocated to product components. This set of product and product component requirements clearly describes the product's performance, design features, verification requirements, and so forth, in terms the developer understands and uses.

The Requirements Development process area supplies requirements to the Technical Solution process area, where the requirements are converted into the product architecture, the product component design, and the product component itself (e.g., coding and fabrication). Requirements are also supplied to the Product Integration process area, where product components are combined and interfaces are verified to ensure that they meet the interface requirements supplied by Requirements Development.

The Requirements Management process area maintains the requirements. It describes activities for obtaining and controlling requirement changes and ensuring that other relevant plans and data are kept current. It provides traceability of requirements from customer to product to product component.

Requirements Management ensures that changes to requirements are reflected in project plans, activities, and work products. This cycle of changes may affect all the other Engineering process areas; thus, requirements management is a dynamic and often recursive sequence of events. The Requirements Management process area is fundamental to a controlled and disciplined engineering design process.

The Technical Solution process area develops technical data packages for product components that will be used by the Product Integration or Supplier Agreement Management process area. Alternative solutions are examined with the intent of selecting the optimum design based on established criteria. These criteria may be significantly different across products, depending on product type, operational environment, performance requirements, support requirements, and cost or delivery schedules. The task of selecting the final solution makes use of the specific practices in the Decision Analysis and Resolution process area.

The Technical Solution process area relies on the specific practices in the Verification process area to perform design verification and peer reviews during design and prior to final build.

The Verification process area ensures that selected work products meet the specified requirements. The Verification process area selects work products and verification methods that will be used to verify work products against specified requirements. Verification is generally an incremental process, starting with product component verification and usually concluding with verification of fully assembled products.

Verification also addresses peer reviews. Peer reviews are a proven method for removing defects early and provide valuable insight into the work products and product components being developed and maintained.

The Validation process area incrementally validates products against the customer's needs. Validation may be performed in the operational environment or in a simulated operational environment. Coordination with the customer on the validation requirements is an important element of this process area.

The scope of the Validation process area includes validation of products, product components, selected intermediate work products, and processes. These validated elements may often require reverification and revalidation. Issues discovered during validation are usually resolved in the Requirements Development or Technical Solution process area.

The Product Integration process area contains the specific practices associated with generating the best possible integration sequence, integrating product components, and delivering the product to the customer.

Product Integration uses the specific practices of both Verification and Validation in implementing the product integration process. Verification practices verify the interfaces and interface requirements of product components prior to product integration. This is an essential event in the integration process. During product integration in the operational environment, the specific practices of the Validation process area are used.

Recursion and Iteration of Engineering Processes

Most process standards agree that there are two ways that processes can be applied. These two ways are called recursion and iteration.

Recursion occurs when a process is applied to successive levels of system elements within a system structure. The outcomes of one application are used as inputs to the next level in the system structure. For example, the verification process is designed to apply to the entire assembled product, the major product components, and even components of components. How far into the product you apply the verification process depends entirely on the size and complexity of the end product.

Iteration occurs when processes are repeated at the same system level. New information is created by the implementation of one process that feeds back into a related process. This new information typically raises questions that must be resolved before completing the processes. For example, iteration will most likely occur between requirements development and technical solution. Reapplication of the processes can resolve the questions that are raised. Iteration can ensure quality prior to applying the next process.

Engineering processes (e.g., requirements development or verification) are implemented repeatedly on a product to ensure that these engineering processes have been adequately addressed before delivery to the customer. Further, engineering processes are applied to components of the product. For example, some questions that are raised by processes associated with the Verification and Validation process areas may be resolved by processes associated with the Requirements Development or Product Integration process area. Recursion and iteration of these processes enable the project to ensure quality in all components of the product, before it is delivered to the customer.

Support

Support process areas cover the activities that support product development and maintenance. The Support process areas address processes that are used in the context of performing other processes. In general, the Support process areas address processes that are targeted toward the project and may address processes that apply more generally to the organization. For example, Process and Product Quality Assurance can be used with all the process areas to provide an objective evaluation of the processes and work products described in all the process areas.

The Support process areas of CMMI are as follows:

- Configuration Management
- Process and Product Quality Assurance
- Measurement and Analysis
- Decision Analysis and Resolution
- Causal Analysis and Resolution

Basic Support Process Areas

The Basic Support process areas address fundamental support functions that are used by all process areas. Although all Support process areas rely on the other process areas for input, the Basic Support process areas provide support functions that also help implement several generic practices.

Figure 4.6 provides a bird's-eye view of the interactions among the Basic Support process areas and with all other process areas.

The Measurement and Analysis process area supports all process areas by providing specific practices that guide projects and organizations in aligning measurement needs and objectives with a measurement approach that will provide objective results. These results can be used in making informed decisions and taking appropriate corrective actions.

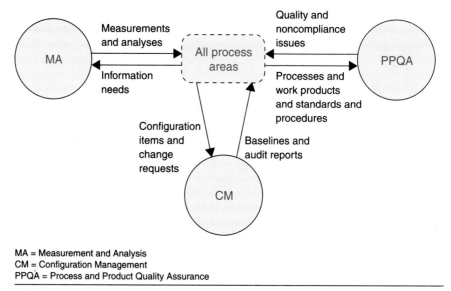

MA = Measurement and Analysis
CM = Configuration Management
PPQA = Process and Product Quality Assurance

FIGURE 4.6
Basic Support Process Areas

Measurement Makes Improvement Meaningful

by David N. Card

Measurement is an essential component of engineering, management, and process improvement. CMMI defines measurement requirements in Measurement and Analysis, Project Planning, Project Monitoring and Control, Quantitative Project Management, and Organizational Process Performance, and to lesser degrees in other process areas. Measurement and analysis are two of the five steps in the Six Sigma DMAIC cycle. Lean is based on the application of the principles of queuing theory to processes. Unless performance can be quantified in terms of productivity, quality, or cycle time, it is hard to gauge improvement, regardless of the improvement approach adopted.

Because the CMMI-based approach to process improvement does not consider measured performance or evaluate the "goodness" of processes during appraisals, an effective measurement and analysis program is essential to the long-term business success of CMMI users. Measurement is the mechanism by which an organization gains insight into its performance and confronts "goodness." A minimal measurement program may pass an appraisal but will limit the organization's opportunities for real improvement. Moreover, without meaningful feedback, a maturity level is not likely to be maintained.

What roles should measurement and analysis play in an organization? Measurement often is defined in terms of collecting data and thus is distinguished from analysis, which is the interpretation and use of data. Clearly, the collection of data must be driven by its intended use. As Mark Twain observed, "Data is like garbage. You better know what you are going to do with it, before you start collecting it." Four classes (or levels) of measurement users or decision-making processes may be defined. CMMI introduces these decision-making processes at different maturity levels. Each class of decision making has a different focus.

- *Enterprise: The long-term survival of the organization.* The enterprise offers products and/or services in a market. Survival typically means maintaining or increasing profitability and market share. (Outside the scope of CMMI.)
- *Process: The efficiency and effectiveness of the organization's means of accomplishing work.* The processes of a typical organization may include software engineering, information technology, marketing, and administration. (CMMI maturity levels 4 and 5.)
- *Project: Realization of a specific product or service for a specific customer or class of customers.* Projects use organizational processes to produce products and/or services for the enterprise to market. (CMMI maturity levels 2 and 3.)
- *Product: Resolution of the technical aspects of the product or service necessary to meet the customer's requirements.* Projects manage

the resources necessary to deliver the desired product or service. (CMMI maturity level 3.)

As indicated in the preceding descriptions, these areas of concern are interrelated. Moreover, measurement and analysis at all of these levels depend on many of the same sources of data. However, the level of detail and the manner in which the data is analyzed or reported for different purposes may vary.[3]

Measurement specialists often focus on the technical challenges of statistical analysis instead of addressing some of the human and social reasons why measurement systems sometimes fail. Many of these problems are common to organizational change initiatives. Three issues specific to measurement are as follows.

- The cost of data collection and processing is always visible, but the benefits of measurement are not. The benefits depend on what decisions are made based on the data. No decisions—no action—no benefits. Organizations must establish an action orientation.
- Measurement and analysis are new to many software and systems engineers and managers. Training and coaching in these new skills are essential to their successful implementation. As the scope of measurement increases with higher maturity, more sophisticated techniques must be mastered, making training even more critical.
- Measurement provides insight into performance. However, gaining and using that insight may be threatening to those whose performance is measured, and even to those who are just the messengers of performance information. Measurement systems must protect the participants.

All of these issues can, and have been, overcome. CMMI's Measurement and Analysis process area provides a good starting point for introducing measurement into an organization. Building on that with skills and techniques appropriate to the target maturity level and intended uses of measurement, as well as confronting the human issues that are sure to be encountered, facilitate the transition to management by fact rather than opinion. Without an appropriate and effective measurement program, maturity levels are insignificant assertions.

---

3. For a more detailed discussion, see Card, D. "A Practical Framework for Software Measurement and Analysis." *Systems Management Strategies* (Auerbach, October 2000).

The Process and Product Quality Assurance process area supports all process areas by providing specific practices for objectively evaluating performed processes, work products, and services against the applicable process descriptions, standards, and procedures, and ensuring that any issues arising from these reviews are addressed. Process and Product Quality Assurance supports the delivery of high-quality products and services by providing the project staff and all levels of managers with appropriate visibility into, and feedback on, the processes and associated work products throughout the life of the project.

Process, People, Technology, and CMMI

by Gargi Keeni

Organizations that have been successful in their process improvement initiatives are known to have taken a holistic approach. Any discussion on process improvement would invariably emphasize the importance of addressing the process, people, and technology (PPT) triangle. However, in reality it is not so common to see synergy among the individuals or groups responsible for these PPT aspects in an organization. Synchronizing the goals of an individual or team with those of the organization is the key for any successful improvement program.

In the context of CMMI, this becomes more evident for the process areas whose activities would have an inherent conflict between individual/team priorities and the organization's priorities. Organizations may unknowingly have reward and recognition systems in which individual incentives and career goals are tied to individual/team performance, thereby inhibiting realization of organizational goals.

Let's take an example of an organization that is trying to implement a Process and Product Quality Assurance (PPQA) process. PPQA is a process area at maturity level 2 whose purpose is to provide objective insight into processes and their associated work products.

Process

It is relatively simple to define the processes that need to be implemented, though that does not always ensure that the intent is achieved. Quite often, individuals/teams work overtime to get records in place just before the compliance check is scheduled!

People

Further probing may highlight the fact that the number of noncompliances is linked to the performance of the project leader or project team. This link motivates the individual or team to spend non-value-added effort (i.e., waste) just to ensure that the number of noncompliances is as low as possible.

The reason for the noncompliance in the first place could have been any of the following.

- The processes are not suitable for the activities done by the individuals/teams.
- The process definition is too complicated to be followed.
- The individuals/teams are not aware of the process and its intent.

So, in this case, the organization cannot reap the benefits of the PPQA activities unless it revisits its people practice of linking the number of noncompliances to the performance of an individual or team. In other words, the organization needs to promote an environment that encourages employee participation in identifying and reporting quality issues, which is subpractice 1 of PPQA SP 1.1.

Technology

To obtain effective and timely conclusions with respect to the preceding reasons cited for noncompliance, organizations need to have systems for tracking and analyzing the noncompliances and the associated corrective actions. This tracking and analysis, in turn, will provide managers at all levels with appropriate visibility into the processes and work products. However, just procuring a tool for managing noncompliances without proper deployment of processes turns out to be counter-productive in most cases.

Objectivity in PPQA evaluations is critical and can be achieved by both independence and use of criteria; however, the profile of the independent entity has a major impact on the quality of PPQA evaluations. In organizations where individuals from other teams conduct the PPQA activities, it is very important to ensure that the right individual is made available for the task. However, as experience says, the right people are usually not available unless the right motivation is provided. If an individual is always evaluated based on the work she does in the team, there is no motivation for her to provide any service external to the team. However, because PPQA is a Support PA which runs across the organization, the organization needs to review its incentive measures to provide the right motivation for these activities which are beyond the individuals'/teams' current functions.

As you can see by this PPQA example, it is important to consider all three dimensions of process, people, and technology when addressing any of the activities described in the process areas in CMMI. The PPT impact becomes even more apparent for PAs at higher maturity levels, which have inherently built-in organizational perspectives regardless of whether it is a large or small organization.

It is essential for an organization to provide an environment that fosters effective deployment of processes. Analysis of the outcome/results on a regular basis provides insights into the effectiveness of the processes and the changes required to meet business objectives.

The PAs at higher maturity levels often directly address people and technology in the practices. However, when implementing these practices, it is important to understand the natural relationships that exist in order to nurture these behaviors so that an organization can readily adapt to the improvement and change which are necessary in today's environment.

The Configuration Management process area supports all process areas by establishing and maintaining the integrity of work products using configuration identification, configuration control, configuration status accounting, and configuration audits. The work products placed under configuration management include the products that are delivered to the customer, designated internal work products, acquired products, tools, and other items that are used in creating and describing these work products. Examples of work products that may be placed under configuration management include plans, process descriptions, requirements, design data, drawings, product specifications, code, compilers, product data files, and product technical publications.

Advanced Support Process Areas

The Advanced Support process areas provide the projects and organization with an improved support capability. Each of these process areas relies on specific inputs or practices from other process areas.

Figure 4.7 provides a bird's-eye view of the interactions among the Advanced Support process areas and with all other process areas.

Using the Causal Analysis and Resolution process area, project members identify causes of selected defects and other problems and

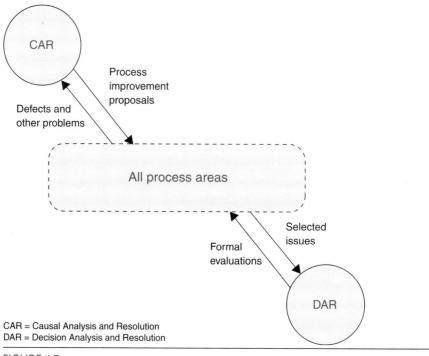

CAR = Causal Analysis and Resolution
DAR = Decision Analysis and Resolution

FIGURE 4.7
Advanced Support Process Areas

take action to prevent them from occurring in the future. While the project's defined processes are the principal targets for identifying the cause of the defect, the process improvement proposals they create target the organization's set of standard processes, which will prevent recurrence of the defect across the organization.

The Decision Analysis and Resolution process area supports all the process areas by determining which issues should be subjected to a formal evaluation process and then applying a formal evaluation process to them.

CHAPTER 5

USING CMMI MODELS

The complexity of today's products demands an integrated view of how organizations do business. CMMI can reduce the cost of process improvement across enterprises that depend on multiple functions or groups to produce products and services.

To achieve this integrated view, the CMMI Framework includes common terminology, common model components, common appraisal methods, and common training materials. This chapter describes how organizations can use the CMMI Product Suite not only to improve their quality, reduce their costs, and optimize their schedules, but also to gauge how well their process improvement program is working.

The Role of Process Standards in Process Definition

by James W. Moore[1]

Suppose you decide to take a physics course at a university. Naturally, you want to get a good grade. So you faithfully attend the lectures, read the textbooks, attend the lab sessions, do the homework, take the final examination, and hope for the best outcome. Alternatively, if you can find a willing instructor, you could ask her for a copy of the final exam on the first day of the course. As time permits, you could figure out the answers to the questions and, by the end of the course, turn in your answers to the exam questions, with a

---

1. ©2006—The MITRE Corporation. All rights reserved. The author's affiliation with The MITRE Corporation is provided for identification purposes only, and is not intended to convey or imply MITRE's concurrence with, or support for, the positions, opinions, or viewpoints expressed by the author.

request for the corresponding grade. Which of these two approaches is the more effective way to learn physics? We'll return to this question at the end of this perspective.

A long tradition of prescriptive process definition standards, such as DoD-Std-2167A, were intended to tell software developers what they must do in order to achieve an acceptable level of professional practice; one conformed to such a standard by implementing processes meeting all of its provisions.[2] In the last dozen or so years, that binary form of pass-fail evaluation has lost favor to a more graded approach of assessing the "maturity" or "capability" of the developer's processes. ISO/IEC 15504, *Process Assessment* (commonly but mistakenly called "SPICE"), describes this approach. ISO/IEC 15504 is "agnostic" with respect to the processes being employed. Methods conforming to the standard can be used to assess any set of processes that are described in a particular stylized manner, called the process reference model. One such process reference model is provided by ISO/IEC/IEEE/EIA 12207, *Software Lifecycle Processes*. Another is provided by ISO/IEC/IEEE 15288, *System Lifecycle Processes*.

The 15504 standard is used in some nations, but CMMI has greater recognition in the U.S. marketplace. Unlike 15504, CMMI provides a great deal of guidance regarding the definition of processes. The criteria that are applied to assess the processes implicitly specify practices that should be embedded in the developer's processes. So this begs the question of whether any other standards are needed for process definition. After all, why not simply implement processes meeting the CMMI criteria and be done with it?

There are four reasons why one should consider using process standards for defining an organization's processes: scope, suitability, communication, and robustness. First, let's look at scope. Although CMMI is broad, it isn't broad enough for all possible uses. An obvious example is quality management. Although CMMI includes provisions addressing the quality of software products and systems, it does not address the organization-level quality Management Systems specified by ISO 9001, *Quality management systems—Requirements*. Since ISO 9001 conformance is regarded as highly important in many countries, multinational suppliers will find it appropriate

---

2. Because they were generally overprescriptive, these standards were often "tailored" by modifying their detailed provisions. Of course, conformance to a tailored standard always begs the question of whether the tailoring was done responsibly, or simply consisted of deleting all inconvenient provisions.

to consider that standard in defining their processes—even software and system processes—related to quality. Although less prominent than ISO 9001, there are many other standards describing processes of various kinds. In particular situations, suppliers should consider the provisions of those standards.

The second reason for considering process standards is suitability. It should be obvious that not every organization needs the same set of processes. After all, every organization has some unique characteristics that cause it to differ from its competitors. That competitive advantage should be addressed in organizational processes so that the advantage is relevantly applied to every project of the organization, thereby enabling the organization to maintain its competitive edge. Defining a set of organizational processes, including those for software and systems engineering, should involve consideration of a number of factors, including the following:

- The size of the organization
- The nature of the products and services provided by the organization
- The competitive structure of the relevant marketplace
- The nature of the competition
- The regulatory structure that is relevant, including regulatory requirements
- Customs, traditions, and regulation in the relevant industry sector
- The "culture" of the organization, including the degree of regimentation that the workforce will tolerate
- Organizational attitudes toward quality
- The amount of investment capital available for process definition and the extent to which it can be amortized over a base of projects
- The uniformity (or diversity) of anticipated project requirements
- The competitive advantages to be "captured" by the processes
- The form in which documentation (either paper or electronic) is to be captured, saved, and possibly delivered

All of these considerations, and many more, affect the definition of organizational processes, leading to the conclusion that the selection and implementation of cost-effective processes require a different solution for every organization.

Of course, process standards do not directly account for all of these factors. They simply provide alternatives to be considered in the overall process definition. In some cases, they describe specific practices that are important in regulatory environments—for example, the Modified Condition Decision Criteria (of RTCA DO-178B, Software Considerations in Airborne Systems and Equipment Certification) that is applied to the testing of avionics systems. More generally, they provide a starting point, a shortcut that allows the process definers to avoid a large volume of relatively straightforward decisions. Perhaps most important is that they provide a baseline of responsible practice, a "safety net," that is omitted only at some risk.

The third reason for considering process standards is communication. Terminology in software engineering is notoriously vague and flexible—a sign of an emerging profession. This can lead to important misunderstandings: "Oh, when you paid me to 'implement' the software, you meant I should 'test' it also? I didn't include that in the price; you have to pay me extra for that!" Even the consideration of proposals is difficult without a baseline of terminology for comparing processes. Suppose the buyer asks the supplier what sort of design review practices are performed by the supplier. One possible answer is to provide dozens of pages of written proposal prose; another possible answer is for the supplier to say, "We use IEEE Std 1028, Software Reviews." The second answer has the advantage of being succinct, of being precise in terms of what is included, and of being generally accepted as responsible practice.[3] The international standards for lifecycle processes, ISO/IEC/IEEE/EIA 12207 and ISO/IEC/IEEE 15288, provide a comprehensive set of processes that span the lifecycles of software products and systems. If a supplier states that its software development process conforms to that of 12207, a buyer knows the answer to a large number of pertinent questions; to pick only one example, the buyer would know that the software requirements, the architectural design, the detailed design, and the code will be evaluated for feasibility of operation and maintenance—important downstream activities.

The final reason for considering process standards is robustness. Reliance upon a single source may lead to defining processes that are inadvertently oriented toward a particular concept of usage. Applying the processes in a different context may lead to unintended results. Despite best attempts at generality, it is impossible to anticipate all possible situations; so it is up to the process designer to

---

3. By the way, I avoid the term "best practice." "Responsible practice" is as good as it gets with me. I simply don't believe that any single practice can be regarded as being the best in all possible situations. I believe that most organizations should strive to use responsible practices that are suited to their particular needs.

consult multiple sources to find processes that are suitable for the particular organization. The level of prescription is an important consideration here. Those who define processes (including the people who wrote CMMI) necessarily have to make a tradeoff of generality versus specificity. Many very good practices were omitted from CMMI because they weren't generally applicable; and many were "watered down" to improve their generality. By consulting multiple sources, including multiple standards, process definers will find practices that are specifically suitable and effective in the intended context, even though they were omitted from CMMI because they could not be generalized to the broad CMMI audience. Those who must practice at a more demanding level (e.g., developing safety-critical software) can supplement their baseline processes by applying standards that provide more detailed or stringent treatments of selected practices (e.g., IEEE Std 1012, *Software Verification and Validation*).

With that said, we are now ready to return to the original question of whether a person who wants to learn physics should sit through the course or should ask for a copy of the final exam on the first day. The answer to the question is, "It depends!" It depends on whether the goal is to gain a broad and useful understanding of physics or to get the highest possible grade with the least possible effort. In business, both answers are reasonable depending on the circumstances.

Applying this analogy to the subject at hand, we can conclude (with some cynicism) that if the organization's goal is to attain the highest possible CMMI rating with the smallest possible investment, it is probably appropriate to accept the final exam on the first day of the course—that is, to define a set of organizational processes that directly and straightforwardly address the evaluation criteria of CMMI. On the other hand, if the organization's goal is to define a set of organizational processes that are robust, descriptive, and suitable to the scope and circumstances of the organization—that is, to gain the intended advantages of process improvement—the organization should consult multiple sources including process definition standards, select suitable ones, and use them as a baseline for defining a cost-effective solution to the organization's needs.

Adopting CMMI

Research has shown that the most powerful initial step to process improvement is to build strong organizational support through strong senior management sponsorship. To gain senior management sponsorship, it is often beneficial to expose senior management to the performance results experienced by others who have used CMMI to improve their processes.

For more information about CMMI performance results, see the SEI Web site at www.sei.cmu.edu/cmmi/results.html [SEI 3].

The senior manager, once committed as the process improvement sponsor, must be actively involved in the CMMI-based process improvement effort. Activities performed by the senior management sponsor include (but are not limited to) the following.

* Influence the organization to adopt CMMI.
* Choose the best people to manage the process improvement effort.
* Monitor the process improvement effort personally.
* Be a visible advocate and spokesperson for the process improvement effort.
* Ensure that adequate resources are available to enable the process improvement effort to be successful.

Executive Responsibilities in Process Improvement

by Bill Curtis

We constantly hear that the primary reason process improvement programs fail is from lack of executive leadership. With that said those responsible for facilitating process improvement programs are hard-pressed to specify exactly what they expect from executives. Herewith are 12 critical actions executives should take to ensure the success of process improvement programs.

1. Take personal responsibility.

   Executives do not deliver systems to customers. Project managers do that. Executives build organizations that deliver systems to customers, and this responsibility cannot be delegated. At the core of Watts Humphrey's Process Maturity Framework that underlies CMMI is a unique model of organizational change and development. Since the responsibility for organizational transformation rests in the executive office, CMMI is a tool for executives to use to improve the performance of their organizations. CMMI will transform not only development practices, but also the organization's culture and the way business results are attained. Executives should not launch an improvement program until they are willing to become personally accountable for its success—or failure.

2. Set realistic goals.

   Executives must initiate process improvement with a clear statement of the issues driving change and the objectives to be achieved. Slogans such as "Level 2 by '02" do little more than reinforce the very behaviors that level 2 was designed to eliminate. If the improvement objectives are unrealistic, the improvement program will be just one more of the organization's chaotic death-march projects. Process improvement must model the behaviors it wants the organization to adopt, especially plan-driven commitments. Schedules for attaining maturity levels should result from planning, not catchy slogans or bonus cycles. Rewards and bonuses should be based on the accomplishment of planned improvement milestones, rather than arbitrary dates for appraisal results.

3. Establish an improvement project.

   Process improvement must be conducted as a project. Executives must assign responsibility for managing the project, provide funding and resources, expect periodic status reports, and measure results. The person assigned to lead the improvement project must be a good role model for other project managers. Executives should ask frequent questions about project plans and the assumptions underlying them. The guidebooks, defined processes, measures, checklists, and other artifacts produced through process improvement are organizational assets. They should be treated as products, albeit for internal use, and be produced with the same discipline used in producing any other product.

4. Manage change.

   How many initiatives can dance on the head of a project manager? Many organizations have multiple improvement programs underway simultaneously. In the initial stages of these programs, the project manager is the person most affected and often is inundated with the number of changes expected. Executives must determine the amount of change the organization can absorb, prioritize the changes to be made, and shield the organization from improvement overkill. The good news is that some improvement programs such as Six Sigma and CMMI can be synthesized, since they evolved from the concepts initiated by Shewhart and Deming.

5. Align management.

Process groups have no power to enforce improvements or change management behavior. If middle managers resist improvements, only executives can force them to align with the program. Executives must build consensus among managers on the objectives and tactics for improvement and hold them accountable for achieving improvement objectives. In particular, middle managers must be developing the skills of the project or program managers who report to them. Management steering committees reporting to executives are one way to ensure that middle and project managers share responsibility for improvement success.

6. Align incentives.

Executives must ensure that incentives are aligned with improvement goals and do not send mixed messages about the behaviors the organization values. Incentives must shift from rewarding heroes to rewarding those whose sound practices avoid the need for heroes. Promotions should go to those who are strong role models of the behaviors the improvement program is trying to instill. Incentives must send a message that management values contributions to building a strong organization just as much as it values individual performance.

7. Establish policies and empower assurance.

Policies that merely regurgitate goals from CMMI process areas represent a lost opportunity for executives to communicate their expectations for behavior in their organizations. Once policies are established, executives need visibility into compliance. Assurance groups have influence only to the extent that executives attend to their reports and address noncompliance. However, the greatest value of assurance groups, and this is subtle in Process and Product Quality Assurance (PPQA), is when they serve as mentors to project managers and technical staff on practices that support compliance. Consequently, assurance groups need to be staffed with competent developers and managers so that they are credible in transferring knowledge of best practices across the organization.

8. Involve customers.

Unless customers understand how they will benefit from new practices, they may perceive the changes as making projects bureaucratic and inflexible. Consequently, project managers are often trapped in a conflict between their improvement objectives and the demands of their customers. Executives own the relationship with customers and must meet with their peers to explain the improvement strategy and how it will make the development organization a more reliable business partner. Involving customers in improving requirements practices is a good initial step for incorporating them into the program.

9. Involve developers.

   The process maturity framework begins the empowerment of developers by involving them in estimating and planning at level 2 and it increases their responsibility at each subsequent level. Executives must understand and encourage this cultural transition. They must also ensure that developers are involved in improvement activities because they have the freshest knowledge of best practices, and are more realistic about how much change they can absorb in an improvement cycle. The role of the process and assurance groups is to assist managers and developers in identifying and deploying best practices.

10. Review status.

    Executives own the organization's commitments. They must approve external commitments and review progress in accomplishing them. Project reviews should focus not only on work status, but also on the progress being made in adopting improvements and addressing impending risks. Executives highlight their commitment through measurement and should add indicators of improvement progress and results to their dashboards. Improvement measures should reflect that benefits accrue project by project, rather than in one big bang.

11. Replace laggards.

    The process group owns responsibility for assisting improvements with the innovators, early adopters, and early and late majority. Executives own the problem of laggards, especially if they are in management. For an improvement program to succeed, executives must be willing to remove anyone who fails to make progress—even friends. Successful organizational change programs often end up with management teams that are different from those that they started with.

12. Never relent.

    True leadership begins under stress. With all the pressures generated by demanding business schedules and cost cutting, executives must nevertheless stand firm in driving the improvements they know the organization must make. If they relent under pressure, the organization learns the art of excuses. The ultimate appraisal of maturity is determined by which practices the organization refuses to sacrifice under grinding pressure.

Executives can assume other responsibilities in supporting process improvement. Nevertheless, these 12 have proven critical, since they require executive authority and represent acts of leadership around which the improvement program can galvanize. Executives with little experience in process-disciplined environments are understandably concerned about risking their careers on practices that have not contributed significantly in their advancement. Fortunately, a growing body of data and a community of mature organizations exist to attest that faith in sensible CMMI-based improvement programs is well placed. It does not take leadership to follow the trodden path. It takes leadership to pursue the promise of new ways.

Given sufficient senior management sponsorship, the next step is establishing a strong, technically competent process group that represents relevant stakeholders to guide process improvement efforts.

For an organization with a mission to develop software-intensive systems, the process group might include engineers representing the different technical disciplines across the organization and other selected members based on the business needs driving improvement. For example, a systems administrator may focus on information-technology support, whereas a marketing representative may focus on integrating customers' needs. Both members could make powerful contributions to the process group.

Once your organization has decided to adopt CMMI, planning can begin with an improvement approach such as the IDEAL (Initiating, Diagnosing, Establishing, Acting, & Learning) model. For more information about the IDEAL model, see the SEI Web site at www.sei.cmu.edu/ideal/ideal.html [SEI 1].

Your Process Improvement Program

Use the CMMI Product Suite to help establish your organization's process improvement program. Using the product suite for this purpose can be a relatively informal process that involves understanding and applying CMMI best practices to your organization. Or, it can be a formal process that involves extensive training, creation of a process improvement infrastructure, appraisals, and more.

Implementing Engineering Culture for Successful Process Improvement

by Tomoo Matsubara

As did most early-day software professionals, I came from another professional area, mechanical engineering. While I worked at Hitachi's machine factory, which manufactured cranes, pumps, and bulldozers, the factory was in the midst of the Kaizen (i.e., improvement) movement that reduced direct and indirect costs and improved quality. Since the factory was an engineering community, all of the improvement activities were done in an engineering way. Engineers are very practical and don't decide anything without seeing, touching, and measuring things.

The typical problem-solving process used in this environment was to identify problems at the factory floor or in front of real things and phenomena, discuss presumable causes, conduct experiments, and build prototypes. For mechanical engineers, conducting experiments, measuring things, and drawing charts is a way of life. In this environment, to understand a problem and to observe the progress of improvement, they produced a lot of charts. For efficient and precise fabrication, they developed and applied jigs (i.e., tools used to create specific shapes) and then used small tools for specific fabrication. In some cases, a component with a complex shape, such as convoluted beams for a monorail, were impossible to fabricate without well-designed jigs.

The culture of the factory was very exciting. Designers and workers were friendly and interacted well together. Once a month there were sports and cultural events, such as lunchtime (one-hour) marathons, boat races, and musical concerts. Twice a year there were work-related competitive games, such as measuring distances, heights, and weights without using gauges, scales, or other measuring devices. Most of the games involved competition among divisions including design, fabrication, and raw materials (i.e., casting and welding). They were like the "constructive disorders" that Tom DeMarco and Tim Lister wrote about in their book, *Peopleware: Productive Projects and Teams* (Dorset House).

After nine years at the machine factory, I moved to a computer factory in 1965. As the general manager of the development organization, I was responsible for developing a banking system. The development organization consisted of hardware makers, software developers, and service providers. I had to anticipate all the risks involved in such a development. One of the biggest potential problems I saw was meeting the systems' high-performance requirements. To begin meeting these requirements, I provided a scheme that consisted of a series of dynamic steps. These steps were allocated to each development group to use, and measures associated with each step were defined. I performed a drastic triage on the requirements to meet time constraints. In the final stage of development, I had to deal with troubleshooting problems created as the result of being saddled with components developed by different organizations. The system was successfully delivered in 1969. While I was in charge, I had to determine the causes of problems that occurred among these intricately interacting components and prioritize action items to address them. I learned much about systems engineering and other fields of engineering from this and other real-world experiences, and thus I became acquainted with a large number of talented individuals having differing expertise.

After a short stint working with banking systems management, I moved again to a software organization called the "software factory" in 1966, immediately after it was formed. It was named by Hitachi's then-CEO, Mr. Komai, since his philosophy was that software should be treated the same as other industrial products. When I started working at the software factory, I experienced a culture shock. Everything seemed to be different from the way the machine factory worked or the computer factory worked. I found no experiment-related approach to problem solving, and in turn, there was minimal use of measurement, numbers, and charts. Designers boldly adopted new ideas and made decisions without conducting any experiments. Tools were rarely used. What most impressed me was that they didn't boast about the products and systems they designed and developed.

When Hitachi created its software subsidiary, Hitachi Software Engineering (HSE), in 1970, I was asked to join and plan for its operation. Just two years later the term "software engineering" was coined as a new engineering field at a NATO conference. At that time, HSE initiated its software development with about 200 programmers who had been working at the software factory. These programmers were scattered over multiple projects in manpower contracts with Hitachi. Since nobody had project management skills and experience, "death-march" projects were rampant. Top management worried about the company's survival. While we were coping with these incessant problems, we were speculating how to eliminate their root causes. Eventually the company improved its practices enough to deserve to call what it was doing "software engineering."

It was obvious that we needed to train project managers and engineers to give them the power to detect, control, and resolve problems. To do this, management (and I) tried to create a culture of self-reliance, engineering attitude, and systematic thinking. The first thing we did was to better align the people. We gathered the people who were scattered over various projects and grouped them into teams that were headed by fledgling HSE project managers. Then, I provided these project managers with three types of charts for them to use, and trained them how to create weekly plots showing current project status. This approach allowed us to see a project's status and its deviation from target curves for schedule, quality, and cost from a controllability point of view (you can see some of these charts, in Tom DeMarco's classic book,[4] *Controlling Software Projects*, and in our papers[5]). This idea is based on my belief that most people spontaneously act to take control if they realize the situation. We trained the project managers to not only plot project statuses on charts, but also discern what is typically going on in the project when specific curve patterns appeared. This strategy also succeeded, and within a few years, we achieved profitable, punctual, and higher-quality projects.

Besides these charts, I introduced a lot of mechanisms and systems to help attack problems. I introduced a tool proposal system, borrowed from the idea of applying jigs that I mentioned earlier. We also introduced war game competitions on coding within the software factory. The primary principles behind these ideas are very simple: First, observe real processes in real projects (i.e., don't decide anything without observation). Second, take an engineering attitude to deal with any and all phenomena. Finally, think systematically and build in feedback mechanisms to lead to steady and stable improvement (i.e., all the principles that I experienced at the

---

4. DeMarco, Tom. *Controlling Software Projects: Management, Measurement & Estimation.* Prentice Hall, 1982.

5. Tajima, D.; and Matsubara, T. "The Computer Software Industry in Japan." *IEEE Computer,* 14, no. 5 (May 1981), pp. 89–96.

machine and computer factories). About 30 years after HSE was created, its four groups achieved CMMI maturity level 3 in 2002, and one of them achieved maturity level 5 in 2004. It was the first such achievement in the world.

The software process is based on software engineering, which is a branch of engineering. However, when I visited some software organizations, I used to be surprised that they lacked engineering expertise as part of software engineering to deal with problems. Developing software requires a complex system in which human beings are critical elements. Consequently, I believe that we must implement appropriate mechanisms for continuous improvement.

Currently, many organizations are coping with integrated process improvement that includes the development of software, hardware, and other related work. To streamline integrated process improvement, an engineering attitude and system-level thinking are common and critical keys.

Selections That Influence Your Program

You must make three selections to apply CMMI to your organization for process improvement:

1. Select a part of the organization.
2. Select a model.
3. Select a representation.

Selecting the projects to be involved in your process improvement program is critical. If you select a group that is too large, it may be too much for the initial improvement effort. The selection should also consider how homogeneous the group is (i.e., whether they all are software engineers, whether they all work on the same product or business line, and so on).

Selecting the model to be used depends on the areas your organization is interested in improving. Not only must you select a constellation (e.g., Development, Acquisition, or Services), but you must also decide whether to include any additions (e.g., IPPD).

The process of selecting the representation to be used has some guidelines because of how CMMI models are built. If your organization likes the idea of maturity levels and the staged representation, your improvement roadmap is already defined. If your organization likes the continuous representation, you can select nearly any process area or group of process areas to guide improvement, although dependencies among process areas should be considered when making such a selection.

As the process improvement plans and activities progress, other important selections must be made, including which appraisal method should be used, which projects should be appraised, how training for personnel should be secured, and which personnel should be trained.

CMMI Models

CMMI models describe what have been determined to be best practices that organizations have found to be productive and useful to achieving their business objectives. Regardless of your type of organization, to apply CMMI best practices, you must use professional judgment when interpreting them for your situation, needs, and business objectives. Although process areas depict the characteristics of an organization committed to process improvement, you must interpret the process areas using an in-depth knowledge of CMMI, your organization, the business environment, and the specific circumstances involved.

As you begin using a CMMI model to improve your organization's processes, map your real-world processes to CMMI process areas. This mapping enables you to initially judge and later track your organization's level of conformance to the CMMI model you are using and to identify opportunities for improvement.

To interpret practices, it is important to consider the overall context in which these practices are used and to determine how well the practices satisfy the goals of a process area in that context. CMMI models do not explicitly prescribe nor imply particular processes that are right for any organization or project. Instead, CMMI describes minimal criteria necessary to plan and implement processes selected by the organization for improvement based on business objectives.

CMMI practices purposely use nonspecific phrases such as "relevant stakeholders," "as appropriate," and "as necessary" to accommodate the needs of different organizations and projects. The specific needs of a project may also differ at various points during its life.

Using CMMI Appraisals

Many organizations find value in measuring their progress by conducting an appraisal and thus earning a maturity level rating or a capability level achievement profile. These appraisals are typically conducted for one or more of the following reasons:

- To determine how well the organization's processes compare to CMMI best practices and identify areas where improvement can be made
- To inform external customers and suppliers about how well the organization's processes compare to CMMI best practices
- To meet the contract requirements of one or more customers

Appraisals of organizations using a CMMI model must conform to the requirements defined in the Appraisal Requirements for CMMI (ARC) document. These appraisals focus on identifying improvement opportunities and comparing the organization's processes to CMMI best practices. Appraisal teams use a CMMI model and ARC-conformant appraisal method to guide their evaluation of the organization as well as how they report their conclusions. The appraisal results are then used (by a process group, for example) to plan improvements for the organization.

Appraisal Requirements for CMMI

The ARC document describes the requirements for several types of appraisals. A full benchmarking class of appraisal is defined as a Class A appraisal. Less formal methods are defined as Class B or Class C methods. The ARC document was designed to help improve consistency across appraisal methods, and to help appraisal method developers, sponsors, and users understand the tradeoffs associated with various methods [SEI 2006a].

Depending on the purpose of the appraisal and the nature of the circumstances, one class may be preferred over the others. Sometimes self-assessments, initial appraisals, quick-look or mini-appraisals, incremental appraisals, or external appraisals are appropriate, and other times a formal benchmarking appraisal is appropriate.

A particular appraisal method is declared an ARC Class A, B, or C appraisal method based on the sets of ARC requirements that the method developer addressed when designing the method.

More information about the ARC is available on the SEI Web site at www.sei.cmu.edu/cmmi/appraisals/appraisals.html.

SCAMPI Appraisal Methods

The SCAMPI appraisal methods are the generally accepted methods used for conducting appraisals using CMMI models. The SCAMPI

Method Definition Document (MDD) defines rules for ensuring the consistency of appraisal ratings. For benchmarking against other organizations, appraisals must ensure consistent ratings. The achievement of a specific maturity level or the satisfaction of a process area must mean the same thing for different appraised organizations.

The SCAMPI family of appraisals includes Class A, B, and C appraisal methods. SCAMPI A is the most rigorous method and the only method that can result in a rating. SCAMPI B provides options in model scope, but the characterization of practices is fixed to one scale and is performed on implemented practices. SCAMPI C provides a wide range of options, including characterization of planned approaches to process implementation according to a scale defined by the user.

More information about SCAMPI methods is available on the SEI Web site at www.sei.cmu.edu/cmmi/appraisals/appraisals.html [SEI 2006b].

Appraisal Considerations

Choices that affect a CMMI-based appraisal include the following:

- Which CMMI model to use for the appraisal (for this constellation, the choice would be between the CMMI for Development model and the CMMI for Development +IPPD model)
- Establishing the appraisal scope, including the organizational unit to be appraised, the CMMI process areas to be investigated, and the maturity level or capability level(s) to be appraised
- Selecting the appraisal method
- Selecting the appraisal team members
- Selecting appraisal participants from the appraisal entities to be interviewed
- Establishing appraisal outputs (e.g., ratings or instantiation-specific findings)
- Establishing appraisal constraints (e.g., time spent on site)

The SCAMPI MDD allows the selection of predefined options for use in an appraisal. These appraisal options are designed to help organizations align CMMI with their business needs and objectives.

Documentation of CMMI appraisal plans and results must always include a description of the appraisal options, model scope, and organizational scope selected. This documentation confirms whether an appraisal meets the requirements for benchmarking.

For organizations that wish to appraise multiple functions or groups, CMMI's integrated approach enables some economy of scale in model and appraisal training. One appraisal method can provide separate or combined results for multiple functions.

The appraisal principles for the CMMI Product Suite[6] remain the same as those used in appraisals for other process improvement models. Those principles are as follows:

- Senior management sponsorship[7]
- A focus on the organization's business objectives
- Confidentiality for interviewees
- Use of a documented appraisal method
- Use of a process reference model (e.g., a CMMI model) as a base
- A collaborative team approach
- A focus on actions for process improvement

How Do You Get the True Value of a CMMI Appraisal?

by Hal Wilson

There appears to be a common belief that earning CMMI appraisal credentials is a guarantee of success in whatever venture might be attempted. Unfortunately, no such guarantee is implied in bestowing CMMI credentials. A CMMI appraisal simply accredits that an organization has demonstrated evidence of the ability to create and follow a set of standard processes that represent industry best practices and, if followed, should provide the basis of success.

It is a documented fact that a set of mature and repeatable processes is an important requirement for success, and the presence of these processes places the organization in the position of having a high probability of achieving success, assuming that other important elements are also present. These other elements include the following:

- Properly funded projects
- Reasonable and achievable schedules

---

6. See the glossary for the definition of "CMMI Product Suite."

7. Experience has shown that the most critical factor influencing successful process improvement and appraisals is senior management sponsorship.

- Committed management
- Meaningful and clearly stated requirements
- A clearly defined scope of work
- Accurately defined interfaces
- Experienced project management
- Trained staff who are experienced in the domain

Of course, typically in today's world, all of these elements are rarely in place at the beginning of a project. Therefore, it is a challenge of the organization to plan for these elements and the risks associated with them.

The SCAMPI method is an effective, repeatable means of gathering and assessing the completeness of an organization's processes, its commitment to execute them on sampled projects, and evidence that these processes are actually employed on projects. Maturity models have always had an unstated presumption that organizations with mature and repeatable processes will use them every time. It would seem logical to assume that organizations that have expended considerable effort to pursue process improvement would also expend effort to employ their processes. From experience, it would seem that some organizations don't always recognize that logic and lose the value of their process investment.

Unfortunately, there is no mechanism in CMMI to validate that such future action will actually occur at the start of a new project. Therefore, it is important that the appraised organization realize that it is the organization's responsibility to ensure that these best practices are actually employed and don't become shelfware.

CMMI appraisals are conducted based on evidence from projects selected by the organization. The next project to be started is an endeavor that is still to come, a potential to be executed in the future. To be successful, the organization must employ its best practices using a newly formed project team to provide the basis for successful execution. When starting a new project, the organization still must ensure that the new project will be able to assemble a team of trained individuals and employ organizational practices with rigor from the outset in order to achieve success. The organization must also ensure that the new project will not apply its practices sloppily or haphazardly and thus do damage to the project's success.

Having good engineering processes in place is an important step along the path to success on new projects. However, much of the critical work that leads to project success is accomplished in the first few months of the project, and employing the organization's processes from the outset by a trained and experienced staff is more important than the processes themselves.

There is evidence that some organizations that spent considerable resources in creating enviable process sets that have been appraised as mature and repeatable have not always invested as heavily in perfecting their ability to roll out those processes rapidly and efficiently when new projects start. To really experience the value of CMMI appraisals and validation of an organization's process, the organization has to learn to deploy its processes early and effectively. Once a project is underway, there is little time for basic process training and for backtracking to rework initial efforts that did not use the best practices.

The positive side of process improvement is that organizations that are truly committed to its tenets are recognizable by their actions, not just by their credentials. The CMMI appraisal provides some insight into the organizational commitment and attitude toward process improvement and its willingness to employ process improvement, not just to attain a credential that will sit on the shelf. Further examination of the organization's methods can add further insight concerning its probability of achieving success.

High-maturity organizations (i.e., those that have achieved CMMI maturity level 4 or 5) willingly demonstrate how they use measurements as a management tool and to determine that their organizations are actually employing their organizational processes effectively. One of the advantages of having a measurement practice and quantitative management behavior ingrained in an organization is that such behaviors help organizations ensure that they are executing effectively. These behaviors are especially suited to monitoring an organization's performance on starting up new projects with the full set of organizational best practices. Such organizational techniques also encourage new projects to adopt the organizational processes from the outset and monitor that they are employing them effectively.

Instead of simply expecting that a CMMI appraisal credential will yield success, organizations still need to promote an environment that will ensure that the best practices will be used in a consistent and disciplined fashion on all projects. CMMI best practices and the SCAMPI methods focus on improving organizational behavior. Without constant attention, it is easy for organizations to slip back into bad habits. Therefore, organizations must be committed to continually invest in monitoring their performance, ensuring employment of its processes, improving processes, providing training, and valuing the experience of the most critical resource in the organization, its people.

A CMMI appraisal provides an outstanding benchmark on the state of an organization's processes. If the organization stops there, it probably won't get the real value of its investment. The biggest return on that investment occurs when the process commitment that resulted in a successful appraisal is continued and exploited on the start of every new project.

CMMI-Related Training

Whether your organization is new to process improvement or is already familiar with process improvement models, training is a key element in the ability of organizations to adopt CMMI. An initial set of courses is provided by the SEI and its Partners, but your organization may wish to supplement these courses with internal instruction. This approach allows your organization to focus on the areas that provide the greatest business value.

The SEI and its Partners offer the *Introduction to CMMI* course, which provides a basic overview of the CMMI models. The SEI also offers the *Intermediate Concepts of CMMI* course to those who plan to become more deeply involved in CMMI adoption or appraisal—for example, those who will guide improvement as part of a process group, those who will lead SCAMPI appraisals, and those who will teach the *Introduction to CMMI* course. Current information about CMMI-related training is available on the SEI Web site at www.sei.cmu.edu/cmmi/training/training.html.

Improving Industrial Practice

by Hans-Jürgen Kugler

"If only we *consequently* applied what we already know about software engineering there would be fewer software problems" is a sentiment that is echoed by all state-of-practice studies. How many software products have a design—maintained over their lifetime—that embodies the principles of good software engineering as, for instance, laid down in Dave Parnas' seminal 1972 paper?[8]

8. Parnas, David L. "On the Criteria to Be Used in Decomposing Systems into Modules." *Communication of the ACM,* 15, no. 12 (1972), pp. 1053–1058.

Such software products are generally *systems* that interact with other systems and thus have the potential for undesired "feature interaction." The "real" software development process, which one "lives" on a daily basis, needs to be considered to be an essential *business* process with direct impact on margin and market share. "Business" and "systems" are key words.

If the "standard" process does not return value to the business, it is bypassed, substituted by waivers, and leads to task forces. CMMI provides valuable guidance as to what a development process needs to address to provide such competitive advantage.

Both of the aforementioned keywords are also a reminder that a development organization is part of a value creation network, and that really generating potential from good practices requires taking a market perspective. My hypothesis is that a difference of more than one level of maturity between supplier and customer will cause difficulties when they try to interface their respective development processes, and therefore, will pose a risk for the overall value chain.

The aim must be to improve industrial practice of the *whole market*. CMMI provides a framework for the evolution of an individual organization, both in maturity and in product or service scope. It does not address the value creation network. I will argue that it is feasible to drive improvements across a whole market segment on the basis of two examples: one from Germany, the home base of my company, and one from Ireland, where the Irish Software Engineering Research Centre investigates some of these aspects.

According to Geoffrey Moore,[9] a market is constituted by "all of those referencing each other in a buying decision." In the automotive market in Germany, according to the manufacturers, 70 percent to 80 percent of the innovation derives from electronics, and 80 percent to 90 percent of that is realized in software.

Our "kingpin" in this domain is Bosch. Bosch is the world's largest tier 1 supplier to the automotive industry, and as such, it strives to master the software challenge comprehensively. Software improvement success here affects the whole supply chain. Bosch's corporate Initiative for Software-determined Systems (BISS)[10] has

---

9. Moore, Geoffrey A. *Crossing the Chasm: Marketing and Selling High-Tech Products to Mainstream Customers.* New York: HarperCollins Publishers, 1991.

10. Wagner, Thomas. Robert Bosch GmbH. "Bringing Software on the Road." SEPG 2004 (Orlando, FL: March 2004).

shown great success with some significant improvements in business units reported publicly.[11]

Awareness creation through public events and specific mentoring of customer-supplier relations allowed Bosch to externalize such achievements, and this externalization resulted in the development process being recognized as a key driver for operational excellence. The relevant automotive industry association (Verband deutscher Automobilindustrie, VDA)[12] issued guidelines, and a software initiative (HIS) was formed by the OEMs.[13]

One key move is to use process maturity to evaluate the ability of suppliers to deliver as committed and to drive industrial best-practice adoption as part of development contracts. The model chosen by the HIS group is based on an automotive adaptation of ISO 15504, "automotive SPICE."[14] The model is designed for assessments in the automotive domain and is compatible with the continuous representation of CMMI.[15]

CMMI remains the foundation of most of the improvement programs. Results show that the market strategy outlined at the beginning does work: Assessments of software development processes show a general trend reflecting improved practices.[16] As a matter of fact, it now reaches the nonautomotive parts of the major industrial players, such as TSS, the IT subsidiary of DaimlerChrysler,[17] which last year reached CMMI level 2 (software), with continuing executive commitment to higher maturity levels. The customer in its market moves the supplier in its own domain and thus goes beyond traditional industry segments.

Lessons learned from this market-based approach form the basis for a wide-scale improvement approach in the Irish software-producing sector. This is a horizontal market mainly consisting of

---

11. Kugler, H.-J.; et. al. "Critical Success Factors for Software Process Improvement at Bosch GS." Electronic Systems for Vehicles, 11th International Congress, VDI (Baden-Baden, 2003).

12. Verband deutscher Automobilindustrie (German Association of Automotive Industry), VDA Volume 13, Development of Software-Driven Systems—Requirements for Processes and Products (1st Edition, 2004); www.vda-qmc.de.

13. HIS—Herstellerinitiative Software (OEM Software Initiative by Audi, BMW, Daimler-Chrysler, Porsche, and Volkswagen); www.automotive-his.de.

14. Automotive SPICE; www.automotive-his.de.

15. Hörmann, Klaus. "Comparison of CMMI and ISO 15504." Kugler Maag CIE white paper.

16. Dittmann, Lars. "Nutzen von SPICE aus der Sicht eines OEM." Volkswagen AG, IAA Workshop (Frankfurt, September 2005).

17. DaimlerChrysler TSS GmbH; http://seir.sei.cmu.edu/pars/pars_list_iframe.asp.

small and medium-size enterprises (SMEs.) Many of the currently targeted 1,300 plus companies have only one dozen or two dozen software-related staff members.

Yet the software sector alone contributes 12 percent of Irish GDP, without even counting those companies whose products and services are also software determined. In this horizontal market, we do not have the uniformity of supply relationships that the automotive market of Germany offers. This has to be compensated for by "clustering." Clusters of SMEs around different aspects, such as domains and target markets, are a concept well supported by Enterprise Ireland,[18] a development agency that now has taken on the objective of increasing the competence of indigenous companies developing software by establishing software process improvement as accepted good practice in industry.[19]

Clusters allow the use of Moore's market definition and strategy. This means working directly with a few kingpins to generate an overall movement. The clusters are still being defined, with one on automotive software in formation and one on medical device applications under consideration. In these domains, the synergy between "local" clusters and international customers can be exploited to create similar market forces to that in the case of Germany.

Process awareness among technical and business leaders is a precondition for active participation in clusters. Creating this awareness is of particular importance in an industry whose growth rates are a measure of their success. So far, three awareness events with international experts and local companies that are recognized good practice leaders and potential kingpins have been held in different regions with great success, and the next ones are scheduled. Here again, the message is that software process improvement is business improvement. It cannot simply be relegated to a sole technical issue.[20]

An initial study of software process issues in a wide range of companies returned interesting results, confirming the overall approach. Creating clusters and "beachheads" requires deployment support, technically and financially. Software process improvement

---

18. See www.enterprise-ireland.com.

19. Connolly, Eugene; and Kugler, H.-J. "Establishing Software Process Improvement in SMEs." Presentation at the First International Research Workshop for Process Improvement in Small Settings (SEI, Pittsburgh: 2005).

20. A key recommended reference at such awareness events is Humphrey, Watts. *Winning with Software: An Executive Strategy* (Boston: Addison-Wesley, 2002).

is supported by a general Productivity Development Fund, but it is recognized that transfer must be actively pursued. Adapting processes and their improvement with the view to the role of SMEs in globally distributed software development is a research topic of Lero, the Irish Software Engineering Research Centre.[21]

A qualification scheme is being studied to ensure a supply of managerially and technically competent mentors, coaches, and "solution teams" that Enterprise Ireland will recommend. Further plans include labs for process modeling and enactment providing demonstration and expert assistance in gathering experience in methods and with tools. This will be a joint user industry, vendor, research, and Enterprise-Ireland initiative to provide what the German automotive industry can afford of its accord. My predictions for the future of process improvement, and therefore for the CMMI, are bright.

---

21. Blowers, Rosario; and Richardson, Ita. "The Capability Maturity Model (SW and Integrated) Tailored in Small Indigenous Software Industries." Proceedings of the First International Research Workshop for Process Improvement in Small Settings (SEI, Pittsburgh: 2005).

CHAPTER 6

CASE STUDY:
APPLYING CMMI TO SERVICES AT RAYTHEON

This case study is but one example of creative, intelligent, and motivated professionals applying CMMI in their organization. We were impressed by this group's summary of their experiences and how they persisted until they found a way to apply CMMI to help them with their process improvement.

We have found that organizations in increasingly diverse industries and environments are using CMMI to help with their process improvement programs in various ways. To respond to this need, some organizations are interpreting CMMI best practices so that they suit their specific environments, just as is described in this case study. The CMMI Product Team has also responded with products to help those in environments that are not strictly product development, to apply CMMI appropriately.

The CMMI Acquisition Module, updated in May 2005, was developed primarily for use in government acquisition program offices. It has been in use since its release in February 2004 and has helped these types of organizations to use CMMI best practices in their environments.

Also, two projects are underway to develop new "constellations" to serve two different applications of CMMI. Although we cannot say at this point what form these constellations will take, their purposes are fairly clear. The purpose of the CMMI for Services constellation is to assist organizations that deliver services. The purpose of the CMMI for Acquisition constellation is to assist organizations that deal with suppliers, including those in government and industry settings. These projects are involving individuals from multiple organizations and viewpoints who are trying to formulate best practices that can be applied across multiple organizations.

As CMMI matures, we will see various ways that it can be used and applied. We hope to learn from all of these approaches and share them with CMMI users and potential users. What is most important is that organizations be able to achieve process improvement, meet their business objectives, and improve their bottom line.

—Mary Beth, Mike, and Sandy

CMMI has historically been applied almost exclusively to organizations engaged in product development as opposed to services. As such, few examples and no practical guidance exist for applying CMMI to service organizations.[1] Increased interest in applying CMMI to services has stimulated discussions surrounding the need for a separate services model. However, in its present form, CMMI does extend the set of industry best practices beyond that of just software, to systems engineering and more, opening the door for greater opportunities in model application.

Raytheon's Pasadena Operations tackled the problem of applying CMMI to services over a six-year period, and the result of its efforts was a methodology for using CMMI in the services sector. In the process of struggling with the application of CMMI (initially the Software CMM) to the operation's service-based business, questions arose about the exact differences between the product development and services sectors. The CMMI model itself affirmed the applicability of applying CMMI to services in its definitions of "product" and "work product" in the glossary.

- The word "product" is used throughout the CMMI Product Suite to mean a work product that is intended for delivery to a customer or end user. The form of a product can vary in different contexts.
- The word "work product" is used to mean a useful result of a process. This can include files, documents, products, parts of a product, **services**, process descriptions, specifications, and invoices. (Emphasis added.)

CMMI for Development, v1.2

In the spirit of these definitions, the Pasadena Operations was able to apply CMMI in an organization in the services sector. This application includes Raytheon's currently patent-pending lifecycle model for services (see Figure 6.4) as well as conceptual insights (see the section titled Epiphanies, later in this chapter) with regard to the CMMI model. Initially, however, the definitions of product and work product, shown earlier, provided little direction or guidance on practical

---

1. Two examples of work done to apply CMMI to services include the following reports, available on the Software Engineering Institute (SEI) Web site: (1) Herndon, Mary Anne; et. al. Interpreting Capability Maturity Model® Integration (CMMI®) for Service Organizations—A Systems Engineering and Integration Services Example (CMU/SEI-2003-TN-005). Pittsburgh: Software Engineering Institute, Carnegie Mellon University, 2003. (2) Gallagher, Brian P. Interpreting Capability Maturity Model Integration (CMMI) for Operational Organizations (CMU/SEI-2002-TN-006). Pittsburgh: Software Engineering Institute, Carnegie Mellon University, 2002.

application. Questions focused on issues concerning the degree of autonomy afforded by the customer in each sector, with services arguably having less autonomy than industries engaged in product development. Varying degrees of autonomy occur in the services sector, ranging from relatively high autonomy where tasks are contracted out by the customer (e.g., information technology), all the way to low autonomy, or "pure services," where the customer typically embeds personnel provided by the contractor directly onto his team. In this pure services case, the customer typically exercises complete control over the personnel as well as the contract, with changes to the latter occurring with only short notice to the contractor.

In addition, with services, the time spent on development versus delivery differs radically when compared to product generation, as illustrated in Figure 6.1. For services, the development phase is relatively brief and is largely performed upfront during the establishment of the initial governing contract. Most of the effort is spent on delivery of the service to the customer. The exact opposite is true for product development, where most of the effort is spent in development and relatively little in delivery. As a result, most of the focus of CMMI best practices (as traditionally applied to product development) is concentrated on *building* the product for delivery, with little or no focus on post-development activities. As such, application of the CMMI model to services is problematic, since many of the practices *require* developing plans, designing solutions, and monitoring progress.

In sharp contrast with the product-oriented organization where most of the lifecycle is spent developing the product, in service-oriented organizations most of the lifecycle is spent delivering the service (product). The development and integration of the service is a relatively brief, although intense, phase.

Services also tend to have lower profit margins than product development and less opportunity exists for passing cost on to the

Product versus Services Development/Delivery Timeline

Product		Develop	Deliver
Service	Develop	Deliver	

FIGURE 6.1
Product versus Services Development/Delivery Timeline

customer by adjusting product pricing. The result is a significantly lower overhead in services companies. The CMMI best practices, however, require performing functions such as quality assurance, configuration management, and process improvement that are traditionally performed as overhead functions in product development organizations.

So, how does a pure services organization of 120 people achieve CMMI maturity level 3, with limited resources for process improvement, staffed with practitioners from standard (product-oriented), high-maturity organizations, with high variation in its technical disciplines and little or no project autonomy from its customers? The answer to this question was found at the Pasadena Operations in 2004 and is detailed in this case study, along with practical solutions. It was found via an evolution of thought that involved the following:

- Studying projects and contracts, realizing that, as a pure services organization, customers have full autonomy over project planning and management
- Acknowledging the necessity for a common solution that was discipline independent and could be applied across all projects
- Employing practical, end-user-based (template-based) solutions

The success of these solutions was demonstrated on December 17, 2004, with the award of a maturity level 3 rating to Raytheon's Pasadena Operations by a third-party SCAMPI A appraisal team led by an independent SEI-authorized lead appraiser.

The Organization and Its Process Dilemma

Raytheon's Pasadena Operations is part of Raytheon Information Solutions (RIS), which is the Federal Information Technology Business Unit of Raytheon Company, a $20 billion aerospace and defense organization. RIS provides a wide range of professional support services to the federal information technology marketplace. Serving government agencies, RIS is dedicated to enabling U.S. civil and defense customers to transform, modernize, and integrate their agencies through the effective use of information technology. RIS consists of five customer-focused business areas and more than 1,400 employees.

The Pasadena Operations consists of a single program office and program manager and is divided into five functional departments. Each department is headed by a department manager who typically oversees several projects.

The work undertaken at the Pasadena Operations encompasses a wide variety of disciplines (from software and systems engineering, to information technology, operations, and scientific analysis) in support of numerous customer projects. Key disciplines include GPS applications, spacecraft navigation and mission analysis, software development for navigation and mission design, science data processing and analysis, information processing systems, ocean data-center operations, information technology, remote sensing, and Web applications. Since the Pasadena Operations is not organized as a matrix organization along functional areas, but rather, is organized across lines of business, a given department might encompass several traditional disciplines (e.g., software engineering, systems engineering, information technology, analysis).

The customer typically acts as the prime project developer, with Raytheon as a subcontractor, providing vital services. Raytheon technical personnel are often integrated directly with the customer team that is engaged in developing the product. As such, the responsibility for overall project planning, risk management, configuration management, and so on, is assumed by the customer, not the services contractor.

Difficulties are readily apparent when attempting a direct application of CMMI to such an organization. Questions arise, such as: How can project planning be done when the customer is running the project? What if the customer decides not to perform one or more practices identified in the CMMI model? How can an organizational standard process be developed that will encompass diverse tasks such as satellite operations, graphic design, and system administration?

History

The history of process improvement and development in Pasadena is as old as the Operations. In 1998, Raytheon opened the Pasadena Operations after it was awarded the Science Data Systems and Implementation and Operations (SDSIO) contract to provide technical and scientific services to the California Institute of Technology and NASA's Jet Propulsion Laboratory. Its success was largely a result of the experience and quality of the staff. Many of these individuals came to the company with many years of experience, often from high-maturity organizations. As a result, a grassroots effort took shape almost immediately to apply process to the work.

Initial obstacles came not from management or the customer, but from the high number of disparate disciplines within the organization and the product-oriented nature of CMMI. With little or no guidance available to aid this effort, the path to successful application would take more than five years.

Process improvement at the Pasadena Operations began shortly after work started. This effort is notable, since it began as and continues to be a grassroots effort that started with the capability maturity model (CMM). A process improvement Special Interest Group (SIG) started up in March 1999 as members of the technical staff discussed the application of formal processes to their current work assignments and to the Pasadena Operations as a whole. Although a number of staff members had come from high-maturity organizations, this was the first time that many were working in a services environment and their experience with formal processes was limited to traditional project-oriented product development. As a result, the focus was on the traditional application of the CMM to current projects and tasks.

This approach immediately encountered obstacles. First, as a services organization, the Pasadena Operations did not have the infrastructure to support a traditional application of a CMMI model. This lack of infrastructure is a direct result of the services business model, which by necessity is designed for direct customer interaction. As a result, the expenses associated with traditional execution of the organization and support process areas of CMMI (i.e., OPF, OPD, OT, CM, PPQA, MA, and DAR) would, for example, need to be passed directly to the customer or funded in such a way that their cost was ultimately billed to the customer. This seemed unlikely if the Pasadena Operations was to remain competitive in the services industry.

Second, most of the Project Management process areas of CMMI (i.e., PP, PMC, IPM, SAM, and RSKM) were "owned" by the customer, since almost all projects undertaken at the Pasadena Operations were run directly by the customer with Raytheon acting in a supporting role (usually by having personnel embedded on the project as team members).

Third, many of the customer's projects were relatively small endeavors (e.g., review a technical paper) and the customer consciously chose not to formally perform many of the engineering practices in CMMI (i.e., RD, REQM, TS, PI, VER, and VAL).

Finally, the diverse nature of the work undertaken by the Pasadena Operations presents its own set of challenges to defining and establishing an organizational standard process that can be applied to all of these activities. For example, how is PI applied to a report containing an analysis of ocean-level and sea-state data? What requirements need managing in routine satellite operations? Is TS applicable for system administration? What risks are associated with generating a graphic design for artwork on a Web page? These questions remained largely unanswered throughout the four-year period from 1999 through 2002.

A top-down approach of building a standard process based on the CMMI model and applying it to selected projects undertaken in a services environment met with failure. Worse, many of the questions of applicability remained unanswered.

As 2002 ended, failure had not dampened enthusiasm for finding a standard process that would work for the Pasadena Operations and the movement to do so remained grassroots. A switch in model focus had begun at the Pasadena Operations in March 2002, with the release of CMMI version 1.1 in January of that year. In August 2002, a new and larger Process SIG was formed with a bottom-up perspective, as well as a charter of analyzing existing processes at the Pasadena Operations and discovering and defining the organization's process identity.

The bottom-up approach to process improvement that started in 2003 focused on conducting a department-by-department analysis of existing processes and procedures. A systematic but unfunded effort began in April 2003 and was supplemented by informal in-house training in the CMMI model. Training in CMMI began in June 2003 with SIG members researching individual process areas and making presentations to the larger group. By the end of 2003, a formal effort had begun to develop a process for the Pasadena Operations and to achieve a level 3 maturity rating against the model by the end of the following year. To this end, a Raytheon Six Sigma project was started in November to achieve this goal. Six Sigma is Raytheon's methodology for process improvement and cultural change and is used throughout the company for all improvement efforts.

At this point, efforts were directed at finding one or more projects in which Raytheon was performing most or all of the practices defined in the model. Three (chiefly software) projects were identified where Raytheon's support included performing many (but not all) of the traditional model processes, and a formal gap analysis was conducted. In addition, the search for a lead appraiser was undertaken and help was sought from other parts of Raytheon, notably the Fullerton Operations.

Although significant areas of conformance between current practices and the model were found during the gap analysis, no single project was found to be in complete compliance. The prospects for bringing any project into full compliance remained problematic due to issues of autonomy, control, and infrastructure. Worse, the projects analyzed represented only a fraction of the Operations' work and the prospects for including other projects seemed unlikely at best. The idea of an aggregate approach to process application dominated the thinking of the process improvement effort through the end of 2003 and into 2004.

The need to continue with process improvement and achieve a maturity rating had also become more urgent. The customer had announced plans to attain a level 2 rating by 2005 and a level 3 rating by 2007. If successful, this might cause the customer to demand a rating of 2 or 3 from contractors. As a result, even a rating limited to only a few projects was desirable from a business survival standpoint.

Success at Last

The effort to achieve a maturity level 3 rating for the Pasadena Operations was established in 2003. At the beginning of 2004, management funded a formal effort to achieve a maturity level 3 model rating before the end of the calendar year. This effort was funded and supported by the local and corporate management teams. However, a strict one-year deadline was imposed by management and the funding allocated was the equivalent of three people working full time. Three major goals were established:

- Achieve a maturity level 3 rating faster and more cost effectively than had previously been accomplished anywhere in the industry.
- Develop appropriate and meaningful solutions for the business.
- Generate solutions that were transferable to other parts of Raytheon.

In early 2004, the current state of the Pasadena Operations with respect to the model had been appraised with the completion of a gap analysis of three software-like projects.

The first breakthrough occurred in early 2004 with the identification of a Contract Work Order (CWO)—each of the individual Task Orders (TO) under our umbrella SDSIO contract—with a *project*. This conceptual breakthrough shifted the process focus away from the traditional technical generation and delivery of a *product* and toward the managing and delivery of a *service*. It also allowed the process to include all work undertaken at the Pasadena Operations, regardless of the type of work or the involvement of the customer in that work. This emulated the approach championed by Raytheon's director of quality and Six Sigma to achieve ISO registration a few years earlier. However, the details of applying all CMMI process areas were far from being worked out. It was clear at the beginning of 2004 that to achieve the ambitious goals established for the effort with the given resources, a well-planned but creative approach would be required. As such, the process improvement effort established the following general approach for achieving its goals:

- A bottom-up approach of mapping CMMI to existing processes and procedures would be used.
- A traditional engineering lifecycle of requirements development, design, implementation, verification, and validation would be used to develop the organization's process.
- An evolutionally or staged approach to the Class C and B appraisals would be employed.
- The solutions developed would be template based, eliminating the need for users to be familiar with the CMMI model, thereby allowing them to focus on their day-to-day work.
- The solution would be sufficiently general to allow direct utilization by other service-oriented organizations.

These five guidelines formed the cornerstone of the approach for achieving a level 3 maturity rating at the Pasadena Operations. These guidelines also proved critical to the success of the effort. In addition, the roles played by key personnel on the process development team proved critical to achieving success.

With these guidelines and the identification of task orders as projects, process improvement proceeded at a rapid pace. The Pasadena Operations standard process was *evolved*, from a set of policies and procedures starting in early May to a fully deployed and mature process by mid-December. With his thorough understanding of the organization and its culture, the lead appraiser recommended a phased-in approach to process deployment (and the SCAMPI appraisals) over this six-month period. This had five advantages:

1. It permitted plans and templates to be thoroughly evaluated and refined before organization-wide deployment.
2. It allowed the appraisal team to participate in this process and provide valuable feedback before deployment.
3. It facilitated piloting new plans and templates on a relatively small number of projects to "debug" new procedures.

4. It provided time for brainstorming of new plans, templates, and procedures that streamlined the organization's process and minimized the impact of changes on behavior.

5. It allowed corrections and refinements to be incorporated at all stages of deployment.

The template-based approach, shown in Figure 6.2, allows abstracting the CMMI model away from the operations process. The project leads select the appropriate templates for the lifecycle from the process asset library (PAL). The practitioners simply use these templates and

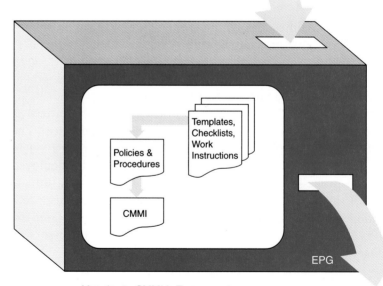

Implementation: Template-Based Process

Organization's defined process is the engineering procedures and templates

Project's defined process is the implementation of the lifecycle and its instantiated templates

Project Leads

Templates,
Checklists,
Work
Instructions

Policies &
Procedures

CMMI

EPG

Mapping to CMMI Is Transparent

Project Process: Templates,
Examples & Training

Project Leads & Project Team

FIGURE 6.2
The Use of Templates for Implementation

associated work instructions to conduct their work. This way, the day-to-day activities map "behind the scenes" into the organizational policies and procedures and these, in turn, map into the model.

The schedule established for the improvement project was the primary driving factor in the approach used. The Earned Value Management System (EVMS) was used to track schedules and costs throughout the project.

Requirements development began by documenting the organization's current process lifecycle. This process was compared with the CMMI model and gaps were identified. A set of policies and procedures was subsequently developed for the organization. These were verified using peer reviews by the management team and focus groups and were later examined by the appraisal team.

After the requirements phase, templates and plans were designed by the process developers and were piloted on a single project (task order). These templates were evaluated by the technical staff and the appraisal team and were refined via the SCAMPI B. As refinements were incorporated into these documents they were deployed across the organization. The design, implementation, verification, and validation phases were therefore staged across the three SCAMPI B events, with a corresponding staged deployment of the process after each event. Figure 6.3 shows a timeline of the project.

Because services have relatively low overhead compared to most product development businesses, the solutions used for process improvement were required to impose no increase in overhead. This is a severe constraint, especially with respect to areas of the model such as PPQA, which in traditional applications is typically implemented as a separate and autonomous group within the organization. Adding one person to the program office at the Pasadena Operations to perform this function (even part time) was precluded from the start.

Likewise, process areas such as IPM, which traditionally require tailoring the organization's standard process to a project, needed to be efficient and quick. With these considerations, a template-based approach was adopted for process solutions. Under this approach, the organization's standard process consists of its lifecycle (see Figure 6.4) and associated templates and governing documents. This approach eliminates almost all of the overhead associated with traditional product-oriented implementations, with the added benefit that only members of the Engineering Process Group (EPG) need to possess a high degree of familiarity with the model.

As such, the template designers (i.e., the EPG) are responsible for ensuring model coverage via the templates. Users of the templates need only be trained in proper utilization. This approach not only decreases the organizational overhead associated with process maintenance, but also increases buy-in from management and the technical staff who can concentrate on work, yet be guaranteed seamless compliance with model practices.

Key Roles That Contributed to Success

The fast-paced development and deployment of process improvement at the Pasadena Operations was facilitated to a high degree by well-defined roles assumed by key participants involved in the project. Each role made a significant contribution to the overall success of the effort and (in future such endeavors) should be given greater consideration upfront.

- **Benevolent/Involved Patron and Sponsor.** The benevolent patron and sponsor was the corporate sponsor and champion of the Pasadena Operations process improvement effort. He not only secured the necessary funding, but also removed obstacles, provided needed resources, made valuable contributions to the process design, and participated on the appraisal team.
- **Steering Committee.** The Steering Committee was the governing body for the process improvement effort. Its membership included the Pasadena Operations program manager (chairman), the department managers, and the EPG.
- **The (Unlikely) EPG.** The Enterprise Process Group consisted of only four people and acted as the process designers and developers. This group included the Manager and the Seer. The membership of this group was augmented at various times by members of the technical staff, especially for data collection prior to the SCAMPI appraisals.
    - **The Manager.** The project manager ran the process improvement initiative as a formal project using formal management techniques, such as EVMS, risk management, and reporting. He oversaw the effort, solved and corrected problems, and acted as a go-between with corporate management.
    - **The Seer.** This individual was responsible for the overall design and implementation of the process solutions, thus ensuring uniformity of solutions and timely development. He worked very closely with the sage and, at periodic milestones, with the lead appraiser to create efficient and pragmatic "out of the box" solutions.
- **The Front Runner.** This role managed process piloting, thereby ensuring that solutions would work once they were deployed.

- **The Sage.** This individual served as the experienced process expert and acted as a counselor to provide guidance during the process improvement effort.
- **Best Practices Communications Committee.** This group (composed of members of the local technical staff) disseminated information and built an overall *esprit de corps* that proved crucial to the overall success of the effort.
- **Focus Groups.** These groups, formed from the local technical staff, provided a "sanity" check on the process as it was developed.

As Figure 6.3 shows, beginning in the second quarter of 2003 a bottom-up approach to process improvement resulted in informal process evaluations by each department, followed by a Raytheon Six Sigma effort to achieve a CMMI level 3 rating by the end of 2004. This effort was ultimately successful following a SCAMPI A in mid-December of 2004, which resulted in the Pasadena Operations achieving a level 3 maturity rating.

Approach to Interpreting CMMI for Services

To provide the reader with an idea of how the CMMI level 3 process areas were mapped to services, the following sampling of the complete mapping is given in this section of the case study. Process areas are grouped into four categories identified by CMMI: Process Management, Project Management, Engineering, and Support. One example is provided within each category. Tables 6.1 through 6.4 list the goals for a process area in each category, the services interpretation, and the Raytheon service solution. (The solutions were used as direct evidence during the SCAMPI A.) Specific practice numbers indicate the specific practices from CMMI version 1.1.

Process Artifacts

The artifacts used as direct evidence during SCAMPI appraisals constitute the process solution set. As such, these documents are divided into three categories: plans, templates, and checklists.

Plans are signed organizational documents whose scope spans projects. That is, plans apply to every project within the organization and are typically signed by the program manager or members of the program office (e.g., EPG, department managers, and training coordinator). They apply to all projects undertaken by the organization and are modified as needed when the method of service delivery changes or when they expire.

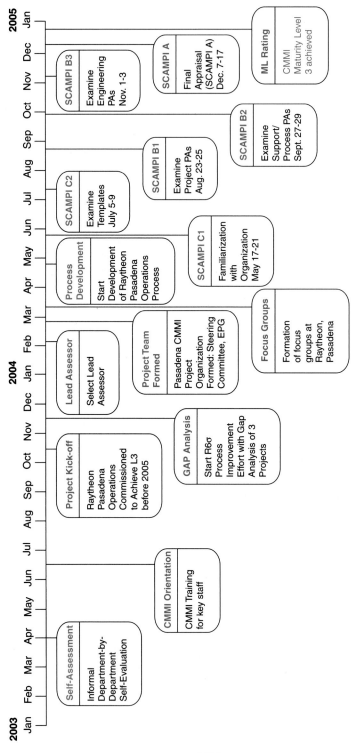

FIGURE 6.3
Process Improvement Timeline 2003–2004

TABLE 6.1 Process Management: Organizational Process Focus (OPF)

CMMI Goal	Services Interpretation	Raytheon Solution (Direct Evidence)
Goal 1: Strengths, weaknesses, and improvement opportunities for the organization's processes are identified periodically and as needed.	(SP 1.1) The Organizational Process Needs and Objectives document specifies process needs and objectives. (SP 1.2) Multiple SCAMPI Bs and site visits culminating in final presentations citing process strengths and weaknesses are conducted periodically. (SP 1.3) Weaknesses identified from SCAMPI Bs and site visits are used to generate and implement improvements. In addition, improvement suggestions from within the organization are collected and used to improve the processes.	Organizational Process Needs and Objectives Business Goals and Objectives Final Presentation from SCAMPI B and C Process Improvement Suggestions
Goal 2: Improvements are planned and implemented, organizational process assets are deployed, and process-related experiences are incorporated into the organizational process assets.	(SP 2.1) Process improvement is conducted according to the Process Improvement Plan. The EPG collects, evaluates, and implements improvement suggestions. Improvements requiring complex analysis are assigned to focus groups where Raytheon Six Sigma is utilized for generating solutions. (SP 2.2 and SP 2.3) Pilot projects are used to test and debug solutions to complex suggestions. Training and announcements support the rollout of changes to processes or templates and to new processes or templates. (SP 2.4) New or improved processes and templates are placed in the PAL for use by all projects within the organization.	Process Improvement Plan Process Improvement Suggestions

TABLE 6.2 Project Management: Integrated Project Management (IPM)

CMMI Goal	Services Interpretation	Raytheon Solution (Direct Evidence)
Goal 1: The project is conducted using a defined process that is tailored from the organization's set of standard processes.	(SP 1.1) The organization's standard process is used *as is* by the project. (SP 1.2) The project's defined process is the implementation of the standard lifecycle model along with the governing documents (procedures and organizational plans) and the associated and completed templates. Labor rates are supplied by finances to projects for estimating cost. (SP 1.3) The standard process supplied by the organization consists of templates (PDP, WBS, RMP, and so on), procedures, plans, and lifecycle, and is preintegrated. (SP 1.4) A stoplight chart in the project status minutes is used to monitor and track the status of all project plans. (SP 1.5) Projects submit metrics (CPI and SPI) to the organizational repository and contribute suggestions, improvements, and examples to the EPG for inclusion in the PAL.	Project Development Plan (PDP) Lifecycle Model Work Breakdown Structure PAL—Templates CM Plan Risk Management Plan (RMP) Project Status Minutes Master Schedule Metrics Repository Process Improvement Suggestions
Goal 2: Coordination and collaboration of the project with relevant stakeholders is conducted.	(SP 2.1) Stakeholder involvement is captured in regular (weekly) status meeting minutes which contain a record of actual attendance versus expected attendance as defined in the RACI matrix[2] in the PDP. (SP 2.2) Project status and critical dependencies (staffing, facilities, and support) are monitored via regular (weekly) meetings. Status is reported to the customer monthly via the Monthly Management Review. Staffing is recorded in the master schedule, which is updated periodically. (SP 2.3) Issues are discussed during regular (weekly) project status meetings and are recorded and tracked as action items to closure in the minutes.	Project Status Minutes Monthly Management Review Master Schedule

2. A RACI matrix is a tool used for assigning cross-functional responsibilities. The letters in RACI stand for Responsible, Accountable, Consulted, and keep Informed.

TABLE 6.3 Engineering: Technical Solution (TS)

CMMI Goal	Services Interpretation	Raytheon Solution (Direct Evidence)
Goal 1: Product or product component solutions are selected from alternative solutions.	(SP 1.2) The design of the service solution is driven by the customer requirements (e.g., facilities, finances, management, support, and personnel) and is documented in a work control plan. (SP 1.1 and SP 1.3) DAR is routinely invoked for evaluation and selection of project staffing. The procedures for generating the service solution are documented in project planning work instructions.	Project Planning Work Instructions Staffing DAR Work Control Plan
Goal 2: Product or product component designs are developed.	(SP 2.3) Service components are derived based on customer requirements (e.g., facilities, finances, management, support, and personnel). (SP 2.1 and SP 2.4) Make/buy (select/hire personnel) decisions are a standard part of the staffing DAR. The design of the service solution is captured in the Work Control Plan. (SP 2.2) The technical data package consists of the WBS, which addresses finances and personnel decisions; the Statement of Work, which contains customer-specific requirements for the project; and the Work Control Plan, which details the service solution.	Work Control Plan Statement of Work Work Breakdown Structure Organizational Requirements *[Department Organizational Chart Lifecycle Model Service Integration Plan]*
Goal 3: Product components and associated support documentation are implemented from their designs.	(SP 3.1) The service is delivered as evidenced by burn rate of funds and work being performed for the customer as documented in the Task Diary. (SP 3.2) Use of the service is documented for the customer in the Work Control Plan.	Task Diary PMiRS (Schedule) Work Control Plan *[Work Authorization Document Engineering Policies]*

TABLE 6.4 Support: Process and Product Quality Assurance (PPQA)

CMMI Goal	Services Interpretation	Raytheon Solution (Direct Evidence)
Goal 1: Adherence of the performed process and associated work products and services to applicable process descriptions, standards, and procedures is objectively evaluated.	(SP 1.1 and SP 1.2) Each month, the organization manager selects one department to audit another department from the six departments in the organization. The manager of the audited department selects three projects to be audited. The audit is conducted using an organizational checklist of items to be examined by the auditing department. Twice per year this audit includes the organizational functions (i.e., purchasing, contracts, finances, training, EPG, and QA). Artifacts are examined and the results are recorded on the QA checklist. Peer reviews (which focus on work product quality) can also be used to ensure work product compliance with standards (i.e., templates).	QA Checklist QA Report Peer Review
Goal 2: Noncompliance issues are objectively tracked and communicated, and resolution is ensured.	(SP 2.1) Upon completion of the audit, the completed checklist is given to the QA manager who records and tracks any deficiencies to completion. The audited department manager works to close any findings and reports closure to the QA manager. (SP 2.2) The QA manager generates a monthly report of the results, along with open findings, and reports these findings to the organization manager, who resolves issues as required. Audit reports and findings are stored by the QA manager for future reference.	QA Plan QA Report

Templates are documents used by projects for (or as part of) providing and delivering services. Templates typically contain substantial content that applies across projects, but they also can contain unspecified project-specific information. The latter is added to the template when it is *instantiated*, thereby transforming it into a document (e.g., Project Development Plan, Work Breakdown Structure). Templates are used for planning, reporting, and recording project information and events. Templates are used by all projects undertaken by the organization and are never modified without prior approval by the EPG. Use of templates encapsulates process activities without requiring users to know the CMMI model.

Checklists are organizational templates used for collecting and logging defined information important to projects or the program office. Checklists ensure that all process steps are performed, and they are typically used for performing quality audits, peer reviews, service (product) integration, and so on. Like templates, checklists are never modified and are used as is.

Of course, new and improved plans, templates, and checklists are designed and released as part of the process improvement activities (OPF).

Lifecycle Model

The Raytheon Pasadena Operations standard process is defined by its currently patent-pending lifecycle model and associated plans, templates, and checklists. Similarly, a project's defined process is defined by the instantiation of the lifecycle and its associated plans, templates, and checklists. The lifecycle captures all of the activities required to establish and deliver technical services from inception to closeout. The roles (stakeholders) associated with these activities are also specified by the lifecycle model. Figure 6.4 shows the Raytheon Pasadena Operations Lifecycle Model and is the basis for mapping the actual work activities into the CMMI model. With this approach, the technical details of the model are abstracted from the day-to-day activities performed by the technical staff.

The lifecycle is divided into seven phases or stages: Explore and Negotiate, Initiate, Cost and Price, Integrate, Perform, Report, and Improve. Each phase contains specific activities that occur as services are defined, designed, constructed, and delivered to the customer. The personnel involved in each phase are also captured in the model. As shown in Figure 6.4, the model is represented as a table whose first column contains the various roles involved throughout the services lifecycle.

Figure 6.4 also shows the participation of each role at every phase of the lifecycle. The EPG only participates in the Improve phase of the lifecycle. Likewise, Raytheon project team members only participate in the Explore and Negotiate and Perform and Report phases.

Each phase is divided into subphases and is numbered in the third row of the table. The numbering is sequential and indicates the order in which these activities take place. The Explore and Negotiate phase is concerned with requirements development and initiating a new task order. In this phase, Raytheon department and task order managers (and sometimes project leads and team members) work with the customer task order manager to develop a Statement of Work. The Statement of Work is the initiating document for all task orders and contains the customer's description of the work to be performed and the services desired.

In the Initiate phase, the Raytheon department and task order managers work to develop a Work Control Plan in response to the customer's request (i.e., Statement of Work). The Raytheon program manager participates in this phase by assigning a new work order to a department, if required. The Cost and Price phase is where pricing is generated by Raytheon finance and the Work Control Plan and Pricing (collectively termed "the proposal") are reviewed both internally and externally. Once the proposal is approved by the customer, the lifecycle enters the Integrate phase. Here, administrative actions are performed to establish the project so that work can begin. Finance enters the work order into its financial tracking tool and creates a charge number and schedule. The task order manager creates the project's Risk Plan and Project Development Plan. Finally, team members are assigned to the project and are provided with authorization by the department manager to work on the contract.

Peer reviews are interspersed throughout these phases to ensure the quality of the service (product) integration, the project (service) plans, and the overall delivered service.

The Perform and Report phases comprise the longest portion of the lifecycle in terms of time required. In these phases, work is performed by the assigned team members, thereby delivering the service to the customer. This phase can last from one month to several years, depending on the work requested. The primary participants in these phases are the project lead, team members, and task order manager. As work is performed by the team members, the project lead monitors their activities via regular (e.g., weekly) status meetings. A Task Diary is used to record tasks assigned by the customer and to track the status of these tasks. This constitutes the core of the verification

FIGURE 6.4   RIS Pasadena Operations Project Lifecycle

	SERVICE DEVELOPMENT				
	EXPLORE & NEGOTIATE				
Role	1	2	3	4	5
Customer	Develop new opportunities	Develop SOW, discuss cost (informal)	Send SOW to customer CTM		
Raytheon Dept. Manager	Develop new opportunities	Develop SOW, discuss cost (informal)			
Raytheon Task Order (TO) Manager	Develop new opportunities	Develop SOW, discuss cost (informal)			
Raytheon Project Lead	Develop new opportunities	Develop SOW, discuss cost (informal)			
Project Team Member	Develop new opportunities				
Customer CTM				Verifies SOW is within contract scope	If not within scope, send back to customer
Raytheon PM					
Customer Contracts					If SOW OK, send to Raytheon contracts
Raytheon Contracts					
Raytheon Finance					
Raytheon EPG					
Model Map	RD, REQM	RD, REQM	RD, REQM	RD, REQM	RD, REQM

Continues

FIGURE 6.4   RIS Pasadena Operations Project Lifecycle *(Continued)*

Role	SERVICE DEVELOPMENT				
	INITIATE				
	6	7	8	9	10
Customer					
Raytheon Dept. Manager		Assign TO manager and lead to project			
Raytheon Task Order (TO) Manager		Instantiate lifecycle model	Select & tailor templates	Create WBS & place under CM	Create WCP & place under CM	Peer reviews WCP
Raytheon Project Lead					Peer reviews WCP
Project Team Member					
Customer CTM					
Raytheon PM	Assign new work to dept. manager				
Customer Contracts					
Raytheon Contracts	Place SOW under CM & forward to dept. manager				
Raytheon Finance					
Raytheon EPG					
Model Map	PI, CM	PI	PI, IPM	PP, DAR, CM	PP, RD, REQM, CM, TS, PI

FIGURE 6.4   RIS Pasadena Operations Project Lifecycle *(Continued)*

	SERVICE DEVELOPMENT					
	COST & PRICE					
Role	11	12	13	14	15	16
Customer					Approve or disapprove WCP and pricing	If WCP & pricing are not approved go to column 11
Raytheon Dept. Manager		Review & approve WCP & pricing				
Raytheon Task Order (TO) Manager		Review & approve WCP & pricing				
Raytheon Project Lead						
Project Team Member						
Customer CTM					If WCP and pricing are not approved, Raytheon TO manager redoes	
Raytheon PM		Review & approve WCP & pricing				
Customer Contracts				Send WCP & pricing to customer		
Raytheon Contracts		Review & approve WCP & pricing	Send WCP and pricing to customer contracts			
Raytheon Finance	Price TO	Review & approve WCP & pricing				
Raytheon EPG						
Model Map	PP, PI	RD, REQM, PI, VER, VAL	VER, VAL	VER, VAL, PI	VER, VAL, PI	VER, VAL, PI

Continues

141

FIGURE 6.4   RIS Pasadena Operations Project Lifecycle *(Continued)*

	SERVICE DEVELOPMENT					
	INTEGRATE					
Role	17	18	19	20	21	22
Customer						
Raytheon Dept. Manager			Update dept. WAD			Peer review PDP & RMP
Raytheon Task Order (TO) Manager			Create charge numbers	Create schedule (in financial tracking tool)		Peer review PDP & RMP
Raytheon Project Lead					Create PDP & place under CM	Create RMP & place under CM	Peer review PDP & RMP	Assign team
Project Team Member						
Customer CTM						
Raytheon PM						
Customer Contracts	Issue TO #					
Raytheon Contracts		Inform TO manager the TO is approved & placed under CM				
Raytheon Finance			Create charge numbers	Create schedule "burn rate"		
Raytheon EPG						
Model Map	PI	PI, CM	PI	PP, PI	PP, PI, CM, RSKM	PI, TS, VER

FIGURE 6.4   RIS Pasadena Operations Project Lifecycle *(Continued)*

| | SERVICE DELIVERY | | | | | |
| | PERFORM | | | | | |
Role	23	24	25	26	27	28
Customer	Request tasks				Agree that tasks are complete	
Raytheon Dept. Manager						
Raytheon Task Order (TO) Manager			Conduct DAR when needed			
Raytheon Project Lead				Agree that tasks are implemented		Change Status of task to "complete" in task diary
Project Team Member	Enter Task in Task Diary	Perform Task		Change Status of task to "implemented" in Task Diary		
Customer CTM						
Raytheon PM						
Customer Contracts						
Raytheon Contracts						
Raytheon Finance						
Raytheon EPG						
Model Map	PMC, MA, IPM	IPM, TS	DAR	VER, VAL	VER, VAL	VER, VAL

Continues

143

FIGURE 6.4   RIS Pasadena Operations Project Lifecycle *(Continued)*

Role	29	30	31	32	33	34	35	36	
SERVICE DELIVERY									
	REPORT						**IMPROVE**		
Customer									
Raytheon Dept. Manager				Meets with TO mgr (pre-MMR)	Brief PM (MMR)			Submit process improvement suggestions	
Raytheon Task Order (TO) Manager				Meets with Dept. mgr (pre-MMR)				Submit process improvement suggestions	
Raytheon Project Lead	Conduct the regular project status review	Record status & metrics						Submit process improvement suggestions	
Project Team Member	Participate in regular project status review							Submit process improvement suggestions	
Customer CTM						Briefed by Raytheon PM at MMR			
Raytheon PM					Briefed by dept. manager (MMR)	Brief customer CTM at MMR		Submit process improvement suggestions	
Customer Contracts									
Raytheon Contracts								Submit process improvement suggestions	
Raytheon Finance			Collect monthly financial data					Submit process improvement suggestions	
Raytheon EPG							Maintain PAL	Evaluate process Improvement suggestions	Insert lessons learned into PAL
Model Map	TS, PMC, MA	PMC, MA, OPF, OPD	PMC, MA	PMC, MA	PMC, MA	PMC, MA	OPF, OPD	OPF, OPD	

and validation process; the project lead verifies that work is finished on schedule and validates its completion with the customer. Completion of tasks is noted in the Task Diary. Status is also reported to the customer task order manager by the Raytheon task order manager each month. Financial, technical, and administrative status is reported and any issues are recorded and tracked to resolution.

In the final phase of the lifecycle, suggestions and examples for improvement are submitted and collected. The EPG is responsible for the analysis, evaluation, and implementation of these suggested improvements. The Improve phase, though listed at the end of the lifecycle, can take place at any phase. It is placed at the end to indicate the final opportunity by the project to submit improvement suggestions when projects are closed out.

Epiphanies

Applying CMMI to services was an intellectually exciting but difficult endeavor. Along the way, key intellectual breakthroughs were made by the process developers that resulted in substantial progress in applying CMMI to services. These intellectual breakthroughs are termed "epiphanies" by the developers and provide insight into the key conceptual milestones in applying the model to the services environment. The following subsections list the major breakthroughs and give a short discussion of their significance.

Epiphany #1: Task Orders Are Equivalent to Projects in the Traditional Application of the Model

This was the first breakthrough in our thinking that enabled all progress in applying CMMI to services. Before this epiphany, the process developers tried to apply the model to (mostly software) projects where substantial opportunities existed for demonstrating various portions of one or more process areas in the model. The difficulty was as obvious as it was frustrating; few or no projects existed that could demonstrate all process areas of the model end to end. Worse, focusing on software projects disenfranchised most of the Pasadena Operations' projects (e.g., analysis, operations, and IT). In addition, customers typically controlled such process areas as Project Planning, Risk Management, and Technical Solution, making it impossible to demonstrate these practices.

A breakthrough was made by shifting the focus away from the traditional technical project application and toward the management and delivery of services. The model could be applied to every Task

Order; no project need be excluded. Planning and other Project Management activities were now identified with planning and managing the delivery of *services* under the contract. This epiphany paved the way for re-identifying each model process area with an equivalent process in the service environment and allowed all projects to be included in the organization's standard process.

Epiphany #2: Every Project Shares the Same (Unchanging) Five Requirements

Originally, thinking about requirements focused on the tasks assigned by the customer to project team members and the recording of these tasks in a log or diary. This ignored the upfront request to provide a service which consisted of staffing, management oversight, financial reporting, facilities, and infrastructure support and led to confusion over the meaning of requirements in the services environment. Furthermore, it left the Product Integration and Technical Solution process areas with a large question mark as to their meaning in the services environment.

With the notion that the requirements applied to the *service*, not to a staff member's assignment on any given day, it was realized that requirements were in fact gathered upfront. These requirements were the same for all projects, and since they were contractually based, they never changed. The umbrella contract was the source of these requirements, since it stated that Raytheon would provide the following services for every Task Order: facilities for personnel and meetings; support in the form of computers, office equipment, and networks; management oversight; adequate and appropriate staffing; and financial oversight and reporting.

Examination of existing Work Control Plans and Statements of Work showed that the details of these requirements (as they pertained to each project) appeared again and again in these documents. Abstracting these five requirements into an organizational requirements document that applied to all projects, and ensuring that templates used for generating Work Control Plans and Statements of Work addressed these requirements, provided a ready solution to developing and managing requirements in the services environment.

Epiphany #3: The Execution and Monitoring of Customer-Assigned Tasks Constitutes the Core of the Verification and Validation Processes

The aforementioned confusion between (traditional) project-specific requirements and contractual service requirements left unanswered the application of verification and validation in the service's lifecycle. This was resolved by realizing that the execution and monitoring of the tasks doled out by the customer were the principal mechanism for verifying and validating the customer's service requirements on a near-continuous basis. All that was needed was to capture these tasks in an official log or diary. This small change in behavior allowed the engineering process areas to be mapped to services.

Epiphany #4: The Relative Time Spent for Development versus Delivery in Services Is Reversed from That of Products

For product-based projects, the development of the product occupies the majority of the time in the project lifecycle, with delivery occurring at the end. In a services environment, the development of the service to be delivered takes place rather quickly and the delivery of the service initiates early and continues for the remainder of the project's life. It should be noted, however, that for both products and services, the majority of the artifacts (e.g., work control plans, project development plans, risk management plans, DAR, peer reviews, and schedules) are generated during the development phase. In the case of the PI process area, "the integration of product components" is the communication between and packaging of the five requirements (see Epiphany #2) that constitute a service, as well as the actual delivery of the service.

Lessons Learned

At the conclusion of this effort, a review was conducted to determine what lessons could be learned from the effort. These lessons learned are presented here as an aid to others considering similar endeavors.

- **Use a bottom-up approach.** Understand existing processes in the organization and how they vary among groups. Derive a lifecycle model from these processes. Let the experts (EPG and other model experts) worry about mapping to the CMMI model, identifying gaps, and filling those gaps. This allows the organization to focus on core capabilities, not on CMMI. The resulting process will provide significant practical improvements to the organization. Results will be achieved faster and less expensively than if using a top-down approach.
- **Employ template-based solutions.** This allows the technical staff to work with solutions that are relevant to their everyday tasks without having to become versed in CMMI. A relatively small group of model

experts can concentrate on ensuring that the CMMI process areas are covered by using the templates, without burdening the technical staff and management with process details that are not directly applicable to their work.

- **Run the implementation as a (serious) project.** Establish a project manager, budget, schedule, and measurable goals. Track and monitor progress regularly using the Earned Value Management System. Use phased deployment, and develop and validate processes before deployment.

- **Implement a "grassroots" communications plan throughout the project.** Start communication with staff and management early to establish and clarify goals. Celebrate small successes publicly at all-hands meetings and other group events. Set up recurring open houses and training sessions with the process developers. Demonstrate the benefits to individuals. Communicate regularly and often with staff.

- **Obtain stakeholders' support and active involvement.** Gain sponsors at the highest level and understand their goals. Involve customers frequently via EPG and steering committee meetings. Communicate the benefit of reaching goals.

- **Use consultants.** Leverage model expertise from other parts of the organization. Choose the lead appraiser wisely (i.e., choose an "out-of-the-box" thinker). Put the appraisal team to work for the organization. Use their feedback to refine processes before deployment.

PART TWO

Generic Goals and Generic Practices and the Process Areas

GENERIC GOALS AND GENERIC PRACTICES

Overview

This section describes, in detail, all the generic goals and generic practices of CMMI—model components that directly address process institutionalization.

In the process areas, generic goals and generic practices appear at the end of each process area. Generic practice elaborations appear after generic practices to show how these practices should uniquely be applied to the process area.

The entire text of the generic goals and generic practices is not repeated in the process areas (i.e., subpractices, notes, examples, and references are omitted). Instead, only the generic goal and generic practice titles and statements appear. As you address each process area, refer to this section for the details of all generic practices.

Process Institutionalization

Institutionalization is an important concept in process improvement. When mentioned in the generic goal and generic practice descriptions, institutionalization implies that the process is ingrained in the way the work is performed and there is commitment and consistency to performing the process.

An institutionalized process is more likely to be retained during times of stress. When the requirements and objectives for the process change, however, the implementation of the process may also need to change to ensure that it remains effective. The generic practices describe activities that address these aspects of institutionalization.

The degree of institutionalization is embodied in the generic goals and expressed in the names of the processes associated with each goal as indicated in Table 7.1.

151

TABLE 7.1   Generic Goals and Process Names

Generic Goal	Progression of Processes
GG 1	Performed process
GG 2	Managed process
GG 3	Defined process
GG 4	Quantitatively managed process
GG 5	Optimizing process

The progression of process institutionalization is characterized in the following descriptions of each process.

Performed Process

A performed process is a process that accomplishes the work necessary to produce work products. The specific goals of the process area are satisfied.

Managed Process

A managed process is a performed process that is planned and executed in accordance with policy; employs skilled people who have adequate resources to produce controlled outputs; involves relevant stakeholders; is monitored, controlled, and reviewed; and is evaluated for adherence to its process description. The process may be instantiated by a project, group, or organizational function. Management of the process is concerned with institutionalization and the achievement of other specific objectives established for the process, such as cost, schedule, and quality objectives. The control provided by a managed process helps to ensure that the established process is retained during times of stress.

The requirements and objectives for the process are established by the organization. The status of the work products and delivery of the services are visible to management at defined points (e.g., at major milestones and completion of major tasks). Commitments are established among those performing the work and the relevant stakeholders and are revised as necessary. Work products are reviewed with relevant stakeholders and are controlled. The work products and services satisfy their specified requirements.

A critical distinction between a performed process and a managed process is the extent to which the process is managed. A managed process is planned (the plan may be part of a more encompassing plan) and the performance of the process is managed against the plan. Corrective actions are taken when the actual results and performance deviate significantly from the plan. A managed process achieves the objectives of the plan and is institutionalized for consistent performance.

Defined Process

A defined process is a managed process that is tailored from the organization's set of standard processes according to the organization's tailoring guidelines; has a maintained process description; and contributes work products, measures, and other process improvement information to the organizational process assets.

The organizational process assets are artifacts that relate to describing, implementing, and improving processes. These artifacts are assets because they are developed or acquired to meet the business objectives of the organization, and they represent investments by the organization that are expected to provide current and future business value.

The organization's set of standard processes, which are the basis of the defined process, are established and improved over time. Standard processes describe the fundamental process elements that are expected in the defined processes. Standard processes also describe the relationships (e.g., the ordering and the interfaces) among these process elements. The organization-level infrastructure to support current and future use of the organization's set of standard processes is established and improved over time. (See the definition of "standard process" in the glossary.)

A project's defined process provides a basis for planning, performing, and improving the project's tasks and activities. A project may have more than one defined process (e.g., one for developing the product and another for testing the product).

A defined process clearly states the following:

- Purpose
- Inputs
- Entry criteria
- Activities
- Roles
- Measures
- Verification steps
- Outputs
- Exit criteria

A critical distinction between a managed process and a defined process is the scope of application of the process descriptions, standards, and procedures. For a managed process, the process descriptions, standards, and procedures are applicable to a particular project, group, or organizational function. As a result, the managed processes of two projects in one organization may be different.

Another critical distinction is that a defined process is described in more detail and is performed more rigorously than a managed process. This means that improvement information is easier to understand, analyze, and use. Finally, management of the defined process is based on the additional insight provided by an understanding of the interrelationships of the process activities and detailed measures of the process, its work products, and its services.

Quantitatively Managed Process

A quantitatively managed process is a defined process that is controlled using statistical and other quantitative techniques. The product quality, service quality, and process-performance attributes are measurable and controlled throughout the project.

Quantitative objectives are established based on the capability of the organization's set of standard processes; the organization's business objectives; and the needs of the customer, end users, organization, and process implementers, subject to the availability of resources. The people performing the process are directly involved in quantitatively managing the process.

Quantitative management is performed on the overall set of processes that produces a product. The subprocesses that are significant contributors to overall process performance are statistically managed. For these selected subprocesses, detailed measures of process performance are collected and statistically analyzed. Special causes of process variation are identified and, where appropriate, the source of the special cause is addressed to prevent its recurrence.

The quality and process-performance measures are incorporated into the organization's measurement repository to support future fact-based decision making.

Activities for quantitatively managing the performance of a process include the following:

- Identifying the subprocesses that are to be brought under statistical management
- Identifying and measuring product and process attributes that are important contributors to quality and process performance
- Identifying and addressing special causes of subprocess variations (based on the selected product and process attributes and subprocesses selected for statistical management)

- Managing each of the selected subprocesses, with the objective of bringing their performance within natural bounds (i.e., making the subprocess performance statistically stable and predictable based on the selected product and process attributes)
- Predicting the ability of the process to satisfy established quantitative quality and process-performance objectives
- Taking appropriate corrective actions when it is determined that the established quantitative quality and process-performance objectives will not be satisfied

These corrective actions include changing the objectives or ensuring that relevant stakeholders have a quantitative understanding of, and have agreed to, the performance shortfall.

A critical distinction between a defined process and a quantitatively managed process is the predictability of process performance. The term quantitatively managed implies using appropriate statistical and other quantitative techniques to manage the performance of one or more critical subprocesses so that the performance of the process can be predicted. A defined process provides only qualitative predictability.

Optimizing Process

An optimizing process is a quantitatively managed process that is changed and adapted to meet relevant current and projected business objectives. An optimizing process focuses on continually improving process performance through both incremental and innovative technological improvements. Process improvements that address common causes of process variation, root causes of defects, and other problems; and those that would measurably improve the organization's processes are identified, evaluated, and deployed as appropriate. These improvements are selected based on a quantitative understanding of their expected contribution to achieving the organization's process improvement objectives versus the cost and impact to the organization.

Selected incremental and innovative technological process improvements are systematically managed and deployed into the organization. The effects of the deployed process improvements are measured and evaluated against the quantitative process improvement objectives.

In a process that is optimized, common causes of process variation are addressed by changing the process in a way that will shift the mean or decrease variation when the process is restabilized. These changes are intended to improve process performance and to achieve the organization's established process improvement objectives.

A critical distinction between a quantitatively managed process and an optimizing process is that the optimizing process is continuously improved by addressing common causes of process variation. A quantitatively managed process is concerned with addressing special causes of process variation and providing statistical predictability of the results. Although the process may produce predictable results, the results may be insufficient to achieve the organization's process improvement objectives.

Relationships among Processes

The generic goals evolve so that each goal provides a foundation for the next. Therefore the following conclusions can be made:

- A managed process is a performed process.
- A defined process is a managed process.
- A quantitatively managed process is a defined process.
- An optimizing process is a quantitatively managed process.

Thus, applied sequentially and in order, the generic goals describe a process that is increasingly institutionalized from a performed process to an optimizing process.

Achieving GG 1 for a process area is equivalent to saying you achieve the specific goals of the process area.

Achieving GG 2 for a process area is equivalent to saying you manage the performance of processes associated with the process area. There is a policy that indicates you will perform it. There is a plan for performing it. There are resources provided, responsibilities assigned, training on how to perform it, selected work products from performing the process are controlled, and so on. In other words, the process is planned and monitored just like any project or support activity.

Achieving GG 3 for a process area assumes that an organizational standard process exists that can be tailored to result in the process you will use. Tailoring might result in making no changes to the standard process. In other words, the process used and the standard process may be identical. Using the standard process "as is" is tailoring because the choice is made that no modification is required.

Each process area describes multiple activities, some of which are repeatedly performed. You may need to tailor the way one of these activities is performed to account for new capabilities or circumstances. For example, you may have a standard for developing or obtaining organizational training that does not consider Web-based training. When preparing to develop or obtain a Web-based course, you may need to tailor the standard process to account for the particular challenges and benefits of Web-based training.

Achieving GG 4 or GG 5 for a process area is conceptually feasible but may not be economical except, perhaps, in situations where the product domain has become stable for an extended period or in situations in which the process area or domain is a critical business driver.

Generic Goals and Generic Practices

This section describes all of the generic goals and generic practices, as well as their associated subpractices, notes, examples, and references. The generic goals are organized in numerical order, GG 1 through GG 5. The generic practices are also organized in numerical order under the generic goal they support.

As mentioned earlier, the subpractices, notes, examples, and references are not repeated in the process areas; the details of each generic goal and generic practice are found only here.

GG 1 *ACHIEVE SPECIFIC GOALS*

The process supports and enables achievement of the specific goals of the process area by transforming identifiable input work products to produce identifiable output work products.

GP 1.1 *PERFORM SPECIFIC PRACTICES*

Perform the specific practices of the process area to develop work products and provide services to achieve the specific goals of the process area.

The purpose of this generic practice is to produce the work products and deliver the services that are expected by performing the process. These practices may be done informally, without following a documented process description or plan. The rigor with which these practices are performed depends on the individuals managing and performing the work and may vary considerably.

GG 2 INSTITUTIONALIZE A MANAGED PROCESS

The process is institutionalized as a managed process.

GP 2.1 ESTABLISH AN ORGANIZATIONAL POLICY

Establish and maintain an organizational policy for planning and performing the process.

The purpose of this generic practice is to define the organizational expectations for the process and make these expectations visible to those in the organization who are affected. In general, senior management is responsible for establishing and communicating guiding principles, direction, and expectations for the organization.

Not all direction from senior management will bear the label "policy." The existence of appropriate organizational direction is the expectation of this generic practice, regardless of what it is called or how it is imparted.

GP 2.2 PLAN THE PROCESS

Establish and maintain the plan for performing the process.

The purpose of this generic practice is to determine what is needed to perform the process and to achieve the established objectives, to prepare a plan for performing the process, to prepare a process description, and to get agreement on the plan from relevant stakeholders.

The practical implications of applying a generic practice vary for each process area. For example, the planning described by this generic practice as applied to the Project Monitoring and Control process area may be carried out in full by the processes associated with the Project Planning process area. However, this generic practice, when applied to the Project Planning process area, sets an expectation that the project planning process itself be planned. Therefore, this generic practice may either reinforce expectations set elsewhere in CMMI or set new expectations that should be addressed.

Refer to the Project Planning process area for more information on establishing and maintaining a project plan.

Establishing a plan includes documenting the plan and a process description. Maintaining the plan includes updating it to reflect corrective actions or changes in requirements or objectives.

The plan for performing the process typically includes the following:

- Process description
- Standards and requirements for the work products and services of the process
- Specific objectives for the performance of the process (e.g., quality, time scale, cycle time, and resource usage)
- Dependencies among the activities, work products, and services of the process
- Resources (including funding, people, and tools) needed to perform the process
- Assignment of responsibility and authority
- Training needed for performing and supporting the process
- Work products to be controlled and the level of control to be applied
- Measurement requirements to provide insight into the performance of the process, its work products, and its services
- Involvement of identified stakeholders
- Activities for monitoring and controlling the process
- Objective evaluation activities of the process
- Management review activities for the process and the work products

Subpractices

1. Define and document the plan for performing the process.

   This plan may be a stand-alone document, embedded in a more comprehensive document, or distributed across multiple documents. In the case of the plan being distributed across multiple documents, ensure that a coherent picture of who does what is preserved. Documents may be hardcopy or softcopy.

2. Define and document the process description.

   The process description, which includes relevant standards and procedures, may be included as part of the plan for performing the process or may be included in the plan by reference.

3. Review the plan with relevant stakeholders and get their agreement.

   This includes reviewing that the planned process satisfies the applicable policies, plans, requirements, and standards to provide assurance to relevant stakeholders.

4. Revise the plan as necessary.

GP 2.3 *PROVIDE RESOURCES*

Provide adequate resources for performing the process, developing the work products, and providing the services of the process.

The purpose of this generic practice is to ensure that the resources necessary to perform the process as defined by the plan are available when they are needed. Resources include adequate funding, appropriate physical facilities, skilled people, and appropriate tools.

The interpretation of the term "adequate" depends on many factors and can change over time. Inadequate resources may be addressed by increasing resources or by removing requirements, constraints, and commitments.

GP 2.4 *ASSIGN RESPONSIBILITY*

Assign responsibility and authority for performing the process, developing the work products, and providing the services of the process.

The purpose of this generic practice is to ensure that there is accountability for performing the process and achieving the specified results throughout the life of the process. The people assigned must have the appropriate authority to perform the assigned responsibilities.

Responsibility can be assigned using detailed job descriptions or in living documents, such as the plan for performing the process. Dynamic assignment of responsibility is another legitimate way to perform this generic practice, as long as the assignment and acceptance of responsibility are ensured throughout the life of the process.

Subpractices

1. Assign overall responsibility and authority for performing the process.
2. Assign responsibility and authority for performing the specific tasks of the process.
3. Confirm that the people assigned to the responsibilities and authorities understand and accept them.

GP 2.5 *TRAIN PEOPLE*

Train the people performing or supporting the process as needed.

The purpose of this generic practice is to ensure that the people have the necessary skills and expertise to perform or support the process.

Appropriate training is provided to the people who will be performing the work. Overview training is provided to orient people who interact with those performing the work.

Examples of methods for providing training include self-study; self-directed training; self-paced, programmed instruction; formalized on-the-job training; mentoring; and formal and classroom training.

Training supports the successful performance of the process by establishing a common understanding of the process and by imparting the skills and knowledge needed to perform the process.

Refer to the Organizational Training process area for more information about training the people performing or supporting the process.

GP 2.6 MANAGE CONFIGURATIONS

Place designated work products of the process under appropriate levels of control.

The purpose of this generic practice is to establish and maintain the integrity of the designated work products of the process (or their descriptions) throughout their useful life.

The designated work products are specifically identified in the plan for performing the process, along with a specification of the appropriate level of control.

Different levels of control are appropriate for different work products and for different points in time. For some work products, it may be sufficient to maintain version control (i.e., the version of the work product in use at a given time, past or present, is known, and changes are incorporated in a controlled manner). Version control is usually under the sole control of the work product owner (which may be an individual, a group, or a team).

Sometimes, it may be critical that work products be placed under formal or baseline configuration management. This type of control includes defining and establishing baselines at predetermined points. These baselines are formally reviewed and agreed on, and serve as the basis for further development of the designated work products.

Refer to the Configuration Management process area for more information about placing work products under configuration management.

Additional levels of control between version control and formal configuration management are possible. An identified work product may be under various levels of control at different points in time.

GP 2.7 *IDENTIFY AND INVOLVE RELEVANT STAKEHOLDERS*

Identify and involve the relevant stakeholders of the process as planned.

The purpose of this generic practice is to establish and maintain the expected involvement of stakeholders during the execution of the process.

Involve relevant stakeholders as described in an appropriate plan for stakeholder involvement. Involve stakeholders appropriately in activities such as the following:

- Planning
- Decisions
- Commitments
- Communications
- Coordination
- Reviews
- Appraisals
- Requirements definitions
- Resolution of problems/issues

Refer to the Project Planning process area for information on the project planning for stakeholder involvement.

The objective of planning stakeholder involvement is to ensure that interactions necessary to the process are accomplished, while not allowing excessive numbers of affected groups and individuals to impede process execution.

Subpractices

1. Identify stakeholders relevant to this process and their appropriate involvement.

   Relevant stakeholders are identified among the suppliers of inputs to, the users of outputs from, and the performers of the activities within the process. Once the relevant stakeholders are identified, the appropriate level of their involvement in process activities is planned.

2. Share these identifications with project planners or other planners as appropriate.

3. Involve relevant stakeholders as planned.

GP 2.8 MONITOR AND CONTROL THE PROCESS

Monitor and control the process against the plan for performing the process and take appropriate corrective action.

The purpose of this generic practice is to perform the direct day-to-day monitoring and controlling of the process. Appropriate visibility into the process is maintained so that appropriate corrective action can be taken when necessary. Monitoring and controlling the process involves measuring appropriate attributes of the process or work products produced by the process.

Refer to the Project Monitoring and Control process area for more information about monitoring and controlling the project and taking corrective action.

Refer to the Measurement and Analysis process area for more information about measurement.

Subpractices

1. Measure actual performance against the plan for performing the process.

   The measures are of the process, its work products, and its services.

2. Review accomplishments and results of the process against the plan for performing the process.

3. Review activities, status, and results of the process with the immediate level of management responsible for the process and identify issues. The reviews are intended to provide the immediate level of management with appropriate visibility into the process. The reviews can be both periodic and event driven.

4. Identify and evaluate the effects of significant deviations from the plan for performing the process.

5. Identify problems in the plan for performing the process and in the execution of the process.

6. Take corrective action when requirements and objectives are not being satisfied, when issues are identified, or when progress differs significantly from the plan for performing the process.

   There are inherent risks that should be considered before any corrective action is taken.

   Corrective action may include the following:

   • Taking remedial action to repair defective work products or services
   • Changing the plan for performing the process
   • Adjusting resources, including people, tools, and other resources
   • Negotiating changes to the established commitments

- Securing change to the requirements and objectives that have to be satisfied
- Terminating the effort

7. Track corrective action to closure.

GP 2.9 OBJECTIVELY EVALUATE ADHERENCE

Objectively evaluate adherence of the process against its process description, standards, and procedures, and address noncompliance.

The purpose of this generic practice is to provide credible assurance that the process is implemented as planned and adheres to its process description, standards, and procedures. This generic practice is implemented, in part, by evaluating selected work products of the process. (See the definition of *objectively evaluate* in the glossary.)

Refer to the Process and Product Quality Assurance process area for more information about objectively evaluating adherence.

People not directly responsible for managing or performing the activities of the process typically evaluate adherence. In many cases, adherence is evaluated by people within the organization, but external to the process or project, or by people external to the organization. As a result, credible assurance of adherence can be provided even during times when the process is under stress (e.g., when the effort is behind schedule or over budget).

GP 2.10   REVIEW STATUS WITH HIGHER LEVEL MANAGEMENT

Review the activities, status, and results of the process with higher level management and resolve issues.

The purpose of this generic practice is to provide higher level management with the appropriate visibility into the process.

Higher level management includes those levels of management in the organization above the immediate level of management responsible for the process. In particular, higher level management includes senior management. These reviews are for managers who provide the policy and overall guidance for the process, and not for those who perform the direct day-to-day monitoring and controlling of the process.

Different managers have different needs for information about the process. These reviews help ensure that informed decisions on the planning and performing of the process can be made. Therefore, these reviews are expected to be both periodic and event driven.

GG 3   **INSTITUTIONALIZE A DEFINED PROCESS**

The process is institutionalized as a defined process.

GP 3.1 **ESTABLISH A DEFINED PROCESS**

Establish and maintain the description of a defined process.

The purpose of this generic practice is to establish and maintain a description of the process that is tailored from the organization's set of standard processes to address the needs of a specific instantiation. The organization should have standard processes that cover the process area, as well as have guidelines for tailoring these standard processes to meet the needs of a project or organizational function. With a defined process, variability in how the processes are performed across the organization is reduced and process assets, data, and learning can be effectively shared.

Refer to the Organizational Process Definition process area for more information about the organization's set of standard processes and tailoring guidelines.

Refer to the Integrated Project Management process area for more information on establishing and maintaining the project's defined process.

The descriptions of the defined processes provide the basis for planning, performing, and managing the activities, work products, and services associated with the process.

Subpractices

1. Select from the organization's set of standard processes those processes that cover the process area and best meet the needs of the project or organizational function.
2. Establish the defined process by tailoring the selected processes according to the organization's tailoring guidelines.
3. Ensure that the organization's process objectives are appropriately addressed in the defined process.
4. Document the defined process and the records of the tailoring.
5. Revise the description of the defined process as necessary.

GP 3.2 **COLLECT IMPROVEMENT INFORMATION**

Collect work products, measures, measurement results, and improvement information derived from planning and performing the process to support the future use and improvement of the organization's processes and process assets.

The purpose of this generic practice is to collect information and artifacts derived from planning and performing the process. This generic practice is performed so that the information and artifacts can be included in the organizational process assets and made available to those who are (or who will be) planning and performing the same or similar processes. The information and artifacts are stored in the organization's measurement repository and the organization's process asset library.

Examples of relevant information include the effort expended for the various activities, defects injected or removed in a particular activity, and lessons learned.

Refer to the Organizational Process Definition process area for more information about the organization's measurement repository and process asset library and for more information about the work products, measures, and improvement information that are incorporated into the organizational process assets.

Refer to the Integrated Project Management process area for more information on contributing work products, measures, and documented experiences to the organizational process assets.

Subpractices

1. Store process and product measures in the organization's measurement repository.

    The process and product measures are primarily those that are defined in the common set of measures for the organization's set of standard processes.

2. Submit documentation for inclusion in the organization's process asset library.

3. Document lessons learned from the process for inclusion in the organization's process asset library.

4. Propose improvements to the organizational process assets.

GG 4 INSTITUTIONALIZE A QUANTITATIVELY MANAGED PROCESS

The process is institutionalized as a quantitatively managed process.

GP 4.1 ESTABLISH QUANTITATIVE OBJECTIVES FOR THE PROCESS

Establish and maintain quantitative objectives for the process, which address quality and process performance, based on customer needs and business objectives.

The purpose of this generic practice is to determine and obtain agreement from relevant stakeholders about specific quantitative objectives for the process. These quantitative objectives can be expressed in terms of product quality, service quality, and process performance.

Refer to the Quantitative Project Management process area for information on how quantitative objectives are set for subprocesses of the project's defined process.

The quantitative objectives may be specific to the process or they may be defined for a broader scope (e.g., for a set of processes). In the latter case, these quantitative objectives may be allocated to some of the included processes.

These quantitative objectives are criteria used to judge whether the products, services, and process performance will satisfy the customers, end users, organization management, and process implementers. These quantitative objectives go beyond the traditional end-product objectives. They also cover intermediate objectives that are used to manage the achievement of the objectives over time. They reflect, in part, the demonstrated performance of the organization's set of standard processes. These quantitative objectives should be set to values that are likely to be achieved when the processes involved are stable and within their natural bounds.

Subpractices

1. Establish the quantitative objectives that pertain to the process.
2. Allocate the quantitative objectives to the process or its subprocesses.

GP 4.2 *STABILIZE SUBPROCESS PERFORMANCE*

Stabilize the performance of one or more subprocesses to determine the ability of the process to achieve the established quantitative quality and process-performance objectives.

The purpose of this generic practice is to stabilize the performance of one or more subprocesses of the defined process, which are critical contributors to overall performance, using appropriate statistical and other quantitative techniques. Stabilizing selected subprocesses supports predicting the ability of the process to achieve the established quantitative quality and process-performance objectives.

Refer to the Quantitative Project Management process area for information on selecting subprocesses for statistical management, monitoring performance of subprocesses, and other aspects of stabilizing subprocess performance.

A stable subprocess shows no significant indication of special causes of process variation. Stable subprocesses are predictable within the limits established by the natural bounds of the subprocess. Variations in the stable subprocess are due to a constant system of chance causes, and the magnitude of the variations can be small or large.

Predicting the ability of the process to achieve the established quantitative objectives requires a quantitative understanding of the contributions of the subprocesses that are critical to achieving these objectives and establishing and managing against interim quantitative objectives over time.

Selected process and product measures are incorporated into the organization's measurement repository to support process-performance analysis and future fact-based decision making.

Subpractices

1. Statistically manage the performance of one or more subprocesses that are critical contributors to the overall performance of the process.
2. Predict the ability of the process to achieve its established quantitative objectives considering the performance of the statistically managed subprocesses.
3. Incorporate selected process-performance measurements into the organization's process-performance baselines.

GG 5 INSTITUTIONALIZE AN OPTIMIZING PROCESS

The process is institutionalized as an optimizing process.

GP 5.1 ENSURE CONTINUOUS PROCESS IMPROVEMENT

Ensure continuous improvement of the process in fulfilling the relevant business objectives of the organization.

The purpose of this generic practice is to select and systematically deploy process and technology improvements that contribute to meeting established quality and process-performance objectives.

Refer to the Organizational Innovation and Deployment process area for information about selecting and deploying incremental and innovative improvements that measurably improve the organization's processes and technologies.

Optimizing the processes that are agile and innovative depends on the participation of an empowered workforce aligned with the business values and objectives of the organization. The organization's ability to rapidly respond to changes and opportunities is enhanced by finding ways to accelerate and share learning. Improvement of the processes is inherently part of everybody's role, resulting in a cycle of continual improvement.

Subpractices

1. Establish and maintain quantitative process improvement objectives that support the organization's business objectives.

    The quantitative process improvement objectives may be specific to the individual process or they may be defined for a broader scope (i.e., for a set of processes), with the individual processes contributing to achieving these objectives. Objectives that are specific to the individual process are typically allocated from quantitative objectives established for a broader scope.

    These process improvement objectives are primarily derived from the organization's business objectives and from a detailed understanding of process capability. These objectives are the criteria used to judge whether the process performance is quantitatively improving the organization's ability to meet its business objectives. These process improvement objectives are often set to values beyond the current process performance, and both incremental and innovative technological improvements may be needed to achieve these objectives. These objectives may also be revised frequently to continue to drive the improvement of the process (i.e., when an objective is achieved, it may be set to a new value that is again beyond the new process performance).

    These process improvement objectives may be the same as, or a refinement of, the objectives established in the "Establish Quantitative Objectives for the Process" generic practice, as long as they can serve as both drivers and criteria for successful process improvement.

2. Identify process improvements that would result in measurable improvements to process performance.

    Process improvements include both incremental changes and innovative technological improvements. The innovative technological improvements are typically pursued as efforts that are separately planned, performed, and managed. Piloting is often performed. These efforts often address specific areas of the processes that are determined by analyzing process performance and identifying specific opportunities for significant measurable improvement.

3. Define strategies and manage deployment of selected process improvements based on the quantified expected benefits, the estimated costs and impacts, and the measured change to process performance.

    The costs and benefits of these improvements are estimated quantitatively, and the actual costs and benefits are measured. Benefits are primarily considered relative to the organization's quantitative process improvement objectives. Improvements are made to both the organization's set of standard processes and the defined processes.

Managing deployment of the process improvements includes piloting changes and implementing adjustments where appropriate, addressing potential and real barriers to deployment, minimizing disruption to ongoing efforts, and managing risks.

GP 5.2 CORRECT ROOT CAUSES OF PROBLEMS

Identify and correct the root causes of defects and other problems in the process.

The purpose of this generic practice is to analyze defects and other problems that were encountered in a quantitatively managed process, to correct the root causes of these types of defects and problems, and to prevent these defects and problems from occurring in the future.

Refer to the Causal Analysis and Resolution process area for more information about identifying and correcting root causes of selected defects. Even though the Causal Analysis and Resolution process area has a project context, it can be applied to processes in other contexts as well.

Root cause analysis can be applied beneficially to processes that are not quantitatively managed. However, the focus of this generic practice is to act on a quantitatively managed process, though the final root causes may be found outside of that process.

Applying Generic Practices

This section helps you to develop a better understanding of the generic practices and provides information for interpreting and applying the generic practices in your organization.

Generic practices are components that are common to all process areas. Think of generic practices as reminders. They serve the purpose of reminding you to do things right, and are expected model components.

For example, when you are achieving the specific goals of the Project Planning process area, you are establishing and maintaining a plan that defines project activities. One of the generic practices that applies to the Project Planning process area is "Establish and maintain the plan for performing the project planning process" (GP 2.2). When applied to this process area, this generic practice reminds you to plan the activities involved in creating the plan for the project.

When you are satisfying the specific goals of the Organizational Training process area, you are developing the skills and knowledge of people in your project and organization so that they can perform their roles effectively and efficiently. When applying the same generic practice (GP 2.2) to the Organizational Training process area, this generic practice reminds you to plan the activities involved in developing the skills and knowledge of people in the organization.

Process Areas That Support Generic Practices

While generic goals and generic practices are the model components that directly address the institutionalization of a process across the organization, many process areas likewise address institutionalization by supporting the implementation of the generic practices. Knowing these relationships will help you effectively implement the generic practices.

Such process areas contain one or more specific practices that when implemented may also fully implement a generic practice or generate a work product that is used in the implementation of a generic practice.

An example is the Configuration Management process area and GP 2.6, "Place designated work products of the process under appropriate levels of control." To implement the generic practice for one or more process areas, you might choose to implement the Configuration Management process area, all or in part, to implement the generic practice.

Another example is the Organizational Process Definition process area and GP 3.1, "Establish and maintain the description of a defined process." To implement this generic practice for one or more process areas, you should first implement the Organizational Process Definition process area, all or in part, to establish the organizational process assets that are needed to implement the generic practice.

Table 7.2 describes (1) the process areas that support the implementation of generic practices, and (2) the recursive relationships between generic practices and their closely related process areas. Both types of relationships are important to remember during process improvement to take advantage of the natural synergies that exist between the generic practices and their related process areas.

TABLE 7.2   Generic Practice and Process Area Relationships

Generic Practice	Roles of Process Areas in Implementation of the Generic Practice	How the Generic Practice Recursively Applies to Its Related Process Area(s)[1]
GP 2.2 Plan the Process	**Project Planning:** The project planning process can implement GP 2.2 in full for all project-related process areas (except for Project Planning itself).	GP 2.2 applied to the project planning process can be characterized as "plan the plan" and covers planning project planning activities.
GP 2.3 Provide Resources GP 2.4 Assign Responsibility	**Project Planning:** The part of the project planning process that implements Project Planning SP 2.4, "Plan for Project Resources," supports the implementation of GP 2.3 and GP 2.4 for all project-related process areas (except perhaps initially for Project Planning itself) by identifying needed processes, roles, and responsibilities to ensure the proper staffing, facilities, equipment, and other assets needed by the project are secured.	
GP 2.5 Train People	**Organizational Training:** The organizational training process supports the implementation of GP 2.5 as applied to all process areas by making the training that addresses strategic or organization-wide training needs available to those who will perform or support the process. **Project Planning:** The part of the project planning process that implements Project Planning SP 2.5, "Plan for Needed Knowledge and Skills," together with the organizational training process, supports the implementation of GP 2.5 in full for all project-related process areas.	GP 2.5 applied to the organizational training process covers training for performing the organizational training activities, which addresses the skills required to manage, create, and accomplish the training.
GP 2.6 Manage Configurations	**Configuration Management:** The configuration management process can implement GP 2.6 in full for all project-related process areas as well as some of the organizational process areas.	GP 2.6 applied to the configuration management process covers change and version control for the work products produced by configuration management activities.

1. When the relationship between a generic practice and a process area is less direct, the risk of confusion is reduced; therefore, we do not describe all recursive relationships in the table (e.g., for generic practices 2.3, 2.4, and 2.10).

TABLE 7.2   Generic Practice and Process Area Relationships *(Continued)*

Generic Practice	Roles of Process Areas in Implementation of the Generic Practice	How the Generic Practice Recursively Applies to Its Related Process Area(s)
GP 2.7 Identify and Involve Relevant Stakeholders	**Project Planning:** The part of the project planning process that implements Project Planning SP 2.6, "Plan Stakeholder involvement," can implement the stakeholder identification part (first two subpractices) of GP 2.7 in full for all project-related process areas. **Project Monitoring and Control:** The part of the project monitoring and control process that implements Project Monitoring and Control SP 1.5, "Monitor Stakeholder Involvement," can aid in implementing the third subpractice of GP 2.7 for all project-related process areas. **Integrated Project Management:** The part of the integrated project management process that implements Integrated Project Management SP 2.1, "Manage Stakeholder Involvement," can aid in implementing the third subpractice of GP 2.7 for all project-related process areas.	GP 2.7 applied to the project planning process covers the involvement of relevant stakeholders in project planning activities. GP 2.7 applied to the project monitoring and control process covers the involvement of relevant stakeholders in project monitoring and control activities. GP 2.7 applied to the integrated project management process covers the involvement of relevant stakeholders in integrated project management activities.
GP 2.8 Monitor and Control the Process	**Project Monitoring and Control:** The project monitoring and control process can implement GP 2.8 in full for all project-related process areas. **Measurement and Analysis:** For all processes, not just project-related processes, the Measurement and Analysis process area provides general guidance about measuring, analyzing, and recording information that can be used in establishing measures for monitoring actual performance of the process.	GP 2.8 applied to the project monitoring and control process covers the monitoring and controlling of the project's monitor and control activities.
GP 2.9 Objectively Evaluate Adherence	**Process and Product Quality Assurance:** The process and product quality assurance process can implement GP 2.9 in full for all process areas (except perhaps for Process and Product Quality Assurance itself).	GP 2.9 applied to the process and product quality assurance process covers the objective evaluation of quality assurance activities.

Continues

TABLE 7.2 Generic Practice and Process Area Relationships *(Continued)*

Generic Practice	Roles of Process Areas in Implementation of the Generic Practice	How the Generic Practice Recursively Applies to Its Related Process Area(s)
GP 2.10 Review Status with Higher Level Management	**Project Monitoring and Control:** The part of the project monitoring and control process that implements Project Monitoring and Control SP 1.6, "Conduct Progress Reviews," and SP 1.7, "Conduct Milestone Reviews," supports the implementation of GP 2.10 for all project-related process areas, perhaps in full, depending on higher level management involvement in these reviews.	
GP 3.1 Establish a Defined Process	**Integrated Project Management:** The part of the integrated project management process that implements Integrated Project Management SP 1.1, "Establish the Project's Defined Process," can implement GP 3.1 in full for all project-related process areas. **Organizational Process Definition:** For all processes, not just project-related processes, the organizational process definition process establishes the organizational process assets needed to implement GP 3.1.	GP 3.1 applied to the integrated project management process covers establishing defined processes for integrated project management activities.
GP 3.2 Collect Improvement Information	**Integrated Project Management:** The part of the integrated project management process that implements Integrated Project Management SP 1.6, "Contribute to the Organizational Process Assets," can implement GP 3.2 in part or full for all project-related process areas. **Organizational Process Focus:** The part of the organizational process focus process that implements Organizational Process Focus SP 3.4, "Incorporate Process-Related Experiences into the Organizational Process Assets," can implement GP 3.2 in part or full for all process areas. **Organizational Process Definition:** For all processes, the organizational process definition process establishes the organizational process assets needed to implement GP 3.2.	GP 3.2 applied to the integrated project management process covers collecting improvement information derived from planning and performing integrated project management activities.

TABLE 7.2   Generic Practice and Process Area Relationships *(Continued)*

Generic Practice	*Roles of Process Areas in Implementation of the Generic Practice*	*How the Generic Practice Recursively Applies to Its Related Process Area(s)*
GP 4.1 Establish Quantitative Objectives for the Process	**Quantitative Project Management:** The part of the quantitative project management process that implements Quantitative Project Management SP 1.1, "Establish the Project's Objectives," supports the implementation of GP 4.1 for all project-related process areas by providing objectives from which the objectives for each particular process can be derived. If these objectives become established as part of implementing subpractices 5 and 8 of Quantitative Project Management SP 1.1, then the quantitative project management process implements GP 4.1 in full. **Organizational Process Performance:** The part of the organizational process-performance process that implements Organizational Process Performance SP 1.3, "Establish Quality and Process-Performance Objectives," supports the implementation of GP 4.1 for all process areas.	GP 4.1 applied to the quantitative project management process covers establishing quantitative objectives for quantitative project management activities. GP 4.1 applied to the organizational process-performance process covers establishing quantitative objectives for organizational process-performance activities.
GP 4.2 Stabilize Subprocess Performance	**Quantitative Project Management:** The part of the quantitative project management process that implements Quantitative Project Management SG 2, "Statistically Manage Subprocess Performance," can implement GP 4.2 in full for all project-related process areas to which a statistically managed subprocess can be mapped. **Organizational Process Performance:** For all processes, not just project-related processes, the organizational process performance process establishes organizational process assets that may be needed to implement GP 4.2.	GP 4.2 applied to the quantitative project management process covers the stabilization of selected subprocesses within quantitative project management activities.

Continues

TABLE 7.2   Generic Practice and Process Area Relationships *(Continued)*

Generic Practice	Roles of Process Areas in Implementation of the Generic Practice	How the Generic Practice Recursively Applies to Its Related Process Area(s)
GP 5.1 Ensure Continuous Process Improvement	**Organizational Innovation and Deployment:** The organizational innovation and deployment process can implement GP 5.1 in full for all process areas providing that quality and process-performance objectives for the organization have been defined. (The latter would be the case, say, if the Organizational Process Performance process area has been implemented.)	GP 5.1 applied to the organizational innovation and deployment process covers ensuring continuous process improvement of organizational innovation and deployment activities.
GP 5.2 Correct Root Causes of Problems	**Causal Analysis and Resolution:** The causal analysis and resolution process can implement GP 5.2 in full for all project-related process areas.	GP 5.2 applied to the causal analysis and resolution process covers identifying root causes of defects and other problems in causal analysis and resolution activities.

Given the dependencies that generic practices have on these process areas, and given the more "holistic" view that many of these process areas provide, these process areas are often implemented early, in whole or in part, before or concurrent with implementing the associated generic practices.

There are also a few situations where the result of applying a generic practice to a particular process area would seem to make a whole process area redundant, but, in fact, it does not. It may be natural to think that applying GP 3.1, Establish a Defined Process, to the Project Planning and Project Monitoring and Control process areas gives the same effect as the first specific goal of Integrated Project Management, "The project is conducted using a defined process that is tailored from the organization's set of standard processes."

Although it is true that there is some overlap, the application of the generic practice to these two process areas provides defined processes covering project planning and project monitoring and control activities. These defined processes do not necessarily cover support activities (such as configuration management), other project management processes (such as supplier agreement management), or the engineering processes. In contrast, the project's defined process, provided by the Integrated Project Management process area, covers all appropriate project management, engineering, and support processes.

CAUSAL ANALYSIS AND RESOLUTION
A Support Process Area at Maturity Level 5

Purpose

The purpose of Causal Analysis and Resolution (CAR) is to identify causes of defects and other problems and take action to prevent them from occurring in the future.

TIP

Although this PA is commonly used for defects, you also can use it for problems such as schedule overruns and inadequate response times that should not be considered defects.

Introductory Notes

The Causal Analysis and Resolution process area involves the following:

- Identifying and analyzing causes of defects and other problems
- Taking specific actions to remove the causes and prevent the occurrence of those types of defects and problems in the future

Causal analysis and resolution improves quality and productivity by preventing the introduction of defects into a product. Reliance on detecting defects after they have been introduced is not cost effective. It is more effective to prevent defects from being introduced by integrating causal analysis and resolution activities into each phase of the project.

HINT

Integrating CAR activities into each project phase will help prevent many defects from being introduced and is thus important to successful implementation of this PA.

Since defects and problems may have been previously encountered on other projects or in earlier phases or tasks of the current project, causal analysis and resolution activities are a mechanism for communicating lessons learned among projects.

The types of defects and other problems encountered are analyzed to identify any trends. Based on an understanding of the defined process and how it is implemented, the root causes of the defects and the future implications of the defects are determined.

Causal analysis may also be performed on problems unrelated to defects. For example, causal analysis may be used to improve quality attributes such as cycle time. Improvement proposals, simulations,

HINT

You also can apply causal analysis to problems of concern to senior management.

HINT

It is impractical to analyze *all* defects and problems; instead, focus on defects and problems that have the largest risk or impact.

TIP

Unlike OID, which looks at many sources to trigger improvement activities, CAR is triggered by actual defects or problems that have been reported.

TIP

Successful implementation of CAR requires significant management commitment and process maturity to ensure that defect and problem data is consistently recorded, causal analysis meetings are adequately supported, and CAR activities are consistently performed across the organization.

dynamic systems models, engineering analyses, new business directives, or other items may initiate such analysis.

When it is impractical to perform causal analysis on all defects, defect targets are selected by tradeoffs on estimated investments and estimated returns of quality, productivity, and cycle time.

A measurement process should already be in place. The defined measures can be used, though in some instances new measures may be needed to analyze the effects of the process change.

Refer to the Measurement and Analysis process area for more information about establishing objectives for measurement and analysis, specifying the measures and analyses to be performed, obtaining and analyzing measures, and reporting results.

Causal Analysis and Resolution activities provide a mechanism for projects to evaluate their processes at the local level and look for improvements that can be implemented.

When improvements are judged to be effective, the information is extended to the organizational level.

Refer to the Organizational Innovation and Deployment process area for more information about improving organizational level processes through proposed improvements and action proposals.

The informative material in this process area is written with the assumption that the specific practices are applied to a quantitatively managed process. The specific practices of this process area may be applicable, but with reduced value, if this assumption is not met.

See the definitions of "stable process" and "common cause of process variation" in the glossary.

Related Process Areas

Refer to the Quantitative Project Management process area for more information about the analysis of process performance and the creation of process capability measures for selected project processes.

Refer to the Organizational Innovation and Deployment process area for more information about the selection and deployment of improvements to organizational processes and technologies.

Refer to the Measurement and Analysis process area for more information about establishing objectives for measurement and analysis, specifying the measures and analyses to be performed, obtaining and analyzing measures, and reporting results.

Specific Goal and Practice Summary

SG 1 Determine Causes of Defects
      SP 1.1   Select Defect Data for Analysis
      SP 1.2   Analyze Causes
SG 2 Address Causes of Defects
      SP 2.1   Implement the Action Proposals
      SP 2.2   Evaluate the Effect of Changes
      SP 2.3   Record Data

Specific Practices by Goal

SG 1 DETERMINE CAUSES OF DEFECTS

Root causes of defects and other problems are systematically determined.

A root cause is a source of a defect such that, if it is removed, the defect is decreased or removed.

SP 1.1 SELECT DEFECT DATA FOR ANALYSIS

Select the defects and other problems for analysis.

Typical Work Products

1. Defect and problem data selected for further analysis

Subpractices

1. Gather relevant defect or problem data.

> Examples of relevant defect data may include the following:
> - Defects reported by the customer
> - Defects reported by end users
> - Defects found in peer reviews
> - Defects found in testing

> Examples of relevant problem data may include the following:
> - Project management problem reports requiring corrective action
> - Process capability problems
> - Process duration measurements
> - Earned value measurements by process (e.g., cost performance index)
> - Resource throughput, utilization, or response time measurements

CAR

HINT

Let your data help you determine which defects, if corrected, will realize the most benefit to your organization. Of course, this approach assumes you have useful and valid data.

TIP

A successful implementation of CAR requires a mature approach to measurement and analysis and the handling of defect and problem data.

It is often impossible to look at every defect. Therefore, you should establish criteria to help you prioritize and categorize defects and problems.

For more information on analyzing and categorizing defects, consult references on Six Sigma. An example method is Orthogonal Defect Classification, which provides standard taxonomies for classifying defects and their resolution.

To identify actions that address a defect or problem, you need to understand its root causes.

An action proposal typically documents the defect or problem to be resolved, when it was introduced and detected, its causes, and specific actions that, when taken, will prevent it from reoccurring.

Action proposals are prioritized, selected, and implemented in Specific Goal (SG) 2.

Refer to the Verification process area for more information about work product verification.

Refer to the Quantitative Project Management process area for more information about statistical management.

2. Determine which defects and other problems will be analyzed further.

When determining which defects to analyze further, consider the impact of the defects, their frequency of occurrence, the similarity between defects, the cost of analysis, the time and resources needed, the safety considerations, etc.

Examples of methods for selecting defects and other problems include the following:
- Pareto analysis
- Histograms
- Process capability analysis

SP 1.2 ANALYZE CAUSES

Perform causal analysis of selected defects and other problems and propose actions to address them.

The purpose of this analysis is to develop solutions to the identified problems by analyzing the relevant data and producing action proposals for implementation.

Typical Work Products

1. Action proposal

Subpractices

1. Conduct causal analysis with the people who are responsible for performing the task.

Causal analysis is performed, typically in meetings, with those people who have an understanding of the selected defect or problem under study. The people who have the best understanding of the selected defect are typically those responsible for performing the task.

Examples of when to perform causal analysis include the following:
- When a stable process does not meet its specified quality and process-performance objectives
- During the task, if and when problems warrant a causal analysis meeting
- When a work product exhibits an unexpected deviation from its requirements

---

Refer to the Quantitative Project Management process area for more information about achieving the project's quality and process-performance objectives.

2. Analyze selected defects and other problems to determine their root causes.

    Depending on the type and number of defects, it may make sense to first group the defects before identifying their root causes.

Examples of methods to determine root causes include the following:

- Cause-and-effect (fishbone) diagrams
- Check sheets

---

3. Group the selected defects and other problems based on their root causes.

Examples of cause groups, or categories, include the following:

- Inadequate training
- Breakdown of communications
- Not accounting for all details of a task
- Making mistakes in manual procedures (e.g., typing)
- Process deficiency

---

4. Propose and document actions that need to be taken to prevent the future occurrence of similar defects or other problems.

Examples of proposed actions include changes to the following:

- The process in question
- Training
- Tools
- Methods
- Communications
- Work products

Examples of specific actions include the following:

- Providing training in common problems and techniques for preventing them
- Changing a process so that error-prone steps do not occur
- Automating all or part of a process
- Reordering process activities
- Adding process steps to prevent defects, such as task kickoff meetings to review common defects and actions to prevent them

---

TIP

There are secondary benefits to causal analysis meetings. Participants develop an appreciation for how upstream activities affect downstream activities, as well as a sense of responsibility and accountability for problems that might otherwise remain unaddressed.

CAR

TIP

By grouping defects together, it is often easier to identify the root cause, rather than just the symptoms that mask it.

TIP

You develop cause-and-effect diagrams using iterative brainstorming (i.e., the "Five Whys"). This process terminates when it reaches root causes outside the experience of the group or outside the control of its management.

An action proposal usually documents the following:
- Originator of the action proposal
- Description of the problem
- Description of the defect cause
- Defect cause category
- Phase when the problem was introduced
- Phase when the defect was identified
- Description of the action proposal
- Action proposal category

SG 2   ADDRESS CAUSES OF DEFECTS

TIP

The real focus of this goal is defect and problem prevention. Defect and problem detection is addressed by verification, validation, and project monitoring activities.

Root causes of defects and other problems are systematically addressed to prevent their future occurrence.

Projects operating according to a well-defined process will systematically analyze the operation where problems still occur and implement process changes to eliminate root causes of selected problems.

SP 2.1   IMPLEMENT THE ACTION PROPOSALS

Implement the selected action proposals that were developed in causal analysis.

Action proposals describe the tasks necessary to remove the root causes of the analyzed defects or problems and avoid their reoccurrence.

TIP

When changes are piloted, measure the results of those changes to determine their value, and whether they should be considered for similar projects.

Only changes that prove to be of value should be considered for broad implementation.

Typical Work Products

1. Action proposals selected for implementation
2. Improvement proposals

Subpractices

1. Analyze the action proposals and determine their priorities.
   Criteria for prioritizing action proposals include the following:
   - Implications of not addressing the defects
   - Cost to implement process improvements to prevent the defects
   - Expected impact on quality

2. Select the action proposals that will be implemented.

3. Create action items for implementing the action proposals.

Examples of information provided in an action item include the following:
- Person responsible for implementing it
- Description of the areas affected by it
- People who are to be kept informed of its status
- Next date that status will be reviewed
- Rationale for key decisions
- Description of implementation actions
- Time and cost for identifying the defect and correcting it
- Estimated cost of not fixing the problem

To implement the action proposals, the following tasks must be done:
- Make assignments
- Coordinate the persons doing the work
- Review the results
- Track the action items to closure

Experiments may be conducted for particularly complex changes.

X-REF

For more information on designing experiments to understand the impact of certain changes, consult references on Six Sigma and Experimental Design.

TIP

Subpractice 4 focuses on the project; Subpractice 5 focuses on the organization.

Examples of experiments include the following:
- Using a temporarily modified process
- Using a new tool

Action items may be assigned to members of the causal analysis team, members of the project team, or other members of the organization.

4. Identify and remove similar defects that may exist in other processes and work products.

5. Identify and document improvement proposals for the organization's set of standard processes.

Refer to the Organizational Innovation and Deployment process area for more information about the selection and deployment of improvement proposals for the organization's set of standard processes.

HINT

When a resolution has more general applicability, don't document the resolution in a lessons learned document; instead document it in an improvement proposal.

X-REF

For more information about improvement proposals, see OPF SP 2.4.

SP 2.2 EVALUATE THE EFFECT OF CHANGES

Evaluate the effect of changes on process performance.

Refer to the Quantitative Project Management process area for more information about analyzing process performance and creating process capability measures for selected processes.

CAR

HINT

Use the measures associated with a process or subprocess (perhaps supplemented by other measures) to evaluate the effect of changes. If the change affects a subprocess being statistically managed, recalculate the natural limits to obtain insight into the effects of the change.

Once the changed process is deployed across the project, the effect of the changes must be checked to gather evidence that the process change has corrected the problem and improved performance.

Typical Work Products

1. Measures of performance and performance change

Subpractices

1. Measure the change in the performance of the project's defined process as appropriate.

    This subpractice determines whether the selected change has positively influenced the process performance and by how much.

    > An example of a change in the performance of the project's defined design process would be the change in the defect density of the design documentation, as statistically measured through peer reviews before and after the improvement has been made. On a statistical process control chart, this would be represented by a change in the mean.

2. Measure the capability of the project's defined process as appropriate.

    This subpractice determines whether the selected change has positively influenced the ability of the process to meet its quality and process-performance objectives, as determined by relevant stakeholders.

    > An example of a change in the capability of the project's defined design process would be a change in the ability of the process to stay within its process-specification boundaries. This can be statistically measured by calculating the range of the defect density of design documentation, as collected in peer reviews before and after the improvement has been made. On a statistical process control chart, this would be represented by lowered control limits.

HINT

It is often too costly to correct every defect or problem. Collect data to know that you are improving project performance relative to your business objectives and to prevent selected defects from reoccurring.

SP 2.3 RECORD DATA

Record causal analysis and resolution data for use across the project and organization.

Data are recorded so that other projects and organizations can make appropriate process changes and achieve similar results.

Record the following:

- Data on defects and other problems that were analyzed
- Rationale for decisions
- Action proposals from causal analysis meetings
- Action items resulting from action proposals
- Cost of the analysis and resolution activities
- Measures of changes to the performance of the defined process resulting from resolutions

Typical Work Products

1. Causal analysis and resolution records

Generic Practices by Goal

GG 1 *ACHIEVE SPECIFIC GOALS*

The process supports and enables achievement of the specific goals of the process area by transforming identifiable input work products to produce identifiable output work products.

GP 1.1 *PERFORM SPECIFIC PRACTICES*

Perform the specific practices of the causal analysis and resolution process to develop work products and provide services to achieve the specific goals of the process area.

GG 2 *INSTITUTIONALIZE A MANAGED PROCESS*

The process is institutionalized as a managed process.

GG 3 *INSTITUTIONALIZE A DEFINED PROCESS*

The process is institutionalized as a defined process.

> *This generic goal's appearance here reflects its location in the staged representation.*

GP 2.1 *ESTABLISH AN ORGANIZATIONAL POLICY*

Establish and maintain an organizational policy for planning and performing the causal analysis and resolution process.

Elaboration:

This policy establishes organizational expectations for identifying and systematically addressing root causes of defects and other problems.

GP 2.2 PLAN THE PROCESS

Establish and maintain the plan for performing the causal analysis and resolution process.

Elaboration:

This plan for performing the causal analysis and resolution process can be included in (or referenced by) the project plan, which is described in the Project Planning process area. This plan differs from the action proposals and associated action items described in several specific practices in this process area. The plan called for in this generic practice would address the project's overall causal analysis and resolution process (perhaps tailored from a standard process maintained by the organization). In contrast, the process action proposals and associated action items address the activities needed to remove a specific root cause under study.

GP 2.3 PROVIDE RESOURCES

Provide adequate resources for performing the causal analysis and resolution process, developing the work products, and providing the services of the process.

Elaboration:

Examples of resources provided include the following tools:
• Database systems
• Process modeling tools
• Statistical analysis packages
• Tools, methods, and analysis techniques (e.g., Ishikawa or fishbone diagram, Pareto analysis, histograms, process capability studies, or control charts)

GP 2.4 ASSIGN RESPONSIBILITY

Assign responsibility and authority for performing the process, developing the work products, and providing the services of the causal analysis and resolution process.

GP 2.5 T*RAIN* P*EOPLE*

Train the people performing or supporting the causal analysis and resolution process as needed.

Elaboration:

> Examples of training topics include the following:
> • Quality management methods (e.g., root cause analysis)

GP 2.6 M*ANAGE* C*ONFIGURATIONS*

Place designated work products of the causal analysis and resolution process under appropriate levels of control.

Elaboration:

> Examples of work products placed under control include the following:
> • Action proposals
> • Action proposals selected for implementation
> • Causal analysis and resolution records

GP 2.7 I*DENTIFY AND* I*NVOLVE* R*ELEVANT* S*TAKEHOLDERS*

Identify and involve the relevant stakeholders of the causal analysis and resolution process as planned.

Elaboration:

> Examples of activities for stakeholder involvement include the following:
> • Conducting causal analysis
> • Assessing the action proposals

GP 2.8 M*ONITOR AND* C*ONTROL THE* P*ROCESS*

Monitor and control the causal analysis and resolution process against the plan for performing the process and take appropriate corrective action.

CAR

Elaboration:

> Examples of measures and work products used in monitoring and controlling include the following:
> - Number of root causes removed
> - Change in quality or process performance per instance of the causal analysis and resolution process
> - Schedule of activities for implementing a selected action proposal

GP 2.9 OBJECTIVELY EVALUATE ADHERENCE

Objectively evaluate adherence of the causal analysis and resolution process against its process description, standards, and procedures, and address non-compliance.

Elaboration:

> Examples of activities reviewed include the following:
> - Determining causes of defects
> - Addressing causes of defects

> Examples of work products reviewed include the following:
> - Action proposals selected for implementation
> - Causal analysis and resolution records

GP 2.10 REVIEW STATUS WITH HIGHER LEVEL MANAGEMENT

Review the activities, status, and results of the causal analysis and resolution process with higher level management and resolve issues.

GG 3 INSTITUTIONALIZE A DEFINED PROCESS

The process is institutionalized as a defined process.

> *This generic goal's appearance here reflects its location in the continuous representation.*

GP 3.1 ESTABLISH A DEFINED PROCESS

Establish and maintain the description of a defined causal analysis and resolution process.

CONTINUOUS ONLY

GP 3.2 COLLECT IMPROVEMENT INFORMATION

Collect work products, measures, measurement results, and improvement information derived from planning and performing the causal analysis and resolution process to support the future use and improvement of the organization's processes and process assets.

Elaboration:

Examples of work products, measures, measurement results, and improvement information include the following:
- Action proposals
- Number of action proposals that are open and for how long
- Action proposal status reports

GG 4   *INSTITUTIONALIZE A QUANTITATIVELY MANAGED PROCESS*

The process is institutionalized as a quantitatively managed process.

GP 4.1 ESTABLISH QUANTITATIVE OBJECTIVES FOR THE PROCESS

Establish and maintain quantitative objectives for the causal analysis and resolution process, which address quality and process performance, based on customer needs and business objectives.

GP 4.2 STABILIZE SUBPROCESS PERFORMANCE

Stabilize the performance of one or more subprocesses to determine the ability of the causal analysis and resolution process to achieve the established quantitative quality and process-performance objectives.

GG 5   *INSTITUTIONALIZE AN OPTIMIZING PROCESS*

The process is institutionalized as an optimizing process.

GP 5.1 ENSURE CONTINUOUS PROCESS IMPROVEMENT

Ensure continuous improvement of the causal analysis and resolution process in fulfilling the relevant business objectives of the organization.

GP 5.2 CORRECT ROOT CAUSES OF PROBLEMS

Identify and correct the root causes of defects and other problems in the causal analysis and resolution process.

CONTINUOUS ONLY

CAR

CONFIGURATION MANAGEMENT
A Support Process Area at Maturity Level 2

Purpose

The purpose of Configuration Management (CM) is to establish and maintain the integrity of work products using configuration identification, configuration control, configuration status accounting, and configuration audits.

TIP

Since this is a support process area, it is up to the project and organization to decide which work products are subject to CM, and the level of control needed.

Introductory Notes

The Configuration Management process area involves the following:

- Identifying the configuration of selected work products that compose the baselines at given points in time
- Controlling changes to configuration items
- Building or providing specifications to build work products from the configuration management system
- Maintaining the integrity of baselines
- Providing accurate status and current configuration data to developers, end users, and customers

HINT

CM should capture enough information to identify and maintain the configuration item after those who have developed it have gone.

The work products placed under configuration management include the products that are delivered to the customer, designated internal work products, acquired products, tools, and other items that are used in creating and describing these work products. (See the definition of "configuration management" in the glossary.)

Acquired products may need to be placed under configuration management by both the supplier and the project. Provisions for conducting configuration management should be established in supplier agreements. Methods to ensure that the data is complete and consistent should be established and maintained.

Refer to the Supplier Agreement Management process area for more information about establishing and maintaining agreements with suppliers.

> Examples of work products that may be placed under configuration management include the following:
> • Plans
> • Process descriptions
> • Requirements
> • Design data
> • Drawings
> • Product specifications
> • Code
> • Compilers
> • Product data files
> • Product technical publications

HINT

Typically, you determine the levels of granularity during planning. Select the configuration to be placed under CM based on technical and business needs.

Configuration management of work products may be performed at several levels of granularity. Configuration items can be decomposed into configuration components and configuration units. Only the term "configuration item" is used in this process area. Therefore, in these practices, "configuration item" may be interpreted as "configuration component" or "configuration unit" as appropriate. (See the definition of "configuration item" in the glossary.)

Baselines provide a stable basis for continuing evolution of configuration items.

> An example of a baseline is an approved description of a product that includes internally consistent versions of requirements, requirement traceability matrices, design, discipline-specific items, and end-user documentation.

HINT

Review and approve baselines before they are added to (or promoted within) the CM system.

Baselines are added to the configuration management system as they are developed. Changes to baselines and the release of work products built from the configuration management system are systematically controlled and monitored via the configuration control, change management, and configuration auditing functions of configuration management.

This process area applies not only to configuration management on projects, but also to configuration management on organizational work products such as standards, procedures, and reuse libraries.

TIP

Any work product whose integrity should be ensured over a period of time might benefit from CM.

Configuration management is focused on the rigorous control of the managerial and technical aspects of work products, including the delivered system.

This process area covers the practices for performing the configuration management function and is applicable to all work products that are placed under configuration management.

Related Process Areas

Refer to the Project Planning process area for information on developing plans and work breakdown structures, which may be useful for determining configuration items.

Refer to the Project Monitoring and Control process area for more information about performance analyses and corrective actions.

Specific Goal and Practice Summary

SG 1 Establish Baselines
    SP 1.1   Identify Configuration Items
    SP 1.2   Establish a Configuration Management System
    SP 1.3   Create or Release Baselines
SG 2 Track and Control Changes
    SP 2.1   Track Change Requests
    SP 2.2   Control Configuration Items
SG 3 Establish Integrity
    SP 3.1   Establish Configuration Management Records
    SP 3.2   Perform Configuration Audits

Specific Practices by Goal

SG 1 ESTABLISH BASELINES

Baselines of identified work products are established.

Specific practices to establish baselines are covered by this specific goal. The specific practices under the Track and Control Changes specific goal serve to maintain the baselines. The specific practices of the Establish Integrity specific goal document and audit the integrity of the baselines.

SP 1.1 IDENTIFY CONFIGURATION ITEMS

Identify the configuration items, components, and related work products that will be placed under configuration management.

Configuration identification is the selection, creation, and specification of the following:

- Products that are delivered to the customer
- Designated internal work products
- Acquired products
- Tools and other capital assets of the project's work environment
- Other items that are used in creating and describing these work products

Items under configuration management will include specifications and interface documents that define the requirements for the product. Other documents, such as test results, may also be included, depending on their criticality to defining the product.

A "configuration item" is an entity designated for configuration management, which may consist of multiple related work products that form a baseline. This logical grouping provides ease of identification and controlled access. The selection of work products for configuration management should be based on criteria established during planning.

Typical Work Products

1. Identified configuration items

Subpractices

1. Select the configuration items and the work products that compose them based on documented criteria.

Example criteria for selecting configuration items at the appropriate work product level include the following:

- Work products that may be used by two or more groups
- Work products that are expected to change over time either because of errors or change of requirements
- Work products that are dependent on each other in that a change in one mandates a change in the others
- Work products that are critical for the project

HINT

When developing your project plan, document what is important for you to control. This part of the plan provides guidance for the project team when identifying configuration items.

HINT

Use criteria to select configuration items to ensure that the selection is consistent and thorough.

Examples of work products that may be part of a configuration item include the following:

- Process descriptions
- Requirements
- Design
- Test plans and procedures
- Test results
- Interface descriptions
- Drawings
- Source code
- Tools (e.g., compilers)

2. Assign unique identifiers to configuration items.
3. Specify the important characteristics of each configuration item.

Example characteristics of configuration items include author, document or file type, and programming language for software code files.

4. Specify when each configuration item is placed under configuration management.

Example criteria for determining when to place work products under configuration management include the following:

- Stage of the project lifecycle
- When the work product is ready for test
- Degree of control desired on the work product
- Cost and schedule limitations
- Customer requirements

5. Identify the owner responsible for each configuration item.

SP 1.2 ESTABLISH A CONFIGURATION MANAGEMENT SYSTEM

Establish and maintain a configuration management and change management system for controlling work products.

A configuration management system includes the storage media, the procedures, and the tools for accessing the configuration system.

A change management system includes the storage media, the procedures, and tools for recording and accessing change requests.

HINT

If you use a CM tool, it will sometimes assign unique identifiers to configuration items for you.

CM

TIP

Specifying when a configuration item must be placed under CM sets expectations among team members as to the control of the project's work products.

TIP

Most organizations use an automated tool for CM. Because of the many aspects to consider, it is difficult to maintain a manual CM process.

HINT

Many software packages are available to help you with CM. Before you purchase one, identify your needs and compare them to the features offered in the software package.

TIP

Not all configuration items require the same level of control. Some may require more control as they move through the project lifecycle.

TIP

A formal CM process is typically change-request based and requires extensive tracking and review of all changes.

TIP

Version control is an important part of CM. There are different ways to identify versions. A standard way is using sequential numbering.

Typical Work Products

1. Configuration management system with controlled work products
2. Configuration management system access control procedures
3. Change request database

Subpractices

1. Establish a mechanism to manage multiple control levels of configuration management.

   The level of control is typically selected based on project objectives, risk, and/or resources. Control levels may vary in relation to the project lifecycle, type of system under development, and specific project requirements.

   Example levels of control include the following:
   - **Create – controlled by author**
   - **Engineering – notification to relevant stakeholders when changes are made**
   - **Development – lower level CCB control**
   - **Formal – higher level CCB control with customer involvement**

   Levels of control can range from informal control that simply tracks changes made when the configuration items are being developed to formal configuration control using baselines that can only be changed as part of a formal configuration management process.

2. Store and retrieve configuration items in a configuration management system.

   Examples of configuration management systems include the following:
   - **Dynamic (or author's) systems contain components currently being created or revised. They are in the author's workspace and are controlled by the author. Configuration items in a dynamic system are under version control.**
   - **Master (or controlled) systems contain current baselines and changes to them. Configuration items in a master system are under full configuration management as described in this process area.**
   - **Static systems contain archives of various baselines released for use. Static systems are under full configuration management as described in this process area.**
   ---

3. Share and transfer configuration items between control levels within the configuration management system.
4. Store and recover archived versions of configuration items.

5. Store, update, and retrieve configuration management records.
6. Create configuration management reports from the configuration management system.
7. Preserve the contents of the configuration management system.

> **HINT**
> To ensure that project members use the CM system, make sure the system is easy to use.

Examples of preservation functions of the configuration management system include the following:
- Backups and restoration of configuration management files
- Archiving of configuration management files
- Recovery from configuration management errors

---

8. Revise the configuration management structure as necessary.

> **HINT**
> Review the CM system regularly to ensure that it is meeting the needs of the projects it serves.

SP 1.3 CREATE OR RELEASE BASELINES

Create or release baselines for internal use and for delivery to the customer.

A baseline is a set of specifications or work products that has been formally reviewed and agreed on, that thereafter serves as the basis for further development or delivery, and that can be changed only through change control procedures. A baseline represents the assignment of an identifier to a configuration item or a collection of configuration items and associated entities. As a product evolves, several baselines may be used to control its development and testing.

FOR SYSTEMS ENGINEERING
One common set of baselines includes the system-level requirements, system-element-level design requirements, and the product definition at the end of development/beginning of production. These are typically referred to as the "functional baseline," "allocated baseline," and "product baseline."

FOR SOFTWARE ENGINEERING
A software baseline can be a set of requirements, design, source code files and the associated executable code, build files, and user documentation (associated entities) that have been assigned a unique identifier.

> **TIP**
> If the baselines released or used do not come from the CM system, the system is not serving its purpose and there is a high risk of losing baseline integrity.

> **TIP**
> If the project or organization uses multiple baselines, it is even more critical to ensure that everyone is using the correct baseline.

Typical Work Products

1. Baselines
2. Description of baselines

CM

TIP

CCB authorization should be formal and documented in some way.

Subpractices

1. Obtain authorization from the configuration control board (CCB) before creating or releasing baselines of configuration items.
2. Create or release baselines only from configuration items in the configuration management system.
3. Document the set of configuration items that are contained in a baseline.
4. Make the current set of baselines readily available.

SG 2 TRACK AND CONTROL CHANGES

TIP

This goal is typically implemented by establishing a change request system and forming a CCB whose primary role is to review and approve baseline changes.

Changes to the work products under configuration management are tracked and controlled.

The specific practices under this specific goal serve to maintain the baselines after they are established by the specific practices under the Establish Baselines specific goal.

SP 2.1 TRACK CHANGE REQUESTS

TIP

Change requests are formally submitted descriptions of desired modifications to work products. If change requests are not documented consistently, they are difficult to analyze and track.

Track change requests for the configuration items.

Change requests address not only new or changed requirements, but also failures and defects in the work products.

Change requests are analyzed to determine the impact that the change will have on the work product, related work products, budget, and schedule.

Typical Work Products

1. Change requests

Subpractices

TIP

A database provides a flexible environment for storing and tracking change requests.

1. Initiate and record change requests in the change request database.
2. Analyze the impact of changes and fixes proposed in the change requests.

   Changes are evaluated through activities that ensure that they are consistent with all technical and project requirements.

   Changes are evaluated for their impact beyond immediate project or contract requirements. Changes to an item used in multiple products can resolve an immediate issue while causing a problem in other applications.

3. Review change requests that will be addressed in the next baseline with the relevant stakeholders and get their agreement.

> Conduct the change request review with appropriate participants. Record the disposition of each change request and the rationale for the decision, including success criteria, a brief action plan if appropriate, and needs met or unmet by the change. Perform the actions required in the disposition, and report the results to relevant stakeholders.

4. Track the status of change requests to closure.

> Change requests brought into the system need to be handled in an efficient and timely manner. Once a change request has been processed, it is critical to close the request with the appropriate approved action as soon as it is practical. Actions left open result in larger than necessary status lists, which in turn result in added costs and confusion.

TIP

A change request system is usually used once an initial baseline is created. A change request system allows you to track every change that is made to a work product.

HINT

Track change requests to closure to ensure that if a change request is not addressed, it was not lost or missed.

SP 2.2 CONTROL CONFIGURATION ITEMS

Control changes to the configuration items.

Control is maintained over the configuration of the work product baseline. This control includes tracking the configuration of each of the configuration items, approving a new configuration if necessary, and updating the baseline.

Typical Work Products

1. Revision history of configuration items
2. Archives of the baselines

TIP

A revision history usually contains not only what was changed, but also who made the changes, and when and why they were made.

Subpractices

1. Control changes to configuration items throughout the life of the product.
2. Obtain appropriate authorization before changed configuration items are entered into the configuration management system.

> For example, authorization may come from the CCB, the project manager, or the customer.

TIP

The life of the product is typically longer than the life of the development project that created it. The responsibility for configuration items may change over time.

3. Check in and check out configuration items from the configuration management system for incorporation of changes in a manner that maintains the correctness and integrity of the configuration items.

HINT

Define authorization procedures so that it is clear how to receive authorization to enter an updated configuration item into the CM system.

CM

TIP

An important part of check in and check out is ensuring that only one copy of a configuration item is authorized for update at one time.

Examples of check-in and check-out steps include the following:
- Confirming that the revisions are authorized
- Updating the configuration items
- Archiving the replaced baseline and retrieving the new baseline

4. Perform reviews to ensure that changes have not caused unintended effects on the baselines (e.g., ensure that the changes have not compromised the safety and/or security of the system).

5. Record changes to configuration items and the reasons for the changes as appropriate.

> If a proposed change to the work product is accepted, a schedule is identified for incorporating the change into the work product and other affected areas.

> Configuration control mechanisms can be tailored to categories of changes. For example, the approval considerations could be less stringent for component changes that do not affect other components.

> Changed configuration items are released after review and approval of configuration changes. Changes are not official until they are released.

SG 3 ESTABLISH INTEGRITY

Integrity of baselines is established and maintained.

TIP

Since baselines are often the "footprints" of a particular product, it is important that they are accurate.

The integrity of the baselines, established by processes associated with the Establish Baselines specific goal, and maintained by processes associated with the Track and Control Changes specific goal, is provided by the specific practices under this specific goal.

SP 3.1 ESTABLISH CONFIGURATION MANAGEMENT RECORDS

Establish and maintain records describing configuration items.

TIP

Without descriptions of the configuration items, it is difficult and time consuming to understand the status of these items relative to the project plan.

Typical Work Products

1. Revision history of configuration items
2. Change log
3. Copy of the change requests
4. Status of configuration items
5. Differences between baselines

Subpractices

1. Record configuration management actions in sufficient detail so the content and status of each configuration item is known and previous versions can be recovered.

2. Ensure that relevant stakeholders have access to and knowledge of the configuration status of the configuration items.

> Examples of activities for communicating configuration status include the following:
> • Providing access permissions to authorized end users
> • Making baseline copies readily available to authorized end users

3. Specify the latest version of the baselines.

4. Identify the version of configuration items that constitute a particular baseline.

5. Describe the differences between successive baselines.

6. Revise the status and history (i.e., changes and other actions) of each configuration item as necessary.

HINT

When describing the differences between baselines, you should be detailed enough so that users of the baselines can differentiate them easily.

CM

SP 3.2 PERFORM CONFIGURATION AUDITS

Perform configuration audits to maintain integrity of the configuration baselines.

Configuration audits confirm that the resulting baselines and documentation conform to a specified standard or requirement. Audit results should be recorded as appropriate. (See the glossary for a definition of "configuration audit.")

TIP

Audits provide an objective way to know that what is supposed to be controlled is controlled and can be retrieved. Retrieval of accurate information is one of CM's many benefits.

> Examples of audit types include the following:
> • Functional Configuration Audits (FCA) – Audits conducted to verify that the as-tested functional characteristics of a configuration item have achieved the requirements specified in its functional baseline documentation and that the operational and support documentation is complete and satisfactory.
> • Physical Configuration Audit (PCA) – Audits conducted to verify that the as-built configuration item conforms to the technical documentation that defines it.
> • Configuration management audits – Audits conducted to confirm that configuration management records and configuration items are complete, consistent, and accurate.

Typical Work Products

1. Configuration audit results
2. Action items

Subpractices

TIP

Integrity includes both accuracy and completeness.

1. Assess the integrity of the baselines.
2. Confirm that the configuration management records correctly identify the configuration items.
3. Review the structure and integrity of the items in the configuration management system.
4. Confirm the completeness and correctness of the items in the configuration management system.

    Completeness and correctness of the content is based on the requirements as stated in the plan and the disposition of approved change requests.

5. Confirm compliance with applicable configuration management standards and procedures.

TIP

An audit is effective only when all action items from the audit are addressed.

6. Track action items from the audit to closure.

Generic Practices by Goal

GG 1 ACHIEVE SPECIFIC GOALS

The process supports and enables achievement of the specific goals of the process area by transforming identifiable input work products to produce identifiable output work products.

GP 1.1 PERFORM SPECIFIC PRACTICES

Perform the specific practices of the configuration management process to develop work products and provide services to achieve the specific goals of the process area.

CONTINUOUS ONLY

GG 2 INSTITUTIONALIZE A MANAGED PROCESS

The process is institutionalized as a managed process.

GP 2.1 ESTABLISH AN ORGANIZATIONAL POLICY

Establish and maintain an organizational policy for planning and performing the configuration management process.

Elaboration:

This policy establishes organizational expectations for establishing and maintaining baselines, tracking and controlling changes to the work products (under configuration management), and establishing and maintaining integrity of the baselines.

GP 2.2 PLAN THE PROCESS

Establish and maintain the plan for performing the configuration management process.

Elaboration:

This plan for performing the configuration management process can be included in (or referenced by) the project plan, which is described in the Project Planning process area.

GP 2.3 PROVIDE RESOURCES

Provide adequate resources for performing the configuration management process, developing the work products, and providing the services of the process.

Elaboration:

Examples of resources provided include the following tools:
- Configuration management tools
- Data management tools
- Archiving and reproduction tools
- Database programs

GP 2.4 ASSIGN RESPONSIBILITY

Assign responsibility and authority for performing the process, developing the work products, and providing the services of the configuration management process.

GP 2.5 TRAIN PEOPLE

Train the people performing or supporting the configuration management process as needed.

CM

Elaboration:

Examples of training topics include the following:
- Roles, responsibilities, and authority of the configuration management staff
- Configuration management standards, procedures, and methods
- Configuration library system

GP 2.6 *MANAGE CONFIGURATIONS*

Place designated work products of the configuration management process under appropriate levels of control.

Elaboration:

Refer to Table 7.2 on page 172 in Generic Goals and Generic Practices for more information about the relationship between generic practice 2.6 and the Configuration Management process area.

Examples of work products placed under control include the following:
- Access lists
- Change status reports
- Change request database
- CCB meeting minutes
- Archived baselines

GP 2.7 *IDENTIFY AND INVOLVE RELEVANT STAKEHOLDERS*

Identify and involve the relevant stakeholders of the configuration management process as planned.

Elaboration:

Examples of activities for stakeholder involvement include the following:
- Establishing baselines
- Reviewing configuration management system reports and resolving issues
- Assessing the impact of changes for the configuration items
- Performing configuration audits
- Reviewing the results of configuration management audits

GP 2.8 *MONITOR AND CONTROL THE PROCESS*

Monitor and control the configuration management process against the plan for performing the process and take appropriate corrective action.

Elaboration:

> Examples of measures and work products used in monitoring and controlling include the following:
> • Number of changes to configuration items
> • Number of configuration audits conducted
> • Schedule of CCB or audit activities

GP 2.9 *OBJECTIVELY EVALUATE ADHERENCE*

Objectively evaluate adherence of the configuration management process against its process description, standards, and procedures, and address non-compliance.

Elaboration:

> Examples of activities reviewed include the following:
> • Establishing baselines
> • Tracking and controlling changes
> • Establishing and maintaining integrity of baselines

> Examples of work products reviewed include the following:
> • Archives of the baselines
> • Change request database

GP 2.10 *REVIEW STATUS WITH HIGHER LEVEL MANAGEMENT*

Review the activities, status, and results of the configuration management process with higher level management and resolve issues.

> GG3 and its practices do not apply for a maturity level 2 rating, but do apply for a maturity level 3 rating and above.

STAGED ONLY

GG 3 *INSTITUTIONALIZE A DEFINED PROCESS*

The process is institutionalized as a defined process.

GP 3.1 *ESTABLISH A DEFINED PROCESS*

Establish and maintain the description of a defined configuration management process.

C/M LEVELS 3–5 ONLY

GP 3.2 COLLECT IMPROVEMENT INFORMATION

Collect work products, measures, measurement results, and improvement information derived from planning and performing the configuration management process to support the future use and improvement of the organization's processes and process assets.

Elaboration:

> Examples of work products, measures, measurement results, and improvement information include the following:
> • Trends in the status of configuration items
> • Configuration audit results
> • Change request aging reports

GG 4 INSTITUTIONALIZE A QUANTITATIVELY MANAGED PROCESS

The process is institutionalized as a quantitatively managed process.

GP 4.1 ESTABLISH QUANTITATIVE OBJECTIVES FOR THE PROCESS

Establish and maintain quantitative objectives for the configuration management process, which address quality and process performance, based on customer needs and business objectives.

GP 4.2 STABILIZE SUBPROCESS PERFORMANCE

Stabilize the performance of one or more subprocesses to determine the ability of the configuration management process to achieve the established quantitative quality and process-performance objectives.

GG 5 INSTITUTIONALIZE AN OPTIMIZING PROCESS

The process is institutionalized as an optimizing process.

GP 5.1 ENSURE CONTINUOUS PROCESS IMPROVEMENT

Ensure continuous improvement of the configuration management process in fulfilling the relevant business objectives of the organization.

GP 5.2 CORRECT ROOT CAUSES OF PROBLEMS

Identify and correct the root causes of defects and other problems in the configuration management process.

DECISION ANALYSIS AND RESOLUTION
A Support Process Area at Maturity Level 3

Purpose

The purpose of Decision Analysis and Resolution (DAR) is to analyze possible decisions using a formal evaluation process that evaluates identified alternatives against established criteria.

TIP

DAR provides organizations with a criterion-based approach to making important decisions objectively.

Introductory Notes

The Decision Analysis and Resolution process area involves establishing guidelines to determine which issues should be subjected to a formal evaluation process and then applying formal evaluation processes to these issues.

A formal evaluation process is a structured approach to evaluating alternative solutions against established criteria to determine a recommended solution to address an issue. A formal evaluation process involves the following actions:

HINT

Initially, learn to use this process for decisions that will have a major impact on the project. Once you are accustomed to using a formal evaluation process, you may find value in using it for selected day-to-day decisions.

- Establishing the criteria for evaluating alternatives
- Identifying alternative solutions
- Selecting methods for evaluating alternatives
- Evaluating the alternative solutions using the established criteria and methods
- Selecting recommended solutions from the alternatives based on the evaluation criteria

Rather than using the phrase "alternative solutions to address issues" each time it is needed, we will use one of two shorter phrases: "alternative solutions" or "alternatives."

A formal evaluation process reduces the subjective nature of the decision and has a higher probability of selecting a solution that meets the multiple demands of relevant stakeholders.

TIP

DAR takes the blame out of decision making. A bad decision is made when all the necessary information that might impact the decision was not considered and relevant stakeholders were not consulted.

TIP

Examples of nontechnical issues include adding additional resources and determining delivery approaches for a training class.

While the primary application of this process area is to technical concerns, formal evaluation processes can also be applied to many nontechnical issues, particularly when a project is being planned. Issues that have multiple alternative solutions and evaluation criteria lend themselves to a formal evaluation process.

> Trade studies of equipment or software are typical examples of formal evaluation processes.

X-REF

Many of the technical issues that may benefit from a formal evaluation process are addressed in TS, PI, VER, and VAL.

During planning, specific issues requiring a formal evaluation process are identified. Typical issues include selection among architectural or design alternatives, use of reusable or commercial off-the-shelf (COTS) components, supplier selection, engineering support environments or associated tools, test environments, delivery alternatives, and logistics and production. A formal evaluation process can also be used to address a make-or-buy decision, the development of manufacturing processes, the selection of distribution locations, and other decisions.

Guidelines are created for deciding when to use formal evaluation processes to address unplanned issues. Guidelines often suggest using formal evaluation processes when issues are associated with medium to high risks or when issues affect the ability to achieve project objectives.

Formal evaluation processes can vary in formality, type of criteria, and methods employed. Less formal decisions can be analyzed in a few hours, use only a few criteria (e.g., effectiveness and cost to implement), and result in a one- or two-page report. More formal decisions may require separate plans, months of effort, meetings to develop and approve criteria, simulations, prototypes, piloting, and extensive documentation.

TIP

Tools such as the Analytic Hierarchy Process (AHP), Quality Function Deployment (QFD), the Pugh Method, the Delphi Method, prioritization matrices, cause-and-effect diagrams, decision trees, weighted criteria spreadsheets, and simulations can incorporate weights in decision making.

Both numeric and non-numeric criteria can be used in a formal evaluation process. Numeric criteria use weights to reflect the relative importance of the criteria. Non-numeric criteria use a more subjective ranking scale (e.g., high, medium, or low). More formal decisions may require a full trade study.

A formal evaluation process identifies and evaluates alternative solutions. The eventual selection of a solution may involve iterative activities of identification and evaluation. Portions of identified alternatives may be combined, emerging technologies may change alternatives, and the business situation of vendors may change during the evaluation period.

A recommended alternative is accompanied by documentation of the selected methods, criteria, alternatives, and rationale for the recommendation. The documentation is distributed to relevant stakeholders; it provides a record of the formal evaluation process and rationale that are useful to other projects that encounter a similar issue.

While some of the decisions made throughout the life of the project involve the use of a formal evaluation process, others do not. As mentioned earlier, guidelines should be established to determine which issues should be subjected to a formal evaluation process.

Related Process Areas

Refer to the Project Planning process area for more information about general planning for projects.

Refer to the Integrated Project Management process area for more information about establishing the project's defined process. The project's defined process includes a formal evaluation process for each selected issue and incorporates the use of guidelines for applying a formal evaluation process to unforeseen issues.

Refer to the Risk Management process area for more information about identifying and mitigating risks. A formal evaluation process is often used to address issues with identified medium or high risks. Selected solutions typically affect risk mitigation plans.

Specific Goal and Practice Summary

SG 1   Evaluate Alternatives
     SP 1.1   Establish Guidelines for Decision Analysis
     SP 1.2   Establish Evaluation Criteria
     SP 1.3   Identify Alternative Solutions
     SP 1.4   Select Evaluation Methods
     SP 1.5   Evaluate Alternatives
     SP 1.6   Select Solutions

Specific Practices by Goal

SG 1   *EVALUATE ALTERNATIVES*

Decisions are based on an evaluation of alternatives using established criteria.

Issues requiring a formal evaluation process may be identified at any time. The objective should be to identify issues as early as possible to maximize the time available to resolve them.

DAR

SP 1.1 ESTABLISH GUIDELINES FOR DECISION ANALYSIS

Establish and maintain guidelines to determine which issues are subject to a formal evaluation process.

TIP

The terms *issues* and *decisions* are used interchangeably here.

Not every decision is significant enough to require a formal evaluation process. The choice between the trivial and the truly important will be unclear without explicit guidance. Whether a decision is significant or not is dependent on the project and circumstances, and is determined by the established guidelines.

Typical guidelines for determining when to require a formal evaluation process include the following:

- When a decision is directly related to topics assessed as being of medium or high risk
- When a decision is related to changing work products under configuration management
- When a decision would cause schedule delays over a certain percentage or specific amount of time
- When a decision affects the ability to achieve project objectives
- When the costs of the formal evaluation process are reasonable when compared to the decision's impact
- When a legal obligation exists during a solicitation

Refer to the Risk Management process area for more information about determining which issues are medium or high risk.

Examples of when to use a formal evaluation process include the following:
- On decisions involving the procurement of material when 20 percent of the material parts constitute 80 percent of the total material costs
- On design-implementation decisions when technical performance failure may cause a catastrophic failure (e.g., safety of flight item)
- On decisions with the potential to significantly reduce design risk, engineering changes, cycle time, response time, and production costs (e.g., to use lithography models to assess form and fit capability before releasing engineering drawings and production builds)

Typical Work Products

1. Guidelines for when to apply a formal evaluation process

Subpractices

1. Establish guidelines.
2. Incorporate the use of the guidelines into the defined process where appropriate.

   Refer to the Integrated Project Management process area for more information about establishing the project's defined process.

HINT

Make sure the guidelines are accessible and understood by everyone in the organization (or project).

SP 1.2 ESTABLISH EVALUATION CRITERIA

Establish and maintain the criteria for evaluating alternatives, and the relative ranking of these criteria.

The evaluation criteria provide the basis for evaluating alternative solutions. The criteria are ranked so that the highest ranked criteria exert the most influence on the evaluation.

This process area is referenced by many other process areas in the model, and there are many contexts in which a formal evaluation process can be used. Therefore, in some situations you may find that criteria have already been defined as part of another process. This specific practice does not suggest that a second development of criteria be conducted.

Document the evaluation criteria to minimize the possibility that decisions will be second-guessed, or that the reason for making the decision will be forgotten. Decisions based on criteria that are explicitly defined and established remove barriers to stakeholder buy-in.

TIP

In less formal cases, all criteria may be roughly equal and ranking may not be necessary.

TIP

Documentation helps to provide an understanding of which criteria were considered and how they were ranked.

DAR

Typical Work Products

1. Documented evaluation criteria
2. Rankings of criteria importance

Subpractices

1. Define the criteria for evaluating alternative solutions.

   Criteria should be traceable to requirements, scenarios, business case assumptions, business objectives, or other documented sources.
   Types of criteria to consider include the following:
   • Technology limitations
   • Environmental impact
   • Risks
   • Total ownership and lifecycle costs

TIP

An example of a non-numeric scale is one that ranks criteria based on low, medium, or high importance.

2. Define the range and scale for ranking the evaluation criteria.

Scales of relative importance for evaluation criteria can be established with non-numeric values or with formulas that relate the evaluation parameter to a numeric weight.

3. Rank the criteria.

The criteria are ranked according to the defined range and scale to reflect the needs, objectives, and priorities of the relevant stakeholders.

4. Assess the criteria and their relative importance.

5. Evolve the evaluation criteria to improve their validity.

6. Document the rationale for the selection and rejection of evaluation criteria.

Documentation of selection criteria and rationale may be needed to justify solutions or for future reference and use.

SP 1.3 *IDENTIFY ALTERNATIVE SOLUTIONS*

Identify alternative solutions to address issues.

HINT

You can use many brainstorming techniques to identify alternative solutions. However, you should establish a few rules before your brainstorming session to ensure that the widest possible range of alternatives is presented.

A wider range of alternatives can surface by soliciting as many stakeholders as practical for input. Input from stakeholders with diverse skills and backgrounds can help teams identify and address assumptions, constraints, and biases. Brainstorming sessions may stimulate innovative alternatives through rapid interaction and feedback. Sufficient candidate solutions may not be furnished for analysis. As the analysis proceeds, other alternatives should be added to the list of potential candidate solutions. The generation and consideration of multiple alternatives early in a decision analysis and resolution process increases the likelihood that an acceptable decision will be made, and that consequences of the decision will be understood.

Typical Work Products

1. Identified alternatives

Subpractices

1. Perform a literature search.

A literature search can uncover what others have done both inside and outside the organization. It may provide a deeper understanding of the problem, alternatives to consider, barriers to implementation, existing trade studies, and lessons learned from similar decisions.

2. Identify alternatives for consideration in addition to those that may be provided with the issue.

Evaluation criteria are an effective starting point for identifying alternatives. The evaluation criteria identify the priorities of the relevant stakeholders and the importance of technical, logistical, or other challenges.

Combining key attributes of existing alternatives can generate additional and sometimes stronger alternatives.

Solicit alternatives from relevant stakeholders. Brainstorming sessions, interviews, and working groups can be used effectively to uncover alternatives.

3. Document the proposed alternatives.

SP 1.4 SELECT EVALUATION METHODS

Select the evaluation methods.

Methods for evaluating alternative solutions against established criteria can range from simulations to the use of probabilistic models and decision theory. These methods need to be carefully selected. The level of detail of a method should be commensurate with cost, schedule, performance, and risk impacts.

> **TIP**
>
> Different evaluation methods require different investments of resources and training.

While many problems may need only one evaluation method, some problems may require multiple methods. For instance, simulations may augment a trade study to determine which design alternative best meets a given criterion.

Typical Work Products

1. Selected evaluation methods

Subpractices

1. Select the methods based on the purpose for analyzing a decision and on the availability of the information used to support the method.

> For example, the methods used for evaluating a solution when requirements are weakly defined may be different from the methods used when the requirements are well defined.

Typical evaluation methods include the following:
- Modeling and simulation
- Engineering studies
- Manufacturing studies
- Cost studies
- Business opportunity studies
- Surveys
- Extrapolations based on field experience and prototypes

DAR

- User review and comment
- Testing
- Judgment provided by an expert or group of experts (e.g., Delphi Method)

2. Select evaluation methods based on their ability to focus on the issues at hand without being overly influenced by side issues.

   Results of simulations can be skewed by random activities in the solution that are not directly related to the issues at hand.

3. Determine the measures needed to support the evaluation method.

   Consider the impact on cost, schedule, performance, and risks.

SP 1.5 EVALUATE ALTERNATIVES

Evaluate alternative solutions using the established criteria and methods.

Evaluating alternative solutions involves analysis, discussion, and review. Iterative cycles of analysis are sometimes necessary. Supporting analyses, experimentation, prototyping, piloting, or simulations may be needed to substantiate scoring and conclusions.

Often, the relative importance of criteria is imprecise and the total effect on a solution is not apparent until after the analysis is performed. In cases where the resulting scores differ by relatively small amounts, the best selection among alternative solutions may not be clear cut. Challenges to criteria and assumptions should be encouraged.

Typical Work Products

1. Evaluation results

Subpractices

1. Evaluate the proposed alternative solutions using the established evaluation criteria and selected methods.
2. Evaluate the assumptions related to the evaluation criteria and the evidence that supports the assumptions.
3. Evaluate whether uncertainty in the values for alternative solutions affects the evaluation and address as appropriate.

   For instance, if the score can vary between two values, is the difference significant enough to make a difference in the final solution set? Does the variation in score represent a high risk? To address these concerns, simulations may be run, further studies may be performed, or evaluation criteria may be modified, among other things.

4. Perform simulations, modeling, prototypes, and pilots as necessary to exercise the evaluation criteria, methods, and alternative solutions.

Untested criteria, their relative importance, and supporting data or functions may cause the validity of solutions to be questioned. Criteria and their relative priorities and scales can be tested with trial runs against a set of alternatives. These trial runs of a select set of criteria allow for the evaluation of the cumulative impact of the criteria on a solution. If the trials reveal problems, different criteria or alternatives might be considered to avoid biases.

5. Consider new alternative solutions, criteria, or methods if the proposed alternatives do not test well; repeat the evaluations until alternatives do test well.

6. Document the results of the evaluation.

    Document the rationale for the addition of new alternatives or methods and changes to criteria, as well as the results of interim evaluations.

SP 1.6 SELECT SOLUTIONS

Select solutions from the alternatives based on the evaluation criteria.

Selecting solutions involves weighing the results from the evaluation of alternatives. Risks associated with implementation of the solutions must be assessed.

> **TIP**
>
> Selecting solutions also involves risk assessment.

Typical Work Products

1. Recommended solutions to address significant issues

Subpractices

1. Assess the risks associated with implementing the recommended solution.

    Refer to the Risk Management process area for more information about identifying and managing risks.

    Decisions must often be made with incomplete information. There can be substantial risk associated with the decision because of having incomplete information.

    When decisions must be made according to a specific schedule, time and resources may not be available for gathering complete information. Consequently, risky decisions made with incomplete information may require re-analysis later. Identified risks should be monitored.

2. Document the results and rationale for the recommended solution.

    It is important to record both why a solution is selected and why another solution was rejected.

DAR

Generic Practices by Goal

GG 1 ACHIEVE SPECIFIC GOALS

The process supports and enables achievement of the specific goals of the process area by transforming identifiable input work products to produce identifiable output work products.

GP 1.1 PERFORM SPECIFIC PRACTICES

Perform the specific practices of the decision analysis and resolution process to develop work products and provide services to achieve the specific goals of the process area.

GG 2 INSTITUTIONALIZE A MANAGED PROCESS

The process is institutionalized as a managed process.

CONTINUOUS ONLY

GG 3 INSTITUTIONALIZE A DEFINED PROCESS

The process is institutionalized as a defined process.

> This generic goal's appearance here reflects its location in the staged representation.

STAGED ONLY

GP 2.1 ESTABLISH AN ORGANIZATIONAL POLICY

Establish and maintain an organizational policy for planning and performing the decision analysis and resolution process.

Elaboration:

This policy establishes organizational expectations for selectively analyzing possible decisions using a formal evaluation process that evaluates identified alternatives against established criteria. The policy should also provide guidance on which decisions require a formal evaluation process.

GP 2.2 PLAN THE PROCESS

Establish and maintain the plan for performing the decision analysis and resolution process.

Elaboration:

This plan for performing the decision analysis and resolution process can be included in (or referenced by) the project plan, which is described in the Project Planning process area.

GP 2.3 PROVIDE RESOURCES

Provide adequate resources for performing the decision analysis and resolution process, developing the work products, and providing the services of the process.

Elaboration:

> Examples of resources provided include the following tools:
> • Simulators and modeling tools
> • Prototyping tools
> • Tools for conducting surveys

GP 2.4 ASSIGN RESPONSIBILITY

Assign responsibility and authority for performing the process, developing the work products, and providing the services of the decision analysis and resolution process.

GP 2.5 TRAIN PEOPLE

Train the people performing or supporting the decision analysis and resolution process as needed.

Elaboration:

> Examples of training topics include the following:
> • Formal decision analysis
> • Methods for evaluating alternative solutions against criteria

GP 2.6 MANAGE CONFIGURATIONS

Place designated work products of the decision analysis and resolution process under appropriate levels of control.

Elaboration:

> Examples of work products placed under control include the following:
> • Guidelines for when to apply a formal evaluation process
> • Evaluation reports containing recommended solutions

GP 2.7 IDENTIFY AND INVOLVE RELEVANT STAKEHOLDERS

Identify and involve the relevant stakeholders of the decision analysis and resolution process as planned.

DAR

Elaboration:

> Examples of activities for stakeholder involvement include the following:
> • Establishing guidelines for which issues are subject to a formal evaluation process
> • Establishing evaluation criteria
> • Identifying and evaluating alternatives
> • Selecting evaluation methods
> • Selecting solutions

GP 2.8 *MONITOR AND CONTROL THE PROCESS*

Monitor and control the decision analysis and resolution process against the plan for performing the process and take appropriate corrective action.

Elaboration:

> Examples of measures and work products used in monitoring and controlling include the following:
> • Cost-to-benefit ratio of using formal evaluation processes
> • Schedule for the execution of a trade study

GP 2.9 *OBJECTIVELY EVALUATE ADHERENCE*

Objectively evaluate adherence of the decision analysis and resolution process against its process description, standards, and procedures, and address noncompliance.

Elaboration:

> Examples of activities reviewed include the following:
> • Evaluating alternatives using established criteria and methods

> Examples of work products reviewed include the following:
> • Guidelines for when to apply a formal evaluation process
> • Evaluation reports containing recommended solutions

GP 2.10 *REVIEW STATUS WITH HIGHER LEVEL MANAGEMENT*

Review the activities, status, and results of the decision analysis and resolution process with higher level management and resolve issues.

GG 3   INSTITUTIONALIZE A DEFINED PROCESS

The process is institutionalized as a defined process.

This generic goal's appearance here reflects its location in the continuous representation.

C ONLY

GP 3.1   ESTABLISH A DEFINED PROCESS

Establish and maintain the description of a defined decision analysis and resolution process.

GP 3.2   COLLECT IMPROVEMENT INFORMATION

Collect work products, measures, measurement results, and improvement information derived from planning and performing the decision analysis and resolution process to support the future use and improvement of the organization's processes and process assets.

Elaboration:

> Examples of work products, measures, measurement results, and improvement information include the following:
> • Number of alternatives considered
> • Evaluation results
> • Recommended solutions to address significant issues

GG 4   INSTITUTIONALIZE A QUANTITATIVELY MANAGED PROCESS

The process is institutionalized as a quantitatively managed process.

GP 4.1   ESTABLISH QUANTITATIVE OBJECTIVES FOR THE PROCESS

Establish and maintain quantitative objectives for the decision analysis and resolution process, which address quality and process performance, based on customer needs and business objectives.

GP 4.2   STABILIZE SUBPROCESS PERFORMANCE

Stabilize the performance of one or more subprocesses to determine the ability of the decision analysis and resolution process to achieve the established quantitative quality and process-performance objectives.

CONTINUOUS ONLY

DAR

GG 5 *Institutionalize an Optimizing Process*

The process is institutionalized as an optimizing process.

GP 5.1 *Ensure Continuous Process Improvement*

Ensure continuous improvement of the decision analysis and resolution process in fulfilling the relevant business objectives of the organization.

GP 5.2 *Correct Root Causes of Problems*

Identify and correct the root causes of defects and other problems in the decision analysis and resolution process.

INTEGRATED PROJECT MANAGEMENT +IPPD
A Project Management Process Area at Maturity Level 3

Purpose

The purpose of Integrated Project Management (IPM) is to establish and manage the project and the involvement of the relevant stakeholders according to an integrated and defined process that is tailored from the organization's set of standard processes.

TIP

IPM matures the project management activities described in PP and PMC so that they address the organizational requirements for projects described in OPF and OPD.

> For IPPD, Integrated Project Management +IPPD also covers the establishment of a shared vision for the project and the establishment of integrated teams that will carry out objectives of the project.

IPPD ADD

Introductory Notes

Integrated Project Management involves the following:

- Establishing the project's defined process at project startup by tailoring the organization's set of standard processes
- Managing the project using the project's defined process
- Establishing the work environment for the project based on the organization's work environment standards
- Using and contributing to the organizational process assets
- Enabling relevant stakeholders' concerns to be identified, considered, and, when appropriate, addressed during the development of the product
- Ensuring that the relevant stakeholders perform their tasks in a coordinated and timely manner (1) to address product and product component requirements, plans, objectives, problems, and risks; (2) to fulfill their commitments; and (3) to identify, track, and resolve coordination issues

IPM +IPPD

Integrated Project Management +IPPD also involves the following:

• Establishing a shared vision for the project

• Establishing integrated teams that are tasked to accomplish project objectives

IPPD ADD

The integrated and defined process that is tailored from the organization's set of standard processes is called the project's defined process.

TIP

Using IPM to guide project management activities enables project plans to be consistent with project activities because they are both derived from standard processes created by the organization. Further, plans tend to be more reliable and are developed more quickly, and new projects learn more quickly.

Managing the project's effort, cost, schedule, staffing, risks, and other factors is tied to the tasks of the project's defined process. The implementation and management of the project's defined process are typically described in the project plan. Certain activities may be covered in other plans that affect the project, such as the quality assurance plan, risk management strategy, and the configuration management plan.

Since the defined process for each project is tailored from the organization's set of standard processes, variability among projects is typically reduced and projects can more easily share process assets, data, and lessons learned.

This process area also addresses the coordination of all activities associated with the project such as the following:

TIP

It is also easier to share resources (e.g., training and software tools) and to "load balance" staff across projects.

- Development activities (e.g., requirements development, design, and verification)
- Service activities (e.g., delivery, help desk, operations, and customer contact)
- Acquisition activities (e.g., solicitation, contract monitoring, and transition to operation)
- Support activities (e.g., configuration management, documentation, marketing, and training)

TIP

A proactive approach to integrating plans and coordinating with relevant stakeholders outside the project is a key activity.

The working interfaces and interactions among relevant stakeholders internal and external to the project are planned and managed to ensure the quality and integrity of the entire product. Relevant stakeholders participate, as appropriate, in defining the project's defined process and the project plan. Reviews and exchanges are regularly conducted with the relevant stakeholders to ensure that coordination issues receive appropriate attention and everyone involved with the project is appropriately aware of the status, plans, and activities. (See the definition of "relevant stakeholder" in the glossary.) In defining the project's defined process, formal interfaces are created as necessary to ensure that appropriate coordination and collaboration occurs.

This process area applies in any organizational structure, including projects that are structured as line organizations, matrix organizations, or integrated teams. The terminology should be appropriately interpreted for the organizational structure in place.

Related Process Areas

Refer to the Project Planning process area for more information about planning the project, which includes identifying relevant stakeholders and their appropriate involvement in the project.

Refer to the Project Monitoring and Control process area for more information about monitoring and controlling the project.

Refer to the Verification process area for more information about peer reviews.

Refer to the Organizational Process Definition process area for more information about organizational process assets and work environment standards.

Refer to the Measurement and Analysis process area for more information about defining a process for measuring and analyzing processes.

> **IPPD ADD**
>
> Refer to the Organizational Process Definition +IPPD process area for more information about creating the organizational rules and guidelines for IPPD.

Specific Goal and Practice Summary

SG 1 Use the Project's Defined Process
- SP 1.1 Establish the Project's Defined Process
- SP 1.2 Use Organizational Process Assets for Planning Project Activities
- SP 1.3 Establish the Project's Work Environment
- SP 1.4 Integrate Plans
- SP 1.5 Manage the Project Using the Integrated Plans
- SP 1.6 Contribute to the Organizational Process Assets

SG 2 Coordinate and Collaborate with Relevant Stakeholders
- SP 2.1 Manage Stakeholder Involvement
- SP 2.2 Manage Dependencies
- SP 2.3 Resolve Coordination Issues

SG 3 Apply IPPD Principles
- SP 3.1 Establish the Project's Shared Vision
- SP 3.2 Establish the Integrated Team Structure
- SP 3.3 Allocate Requirements to Integrated Teams
- SP 3.4 Establish Integrated Teams
- SP 3.5 Ensure Collaboration among Interfacing Teams

IPPD ADDITION

IPM +IPPD

> **TIP**
>
> In going from Version 1.1 to 1.2, IPPD material was consolidated and moved. The IPM addition now has only one IPPD goal. SP 1.3 is derived from OEI SP 1.2, but suitably generalized to apply in all project situations. SP 3.1 is a consolidation of IPM SP 3.1 and 3.2. SP 3.2 is derived from IPM SP 4.1; SP 3.3 is derived from IPM SP 4.2; and SP 3.5 is derived from IT SP 2.5. Finally, SP 3.4 is a consolidation of IPM SP 4.3 and several IT SG 2 SPs. (OEI and IT are abbreviations of V1.1 process areas no longer appearing in V1.2.)

Specific Practices by Goal

SG 1 USE THE PROJECT'S DEFINED PROCESS

The project is conducted using a defined process that is tailored from the organization's set of standard processes.

TIP
All projects that use IPM have the organization's set of standard processes as a basis to begin planning all project activities.

The project's defined process must include those processes from the organization's set of standard processes that address all processes necessary to acquire or develop and maintain the product. The product-related lifecycle processes, such as the manufacturing and support processes, are developed concurrently with the product.

SP 1.1 ESTABLISH THE PROJECT'S DEFINED PROCESS

Establish and maintain the project's defined process from project startup through the life of the project.

Refer to the Organizational Process Definition process area for more information about the organizational process assets.

Refer to the Organizational Process Focus process area for more information about organizational process needs and objectives and deploying the organization's set of standard processes on projects.

The project's defined process consists of defined processes that form an integrated, coherent lifecycle for the project.

> The project's defined process supports IPPD with processes that
> - Make the integrated project management environment more amenable to collocated or distributed teams
> - Select the project's integrated team structure
> - Allocate limited personnel resources
> - Implement cross-integrated team communication
>
> *IPPD ADDITION*

The project's defined process should satisfy the project's contractual and operational needs, opportunities, and constraints. It is designed to provide a best fit for the project's needs. A project's defined process is based on the following factors:

- Customer requirements
- Product and product component requirements
- Commitments

- Organizational process needs and objectives
- Organization's set of standard processes and tailoring guidelines
- Operational environment
- Business environment

Establishing the project's defined process at project startup helps to ensure that project staff and stakeholders implement a set of activities needed to efficiently establish an initial set of requirements and plans for the project. As the project progresses, the description of the project's defined process is elaborated and revised to better meet the project's requirements and the organization's process needs and objectives. Also, as the organization's set of standard processes change, the project's defined process may need to be revised.

> **TIP**
>
> IPM depends strongly on OPD. It is impossible to implement the specific practices in IPM without having in place the organizational infrastructure described in OPD.

Typical Work Products

1. The project's defined process

Subpractices

1. Select a lifecycle model from those available from the organizational process assets.

> Examples of project characteristics that could affect the selection of lifecycle models include the following:
> - Size of the project
> - Experience and familiarity of staff in implementing the process
> - Constraints such as cycle time and acceptable defect levels

2. Select the standard processes from the organization's set of standard processes that best fit the needs of the project.
3. Tailor the organization's set of standard processes and other organizational process assets according to the tailoring guidelines to produce the project's defined process.

    Sometimes the available lifecycle models and standard processes are inadequate to meet a specific project's needs. Sometimes the project will be unable to produce required work products or measures. In such circumstances, the project will need to seek approval to deviate from what is required by the organization. Waivers are provided for this purpose.
4. Use other artifacts from the organization's process asset library as appropriate.

> **TIP**
>
> The organization's set of standard processes are tailored to address the project's specific needs and situation. For example, are stringent quality, safety, or security requirements in place? Is the risk of delivering the wrong product high? Are we working with a new customer, product line, or line of business? Are there stringent schedule constraints?

HINT

Maintain the process asset library to keep it current, or else it could become the dumping ground for all project information and quickly become unusable.

Other artifacts may include the following:
- Lessons-learned documents
- Templates
- Example documents
- Estimating models

5. Document the project's defined process.

   The project's defined process covers all of the activities for the project and its interfaces to relevant stakeholders.

> Examples of project activities include the following:
> - Project planning
> - Project monitoring
> - Requirements development
> - Requirements management
> - Supplier management
> - Configuration management
> - Quality assurance
> - Risk management
> - Decision analysis and resolution
> - Product development and support
> - Solicitation

TIP

Remember the point from the Introductory Notes that states, "Relevant stakeholders participate, as appropriate, in defining the project's defined process and the project plan."

6. Conduct peer reviews of the project's defined process.

   Refer to the Verification process area for more information about conducting peer reviews.

7. Revise the project's defined process as necessary.

SP 1.2 USE ORGANIZATIONAL PROCESS ASSETS FOR PLANNING PROJECT ACTIVITIES

Use the organizational process assets and measurement repository for estimating and planning the project's activities.

Refer to the Organizational Process Definition process area for more information about organizational process assets and the organization's measurement repository.

TIP

These activities may be similar to what you were doing to address PP, but because data and experiences from other projects are now more readily available and applicable, the accuracy of project planning should improve.

Typical Work Products

1. Project estimates
2. Project plans

Subpractices

1. Use the tasks and work products of the project's defined process as a basis for estimating and planning the project's activities.

   An understanding of the relationships among the various tasks and work products of the project's defined process, and of the roles to be performed by the relevant stakeholders, is a basis for developing a realistic plan.

2. Use the organization's measurement repository in estimating the project's planning parameters.

   This estimate typically includes the following:

   - Using appropriate historical data from this project or similar projects
   - Accounting for and recording similarities and differences between the current project and those projects whose historical data will be used
   - Independently validating the historical data
   - Recording the reasoning, assumptions, and rationale used to select the historical data

TIP

Independent validation of data confirms that the historical data used is applicable to the project.

Examples of parameters that are considered for similarities and differences include the following:
- Work product and task attributes
- Application domain
- Design approach
- Operational environment
- Experience of the people

Examples of data contained in the organization's measurement repository include the following:
- Size of work products or other work product attributes
- Effort
- Cost
- Schedule
- Staffing
- Defects
- Response time
- Service capacity
- Supplier performance

IPM +IPPD

SP 1.3 *Establish the Project's Work Environment*

Establish and maintain the project's work environment based on the organization's work environment standards.

TIP

Often the project's work environment contains components that are common to the organization's overall work environment. Many of these components may be provided by IT or the facilities group.

An appropriate work environment for a project comprises an infrastructure of facilities, tools, and equipment that people need to perform their jobs effectively in support of business and project objectives. The work environment and its components are maintained at a level of performance and reliability indicated by the organizational work environment standards. As required, the project's work environment or some of its components can be developed internally or acquired from external sources.

An effective work environment helps projects employing IPPD to conduct work using collocated or distributed integrated teams. Two-way communications media should be readily accessible by all relevant stakeholders in the project.

IPPD ADD

The project's work environment might encompass environments for product integration, verification, and validation or they might be separate environments.

Refer to the Establish Work Environment Standards specific practice in the Organizational Process Definition process area for more information about work environment standards.

Refer to the Establish the Product Integration Environment specific practice of the Product Integration process area for more information about establishing and maintaining the product integration environment for the project.

Refer to the Establish the Verification Environment specific practice of the Verification process area for more information about establishing and maintaining the verification environment for the project.

Refer to the Establish the Validation Environment specific practice of the Validation process area for more information about establishing and maintaining the validation environment for the project.

Typical Work Products

1. Equipment and tools for the project
2. Installation, operation, and maintenance manuals for the project work environment
3. User surveys and results
4. Usage, performance, and maintenance records
5. Support services for the project's work environment

Subpractices

1. Plan, design, and install a work environment for the project.

   The critical aspects of the project work environment are, like any other product, requirements driven. Work environment functionality and operations are explored with the same rigor as is done for any other product development.

TIP

A facilities group can use input from the project to create the work environment.

It may be necessary to make tradeoffs among performance, costs, and risks. The following are examples of each:

• Performance considerations may include timely interoperable communications, safety, security, and maintainability.
• Costs may include capital outlays, training, support structure, disassembly and disposal of existing environments, and operation and maintenance of the environment.
• Risks may include workflow and project disruptions.

Examples of equipment and tools include the following:

• Office software
• Decision support software
• Project management tools
• Requirements management tools, design tools
• Configuration management tools
• Evaluation tools
• Test and/or evaluation equipment

---

2. Provide ongoing maintenance and operational support for the project's work environment.

   Maintenance and support of the work environment can be accomplished either with capabilities found inside the organization or hired from outside the organization.

Examples of maintenance and support approaches include the following:

• Hiring people to perform the maintenance and support
• Training people to perform the maintenance and support
• Contracting the maintenance and support
• Developing expert users for selected tools

---

3. Maintain the qualification of the components of the project's work environment.

   Components include software, databases, hardware, tools, test equipment, and appropriate documentation. Qualification of software includes appropriate certifications. Hardware and test equipment qualification includes calibration and adjustment records and traceability to calibration standards.

4. Periodically review how well the work environment is meeting the project's needs and supporting collaboration, and take action as appropriate.

Examples of actions that might be taken include the following:
• Adding new tools
• Acquiring additional networks, equipment, training, and support

---

SP 1.4 INTEGRATE PLANS

Integrate the project plan and the other plans that affect the project to describe the project's defined process.

Refer to the Project Planning process area for more information about establishing and maintaining a project plan.

Refer to the Organizational Process Definition process area for more information about organizational process assets and, in particular, the organization's measurement repository.

Refer to the Measurement and Analysis process area for more information about defining measures and measurement activities and using analytic techniques.

Refer to the Risk Management process area for more information about identifying and analyzing risks.

Refer to the Organizational Process Focus process area for more information about organizational process needs and objectives.

TIP

One of the main differences between IPM and PP is that IPM is more proactive in coordinating with relevant stakeholders, both internal (different teams) and external (organizational functions and support groups) to the project, and is concerned with the integration of plans.

TIP

To formulate estimates, data should be available from the organization's measurement repository. Additionally, templates, examples, and lessons-learned documents should be available from the organization's process asset library.

This specific practice extends the specific practices for establishing and maintaining a project plan to address additional planning activities such as incorporating the project's defined process, coordinating with relevant stakeholders, using organizational process assets, incorporating plans for peer reviews, and establishing objective entry and exit criteria for tasks.

The development of the project plan should account for current and projected needs, objectives, and requirements of the organization, customer, suppliers, and end users, as appropriate.

The plans of the integrated teams are included in this integration. Developing a complete project plan and the project's defined process may require an iterative effort if a complex, multi-layered, integrated team structure is being deployed.

IPPD ADD

Typical Work Products

1. Integrated plans

Subpractices

1. Integrate other plans that affect the project with the project plan.

    Other plans that affect the project may include the following:
    - Quality assurance plans
    - Configuration management plans
    - Risk management strategy
    - Documentation plans

2. Incorporate into the project plan the definitions of measures and measurement activities for managing the project.

Examples of measures that would be incorporated include the following:
- Organization's common set of measures
- Additional project-specific measures

---

3. Identify and analyze product and project interface risks.

Examples of product and project interface risks include the following:
- Incomplete interface descriptions
- Unavailability of tools or test equipment
- Availability of COTS components
- Inadequate or ineffective team interfaces

---

4. Schedule the tasks in a sequence that accounts for critical development factors and project risks.

Examples of factors considered in scheduling include the following:
- Size and complexity of the tasks
- Integration and test issues
- Needs of the customer and end users
- Availability of critical resources
- Availability of key personnel

---

5. Incorporate the plans for performing peer reviews on the work products of the project's defined process.

    Refer to the Verification process area for more information about peer reviews.

6. Incorporate the training needed to perform the project's defined process in the project's training plans.

> This task typically involves negotiating with the organizational training group the support they will provide.

7. Establish objective entry and exit criteria to authorize the initiation and completion of the tasks described in the work breakdown structure (WBS).

> *Refer to the Project Planning process area for more information about the WBS.*

8. Ensure that the project plan is appropriately compatible with the plans of relevant stakeholders.

> Typically the plan and changes to the plan will be reviewed for compatibility.

9. Identify how conflicts will be resolved that arise among relevant stakeholders.

X-REF

Refer to OT for more information about organizational training.

TIP

Because of the organizational inputs from the OSSP, many of the activities in PP are performed in more detail; and because of the historical data and experiences captured in the other organizational process assets, this detail is more reliable.

TIP

Walk your talk. The prior SPs established the plan—this SP implements and manages the project against that plan.

SP 1.5 MANAGE THE PROJECT USING THE INTEGRATED PLANS

Manage the project using the project plan, the other plans that affect the project, and the project's defined process.

Refer to the Organizational Process Definition process area for more information about the organizational process assets.

Refer to the Organizational Process Focus process area for more information about organizational process needs and objectives and coordinating process improvement activities with the rest of the organization.

Refer to the Risk Management process area for more information about managing risks.

Refer to the Project Monitoring and Control process area for more information about monitoring and controlling the project.

Typical Work Products

1. Work products created by performing the project's defined process
2. Collected measures ("actuals") and progress records or reports
3. Revised requirements, plans, and commitments
4. Integrated plans

Subpractices

1. Implement the project's defined process using the organization's process asset library.

This task typically includes the following:

- Incorporating artifacts from the organization's process asset library into the project as appropriate
- Using lessons learned from the organization's process asset library to manage the project

2. Monitor and control the project's activities and work products using the project's defined process, project plan, and other plans that affect the project.

TIP

The organization's process improvement plan is another plan that might affect the project.

This task typically includes the following:

- Using the defined entry and exit criteria to authorize the initiation and determine the completion of the tasks
- Monitoring the activities that could significantly affect the actual values of the project's planning parameters
- Tracking the project's planning parameters using measurable thresholds that will trigger investigation and appropriate actions
- Monitoring product and project interface risks
- Managing external and internal commitments based on the plans for the tasks and work products of the project's defined process

An understanding of the relationships among the various tasks and work products of the project's defined process, and of the roles to be performed by the relevant stakeholders, along with well-defined control mechanisms (e.g., peer reviews) achieves better visibility into the project's performance and better control of the project.

3. Obtain and analyze the selected measures to manage the project and support the organization's needs.

Refer to the Measurement and Analysis process area for more information about defining a process for obtaining and analyzing measures.

4. Periodically review and align the project's performance with the current and anticipated needs, objectives, and requirements of the organization, customer, and end users, as appropriate.

This review includes alignment with the organizational process needs and objectives.

Examples of actions that achieve alignment include the following:

- Accelerating the schedule, with appropriate adjustments to other planning parameters and the project risks
- Changing the requirements in response to a change in market opportunities or customer and end-user needs
- Terminating the project

IPM +IPPD

SP 1.6 CONTRIBUTE TO THE ORGANIZATIONAL PROCESS ASSETS

TIP

This SP provides feedback to the organization so that the organizational assets can be improved, and data and experiences can be shared with other projects.

Contribute work products, measures, and documented experiences to the organizational process assets.

Refer to the Organizational Process Focus process area for more information about process improvement proposals.

Refer to the Organizational Process Definition process area for more information about the organizational process assets, the organization's measurement repository, and the organization's process asset library.

This specific practice addresses collecting information from processes in the project's defined process.

Typical Work Products

1. Proposed improvements to the organizational process assets
2. Actual process and product measures collected from the project
3. Documentation (e.g., exemplary process descriptions, plans, training modules, checklists, and lessons learned)
4. Process artifacts associated with tailoring and implementing the organization's set of standard processes on the project

Subpractices

X-REF

Improvements are proposed using "process improvement proposals." For more information, see OPF SP 2.4.

1. Propose improvements to the organizational process assets.
2. Store process and product measures in the organization's measurement repository.

    Refer to the Project Planning process area for more information about recording planning and replanning data.

    Refer to the Project Monitoring and Control process area for more information about recording measures.

    This typically includes the following:
    • Planning data
    • Replanning data
    • Measures

Examples of data recorded by the project include the following:
- Task descriptions
- Assumptions
- Estimates
- Revised estimates
- Definitions of recorded data and measures
- Measures
- Context information that relates the measures to the activities performed and work products produced
- Associated information needed to reconstruct the estimates, assess their reasonableness, and derive estimates for new work

---

3. Submit documentation for possible inclusion in the organization's process asset library.

Examples of documentation include the following:
- Exemplary process descriptions
- Training modules
- Exemplary plans
- Checklists

---

4. Document lessons learned from the project for inclusion in the organization's process asset library.
5. Provide process artifacts associated with tailoring and implementing the organization's set of standard processes in support of the organization's process monitoring activities.

> *Refer to the Monitor Implementation specific practice of the Organization Process Focus process area for more information about the organization's activities to understand the extent of deployment of standard processes on new and existing projects.*

SG 2 COORDINATE AND COLLABORATE WITH RELEVANT STAKEHOLDERS

Coordination and collaboration of the project with relevant stakeholders is conducted.

X-REF

Relevant stakeholders are identified in GP 2.7 and PP SP 2.6.

SP 2.1 MANAGE STAKEHOLDER INVOLVEMENT

Manage the involvement of the relevant stakeholders in the project.

Stakeholder involvement is managed according to the project's integrated and defined process.

Refer to the Project Planning process area for more information about identifying stakeholders and their appropriate involvement and about establishing and maintaining commitments.

Typical Work Products

1. Agendas and schedules for collaborative activities
2. Documented issues (e.g., issues with customer requirements, product and product component requirements, product architecture, and product design)
3. Recommendations for resolving relevant stakeholder issues

Subpractices

1. Coordinate with the relevant stakeholders who should participate in the project's activities.

   The relevant stakeholders should already be identified in the project plan.

2. Ensure that work products that are produced to satisfy commitments meet the requirements of the recipient projects.

   Refer to the Verification process area for more information about verifying work products against their requirements.

   This task typically includes the following:

   • Reviewing, demonstrating, or testing, as appropriate, each work product produced by relevant stakeholders
   • Reviewing, demonstrating, or testing, as appropriate, each work product produced by the project for other projects with representatives of the projects receiving the work product
   • Resolving issues related to the acceptance of the work products

3. Develop recommendations and coordinate the actions to resolve misunderstandings and problems with the product and product component requirements, product and product component architecture, and product and product component design.

SP 2.2 MANAGE DEPENDENCIES

Participate with relevant stakeholders to identify, negotiate, and track critical dependencies.

Refer to the Project Planning process area for more information about identifying stakeholders and their appropriate involvement and about establishing and maintaining commitments.

Typical Work Products

1. Defects, issues, and action items resulting from reviews with relevant stakeholders

TIP

These commitments may be external commitments that project staff is addressing.

TIP

Too often, individuals assume critical dependencies identified at the beginning of a project don't change and are someone else's job.

2. Critical dependencies

3. Commitments to address critical dependencies

4. Status of critical dependencies

Subpractices

1. Conduct reviews with relevant stakeholders.

2. Identify each critical dependency.

3. Establish need dates and plan dates for each critical dependency based on the project schedule.

4. Review and get agreement on the commitments to address each critical dependency with the people responsible for providing the work product and the people receiving the work product.

5. Document the critical dependencies and commitments.

   Documentation of commitments typically includes the following:

   • Describing the commitment
   • Identifying who made the commitment
   • Identifying who is responsible for satisfying the commitment
   • Specifying when the commitment will be satisfied
   • Specifying the criteria for determining if the commitment has been satisfied

6. Track the critical dependencies and commitments and take corrective action as appropriate.

   Refer to the Project Monitoring and Control process area for more information about tracking commitments.

   Tracking the critical dependencies typically includes the following:

   • Evaluating the effects of late and early completion for impacts on future activities and milestones
   • Resolving actual and potential problems with the responsible people whenever possible
   • Escalating to the appropriate managers the actual and potential problems not resolvable with the responsible people

SP 2.3 RESOLVE COORDINATION ISSUES

Resolve issues with relevant stakeholders.

Examples of coordination issues include the following:
• Late critical dependencies and commitments
• Product and product component requirements and design defects
• Product-level problems
• Unavailability of critical resources or personnel

TIP

Ironically, when time and money are limited, integration, coordination, and collaboration activities become more critical. Coordination helps ensure that all involved parties contribute to the product in a timely way to minimize rework and delays.

HINT

You can facilitate coordination on critical dependencies by determining need and plan dates for each critical dependency and then establishing and managing commitments as described in these subpractices and in PP and PMC.

TIP

These issues are expected to be resolved at the project level. However, since stakeholders may be from outside the project, issues may need to be escalated to the appropriate level of management to be resolved.

IPM +IPPD

TIP

For projects implementing IPPD, this SP is critical if project teams are to perform in a manner that is consistent with the project's shared vision.

Typical Work Products

1. Relevant stakeholder coordination issues
2. Status of relevant stakeholder coordination issues

Subpractices

1. Identify and document issues.
2. Communicate issues to the relevant stakeholders.
3. Resolve issues with the relevant stakeholders.
4. Escalate to the appropriate managers those issues not resolvable with the relevant stakeholders.
5. Track the issues to closure.
6. Communicate with the relevant stakeholders on the status and resolution of the issues.

TIP

The SPs that follow SG 3 should prove useful to any project that needs to bring individuals of differing views, cultures, and expertise together as a team.

SG 3 APPLY IPPD PRINCIPLES

The project is managed using IPPD principles.

The purpose of this specific goal and its practices is to create an IPPD environment that enables integrated teams to efficiently meet the project's requirements and produce a quality product.

TIP

The first four specific practices of SG 3 are performed concurrently with the first four specific practices of SG 1.

SP 3.1 ESTABLISH THE PROJECT'S SHARED VISION

Establish and maintain a shared vision for the project.

A project does not operate in isolation. Understanding organizational mission, goals, expectations and constraints allows the project to align its direction, activities, and shared vision with the organization and helps create a common purpose within which project activities can be coordinated. To enable this, it is critical to understand the interfaces between the project and stakeholders external to the project and the objectives and expectations of all relevant stakeholders (internal and external).

When creating a shared vision, consider:

TIP

Each member of the IPPD project should have dual aspirations and expectations: those specific to the project and those related to their home organization.

- external stakeholder expectations and requirements
- the aspirations and expectations of the project leader, team leaders, and team members
- the project's objectives
- the conditions and outcomes the project will create
- interfaces the project needs to maintain

IPPD ADDITION

- the visions created by interfacing groups
- the constraints imposed by outside authorities (e.g., environmental regulations)
- project operation while working to achieve its objectives (both principles and behaviors)

When creating a shared vision, all people in the project should be invited to participate. Although there may be a draft proposal, the larger population must have an opportunity to speak and be heard about what really matters to them. The shared vision is articulated in terms of both the core ideology (values, principles, and behaviors) and the desired future to which each member of the project can commit.

An effective communications strategy is key to implementing and focusing the shared vision throughout the project. Promulgation of the shared vision is a public declaration of the commitment of the project to their shared vision and provides the opportunity for others to examine, understand, and align their activities in a common direction. The shared vision should be communicated, and agreement and commitment of the relevant stakeholders should be obtained.

Effective communications are also especially important when incorporating new project members. New members of the project often need more or special attention to ensure that they understand the shared vision, have a stake in it, and are prepared to follow it in doing their work.

Typical Work Products

1. Documented shared vision
2. Communications strategy
3. Published principles, shared vision statement, mission statement, and objectives (e.g., posters, wallet cards, and presentations)

Subpractices

1. Articulate the project's shared vision in terms of purpose or mission, vision, values, and objectives.
2. Reach consensus on the project's shared vision.
3. Establish a strategy to communicate the project's shared vision both externally and internally.
4. Create presentations suitable for the various audiences that need to be informed about the project's shared vision.
5. Ensure that project and individual activities and tasks are aligned with the project's shared vision.

IPPD ADDITION

TIP

CMMI development is one example of an IPPD project. The CMMI project communicated its shared vision broadly so that the management team guiding CMMI activities, the home organizations that sponsored project team members, and the community had a clear understanding of the project's objectives, values, and intended outcomes.

TIP

Continuing the story of CMMI, presentations targeting different audiences were created and repeatedly delivered early on, and continue today.

TIP

"Foundational documents" (e.g., requirements, architecture, and change criteria) for CMMI have rarely changed, except to address new opportunities and risks, and they continue to guide the project today.

IPM +IPPD

SP 3.2 *ESTABLISH THE INTEGRATED TEAM STRUCTURE*

Establish and maintain the integrated team structure for the project.

Product requirements, cost, schedule, risk, resource projections, business processes, the project's defined process, and organizational guidelines are evaluated to establish the basis for defining integrated teams and their responsibilities, authorities, and interrelationships.

A typical integrated team structure may be based on the product-oriented hierarchy found in the WBS. More complex structuring occurs when the WBS is not product oriented, product risks are not uniform, and resources are constrained.

The integrated team structure is a dynamic entity that is adjusted to changes in people, requirements, and the nature of tasks, and to tackle many difficulties. For small projects, the integrated team structure can treat the whole project as an integrated team. The integrated team structure should be continuously monitored to detect malfunctions, mismanaged interfaces, and mismatches of the work to the staff. Corrective action should be taken when performance does not meet expectations.

Refer to the Establish Rules and Guidelines for Integrated Teams specific practice in the Organizational Process Definition +IPPD process area for more information about establishing organizational rules and guidelines for structuring and forming integrated teams.

Typical Work Products

1. Assessments of the product and product architectures, including risk and complexity
2. Integrated team structure

Subpractices

1. Establish an integrated team structure.

    An integrated team structure is dependent on:

    - An assessment of product risk and complexity
    - Location and types of risks
    - Integration risks, including product component interfaces and inter-team communication
    - Resources, including availability of appropriately skilled people
    - Limitations on team size for effective collaboration
    - Need for team membership of stakeholders external to the project
    - Business processes
    - Organizational structure

IPPD ADDITION

TIP

Establishing the right team structure aids in planning, coordination, and risk management. Projects sometimes choose something between full IPPD and no IPPD: A single, top-level, integrated team is in place for the duration of the project, but the rest of the project work is performed within traditional organizational boundaries. Such an approach can improve efficiency and be pursued if the product architecture aligns well with existing organizational boundaries.

TIP

Over the life of CMMI development, different integrated team structures have been used.

The integrated team structure should be based on an understanding of the project's defined process and shared vision, the organization's standard processes, and the organizational process assets applicable to teams and team structures.

2. Periodically evaluate and modify the integrated team structure to best meet project needs.

Changes to the product requirements or architecture could affect the team structure.

Continuously monitor the integrated team structure to detect problems such as mismanaged interfaces, and mismatches between the work assigned and the staff performing the work. Take corrective action, including assessing the deployed teams and structures, when performance does not meet expectations.

Changes in team structure can include the following:

- Retiring a team for a period of time (e.g., while long-duration manufacturing or verifications are done)
- Disbanding a team when it is no longer cost effective in serving the project
- Combining teams to achieve operating efficiencies
- Adding teams as new product components are identified for development

SP 3.3 ALLOCATE REQUIREMENTS TO INTEGRATED TEAMS

Allocate requirements, responsibilities, tasks, and interfaces to teams in the integrated team structure.

This allocation of requirements to integrated teams is done before any teams are formed to verify that the integrated team structure is workable and covers all the necessary requirements, responsibilities, authorities, tasks, and interfaces. Once the structure is confirmed, integrated team sponsors are chosen to establish the individual teams in the structure.

Typical Work Products

1. Responsibilities allocated to each integrated team
2. Work product requirements, technical interfaces, and business (e.g., cost accounting and project management) interfaces each integrated team will be responsible for satisfying
3. List of integrated team sponsors

IPPD ADDITION

HINT

Achieve the right allocation before teams are formed, because deciding which requirements to allocate to which team determines how the teams are staffed.

IPM +IPPD

Subpractices

1. Allocate the tasks, responsibilities, work products to be delivered, and the associated requirements and interfaces to the appropriate integrated teams.

    Business, management, and other nontechnical responsibilities and authorities for each integrated team are necessary elements to proper team function. Integrated team responsibilities and authorities are normally developed by the project and are consistent with established organization practices.

    Example responsibilities and authorities, include the following:
    - Authority of teams to pick their own leader
    - Authority of teams to implement subteams (e.g., a product team forming an integration subteam)
    - Reporting chains
    - Reporting requirements (cost, schedule, and performance status)
    - Progress reporting measures and methods

2. Check that the distribution of requirements and interfaces covers all specified product requirements and other requirements.

    In the event that complete coverage of requirements is not achieved, corrective action should be taken to redistribute requirements or to alter the integrated team structure.

3. Designate the sponsor for each integrated team.

    An integrated team sponsor is a manager (individual or team) who is responsible for establishing and providing resources to an integrated team, monitoring its activities and progress, and taking corrective action when needed. A sponsor may manage one or many teams. Team sponsors can be project managers.

SP 3.4 ESTABLISH INTEGRATED TEAMS

Establish and maintain integrated teams in the structure.

TIP
Although the sponsor helps to form the team, he is usually not involved in daily activities. The sponsor may be part of the management team.

The integrated teams within the integrated team structure are established by the team sponsors. This process encompasses choosing team leaders and team members, and establishing the team charter for each integrated team based on the allocation of requirements. It also involves providing the resources required to accomplish the tasks assigned to the team.

Refer to the Establish Rules and Guidelines for Integrated Teams specific practice in the Organizational Process Definition +IPPD process area for more information about establishing organizational rules and guidelines for structuring and forming integrated teams.

IPPD ADDITION

Typical Work Products

1. List of team leaders
2. List of team members assigned to each integrated team
3. Integrated team charters
4. Measures for evaluating the performance of integrated teams
5. Periodic integrated team status reports

Subpractices

1. Choose a leader for each integrated team.

   The extent of organizational and project direction in selecting the leader is often a function of product risk and complexity or an organization's need to "grow" new leaders. Team sponsors may select the team leader, or team members may vote on a leader from within the team, depending on organizational policies.

2. Allocate resources to each integrated team.

   The people and other resources are allocated to each integrated team. These items are discussed with the team to ensure that the resources are adequate and that the people are adequate to carry out the tasks and are compatible with other members of the team.

3. Charter each integrated team.

   The team charter is the contract among the team members and between the team and its sponsor for the expected work and level of performance. Charters establish the rights, guarantees, privileges, and permissions for organizing and performing the team's assigned requirements and interfaces, responsibilities and tasks. The integrated team and its sponsor develop the team charter as a negotiation activity. When both approve it, the team charter constitutes a recognized agreement with management authority.

   Charters can include the following aspects:
   - How assignments are accepted
   - How resources and input are accessed
   - How work gets done
   - Who checks and reviews work
   - How work is approved
   - How work is delivered and communicated

4. Review the composition of an integrated team and its place in the integrated team structure when its team leader changes or another significant change of membership occurs.

   A change of this kind may significantly affect the ability of the team to accomplish its objectives. A review of the match between the new composition and the current responsibilities should be made. If the match is not satisfactory, the team composition should be changed or the team's responsibility should be modified.

IPPD ADDITION

TIP

The leader of an integrated team is often a member of the integrated team one layer up in the product hierarchy.

TIP

The charter is reviewed by all members of the team to ensure buy-in.

TIP

Often each team member represents a specific and essential perspective. When team composition changes, you must review the roles of departing team members to see whether their perspectives are still represented.

IPM +IPPD

5. Review the composition of a team and its tasking when a change in team responsibility occurs.

   Changes in responsibilities often occur as the project moves from one phase to the next. For example, less design expertise on teams may be needed when detailed design is completed and fabrication and integration of product components begins.

6. Manage the overall performance of the teams.

   The charter should specify how both team and individual performance will be measured and should include the critical success factors for the team within the project.

SP 3.5 ENSURE COLLABORATION AMONG INTERFACING TEAMS

Ensure collaboration among interfacing teams.

TIP

This SP addresses the tendency of team members to become insular in outlook and not feel responsible for larger project issues. This SP complements the specific practices of SG 2.

The success of an integrated team-based project is a function of how effectively and successfully the integrated teams collaborate with one another to achieve project objectives. This collaboration may be accomplished using interface control working groups.

See the Coordinate and Collaborate with Relevant Stakeholders specific goal of this process area for more information about managing stakeholder involvement, critical dependencies, and resolving coordination issues.

Refer to the Establish Rules and Guidelines for Integrated Teams specific practice in the Organizational Process Definition +IPPD process area for more information about establishing organizational expectations and rules that will guide how the integrated teams work collectively.

IPPD ADDITION

Typical Work Products

1. Work product ownership agreements
2. Team work plans
3. Commitment lists

Subpractices

1. Establish and maintain the boundaries of work product ownership among interfacing teams within the project or organization.
2. Establish and maintain interfaces and processes among interfacing teams for the exchange of inputs, outputs, or work products.
3. Develop, communicate, and distribute among interfacing teams the commitment lists and work plans that are related to work product or team interfaces.

Generic Practices by Goal

GG 1 ACHIEVE SPECIFIC GOALS

The process supports and enables achievement of the specific goals of the process area by transforming identifiable input work products to produce identifiable output work products.

GP 1.1 PERFORM SPECIFIC PRACTICES

Perform the specific practices of the integrated project management process to develop work products and provide services to achieve the specific goals of the process area.

GG 2 INSTITUTIONALIZE A MANAGED PROCESS

The process is institutionalized as a managed process.

GG 3 INSTITUTIONALIZE A DEFINED PROCESS

The process is institutionalized as a defined process.

This generic goal's appearance here reflects its location in the staged representation.

CONTINUOUS ONLY

STAGED ONLY

GP 2.1 ESTABLISH AN ORGANIZATIONAL POLICY

Establish and maintain an organizational policy for planning and performing the integrated project management process.

Elaboration:

This policy establishes organizational expectations for establishing and maintaining the project's defined process from project startup through the life of the project, using the project's defined process in managing the project, and coordinating and collaborating with relevant stakeholders.

This policy also establishes organizational expectations for applying IPPD principles.

IPPD ADD

GP 2.2 PLAN THE PROCESS

Establish and maintain the plan for performing the integrated project management process.

IPM +IPPD

Elaboration:

This plan for the integrated project management process unites the planning for the project planning and monitor and control processes. The planning for performing the planning-related practices in Integrated Project Management is addressed as part of planning the project planning process. This plan for performing the monitor-and-control-related practices in Integrated Project Management can be included in (or referenced by) the project plan, which is described in the Project Planning process area.

Refer to Table 7.2 on page 172 in Generic Goals and Generic Practices for more information about the relationship between generic practice 2.2 and project planning processes.

GP 2.3 PROVIDE RESOURCES

Provide adequate resources for performing the integrated project management process, developing the work products, and providing the services of the process.

Elaboration:

> Examples of resources provided include the following tools:
> • Problem-tracking and trouble-reporting packages
> • Groupware
> • Video conferencing
> • Integrated decision database
> • Integrated product support environments

GP 2.4 ASSIGN RESPONSIBILITY

Assign responsibility and authority for performing the process, developing the work products, and providing the services of the integrated project management process.

GP 2.5 TRAIN PEOPLE

Train the people performing or supporting the integrated project management process as needed.

Elaboration:

Examples of training topics include the following:
- Tailoring the organization's set of standard processes to meet the needs of the project
- Procedures for managing the project based on the project's defined process
- Using the organization's measurement repository
- Using the organizational process assets
- Integrated management
- Intergroup coordination
- Group problem solving

Examples of training topics also include the following:
- Building the project's shared vision
- Team building

IPPD ADD

GP 2.6 MANAGE CONFIGURATIONS

Place designated work products of the integrated project management process under appropriate levels of control.

Elaboration:

Examples of work products placed under control include the following:
- The project's defined process
- Project plans
- Other plans that affect the project
- Integrated plans
- Actual process and product measures collected from the project

Examples of work products placed under control also include the following:
- Project's shared vision
- Integrated team structure
- Integrated team charters

IPPD ADDITION

IPM +IPPD

GP 2.7 IDENTIFY AND INVOLVE RELEVANT STAKEHOLDERS

Identify and involve the relevant stakeholders of the integrated project management process as planned.

Elaboration:

Refer to Table 7.2 on page 172 in Generic Goals and Generic Practices for more information about the relationship between generic practice 2.7 and the Manage Stakeholder Involvement practice in this process area.

Examples of activities for stakeholder involvement include the following:
- Resolving issues about the tailoring of the organizational process assets
- Resolving issues among the project plan and the other plans that affect the project
- Reviewing project performance to align with current and projected needs, objectives, and requirements

---

Examples of activities for stakeholder involvement also include the following:
- Creating the project's shared vision
- Defining the integrated team structure for the project
- Populating the integrated teams

IPPD Addition

GP 2.8 MONITOR AND CONTROL THE PROCESS

Monitor and control the integrated project management process against the plan for performing the process and take appropriate corrective action.

Elaboration:

Examples of measures and work products used in monitoring and controlling include the following:
- Number of changes to the project's defined process
- Schedule and effort to tailor the organization's set of standard processes
- Interface coordination issue trends (i.e., number identified and number closed)
- Schedule for project tailoring activities

Examples of measures and work products used in monitoring and controlling also include the following:
- Project's shared vision usage and effectiveness
- Integrated team-structure usage and effectiveness
- Integrated team charters usage and effectiveness

IPPD Addition

GP 2.9 OBJECTIVELY EVALUATE ADHERENCE

Objectively evaluate adherence of the integrated project management process against its process description, standards, and procedures, and address non-compliance.

Elaboration:

> Examples of activities reviewed include the following:
> - Establishing, maintaining, and using the project's defined process
> - Coordinating and collaborating with relevant stakeholders

Examples of activities reviewed also include the following:
- Using the project's shared vision
- Organizing integrated teams

IPPD ADD

> Examples of work products reviewed include the following:
> - Project's defined process
> - Project plans
> - Other plans that affect the project

Examples of work products reviewed also include the following:
- Integrated team structure
- Integrated team charters
- Shared vision statements

IPPD ADDITION

GP 2.10 REVIEW STATUS WITH HIGHER LEVEL MANAGEMENT

Review the activities, status, and results of the integrated project management process with higher level management and resolve issues.

GG 3 INSTITUTIONALIZE A DEFINED PROCESS

The process is institutionalized as a defined process.

> *This generic goal's appearance here reflects its location in the continuous representation.*

CONT. ONLY

IPM +IPPD

GP 3.1 *ESTABLISH A DEFINED PROCESS*

Establish and maintain the description of a defined integrated project management process.

Elaboration:

Refer to Table 7.2 on page 172 in Generic Goals and Generic Practices for more information about the relationship between generic practice 3.1 and the Integrated Project Management process area.

GP 3.2 *COLLECT IMPROVEMENT INFORMATION*

Collect work products, measures, measurement results, and improvement information derived from planning and performing the integrated project management process to support the future use and improvement of the organization's processes and process assets.

Elaboration:

Refer to Table 7.2 on page 172 in Generic Goals and Generic Practices for more information about the relationship between generic practice 3.2 and the Integrated Project Management process area.

Examples of work products, measures, measurement results, and improvement information include the following:

- Project's defined process
- Number of tailoring options exercised by the project to create its defined process
- Interface coordination issue trends (i.e., number identified and number closed)
- Number of times the PAL is accessed for assets related to project planning by project personnel
- Records of expenses related to holding face-to-face meetings versus holding meetings using collaborative equipment such as teleconferencing and videoconferencing

---

Examples of work products, measures, measurement results, and improvement information also include the following:

- Integrated team charters
- Project shared vision

IPPD ADDITION

GG 4 *INSTITUTIONALIZE A QUANTITATIVELY MANAGED PROCESS*

The process is institutionalized as a quantitatively managed process.

GP 4.1 *ESTABLISH QUANTITATIVE OBJECTIVES FOR THE PROCESS*

Establish and maintain quantitative objectives for the integrated project management process, which address quality and process performance, based on customer needs and business objectives.

GP 4.2 *STABILIZE SUBPROCESS PERFORMANCE*

Stabilize the performance of one or more subprocesses to determine the ability of the integrated project management process to achieve the established quantitative quality and process-performance objectives.

GG 5 *INSTITUTIONALIZE AN OPTIMIZING PROCESS*

The process is institutionalized as an optimizing process.

GP 5.1 *ENSURE CONTINUOUS PROCESS IMPROVEMENT*

Ensure continuous improvement of the integrated project management process in fulfilling the relevant business objectives of the organization.

GP 5.2 *CORRECT ROOT CAUSES OF PROBLEMS*

Identify and correct the root causes of defects and other problems in the integrated project management process.

CONTINUOUS ONLY

IPM +IPPD

MEASUREMENT AND ANALYSIS
A Support Process Area at Maturity Level 2

Purpose

The purpose of Measurement and Analysis (MA) is to develop and sustain a measurement capability that is used to support management information needs.

HINT

Use this process area whenever you need to measure project progress, product size or quality, or process performance in support of making decisions and taking corrective action.

Introductory Notes

The Measurement and Analysis process area involves the following:

- Specifying the objectives of measurement and analysis such that they are aligned with identified information needs and objectives
- Specifying the measures, analysis techniques, and mechanism for data collection, data storage, reporting, and feedback
- Implementing the collection, storage, analysis, and reporting of the data
- Providing objective results that can be used in making informed decisions, and taking appropriate corrective actions

TIP

This process area uses the term *objective* both as a noun meaning "a goal to be attained" (first bullet) and as an adjective meaning "unbiased" (fourth bullet).

The integration of measurement and analysis activities into the processes of the project supports the following:

- Objective planning and estimating
- Tracking actual performance against established plans and objectives
- Identifying and resolving process-related issues
- Providing a basis for incorporating measurement into additional processes in the future

The staff required to implement a measurement capability may or may not be employed in a separate organization-wide program. Measurement capability may be integrated into individual projects or other organizational functions (e.g., quality assurance).

TIP

Measurement involves everyone. A centralized group, such as a process group or a measurement group, may provide help in defining the measures, the analyses to perform, and the reporting content and charts used.

MA

The initial focus for measurement activities is at the project level. However, a measurement capability may prove useful for addressing organization- and/or enterprise-wide information needs. To support this capability, the measurement activities *should support information needs at multiple levels including the business, organizational unit, and project to minimize re-work as the organization matures.*

Projects may choose to store project-specific data and results in a project-specific repository. When data are shared more widely across projects, the data may reside in the organization's measurement repository.

Measurement and analysis of the product components provided by suppliers is essential for effective management of the quality and costs of the project. It is possible, with careful management of supplier agreements, to provide insight into the data that support supplier-performance analysis.

X-REF

Refer to SP 1.4 in OPD for more information about the organization's measurement repository.

TIP

It is important to include in the supplier agreement any measurement and analysis activities that you want the supplier to perform. Refer to SAM for more information about supplier activities.

Related Process Areas

Refer to the Project Planning process area for more information about estimating project attributes and other planning information needs.

Refer to the Project Monitoring and Control process area for more information about monitoring project performance information needs.

Refer to the Configuration Management process area for more information about managing measurement work products.

Refer to the Requirements Development process area for more information about meeting customer requirements and related information needs.

Refer to the Requirements Management process area for more information about maintaining requirements traceability and related information needs.

Refer to the Organizational Process Definition process area for more information about establishing the organization's measurement repository.

Refer to the Quantitative Project Management process area for more information about understanding variation and the appropriate use of statistical analysis techniques.

Specific Goal and Practice Summary

SG 1 Align Measurement and Analysis Activities
  SP 1.1 Establish Measurement Objectives
  SP 1.2 Specify Measures
  SP 1.3 Specify Data Collection and Storage Procedures
  SP 1.4 Specify Analysis Procedures
SG 2 Provide Measurement Results
  SP 2.1 Collect Measurement Data
  SP 2.2 Analyze Measurement Data
  SP 2.3 Store Data and Results
  SP 2.4 Communicate Results

Specific Practices by Goal

SG 1 *ALIGN MEASUREMENT AND ANALYSIS ACTIVITIES*

Measurement objectives and activities are aligned with identified information needs and objectives.

The specific practices covered under this specific goal may be addressed concurrently or in any order:

- When establishing measurement objectives, experts often think ahead about necessary criteria for specifying measures and analysis procedures. They also think concurrently about the constraints imposed by data collection and storage procedures.
- It often is important to specify the essential analyses that will be conducted before attending to details of measurement specification, data collection, or storage.

TIP

When starting a measurement program, an iterative process is usually helpful since you often do not know all of your objectives initially.

SP 1.1 *ESTABLISH MEASUREMENT OBJECTIVES*

Establish and maintain measurement objectives that are derived from identified information needs and objectives.

Measurement objectives document the purposes for which measurement and analysis are done, and specify the kinds of actions that may be taken based on the results of data analyses.

  The sources for measurement objectives may be management, technical, project, product, or process implementation needs.

  The measurement objectives may be constrained by existing processes, available resources, or other measurement considerations.

HINT

When establishing measurement objectives, ask yourself what question you are answering with the data, why you are measuring something, and how these measurements will affect project behavior.

MA

HINT

Measurement can be an expensive activity. Think about why you are collecting the measures and try to ensure that the measures will be used.

TIP

It is important to consider staff in these interviews. You want everyone to feel ownership of your measurement program.

Judgments may need to be made about whether the value of the results will be commensurate with the resources devoted to doing the work.

Modifications to identified information needs and objectives may, in turn, be indicated as a consequence of the process and results of measurement and analysis.

Sources of information needs and objectives may include the following:

- Project plans
- Monitoring of project performance
- Interviews with managers and others who have information needs
- Established management objectives
- Strategic plans
- Business plans
- Formal requirements or contractual obligations
- Recurring or other troublesome management or technical problems
- Experiences of other projects or organizational entities
- External industry benchmarks
- Process improvement plans

Example measurement objectives include the following:
- Reduce time to delivery
- Reduce total lifecycle cost
- Deliver specified functionality completely
- Improve prior levels of quality
- Improve prior customer satisfaction ratings
- Maintain and improve the acquirer/supplier relationships

Refer to the Project Planning process area for more information about estimating project attributes and other planning information needs.

Refer to the Project Monitoring and Control process area for more information about project performance information needs.

Refer to the Requirements Development process area for more information about meeting customer requirements and related information needs.

Refer to the Requirements Management process area for more information about maintaining requirements traceability and related information needs.

Typical Work Products

1. Measurement objectives

Subpractices

1. Document information needs and objectives.

   Information needs and objectives are documented to allow traceability to subsequent measurement and analysis activities.

2. Prioritize information needs and objectives.

   It may be neither possible nor desirable to subject all initially identified information needs to measurement and analysis. Priorities may also need to be set within the limits of available resources.

3. Document, review, and update measurement objectives.

   It is important to carefully consider the purposes and intended uses of measurement and analysis.

   The measurement objectives are documented, reviewed by management and other relevant stakeholders, and updated as necessary. Doing so enables traceability to subsequent measurement and analysis activities, and helps ensure that the analyses will properly address identified information needs and objectives.

   It is important that users of measurement and analysis results be involved in setting measurement objectives and deciding on plans of action. It may also be appropriate to involve those who provide the measurement data.

> **TIP**
>
> Many times measures are collected and are not used. If you have adequate reviews of the objectives, you will minimize the risk of a measure not being used.

4. Provide feedback for refining and clarifying information needs and objectives as necessary.

   Identified information needs and objectives may need to be refined and clarified as a result of setting measurement objectives. Initial descriptions of information needs may be unclear or ambiguous. Conflicts may arise between existing needs and objectives. Precise targets on an already existing measure may be unrealistic.

5. Maintain traceability of the measurement objectives to the identified information needs and objectives.

   There must always be a good answer to the question, "Why are we measuring this?"

   Of course, the measurement objectives may also change to reflect evolving information needs and objectives.

SP 1.2 SPECIFY MEASURES

Specify measures to address the measurement objectives.

Measurement objectives are refined into precise, quantifiable measures.

   Measures may be either "base" or "derived." Data for base measures are obtained by direct measurement. Data for derived measures come from other data, typically by combining two or more base measures.

> **HINT**
>
> When specifying measures, ask yourself which specific measures you will collect.

MA

> Examples of commonly used base measures include the following:
> • Estimates and actual measures of work product size (e.g., number of pages)
> • Estimates and actual measures of effort and cost (e.g., number of person hours)
> • Quality measures (e.g., number of defects by severity)

> Examples of commonly used derived measures include the following:
> • Earned Value
> • Schedule Performance Index
> • Defect density
> • Peer review coverage
> • Test or verification coverage
> • Reliability measures (e.g., mean time to failure)
> • Quality measures (e.g., number of defects by severity/total number of defects)

TIP

An example of a derived measure that is typically expressed as a ratio is a productivity measure (e.g., lines of code per hour). An example of a derived measure that is typically expressed as a composite index is a process capability index (e.g., Cpk, which indicates how well centered and tightly distributed a stable process is relative to a customer's specification limits).

Derived measures typically are expressed as ratios, composite indices, or other aggregate summary measures. They are often more quantitatively reliable and meaningfully interpretable than the base measures used to generate them.

Typical Work Products

1. Specifications of base and derived measures

Subpractices

1. Identify candidate measures based on documented measurement objectives.

   The measurement objectives are refined into specific measures. The identified candidate measures are categorized and specified by name and unit of measure.

2. Identify existing measures that already address the measurement objectives.

   Specifications for measures may already exist, perhaps established for other purposes earlier or elsewhere in the organization.

3. Specify operational definitions for the measures.

   Operational definitions are stated in precise and unambiguous terms. They address two important criteria as follows:

   • Communication: What has been measured, how was it measured, what are the units of measure, and what has been included or excluded?

TIP

Operational definitions are a key to effective specification of measures.

- Repeatability: Can the measurement be repeated, given the same definition, to get the same results?

4. Prioritize, review, and update measures.

   Proposed specifications of the measures are reviewed for their appropriateness with potential end users and other relevant stakeholders. Priorities are set or changed, and specifications of the measures are updated as necessary.

SP 1.3 SPECIFY DATA COLLECTION AND STORAGE PROCEDURES

Specify how measurement data will be obtained and stored.

Explicit specification of collection methods helps ensure that the right data are collected properly. It may also aid in further clarifying information needs and measurement objectives.

 Proper attention to storage and retrieval procedures helps ensure that data are available and accessible for future use.

Typical Work Products

1. Data collection and storage procedures
2. Data collection tools

Subpractices

1. Identify existing sources of data that are generated from current work products, processes, or transactions.

   Existing sources of data may already have been identified when specifying the measures. Appropriate collection mechanisms may exist whether or not pertinent data have already been collected.

2. Identify measures for which data are needed, but are not currently available.

3. Specify how to collect and store the data for each required measure.

   Explicit specifications are made of how, where, and when the data will be collected. Procedures for collecting valid data are specified. The data are stored in an accessible manner for analysis, and it is determined whether they will be saved for possible reanalysis or documentation purposes.

   Questions to be considered typically include the following:
   - Have the frequency of collection and the points in the process where measurements will be made been determined?
   - Has the timeline that is required to move measurement results from the points of collection to repositories, other databases, or end users been established?
   - Who is responsible for obtaining the data?

X-REF

For additional information on specifying measures, see SEI's Software Engineering Measurement and Analysis Web site (www.sei.cmu.edu/sema), the Practical Software & Systems Measurement Web site (www.psmsc.com), and the iSixSigma Web site (www.isixsigma.com).

TIP

Ensuring appropriate accessibility and maintenance of data integrity are two key concerns related to data storage and retrieval.

MA

- Who is responsible for data storage, retrieval, and security?
- Have necessary supporting tools been developed or acquired?

4. Create data collection mechanisms and process guidance.

Data collection and storage mechanisms are well integrated with other normal work processes. Data collection mechanisms may include manual or automated forms and templates. Clear, concise guidance on correct procedures is available to those responsible for doing the work. Training is provided as necessary to clarify the processes necessary for collection of complete and accurate data and to minimize the burden on those who must provide and record the data.

5. Support automatic collection of the data where appropriate and feasible.

Automated support can aid in collecting more complete and accurate data.

> Examples of such automated support include the following:
> - Time stamped activity logs
> - Static or dynamic analyses of artifacts

However, some data cannot be collected without human intervention (e.g., customer satisfaction or other human judgments), and setting up the necessary infrastructure for other automation may be costly.

6. Prioritize, review, and update data collection and storage procedures.

Proposed procedures are reviewed for their appropriateness and feasibility with those who are responsible for providing, collecting, and storing the data. They also may have useful insights about how to improve existing processes, or be able to suggest other useful measures or analyses.

7. Update measures and measurement objectives as necessary.

Priorities may need to be reset based on the following:

- The importance of the measures
- The amount of effort required to obtain the data

Considerations include whether new forms, tools, or training would be required to obtain the data.

SP 1.4 SPECIFY ANALYSIS PROCEDURES

Specify how measurement data will be analyzed and reported.

Specifying the analysis procedures in advance ensures that appropriate analyses will be conducted and reported to address the documented measurement objectives (and thereby the information needs and objectives on which they are based). This approach also provides a check that the necessary data will in fact be collected.

TIP

In today's environment, automation is often used. However, some organizations use several tools and databases to address their measurement needs. You need to manage the compatibility among the tools and databases carefully.

TIP

Often someone can manipulate data to provide the picture they want to convey. By specifying the analysis procedures in advance, you can minimize this type of abuse.

Typical Work Products

1. Analysis specifications and procedures
2. Data analysis tools

Subpractices

1. Specify and prioritize the analyses that will be conducted and the reports that will be prepared.

    Early attention should be paid to the analyses that will be conducted and to the manner in which the results will be reported. These should meet the following criteria:

    - The analyses explicitly address the documented measurement objectives
    - Presentation of the results is clearly understandable by the audiences to whom the results are addressed

    Priorities may have to be set within available resources.

2. Select appropriate data analysis methods and tools.

    Refer to the Select Measures and Analytic Techniques and Apply Statistical Methods to Understand Variation specific practices of the Quantitative Project Management process area for more information about the appropriate use of statistical analysis techniques and understanding variation, respectively.

    Issues to be considered typically include the following:

    - Choice of visual display and other presentation techniques (e.g., pie charts, bar charts, histograms, radar charts, line graphs, scatter plots, or tables)
    - Choice of appropriate descriptive statistics (e.g., arithmetic mean, median, or mode)
    - Decisions about statistical sampling criteria when it is impossible or unnecessary to examine every data element
    - Decisions about how to handle analysis in the presence of missing data elements
    - Selection of appropriate analysis tools

    Descriptive statistics are typically used in data analysis to do the following:

    - Examine distributions on the specified measures (e.g., central tendency, extent of variation, or data points exhibiting unusual variation)
    - Examine the interrelationships among the specified measures (e.g., comparisons of defects by phase of the product's lifecycle or by product component)
    - Display changes over time

3. Specify administrative procedures for analyzing the data and communicating the results.

MA

Issues to be considered typically include the following:

- Identifying the persons and groups responsible for analyzing the data and presenting the results
- Determining the timeline to analyze the data and present the results
- Determining the venues for communicating the results (e.g., progress reports, transmittal memos, written reports, or staff meetings)

4. Review and update the proposed content and format of the specified analyses and reports.

All of the proposed content and format are subject to review and revision, including analytic methods and tools, administrative procedures, and priorities. The relevant stakeholders consulted should include intended end users, sponsors, data analysts, and data providers.

5. Update measures and measurement objectives as necessary.

Just as measurement needs drive data analysis, clarification of analysis criteria can affect measurement. Specifications for some measures may be refined further based on the specifications established for data analysis procedures. Other measures may prove to be unnecessary, or a need for additional measures may be recognized.

The exercise of specifying how measures will be analyzed and reported may also suggest the need for refining the measurement objectives themselves.

6. Specify criteria for evaluating the utility of the analysis results and for evaluating the conduct of the measurement and analysis activities.

Criteria for evaluating the utility of the analysis might address the extent to which the following apply:

- The results are (1) provided on a timely basis, (2) understandable, and (3) used for decision making.
- The work does not cost more to perform than is justified by the benefits that it provides.

Criteria for evaluating the conduct of the measurement and analysis might include the extent to which the following apply:

- The amount of missing data or the number of flagged inconsistencies is beyond specified thresholds.
- There is selection bias in sampling (e.g., only satisfied end users are surveyed to evaluate end-user satisfaction, or only unsuccessful projects are evaluated to determine overall productivity).
- The measurement data are repeatable (e.g., statistically reliable).
- Statistical assumptions have been satisfied (e.g., about the distribution of data or about appropriate measurement scales).

TIP

Those responsible for analyzing the data and presenting the results should include those whose activities generated the measurement data or their management whenever possible, with support provided by a process group, QA group, or measurement experts.

X-REF

Refer to SP 1.1 when refining your measurement objectives.

TIP

The criteria are divided into two lists. The first comprises criteria that any organization can use. The second is a bit more sophisticated and might be used by organizations once they establish their measurement program.

SG 2 PROVIDE MEASUREMENT RESULTS

Measurement results, which address identified information needs and objectives, are provided.

The primary reason for doing measurement and analysis is to address identified information needs and objectives. Measurement results based on objective evidence can help to monitor performance, fulfill contractual obligations, make informed management and technical decisions, and enable corrective actions to be taken.

TIP

MA provides the foundation for the behavior required in high-maturity organizations. By the time organizations reach maturity level 4, management and staff will use measurement results as part of their daily work.

SP 2.1 COLLECT MEASUREMENT DATA

Obtain specified measurement data.

The data necessary for analysis are obtained and checked for completeness and integrity.

Typical Work Products

1. Base and derived measurement data sets
2. Results of data integrity tests

Subpractices

1. Obtain the data for base measures.

    Data are collected as necessary for previously used as well as for newly specified base measures. Existing data are gathered from project records or from elsewhere in the organization.

    Note that data that were collected earlier may no longer be available for reuse in existing databases, paper records, or formal repositories.

2. Generate the data for derived measures.

    Values are newly calculated for all derived measures.

3. Perform data integrity checks as close to the source of the data as possible.

    All measurements are subject to error in specifying or recording data. It is always better to identify such errors and to identify sources of missing data early in the measurement and analysis cycle.

    Checks can include scans for missing data, out-of-bounds data values, and unusual patterns and correlation across measures. It is particularly important to do the following:

    • Test and correct for inconsistency of classifications made by human judgment (i.e., to determine how frequently people make differing classification decisions based on the same information, otherwise known as "inter-coder reliability").

TIP

If too much time has passed, it may be inefficient or even impossible to verify the integrity of a measure or to identify the source of missing data.

MA

- Empirically examine the relationships among the measures that are used to calculate additional derived measures. Doing so can ensure that important distinctions are not overlooked and that the derived measures convey their intended meanings (otherwise known as "criterion validity").

SP 2.2 ANALYZE MEASUREMENT DATA

Analyze and interpret measurement data.

The measurement data are analyzed as planned, additional analyses are conducted as necessary, results are reviewed with relevant stakeholders, and necessary revisions for future analyses are noted.

Typical Work Products

1. Analysis results and draft reports

Subpractices

1. Conduct initial analyses, interpret the results, and draw preliminary conclusions.

    The results of data analyses are rarely self-evident. Criteria for interpreting the results and drawing conclusions should be stated explicitly.

2. Conduct additional measurement and analysis as necessary, and prepare results for presentation.

    The results of planned analyses may suggest (or require) additional, unanticipated analyses. In addition, they may identify needs to refine existing measures, to calculate additional derived measures, or even to collect data for additional base measures to properly complete the planned analysis. Similarly, preparing the initial results for presentation may identify the need for additional, unanticipated analyses.

3. Review the initial results with relevant stakeholders.

    It may be appropriate to review initial interpretations of the results and the way in which they are presented before disseminating and communicating them more widely.

    Reviewing the initial results before their release may prevent needless misunderstandings and lead to improvements in the data analysis and presentation.

    Relevant stakeholders with whom reviews may be conducted include intended end users and sponsors, as well as data analysts and data providers.

4. Refine criteria for future analyses.

    Valuable lessons that can improve future efforts are often learned from conducting data analyses and preparing results. Similarly, ways

> **TIP**
>
> Often someone can misinterpret analyses and draw incorrect conclusions. By specifying criteria for interpreting results in advance, you can minimize the risk of drawing incorrect conclusions.

> **TIP**
>
> Measurement and analysis is a learning process. You will typically go through many cycles before the measures and analyses are fine-tuned.

to improve measurement specifications and data collection procedures may become apparent, as may ideas for refining identified information needs and objectives.

SP 2.3 STORE DATA AND RESULTS

Manage and store measurement data, measurement specifications, and analysis results.

Storing measurement-related information enables the timely and cost-effective future use of historical data and results. The information also is needed to provide sufficient context for interpretation of the data, measurement criteria, and analysis results.

Information stored typically includes the following:

- Measurement plans
- Specifications of measures
- Sets of data that have been collected
- Analysis reports and presentations

The stored information contains or references the information needed to understand and interpret the measures and to assess them for reasonableness and applicability (e.g., measurement specifications used on different projects when comparing across projects).

Data sets for derived measures typically can be recalculated and need not be stored. However, it may be appropriate to store summaries based on derived measures (e.g., charts, tables of results, or report prose).

Interim analysis results need not be stored separately if they can be efficiently reconstructed.

Projects may choose to store project-specific data and results in a project-specific repository. When data are shared more widely across projects, the data may reside in the organization's measurement repository.

> **HINT**
> Understand what to store, what can be recalculated or reconstructed, and what to discard.

Refer to the Establish the Organization's Measurement Repository specific practice of the Organizational Process Definition process area for more information about establishing the organization's measurement repository.

Refer to the Configuration Management process area for information about managing measurement work products.

Typical Work Products

1. Stored data inventory

MA

Subpractices

1. Review the data to ensure their completeness, integrity, accuracy, and currency.
2. Store the data according to the data storage procedures.
3. Make the stored contents available for use only by appropriate groups and personnel.
4. Prevent the stored information from being used inappropriately.

TIP

Inappropriate use of data will seriously undermine the credibility of your MA implementation.

> Examples of ways to prevent inappropriate use of the data and related information include controlling access to data and educating people on the appropriate use of data.

> Examples of inappropriate use include the following:
> • Disclosure of information that was provided in confidence
> • Faulty interpretations based on incomplete, out-of-context, or otherwise misleading information
> • Measures used to improperly evaluate the performance of people or to rank projects
> • Impugning the integrity of specific individuals

SP 2.4 COMMUNICATE RESULTS

Report results of measurement and analysis activities to all relevant stakeholders.

TIP

An indicator of a mature organization is the daily use of measurement data by both staff and management to guide their activities. This requires effective communication of measurement data and the results of analyses.

The results of the measurement and analysis process are communicated to relevant stakeholders in a timely and usable fashion to support decision making and assist in taking corrective action.

Relevant stakeholders include intended users, sponsors, data analysts, and data providers.

Typical Work Products

1. Delivered reports and related analysis results
2. Contextual information or guidance to aid in the interpretation of analysis results

Subpractices

1. Keep relevant stakeholders apprised of measurement results on a timely basis.

   Measurement results are communicated in time to be used for their intended purposes. Reports are unlikely to be used if they are distributed with little effort to follow up with those who need to know the results.

To the extent possible and as part of the normal way they do business, users of measurement results are kept personally involved in setting objectives and deciding on plans of action for measurement and analysis. The users are regularly kept apprised of progress and interim results.

Refer to the Project Monitoring and Control process area for more information about the use of measurement results.

2. Assist relevant stakeholders in understanding the results.

   Results are reported in a clear and concise manner appropriate to the methodological sophistication of the relevant stakeholders. They are understandable, easily interpretable, and clearly tied to identified information needs and objectives.

   The data are often not self-evident to practitioners who are not measurement experts. Measurement choices should be explicitly clear about the following:

   - How and why the base and derived measures were specified
   - How the data were obtained
   - How to interpret the results based on the data analysis methods that were used
   - How the results address information needs

TIP

As organizations mature, management and staff should become more comfortable with measurement, be more likely to interpret the analyses correctly, and be able to ask the right questions to help them draw the right conclusions.

Examples of actions to assist in understanding of results include the following:
- Discussing the results with the relevant stakeholders
- Providing a transmittal memo that provides background and explanation
- Briefing users on the results
- Providing training on the appropriate use and understanding of measurement results

---

Generic Practices by Goal

GG 1 ACHIEVE SPECIFIC GOALS

The process supports and enables achievement of the specific goals of the process area by transforming identifiable input work products to produce identifiable output work products.

GP 1.1 PERFORM SPECIFIC PRACTICES

Perform the specific practices of the measurement and analysis process to develop work products and provide services to achieve the specific goals of the process area.

CONTINUOUS ONLY

MA

GG 2 INSTITUTIONALIZE A MANAGED PROCESS

The process is institutionalized as a managed process.

GP 2.1 ESTABLISH AN ORGANIZATIONAL POLICY

Establish and maintain an organizational policy for planning and performing the measurement and analysis process.

Elaboration:

This policy establishes organizational expectations for aligning measurement objectives and activities with identified information needs and objectives and for providing measurement results.

GP 2.2 PLAN THE PROCESS

Establish and maintain the plan for performing the measurement and analysis process.

Elaboration:

This plan for performing the measurement and analysis process can be included in (or referenced by) the project plan, which is described in the Project Planning process area.

GP 2.3 PROVIDE RESOURCES

Provide adequate resources for performing the measurement and analysis process, developing the work products, and providing the services of the process.

Elaboration:

Measurement personnel may be employed full time or part time. A measurement group may or may not exist to support measurement activities across multiple projects.

> Examples of other resources provided include the following tools:
> - Statistical packages
> - Packages that support data collection over networks

GP 2.4 ASSIGN RESPONSIBILITY

Assign responsibility and authority for performing the process, developing the work products, and providing the services of the measurement and analysis process.

GP 2.5 TRAIN PEOPLE

Train the people performing or supporting the measurement and analysis process as needed.

Elaboration:

Examples of training topics include the following:
- Statistical techniques
- Data collection, analysis, and reporting processes
- Development of goal-related measurements (e.g., Goal Question Metric)

GP 2.6 MANAGE CONFIGURATIONS

Place designated work products of the measurement and analysis process under appropriate levels of control.

Elaboration:

Examples of work products placed under control include the following:
- Specifications of base and derived measures
- Data collection and storage procedures
- Base and derived measurement data sets
- Analysis results and draft reports
- Data analysis tools

GP 2.7 IDENTIFY AND INVOLVE RELEVANT STAKEHOLDERS

Identify and involve the relevant stakeholders of the measurement and analysis process as planned.

Elaboration:

Examples of activities for stakeholder involvement include the following:
- Establishing measurement objectives and procedures
- Assessing measurement data
- Providing meaningful feedback to those responsible for providing the raw data on which the analysis and results depend

GP 2.8 MONITOR AND CONTROL THE PROCESS

Monitor and control the measurement and analysis process against the plan for performing the process and take appropriate corrective action.

MA

Elaboration:

> Examples of measures and work products used in monitoring and controlling include the following:
> • Percentage of projects using progress and performance measures
> • Percentage of measurement objectives addressed
> • Schedule for collection and review of measurement data

GP 2.9 OBJECTIVELY EVALUATE ADHERENCE

Objectively evaluate adherence of the measurement and analysis process against its process description, standards, and procedures, and address noncompliance.

Elaboration:

> Examples of activities reviewed include the following:
> • Aligning measurement and analysis activities
> • Providing measurement results

> Examples of work products reviewed include the following:
> • Specifications of base and derived measures
> • Data collection and storage procedures
> • Analysis results and draft reports

GP 2.10 REVIEW STATUS WITH HIGHER LEVEL MANAGEMENT

Review the activities, status, and results of the measurement and analysis process with higher level management and resolve issues.

> GG3 and its practices do not apply for a maturity level 2 rating, but do apply for a maturity level 3 rating and above.

S ONLY

GG 3 INSTITUTIONALIZE A DEFINED PROCESS

The process is institutionalized as a defined process.

GP 3.1 ESTABLISH A DEFINED PROCESS

Establish and maintain the description of a defined measurement and analysis process.

C/M LEVELS 3 – 5 ONLY

GP 3.2 *COLLECT IMPROVEMENT INFORMATION*

Collect work products, measures, measurement results, and improvement information derived from planning and performing the measurement and analysis process to support the future use and improvement of the organization's processes and process assets.

Elaboration:

Examples of work products, measures, measurement results, and improvement information include the following:
- Data currency status
- Results of data integrity tests
- Data analysis reports

GG 4 *INSTITUTIONALIZE A QUANTITATIVELY MANAGED PROCESS*

The process is institutionalized as a quantitatively managed process.

GP 4.1 *ESTABLISH QUANTITATIVE OBJECTIVES FOR THE PROCESS*

Establish and maintain quantitative objectives for the measurement and analysis process, which address quality and process performance, based on customer needs and business objectives.

GP 4.2 *STABILIZE SUBPROCESS PERFORMANCE*

Stabilize the performance of one or more subprocesses to determine the ability of the measurement and analysis process to achieve the established quantitative quality and process-performance objectives.

GG 5 *INSTITUTIONALIZE AN OPTIMIZING PROCESS*

The process is institutionalized as an optimizing process.

GP 5.1 *ENSURE CONTINUOUS PROCESS IMPROVEMENT*

Ensure continuous improvement of the measurement and analysis process in fulfilling the relevant business objectives of the organization.

GP 5.2 *CORRECT ROOT CAUSES OF PROBLEMS*

Identify and correct the root causes of defects and other problems in the measurement and analysis process.

ORGANIZATIONAL INNOVATION AND DEPLOYMENT
A Process Management Process Area at Maturity Level 5

Purpose

The purpose of Organizational Innovation and Deployment (OID) is to select and deploy incremental and innovative improvements that measurably improve the organization's processes and technologies. The improvements support the organization's quality and process-performance objectives as derived from the organization's business objectives.

TIP

OID potentially improves the value of *all* processes and technology, through both innovative as well as incremental improvements.

Introductory Notes

The Organizational Innovation and Deployment process area enables the selection and deployment of improvements that can enhance the organization's ability to meet its quality and process-performance objectives. (See the definition of "quality and process-performance objectives" in the glossary.) The term "improvement," as used in this process area, refers to all of the ideas (proven and unproven) that would change the organization's processes and technologies to better meet the organization's quality and process-performance objectives.

TIP

Changes must be measurably better, not just different. In early improvement efforts, it is often difficult to measure the effects of changes, so sometimes things are just different not better. This is one of the main reasons this process area is staged at the highest maturity level.

Quality and process-performance objectives that this process area might address include the following:

- Improved product quality (e.g., functionality, performance)
- Increased productivity
- Decreased cycle time
- Greater customer and end-user satisfaction
- Shorter development or production time to change functionality or add new features, or adapt to new technologies
- Reduce delivery time
- Reduce time to adapt to new technologies and business needs

Achievement of these objectives depends on the successful establishment of an infrastructure that enables and encourages all people

TIP

Those closest to a process are most familiar with its details and can identify incremental improvement opportunities. That is why everyone in the organization should be empowered and encouraged to suggest potential improvements.

TIP

Change and the ability to manage change is one of the key characteristics of a mature organization; another is when the majority (70% to 90%) of the workforce is involved in proposing and evaluating changes.

HINT

If a proposed improvement is unrelated to the organization's objectives, it probably is not worth pursuing. However, occasionally it may indicate an opportunity missed by those who created the objectives, so if appropriate, revisit the objectives to see if they should be updated.

HINT

Although many changes may individually have merit, consider their cumulative impact on the organization.

in the organization to propose potential improvements to the organization's processes and technologies. Achievement of these objectives also depends on being able to effectively evaluate and deploy proposed improvements to the organization's processes and technologies. All members of the organization can participate in the organization's process- and technology-improvement activities. Their proposals are systematically gathered and addressed.

Pilots are conducted to evaluate significant changes involving untried, high-risk, or innovative improvements before they are broadly deployed.

Process and technology improvements that will be deployed across the organization are selected from process- and technology-improvement proposals based on the following criteria:

- A quantitative understanding of the organization's current quality and process performance
- The organization's quality and process-performance objectives
- Estimates of the improvement in quality and process performance resulting from deploying the process and technology improvements
- Estimated costs of deploying process and technology improvements, and the resources and funding available for such deployment

The expected benefits added by the process and technology improvements are weighed against the cost and impact to the organization. Change and stability must be balanced carefully. Change that is too great or too rapid can overwhelm the organization, destroying its investment in organizational learning represented by organizational process assets. Rigid stability can result in stagnation, allowing the changing business environment to erode the organization's business position.

Improvements are deployed, as appropriate, to new and ongoing projects.

In this process area, the term "process and technology improvements" refers to incremental and innovative improvements to processes and also to process or product technologies (including project work environments).

The informative material in this process area is written with the assumption that the specific practices are applied to a quantitatively managed process. The specific practices of this process area may be applicable, but with reduced value, if the assumption is not met.

The specific practices in this process area complement and extend those found in the Organizational Process Focus process area. The focus of this process area is process improvement that is based on a quantitative knowledge of the organization's set of standard processes and technologies and their expected quality and performance in predictable situations. In the Organizational Process Focus process area, no assumptions are made about the quantitative basis of improvement.

HINT

Select OID for use in your improvement program after most of the other process areas, because it relies on the organization's ability to statistically manage its critical subprocesses as a basis for estimating and determining the impact of a change.

OID

Related Process Areas

Refer to the Organizational Process Definition process area for more information about incorporating the deployed process improvements into organizational process assets.

Refer to the Organizational Process Focus process area for more information about soliciting, collecting, and handling process improvement proposals and coordinating the deployment of process improvement into the project's defined processes.

Refer to the Organizational Training process area for more information about providing updated training to support deployment of process and technology improvements.

Refer to the Organizational Process Performance process area for more information about quality and process-performance objectives and process-performance models. Quality and process-performance objectives are used to analyze and select process- and technology-improvement proposals for deployment. Process-performance models are used to quantify the impact and benefits of innovations.

Refer to the Measurement and Analysis process area for more information about establishing objectives for measurement and analysis, specifying the measures and analyses to be performed, obtaining and analyzing measures, and reporting results.

Refer to the Integrated Project Management process area for more information about coordinating the deployment of process and technology improvements into the project's defined process and project work environment.

Refer to the Decision Analysis and Resolution process area for more information about formal evaluations related to improvement proposals and innovations.

Specific Goal and Practice Summary

SG 1 Select Improvements
    SP 1.1   Collect and Analyze Improvement Proposals
    SP 1.2   Identify and Analyze Innovations
    SP 1.3   Pilot Improvements
    SP 1.4   Select Improvements for Deployment
SG 2 Deploy Improvements
    SP 2.1   Plan the Deployment
    SP 2.2   Manage the Deployment
    SP 2.3   Measure Improvement Effects

Specific Practices by Goal

SG 1 SELECT IMPROVEMENTS

Process and technology improvements, which contribute to meeting quality and process-performance objectives, are selected.

SP 1.1 COLLECT AND ANALYZE IMPROVEMENT PROPOSALS

Collect and analyze process- and technology-improvement proposals.

Each process- and technology-improvement proposal must be analyzed.
    Simple process and technology improvements, with well-understood benefits and effects, will not usually undergo detailed evaluations.

> Examples of simple process and technology improvements include the following:
> - Add an item to a peer review checklist.
> - Combine the technical review and management review for suppliers into a single technical/management review.

Typical Work Products

1. Analyzed process- and technology-improvement proposals

Subpractices

1. Collect process- and technology-improvement proposals.

    A process- and technology-improvement proposal documents proposed incremental and innovative improvements to specific processes and technologies. Managers and staff in the organization, as well as customers, end users, and suppliers can submit process- and technology-improvement proposals. Process and technology

---

HINT

Everyone in the organization must be aware that they can submit an improvement proposal, and know how to submit one.

TIP

Ideas for incremental improvements often originate from within the organization; ideas for innovative improvements often originate from outside the organization.

HINT

You can collect proposals using open-ended mechanisms, surveys, or focus groups.

improvements may be implemented at the local level before being proposed for the organization.

TIP

"Local level" refers to an individual project.

OID

Examples of sources for process- and technology-improvement proposals include the following:

- Findings and recommendations from process appraisals
- The organization's quality and process-performance objectives
- Analysis of data about customer and end-user problems as well as customer and end-user satisfaction
- Analysis of data about project performance compared to quality and productivity objectives
- Analysis of technical performance measures
- Results of process and product benchmarking efforts
- Analysis of data on defect causes
- Measured effectiveness of process activities
- Measured effectiveness of project work environments
- Examples of process- and technology-improvement proposals that were successfully adopted elsewhere
- Feedback on previously submitted process- and technology-improvement proposals
- Spontaneous ideas from managers and staff

Refer to the Organizational Process Focus process area for more information about process- and technology-improvement proposals.

2. Analyze the costs and benefits of process- and technology-improvement proposals as appropriate.

TIP

Without a quantitative understanding of current performance, it is difficult to evaluate the effect of an improvement.

   Process- and technology-improvement proposals that have a large cost-to-benefit ratio are rejected.

   Criteria for evaluating costs and benefits include the following:
   - Contribution toward meeting the organization's quality and process-performance objectives
   - Effect on mitigating identified project and organizational risks
   - Ability to respond quickly to changes in project requirements, market situations, and the business environment
   - Effect on related processes and associated assets
   - Cost of defining and collecting data that supports the measurement and analysis of the process- and technology-improvement proposal
   - Expected life span of the proposal

   Process- and technology-improvement proposals that would not improve the organization's processes are rejected.

   Process-performance models provide insight into the effect of process changes on process capability and performance.

Refer to the Organizational Process Performance process area for more information about process-performance models.

3. Identify the process- and technology-improvement proposals that are innovative.

Innovative improvements are also identified and analyzed in the Identify and Analyze Innovations specific practice.

Whereas this specific practice analyzes proposals that have been passively collected, the purpose of the Identify and Analyze Innovations specific practice is to actively search for and locate innovative improvements. The search primarily involves looking outside the organization.

Innovative improvements are typically identified by reviewing process- and technology-improvement proposals or by actively investigating and monitoring innovations that are in use in other organizations or are documented in research literature. Innovation may be inspired by internal improvement objectives or by the external business environment.

Innovative improvements are typically major changes to the process that represent a break from the old way of doing things (e.g., changing the lifecycle model). Innovative improvements may also include changes in the products that support, enhance, or automate the process (e.g., using off-the-shelf products to support the process).

Examples of innovative improvements include the following:
- Advances in computer and related hardware products
- New support tools
- New techniques, methodologies, processes, or lifecycle models
- New interface standards
- New reusable components
- New management techniques
- New quality-improvement techniques
- New process development and deployment support tools

TIP

To identify barriers to deployment, it is helpful to understand the organization's attitude toward change and its ability to change. Such knowledge influences whether and how changes, especially large ones, are implemented.

4. Identify potential barriers and risks to deploying each process- and technology-improvement proposal.

Examples of barriers to deploying process and technology improvements include the following:
- Turf guarding and parochial perspectives
- Unclear or weak business rationale
- Lack of short-term benefits and visible successes
- Unclear picture of what is expected from everyone
- Too many changes at the same time
- Lack of involvement and support of relevant stakeholders

Examples of risk factors that affect the deployment of process and technology improvements include the following:
- Compatibility of the improvement with existing processes, values, and skills of potential end users
- Complexity of the improvement
- Difficulty implementing the improvement
- Ability to demonstrate the value of the improvement before widespread deployment
- Justification for large, up-front investments in areas such as tools and training
- Inability to overcome "technology drag" where the current implementation is used successfully by a large and mature installed base of end users

5. Estimate the cost, effort, and schedule required for deploying each process- and technology-improvement proposal.

6. Select the process- and technology-improvement proposals to be piloted before broadscale deployment.

    Since innovations, by definition, usually represent a major change, most innovative improvements will be piloted.

7. Document the results of the evaluation of each process- and technology-improvement proposal.

8. Monitor the status of each process- and technology-improvement proposal.

TIP

These subpractices represent the rigor that is expected of high-maturity organizations and is typically not possible at earlier stages of process improvement.

SP 1.2 IDENTIFY AND ANALYZE INNOVATIONS

Identify and analyze innovative improvements that could increase the organization's quality and process performance.

The specific practice, Collect and Analyze Improvement Proposals, analyzes proposals that are passively collected. The purpose of this specific practice is to actively search for, locate, and analyze innovative improvements. This search primarily involves looking outside the organization.

TIP

This practice is similar in approach to the Elicit Requirements specific practice in RD. Potential innovative improvements are proactively sought after rather than passively collecting proposals.

Typical Work Products

1. Candidate innovative improvements
2. Analysis of proposed innovative improvements

Subpractices

1. Analyze the organization's set of standard processes to determine areas where innovative improvements would be most helpful.

These analyses are performed to determine which subprocesses are critical to achieving the organization's quality and process-performance objectives and which ones are good candidates to be improved.

2. Investigate innovative improvements that may improve the organization's set of standard processes.

Investigating innovative improvements involves the following:

- Systematically maintaining awareness of leading relevant technical work and technology trends
- Periodically searching for commercially available innovative improvements
- Collecting proposals for innovative improvements from the projects and the organization
- Systematically reviewing processes and technologies used externally and comparing them to those used within the organization
- Identifying areas where innovative improvements have been used successfully, and reviewing data and documentation of experience using these improvements
- Identifying improvements that integrate new technology into products and project work environments

3. Analyze potential innovative improvements to understand their effects on process elements and predict their influence on the process.

Process-performance models can provide a basis for analyzing possible effects of changes to process elements.

Refer to the Organizational Process Performance process area for more information about process-performance models.

4. Analyze the costs and benefits of potential innovative improvements.

Innovative improvements that have a very large cost-to-benefit ratio are rejected.

5. Create process- and technology-improvement proposals for those innovative improvements that would result in improving the organization's processes or technologies.

6. Select the innovative improvements to be piloted before broadscale deployment.

Since innovations, by definition, usually represent a major change, most innovative improvements will be piloted.

7. Document the results of the evaluations of innovative improvements.

SP 1.3 PILOT IMPROVEMENTS

Pilot process and technology improvements to select which ones to implement.

Pilots are performed to assess new and unproven major changes before they are broadly deployed, as appropriate.

TIP

Investigating innovative improvements is an ongoing activity that involves monitoring the marketplace for innovations that could benefit the organization and help it reach its objectives.

X-REF

When analyzing innovations, it is important to consider their role in business strategy and growth. For example, see Christensen, Clayton M., and Michael E. Raynor, "The Innovator's Solution: Creating and Sustaining Successful Growth," Harvard Business School Press (September 2003).

The implementation of this specific practice may overlap with the implementation of the Implement the Action Proposals specific practice in the Causal Analysis and Resolution process area (e.g., when causal analysis and resolution is implemented organizationally or across multiple projects).

Typical Work Products

1. Pilot evaluation reports
2. Documented lessons learned from pilots

Subpractices

1. Plan the pilots.

   When planning pilots, it is critical to define quantitative criteria to be used for evaluating pilot results.

2. Review and get relevant stakeholder agreement on the plans for the pilots.

3. Consult with and assist the people performing the pilots.

4. Perform each pilot in an environment that is characteristic of the environment present in a broadscale deployment.

5. Track the pilots against their plans.

6. Review and document the results of pilots.

   Pilot results are evaluated using the quantitative criteria defined during pilot planning. Reviewing and documenting the results of pilots usually involves the following:

   • Deciding whether to terminate the pilot, replan and continue the pilot, or proceed with deploying the process and technology improvement

   • Updating the disposition of process- and technology-improvement proposals associated with the pilot

   • Identifying and documenting new process- and technology-improvement proposals as appropriate

   • Identifying and documenting lessons learned and problems encountered during the pilot

SP 1.4 *Select Improvements for Deployment*

Select process and technology improvements for deployment across the organization.

Selection of process and technology improvements for deployment across the organization is based on quantifiable criteria derived from the organization's quality and process-performance objectives.

TIP

Another purpose of a pilot is to gauge a change's applicability to other projects.

TIP

A pilot may involve a single project or a group of projects.

TIP

Because of the need for careful coordination, pilots are often planned in the same manner as projects.

HINT

When planning a pilot, decide who will participate, how to conduct the pilot, how to collect results, and what information to collect to decide on broad-scale deployment.

OID

Typical Work Products

1. Process and technology improvements selected for deployment

Subpractices

1. Prioritize the candidate process and technology improvements for deployment.

   > Priority is based on an evaluation of the estimated cost-to-benefit ratio with regard to the quality and process-performance objectives.
   >
   > *Refer to the Organizational Process Performance process area for more information about quality and process-performance objectives.*

2. Select the process and technology improvements to be deployed.

   > The selection of the process improvements is based on their priorities and the available resources.

3. Determine how each process and technology improvement will be deployed.

Examples of where the process and technology improvements may be deployed include the following:

- Organizational process assets
- Project-specific or common work environments
- Organization's product families
- Organization's capabilities
- Organization's projects
- Organizational groups

---

4. Document the results of the selection process.

   > The results of the selection process usually include the following:
   >
   > - The selection criteria for candidate improvements
   > - The disposition of each improvement proposal
   > - The rationale for the disposition of each improvement proposal
   > - The assets to be changed for each selected improvement

SG 2 DEPLOY IMPROVEMENTS

Measurable improvements to the organization's processes and technologies are continually and systematically deployed.

SP 2.1 PLAN THE DEPLOYMENT

Establish and maintain the plans for deploying the selected process and technology improvements.

TIP

There is a need to balance stability with change. You can't afford to make every promising change; therefore, you must be selective about which changes you deploy across the organization.

TIP

The point of this subpractice is to determine the deployment approach in greater detail than was described in earlier steps (e.g., where the improvement will need to be incorporated).

TIP

Documenting the results of selection can help if the business environment changes enough for you to reconsider the decision and make a different selection.

TIP

The identification and analysis of improvement proposals and innovations (SG 1 SPs) are typically ongoing activities. In contrast, the detailed planning for and deployment of improvements may be done periodically (e.g., quarterly or annually).

The plans for deploying each process and technology improvement may be included in the organization's plan for organizational innovation and deployment or they may be documented separately.

The implementation of this specific practice complements the Deploy Organizational Process Assets specific practice in the Organizational Process Focus process area, and adds the use of quantitative data to guide the deployment and to determine the value of the improvements with respect to quality and process-performance objectives.

Refer to the Organizational Process Focus process area for more information about deploying organizational process assets.

This specific practice plans the deployment of individual process and technology improvements. The Plan the Process generic practice addresses comprehensive planning that covers the specific practices in this process area.

TIP

Depending on the magnitude of the change, it could take months or years before the change is fully deployed. Therefore, it is important to think about the retirement of those processes and products that the change will replace.

Typical Work Products

1. Deployment plan for selected process and technology improvements

Subpractices

1. Determine how each process and technology improvement must be adjusted for organization-wide deployment.

    Process and technology improvements proposed within a limited context (e.g., for a single project) might have to be modified to work across the organization.

2. Determine the changes necessary to deploy each process and technology improvement.

Examples of changes needed to deploy a process and technology improvement include the following:
- Process descriptions, standards, and procedures
- Work environments
- Education and training
- Skills
- Existing commitments
- Existing activities
- Continuing support to end users
- Organizational culture and characteristics

---

3. Identify strategies to address potential barriers to deploying each process and technology improvement.

4. Establish measures and objectives for determining the value of each process and technology improvement with respect to the organization's quality and process-performance objectives.

Examples of measures for determining the value of a process and technology improvement include the following:

- Return on investment
- Time to recover the cost of the process or technology improvement
- Measured improvement in the project's or organization's process performance
- Number and types of project and organizational risks mitigated by the process or technology improvement
- Average time required to respond to changes in project requirements, market situations, and the business environment

---

Refer to the Measurement and Analysis process area for more information about establishing objectives for measurement and analysis, specifying the measures and analyses to be performed, obtaining and analyzing measures, and reporting results.

5. Document the plan for deploying each process and technology improvement.
6. Review and get agreement with relevant stakeholders on the plan for deploying each process and technology improvement.
7. Revise the plan for deploying each process and technology improvement as necessary.

SP 2.2 MANAGE THE DEPLOYMENT

Manage the deployment of the selected process and technology improvements.

The implementation of this specific practice may overlap with the implementation of the Implement the Action Proposals specific practice in the Causal Analysis and Resolution process area (e.g., when causal analysis and resolution is implemented organizationally or across multiple projects). The primary difference is that in the Causal Analysis and Resolution process area, planning is done to manage the removal of the root causes of defects or problems from the project's defined processes. In the Organizational Innovation and Deployment process area, planning is done to manage the deployment of improvements to the organization's processes and technologies that can be quantified against the organization's business objectives.

Typical Work Products

1. Updated training materials (to reflect deployed process and technology improvements)
2. Documented results of process- and technology-improvement deployment activities
3. Revised process- and technology-improvement measures, objectives, priorities, and deployment plans

Subpractices

1. Monitor the deployment of the process and technology improvements using the deployment plan.
2. Coordinate the deployment of process and technology improvements across the organization.

    Coordinating deployment includes the following activities:

    - Coordinating the activities of projects, support groups, and organizational groups for each process and technology improvement
    - Coordinating the activities for deploying related process and technology improvements

3. Quickly deploy process and technology improvements in a controlled and disciplined manner, as appropriate.

> **TIP**
>
> One of the goals of most organizations is to be nimble and agile. Therefore, it is necessary to introduce small changes quickly, especially when they are limited and address an error.

Examples of methods for quickly deploying process and technology improvements include the following:

- Using red-lines, process change notices, or other controlled process documentation as interim process descriptions
- Deploying process and technology improvements incrementally, rather than as a single deployment
- Providing comprehensive consulting to early adopters of the process and technology improvement in lieu of revised formal training

---

4. Incorporate the process and technology improvements into organizational process assets, as appropriate.

    Refer to the Organizational Process Definition process area for more information about organizational process assets.

5. Coordinate the deployment of the process and technology improvements into the projects' defined processes as appropriate.

    Refer to the Organizational Process Focus process area for more information about deploying organizational process assets.

6. Provide consulting, as appropriate, to support deployment of the process and technology improvements.

> **TIP**
>
> Extensive or complex improvements may require help, such as training, user support, or feedback on use of the new or updated process.

7. Provide updated training materials to reflect the improvements to the organizational process assets.

   Refer to the Organizational Training process area for more information about training materials.

8. Confirm that the deployment of all process and technology improvements is completed.

9. Determine whether the ability of the defined process to meet quality and process-performance objectives is adversely affected by the process and technology improvement, and take corrective action as necessary.

   Refer to the Quantitative Project Management process area for more information about quantitatively managing the project's defined process to achieve the project's established quality and process-performance objectives.

10. Document and review the results of process- and technology-improvement deployment.

    Documenting and reviewing the results includes the following:

    • Identifying and documenting lessons learned
    • Identifying and documenting new process- and technology-improvement proposals
    • Revising process- and technology-improvement measures, objectives, priorities, and deployment plans

TIP

This should not be the first time the defined process with the improvement incorporated is analyzed to evaluate its impact on the organization's ability to meet its objectives. However, this further evaluation ensures that no unanticipated consequences have occurred.

SP 2.3 MEASURE IMPROVEMENT EFFECTS

Measure the effects of the deployed process and technology improvements.

Refer to the Measurement and Analysis process area for more information about establishing objectives for measurement and analysis, specifying the measures and analyses to be performed, obtaining and analyzing measures, and reporting results.

The implementation of this specific practice may overlap with the implementation of the Evaluate the Effect of Changes specific practice in the Causal Analysis and Resolution process area (e.g., when causal analysis and resolution is implemented organizationally or across multiple projects).

TIP

CAR addresses only the changes that were identified to prevent reoccurrence of a defect or problem. This specific practice looks at measuring the effects of all improvements that you are deploying across the organization.

Typical Work Products

1. Documented measures of the effects resulting from the deployed process and technology improvements

Subpractices

1. Measure the actual cost, effort, and schedule for deploying each process and technology improvement.

2. Measure the value of each process and technology improvement.

3. Measure the progress toward achieving the organization's quality and process-performance objectives.

4. Analyze the progress toward achieving the organization's quality and process-performance objectives and take corrective action as needed.

> *Refer to the Organizational Process Performance process area for more information about process-performance analyses.*

5. Store the measures in the organization's measurement repository.

TIP

Having measures available for reference may help evaluate newly proposed improvements that are similar to this one.

Generic Practices by Goal

GG 1 *ACHIEVE SPECIFIC GOALS*

The process supports and enables achievement of the specific goals of the process area by transforming identifiable input work products to produce identifiable output work products.

GP 1.1 *PERFORM SPECIFIC PRACTICES*

Perform the specific practices of the organizational innovation and deployment process to develop work products and provide services to achieve the specific goals of the process area.

GG 2 *INSTITUTIONALIZE A MANAGED PROCESS*

The process is institutionalized as a managed process.

GG 3 *INSTITUTIONALIZE A DEFINED PROCESS*

The process is institutionalized as a defined process.

> *This generic goal's appearance here reflects its location in the staged representation.*

CONTINUOUS ONLY

STAGED ONLY

GP 2.1 *ESTABLISH AN ORGANIZATIONAL POLICY*

Establish and maintain an organizational policy for planning and performing the organizational innovation and deployment process.

Elaboration:

This policy establishes organizational expectations for identifying and deploying process and technology improvements that contribute to meeting quality and process-performance objectives.

GP 2.2 PLAN THE PROCESS

Establish and maintain the plan for performing the organizational innovation and deployment process.

Elaboration:

This plan for performing the organizational innovation and deployment process differs from the deployment plans described in a specific practice in this process area. The plan called for in this generic practice would address the comprehensive planning for all of the specific practices in this process area, from collecting and analyzing improvement proposals all the way through to the measurement of improvement effects. In contrast, the deployment plans called for in the specific practice would address the planning needed for the deployment of individual process and technology improvements.

GP 2.3 PROVIDE RESOURCES

Provide adequate resources for performing the organizational innovation and deployment process, developing the work products, and providing the services of the process.

Elaboration:

Examples of resources provided include the following tools:
- Simulation packages
- Prototyping tools
- Statistical packages
- Dynamic systems modeling
- Subscriptions to online technology databases and publications
- Process modeling tools

GP 2.4 ASSIGN RESPONSIBILITY

Assign responsibility and authority for performing the process, developing the work products, and providing the services of the organizational innovation and deployment process.

GP 2.5 TRAIN PEOPLE

Train the people performing or supporting the organizational innovation and deployment process as needed.

OID

Elaboration:

Examples of training topics include the following:
- Planning, designing, and conducting pilots
- Cost/benefit analysis
- Technology transition
- Change management

GP 2.6 MANAGE CONFIGURATIONS

Place designated work products of the organizational innovation and deployment process under appropriate levels of control.

Elaboration:

Examples of work products placed under control include the following:
- Documented lessons learned from pilots
- Revised process- and technology-improvement measures, objectives, priorities, and deployment plans
- Updated training material

GP 2.7 IDENTIFY AND INVOLVE RELEVANT STAKEHOLDERS

Identify and involve the relevant stakeholders of the organizational innovation and deployment process as planned.

Elaboration:

Examples of activities for stakeholder involvement include the following:
- Reviewing process- and technology-improvement proposals that may have major impacts on process performance or on customer and end-user satisfaction
- Providing feedback to the organization on the status and results of the process- and technology-improvement deployment activities
---

The feedback typically involves:

- Informing the people who submit process- and technology-improvement proposals about the disposition of their proposals
- Regularly informing relevant stakeholders about the plans and status for selecting and deploying process and technology improvements
- Preparing and distributing a summary of process- and technology-improvement selection and deployment activities

GP 2.8 MONITOR AND CONTROL THE PROCESS

Monitor and control the organizational innovation and deployment process against the plan for performing the process and take appropriate corrective action.

Elaboration:

> Examples of measures and work products used in monitoring and controlling include the following:
> - Change in quality
> - Change in process performance
> - Schedule for activities to deploy a selected improvement

GP 2.9 OBJECTIVELY EVALUATE ADHERENCE

Objectively evaluate adherence of the organizational innovation and deployment process against its process description, standards, and procedures, and address noncompliance.

Elaboration:

> Examples of activities reviewed include the following:
> - Selecting improvements
> - Deploying improvements

> Examples of work products reviewed include the following:
> - Deployment plans
> - Revised process- and technology-improvement measures, objectives, priorities, and deployment plans
> - Updated training material

GP 2.10 REVIEW STATUS WITH HIGHER LEVEL MANAGEMENT

Review the activities, status, and results of the organizational innovation and deployment process with higher level management and resolve issues.

GG 3   INSTITUTIONALIZE A DEFINED PROCESS

The process is institutionalized as a defined process.

> *This generic goal's appearance here reflects its location in the continuous representation.*

CONTINUOUS ONLY

GP 3.1 ESTABLISH A DEFINED PROCESS

Establish and maintain the description of a defined organizational innovation and deployment process.

GP 3.2 COLLECT IMPROVEMENT INFORMATION

Collect work products, measures, measurement results, and improvement information derived from planning and performing the organizational innovation and deployment process to support the future use and improvement of the organization's processes and process assets.

Elaboration:

> Examples of work products, measures, measurement results, and improvement information include the following:
> - Lessons learned captured from relevant stakeholders that identify barriers to deployment from previous technology insertions
> - Documented measures of the costs and benefits resulting from deploying innovations
> - Report of a comparison of similar development processes to identify the potential for improving efficiency

GG 4 INSTITUTIONALIZE A QUANTITATIVELY MANAGED PROCESS

The process is institutionalized as a quantitatively managed process.

GP 4.1 ESTABLISH QUANTITATIVE OBJECTIVES FOR THE PROCESS

Establish and maintain quantitative objectives for the organizational innovation and deployment process, which address quality and process performance, based on customer needs and business objectives.

GP 4.2 STABILIZE SUBPROCESS PERFORMANCE

Stabilize the performance of one or more subprocesses to determine the ability of the organizational innovation and deployment process to achieve the established quantitative quality and process-performance objectives.

GG 5 INSTITUTIONALIZE AN OPTIMIZING PROCESS

The process is institutionalized as an optimizing process.

CONTINUOUS ONLY

GP 5.1 ENSURE CONTINUOUS PROCESS IMPROVEMENT

Ensure continuous improvement of the organizational innovation and deployment process in fulfilling the relevant business objectives of the organization.

GP 5.2 CORRECT ROOT CAUSES OF PROBLEMS

Identify and correct the root causes of defects and other problems in the organizational innovation and deployment process.

CONTINUOUS ONLY

ORGANIZATIONAL PROCESS DEFINITION +IPPD
A Process Management Process Area at Maturity Level 3

Purpose

The purpose of Organizational Process Definition (OPD) is to establish and maintain a usable set of organizational process assets and work environment standards.

IPPD ADD

For IPPD, Organizational Process Definition +IPPD also covers the establishment of organizational rules and guidelines that enable conducting work using integrated teams.

TIP

The IPPD additions OPD SG 2 (new to Version 1.2) and IPM SG 3 address the use of integrated teams.

Introductory Notes

Organizational process assets enable consistent process performance across the organization and provide a basis for cumulative, long-term benefits to the organization. (See the definition of "organizational process assets" in the glossary.)

The organization's process asset library is a collection of items maintained by the organization for use by the people and projects of the organization. This collection of items includes descriptions of processes and process elements, descriptions of lifecycle models, process tailoring guidelines, process-related documentation, and data. The organization's process asset library supports organizational learning and process improvement by allowing the sharing of best practices and lessons learned across the organization.

The organization's set of standard processes is tailored by projects to create their defined processes. The other organizational process assets are used to support tailoring as well as the implementation of the defined processes. The work environment standards are used to guide creation of project work environments.

A standard process is composed of other processes (i.e., subprocesses) or process elements. A process element is the fundamental (e.g., atomic) unit of process definition and describes the activities and tasks to consistently perform work. Process architecture provides

TIP

OPD contains the specific practices that capture the organization's requirements, standards, and guidelines, to be used by all projects across the organization.

HINT

As with any library, a key challenge is to enable staff to locate information quickly. Therefore, it is necessary to catalog, maintain, and archive information.

rules for connecting the process elements of a standard process. The organization's set of standard processes may include multiple process architectures.

(See the definitions of "standard process," "process architecture," "subprocess," and "process element" in the glossary.)

TIP

CMMI models try to capture the "what" and not the "how." However, in notes and examples, guidance is provided to give you some tips on the interpretation and implementation of the concepts.

> The organizational process assets may be organized in many ways, depending on the implementation of the Organizational Process Definition process area. Examples include the following:
> - Descriptions of lifecycle models may be documented as part of the organization's set of standard processes, or they may be documented separately.
> - The organization's set of standard processes may be stored in the organization's process asset library, or they may be stored separately.
> - A single repository may contain both the measurements and the process-related documentation, or they may be stored separately.

Related Process Areas

Refer to the Organizational Process Focus process area for more information about organizational process-related matters.

Specific Goal and Practice Summary

TIP

In going from Version 1.1 to 1.2, IPPD material was consolidated and moved. SP 1.6 is a new specific practice in Version 1.2 that addresses work environment standards. It is derived in part from OEI SP 1.2 but is no longer limited in application to IPPD.

SG 1 Establish Organizational Process Assets
    SP 1.1   Establish Standard Processes
    SP 1.2   Establish Lifecycle Model Descriptions
    SP 1.3   Establish Tailoring Criteria and Guidelines
    SP 1.4   Establish the Organization's Measurement Repository
    SP 1.5   Establish the Organization's Process Asset Library
    SP 1.6   Establish Work Environment Standards
SG 2 Enable IPPD Management
    SP 2.1   Establish Empowerment Mechanisms
    SP 2.2   Establish Rules and Guidelines for Integrated Teams
    SP 2.3   Balance Team and Home Organization Responsibilities

IPPD ADD

Specific Practices by Goal

TIP

OPD now has an IPPD addition. SP 2.1 is derived from OEI SP 2.1. SP 2.2 is derived from several IT SG 2 SPs and IPM SG 4 SPs. SP 2.3 is derived from OEI SP 2.3. (IT and OEI are abbreviations of process areas in V1.1 not found in V1.2.)

SG 1   *ESTABLISH ORGANIZATIONAL PROCESS ASSETS*

A set of organizational process assets is established and maintained.

OPD +IPPD

IPPD ADDITION

Integrated processes that emphasize parallel rather than serial development are a cornerstone of IPPD implementation. The processes for developing the product and for developing product-related lifecycle processes, such as the manufacturing process and the support process, are integrated and conducted concurrently. Such integrated processes should accommodate the information provided by stakeholders representing all phases of the product lifecycle from both business and technical functions. Processes for effective teamwork are also needed.

TIP

For more information about IPPD, see the annotated IPPD bibliography and the People CMM on the SEI Web site.

SP 1.1 ESTABLISH STANDARD PROCESSES

Establish and maintain the organization's set of standard processes.

Standard processes may be defined at multiple levels in an enterprise and they may be related in a hierarchical manner. For example, an enterprise may have a set of standard processes that is tailored by individual organizations (e.g., a division or site) in the enterprise to establish their set of standard processes. The set of standard processes may also be tailored for each of the organization's business areas or product lines. Thus "the organization's set of standard processes" can refer to the standard processes established at the organization level and standard processes that may be established at lower levels, although some organizations may only have a single level of standard processes. (See the definitions of "standard process" and "organization's set of standard processes" in the glossary.)

Multiple standard processes may be needed to address the needs of different application domains, lifecycle models, methodologies, and tools. The organization's set of standard processes contains process elements (e.g., a work product size-estimating element) that may be interconnected according to one or more process architectures that describe the relationships among these process elements.

The organization's set of standard processes typically includes technical, management, administrative, support, and organizational processes.

TIP

Organizational process assets support a fundamental change in behavior. Projects no longer create their processes from scratch but instead use the best practices of the organization, thus improving quality and saving time and money.

TIP

Standard processes define the key activities performed in an organization. Some examples of standard processes include requirements elicitation, design, and testing; planning, estimating, monitoring, and control; and product delivery and support.

TIP

The OSSP can include processes that are not directly addressed by CMMI, such as proposal development, project approval, financial management, and procurement.

IPPD ADD

In an IPPD environment, the organization's set of standard processes includes a process that projects use to establish a shared vision.

The organization's set of standard processes should collectively cover all processes needed by the organization and projects, including those processes addressed by the process areas at Maturity Level 2.

TIP

Often organizations look at the exemplar processes from their projects as a starting point to populate the OSSP.

Typical Work Products

1. Organization's set of standard processes

Subpractices

1. Decompose each standard process into constituent process elements to the detail needed to understand and describe the process.

TIP

The objective is to decompose and define the process so that it can be performed consistently across projects but will allow enough flexibility to meet the unique requirements of each project.

   Each process element covers a bounded and closely related set of activities. The descriptions of the process elements may be templates to be filled in, fragments to be completed, abstractions to be refined, or complete descriptions to be tailored or used unmodified. These elements are described in sufficient detail such that the process, when fully defined, can be consistently performed by appropriately trained and skilled people.

> Examples of process elements include the following:
> • Template for generating work product size estimates
> • Description of work product design methodology
> • Tailorable peer review methodology
> • Template for conduct of management reviews

2. Specify the critical attributes of each process element.

> Examples of critical attributes include the following:
> • Process roles
> • Applicable standards
> • Applicable procedures, methods, tools, and resources
> • Process-performance objectives
> • Entry criteria
> • Inputs
> • Product and process measures to be collected and used
> • Verification points (e.g., peer reviews)
> • Outputs
> • Interfaces
> • Exit criteria

3. Specify the relationships of the process elements.

> Examples of relationships include the following:
> • Ordering of the process elements
> • Interfaces among the process elements
> • Interfaces with external processes
> • Interdependencies among the process elements

The rules for describing the relationships among process elements are referred to as "process architecture." The process architecture covers the essential requirements and guidelines. The detailed specifications of these relationships are covered in the descriptions of the defined processes that are tailored from the organization's set of standard processes.

4. Ensure that the organization's set of standard processes adheres to applicable policies, standards, and models.

    Adherence to applicable process standards and models is typically demonstrated by developing a mapping from the organization's set of standard processes to the relevant process standards and models. In addition, this mapping will be a useful input to future appraisals.

5. Ensure that the organization's set of standard processes satisfies the process needs and objectives of the organization.

    Refer to the Organizational Process Focus process area for more information about establishing and maintaining the organization's process needs and objectives.

6. Ensure that there is appropriate integration among the processes that are included in the organization's set of standard processes.

7. Document the organization's set of standard processes.

8. Conduct peer reviews on the organization's set of standard processes.

    Refer to the Verification process area for more information about peer review.

9. Revise the organization's set of standard processes as necessary.

SP 1.2 ESTABLISH LIFECYCLE MODEL DESCRIPTIONS

Establish and maintain descriptions of the lifecycle models approved for use in the organization.

Lifecycle models may be developed for a variety of customers or in a variety of situations, since one lifecycle model may not be appropriate for all situations. Lifecycle models are often used to define the phases of the project. Also, the organization may define different lifecycle models for each type of product and service it delivers.

Typical Work Products

1. Descriptions of lifecycle models

Subpractices

1. Select lifecycle models based on the needs of projects and the organization.

HINT

Your initial focus should first be on standardizing what you already do well.

HINT

Break down stovepipes: When capabilities residing in different organizations are routinely needed to understand tradeoffs and resolve system-level problems, consider establishing a standard end-to-end process for performing joint work.

TIP

When managing a project, it is helpful to have a standard description for the phases the project moves through (i.e., project lifecycle model) to organize and assess the adequacy of project activities and to monitor progress.

> For example, project lifecycle models include the following:
> • Waterfall
> • Spiral
> • Evolutionary
> • Incremental
> • Iterative

2. Document the descriptions of the lifecycle models.

> The lifecycle models may be documented as part of the organization's standard process descriptions or they may be documented separately.

3. Conduct peer reviews on the lifecycle models.

> *Refer to the Verification process area for more information about conducting peer reviews.*

4. Revise the descriptions of the lifecycle models as necessary.

SP 1.3 ESTABLISH TAILORING CRITERIA AND GUIDELINES

Establish and maintain the tailoring criteria and guidelines for the organization's set of standard processes.

> In creating the tailoring criteria and guidelines, include considerations for concurrent development and operating with integrated teams. For example, how one tailors the manufacturing process will be different depending on whether it is developed serially after the product has been developed or in parallel with the development of the product, as in IPPD. Processes, such as resource allocation, will also be tailored differently if the project is operating with integrated teams.
>
> *IPPD ADDITION*

The tailoring criteria and guidelines describe the following:

- How the organization's set of standard processes and organizational process assets are used to create the defined processes
- Mandatory requirements that must be satisfied by the defined processes (e.g., the subset of the organizational process assets that are essential for any defined process)
- Options that can be exercised and criteria for selecting among the options
- Procedures that must be followed in performing and documenting process tailoring

---

TIP

It helps to provide guidance about which lifecycle models work best with which types of projects.

TIP

Tailoring allows projects to adapt the OSSP and other assets to meet their needs. The challenge is to provide guidance that has sufficient flexibility to meet the unique needs of each project but at the same time ensure meaningful consistency.

Examples of reasons for tailoring include the following:

- Adapting the process for a new product line or work environment
- Customizing the process for a specific application or class of similar applications
- Elaborating the process description so that the resulting defined process can be performed

---

Flexibility in tailoring and defining processes is balanced with ensuring appropriate consistency in the processes across the organization. Flexibility is needed to address contextual variables such as the domain; nature of the customer; cost, schedule, and quality tradeoffs; technical difficulty of the work; and experience of the people implementing the process. Consistency across the organization is needed so that organizational standards, objectives, and strategies are appropriately addressed, and process data and lessons learned can be shared.

Tailoring criteria and guidelines may allow for using a standard process "as is," with no tailoring.

TIP

Finding this balance usually takes time, as the organization gains experience from using these assets.

OPD +IPPD

Typical Work Products

1. Tailoring guidelines for the organization's set of standard processes

Subpractices

1. Specify the selection criteria and procedures for tailoring the organization's set of standard processes.

Examples of criteria and procedures include the following:

- Criteria for selecting lifecycle models from those approved by the organization
- Criteria for selecting process elements from the organization's set of standard processes
- Procedures for tailoring the selected lifecycle models and process elements to accommodate specific process characteristics and needs

---

Examples of tailoring actions include the following:

- Modifying a lifecycle model
- Combining elements of different lifecycle models
- Modifying process elements
- Replacing process elements
- Reordering process elements

---

2. Specify the standards for documenting the defined processes.

3. Specify the procedures for submitting and obtaining approval of waivers from the requirements of the organization's set of standard processes.

4. Document the tailoring guidelines for the organization's set of standard processes.

5. Conduct peer reviews on the tailoring guidelines.

> Refer to the Verification process area for more information about conducting peer reviews.

6. Revise the tailoring guidelines as necessary.

SP 1.4 ESTABLISH THE ORGANIZATION'S MEASUREMENT REPOSITORY

Establish and maintain the organization's measurement repository.

Refer to the Use Organizational Process Assets for Planning Project Activities specific practice of the Integrated Project Management process area for more information about the use of the organization's measurement repository in planning project activities.

The repository contains both product and process measures that are related to the organization's set of standard processes. It also contains or refers to the information needed to understand and interpret the measures and assess them for reasonableness and applicability. For example, the definitions of the measures are used to compare similar measures from different processes.

Typical Work Products

1. Definition of the common set of product and process measures for the organization's set of standard processes

2. Design of the organization's measurement repository

3. Organization's measurement repository (that is, the repository structure and support environment)

4. Organization's measurement data

Subpractices

1. Determine the organization's needs for storing, retrieving, and analyzing measurements.

2. Define a common set of process and product measures for the organization's set of standard processes.

   The measures in the common set are selected based on the organization's set of standard processes. *They are selected for their ability to provide visibility into process performance to support expected business objectives.* The common set of measures may vary for different standard processes.

HINT

Streamline the waiver process to enable new projects to establish their defined process quickly, and to avoid stalling.

TIP

Both the tailoring process and guidelines may be documented as part of the OSSP.

TIP

The organization's measurement repository is a critical resource that helps new projects plan by providing answers to questions about projects similar to their own (e.g., How long did it take? How much effort was expended? What was the resulting quality?).

TIP

Although this practice concentrates on repository establishment and maintenance, the real value occurs when the people in the organization begin using the data when establishing defined processes and plans.

TIP

These measures change over time and therefore should be reviewed periodically.

Operational definitions for the measures specify the procedures for collecting valid data and the point in the process where the data will be collected.

Examples of classes of commonly used measures include the following:
- Estimates of work product size (e.g., pages)
- Estimates of effort and cost (e.g., person hours)
- Actual measures of size, effort, and cost
- Quality measures (e.g., number of defects found or severity of defects)
- Peer review coverage
- Test coverage
- Reliability measures (e.g., mean time to failure)

Refer to the Measurement and Analysis process area for more information about defining measures.

3. Design and implement the measurement repository.

4. Specify the procedures for storing, updating, and retrieving measures.

5. Conduct peer reviews on the definitions of the common set of measures and the procedures for storing and retrieving measures.

   Refer to the Verification process area for more information about conducting peer reviews.

6. Enter the specified measures into the repository.

   Refer to the Measurement and Analysis process area for more information about collecting and analyzing data.

7. Make the contents of the measurement repository available for use by the organization and projects as appropriate.

8. Revise the measurement repository, common set of measures, and procedures as the organization's needs change.

   Examples of when the common set of measures may need to be revised include the following:
   - New processes are added
   - Processes are revised and new measures are needed
   - Finer granularity of data is required
   - Greater visibility into the process is required
   - Measures are retired

TIP

Measurement and analysis practices (see MA) are a prerequisite to establishing the organization's measurement repository.

TIP

Entering measurements into a repository is commonly an automated process; however, when not automated, it should be done by the person collecting the measurements.

SP 1.5 ESTABLISH THE ORGANIZATION'S PROCESS ASSET LIBRARY

Establish and maintain the organization's process asset library.

TIP

Think of why you are storing this information and how often it will be retrieved.

> Examples of items to be stored in the organization's process asset library include the following:
> - Organizational policies
> - Defined process descriptions
> - Procedures (e.g., estimating procedure)
> - Development plans
> - Acquisition plans
> - Quality assurance plans
> - Training materials
> - Process aids (e.g., checklists)
> - Lessons-learned reports

Typical Work Products

1. Design of the organization's process asset library
2. Organization's process asset library
3. Selected items to be included in the organization's process asset library
4. Catalog of items in the organization's process asset library

Subpractices

HINT

A major objective of the process asset library (PAL) is to ensure that information is easy to locate and use.

1. Design and implement the organization's process asset library, including the library structure and support environment.
2. Specify the criteria for including items in the library.
   The items are selected based primarily on their relationship to the organization's set of standard processes.
3. Specify the procedures for storing and retrieving items.
4. Enter the selected items into the library and catalog them for easy reference and retrieval.
5. Make the items available for use by the projects.
6. Periodically review the use of each item and use the results to maintain the library contents.
7. Revise the organization's process asset library as necessary.
   Examples of when the library may need to be revised include the following:
   - New items are added
   - Items are retired
   - Current versions of items are changed

TIP

Library maintenance can quickly become an issue if all documents from every project are stored in the library.

TIP

Some organizations regularly review their PAL contents every 12 to 18 months to decide what to discard or archive.

SP 1.6 *ESTABLISH WORK ENVIRONMENT STANDARDS*

Establish and maintain work environment standards.

Work environment standards allow the organization and projects to benefit from common tools, training, and maintenance, as well as cost savings from volume purchases. Work environment standards address the needs of all stakeholders and consider productivity, cost, availability, security, and workplace health, safety, and ergonomic factors. Work environment standards can include guidelines for tailoring and/or the use of waivers that allow adaptation of the project's work environment to meet specific needs.

> Examples of work environment standards include
> - Procedures for operation, safety, and security of the work environment
> - Standard workstation hardware and software
> - Standard application software and tailoring guidelines for it
> - Standard production and calibration equipment
> - Process for requesting and approving tailoring or waivers

Typical Work Products

1. Work environment standards

Subpractices

1. Evaluate commercially-available work environment standards appropriate for the organization.
2. Adopt existing work environment standards and develop new ones to fill gaps based on the organization's process needs and objectives.

SG 2 ENABLE IPPD MANAGEMENT

Organizational rules and guidelines, which govern the operation of integrated teams, are provided.

An organizational infrastructure that supports and promotes IPPD concepts is critical if it is to be successfully sustained over the long term. These rules and guidelines promote concepts such as integrated teaming and allow for empowered decision making at many levels. Through its rules and guidelines, the organization demonstrates commitment to IPPD and the success of its integrated teams.

IPPD rules and guidelines become part of the organization's set of standard processes and the project's defined process. The organization's standard processes enable, promote, and reinforce the behaviors expected from projects, integrated teams, and people. These expected

IPPD ADDITION

OPD +IPPD

TIP

Work environment standards must make sense for your organization, its line of business, the degree of collaboration to be supported, and so on.

HINT

If your organization has a shared vision, your work environment must support it.

TIP

Typically, projects have additional requirements for their work environment. This specific practice establishes the standards to be addressed across the organization.

TIP

This goal establishes an organizational infrastructure for successful IPPD performance.

TIP

The specific practices that follow should prove useful to any organization with a frequent need to bring individuals of differing views, cultures, and expertise together as a *team*.

behaviors are typically communicated in the form of policies, operating procedures, guidelines, and other organizational process assets.

SP 2.1 ESTABLISH EMPOWERMENT MECHANISMS

Establish and maintain empowerment mechanisms to enable timely decision making.

In a successful IPPD environment, clear channels of responsibility and authority must be established. Issues can arise at any level of the organization when integrated teams assume too much or too little authority and when it is unclear who is responsible for making decisions. Documenting and deploying organizational guidelines that clearly define the empowerment of integrated teams can prevent these issues.

Implementing IPPD introduces challenges to leadership because of the cultural changes required when people and integrated teams are empowered and decisions are driven to the lowest level appropriate. Effective and efficient communication mechanisms are critical to timely and sound decision making in the integrated work environment. Once an integrated team project structure is established and training is provided, mechanisms to handle empowerment, decision making, and issue resolution also need to be provided.

Refer to the Decision Analysis and Resolution process area for more information about decision making.

Typical Work Products

1. Empowerment rules and guidelines for people and integrated teams
2. Decision-making rules and guidelines
3. Issue resolution documentation

Subpractices

1. Determine rules and guidelines for the degree of empowerment provided to people and integrated teams.

    Factors to consider regarding integrated team empowerment include the following:

    - Authority of teams to pick their own leader
    - Authority of teams to implement subteams (e.g., a product team forming an integration subteam)
    - The degree of collective decision making
    - The level of consensus needed for integrated team decisions
    - How conflicts and differences of opinion within the integrated teams are addressed and resolved

---

TIP

Teams cannot operate as "high-performance teams" if they have to go to management for approval of every action or decision.

TIP

This specific practice also addresses issue resolution.

IPPD ADDITION

Sometimes teams persist beyond their productive life in organizations that do not have a home organization for the team members to return to after the integrated team is dissolved. Therefore, there should be guidelines for disbanding the integrated teams and maintaining home organizations.

Typical Work Products

1. Organizational guidelines for balancing team and home organization responsibilities
2. Performance review process that considers both functional supervisor and team leader input

Subpractices

1. Establish guidelines for home organization responsibilities that promote integrated team behavior.
2. Establish guidelines for team management responsibilities to ensure integrated team members report appropriately to their home organizations.
3. Establish a performance review process that considers input from both home organization and integrated team leaders.
4. Maintain the guidelines for balancing team and home organization responsibilities.

Generic Practices by Goal

GG 1 ACHIEVE SPECIFIC GOALS

The process supports and enables achievement of the specific goals of the process area by transforming identifiable input work products to produce identifiable output work products.

GP 1.1 PERFORM SPECIFIC PRACTICES

Perform the specific practices of the organizational process definition process to develop work products and provide services to achieve the specific goals of the process area.

GG 2 INSTITUTIONALIZE A MANAGED PROCESS

The process is institutionalized as a managed process.

GG 3 *INSTITUTIONALIZE A DEFINED PROCESS*

The process is institutionalized as a defined process.

This generic goal's appearance here reflects its location in the staged representation.

GP 2.1 *ESTABLISH AN ORGANIZATIONAL POLICY*

Establish and maintain an organizational policy for planning and performing the organizational process definition process.

Elaboration:

This policy establishes organizational expectations for establishing and maintaining a set of standard processes for use by the organization and making organizational process assets available across the organization.

GP 2.2 *PLAN THE PROCESS*

Establish and maintain the plan for performing the organizational process definition process.

Elaboration:

This plan for performing the organizational process definition process can be part of (or referenced by) the organization's process improvement plan.

GP 2.3 *PROVIDE RESOURCES*

Provide adequate resources for performing the organizational process definition process, developing the work products, and providing the services of the process.

Elaboration:

A process group typically manages the organizational process definition activities. This group typically is staffed by a core of professionals whose primary responsibility is coordinating organizational process improvement. This group is supported by process owners and people with expertise in various disciplines such as the following:

- Project management
- The appropriate engineering disciplines
- Configuration management
- Quality assurance

Examples of other resources provided include the following tools:
- Database management systems
- Process modeling tools
- Web page builders and browsers

GP 2.4 ASSIGN RESPONSIBILITY

Assign responsibility and authority for performing the process, developing the work products, and providing the services of the organizational process definition process.

GP 2.5 TRAIN PEOPLE

Train the people performing or supporting the organizational process definition process as needed.

Elaboration:

Examples of training topics include the following:
- CMMI and other process and process improvement reference models
- Planning, managing, and monitoring processes
- Process modeling and definition
- Developing a tailorable standard process
- Developing work environment standards
- Ergonomics

GP 2.6 MANAGE CONFIGURATIONS

Place designated work products of the organizational process definition process under appropriate levels of control.

Elaboration:

Examples of work products placed under control include the following:
- Organization's set of standard processes
- Descriptions of the lifecycle models
- Tailoring guidelines for the organization's set of standard processes
- Definitions of the common set of product and process measures
- Organization's measurement data

Examples of work products placed under control include the following:
• Empowerment rules and guidelines for people and integrated teams
• Organizational process documentation for issue resolution

GP 2.7 *IDENTIFY AND INVOLVE RELEVANT STAKEHOLDERS*

Identify and involve the relevant stakeholders of the organizational process definition process as planned.

Elaboration:

Examples of activities for stakeholder involvement include the following:
• Reviewing the organization's set of standard processes
• Reviewing the organization's lifecycle models
• Resolving issues on the tailoring guidelines
• Assessing the definitions of the common set of process and product measures
• Reviewing the work environment standards

Examples of activities for stakeholder involvement also include the following:
• Establishing and maintaining IPPD empowerment mechanisms
• Establishing and maintaining organizational rules and guidelines for the structuring and forming of integrated teams

GP 2.8 *MONITOR AND CONTROL THE PROCESS*

Monitor and control the organizational process definition process against the plan for performing the process and take appropriate corrective action.

Elaboration:

Examples of measures and work products used in monitoring and controlling include the following:
• Percentage of projects using the process architectures and process elements of the organization's set of standard processes
• Defect density of each process element of the organization's set of standard processes
• Number of worker's compensation claims due to ergonomic problems
• Schedule for development of a process or process change

GP 2.9 OBJECTIVELY EVALUATE ADHERENCE

Objectively evaluate adherence of the organizational process definition process against its process description, standards, and procedures, and address noncompliance.

Elaboration:

Examples of activities reviewed include the following:
• Establishing organizational process assets

Examples of activities reviewed also include the following:
• Determining rules and guidelines for the degree of empowerment provided to people and integrated teams
• Establishing and maintaining an issue resolution process

IPPD ADD

Examples of work products reviewed include the following:
• Organization's set of standard processes
• Descriptions of the lifecycle models
• Tailoring guidelines for the organization's set of standard processes
• Organization's measurement data

Examples of work products reviewed also include the following:
• Empowerment rules and guidelines for people and integrated teams
• Organizational process documentation

IPPD ADD

GP 2.10 REVIEW STATUS WITH HIGHER LEVEL MANAGEMENT

Review the activities, status, and results of the organizational process definition process with higher level management and resolve issues.

GG 3 INSTITUTIONALIZE A DEFINED PROCESS

The process is institutionalized as a defined process.

> *This generic goal's appearance here reflects its location in the continuous representation.*

CONTINUOUS ONLY

GP 3.1 ESTABLISH A DEFINED PROCESS

Establish and maintain the description of a defined organizational process definition process.

GP 3.2 COLLECT IMPROVEMENT INFORMATION

Collect work products, measures, measurement results, and improvement information derived from planning and performing the organizational process definition process to support the future use and improvement of the organization's processes and process assets.

Elaboration:

Examples of work products, measures, measurement results, and improvement information include the following:
- Submission of lessons learned to the organization's process asset library
- Submission of measurement data to the organization's measurement repository
- Status of the change requests submitted to modify the organization's standard process
- Record of non-standard tailoring requests

Examples of work products, measures, measurement results, and improvement information also include the following:
- Status of performance review input from integrated teams

IPPD ADD

GG 4 INSTITUTIONALIZE A QUANTITATIVELY MANAGED PROCESS

The process is institutionalized as a quantitatively managed process.

GP 4.1 ESTABLISH QUANTITATIVE OBJECTIVES FOR THE PROCESS

Establish and maintain quantitative objectives for the organizational process definition process, which address quality and process performance, based on customer needs and business objectives.

GP 4.2 STABILIZE SUBPROCESS PERFORMANCE

Stabilize the performance of one or more subprocesses to determine the ability of the organizational process definition process to achieve the established quantitative quality and process-performance objectives.

CONTINUOUS ONLY

GG 5 *INSTITUTIONALIZE AN OPTIMIZING PROCESS*

The process is institutionalized as an optimizing process.

GP 5.1 *ENSURE CONTINUOUS PROCESS IMPROVEMENT*

Ensure continuous improvement of the organizational process definition process in fulfilling the relevant business objectives of the organization.

GP 5.2 *CORRECT ROOT CAUSES OF PROBLEMS*

Identify and correct the root causes of defects and other problems in the organizational process definition process.

CONTINUOUS ONLY

OPD +IPPD

ORGANIZATIONAL PROCESS FOCUS
A Process Management Process Area at Maturity Level 3

Purpose

The purpose of Organizational Process Focus (OPF) is to plan, implement, and deploy organizational process improvements based on a thorough understanding of the current strengths and weaknesses of the organization's processes and process assets.

Introductory Notes

The organization's processes include all the processes used by the organization and its projects. Candidate improvements to the organization's processes and process assets are obtained from various sources, including measurement of the processes, lessons learned in implementing the processes, results of process appraisals, results of product evaluation activities, results of benchmarking against other organizations' processes, and recommendations from other improvement initiatives in the organization.

Process improvement occurs within the context of the organization's needs and is used to address the organization's objectives. The organization encourages participation in process improvement activities by those who will perform the process. The responsibility for facilitating and managing the organization's process improvement activities, including coordinating the participation of others, is typically assigned to a process group. The organization provides the long-term commitment and resources required to sponsor this group and to ensure the effective and timely deployment of the improvements.

Careful planning is required to ensure that process improvement efforts across the organization are adequately managed and implemented. The organization's planning for process improvement results in a process improvement plan.

The organization's process improvement plan will address appraisal planning, process action planning, pilot planning, and

TIP

As Watts Humphrey points out, "If you don't know where you are, a map won't help." Benchmark the processes and practices in your organization before you begin to improve them.

TIP

Although CMMI describes many of the processes that are critical to success, it does not contain everything. Therefore, you may improve processes, such as meeting management and proposal development, which might not be discussed in CMMI.

TIP

Project participation is essential to any process improvement effort.

TIP

Especially in the early phases of process improvement, the process group must visibly demonstrate the organization's investment in process improvement.

HINT

Run your process improvement like a project or series of projects. Use CMMI practices to help you plan, implement, and manage your process improvement activities.

TIP

With any type of change, an investment is required. These activities may require weeks, months, or even years. One challenge is to demonstrate improvements the organization can see quickly.

deployment planning. Appraisal plans describe the appraisal timeline and schedule, the scope of the appraisal, the resources required to perform the appraisal, the reference model against which the appraisal will be performed, and the logistics for the appraisal.

Process action plans usually result from appraisals and document how specific improvements targeting the weaknesses uncovered by an appraisal will be implemented. In cases in which it is determined that the improvement described in the process action plan should be tested on a small group before deploying it across the organization, a pilot plan is generated.

Finally, when the improvement is to be deployed, a deployment plan is used. This plan describes when and how the improvement will be deployed across the organization.

Organizational process assets are used to describe, implement, and improve the organization's processes (see the definition of "organizational process assets" in the glossary).

Related Process Areas

Refer to the Organizational Process Definition process area for more information about the organizational process assets.

Specific Goal and Practice Summary

SG 1 Determine Process Improvement Opportunities
    SP 1.1   Establish Organizational Process Needs
    SP 1.2   Appraise the Organization's Processes
    SP 1.3   Identify the Organization's Process Improvements
SG 2 Plan and Implement Process Improvements
    SP 2.1   Establish Process Action Plans
    SP 2.2   Implement Process Action Plans
SG 3 Deploy Organizational Process Assets and Incorporate Lessons Learned
    SP 3.1   Deploy Organizational Process Assets
    SP 3.2   Deploy Standard Processes
    SP 3.3   Monitor Implementation
    SP 3.4   Incorporate Process-Related Experiences into the Organizational Process Assets

Specific Practices by Goal

SG 1   *DETERMINE PROCESS IMPROVEMENT OPPORTUNITIES*

Strengths, weaknesses, and improvement opportunities for the organization's processes are identified periodically and as needed.

Strengths, weaknesses, and improvement opportunities may be determined relative to a process standard or model such as a CMMI model or International Organization for Standardization (ISO) standard. The process improvements should be selected specifically to address the organization's needs.

SP 1.1 ESTABLISH ORGANIZATIONAL PROCESS NEEDS

Establish and maintain the description of the process needs and objectives for the organization.

> Integrated processes that emphasize parallel rather than serial development are a cornerstone of IPPD implementation. The processes for developing the product and for developing product-related lifecycle processes, such as the manufacturing process and the support process processes, are integrated and conducted concurrently. Such integrated processes need to accommodate the information provided by stakeholders representing all phases of the product lifecycle from both business and technical functions. Processes for effective teamwork will also be needed.

IPPD ADDITION

> Examples of processes for effective teamwork include the following:
> • Communications
> • Collaborative decision making
> • Issue resolution
> • Team building

IPPD ADDITION

The organization's processes operate in a business context that must be understood. The organization's business objectives, needs, and constraints determine the needs and objectives for the organization's processes. Typically, the issues related to finance, technology, quality, human resources, and marketing are important process considerations.

TIP

Process improvement must relate directly to the business's objectives.

The organization's process needs and objectives cover aspects that include the following:

• Characteristics of the processes
• Process-performance objectives, such as time-to-market and delivered quality
• Process effectiveness

Typical Work Products

1. Organization's process needs and objectives

Subpractices

1. Identify the policies, standards, and business objectives that are applicable to the organization's processes.
2. Examine relevant process standards and models for best practices.
3. Determine the organization's process-performance objectives.

   Process-performance objectives may be expressed in quantitative or qualitative terms.

   Refer to the Measurement and Analysis process area for more information about establishing measurement objectives.

TIP

Examples of process-performance objectives include reducing defects identified in the field by 20% per year (quantitative) and increasing customer satisfaction (qualitative).

> Examples of process-performance objectives include the following:
> - Cycle time
> - Defect removal rates
> - Productivity

4. Define the essential characteristics of the organization's processes.

   The essential characteristics of the organization's processes are determined based on the following:

   - Processes currently being used in the organization
   - Standards imposed by the organization
   - Standards commonly imposed by customers of the organization

> Examples of process characteristics include the following:
> - Level of detail used to describe the processes
> - Process notation used
> - Granularity of the processes

5. Document the organization's process needs and objectives.
6. Revise the organization's process needs and objectives as needed.

HINT

Select the appraisal method that matches the purpose and information needed. Guide your selection by knowing the amount of information needed and the importance of its accuracy.

SP 1.2 *APPRAISE THE ORGANIZATION'S PROCESSES*

Appraise the organization's processes periodically and as needed to maintain an understanding of their strengths and weaknesses.

Process appraisals may be performed for the following reasons:

- To identify processes that should be improved
- To confirm progress and make the benefits of process improvement visible
- To satisfy the needs of a customer-supplier relationship
- To motivate and facilitate buy-in

The buy-in gained during a process appraisal can be eroded significantly if it is not followed by an appraisal-based action plan.

Typical Work Products

1. Plans for the organization's process appraisals
2. Appraisal findings that address strengths and weaknesses of the organization's processes
3. Improvement recommendations for the organization's processes

Subpractices

1. Obtain sponsorship of the process appraisal from senior management.

   Senior management sponsorship includes the commitment to have the organization's managers and staff participate in the process appraisal and to provide the resources and funding to analyze and communicate the findings of the appraisal.

   TIP

   The commitment of resources to the appraisal must be visible throughout the organization.

2. Define the scope of the process appraisal.

   Process appraisals may be performed on the entire organization or may be performed on a smaller part of an organization such as a single project or business area.

   The scope of the process appraisal addresses the following:

   - Definition of the organization (e.g., sites or business areas) that will be covered by the appraisal
   - Identification of the project and support functions that will represent the organization in the appraisal
   - Processes that will be appraised

3. Determine the method and criteria for process appraisal.

   Process appraisals can occur in many forms. Process appraisals should address the needs and objectives of the organization, which may change over time. For example, the appraisal may be based on a process model, such as a CMMI model, or on a national or international standard, such as ISO 9001 [ISO 2000]. The appraisals may also be based on a benchmark comparison with other organizations. The appraisal method may assume a variety of characteristics in terms of time and effort expended, makeup of the appraisal team, and the method and depth of investigation.

   TIP

   Examples of appraisal methods include SCAMPI A, B, and C, as well as gap analysis and surveys.

4. Plan, schedule, and prepare for the process appraisal.

5. Conduct the process appraisal.
6. Document and deliver the appraisal's activities and findings.

SP 1.3 IDENTIFY THE ORGANIZATION'S PROCESS IMPROVEMENTS

Identify improvements to the organization's processes and process assets.

Typical Work Products

1. Analysis of candidate process improvements
2. Identification of improvements for the organization's processes

Subpractices

1. Determine candidate process improvements.

   Candidate process improvements are typically determined by doing the following:
   - Measure the processes and analyze the measurement results
   - Review the processes for effectiveness and suitability
   - Review the lessons learned from tailoring the organization's set of standard processes
   - Review the lessons learned from implementing the processes
   - Review process improvement proposals submitted by the organization's managers, staff, and other relevant stakeholders
   - Solicit inputs on process improvements from senior management and leaders in the organization
   - Examine the results of process appraisals and other process-related reviews
   - Review results of other organizational improvement initiatives

2. Prioritize the candidate process improvements.

   Criteria for prioritization are as follows:
   - Consider the estimated cost and effort to implement the process improvements
   - Appraise the expected improvement against the organization's improvement objectives and priorities
   - Determine the potential barriers to the process improvements and develop strategies for overcoming these barriers

> **HINT**
>
> In the early stages of process improvement, there are more candidate improvements than resources to address them. Prioritize these opportunities to be most effective.

> **HINT**
>
> Choose improvements that are visible to the organization, have a defined scope, and can be addressed successfully by available resources. If you try to do too much too quickly, it may result in failure and cause the improvement program to be questioned.

Examples of techniques to help determine and prioritize the possible improvements to be implemented include the following:
- A gap analysis that compares current conditions in the organization with optimal conditions
- Force-field analysis of potential improvements to identify potential barriers and strategies for overcoming those barriers
- Cause-and-effect analyses to provide information on the potential effects of different improvements that can then be compared

3. Identify and document the process improvements that will be implemented.

4. Revise the list of planned process improvements to keep it current.

SG 2 PLAN AND IMPLEMENT PROCESS IMPROVEMENTS

Process actions that address improvements to the organization's processes and process assets are planned and implemented.

Successful implementation of improvements requires participation in process action planning and implementation by process owners, those performing the process, and support organizations.

SP 2.1 ESTABLISH PROCESS ACTION PLANS

Establish and maintain process action plans to address improvements to the organization's processes and process assets.

Establishing and maintaining process action plans typically involves the following roles:

- Management steering committees to set strategies and oversee process improvement activities
- Process group staff to facilitate and manage process improvement activities
- Process action teams to define and implement process actions
- Process owners to manage deployment
- Practitioners to perform the process

This involvement helps to obtain buy-in on the process improvements and increases the likelihood of effective deployment.

Process action plans are detailed implementation plans. These plans differ from the organization's process improvement plan in that they are plans targeting specific improvements that have been defined to address weaknesses usually uncovered by appraisals.

Typical Work Products

1. Organization's approved process action plans

Subpractices

1. Identify strategies, approaches, and actions to address the identified process improvements.

   New, unproven, and major changes are piloted before they are incorporated into normal use.

TIP

Organizational process assets are those created by the activities in OPD.

TIP

Most of the organization should be involved in these activities.

TIP

Depending on the magnitude of the improvement, a process action plan can look similar to a project plan. If the improvement is small, the plan can look similar to a plan for a routine maintenance activity.

OPF

2. Establish process action teams to implement the actions.

The teams and people performing the process improvement actions are called "process action teams." Process action teams typically include process owners and those who perform the process.

3. Document process action plans.

Process action plans typically cover the following:

- Process improvement infrastructure
- Process improvement objectives
- Process improvements that will be addressed
- Procedures for planning and tracking process actions
- Strategies for piloting and implementing the process actions
- Responsibility and authority for implementing the process actions
- Resources, schedules, and assignments for implementing the process actions
- Methods for determining the effectiveness of the process actions
- Risks associated with process action plans

4. Review and negotiate process action plans with relevant stakeholders.

5. Review process action plans as necessary.

SP 2.2 IMPLEMENT PROCESS ACTION PLANS

Implement process action plans.

Typical Work Products

1. Commitments among the various process action teams
2. Status and results of implementing process action plans
3. Plans for pilots

Subpractices

1. Make process action plans readily available to relevant stakeholders.
2. Negotiate and document commitments among the process action teams and revise their process action plans as necessary.
3. Track progress and commitments against process action plans.
4. Conduct joint reviews with the process action teams and relevant stakeholders to monitor the progress and results of the process actions.
5. Plan pilots needed to test selected process improvements.
6. Review the activities and work products of process action teams.
7. Identify, document, and track to closure issues in implementing process action plans.
8. Ensure that the results of implementing process action plans satisfy the organization's process improvement objectives.

TIP

Depending on the size of the organization and the extent of the change, the implementation activity can take days, weeks, months, or even years.

SG 3 DEPLOY ORGANIZATIONAL PROCESS ASSETS AND INCORPORATE LESSONS LEARNED

The organizational process assets are deployed across the organization and process-related experiences are incorporated into the organizational process assets.

The specific practices within this specific goal describe ongoing activities. New opportunities to benefit from the organizational process assets and changes to them may arise throughout the life of each project. Deployment of the standard processes and other organizational process assets must be continually supported within the organization, particularly for new projects at startup.

SP 3.1 DEPLOY ORGANIZATIONAL PROCESS ASSETS

Deploy organizational process assets across the organization.

Deploying organizational process assets or changes to organizational process assets should be performed in an orderly manner. Some organizational process assets or changes to organizational process assets may not be appropriate for use in some parts of the organization (because of customer requirements or the current lifecycle phase being implemented, for example). It is therefore important that those that are or will be executing the process, as well as other organization functions (such as training and quality assurance), be involved in the deployment as necessary.

Refer to the Organizational Process Definition process area for more information about how the deployment of organizational process assets is supported and enabled by the organization's process asset library.

> **HINT**
> Be sure to think about retiring the assets and work products that the change replaces.

> OPF

Typical Work Products

1. Plans for deploying organizational process assets and changes to them across the organization
2. Training materials for deploying organizational process assets and changes to them
3. Documentation of changes to organizational process assets
4. Support materials for deploying organizational process assets and changes to them

Subpractices

1. Deploy organizational process assets across the organization.

   Typical activities performed as a part of this deployment include the following:

- Identifying the organizational process assets that should be adopted by those who perform the process
- Determining how the organizational process assets are made available (e.g., via Web site)
- Identifying how changes to the organizational process assets are communicated
- Identifying the resources (e.g., methods and tools) needed to support the use of the organizational process assets
- Planning the deployment
- Assisting those who use the organizational process assets
- Ensuring that training is available for those who use the organizational process assets

Refer to the Organizational Training process area for more information about coordination of training.

2. Document the changes to the organizational process assets.

   Documenting changes to the organizational process assets serves two main purposes:

   - To enable communication of the changes
   - To understand the relationship of changes in the organizational process assets to changes in process performance and results

3. Deploy the changes that were made to the organizational process assets across the organization.

   Typical activities performed as a part of deploying changes include the following:

   - Determining which changes are appropriate for those who perform the process
   - Planning the deployment
   - Arranging for the associated support needed to successfully transition the changes

4. Provide guidance and consultation on the use of the organizational process assets.

SP 3.2 DEPLOY STANDARD PROCESSES

Deploy the organization's set of standard processes to projects at their startup and deploy changes to them as appropriate throughout the life of each project.

It is important that new projects use proven and effective processes to perform critical early activities (e.g., project planning, receiving requirements, and obtaining resources).

Projects should also periodically update their defined processes to incorporate the latest changes made to the organization's set of standard processes when it will benefit them. This periodic updating helps to ensure that all project activities derive the full benefit of what other projects have learned.

Refer to the Organizational Process Definition process area for more information about the organization's set of standard processes and tailoring guidelines.

Typical Work Products

1. Organization's list of projects and status of process deployment on each project (i.e., existing and planned projects)
2. Guidelines for deploying the organization's set of standard processes on new projects
3. Records of tailoring the organization's set of standard processes and implementing them on identified projects

Subpractices

1. Identify projects within the organization that are starting up.
2. Identify active projects that would benefit from implementing the organization's current set of standard processes.
3. Establish plans to implement the organization's current set of standard processes on the identified projects.
4. Assist projects in tailoring the organization's set of standard processes to meet project needs.

   Refer to the Integrated Project Management process area for more information about tailoring the organization's set of standard processes to meet the unique needs and objectives of the project.

5. Maintain records of tailoring and implementing processes on the identified projects.
6. Ensure that the defined processes resulting from process tailoring are incorporated into the plans for process-compliance evaluations.

   Process-compliance evaluations address objective evaluations of project activities against the project's defined processes.

7. As the organization's set of standard processes are updated, identify which projects should implement the changes.

SP 3.3 MONITOR IMPLEMENTATION

Monitor the implementation of the organization's set of standard processes and use of process assets on all projects.

By monitoring implementation, the organization ensures that the organization's set of standard processes and other process assets are appropriately deployed to all projects. Monitoring implementation also helps the organization develop an understanding of the organizational process assets being used and where they are used within the organization. Monitoring also helps to establish a broader context for interpreting and using process and product measures, lessons learned, and improvement information obtained from projects.

Typical Work Products

1. Results of monitoring process implementation on projects
2. Status and results of process-compliance evaluations
3. Results of reviewing selected process artifacts created as part of process tailoring and implementation

Subpractices

1. Monitor projects for their use of the organization's process assets and changes to them.
2. Review selected process artifacts created during the life of each project.

   Reviewing selected process artifacts created during the life of a project ensures that all projects are making appropriate use of the organization's set of standard processes.

3. Review the results of process-compliance evaluations to determine how well the organization's set of standard processes has been deployed.

   Refer to the Process and Product Quality Assurance process area for more information about objectively evaluating processes against applicable process descriptions, standards, and procedures.

4. Identify, document, and track to closure issues related to implementing the organization's set of standard processes.

SP 3.4 *INCORPORATE PROCESS-RELATED EXPERIENCES INTO THE ORGANIZATIONAL PROCESS ASSETS*

TIP

This practice relates to practices in IPM. IPM, OPF, and OPD are tightly related. OPD defines the organizational assets. OPF manages them, deploys them across the organization, and collects feedback. IPM uses the assets on the project and provides feedback to the organization.

Incorporate process-related work products, measures, and improvement information derived from planning and performing the process into the organizational process assets.

Typical Work Products

1. Process improvement proposals
2. Process lessons learned
3. Measurements on the organizational process assets
4. Improvement recommendations for the organizational process assets
5. Records of the organization's process improvement activities
6. Information on the organizational process assets and improvements to them

Subpractices

1. Conduct periodic reviews of the effectiveness and suitability of the organization's set of standard processes and related organizational process assets relative to the organization's business objectives.

2. Obtain feedback about the use of the organizational process assets.

3. Derive lessons learned from defining, piloting, implementing, and deploying the organizational process assets.

TIP

Some feedback may be collected as part of QA activities.

4. Make available lessons learned to the people in the organization as appropriate.

   Actions may have to be taken to ensure that lessons learned are used appropriately.

TIP

Lessons learned are usually made available through the library established in OPD.

> Examples of inappropriate use of lessons learned include the following:
> • Evaluating the performance of people
> • Judging process performance or results

> Examples of ways to prevent inappropriate use of lessons learned include the following:
> • Controlling access to the lessons learned
> • Educating people about the appropriate use of lessons learned

5. Analyze the organization's common set of measures.

   Refer to the Measurement and Analysis process area for more information about analyzing measures.

   Refer to the Organizational Process Definition process area for more information about establishing an organizational measurement repository, including common measures.

TIP

Common sets of measures are usually kept in the organization's measurement repository, established in OPD.

6. Appraise the processes, methods, and tools in use in the organization and develop recommendations for improving the organizational process assets.

   This appraisal typically includes the following:
   • Determining which of the processes, methods, and tools are of potential use to other parts of the organization
   • Appraising the quality and effectiveness of the organizational process assets
   • Identifying candidate improvements to the organizational process assets
   • Determining compliance with the organization's set of standard processes and tailoring guidelines

TIP

We use the word *appraise* here more in line with Webster's definition of the word, rather than the appraisal term we use in CMMI.

OPF

7. Make the best of the organization's processes, methods, and tools available to the people in the organization as appropriate.

8. Manage process improvement proposals.

> Process improvement proposals can address both process and technology improvements.

> The activities for managing process improvement proposals typically include the following:
> - Soliciting process improvement proposals
> - Collecting process improvement proposals
> - Reviewing process improvement proposals
> - Selecting the process improvement proposals that will be implemented
> - Tracking the implementation of process improvement proposals

> Process improvement proposals are documented as process change requests or problem reports, as appropriate.

> Some process improvement proposals may be incorporated into the organization's process action plans.

9. Establish and maintain records of the organization's process improvement activities.

Generic Practices by Goal

GG 1 ACHIEVE SPECIFIC GOALS

The process supports and enables achievement of the specific goals of the process area by transforming identifiable input work products to produce identifiable output work products.

GP 1.1 PERFORM SPECIFIC PRACTICES

Perform the specific practices of the organizational process focus process to develop work products and provide services to achieve the specific goals of the process area.

GG 2 INSTITUTIONALIZE A MANAGED PROCESS

The process is institutionalized as a managed process.

GG 3 INSTITUTIONALIZE A DEFINED PROCESS

The process is institutionalized as a defined process.

> This generic goal's appearance here reflects its location in the staged representation.

CONTINUOUS ONLY

STAGED ONLY

GP 2.1 *ESTABLISH AN ORGANIZATIONAL POLICY*

Establish and maintain an organizational policy for planning and performing the organizational process focus process.

Elaboration:

This policy establishes organizational expectations for determining process improvement opportunities for the processes being used and for planning, implementing, and deploying process improvements across the organization.

GP 2.2 *PLAN THE PROCESS*

Establish and maintain the plan for performing the organizational process focus process.

Elaboration:

This plan for performing the organizational process focus process, which is often called "the process improvement plan," differs from the process action plans described in specific practices in this process area. The plan called for in this generic practice addresses the comprehensive planning for all of the specific practices in this process area, from the establishment of organizational process needs all the way through to the incorporation of process-related experiences into the organizational process assets.

GP 2.3 *PROVIDE RESOURCES*

Provide adequate resources for performing the organizational process focus process, developing the work products, and providing the services of the process.

Elaboration:

Examples of resources provided include the following tools:
- Database management systems
- Process improvement tools
- Web page builders and browsers
- Groupware
- Quality-improvement tools (e.g., cause-and-effect diagrams, affinity diagrams, and Pareto charts)

GP 2.4 ASSIGN RESPONSIBILITY

Assign responsibility and authority for performing the process, developing the work products, and providing the services of the organizational process focus process.

Elaboration:

Two groups are typically established and assigned responsibility for process improvement: (1) a management steering committee for process improvement to provide senior management sponsorship, and (2) a process group to facilitate and manage the process improvement activities.

GP 2.5 TRAIN PEOPLE

Train the people performing or supporting the organizational process focus process as needed.

Elaboration:

> Examples of training topics include the following:
> • CMMI and other process improvement reference models
> • Planning and managing process improvement
> • Tools, methods, and analysis techniques
> • Process modeling
> • Facilitation techniques
> • Change management

GP 2.6 MANAGE CONFIGURATIONS

Place designated work products of the organizational process focus process under appropriate levels of control.

Elaboration:

> Examples of work products placed under control include the following:
> • Process improvement proposals
> • Organization's approved process action plans
> • Training materials for deploying organizational process assets
> • Guidelines for deploying the organization's set of standard processes on new projects
> • Plans for the organization's process appraisals

GP 2.7 *IDENTIFY AND INVOLVE RELEVANT STAKEHOLDERS*

Identify and involve the relevant stakeholders of the organizational process focus process as planned.

Elaboration:

Examples of activities for stakeholder involvement include the following:
- Coordinating and collaborating on process improvement activities with process owners, those who are or will be performing the process, and support organizations (e.g., training staff and quality assurance representatives)
- Establishing the organizational process needs and objectives
- Appraising the organization's processes
- Implementing process action plans
- Coordinating and collaborating on the execution of pilots to test selected improvements
- Deploying organizational process assets and changes to organizational process assets
- Communicating the plans, status, activities, and results related to planning, implementing, and deploying process improvements

GP 2.8 *MONITOR AND CONTROL THE PROCESS*

Monitor and control the organizational process focus process against the plan for performing the process and take appropriate corrective action.

Elaboration:

Examples of measures and work products used in monitoring and controlling include the following:
- Number of process improvement proposals submitted, accepted, or implemented
- CMMI maturity level or capability level
- Schedule for deployment of an organizational process asset
- Percentage of projects using the current organization's set of standard processes (or tailored version of same)
- Issue trends associated with implementing the organization's set of standard processes (i.e., number of issues identified and number closed)

OPF

GP 2.9 *Objectively Evaluate Adherence*

Objectively evaluate adherence of the organizational process focus process against its process description, standards, and procedures, and address non-compliance.

Elaboration:

Examples of activities reviewed include the following:
- Determining process improvement opportunities
- Planning and coordinating process improvement activities
- Deploying the organization's set of standard processes on projects at their startup

---

Examples of work products reviewed include the following:
- Process improvement plans
- Process action plans
- Process deployment plans
- Plans for the organization's process appraisals

GP 2.10 *Review Status with Higher Level Management*

Review the activities, status, and results of the organizational process focus process with higher level management and resolve issues.

Elaboration:

These reviews are typically in the form of a briefing presented to the management steering committee by the process group and the process action teams.

Examples of presentation topics include the following:
- Status of improvements being developed by process action teams
- Results of pilots
- Results of deployments
- Schedule status for achieving significant milestones (e.g., readiness for an appraisal, or progress toward achieving a targeted organizational maturity level or capability level profile)

GG 3 *INSTITUTIONALIZE A DEFINED PROCESS*

CONT. ONLY

The process is institutionalized as a defined process.

This generic goal's appearance here reflects its location in the continuous representation.

GP 3.1 *ESTABLISH A DEFINED PROCESS*

Establish and maintain the description of a defined organizational process focus process.

GP 3.2 *COLLECT IMPROVEMENT INFORMATION*

Collect work products, measures, measurement results, and improvement information derived from planning and performing the organizational process focus process to support the future use and improvement of the organization's processes and process assets.

Elaboration:

> Examples of work products, measures, measurement results, and improvement information include the following:
> - Criteria used for prioritizing candidate process improvements
> - Appraisal findings that address strengths and weaknesses of the organization's processes
> - Status of improvement activities against the schedule
> - Records of tailoring the organization's set of standard processes and implementing them on identified projects

GG 4 *INSTITUTIONALIZE A QUANTITATIVELY MANAGED PROCESS*

The process is institutionalized as a quantitatively managed process.

GP 4.1 *ESTABLISH QUANTITATIVE OBJECTIVES FOR THE PROCESS*

Establish and maintain quantitative objectives for the organizational process focus process, which address quality and process performance, based on customer needs and business objectives.

GP 4.2 *STABILIZE SUBPROCESS PERFORMANCE*

Stabilize the performance of one or more subprocesses to determine the ability of the organizational process focus process to achieve the established quantitative quality and process-performance objectives.

CONTINUOUS ONLY

OPF

GG 5 *Institutionalize an Optimizing Process*

The process is institutionalized as an optimizing process.

GP 5.1 *Ensure Continuous Process Improvement*

Ensure continuous improvement of the organizational process focus process in fulfilling the relevant business objectives of the organization.

GP 5.2 *Correct Root Causes of Problems*

Identify and correct the root causes of defects and other problems in the organizational process focus process.

ORGANIZATIONAL PROCESS PERFORMANCE
A Process Management Process Area at Maturity Level 4

Purpose

The purpose of Organizational Process Performance (OPP) is to establish and maintain a quantitative understanding of the performance of the organization's set of standard processes in support of quality and process-performance objectives, and to provide the process-performance data, baselines, and models to quantitatively manage the organization's projects.

Introductory Notes

Process performance is a measure of the actual results achieved by following a process. Process performance is characterized by process measures (e.g., effort, cycle time, and defect removal effectiveness) and product measures (e.g., reliability, defect density, capacity, response time, and cost).

The common measures for the organization are composed of process and product measures that can be used to summarize the actual performance of processes in individual projects in the organization. The organizational data for these measures are analyzed to establish a distribution and range of results, which characterize the expected performance of the process when used on any individual project in the organization.

In this process area, the phrase "quality and process-performance objectives" covers objectives and requirements for product quality, service quality, and process performance. As indicated above, the term "process performance" includes quality; however, to emphasize the importance of quality, the phrase "quality and process-performance objectives" is used rather than just "process-performance objectives."

The expected process performance can be used in establishing the project's quality and process-performance objectives and can be used as a baseline against which actual project performance can be compared.

TIP

QPM and OPP are tightly coupled process areas. An organization seeking to implement one of these should implement both of them.

X-REF

The concept of "common measures" is further described in OPD SP 1.4.

TIP

A subprocess measure's "central tendency and spread," normalized appropriately (e.g., for work product size), can serve as its process-performance baseline (PPB). Such a PPB can be displayed different ways, such as by a control chart, box plot, or histogram. OPP practices assume, at a minimum, that PPBs are established for selected subprocess measures, but the organization and projects may benefit from establishing PPBs for other measures too.

TIP

This paragraph describes in a simplified way how the organization's process-performance baselines (referred to here as "expected process performance") support quantitative project management (QPM) that, in turn, provide the data used to refine these baselines.

OPP

This information is used to quantitatively manage the project. Each quantitatively managed project, in turn, provides actual performance results that become a part of the baseline data for the organizational process assets.

The associated process-performance models are used to represent past and current process performance and to predict future results of the process. For example, the latent defects in the delivered product can be predicted using measurements of defects identified during product verification activities.

When the organization has measures, data, and analytical techniques for critical process, product, and service characteristics, it is able to do the following:

X-REF

See the Brad Clark and Dave Zubrow presentation, "How Good is the Software: A Review of Defect Prediction Techniques," from the SEPG 2001 conference (www.sei.cmu.edu/sema/pdf /defect-prediction-tech-niques.pdf). Some of these techniques can be the basis for process-performance models.

- Determine whether processes are behaving consistently or have stable trends (i.e., are predictable)
- Identify processes where the performance is within natural bounds that are consistent across process implementation teams
- Establish criteria for identifying whether a process or subprocess should be statistically managed, and determine pertinent measures and analytical techniques to be used in such management
- Identify processes that show unusual (e.g., sporadic or unpredictable) behavior
- Identify any aspects of the processes that can be improved in the organization's set of standard processes
- Identify the implementation of a process which performs best

Related Process Areas

TIP

Much of what is described in OPP (and in QPM) utilizes the practices described in MA. Mastering many of the practices in MA is a prerequisite to implementing OPP and QPM.

Refer to the Quantitative Project Management process area for more information about the use of process-performance baselines and models.

Refer to the Measurement and Analysis process area for more information about specifying measures and collecting and analyzing data.

Specific Goal and Practice Summary

SG 1 Establish Performance Baselines and Models
  SP 1.1   Select Processes
  SP 1.2   Establish Process-Performance Measures
  SP 1.3   Establish Quality and Process-Performance Objectives
  SP 1.4   Establish Process-Performance Baselines
  SP 1.5   Establish Process-Performance Models

Specific Practices by Goal

SG 1   ESTABLISH PERFORMANCE BASELINES AND MODELS

X-REF

The 2001 NDIA presentation by Doug Smith and Craig Hollenbach (www.dtic.mil/ndia/2001cmmi/hollenbach.pdf) provides examples of process-performance baselines and models.

Baselines and models, which characterize the expected process performance of the organization's set of standard processes, are established and maintained.

Prior to establishing process-performance baselines and models, it is necessary to determine which processes are suitable to be measured (the Select Processes specific practice), which measures are useful for determining process performance (the Establish Process-Performance Measures specific practice), and the quality and process-performance objectives for those processes (the Establish Quality and Process-Performance Objectives specific practice). These specific practices are often interrelated and may need to be performed concurrently to select the appropriate processes, measures, and quality and process-performance objectives. Often, the selection of one process, measure, or objective will constrain the selection of the others. For example, if a certain process is selected, the measures and objectives for that process may be constrained by the process itself.

SP 1.1   SELECT PROCESSES

Select the processes or subprocesses in the organization's set of standard processes that are to be included in the organization's process-performance analyses.

Refer to the Organizational Process Definition process area for more information about the structure of the organizational process assets.

The organization's set of standard processes consists of a set of standard processes that, in turn, are composed of subprocesses.

Typically, it will not be possible, useful, or economically justifiable to apply statistical management techniques to all processes or subprocesses of the organization's set of standard processes. Selection of the processes and/or subprocesses is based on the needs and objectives of both the organization and projects.

HINT

Select process elements, not processes composed of multiple elements. Multiple sources of variation hidden in a process are not easily analyzed. What might appear to be a stable process may in fact be a collection of unstable process elements; leaving you unable to predict future behavior or find opportunities for improvement.

TIP

These examples of criteria used to select subprocesses are fairly sophisticated and are typical of organizations almost at ML4-5. At lower MLs, only a few of the criteria may be practical. The criteria used will grow in sophistication and the selection evolves as more experience and data are gained.

> Examples of criteria which may be used for the selection of a process or subprocess for organizational analysis include the following:
> - The relationship of the subprocess to key business objectives
> - Current availability of valid historical data relevant to the subprocess
> - The current degree of variability of this data
> - Subprocess stability (e.g. stable performance in comparable instances)
> - The availability of corporate or commercial information that can be used to build predictive models

OPP

The existence of project data that indicates the process or subprocess has been or can be stabilized is a useful criterion for selection of a process or subprocess.

Typical Work Products

1. List of processes or subprocesses identified for process-performance analyses

SP 1.2 ESTABLISH PROCESS-PERFORMANCE MEASURES

Establish and maintain definitions of the measures that are to be included in the organization's process-performance analyses.

Refer to the Measurement and Analysis process area for more information about selecting measures.

Typical Work Products

1. Definitions for the selected measures of process performance

Subpractices

1. Determine which of the organization's business objectives for quality and process performance need to be addressed by the measures.
2. Select measures that provide appropriate insight into the organization's quality and process performance.

    The Goal Question Metric paradigm is an approach that can be used to select measures that provide insight into the organization's business objectives.

Examples of criteria used to select measures include the following:
- Relationship of the measures to the organization's business objectives
- Coverage that the measures provide over the entire life of the product or service
- Visibility that the measures provide into the process performance
- Availability of the measures
- Extent to which the measures are objective
- Frequency at which the observations of the measure can be collected
- Extent to which the measures are controllable by changes to the process or subprocess
- Extent to which the measures represent the users' view of effective process performance

---

3. Incorporate the selected measures into the organization's set of common measures.

HINT

Because not all processes contribute equally to a business objective, and all such analyses consume time, effort, and money, you should start with a small selection, and as you learn more, modify and expand the selection accordingly.

HINT

Analyze business objectives to identify process measures that give insight into quality and process performance.

X-REF

Goal Question Metric (GQM) is a well-known approach to deriving measures that provide insight into issues of interest. See www.cs.umd.edu/~mvz/handouts/gqm.pdf. The SEI's variant of GQM is called the Goal Question Indicator Metric (GQIM). See www.sei.cmu.edu/products/courses/implement.goal-driven.sw.meas.html.

HINT

To begin systematic collection of these measures from new projects, incorporate them into the organization's set of common measures (OPD SP 1.4).

Refer to the Organizational Process Definition process area for more information about establishing organizational process assets.

4. Revise the set of measures as necessary.

SP 1.3 ESTABLISH QUALITY AND PROCESS-PERFORMANCE OBJECTIVES

Establish and maintain quantitative objectives for quality and process performance for the organization.

The organization's quality and process-performance objectives should have the following attributes:

- Based on the organization's business objectives
- Based on the past performance of projects
- Defined to gauge process performance in areas such as product quality, productivity, cycle time, or response time
- Constrained by the inherent variability or natural bounds of the selected process or subprocess

> **TIP**
>
> Objectives based on the organization's business objectives may set the bar too high to motivate projects to identify process improvements. From a practical standpoint, what does the performance data show about how well a project can do relative to a particular process? In summary, there is need for "balance" between "desires" and "reality."

Typical Work Products

1. Organization's quality and process-performance objectives

Subpractices

1. Review the organization's business objectives related to quality and process performance.

> **TIP**
>
> OPP *aligns* the organization's process-performance analyses and management of projects with business objectives.

Examples of business objectives include the following:
- Achieve a development cycle of a specified duration for a specified release of a product
- Achieve an average response time less than a specified duration for a specified version of a service
- Deliver functionality of the product to a target percentage of estimated cost
- Decrease the cost of maintenance of the products by a specified percent

---

2. Define the organization's quantitative objectives for quality and process performance.

Objectives may be established for process or subprocess measurements (e.g., effort, cycle time, and defect removal effectiveness) as well as for product measurements (e.g., reliability and defect density) and service measurements (e.g., capacity and response times) where appropriate.

> **TIP**
>
> The quantitative objectives for quality and process performance should be related to the organization's business objectives.

OPP

> Examples of quality and process-performance objectives include the following:
> • Achieve a specified productivity
> • Deliver work products with no more than a specified number of latent defects
> • Shorten time to delivery to a specified percentage of the process-performance baseline
> • Reduce the total lifecycle cost of new and existing products by a percentage
> • Deliver a percentage of the specified product functionality

3. Define the priorities of the organization's objectives for quality and process performance.
4. Review, negotiate, and obtain commitment for the organization's quality and process-performance objectives and their priorities from the relevant stakeholders.
5. Revise the organization's quantitative objectives for quality and process performance as necessary.

> Examples of when the organization's quantitative objectives for quality and process performance may need to be revised include the following:
> • When the organization's business objectives change
> • When the organization's processes change
> • When actual quality and process performance differs significantly from the objectives

SP 1.4 ESTABLISH PROCESS-PERFORMANCE BASELINES

Establish and maintain the organization's process-performance baselines.

The organization's process-performance baselines are a measurement of performance for the organization's set of standard processes at various levels of detail, as appropriate. The processes include the following:

- Sequence of connected processes
- Processes that cover the entire life of the project
- Processes for developing individual work products

There may be several process-performance baselines to characterize performance for subgroups of the organization.

TIP

Commitment to the organization's quality and process-performance objectives means senior management supports them by periodically reviewing how well projects are performing relative to them. Project management and senior technical staff incorporate them into their projects and strive hard to achieve them.

TIP

The term *process-performance baseline* is used instead of *process capability baseline* because *process capability* assumes the events are generated from the same process (and people). This may be a correct assumption in the case of a single project (*or team*), but not for the whole organization.

> Examples of criteria used to categorize subgroups include the following:
> - Product line
> - Line of business
> - Application domain
> - Complexity
> - Team size
> - Work product size
> - Process elements from the organization's set of standard processes

Allowable tailoring of the organization's set of standard processes may significantly affect the comparability of the data for inclusion in process-performance baselines. The effects of tailoring should be considered in establishing baselines. Depending on the tailoring allowed, separate performance baselines may exist for each type of tailoring.

Refer to the Quantitative Project Management process area for more information about the use of process-performance baselines.

Typical Work Products

1. Baseline data on the organization's process performance

Subpractices

1. Collect measurements from the organization's projects.

   The process or subprocess in use when the measurement was taken is recorded to enable appropriate use later.

   Refer to the Measurement and Analysis process area for information about collecting and analyzing data.

2. Establish and maintain the organization's process-performance baselines from the collected measurements and analyses.

   Refer to the Measurement and Analysis process area for information about establishing objectives for measurement and analysis, specifying the measures and analyses to be performed, obtaining and analyzing measures, and reporting results.

   Process-performance baselines are derived by analyzing the collected measures to establish a distribution and range of results that characterize the expected performance for selected processes or subprocesses when used on any individual project in the organization.

   The measurements from stable subprocesses from projects should be used; other data may not be reliable.

3. Review and get agreement with relevant stakeholders about the organization's process-performance baselines.

HINT

Record sufficient contextual information with a measurement to enable identification of the process-performance baseline it should be included in, when it was generated, and by whom.

TIP

Unless the process is stable, process-performance baselines will actually be a mixture of measurements taken from *different* processes. This severely limits their usefulness to projects (e.g., trial natural bounds are likely to be far apart).

HINT

Investigate subgrouping when incorporating data from multiple projects (and teams) into the same process-performance baseline. Even if the process is stable in individual projects, it still might be executed sufficiently differently across projects to make establishment of a single baseline inappropriate.

OPP

4. Make the organization's process-performance information available across the organization in the organization's measurement repository.

> The organization's process-performance baselines are used by the projects to estimate the natural bounds for process performance.

> *Refer to the Organizational Process Definition process area for more information about establishing the organization's measurement repository.*

5. Compare the organization's process-performance baselines to the associated objectives.

6. Revise the organization's process-performance baselines as necessary.

TIP

OPP does not directly say what to do with the results of the comparison of the baseline to the objectives. Ideally, the objectives are attainable, but a stretch beyond the baseline. This comparison establishes feasible objectives. If the objectives are infeasible, revise them using CAR or OID to search for ways to improve performance.

HINT

Establish process-performance models that give insight at different points in a project (e.g., at the end of each phase) to track progress.

> Examples of when the organization's process-performance baselines may need to be revised include the following:
> • When the processes change
> • When the organization's results change
> • When the organization's needs change

SP 1.5 ESTABLISH PROCESS-PERFORMANCE MODELS

Establish and maintain the process-performance models for the organization's set of standard processes.

Process-performance models are used to estimate or predict the value of a process-performance measure from the values of other process, product, and service measurements. These process-performance models typically use process and product measurements collected throughout the life of the project to estimate progress toward achieving objectives that cannot be measured until later in the project's life.

The process-performance models are used as follows:

• The organization uses them for estimating, analyzing, and predicting the process performance associated with the processes in the organization's set of standard processes.

• The organization uses them to assess the (potential) return on investment for process improvement activities.

• Projects use them for estimating, analyzing, and predicting the process performance for their defined processes.

• Projects use them for selecting processes or subprocesses for use.

These measures and models are defined to provide insight into, and to provide the ability to predict, critical process and product characteristics that are relevant to business value.

Examples of areas of concern to projects in which models may be useful include the following:
- Schedule and cost
- Reliability
- Defect identification and removal rates
- Defect removal effectiveness
- Latent defect estimation
- Response time
- Project progress
- Combinations of these areas

Examples of process-performance models include the following:
- System dynamics models
- Reliability growth models
- Complexity models

Refer to the Quantitative Project Management process area for more information about the use of process-performance models.

Typical Work Products

1. Process-performance models

Subpractices

1. Establish the process-performance models based on the organization's set of standard processes and the organization's process-performance baselines.
2. Calibrate the process-performance models based on the organization's past results and current needs.
3. Review the process-performance models and get agreement with relevant stakeholders.
4. Support the projects' use of the process-performance models.
5. Revise the process-performance models as necessary.

Examples of when the process-performance models may need to be revised include the following:
- When the processes change
- When the organization's results change
- When the organization's needs change

X-REF

A paper by Tobias Häberlein, located at http://prosim.pdx.edu/prosim2003/paper/prosim03_haeberlein.pdf, concerns the application of system dynamics to acquisition, but much of what is said has broader applicability. (System dynamics models were first used to model software.) The paper also has a good collection of references.

TIP

A review of the organization's set of standard processes helps to identify process and product characteristics that might assist you in constructing a process-performance model. Process-performance baselines provide a primary source of the information needed to quantify and calibrate the model.

OPP

HINT

Meet with relevant stakeholders to discuss the process-performance models (e.g., their usefulness and limitations) and the support required to make effective use of such models on projects.

X-REF

To use process-performance models effectively, project staff and management may need significant support. The subpractices of OID SP 2.2 provide some example forms of support.

Generic Practices by Goal

GG 1 ACHIEVE SPECIFIC GOALS

The process supports and enables achievement of the specific goals of the process area by transforming identifiable input work products to produce identifiable output work products.

GP 1.1 PERFORM SPECIFIC PRACTICES

Perform the specific practices of the organizational process-performance process to develop work products and provide services to achieve the specific goals of the process area.

GG 2 INSTITUTIONALIZE A MANAGED PROCESS

The process is institutionalized as a managed process.

GG 3 INSTITUTIONALIZE A DEFINED PROCESS

The process is institutionalized as a defined process.

This generic goal's appearance here reflects its location in the staged representation.

CONTINUOUS ONLY

STAGED ONLY

GP 2.1 ESTABLISH AN ORGANIZATIONAL POLICY

Establish and maintain an organizational policy for planning and performing the organizational process-performance process.

Elaboration:

This policy establishes organizational expectations for establishing and maintaining process-performance baselines for the organization's set of standard processes.

GP 2.2 PLAN THE PROCESS

Establish and maintain the plan for performing the organizational process-performance process.

Elaboration:

This plan for performing the organizational process-performance process can be included in (or referenced by) the organization's process improvement plan, which is described in the Organizational Process Focus process area, or it may be documented in a separate plan that describes only the plan for the organizational process performance process.

GP 2.3 *PROVIDE RESOURCES*

Provide adequate resources for performing the organizational process per-formance process, developing the work products, and providing the services of the process.

Elaboration:

Special expertise in statistics and statistical process control may be needed to establish the process-performance baselines for the organization's set of standard processes.

Examples of other resources provided include the following tools:
- Database management systems
- System dynamics model
- Process modeling tools
- Statistical analysis packages
- Problem-tracking packages

GP 2.4 *ASSIGN RESPONSIBILITY*

Assign responsibility and authority for performing the process, developing the work products, and providing the services of the organizational process-per-formance process.

GP 2.5 *TRAIN PEOPLE*

Train the people performing or supporting the organizational process per-formance process as needed.

Elaboration:

Examples of training topics include the following:
- Process and process improvement modeling
- Quantitative and statistical methods (e.g., estimating models, Pareto analysis, and control charts)

GP 2.6 *MANAGE CONFIGURATIONS*

Place designated work products of the organizational process performance process under appropriate levels of control.

OPP

Elaboration:

> Examples of work products placed under control include the following:
> • Organization's quality and process-performance objectives
> • Definitions of the selected measures of process performance
> • Baseline data on the organization's process performance

GP 2.7 *IDENTIFY AND INVOLVE RELEVANT STAKEHOLDERS*

Identify and involve the relevant stakeholders of the organizational process performance process as planned.

Elaboration:

> Examples of activities for stakeholder involvement include the following:
> • Establishing the organization's quality and process-performance objectives and their priorities
> • Reviewing and resolving issues on the organization's process-performance baselines
> • Reviewing and resolving issues on the organization's process-performance models

GP 2.8 *MONITOR AND CONTROL THE PROCESS*

Monitor and control the organizational process performance process against the plan for performing the process and take appropriate corrective action.

Elaboration:

> Examples of measures and work products used in monitoring and controlling include the following:
> • Trends in the organization's process performance with respect to changes in work products and task attributes (e.g., size growth, effort, schedule, and quality)
> • Schedule for collecting and reviewing measures to be used for establishing a process-performance baseline

GP 2.9 *OBJECTIVELY EVALUATE ADHERENCE*

Objectively evaluate adherence of the organizational process performance process against its process description, standards, and procedures, and address noncompliance.

Elaboration:

> Examples of activities reviewed include the following:
> • Establishing process-performance baselines and models

> Examples of work products reviewed include the following:
> • Process-performance plans
> • Organization's quality and process-performance objectives
> • Definitions of the selected measures of process performance

GP 2.10 REVIEW STATUS WITH HIGHER LEVEL MANAGEMENT

Review the activities, status, and results of the organizational process performance process with higher level management and resolve issues.

GG 3 INSTITUTIONALIZE A DEFINED PROCESS

The process is institutionalized as a defined process.

> *This generic goal's appearance here reflects its location in the continuous representation.*

CONT. ONLY

GP 3.1 ESTABLISH A DEFINED PROCESS

Establish and maintain the description of a defined organizational process performance process.

GP 3.2 COLLECT IMPROVEMENT INFORMATION

Collect work products, measures, measurement results, and improvement information derived from planning and performing the organizational process performance process to support the future use and improvement of the organization's processes and process assets.

Elaboration:

> Examples of work products, measures, measurement results, and improvement information include the following:
> • Process-performance baselines
> • Percent of measurement data that is rejected because of inconsistencies with the process-performance measurement definitions

OPP

GG 4　*INSTITUTIONALIZE A QUANTITATIVELY MANAGED PROCESS*

The process is institutionalized as a quantitatively managed process.

GP 4.1　*ESTABLISH QUANTITATIVE OBJECTIVES FOR THE PROCESS*

Establish and maintain quantitative objectives for the organizational process performance process, which address quality and process performance, based on customer needs and business objectives.

GP 4.2　*STABILIZE SUBPROCESS PERFORMANCE*

Stabilize the performance of one or more subprocesses to determine the ability of the organizational process performance process to achieve the established quantitative quality and process-performance objectives.

GG 5　*INSTITUTIONALIZE AN OPTIMIZING PROCESS*

The process is institutionalized as an optimizing process.

GP 5.1　*ENSURE CONTINUOUS PROCESS IMPROVEMENT*

Ensure continuous improvement of the organizational process-performance process in fulfilling the relevant business objectives of the organization.

GP 5.2　*CORRECT ROOT CAUSES OF PROBLEMS*

Identify and correct the root causes of defects and other problems in the organizational process-performance process.

ORGANIZATIONAL TRAINING

A Process Management Process Area at Maturity Level 3

Purpose

The purpose of Organizational Training (OT) is to develop the skills and knowledge of people so they can perform their roles effectively and efficiently.

Introductory Notes

Organizational Training includes training to support the organization's strategic business objectives and to meet the tactical training needs that are common across projects and support groups. Specific training needs identified by individual projects and support groups are handled at the project and support group level and are outside the scope of Organizational Training. Project and support groups are responsible for identifying and addressing their specific training needs.

Refer to the Project Planning process area for more information about the specific training needs identified by projects.

An organizational training program involves the following:

- Identifying the training needed by the organization
- Obtaining and providing training to address those needs
- Establishing and maintaining training capability
- Establishing and maintaining training records
- Assessing training effectiveness

Effective training requires assessment of needs, planning, instructional design, and appropriate training media (e.g., workbooks and computer software), as well as a repository of training process data. As an organizational process, the main components of training include a managed training development program, documented plans, personnel with appropriate mastery of specific disciplines and other areas of

TIP

OT addresses the organization's training needs. The project's training needs are addressed in PP, PMC, and IPM.

TIP

Training data includes student training records, dates of classes, and other training information.

OT

knowledge, and mechanisms for measuring the effectiveness of the training program.

The identification of process training needs is primarily based on the skills that are required to perform the organization's set of standard processes.

Refer to the Organizational Process Definition process area for more information about the organization's set of standard processes.

TIP

Remember, CMMI sets expectations on *what* needs to be done, not *how* to do it. Therefore, each organization must decide what type of training is best for any situation.

TIP

To deploy these processes effectively across the organization, training is typically required.

Certain skills may be effectively and efficiently imparted through vehicles other than in-class training experiences (e.g., informal mentoring). Other skills require more formalized training vehicles, such as in a classroom, by Web-based training, through guided self-study, or via a formalized on-the-job training program. The formal or informal training vehicles employed for each situation should be based on an assessment of the need for training and the performance gap to be addressed. The term "training" used throughout this process area is used broadly to include all of these learning options.

Success in training can be measured in terms of the availability of opportunities to acquire the skills and knowledge needed to perform new and ongoing enterprise activities.

Skills and knowledge may be technical, organizational, or contextual. Technical skills pertain to the ability to use the equipment, tools, materials, data, and processes required by a project or a process. Organizational skills pertain to behavior within and according to the employee's organization structure, role and responsibilities, and general operating principles and methods. Contextual skills are the self-management, communication, and interpersonal abilities needed to successfully perform in the organizational and social context of the project and support groups.

The phrase "project and support groups" is used frequently in the text of the process area description to indicate an organization-level perspective.

Related Process Areas

Refer to the Organizational Process Definition process area for more information about the organization's process assets.

Refer to the Project Planning process area for more information about the specific training needs identified by projects.

Refer to the Decision Analysis and Resolution process area for how to apply decision-making criteria when determining training approaches.

Specific Goal and Practice Summary

SG 1 Establish an Organizational Training Capability
    SP 1.1   Establish the Strategic Training Needs
    SP 1.2   Determine Which Training Needs Are the Responsibility of the Organization
    SP 1.3   Establish an Organizational Training Tactical Plan
    SP 1.4   Establish Training Capability
SG 2 Provide Necessary Training
    SP 2.1   Deliver Training
    SP 2.2   Establish Training Records
    SP 2.3   Assess Training Effectiveness

Specific Practices by Goal

SG 1 *ESTABLISH AN ORGANIZATIONAL TRAINING CAPABILITY*

A training capability, which supports the organization's management and technical roles, is established and maintained.

The organization identifies the training required to develop the skills and the knowledge necessary to perform enterprise activities. Once the needs are identified, a training program addressing those needs is developed.

> Cross-functional training, leadership training, interpersonal skills training, and training in the skills needed to integrate appropriate business and technical functions is needed by integrated team members. The potentially wider range of requirements and participant backgrounds may require relevant stakeholders who were not involved in requirements development to take cross training in the disciplines involved in product design in order to commit to requirements with a full understanding of the range of requirements and their interrelationships.

IPPD ADDITION

SP 1.1 *ESTABLISH THE STRATEGIC TRAINING NEEDS*

Establish and maintain the strategic training needs of the organization.

Strategic training needs address long-term objectives to build a capability by filling significant knowledge gaps, introducing new technologies, or implementing major changes in behavior. Strategic planning typically looks two to five years into the future.

HINT

Use strategic training to ensure that the organization continues as a learning organization, strengthens its core competencies, and remains competitive.

OT

Examples of sources of strategic training needs include the following:
- Organization's standard processes
- Organization's strategic business plan
- Organization's process improvement plan
- Enterprise-level initiatives
- Skill assessments
- Risk analyses

IPPD requires leadership and interpersonal skills beyond those typically found in traditional development environments. Specific skills emphasized in an IPPD environment include the following:
- The ability to integrate all appropriate business and technical functions and their processes
- The ability to coordinate and collaborate with others

IPPD Addition

Typical Work Products

1. Training needs
2. Assessment analysis

Subpractices

1. Analyze the organization's strategic business objectives and process improvement plan to identify potential future training needs.
2. Document the strategic training needs of the organization.

Examples of categories of training needs include (but are not limited to) the following:
- Process analysis and documentation
- Engineering (e.g., requirements analysis, design, testing, configuration management, and quality assurance)
- Service delivery
- Selection and management of suppliers
- Management (e.g., estimating, tracking, and risk management)
- Disaster recovery and continuity of operations

3. Determine the roles and skills needed to perform the organization's set of standard processes.
4. Document the training needed to perform the roles in the organization's set of standard processes.

5. Document the training needed to maintain the safe, secure and continued operation of the business.

6. Revise the organization's strategic needs and required training as necessary.

SP 1.2 DETERMINE WHICH TRAINING NEEDS ARE THE RESPONSIBILITY OF THE ORGANIZATION

Determine which training needs are the responsibility of the organization and which will be left to the individual project or support group.

Refer to the Project Planning process area for more information about project- and support-group-specific plans for training.

In addition to strategic training needs, organizational training addresses training requirements that are common across projects and support groups. Projects and support groups have the primary responsibility for identifying and addressing their specific training needs. The organization's training staff is only responsible for addressing common cross-project and support group training needs (e.g., training in work environments common to multiple projects). In some cases, however, the organization's training staff may address additional training needs of projects and support groups, as negotiated with them, within the context of the training resources available and the organization's training priorities.

> **TIP**
>
> Small organizations may choose to use the practices in this PA to address all of their training. If so, the scope and intent of the practices should be expanded appropriately.

Typical Work Products

1. Common project and support group training needs
2. Training commitments

Subpractices

1. Analyze the training needs identified by the various projects and support groups.

   Analysis of project and support group needs is intended to identify common training needs that can be most efficiently addressed organization-wide. These needs-analysis activities are used to anticipate future training needs that are first visible at the project and support group level.

2. Negotiate with the various projects and support groups on how their specific training needs will be satisfied.

   The support provided by the organization's training staff depends on the training resources available and the organization's training priorities.

OT

> Examples of training appropriately performed by the project or support
> group include the following:
> • Training in the application or service domain of the project
> • Training in the unique tools and methods used by the project or support
> group
> • Training in safety, security, and human factors

3. Document the commitments for providing training support to the
projects and support groups.

SP 1.3 ESTABLISH AN ORGANIZATIONAL TRAINING TACTICAL PLAN

Establish and maintain an organizational training tactical plan.

TIP

For many organizations, this
planning is performed annually,
with a review each quarter.

The organizational training tactical plan is the plan to deliver the
training that is the responsibility of the organization and is necessary
for individuals to perform their roles effectively. This plan addresses
the near-term execution of training and is adjusted periodically in
response to changes (e.g., in needs or resources) and to evaluations
of effectiveness.

Typical Work Products

1. Organizational training tactical plan

Subpractices

1. Establish plan content.

Organizational training tactical plans typically contain the following:
- Training needs
- Training topics
- Schedules based on training activities and their dependencies
- Methods used for training
- Requirements and quality standards for training materials
- Training tasks, roles, and responsibilities
- Required resources including tools, facilities, environments,
staffing, and skills and knowledge

2. Establish commitments to the plan.

Documented commitments by those responsible for implementing
and supporting the plan are essential for the plan to be effective.

3. Revise plan and commitments as necessary.

SP 1.4 *ESTABLISH TRAINING CAPABILITY*

Establish and maintain training capability to address organizational training needs.

Refer to the Decision Analysis and Resolution process area for how to apply decision-making criteria when selecting training approaches and developing training materials.

Typical Work Products

1. Training materials and supporting artifacts

Subpractices

1. Select the appropriate approaches to satisfy specific organizational training needs.

   Many factors may affect the selection of training approaches, including audience-specific knowledge, costs and schedule, work environment, and so on. Selection of an approach requires consideration of the means to provide skills and knowledge in the most effective way possible given the constraints.

   > Examples of training approaches include the following:
   > - Classroom training
   > - Computer-aided instruction
   > - Guided self-study
   > - Formal apprenticeship and mentoring programs
   > - Facilitated videos
   > - Chalk talks
   > - Brown-bag lunch seminars
   > - Structured on-the-job training

2. Determine whether to develop training materials internally or acquire them externally.

   Determine the costs and benefits of internal training development or of obtaining training externally.

   > Example criteria that can be used to determine the most effective mode of knowledge or skill acquisition include the following:
   > - Performance objectives
   > - Time available to prepare for project execution
   > - Business objectives
   > - Availability of in-house expertise
   > - Availability of training from external sources

OT

> Examples of external sources of training include the following:
> - Customer-provided training
> - Commercially available training courses
> - Academic programs
> - Professional conferences
> - Seminars

3. Develop or obtain training materials.

   Training may be provided by the project, by support groups, by the organization, or by an external organization. The organization's training staff coordinates the acquisition and delivery of training regardless of its source.

> Examples of training materials include the following:
> - Courses
> - Computer-aided instruction
> - Videos

4. Develop or obtain qualified instructors.

   To ensure that internally provided training instructors have the necessary knowledge and training skills, criteria can be defined to identify, develop, and qualify them. In the case of externally provided training, the organization's training staff can investigate how the training provider determines which instructors will deliver the training. This can also be a factor in selecting or continuing to use a specific training provider.

5. Describe the training in the organization's training curriculum.

> Examples of the information provided in the training descriptions for each course include the following:
> - Topics covered in the training
> - Intended audience
> - Prerequisites and preparation for participating
> - Training objectives
> - Length of the training
> - Lesson plans
> - Completion criteria for the course
> - Criteria for granting training waivers

6. Revise the training materials and supporting artifacts as necessary.

> Examples of situations in which the training materials and supporting artifacts may need to be revised include the following:
> • Training needs change (e.g., when new technology associated with the training topic is available)
> • An evaluation of the training identifies the need for change (e.g., evaluations of training effectiveness surveys, training program performance assessments, or instructor evaluation forms)

SG 2   PROVIDE NECESSARY TRAINING

Training necessary for individuals to perform their roles effectively is provided.

In selecting people to be trained, the following should be taken into consideration:

- Background of the target population of training participants
- Prerequisite background to receive training
- Skills and abilities needed by people to perform their roles
- Need for cross-discipline technical management training for all disciplines, including project management
- Need for managers to have training in appropriate organizational processes
- Need for training in the basic principles of all appropriate disciplines to support personnel in quality management, configuration management, and other related support functions
- Need to provide competency development for critical functional areas
- Need to maintain the competencies and qualifications of personnel to operate and maintain work environments common to multiple projects

SP 2.1 DELIVER TRAINING

Deliver the training following the organizational training tactical plan.

Typical Work Products

1. Delivered training course

Subpractices

1. Select the people who will receive the training necessary to perform their roles effectively.

    Training is intended to impart knowledge and skills to people performing various roles within the organization. Some people already possess the knowledge and skills required to perform well in their designated roles. Training can be waived for these people, but care should be taken that training waivers are not abused.

2. Schedule the training, including any resources, as necessary (e.g., facilities and instructors).

   Training should be planned and scheduled. Training is provided that has a direct bearing on the expectations of work performance. Therefore, optimal training occurs in a timely manner with regard to imminent job-performance expectations. These expectations often include the following:

   • Training in the use of specialized tools
   • Training in procedures that are new to the individual who will perform them

3. Conduct the training.

   Experienced instructors should perform training. When possible, training is conducted in settings that closely resemble actual performance conditions and includes activities to simulate actual work situations. This approach includes integration of tools, methods, and procedures for competency development. Training is tied to work responsibilities so that on-the-job activities or other outside experiences will reinforce the training within a reasonable time after the training.

4. Track the delivery of training against the plan.

SP 2.2 ESTABLISH TRAINING RECORDS

Establish and maintain records of the organizational training.

Refer to the Project Monitoring and Control process area for information about how project or support group training records are maintained.

The scope of this practice is for the training performed at the organizational level. Establishment and maintenance of training records for project- or support-group-sponsored training is the responsibility of each individual project or support group.

Typical Work Products

1. Training records
2. Training updates to the organizational repository

Subpractices

1. Keep records of all students who successfully complete each training course or other approved training activity as well as those who are unsuccessful.

TIP

To provide consistent and complete information on each employee, the training records may include all training, whether performed at the organization's level or by a project or support group.

TIP

To ensure that training records are accurate, you may want to use some CM practices.

2. Keep records of all staff who have been waived from specific training.

    The rationale for granting a waiver should be documented, and both the manager responsible and the manager of the excepted individual should approve the waiver for organizational training.

3. Keep records of all students who successfully complete their designated required training.

4. Make training records available to the appropriate people for consideration in assignments.

    Training records may be part of a skills matrix developed by the training organization to provide a summary of the experience and education of people, as well as training sponsored by the organization.

SP 2.3 ASSESS TRAINING EFFECTIVENESS

Assess the effectiveness of the organization's training program.

A process should exist to determine the effectiveness of training (i.e., how well the training is meeting the organization's needs).

> Examples of methods used to assess training effectiveness include the following:
> - Testing in the training context
> - Post-training surveys of training participants
> - Surveys of managers' satisfaction with post-training effects
> - Assessment mechanisms embedded in courseware

TIP

Training effectiveness can change over time. Initially, training may be done using one medium or mode of delivery to train large numbers of people and another medium or mode of delivery to train the "stragglers."

Measures may be taken to assess the benefit of the training against both the project's and organization's objectives. Particular attention should be paid to the need for various training methods, such as training teams as integral work units. When used, performance objectives should be shared with course participants, and should be unambiguous, observable, and verifiable. The results of the training-effectiveness assessment should be used to revise training materials as described in the Establish Training Capability specific practice.

Typical Work Products

1. Training-effectiveness surveys
2. Training program performance assessments
3. Instructor evaluation forms
4. Training examinations

OT

Subpractices

1. Assess in-progress or completed projects to determine whether staff knowledge is adequate for performing project tasks.
2. Provide a mechanism for assessing the effectiveness of each training course with respect to established organizational, project, or individual learning (or performance) objectives.
3. Obtain student evaluations of how well training activities met their needs.

Generic Practices by Goal

GG 1 ACHIEVE SPECIFIC GOALS

The process supports and enables achievement of the specific goals of the process area by transforming identifiable input work products to produce identifiable output work products.

GP 1.1 PERFORM SPECIFIC PRACTICES

Perform the specific practices of the organizational training process to develop work products and provide services to achieve the specific goals of the process area.

GG 2 INSTITUTIONALIZE A MANAGED PROCESS

The process is institutionalized as a managed process.

GG 3 INSTITUTIONALIZE A DEFINED PROCESS

The process is institutionalized as a defined process.

> This generic goal's appearance here reflects its location in the staged representation.

CONTINUOUS ONLY

STAGED ONLY

GP 2.1 ESTABLISH AN ORGANIZATIONAL POLICY

Establish and maintain an organizational policy for planning and performing the organizational training process.

Elaboration:

This policy establishes organizational expectations for identifying the strategic training needs of the organization, and providing that training.

GP 2.2 PLAN THE PROCESS

Establish and maintain the plan for performing the organizational training process.

Elaboration:

This plan for performing the organizational training process differs from the tactical plan for organizational training described in a specific practice in this process area. The plan called for in this generic practice would address the comprehensive planning for all of the specific practices in this process area, from the establishment of strategic training needs all the way through to the assessment of the effectiveness of the organizational training effort. In contrast, the organizational training tactical plan called for in the specific practice would address the periodic planning for the delivery of individual training offerings.

GP 2.3 PROVIDE RESOURCES

Provide adequate resources for performing the organizational training process, developing the work products, and providing the services of the process.

Elaboration:

Examples of people (full or part time, internal or external), and skills needed include the following:
- Subject-matter experts
- Curriculum designers
- Instructional designers
- Instructors
- Training administrators

Special facilities may be required for training. When necessary, the facilities required for the activities in the Organizational Training process area are developed or purchased.

Examples of other resources provided include the following tools:
- Instruments for analyzing training needs
- Workstations to be used for training
- Instructional design tools
- Packages for developing presentation materials

OT

GP 2.4 ASSIGN RESPONSIBILITY

Assign responsibility and authority for performing the process, developing the work products, and providing the services of the organizational training process.

GP 2.5 TRAIN PEOPLE

Train the people performing or supporting the organizational training process as needed.

Elaboration:

Refer to Table 7.2 on page 172 in Generic Goals and Generic Practices for more information about the relationship between generic practice 2.5 and the Organizational Training process area.

Examples of training topics include the following:
- Knowledge and skills needs analysis
- Instructional design
- Instructional techniques (e.g., train the trainer)
- Refresher training on subject matter

GP 2.6 MANAGE CONFIGURATIONS

Place designated work products of the organizational training process under appropriate levels of control.

Elaboration:

Examples of work products placed under control include the following:
- Organizational training tactical plan
- Training records
- Training materials and supporting artifacts
- Instructor evaluation forms

GP 2.7 IDENTIFY AND INVOLVE RELEVANT STAKEHOLDERS

Identify and involve the relevant stakeholders of the organizational training process as planned.

Elaboration:

> Examples of activities for stakeholder involvement include the following:
> - Establishing a collaborative environment for discussion of training needs and training effectiveness to ensure that the organization's training needs are met
> - Identifying training needs
> - Reviewing the organizational training tactical plan
> - Assessing training effectiveness

GP 2.8 MONITOR AND CONTROL THE PROCESS

Monitor and control the organizational training process against the plan for performing the process and take appropriate corrective action.

Elaboration:

> Examples of measures and work products used in monitoring and controlling include the following:
> - Number of training courses delivered (e.g., planned versus actual)
> - Post-training evaluation ratings
> - Training program quality survey ratings
> - Schedule for delivery of training
> - Schedule for development of a course

GP 2.9 OBJECTIVELY EVALUATE ADHERENCE

Objectively evaluate adherence of the organizational training process against its process description, standards, and procedures, and address noncompliance.

Elaboration:

> Examples of activities reviewed include the following:
> - Identifying training needs and making training available
> - Providing necessary training

> Examples of work products reviewed include the following:
> - Organizational training tactical plan
> - Training materials and supporting artifacts
> - Instructor evaluation forms

OT

GP 2.10 REVIEW STATUS WITH HIGHER LEVEL MANAGEMENT

Review the activities, status, and results of the organizational training process with higher level management and resolve issues.

GG 3 INSTITUTIONALIZE A DEFINED PROCESS

The process is institutionalized as a defined process.

This generic goal's appearance here reflects its location in the continuous representation.

CONT. ONLY

GP 3.1 ESTABLISH A DEFINED PROCESS

Establish and maintain the description of a defined organizational training process.

GP 3.2 COLLECT IMPROVEMENT INFORMATION

Collect work products, measures, measurement results, and improvement information derived from planning and performing the organizational training process to support the future use and improvement of the organization's processes and process assets.

Elaboration:

> Examples of work products, measures, measurement results, and improvement information include the following:
> • Results of training effectiveness surveys
> • Training program performance assessment results
> • Course evaluations
> • Training requirements from an advisory group

GG 4 INSTITUTIONALIZE A QUANTITATIVELY MANAGED PROCESS

The process is institutionalized as a quantitatively managed process.

GP 4.1 ESTABLISH QUANTITATIVE OBJECTIVES FOR THE PROCESS

Establish and maintain quantitative objectives for the organizational training process, which address quality and process performance, based on customer needs and business objectives.

CONTINUOUS ONLY

GP 4.2 STABILIZE SUBPROCESS PERFORMANCE

Stabilize the performance of one or more subprocesses to determine the ability of the organizational training process to achieve the established quantitative quality and process-performance objectives.

GG 5 INSTITUTIONALIZE AN OPTIMIZING PROCESS

The process is institutionalized as an optimizing process.

GP 5.1 ENSURE CONTINUOUS PROCESS IMPROVEMENT

Ensure continuous improvement of the organizational training process in fulfilling the relevant business objectives of the organization.

GP 5.2 CORRECT ROOT CAUSES OF PROBLEMS

Identify and correct the root causes of defects and other problems in the organizational training process.

CONTINUOUS ONLY

OT

PRODUCT INTEGRATION
An Engineering Process Area at Maturity Level 3

Purpose

The purpose of Product Integration (PI) is to assemble the product from the product components, ensure that the product, as integrated, functions properly, and deliver the product.

HINT

To achieve problem-free integration, you need to prepare for product integration activities early in the project.

Introductory Notes

This process area addresses the integration of product components into more complex product components or into complete products.

The scope of this process area is to achieve complete product integration through progressive assembly of product components, in one stage or in incremental stages, according to a defined integration sequence and procedures. Throughout the process areas, where we use the terms product and product component, their intended meanings also encompass services and their components.

A critical aspect of product integration is the management of internal and external interfaces of the products and product components to ensure compatibility among the interfaces. Attention should be paid to interface management throughout the project.

Product integration is more than just a one-time assembly of the product components at the conclusion of design and fabrication. Product integration can be conducted incrementally, using an iterative process of assembling product components, evaluating them, and then assembling more product components. This process may begin with analysis and simulations (e.g., threads, rapid prototypes, virtual prototypes, and physical prototypes) and steadily progress through increasingly more realistic incremental functionality until the final product is achieved. In each successive build, prototypes (virtual, rapid, or physical) are constructed, evaluated, improved, and reconstructed based on knowledge gained in the evaluation

TIP

In PI, the word *integration* refers only to product integration. In some engineering disciplines (e.g., mechanical engineering), the term *assembly* is generally preferred over *integration*. In PI, these two words are used interchangeably.

HINT

Many problems encountered in product integration are due to interface incompatibilities. Therefore, PI covers interface management.

PI

TIP

Product integration typically proceeds in incremental stages. At each stage, a partial assembly is followed by evaluation. In early stages, prototypes may be used in place of product components that are unavailable. The last stage may integrate the complete product with the end user in the intended environment.

process. The degree of virtual versus physical prototyping required depends on the functionality of the design tools, the complexity of the product, and its associated risk. There is a high probability that the product, integrated in this manner, will pass product verification and validation. For some products and services, the last integration phase will occur when they are deployed at the intended operational site.

Related Process Areas

Refer to the Requirements Development process area for more information about identifying interface requirements.

Refer to the Technical Solution process area for more information about defining the interfaces and the integration environment (when the integration environment needs to be developed).

Refer to the Verification process area for more information about verifying the interfaces, the integration environment, and the progressively assembled product components.

Refer to the Validation process area for more information about performing validation of the product components and the integrated product.

Refer to the Risk Management process area for more information about identifying risks and the use of prototypes in risk mitigation for both interface compatibility and product component integration.

Refer to the Decision Analysis and Resolution process area for more information about using a formal evaluation process for selecting the appropriate integration sequence and procedures and for deciding whether the integration environment should be acquired or developed.

Refer to the Configuration Management process area for more information about managing changes to interface definitions and about the distribution of information.

Refer to the Supplier Agreement Management process area for more information about acquiring product components or parts of the integration environment.

Specific Goal and Practice Summary

SG 1 Prepare for Product Integration
    SP 1.1   Determine Integration Sequence
    SP 1.2   Establish the Product Integration Environment
    SP 1.3   Establish Product Integration Procedures and Criteria
SG 2 Ensure Interface Compatibility
    SP 2.1   Review Interface Descriptions for Completeness
    SP 2.2   Manage Interfaces
SG 3 Assemble Product Components and Deliver the Product
    SP 3.1   Confirm Readiness of Product Components for Integration
    SP 3.2   Assemble Product Components
    SP 3.3   Evaluate Assembled Product Components
    SP 3.4   Package and Deliver the Product or Product Component

Specific Practices by Goal

SG 1 PREPARE FOR PRODUCT INTEGRATION

Preparation for product integration is conducted.

Preparing for integration of product components involves establishing and maintaining an integration sequence, the environment for performing the integration, and integration procedures. The specific practices of the Prepare for Product Integration specific goal build on each other in the following way. The first specific practice determines the sequence for product and product component integration. The second determines the environment that will be used to carry out the product and product component integration. The third develops procedures and criteria for product and product component integration. Preparation for integration starts early in the project and the integration sequence is developed concurrently with the practices in the Technical Solution process area.

> **TIP**
>
> A passive approach to product integration is to wait until product components are ready to integrate to begin assembly and testing. PI recommends a proactive approach that initiates integration activities early in the project and performs integration activities concurrently with the practices of TS and SAM. Such an approach affects the development schedules of the project and its suppliers.

SP 1.1 DETERMINE INTEGRATION SEQUENCE

Determine the product component integration sequence.

The product components that are integrated may include those that are a part of the product to be delivered along with test equipment, test software, or other integration items such as fixtures. Once you have analyzed alternative test and assembly integration sequences, select the best integration sequence.

The product integration sequence can provide for incremental assembly and evaluation of product components that provide a

> **TIP**
>
> Besides product components, the integration sequence can address integration with test equipment and assembly fixtures.

PI

problem-free foundation for incorporation of other product components as they become available, or for prototypes of high-risk product components.

The integration sequence should be harmonized with the selection of solutions and the design of product and product components in the Technical Solution process area.

Refer to the Decision Analysis and Resolution process area for more information about using a formal evaluation process to select the appropriate product integration sequence.

Refer to the Risk Management process area for more information about identifying and handling risks associated with the integration sequence.

Refer to the Supplier Agreement Management process area for more information about transitioning acquired product components and the need for handling those product components in the product integration sequence.

Typical Work Products

1. Product integration sequence
2. Rationale for selecting or rejecting integration sequences

Subpractices

1. Identify the product components to be integrated.
2. Identify the verifications to be performed during the integration of the product components.
3. Identify alternative product component integration sequences.

    This can include defining the specific tools and test equipment to support the product integration.
4. Select the best integration sequence.
5. Periodically review the product integration sequence and revise as needed.

    Assess the product integration sequence to ensure that variations in production and delivery schedules have not had an adverse impact on the sequence or compromised the factors on which earlier decisions were made.
6. Record the rationale for decisions made and deferred.

SP 1.2 ESTABLISH THE PRODUCT INTEGRATION ENVIRONMENT

Establish and maintain the environment needed to support the integration of the product components.

Refer to the Technical Solution process area for more information about make-or-buy decisions.

HINT

At each stage following an assembly, test whether the resulting assembly behaves as expected.

TIP

You can use a formal evaluation process to select an integration sequence from among alternatives. Criteria for selection can include the impact of the alternative sequence on cost, schedule, performance, and risk.

TIP

Providing an integration environment to support product integration may be a significant endeavor best treated as a project.

The environment for product integration can either be acquired or developed. To establish an environment, requirements for the purchase or development of equipment, software, or other resources will need to be developed. These requirements are gathered when implementing the processes associated with the Requirements Development process area. The product integration environment may include the reuse of existing organizational resources. The decision to acquire or develop the product integration environment is addressed in the processes associated with the Technical Solution process area.

The environment required at each step of the product integration process may include test equipment, simulators (taking the place of unavailable product components), pieces of real equipment, and recording devices.

Typical Work Products

1. Verified environment for product integration
2. Support documentation for the product integration environment

Subpractices

1. Identify the requirements for the product integration environment.
2. Identify verification criteria and procedures for the product integration environment.
3. Decide whether to make or buy the needed product integration environment.

    Refer to the Supplier Agreement Management process area for more information about acquiring parts of the integration environment.

4. Develop an integration environment if a suitable environment cannot be acquired.

    For unprecedented, complex projects, the product integration environment can be a major development. As such, it would involve project planning, requirements development, technical solutions, verification, validation, and risk management.

5. Maintain the product integration environment throughout the project.
6. Dispose of those portions of the environment that are no longer useful.

SP 1.3 *ESTABLISH PRODUCT INTEGRATION PROCEDURES AND CRITERIA*

Establish and maintain procedures and criteria for integration of the product components.

> **TIP**
>
> Consider what is required of the integration environment at each stage of integration according to the integration sequence established in SP 1.1.

> **HINT**
>
> Revise the integration environment if the integration sequence changes, additional prototypes and simulations are needed to replace product components that are to be delivered late, or the understanding of the operational environment changes significantly.

PI

TIP

This specific practice answers questions such as how to obtain product components to be assembled, how to assemble them, and what testing to perform. Also, criteria are established to answer questions such as when a component is ready, what level of performance is required on each test, and what is acceptable validation and delivery of the final product.

Procedures for the integration of the product components can include such things as the number of incremental iterations to be performed and details of the expected tests and other evaluations to be carried out at each stage.

Criteria can indicate the readiness of a product component for integration or its acceptability.

Procedures and criteria for product integration address the following:

- Level of testing for build components
- Verification of interfaces
- Thresholds of performance deviation
- Derived requirements for the assembly and its external interfaces
- Allowable substitutions of components
- Testing environment parameters
- Limits on cost of testing
- Quality/cost tradeoffs for integration operations
- Probability of proper functioning
- Delivery rate and its variation
- Lead time from order to delivery
- Personnel availability
- Availability of the integration facility/line/environment

TIP

Criteria may impose limits or constraints on how testing is performed.

Criteria can be defined for how the product components are to be verified and the functions they are expected to have. Criteria can be defined for how the assembled product components and final integrated product are to be validated and delivered.

Criteria may also constrain the degree of simulation permitted for a product component to pass a test, or may constrain the environment to be used for the integration test.

Pertinent parts of the schedule and criteria for assembly should be shared with suppliers of work products to reduce the occurrence of delays and component failure.

Refer to the Supplier Agreement Management process area for more information about communicating with suppliers.

Typical Work Products

1. Product integration procedures
2. Product integration criteria

Subpractices

1. Establish and maintain product integration procedures for the product components.
2. Establish and maintain criteria for product component integration and evaluation.
3. Establish and maintain criteria for validation and delivery of the integrated product.

SG 2   ENSURE INTERFACE COMPATIBILITY

The product component interfaces, both internal and external, are compatible.

Many product integration problems arise from unknown or uncontrolled aspects of both internal and external interfaces. Effective management of product component interface requirements, specifications, and designs helps ensure that implemented interfaces will be complete and compatible.

SP 2.1 REVIEW INTERFACE DESCRIPTIONS FOR COMPLETENESS

Review interface descriptions for coverage and completeness.

The interfaces should include, in addition to product component interfaces, all the interfaces with the product integration environment.

Typical Work Products

1. Categories of interfaces
2. List of interfaces per category
3. Mapping of the interfaces to the product components and the product integration environment

Subpractices

1. Review interface data for completeness and ensure complete coverage of all interfaces.

   Consider all the product components and prepare a relationship table. Interfaces are usually classified in three main classes: environmental, physical, and functional. Typical categories for these classes include the following: mechanical, fluid, sound, electrical, climatic, electromagnetic, thermal, message, and the human-machine or human interface.

TIP

The source of many product integration problems lies in incompatible interfaces. SG 2 is designed to help ensure that interfaces are compatible.

X-REF

Interfaces are also addressed in RD SP 2.3, Interface Requirements, and TS SP 2.3, Interface Designs. Interfaces are important in the development of a product.

TIP

These reviews should be *periodic* to ensure consistency is maintained between interface descriptions and product components (see Subpractice 3) and that new interfaces are not overlooked.

TIP

Interfaces with environments such as product integration, verification, and validation environments, as well as operational, maintenance, and support environments, should be addressed.

TIP

Interface data is all the data associated with product component interfaces, including requirements, designs, and interface descriptions.

PI

HINT

To know which interfaces to describe, maintain, and periodically review, prepare a relationship table to identify interfaces between product components (or between a product component and an environment). The objectives are to achieve coverage of all interfaces and ensure completeness.

TIP

Overlooked or incompletely described interfaces are risks to be identified and managed (RSKM). The realization of these risks may lead to safety recalls and has proven very costly.

HINT

Use these examples to ensure that all aspects of an interface are addressed in an interface description.

TIP

For mechanical or electrical product components, markings can help ensure correct connections.

HINT

Include stakeholders internal and external to the project (e.g., suppliers).

Examples of interfaces (e.g., for mechanical or electronic components) that may be classified within these three classes include the following:

- Mechanical interfaces (e.g., weight and size, center of gravity, clearance of parts in operation, space required for maintenance, fixed links, mobile links, and shocks and vibrations received from the bearing structure)
- Noise interfaces (e.g., noise transmitted by the structure, noise transmitted in the air, and acoustics)
- Climatic interfaces (e.g., temperature, humidity, pressure, and salinity)
- Thermal interfaces (e.g., heat dissipation, transmission of heat to the bearing structure, and air conditioning characteristics)
- Fluid interfaces (e.g., fresh water inlet/outlet, seawater inlet/outlet for a naval/coastal product, air conditioning, compressed air, nitrogen, fuel, lubricating oil, and exhaust gas outlet)
- Electrical interfaces (e.g., power supply consumption by network with transients and peak values; nonsensitive control signal for power supply and communications; sensitive signal [e.g., analog links]; disturbing signal [e.g., microwave]; and grounding signal to comply with the TEMPEST standard)
- Electromagnetic interfaces (e.g., magnetic field, radio and radar links, optical band link wave guides, and coaxial and optical fibers)
- Human-machine interface (e.g., audio or voice synthesis, audio or voice recognition, display [analog dial, television screen, or liquid-crystal display, indicators' light-emitting diodes], and manual controls [pedal, joystick, ball, keys, push buttons, or touch screen])
- Message interfaces (e.g., origination, destination, stimulus, protocols, and data characteristics)

2. Ensure that product components and interfaces are marked to ensure easy and correct connection to the joining product component.
3. Periodically review the adequacy of interface descriptions.

   Once established, the interface descriptions must be periodically reviewed to ensure there is no deviation between the existing descriptions and the products being developed, processed, produced, or bought.

   The interface descriptions for product components should be reviewed with relevant stakeholders to avoid misinterpretations, reduce delays, and prevent the development of interfaces that do not work properly.

SP 2.2 MANAGE INTERFACES

Manage internal and external interface definitions, designs, and changes for products and product components.

Interface requirements drive the development of the interfaces necessary to integrate product components. Managing product and product component interfaces starts very early in the development of the product. The definitions and designs for interfaces affect not only the product components and external systems, but can also affect the verification and validation environments.

Refer to the Requirements Development process area for more information about requirements for interfaces.

Refer to the Technical Solution process area for more information about design of interfaces between product components.

Refer to the Requirements Management process area for more information about managing the changes to the interface requirements.

Refer to the Configuration Management process area for more information about distributing changes to the interface descriptions (specifications) so that everyone can know the current state of the interfaces.

Management of the interfaces includes maintenance of the consistency of the interfaces throughout the life of the product, and resolution of conflict, noncompliance, and change issues. The management of interfaces between products acquired from suppliers and other products or product components is critical for success of the project.

Refer to the Supplier Agreement Management process area for more information about managing suppliers.

The interfaces should include, in addition to product component interfaces, all the interfaces with the environment as well as other environments for verification, validation, operations, and support.

The interface changes are documented, maintained, and readily accessible.

Typical Work Products

1. Table of relationships among the product components and the external environment (e.g., main power supply, fastening product, and computer bus system)
2. Table of relationships among the different product components
3. List of agreed-to interfaces defined for each pair of product components, when applicable
4. Reports from the interface control working group meetings
5. Action items for updating interfaces
6. Application program interface (API)
7. Updated interface description or agreement

HINT

Manage interfaces early in the project to help prevent inconsistencies from arising between product components.

X-REF

Interface descriptions are typically placed under configuration management (see GP 2.6) so that changes in status are recorded and communicated (see CM SP 3.1).

TIP

These tables in the typical work products are developed as part of the previous specific practice (SP 2.1), but here they have a role in managing interfaces.

TIP

An API is the interface that a computer system, library, or application provides to allow other computer programs to make requests for service and/or exchange data.

PI

Subpractices

1. Ensure the compatibility of the interfaces throughout the life of the product.

2. Resolve conflict, noncompliance, and change issues.

3. Maintain a repository for interface data accessible to project participants.

> A common accessible repository for interface data provides a mechanism to ensure that everyone knows where the current interface data resides and can access it for use.

TIP

A repository for interface data provides access to interface descriptions so that deviations from these definitions are less likely.

SG 3 ASSEMBLE PRODUCT COMPONENTS AND DELIVER THE PRODUCT

Verified product components are assembled and the integrated, verified, and validated product is delivered.

X-REF

While the primary focus of SG 3 is on PI, it summarizes concepts from three PAs: PI, VER, and VAL.

Integration of product components proceeds according to the product integration sequence and available procedures. Before integration, each product component should be confirmed to be compliant with its interface requirements. Product components are assembled into larger, more complex product components. These assembled product components are checked for correct interoperation. This process continues until product integration is complete. If, during this process, problems are identified, the problem should be documented and a corrective action process initiated.

TIP

If problems are identified before, during, or after an integration stage, an exception report is written (see PMC SG 2).

Ensure that the assembly of the product components into larger and more complex product components is conducted according to the product integration sequence and available procedures. The timely receipt of needed product components and the involvement of the right people contribute to the successful integration of the product components that compose the product.

X-REF

The first three specific practices of SG 3 progressively integrate product components in the integration environment using the integration sequence, procedures, and criteria established in SG 1 until the complete product is assembled. The final specific practice is responsible for product packaging, delivery, and installation.

SP 3.1 CONFIRM READINESS OF PRODUCT COMPONENTS FOR INTEGRATION

Confirm, prior to assembly, that each product component required to assemble the product has been properly identified, functions according to its description, and that the product component interfaces comply with the interface descriptions.

Refer to the Verification process area for more information about verifying product components.

Refer to the Technical Solution process area for more information about unit test of product components.

The purpose of this specific practice is to ensure that the properly identified product component that meets its description can actually be assembled according to the product integration sequence and available procedures. The product components are checked for quantity, obvious damage, and consistency between the product component and interface descriptions.

Those conducting product integration are ultimately responsible for checking to make sure everything is proper with the product components before assembly.

TIP

It may seem as if these practices were written for assembling mechanical or electronic product components, but with the exception of a few notes and subpractices, they also apply more generally, including to software.

Typical Work Products

1. Acceptance documents for the received product components
2. Delivery receipts
3. Checked packing lists
4. Exception reports
5. Waivers

Subpractices

1. Track the status of all product components as soon as they become available for integration.
2. Ensure that product components are delivered to the product integration environment in accordance with the product integration sequence and available procedures.
3. Confirm the receipt of each properly identified product component.
4. Ensure that each received product component meets its description.
5. Check the configuration status against the expected configuration.
6. Perform a pre-check (e.g., by a visual inspection and using basic measures) of all the physical interfaces before connecting product components together.

SP 3.2 ASSEMBLE PRODUCT COMPONENTS

Assemble product components according to the product integration sequence and available procedures.

The assembly activities of this specific practice and the evaluation activities of the next specific practice are conducted iteratively, from the initial product components, through the interim assemblies of product components, to the product as a whole.

HINT

Assembly (SP 3.2) and evaluation (SP 3.3) occur at each integration stage. Evaluate the assembled product components before proceeding to the next integration stage.

Typical Work Products

1. Assembled product or product components

PI

Subpractices

1. Ensure the readiness of the product integration environment.
2. Ensure that the assembly sequence is properly performed.

   Record all appropriate information (e.g., configuration status, serial numbers of the product components, types, and calibration date of the meters).

3. Revise the product integration sequence and available procedures as appropriate.

SP 3.3 *Evaluate Assembled Product Components*

Evaluate assembled product components for interface compatibility.

Refer to the Verification process area for more information about verifying assembled product components.

Refer to the Validation process area for more information about validating assembled product components.

This evaluation involves examining and testing assembled product components for performance, suitability, or readiness using the available procedures and environment. It is performed as appropriate for different stages of assembly of product components as identified in the product integration sequence and available procedures. The product integration sequence and available procedures may define a more refined integration and evaluation sequence than might be envisioned just by examining the product architecture. For example, if an assembly of product components is composed of four less complex product components, the integration sequence will not necessarily call for the simultaneous integration and evaluation of the four units as one. Rather, the four less complex units may be integrated progressively, one at a time, with an evaluation after each assembly operation prior to realizing the more complex product component that matched the specification in the product architecture. Alternatively, the product integration sequence and available procedures could have determined that only a final evaluation was the best one to perform.

Typical Work Products

1. Exception reports
2. Interface evaluation reports
3. Product integration summary reports

HINT

If the integration does not proceed as planned (e.g., a product component is not ready for integration), you may have to revise the integration sequence, procedures, and plans.

X-REF

We also addressed interface compatibility in SG 2. Here in SP 3.3, the focus is on evaluating an assembly for interface compatibility. In this practice, the evaluations indicated by the integration procedures established in SP 1.3 are conducted.

TIP

While the integration sequence must eventually lead to integration of all product components, this complete integration may be accomplished in multiple stages as opposed to a single stage.

Subpractices

1. Conduct the evaluation of assembled product components following the product integration sequence and available procedures.
2. Record the evaluation results.

> Example results include the following:
> • Any adaptation required to the integration procedure
> • Any change to the product configuration (spare parts, new release)
> • Evaluation procedure deviations

SP 3.4 PACKAGE AND DELIVER THE PRODUCT OR PRODUCT COMPONENT

Package the assembled product or product component and deliver it to the appropriate customer.

Refer to the Verification process area for more information about verifying the product or an assembly of product components before packaging.

Refer to the Validation process area for more information about validating the product or an assembly of product components before packaging.

The packaging requirements for some products can be addressed in their specifications and verification criteria. This is especially important when items are stored and transported by the customer. In such cases, there may be a spectrum of environmental and stress conditions specified for the package. In other circumstances, factors such as the following may become important:

- Economy and ease of transportation (e.g., containerization)
- Accountability (e.g., shrink wrapping)
- Ease and safety of unpacking (e.g., sharp edges, strength of binding methods, childproofing, environmental friendliness of packing material, and weight)

The adjustment required to fit product components together in the factory could be different from the one required to fit product components together when installed on the operational site. In that case, the product's logbook for the customer should be used to record such specific parameters.

Typical Work Products

1. Packaged product or product components
2. Delivery documentation

TIP

Evaluations include tests for interface compatibility, tests of how well the assembled product components interoperate, and tests involving end users. Thus, the evaluations may involve both verification and validation.

HINT

Remember to document any adaptation, change, or deviation from the established integration procedure.

X-REF

Verification and validation before packaging really fall within the scope of SP 3.3. References to VAL and VER are here for emphasis.

TIP

Depending on the nature of the product, packaging may be relatively straightforward (e.g., distributing software on CDs), or complicated (e.g., packaging and transporting large HVAC systems to office buildings).

PI

Subpractices

1. Review the requirements, design, product, verification results, and documentation to ensure that issues affecting the packaging and delivery of the product are identified and resolved.

2. Use effective methods to package and deliver the assembled product.

> **FOR SOFTWARE ENGINEERING**
>
> Examples of software packaging and delivery methods include the following:
> - Magnetic tape
> - Diskettes
> - Hardcopy documents
> - Compact disks
> - Other electronic distribution such as the Internet

3. Satisfy the applicable requirements and standards for packaging and delivering the product.

> Examples of requirements and standards include those for safety, the environment, security, transportability, and disposal.

> **FOR SOFTWARE ENGINEERING**
>
> Examples of requirements and standards for packaging and delivering software include the following:
> - Type of storage and delivery media
> - Custodians of the master and backup copies
> - Required documentation
> - Copyrights
> - License provisions
> - Security of the software

X-REF

A product installation process (TS SP 3.2) should describe how to prepare a site for product installation.

4. Prepare the operational site for installation of the product.

   Preparing the operational site may be the responsibility of the customer or end users.

5. Deliver the product and related documentation and confirm receipt.

6. Install the product at the operational site and confirm correct operation.

   Installing the product may be the responsibility of the customer or the end users. In some circumstances, very little may need to be done to confirm correct operation. In other circumstances, final verification of the integrated product occurs at the operational site.

Generic Practices by Goal

GG 1 ACHIEVE SPECIFIC GOALS

The process supports and enables achievement of the specific goals of the process area by transforming identifiable input work products to produce identifiable output work products.

GP 1.1 PERFORM SPECIFIC PRACTICES

Perform the specific practices of the product integration process to develop work products and provide services to achieve the specific goals of the process area.

GG 2 INSTITUTIONALIZE A MANAGED PROCESS

The process is institutionalized as a managed process.

GG 3 INSTITUTIONALIZE A DEFINED PROCESS

The process is institutionalized as a defined process.

This generic goal's appearance here reflects its location in the staged representation.

CONTINUOUS ONLY

STAGED ONLY

GP 2.1 ESTABLISH AN ORGANIZATIONAL POLICY

Establish and maintain an organizational policy for planning and performing the product integration process.

Elaboration:

This policy establishes organizational expectations for developing product integration sequences, procedures, and an environment; ensuring interface compatibility among product components; assembling the product components; and delivering the product and product components.

GP 2.2 PLAN THE PROCESS

Establish and maintain the plan for performing the product integration process.

Elaboration:

This plan for performing the product integration process addresses the comprehensive planning for all of the specific practices in this process area, from the preparation for product integration all the way through to the delivery of the final product.

PI

GP 2.3 PROVIDE RESOURCES

Provide adequate resources for performing the product integration process, developing the work products, and providing the services of the process.

Elaboration:

Product component interface coordination may be accomplished with an Interface Control Working Group consisting of people who represent external and internal interfaces. Such groups can be used to elicit needs for interface requirements development.

Special facilities may be required for assembling and delivering the product. When necessary, the facilities required for the activities in the Product Integration process area are developed or purchased.

Examples of other resources provided include the following tools:
- Prototyping tools
- Analysis tools
- Simulation tools
- Interface management tools
- Assembly tools (e.g., compilers, make files, joining tools, jigs, and fixtures)

GP 2.4 ASSIGN RESPONSIBILITY

Assign responsibility and authority for performing the process, developing the work products, and providing the services of the product integration process.

GP 2.5 TRAIN PEOPLE

Train the people performing or supporting the product integration process as needed.

Elaboration:

Examples of training topics include the following:
- Application domain
- Product integration procedures and criteria
- Organization's facilities for integration and assembly
- Assembly methods
- Packaging standards

GP 2.6 MANAGE CONFIGURATIONS

Place designated work products of the product integration process under appropriate levels of control.

Elaboration:

> Examples of work products placed under control include the following:
> • Acceptance documents for the received product components
> • Evaluated assembled product and product components
> • Product integration sequence
> • Product integration procedures and criteria
> • Updated interface description or agreement

GP 2.7 IDENTIFY AND INVOLVE RELEVANT STAKEHOLDERS

Identify and involve the relevant stakeholders of the product integration process as planned.

Elaboration:

Select relevant stakeholders from customers, end users, developers, producers, testers, suppliers, marketers, maintainers, disposal personnel, and others who may be affected by, or may affect, the product as well as the process.

> Examples of activities for stakeholder involvement include the following:
> • Reviewing interface descriptions for completeness
> • Establishing the product integration sequence
> • Establishing the product integration procedures and criteria
> • Assembling and delivering the product and product components
> • Communicating the results after evaluation
> • Communicating new, effective product integration processes to give affected people the opportunity to improve their performance

GP 2.8 MONITOR AND CONTROL THE PROCESS

Monitor and control the product integration process against the plan for performing the process and take appropriate corrective action.

Elaboration:

> Examples of measures and work products used in monitoring and controlling include the following:
> - Product component integration profile (e.g., product component assemblies planned and performed, and number of exceptions found)
> - Integration evaluation problem report trends (e.g., number written and number closed)
> - Integration evaluation problem report aging (i.e., how long each problem report has been open)
> - Schedule for conduct of specific integration activities

GP 2.9 OBJECTIVELY EVALUATE ADHERENCE

Objectively evaluate adherence of the product integration process against its process description, standards, and procedures, and address noncompliance.

Elaboration:

> Examples of activities reviewed include the following:
> - Establishing and maintaining a product integration sequence
> - Ensuring interface compatibility
> - Assembling product components and delivering the product

> Examples of work products reviewed include the following:
> - Product integration sequence
> - Product integration procedures and criteria
> - Acceptance documents for the received product components
> - Assembled product and product components

GP 2.10 REVIEW STATUS WITH HIGHER LEVEL MANAGEMENT

Review the activities, status, and results of the product integration process with higher level management and resolve issues.

GG 3 INSTITUTIONALIZE A DEFINED PROCESS

The process is institutionalized as a defined process.

> *This generic goal's appearance here reflects its location in the continuous representation.*

CONT. ONLY

GP 3.1 Establish a Defined Process

Establish and maintain the description of a defined product integration process.

GP 3.2 Collect Improvement Information

Collect work products, measures, measurement results, and improvement information derived from planning and performing the product integration process to support the future use and improvement of the organization's processes and process assets.

Elaboration:

Examples of work products, measures, measurement results, and improvement information include the following:

- Records of the receipt of product components, exception reports, confirmation of configuration status, and results of readiness checking
- Percent of total development effort spent in product integration (actual to date plus estimate to complete)
- Defects found in the product and test environment during product integration
- Problem reports resulting from product integration

GG 4 INSTITUTIONALIZE A QUANTITATIVELY MANAGED PROCESS

The process is institutionalized as a quantitatively managed process.

GP 4.1 Establish Quantitative Objectives for the Process

Establish and maintain quantitative objectives for the product integration process, which address quality and process performance, based on customer needs and business objectives.

GP 4.2 Stabilize Subprocess Performance

Stabilize the performance of one or more subprocesses to determine the ability of the product integration process to achieve the established quantitative quality and process-performance objectives.

GG 5 INSTITUTIONALIZE AN OPTIMIZING PROCESS

The process is institutionalized as an optimizing process.

CONTINUOUS ONLY

PI

GP 5.1 ENSURE CONTINUOUS PROCESS IMPROVEMENT

Ensure continuous improvement of the product integration process in fulfilling the relevant business objectives of the organization.

GP 5.2 CORRECT ROOT CAUSES OF PROBLEMS

Identify and correct the root causes of defects and other problems in the product integration process.

CONTINUOUS ONLY

PROJECT MONITORING AND CONTROL
A Project Management Process Area at Maturity Level 2

Purpose

The purpose of Project Monitoring and Control (PMC) is to provide an understanding of the project's progress so that appropriate corrective actions can be taken when the project's performance deviates significantly from the plan.

TIP

PP provides the overall plan and PMC tracks activities against the plan.

Introductory Notes

A project's documented plan is the basis for monitoring activities, communicating status, and taking corrective action. Progress is primarily determined by comparing actual work product and task attributes, effort, cost, and schedule to the plan at prescribed milestones or control levels within the project schedule or work breakdown structure (WBS). Appropriate visibility enables timely corrective action to be taken when performance deviates significantly from the plan. A deviation is significant if, when left unresolved, it precludes the project from meeting its objectives.

The term "project plan" is used throughout these practices to refer to the overall plan for controlling the project.

When actual status deviates significantly from the expected values, corrective actions are taken as appropriate. These actions may require replanning, which may include revising the original plan, establishing new agreements, or including additional mitigation activities within the current plan.

TIP

Initially, as processes based on PMC are introduced, project managers and staff are reactive. However, as monitoring and control of activities become routine, project managers and staff begin to anticipate problems and success in advance.

HINT

Variation will normally occur. Perform corrective action only when a significant deviation occurs.

TIP

Throughout the other PAs, when corrective action is needed, PMC is referenced.

Related Process Areas

Refer to the Project Planning process area for more information about the project plan, including how it specifies the appropriate level of project monitoring, the measures used to monitor progress, and known risks.

Refer to the Measurement and Analysis process area for information about the process of measuring, analyzing, and recording information.

Specific Goal and Practice Summary

SG 1 Monitor Project Against Plan
      SP 1.1   Monitor Project Planning Parameters
      SP 1.2   Monitor Commitments
      SP 1.3   Monitor Project Risks
      SP 1.4   Monitor Data Management
      SP 1.5   Monitor Stakeholder Involvement
      SP 1.6   Conduct Progress Reviews
      SP 1.7   Conduct Milestone Reviews
SG 2 Manage Corrective Action to Closure
      SP 2.1   Analyze Issues
      SP 2.2   Take Corrective Action
      SP 2.3   Manage Corrective Action

Specific Practices by Goal

SG 1 MONITOR PROJECT AGAINST PLAN

X-REF

The project plan was developed in PP.

Actual performance and progress of the project are monitored against the project plan.

SP 1.1 MONITOR PROJECT PLANNING PARAMETERS

Monitor the actual values of the project planning parameters against the project plan.

Project planning parameters constitute typical indicators of project progress and performance and include attributes of work products and tasks, cost, effort, and schedule. Attributes of the work products and tasks include such items as size, complexity, weight, form, fit, or function.

TIP

Actual values are used as "historical data" to provide a basis for estimates in planning.

Monitoring typically involves measuring the actual values of project planning parameters, comparing actual values to the estimates in the plan, and identifying significant deviations. Recording actual values of the project planning parameters includes recording associated contextual information to help understand the measures. An analysis of the impact that significant deviations have on determining what corrective actions to take is handled in the second specific goal and its specific practices in this process area.

Typical Work Products

1. Records of project performance
2. Records of significant deviations

Subpractices

1. Monitor progress against the schedule.

   Progress monitoring typically includes the following:

   - Periodically measuring the actual completion of activities and milestones
   - Comparing actual completion of activities and milestones against the schedule documented in the project plan
   - Identifying significant deviations from the schedule estimates in the project plan

TIP

These subpractices mirror the specific practices in PP.

2. Monitor the project's cost and expended effort.

   Effort and cost monitoring typically includes the following:

   - Periodically measuring the actual effort and cost expended and staff assigned
   - Comparing actual effort, costs, staffing, and training to the estimates and budget documented in the project plan
   - Identifying significant deviations from the budget in the project plan

3. Monitor the attributes of the work products and tasks.

   Refer to the Project Planning process area for information about the attributes of work products and tasks.

   Monitoring the attributes of the work products and tasks typically includes the following:

   - Periodically measuring the actual attributes of the work products and tasks, such as size or complexity (and the changes to the attributes)
   - Comparing the actual attributes of the work products and tasks (and the changes to the attributes) to the estimates documented in the project plan
   - Identifying significant deviations from the estimates in the project plan

4. Monitor resources provided and used.

   Refer to the Project Planning process area for information about planned resources.

   Examples of resources include the following:
   - Physical facilities
   - Computers, peripherals, and software used in design, manufacturing, testing, and operation
   - Networks
   - Security environment
   - Project staff
   - Processes

5. Monitor the knowledge and skills of project personnel.

   Refer to the Project Planning process area for information about planning for knowledge and skills needed to perform the project.

   Monitoring the knowledge and skills of the project personnel typically includes the following:
   - Periodically measuring the acquisition of knowledge and skills by project personnel
   - Comparing actual training obtained to that documented in the project plan
   - Identifying significant deviations from estimates in the project plan

6. Document the significant deviations in the project planning parameters.

SP 1.2 MONITOR COMMITMENTS

Monitor commitments against those identified in the project plan.

TIP

Things happen that prevent appropriate follow-through with commitments, especially in an immature organization. Therefore, it is necessary to monitor commitments and take corrective action when commitments change.

Typical Work Products

1. Records of commitment reviews

Subpractices

1. Regularly review commitments (both external and internal).
2. Identify commitments that have not been satisfied or that are at significant risk of not being satisfied.
3. Document the results of the commitment reviews.

SP 1.3 MONITOR PROJECT RISKS

Monitor risks against those identified in the project plan.

Refer to the Project Planning process area for more information about identifying project risks.

Refer to the Risk Management process area for more information about risk management activities.

TIP

SP 1.3 is the handshake with the risks that were identified in PP. This practice is reactive and involves minimal risk management activities. For more complete and proactive handling of project risks, refer to RSKM.

Typical Work Products

1. Records of project risk monitoring

Subpractices

1. Periodically review the documentation of the risks in the context of the project's current status and circumstances.
2. Revise the documentation of the risks, as additional information becomes available, to incorporate changes.

3. Communicate risk status to relevant stakeholders.

> Examples of risk status include the following:
> • A change in the probability that the risk occurs
> • A change in risk priority

SP 1.4 MONITOR DATA MANAGEMENT

Monitor the management of project data against the project plan.

Refer to the Plan for Data Management specific practice in the Project Planning process area for more information about identifying the types of data that should be managed and how to plan for their management.

Once the plans for the management of project data are made, the management of that data must be monitored to ensure that those plans are accomplished.

Typical Work Products

1. Records of data management

Subpractices

1. Periodically review data management activities against their description in the project plan.
2. Identify and document significant issues and their impacts.
3. Document the results of data management activity reviews.

SP 1.5 MONITOR STAKEHOLDER INVOLVEMENT

Monitor stakeholder involvement against the project plan.

Refer to the Plan Stakeholder Involvement specific practice in the Project Planning process area for more information about identifying relevant stakeholders and planning the appropriate involvement with them.

Once the stakeholders are identified and the extent of their involvement within the project is specified in project planning, that involvement must be monitored to ensure that the appropriate interactions are occurring.

Typical Work Products

1. Records of stakeholder involvement

Subpractices

1. Periodically review the status of stakeholder involvement.

2. Identify and document significant issues and their impacts.

3. Document the results of the stakeholder involvement status reviews.

SP 1.6 CONDUCT PROGRESS REVIEWS

Periodically review the project's progress, performance, and issues.

TIP

Progress reviews are held regularly (e.g., weekly, monthly, or quarterly).

Progress reviews are reviews on the project to keep stakeholders informed. These project reviews can be informal reviews and may not be specified explicitly in the project plans.

Typical Work Products

1. Documented project review results

Subpractices

1. Regularly communicate status on assigned activities and work products to relevant stakeholders.

   Managers, staff members, customers, end users, suppliers, and other relevant stakeholders within the organization are included in the reviews as appropriate.

2. Review the results of collecting and analyzing measures for controlling the project.

   Refer to the Measurement and Analysis process area for more information about the process for measuring and analyzing project performance data.

3. Identify and document significant issues and deviations from the plan.

4. Document change requests and problems identified in any of the work products and processes.

   Refer to the Configuration Management process area for more information about how changes are managed.

5. Document the results of the reviews.

6. Track change requests and problem reports to closure.

SP 1.7 CONDUCT MILESTONE REVIEWS

TIP

Milestones are major events in a project. If you are using a project lifecycle model, milestones may be predetermined.

Review the accomplishments and results of the project at selected project milestones.

Refer to the Project Planning process area for more information about milestone planning.

Milestone reviews are planned during project planning and are typically formal reviews.

Typical Work Products

1. Documented milestone review results

Subpractices

1. Conduct reviews at meaningful points in the project's schedule, such as the completion of selected stages, with relevant stakeholders.

   Managers, staff members, customers, end users, suppliers, and other relevant stakeholders within the organization are included in the milestone reviews as appropriate.

2. Review the commitments, plan, status, and risks of the project.

3. Identify and document significant issues and their impacts.

4. Document the results of the review, action items, and decisions.

5. Track action items to closure.

SG 2 MANAGE CORRECTIVE ACTION TO CLOSURE

Corrective actions are managed to closure when the project's performance or results deviate significantly from the plan.

SP 2.1 ANALYZE ISSUES

Collect and analyze the issues and determine the corrective actions necessary to address the issues.

> **HINT**
>
> Managing corrective action to closure is critical. It is not enough to identify the action item; you must confirm that it has been completed.

Typical Work Products

1. List of issues needing corrective actions

Subpractices

1. Gather issues for analysis.

   Issues are collected from reviews and the execution of other processes.

Examples of issues to be gathered include the following:
- Issues discovered through performing verification and validation activities
- Significant deviations in the project planning parameters from the estimates in the project plan
- Commitments (either internal or external) that have not been satisfied
- Significant changes in risk status
- Data access, collection, privacy, or security issues
- Stakeholder representation or involvement issues

---

2. Analyze issues to determine need for corrective action.

Refer to the Project Planning process area for information about corrective action criteria.

Corrective action is required when the issue, if left unresolved, may prevent the project from meeting its objectives.

SP 2.2 *TAKE CORRECTIVE ACTION*

Take corrective action on identified issues.

Typical Work Products

1. Corrective action plan

Subpractices

1. Determine and document the appropriate actions needed to address the identified issues.

Refer to the Project Planning process area for more information about the project plan when replanning is needed.

TIP

In some cases, the corrective action can be to monitor the situation. A corrective action does not always result in a complete solution to the problem.

Examples of potential actions include the following:
- Modifying the statement of work
- Modifying requirements
- Revising estimates and plans
- Renegotiating commitments
- Adding resources
- Changing processes
- Revising project risks

---

2. Review and get agreement with relevant stakeholders on the actions to be taken.
3. Negotiate changes to internal and external commitments.

SP 2.3 *MANAGE CORRECTIVE ACTION*

Manage corrective actions to closure.

Typical Work Products

1. Corrective action results

Subpractices

1. Monitor corrective actions for completion.

2. Analyze results of corrective actions to determine the effectiveness of the corrective actions.

3. Determine and document appropriate actions to correct deviations from planned results for corrective actions.

> Lessons learned as a result of taking corrective action can be inputs to planning and risk management processes.

Generic Practices by Goal

GG 1 ACHIEVE SPECIFIC GOALS

The process supports and enables achievement of the specific goals of the process area by transforming identifiable input work products to produce identifiable output work products.

GP 1.1 PERFORM SPECIFIC PRACTICES

Perform the specific practices of the project monitoring and control process to develop work products and provide services to achieve the specific goals of the process area.

CONTINUOUS ONLY

GG 2 INSTITUTIONALIZE A MANAGED PROCESS

The process is institutionalized as a managed process.

GP 2.1 ESTABLISH AN ORGANIZATIONAL POLICY

Establish and maintain an organizational policy for planning and performing the project monitoring and control process.

Elaboration:

This policy establishes organizational expectations for monitoring performance against the project plan and managing corrective action to closure when actual performance or results deviate significantly from the plan.

GP 2.2 PLAN THE PROCESS

Establish and maintain the plan for performing the project monitoring and control process.

Elaboration:

This plan for performing the project monitoring and control process can be part of (or referenced by) the project plan, as described in the Project Planning process area.

GP 2.3 *PROVIDE RESOURCES*

Provide adequate resources for performing the project monitoring and control process, developing the work products, and providing the services of the process.

Elaboration:

Examples of resources provided include the following tools:
- Cost tracking systems
- Effort reporting systems
- Action item tracking systems
- Project management and scheduling programs

GP 2.4 *ASSIGN RESPONSIBILITY*

Assign responsibility and authority for performing the process, developing the work products, and providing the services of the project monitoring and control process.

GP 2.5 *TRAIN PEOPLE*

Train the people performing or supporting the project monitoring and control process as needed.

Elaboration:

Examples of training topics include the following:
- Monitoring and control of projects
- Risk management
- Data management

GP 2.6 *MANAGE CONFIGURATIONS*

Place designated work products of the project monitoring and control process under appropriate levels of control.

Elaboration:

Examples of work products placed under control include the following:
- Project schedules with status
- Project measurement data and analysis
- Earned value reports

GP 2.7 *IDENTIFY AND INVOLVE RELEVANT STAKEHOLDERS*

Identify and involve the relevant stakeholders of the project monitoring and control process as planned.

Elaboration:

Refer to Table 7.2 on page 172 in Generic Goals and Generic Practices for more information about the relationship between generic practice 2.7 and the Monitor Stakeholder Involvement practice in the Project Monitoring and Control process area.

Examples of activities for stakeholder involvement include the following:
- Assessing the project against the plan
- Reviewing commitments and resolving issues
- Reviewing project risks
- Reviewing data management activities
- Reviewing project progress
- Managing corrective actions to closure

GP 2.8 *MONITOR AND CONTROL THE PROCESS*

Monitor and control the project monitoring and control process against the plan for performing the process and take appropriate corrective action.

Elaboration:

Refer to Table 7.2 on page 172 in Generic Goals and Generic Practices for more information about the relationship between generic practice 2.8 and the Project Monitoring and Control process area.

Examples of measures and work products used in monitoring and controlling include the following:
- Number of open and closed corrective actions
- Schedule with status for monthly financial data collection, analysis, and reporting
- Number and types of reviews performed
- Review schedule (planned versus actual and slipped target dates)
- Schedule for collection and analysis of monitoring data

GP 2.9 *OBJECTIVELY EVALUATE ADHERENCE*

Objectively evaluate adherence of the project monitoring and control process against its process description, standards, and procedures, and address noncompliance.

Elaboration:

Examples of activities reviewed include the following:
- Monitoring project performance against the project plan
- Managing corrective actions to closure

Examples of work products reviewed include the following:
- Records of project performance
- Project review results

GP 2.10 REVIEW STATUS WITH HIGHER LEVEL MANAGEMENT

Review the activities, status, and results of the project monitoring and control process with higher level management and resolve issues.

GG3 and its practices do not apply for a maturity level 2 rating, but do apply for a maturity level 3 rating and above.

S ONLY

GG 3 **INSTITUTIONALIZE A DEFINED PROCESS**

The process is institutionalized as a defined process.

GP 3.1 ESTABLISH A DEFINED PROCESS

Establish and maintain the description of a defined project monitoring and control process.

GP 3.2 COLLECT IMPROVEMENT INFORMATION

Collect work products, measures, measurement results, and improvement information derived from planning and performing the project monitoring and control process to support the future use and improvement of the organization's processes and process assets.

Elaboration:

Examples of work products, measures, measurement results, and improvement information include the following:
- Records of significant deviations
- Criteria for what constitutes a deviation
- Corrective action results

CONTINUOUS/MATURITY LEVELS 3–5 ONLY

GG 4 *Institutionalize a Quantitatively Managed Process*

The process is institutionalized as a quantitatively managed process.

GP 4.1 *Establish Quantitative Objectives for the Process*

Establish and maintain quantitative objectives for the project monitoring and control process, which address quality and process performance, based on customer needs and business objectives.

GP 4.2 *Stabilize Subprocess Performance*

Stabilize the performance of one or more subprocesses to determine the ability of the project monitoring and control process to achieve the established quantitative quality and process-performance objectives.

GG 5 *Institutionalize an Optimizing Process*

The process is institutionalized as an optimizing process.

GP 5.1 *Ensure Continuous Process Improvement*

Ensure continuous improvement of the project monitoring and control process in fulfilling the relevant business objectives of the organization.

GP 5.2 *Correct Root Causes of Problems*

Identify and correct the root causes of defects and other problems in the project monitoring and control process.

PROJECT PLANNING
A Project Management Process Area at Maturity Level 2

PP

Purpose

The purpose of Project Planning (PP) is to establish and maintain plans that define project activities.

Introductory Notes

The Project Planning process area involves the following:

- Developing the project plan
- Interacting with stakeholders appropriately
- Getting commitment to the plan
- Maintaining the plan

Planning begins with requirements that define the product and project.

Planning includes estimating the attributes of the work products and tasks, determining the resources needed, negotiating commitments, producing a schedule, and identifying and analyzing project risks. Iterating through these activities may be necessary to establish the project plan. The project plan provides the basis for performing and controlling the project's activities that address the commitments with the project's customer.

The project plan will usually need to be revised as the project progresses to address changes in requirements and commitments, inaccurate estimates, corrective actions, and process changes. Specific practices describing both planning and replanning are contained in this process area.

The term "project plan" is used throughout the generic and specific practices in this process area to refer to the overall plan for controlling the project.

TIP

In planning, you determine the requirements to be fulfilled, the tasks to perform, and the resources and coordination required, and then you document all of this to obtain the needed resources and commitments.

TIP

The plan is a declaration that the work has been rationally thought through and requests for resources are credible. If you ask management to commit resources, they want to know it is worth the investment. A project plan helps you convince them.

X-REF

PMC addresses tracking of project activities in the plan.

TIP

Project planning is not just for large projects. Research with PSP has demonstrated that individuals working on tasks lasting only a few hours increase overall quality and productivity by making time to plan.

HINT

To limit change in the plan, determine early in the project when and what kind of changes will be accepted.

HINT

Both the organization and the project should define triggers for replanning.

Related Process Areas

Refer to the Requirements Development process area for more information about developing requirements that define the product and product components. Product and product component requirements and changes to those requirements serve as a basis for planning and replanning.

Refer to the Requirements Management process area for more information about managing requirements needed for planning and replanning.

Refer to the Risk Management process area for more information about identifying and managing risks.

Refer to the Technical Solution process area for more information about transforming requirements into product and product component solutions.

Specific Goal and Practice Summary

SG 1 Establish Estimates
    SP 1.1   Estimate the Scope of the Project
    SP 1.2   Establish Estimates of Work Product and Task Attributes
    SP 1.3   Define Project Lifecycle
    SP 1.4   Determine Estimates of Effort and Cost

SG 2 Develop a Project Plan
    SP 2.1   Establish the Budget and Schedule
    SP 2.2   Identify Project Risks
    SP 2.3   Plan for Data Management
    SP 2.4   Plan for Project Resources
    SP 2.5   Plan for Needed Knowledge and Skills
    SP 2.6   Plan Stakeholder Involvement
    SP 2.7   Establish the Project Plan

SG 3 Obtain Commitment to the Plan
    SP 3.1   Review Plans That Affect the Project
    SP 3.2   Reconcile Work and Resource Levels
    SP 3.3   Obtain Plan Commitment

Specific Practices by Goal

SG 1   *ESTABLISH ESTIMATES*

X-REF

SG 1 focuses on providing estimates of project planning parameters; actual values are monitored in PMC SP 1.1.

Estimates of project planning parameters are established and maintained.

Project planning parameters include all information needed by the project to perform the necessary planning, organizing, staffing, directing, coordinating, reporting, and budgeting.

Estimates of planning parameters should have a sound basis to instill confidence that any plans based on these estimates are capable of supporting project objectives.

Factors that are typically considered when estimating these parameters include the following:

- Project requirements, including the product requirements, the requirements imposed by the organization, the requirements imposed by the customer, and other requirements that impact the project
- Scope of the project
- Identified tasks and work products
- Technical approach
- Selected project lifecycle model (e.g., waterfall, incremental, or spiral)
- Attributes of the work products and tasks (e.g., size or complexity)
- Schedule
- Models or historical data for converting the attributes of the work products and tasks into labor hours and cost
- Methodology (e.g., models, data, algorithms) used to determine needed material, skills, labor hours, and cost

Documentation of the estimating rationale and supporting data is needed for stakeholders' review and commitment to the plan and for maintenance of the plan as the project progresses.

SP 1.1 ESTIMATE THE SCOPE OF THE PROJECT

Establish a top-level work breakdown structure (WBS) to estimate the scope of the project.

The WBS evolves with the project. Initially a top-level WBS can serve to structure the initial estimating. The development of a WBS divides the overall project into an interconnected set of manageable components. Typically, the WBS is a product oriented structure that provides a scheme for identifying and organizing the logical units of work to be managed, which are called "work packages." The WBS provides a reference and organizational mechanism for assigning effort, schedule, and responsibility and is used as the underlying framework to plan, organize, and control the work done on the project. Some projects use the term "contract WBS" to refer to the portion of the WBS placed under contract (possibly the entire WBS). Not all projects have a contract WBS (e.g., internally funded development).

TIP

Project planning parameters are a key to managing a project. Planning parameters primarily include size, effort, and cost.

TIP

The basis for estimates can include historical data, the judgment of experienced estimators, and other factors.

PP

HINT

Use this rationale to help justify to management why you need resources and why the effort and schedule estimates are appropriate.

HINT

To develop estimates, decompose the project into smaller work items (the WBS), estimate the resources needed by each item, and then roll these up. This will result in more accurate estimates.

TIP

Interaction and iteration among planning, requirements definition, and design are often necessary. A project can learn a lot from each iteration and can use this knowledge to update the plan, requirements, and design for the next iteration.

TIP

The WBS is the basis for many management-related tasks (not just estimating). The Product Breakdown Structure (PBS) is usually a part of the WBS and defines the structure of products and product components that will be developed for a specific project.

HINT

Use the WBS to help you define the product architecture.

TIP

The level of detail often depends on the level and completeness of the requirements. Often the work packages and estimates evolve as the requirements evolve.

HINT

Consider establishing a management reserve commensurate to the overall uncertainty that allows for the efficient allocation of resources to address the uncertainty of estimates.

X-REF

Reuse is also addressed in TS.

HINT

Learn to quantify the resources needed for particular tasks by associating size measures with each type of work product and building historical data. By collecting historical data from projects, you can learn how measured size relates to the resources consumed by tasks. This knowledge can then be used when planning the next project.

Typical Work Products

1. Task descriptions
2. Work package descriptions
3. WBS

Subpractices

1. Develop a WBS based on the product architecture.

   The WBS provides a scheme for organizing the project's work around the product and product components that the work supports. The WBS should permit the identification of the following items:

   • Identified risks and their mitigation tasks
   • Tasks for deliverables and supporting activities
   • Tasks for skill and knowledge acquisition
   • Tasks for development of needed support plans, such as configuration management, quality assurance, and verification plans
   • Tasks for integration and management of nondevelopmental items

2. Identify the work packages in sufficient detail to specify estimates of project tasks, responsibilities, and schedule.

   The top-level WBS is intended to help in gauging the project work effort in terms of tasks and organizational roles and responsibilities. The amount of detail in the WBS at this more detailed level helps in developing realistic schedules, thereby minimizing the need for management reserve.

3. Identify product or product components that will be externally acquired.

   Refer to the Supplier Agreement Management process area for more information about acquiring products from sources external to the project.

4. Identify work products that will be reused.

SP 1.2 ESTABLISH ESTIMATES OF WORK PRODUCT AND TASK ATTRIBUTES

Establish and maintain estimates of the attributes of the work products and tasks.

Size is the primary input to many models used to estimate effort, cost, and schedule. The models can also be based on inputs such as connectivity, complexity, and structure.

> Examples of types of work products for which size estimates are made include the following:
> • Deliverable and nondeliverable work products
> • Documents and files
> • Operational and support hardware, firmware, and software

Examples of size measures include the following:
- Number of functions
- Function points
- Source lines of code
- Number of classes and objects
- Number of requirements
- Number and complexity of interfaces
- Number of pages
- Number of inputs and outputs
- Number of technical risk items
- Volume of data
- Number of logic gates for integrated circuits
- Number of parts (e.g., printed circuit boards, components, and mechanical parts)
- Physical constraints (e.g., weight and volume)

X-REF

For more information on estimating, see Stutzke, Richard D., "Estimating Software-Intensive Systems: Projects, Products, and Processes," SEI Series in Software Engineering, 2005.

PP

The estimates should be consistent with project requirements to determine the project's effort, cost, and schedule. A relative level of difficulty or complexity should be assigned for each size attribute.

HINT

Consider providing guidelines on how to estimate the difficulty or complexity of a task to improve estimation accuracy, especially when size measures are not available.

Typical Work Products

1. Technical approach
2. Size and complexity of tasks and work products
3. Estimating models
4. Attribute estimates

Subpractices

1. Determine the technical approach for the project.

   The technical approach defines a top-level strategy for development of the product. It includes decisions on architectural features, such as distributed or client/server; state-of-the-art or established technologies to be applied, such as robotics, composite materials, or artificial intelligence; and breadth of the functionality expected in the final products, such as safety, security, and ergonomics.

2. Use appropriate methods to determine the attributes of the work products and tasks that will be used to estimate the resource requirements.

   Methods for determining size and complexity should be based on validated models or historical data.

   The methods for determining attributes evolve as our understanding of the relationship of product characteristics to attributes increases.

TIP

Mature organizations maintain historical data to help projects establish reasonable estimates (see SP 1.4, MA, and IPM SP 1.2).

> Examples of current methods include the following:
> • Number of logic gates for integrated circuit design
> • Lines of code or function points for software
> • Number/complexity of requirements for systems engineering
> • Number of square feet for standard-specified residential homes

3. Estimate the attributes of the work products and tasks.

SP 1.3 DEFINE PROJECT LIFECYCLE

Define the project lifecycle phases on which to scope the planning effort.

TIP

For example, in waterfall development, at the end of the requirements analysis phase, the requirements are evaluated to assess consistency, completeness, and feasibility, and to decide whether the project is ready (from a technical and risk perspective) to commit resources to the design phase.

The determination of a project's lifecycle phases provides for planned periods of evaluation and decision making. These are normally defined to support logical decision points at which significant commitments are made concerning resources and technical approach. Such points provide planned events at which project course corrections and determinations of future scope and cost can be made.

The project lifecycle phases need to be defined depending on the scope of requirements, the estimates for project resources, and the nature of the project. Larger projects may contain multiple phases, such as concept exploration, development, production, operations, and disposal. Within these phases, subphases may be needed. A development phase may include subphases such as requirements analysis, design, fabrication, integration, and verification. The determination of project phases typically includes selection and refinement of one or more development models to address interdependencies and appropriate sequencing of the activities in the phases.

Depending on the strategy for development, there may be intermediate phases for the creation of prototypes, increments of capability, or spiral model cycles.

Understanding the project lifecycle is crucial in determining the scope of the planning effort and the timing of the initial planning, as well as the timing and criteria (critical milestones) for replanning.

Typical Work Products

1. Project lifecycle phases

SP 1.4 DETERMINE ESTIMATES OF EFFORT AND COST

Estimate the project effort and cost for the work products and tasks based on estimation rationale.

Estimates of effort and cost are generally based on the results of analysis using models or historical data applied to size, activities, and other planning parameters. Confidence in these estimates is based on the rationale for the selected model and the nature of the data. There may be occasions when the available historical data does not apply, such as where efforts are unprecedented or where the type of task does not fit available models. An effort is unprecedented (to some degree) if a similar product or component has never been built. An effort may also be unprecedented if the development group has never built such a product or component.

Unprecedented efforts are more risky, require more research to develop reasonable bases of estimate, and require more management reserve. The uniqueness of the project must be documented when using these models to ensure a common understanding of any assumptions made in the initial planning stages.

Typical Work Products

1. Estimation rationale
2. Project effort estimates
3. Project cost estimates

Subpractices

1. Collect the models or historical data that will be used to transform the attributes of the work products and tasks into estimates of the labor hours and cost.

    Many parametric models have been developed to aid in estimating cost and schedule. The use of these models as the sole source of estimation is not recommended because these models are based on historical project data that may or may not be pertinent to your project. Multiple models and/or methods can be used to ensure a high level of confidence in the estimate.

    Historical data include the cost, effort, and schedule data from previously executed projects, plus appropriate scaling data to account for differing sizes and complexity.

2. Include supporting infrastructure needs when estimating effort and cost.

    The supporting infrastructure includes resources needed from a development and sustainment perspective for the product.

    Consider the infrastructure resource needs in the development environment, the test environment, the production environment, the target environment, or any appropriate combination of these when estimating effort and cost.

X-REF

An example of a parametric software cost estimation model is COCOMO II (see http://csse.usc.edu/research/ COCOMOII).

HINT

Calibrate estimation techniques and methods to take into consideration the project's specific characteristics.

TIP

Unprecedented efforts require an iterative or spiral development model that provides frequent opportunities for feedback used to resolve issues or risks and to plan the next iteration.

HINT

If you are using only one parametric model, make sure it is calibrated to your project's characteristics.

TIP

Scaling can be reliable when applied from experiences similar to the one at hand.

PP

> Examples of infrastructure resources include the following:
> • Critical computer resources (e.g., memory, disk and network capacity, peripherals, communication channels, and the capacities of these)
> • Engineering environments and tools (e.g., tools for prototyping, assembly, computer-aided design [CAD], and simulation)
> • Facilities, machinery, and equipment (e.g., test benches and recording devices)

3. Estimate effort and cost using models and/or historical data.

Effort and cost inputs used for estimating typically include the following:

- Judgmental estimates provided by an expert or group of experts (e.g., Delphi Method)
- Risks, including the extent to which the effort is unprecedented
- Critical competencies and roles needed to perform the work
- Product and product component requirements
- Technical approach
- WBS
- Size estimates of work products and anticipated changes
- Cost of externally acquired products
- Selected project lifecycle model and processes
- Lifecycle cost estimates
- Capability of tools provided in engineering environment
- Skill levels of managers and staff needed to perform the work
- Knowledge, skill, and training needs
- Facilities needed (e.g., office and meeting space and workstations)
- Engineering facilities needed
- Capability of manufacturing process(es)
- Travel
- Level of security required for tasks, work products, hardware, software, personnel, and work environment
- Service level agreements for call centers and warranty work
- Direct labor and overhead

TIP

The common phrase "walk the talk" is often used when talking about how a project is conducted. The project plan is "the talk."

TIP

In some cases, each project phase may have a more detailed and focused plan of its own, in addition to the overall project plan. Also, a detailed plan typically is provided for each iteration or spiral of development focused on particular requirements issues, design issues, or other risks.

SG 2 DEVELOP A PROJECT PLAN

A project plan is established and maintained as the basis for managing the project.

A project plan is a formal, approved document used to manage and control the execution of the project. It is based on the project requirements and the established estimates.

The project plan should consider all phases of the project lifecycle. Project planning should ensure that all plans affecting the project are consistent with the overall project plan.

SP 2.1 ESTABLISH THE BUDGET AND SCHEDULE

Establish and maintain the project's budget and schedule.

The project's budget and schedule are based on the developed estimates and ensure that budget allocation, task complexity, and task dependencies are appropriately addressed.

Event-driven, resource-limited schedules have proven to be effective in dealing with project risk. Identifying accomplishments to be demonstrated before initiation of the event provides some flexibility in the timing of the event, a common understanding of what is expected, a better vision of the state of the project, and a more accurate status of the project's tasks.

Typical Work Products

1. Project schedules
2. Schedule dependencies
3. Project budget

Subpractices

1. Identify major milestones.

   Milestones are often imposed to ensure completion of certain deliverables by the milestone. Milestones can be event based or calendar based. If calendar based, once milestone dates have been agreed on, it is often very difficult to change them.

2. Identify schedule assumptions.

   When schedules are initially developed, it is common to make assumptions about the duration of certain activities. These assumptions are frequently made on items for which little if any estimation data is available. Identifying these assumptions provides insight into the level of confidence (uncertainties) in the overall schedule.

3. Identify constraints.

   Factors that limit the flexibility of management options need to be identified as early as possible. The examination of the attributes of the work products and tasks often will bring these issues to the surface. Such attributes can include task duration, resources, inputs, and outputs.

TIP

The use of agile software methods is an important variation. Agile software methods utilize user or customer feedback in one phase to drive what takes place in the next.

TIP

Plans that may affect the project plan include configuration management plans, quality assurance plans, the organization's process improvement plan, and the organization's training plan.

HINT

If the budget is dictated by others and it doesn't cover your estimated resource needs, replan to ensure that the project will be within budget. Likewise, if the schedule is dictated by others and it isn't consistent with your plan, replan to ensure that the project will be able to deliver the product on time (perhaps with fewer features).

TIP

In an event-driven schedule, tasks can be initiated only after certain criteria are met.

TIP

Defining event-based milestones and monitoring their completion (PMC SP 1.1 Subpractice 1) provides visibility into the project's progress.

PP

4. Identify task dependencies.

   Typically, the tasks for a project can be accomplished in some ordered sequence that will minimize the duration of the project. This involves the identification of predecessor and successor tasks to determine the optimal ordering.

Examples of tools that can help determine an optimal ordering of task activities include the following:

- Critical Path Method (CPM)
- Program Evaluation and Review Technique (PERT)
- Resource-limited scheduling

---

5. Define the budget and schedule.

   Establishing and maintaining the project's budget and schedule typically includes the following:

   - Defining the committed or expected availability of resources and facilities
   - Determining time phasing of activities
   - Determining a breakout of subordinate schedules
   - Defining the dependencies between the activities (predecessor or successor relationships)
   - Defining the schedule activities and milestones to support accuracy in progress measurement
   - Identifying milestones for delivery of products to the customer
   - Defining activities of appropriate duration
   - Defining milestones of appropriate time separation
   - Defining a management reserve based on the confidence level in meeting the schedule and budget
   - Using appropriate historical data to verify the schedule
   - Defining incremental funding requirements
   - Documenting project assumptions and rationale

6. Establish corrective action criteria.

HINT

Establish corrective action criteria early in the project to ensure that issues are addressed appropriately and consistently.

   Criteria are established for determining what constitutes a significant deviation from the project plan. A basis for gauging issues and problems is necessary to determine when a corrective action should be taken. The corrective actions may require replanning, which may include revising the original plan, establishing new agreements, or including mitigation activities within the current plan.

SP 2.2 IDENTIFY PROJECT RISKS

TIP

Risk management is a key to project success.

Identify and analyze project risks.

Refer to the Risk Management process area for more information about risk management activities.

Refer to the Monitor Project Risks specific practice in the Project Monitoring and Control process area for more information about risk monitoring activities.

Risks are identified or discovered and analyzed to support project planning. This specific practice should be extended to all the plans that affect the project to ensure that the appropriate interfacing is taking place between all relevant stakeholders on identified risks. Project planning risk identification and analysis typically include the following:

- Identifying risks
- Analyzing the risks to determine the impact, probability of occurrence, and time frame in which problems are likely to occur
- Prioritizing risks

Typical Work Products

1. Identified risks
2. Risk impacts and probability of occurrence
3. Risk priorities

Subpractices

1. Identify risks.

    The identification of risks involves the identification of potential issues, hazards, threats, vulnerabilities, and so on that could negatively affect work efforts and plans. Risks must be identified and described in an understandable way before they can be analyzed. When identifying risks, it is a good idea to use a standard method for defining risks. Risk identification and analysis tools can be used to help identify possible problems.

Examples of risk identification and analysis tools include the following:
- Risk taxonomies
- Risk assessments
- Checklists
- Structured interviews
- Brainstorming
- Performance models
- Cost models
- Network analysis
- Quality factor analysis

TIP

Risk identification and analysis tools help to identify risks by identifying them more completely and rapidly, analyzing them more consistently, and allowing what has been learned on previous projects to be applied to new projects.

2. Document the risks.

3. Review and obtain agreement with relevant stakeholders on the completeness and correctness of the documented risks.

4. Revise the risks as appropriate.

> Examples of when identified risks may need to be revised include the following:
> • When new risks are identified
> • When risks become problems
> • When risks are retired
> • When project circumstances change significantly

SP 2.3 PLAN FOR DATA MANAGEMENT

Plan for the management of project data.

> When integrated teams are formed, project data includes data developed and used solely within a particular team as well as data applicable across integrated team boundaries, if there are multiple integrated teams.
>
> *IPPD ADD*

TIP

This SP helps answer questions such as what data the project should collect, distribute, deliver, and archive; how and when it should do this; who should be able to access it; and how data will be stored to address the need for privacy and security, yet give access to those who need it.

HINT

Interpret data broadly to benefit from data management more fully.

Data are the various forms of documentation required to support a program in all of its areas (e.g., administration, engineering, configuration management, finance, logistics, quality, safety, manufacturing, and procurement). The data can take any form (e.g., reports, manuals, notebooks, charts, drawings, specifications, files, or correspondence). The data may exist in any medium (e.g., printed or drawn on various materials, photographs, electronic, or multimedia). Data may be deliverable (e.g., items identified by a program's contract data requirements) or data may be nondeliverable (e.g., informal data, trade studies and analyses, internal meeting minutes, internal design review documentation, lessons learned, and action items). Distribution can take many forms, including electronic transmission.

The data requirements for the project should be established for both the data items to be created and their content and form, based on a common or standard set of data requirements. Uniform content and format requirements for data items facilitate understanding of data content and help with consistent management of the data resources.

TIP

Selecting a standard form can facilitate communication and understanding.

The reason for collecting each document should be clear. This task includes the analysis and verification of project deliverables and nondeliverables, contract and noncontract data requirements, and customer-supplied data. Often, data is collected with no clear understanding of how it will be used. Data is costly and should be collected only when needed.

Typical Work Products

1. Data management plan
2. Master list of managed data
3. Data content and format description
4. Data requirements lists for acquirers and for suppliers
5. Privacy requirements
6. Security requirements
7. Security procedures
8. Mechanism for data retrieval, reproduction, and distribution
9. Schedule for collection of project data
10. Listing of project data to be collected

Subpractices

1. Establish requirements and procedures to ensure privacy and security of the data.

   Not everyone will have the need or clearance necessary to access the project data. Procedures must be established to identify who has access to what data as well as when they have access to the data.

2. Establish a mechanism to archive data and to access archived data.

   Accessed information should be in an understandable form (e.g., electronic or computer output from a database) or represented as originally generated.

3. Determine the project data to be identified, collected, and distributed.

SP 2.4 PLAN FOR PROJECT RESOURCES

Plan for necessary resources to perform the project.

> When integrated teams are formed, planning for project resources should consider staffing of the integrated teams. **IPPD ADD**

Defining project resources (labor, machinery/equipment, materials, and methods) and quantities needed to perform project activities builds on the initial estimates and provides additional information that can be applied to expand the WBS used to manage the project.

   The top-level WBS developed earlier as an estimation mechanism is typically expanded by decomposing these top levels into work

TIP

Providing a reason for the data being collected encourages cooperation from those providing the data.

TIP

The data management plan defines the data necessary for the project, who owns it, where it is stored, and how it is used. It may even specify what happens to the data after the project terminates.

PP

TIP

Data privacy and security should be considered, but may not be an applicable consideration for certain types of projects.

X-REF

Measurement data is a subset of project data. See MA SPs 1.3 and 2.3 for more information on collecting, storing, and controlling access to measurement data.

TIP

This practice addresses *all* resources, not just personnel.

TIP

The WBS established in SP 1.1 is expanded to help identify roles as well as staffing, process, facility, and tool requirements; assign work; obtain commitment to perform the work; and track it to completion. Automated tools can help you with this activity.

packages that represent singular work units that can be separately assigned, performed, and tracked. This subdivision is done to distribute management responsibility and provide better management control. Each work package or work product in the WBS should be assigned a unique identifier (e.g., number) to permit tracking. A WBS can be based on requirements, activities, work products, or a combination of these items. A dictionary that describes the work for each work package in the WBS should accompany the work breakdown structure.

Typical Work Products

1. WBS work packages
2. WBS task dictionary
3. Staffing requirements based on project size and scope
4. Critical facilities/equipment list
5. Process/workflow definitions and diagrams
6. Program administration requirements list

Subpractices

TIP

At maturity level 3, the organization is typically the main source of process requirements, standard processes, and process assets that aid in their use (see OPF SP 2.3 and OPD).

1. Determine process requirements.

   The processes used to manage a project must be identified, defined, and coordinated with all the relevant stakeholders to ensure efficient operations during project execution.

2. Determine staffing requirements.

   The staffing of a project depends on the decomposition of the project requirements into tasks, roles, and responsibilities for accomplishing the project requirements as laid out within the work packages of the WBS.

   Staffing requirements must consider the knowledge and skills required for each of the identified positions, as defined in the Plan for Needed Knowledge and Skills specific practice.

3. Determine facilities, equipment, and component requirements.

   Most projects are unique in some sense and require some set of unique assets to accomplish the objectives of the project. The determination and acquisition of these assets in a timely manner are crucial to project success.

TIP

Some items (e.g., unusual skills) take time to obtain, and need for these should be identified early.

   Lead-time items need to be identified early to determine how they will be addressed. Even when the required assets are not unique, compiling a list of all of the facilities, equipment, and parts (e.g., number of computers for the personnel working on the project, software applications, and office space) provides insight into aspects of the scope of an effort that are often overlooked.

SP 2.5 PLAN FOR NEEDED KNOWLEDGE AND SKILLS

Plan for knowledge and skills needed to perform the project.

Refer to the Organizational Training process area for more information about knowledge and skills information to be incorporated into the project plan.

Knowledge delivery to projects involves both training of project personnel and acquisition of knowledge from outside sources.

Staffing requirements are dependent on the knowledge and skills available to support the execution of the project.

Typical Work Products

1. Inventory of skill needs
2. Staffing and new hire plans
3. Databases (e.g., skills and training)

Subpractices

1. Identify the knowledge and skills needed to perform the project.
2. Assess the knowledge and skills available.
3. Select mechanisms for providing needed knowledge and skills.

> Example mechanisms include the following:
> - In-house training (both organizational and project)
> - External training
> - Staffing and new hires
> - External skill acquisition

The choice of in-house training or outsourced training for the needed knowledge and skills is determined by the availability of training expertise, the project's schedule, and the business objectives.

4. Incorporate selected mechanisms into the project plan.

SP 2.6 PLAN STAKEHOLDER INVOLVEMENT

Plan the involvement of identified stakeholders.

> When integrated teams are formed, stakeholder involvement should be planned down to the integrated team level.

IPPD ADD

Stakeholders are identified from all phases of the project lifecycle by identifying the type of people and functions needing representation in the project and describing their relevance and the degree of interaction

---

TIP

This practice addresses the training that is specific to the project.

TIP

At maturity level 2, the organization may not be capable of providing much training for its projects. Each project might address all of its knowledge and skill needs. At maturity level 3, the organization takes responsibility for addressing common training needs (e.g., training in the organization's set of standard processes).

TIP

Either the project or the organization can maintain these typical work products.

HINT

Consider all knowledge and skills required for the project, not just the technical aspects.

TIP

If a skill is needed for the current project, but is not expected to be needed for future projects, external skill acquisition may be the best choice. However, if the skill needed for the project is expected to continue, training existing employees or hiring a new employee should be explored.

X-REF

Identifying and involving relevant stakeholders is also addressed in PMC SP 1.5, IPM, and GP 2.7.

PP

HINT

For each project phase, identify stakeholders important to the success of that phase and their role (e.g., implementer, reviewer, or consultant). Arrange this information into a matrix to aid in communication, obtain their commitment (SP 3.3), and monitor status (PMC SP 1.5).

TIP

Not all stakeholders identified will be relevant stakeholders. Only a limited number of stakeholders are selected for interaction with the project as work progresses.

for specific project activities. A two-dimensional matrix with stakeholders along one axis and project activities along the other axis is a convenient format for accomplishing this identification. Relevance of the stakeholder to the activity in a particular project phase and the amount of interaction expected would be shown at the intersection of the project phase activity axis and the stakeholder axis.

For the inputs of stakeholders to be useful, careful selection of relevant stakeholders is necessary. For each major activity, identify the stakeholders who are affected by the activity and those who have expertise that is needed to conduct the activity. This list of relevant stakeholders will probably change as the project moves through the phases of the project lifecycle. It is important, however, to ensure that relevant stakeholders in the latter phases of the lifecycle have early input to requirements and design decisions that affect them.

Examples of the type of material that should be included in a plan for stakeholder interaction include the following:
• List of all relevant stakeholders
• Rationale for stakeholder involvement
• Roles and responsibilities of the relevant stakeholders with respect to the project, by project lifecycle phase
• Relationships between stakeholders
• Relative importance of the stakeholder to success of the project, by project lifecycle phase
• Resources (e.g., training, materials, time, and funding) needed to ensure stakeholder interaction
• Schedule for phasing of stakeholder interaction

Conduct of this specific practice relies on shared or exchanged information with the previous Plan for Needed Knowledge and Skills specific practice.

Typical Work Products

1. Stakeholder involvement plan

SP 2.7 ESTABLISH THE PROJECT PLAN

Establish and maintain the overall project plan content.

A documented plan that addresses all relevant planning items is necessary to achieve the mutual understanding, commitment, and performance of individuals, groups, and organizations that must execute

HINT

Most project plans change over time as requirements are better understood, so plan how and when you will maintain the plan.

or support the plans. The plan generated for the project defines all aspects of the effort, tying together in a logical manner: project lifecycle considerations; technical and management tasks; budgets and schedules; milestones; data management, risk identification, resource and skill requirements; and stakeholder identification and interaction. Infrastructure descriptions include responsibility and authority relationships for project staff, management, and support organizations.

TIP

The plan document should reflect the project's status as requirements and the project environment change.

FOR SOFTWARE ENGINEERING

For software, the planning document is often referred to as one of the following:

- Software development plan
- Software project plan
- Software plan

FOR HARDWARE ENGINEERING

For hardware, the planning document is often referred to as a hardware development plan. Development activities in preparation for production may be included in the hardware development plan or defined in a separate production plan.

TIP

A documented plan communicates resources needed, expectations, and commitments; contains a game plan for relevant stakeholders, including the project team (SP 3.3); documents the commitment to management and other providers of resources; and is the basis for managing the project.

PP

Examples of plans that have been used in the U.S. Department of Defense community include the following:

- Integrated Master Plan—an event-driven plan that documents significant accomplishments with pass/fail criteria for both business and technical elements of the project and that ties each accomplishment to a key program event.
- Integrated Master Schedule—an integrated and networked multi-layered schedule of program tasks required to complete the work effort documented in a related Integrated Master Plan.
- Systems Engineering Management Plan—a plan that details the integrated technical effort across the project.
- Systems Engineering Master Schedule—an event-based schedule that contains a compilation of key technical accomplishments, each with measurable criteria, requiring successful completion to pass identified events.
- Systems Engineering Detailed Schedule—a detailed, time-dependent, task-oriented schedule that associates specific dates and milestones with the Systems Engineering Master Schedule.

TIP

Before making a commitment, a project member analyzes what it will take to meet it. Project members who make commitments should continually evaluate their ability to meet their commitments, communicate immediately to those affected when they cannot meet their commitments, and mitigate the impacts of being unable to meet their commitments.

TIP

Commitments are a recurring theme in CMMI. Requirements are committed to in REQM, documented and reconciled in PP, monitored in PMC, and addressed more thoroughly in IPM.

HINT

Beware of commitments that are not given freely. A favorite quote that applies is "How bad do you want it? That is how bad you will get it!" If you do not allow commitments to be made freely, staff most likely will try to provide the commitment you want to hear instead of a well-thought out answer that is accurate.

HINT

Plans that affect a project can vary from one project to another. Consider the relevant stakeholders and tasks to be performed to understand what other plans affect the project.

Typical Work Products

1. Overall project plan

SG 3   OBTAIN COMMITMENT TO THE PLAN

Commitments to the project plan are established and maintained.

To be effective, plans require commitment by those responsible for implementing and supporting the plan.

SP 3.1   REVIEW PLANS THAT AFFECT THE PROJECT

Review all plans that affect the project to understand project commitments.

> When integrated teams are formed, their integrated work plans are among the plans to review.
>
> IPPD ADD

Plans developed within other process areas will typically contain information similar to that called for in the overall project plan. These plans may provide additional detailed guidance and should be compatible with and support the overall project plan to indicate who has the authority, responsibility, accountability, and control. All plans that affect the project should be reviewed to ensure a common understanding of the scope, objectives, roles, and relationships that are required for the project to be successful. Many of these plans are described by the Plan the Process generic practice in each of the process areas.

Typical Work Products

1. Record of the reviews of plans that affect the project

SP 3.2 RECONCILE WORK AND RESOURCE LEVELS

Reconcile the project plan to reflect available and estimated resources.

> When integrated teams are formed, special attention should be paid to resource commitments in circumstances of distributed integrated teams and when people are on multiple integrated teams in one or more projects.

IPPD ADD

To establish a project that is feasible, obtain commitment from relevant stakeholders and reconcile any differences between the estimates and the available resources. Reconciliation is typically accomplished by lowering or deferring technical performance requirements, negotiating more resources, finding ways to increase productivity, outsourcing, adjusting the staff skill mix, or revising all plans that affect the project or schedules.

Typical Work Products

1. Revised methods and corresponding estimating parameters (e.g., better tools and use of off-the-shelf components)
2. Renegotiated budgets
3. Revised schedules
4. Revised requirements list
5. Renegotiated stakeholder agreements

SP 3.3 OBTAIN PLAN COMMITMENT

Obtain commitment from relevant stakeholders responsible for performing and supporting plan execution.

> When integrated teams are formed, the integrated team plans should have buy-in from the team members, the interfacing teams, the project, and the process owners of the standard processes that the team has selected for tailored application.

IPPD ADD

Obtaining commitment involves interaction among all relevant stakeholders both internal and external to the project. The individual or group making a commitment should have confidence that the work can be performed within cost, schedule, and performance constraints. Often, a provisional commitment is adequate to allow the effort to begin and to permit research to be performed to increase confidence to the appropriate level needed to obtain a full commitment.

TIP

How related plans are documented is up to the project. Sometimes it makes sense to have all plans in one document. Other times it doesn't. However, all the plans must be consistent and be consistently updated.

TIP

A well-written plan includes estimates of the resources needed to complete the project successfully. When the estimates are higher than the resources available, the situation must be reconciled so that all relevant stakeholders can commit to a feasible plan (SP 3.3).

TIP

Since resource availability can change, such reconciliation will likely need to be done multiple times during the life of the project.

TIP

Commitments are a two-way form of communication.

TIP

In maturity level 1 organizations, management often communicates a different picture of the project than the staff does. This inconsistency indicates that commitments were not obtained.

PP

TIP

Documenting commitments makes clear the responsibilities of those involved with the project.

HINT

Use the WBS to ensure that all tasks are considered when obtaining commitments. Use the stakeholder involvement plan (or matrix) to ensure that all relevant stakeholders are considered.

TIP

A commitment not documented is a commitment not made (memories are imperfect and thus unreliable).

TIP

Senior management must be informed of external commitments (especially those with customers, end users, and suppliers), as they can expose the organization to unnecessary risk.

X-REF

For more information on managing commitments, dependencies, and coordination issues among relevant stakeholders, see IPM SG 2. For more information on identifying and managing interfaces, see PI SG 2.

Typical Work Products

1. Documented requests for commitments
2. Documented commitments

Subpractices

1. Identify needed support and negotiate commitments with relevant stakeholders.

   The WBS can be used as a checklist for ensuring that commitments are obtained for all tasks.

   The plan for stakeholder interaction should identify all parties from whom commitment should be obtained.

2. Document all organizational commitments, both full and provisional, ensuring appropriate level of signatories.

   Commitments must be documented to ensure a consistent mutual understanding as well as for tracking and maintenance. Provisional commitments should be accompanied by a description of the risks associated with the relationship.

3. Review internal commitments with senior management as appropriate.

4. Review external commitments with senior management as appropriate.

   Management may have the necessary insight and authority to reduce risks associated with external commitments.

5. Identify commitments on interfaces between elements in the project, and with other projects and organizational units so that they can be monitored.

   Well-defined interface specifications form the basis for commitments.

Generic Practices by Goal

GG 1 ACHIEVE SPECIFIC GOALS

The process supports and enables achievement of the specific goals of the process area by transforming identifiable input work products to produce identifiable output work products.

GP 1.1 PERFORM SPECIFIC PRACTICES

Perform the specific practices of the project planning process to develop work products and provide services to achieve the specific goals of the process area.

GG 2 INSTITUTIONALIZE A MANAGED PROCESS

The process is institutionalized as a managed process.

CONTINUOUS ONLY

GP 2.1 ESTABLISH AN ORGANIZATIONAL POLICY

Establish and maintain an organizational policy for planning and performing the project planning process.

Elaboration:

This policy establishes organizational expectations for estimating the planning parameters, making internal and external commitments, and developing the plan for managing the project.

GP 2.2 PLAN THE PROCESS

Establish and maintain the plan for performing the project planning process.

Elaboration:

Refer to Table 7.2 on page 172 in Generic Goals and Generic Practices for more information about the relationship between generic practice 2.2 and the Project Planning process area.

GP 2.3 PROVIDE RESOURCES

Provide adequate resources for performing the project planning process, developing the work products, and providing the services of the process.

Elaboration:

Special expertise, equipment, and facilities in project planning may be required. Special expertise in project planning may include the following:

- Experienced estimators
- Schedulers
- Technical experts in applicable areas (e.g., product domain and technology)

Examples of other resources provided include the following tools:
- Spreadsheet programs
- Estimating models
- Project planning and scheduling packages

GP 2.4 ASSIGN RESPONSIBILITY

Assign responsibility and authority for performing the process, developing the work products, and providing the services of the project planning process.

GP 2.5 T*RAIN* P*EOPLE*

Train the people performing or supporting the project planning process as needed.

Elaboration:

Examples of training topics include the following:
- Estimating
- Budgeting
- Negotiating
- Risk identification and analysis
- Data management
- Planning
- Scheduling

GP 2.6 M*ANAGE* C*ONFIGURATIONS*

Place designated work products of the project planning process under appropriate levels of control.

Elaboration:

Examples of work products placed under control include the following:
- Work breakdown structure
- Project plan
- Data management plan
- Stakeholder involvement plan

GP 2.7 I*DENTIFY AND* I*NVOLVE* R*ELEVANT* S*TAKEHOLDERS*

Identify and involve the relevant stakeholders of the project planning process as planned.

Elaboration:

Refer to Table 7.2 on page 172 in Generic Goals and Generic Practices for more information about the relationship between generic practice 2.7 and the Plan Stakeholder Involvement practice in the Project Planning process area.

PP

> Examples of activities for stakeholder involvement include the following:
> - Establishing estimates
> - Reviewing and resolving issues on the completeness and correctness of the project risks
> - Reviewing data management plans
> - Establishing project plans
> - Reviewing project plans and resolving issues on work and resource issues

GP 2.8 MONITOR AND CONTROL THE PROCESS

Monitor and control the project planning process against the plan for performing the process and take appropriate corrective action.

Elaboration:

> Examples of measures and work products used in monitoring and controlling include the following:
> - Number of revisions to the plan
> - Cost, schedule, and effort variance per plan revision
> - Schedule for development and maintenance of program plans

GP 2.9 OBJECTIVELY EVALUATE ADHERENCE

Objectively evaluate adherence of the project planning process against its process description, standards, and procedures, and address noncompliance.

Elaboration:

> Examples of activities reviewed include the following:
> - Establishing estimates
> - Developing the project plan
> - Obtaining commitments to the project plan

> Examples of work products reviewed include the following:
> - WBS
> - Project plan
> - Data management plan
> - Stakeholder involvement plan

GP 2.10 *Review Status with Higher Level Management*

Review the activities, status, and results of the project planning process with higher level management and resolve issues.

S ONLY

GG3 and its practices do not apply for a maturity level 2 rating, but do apply for a maturity level 3 rating and above.

GG 3 *Institutionalize a Defined Process*

The process is institutionalized as a defined process.

GP 3.1 *Establish a Defined Process*

Establish and maintain the description of a defined project planning process.

CONTINUOUS/MATURITY LEVELS 3 – 5 ONLY

GP 3.2 *Collect Improvement Information*

Collect work products, measures, measurement results, and improvement information derived from planning and performing the project planning process to support the future use and improvement of the organization's processes and process assets.

Elaboration:

> Examples of work products, measures, measurement results, and improvement information include the following:
> - Project data library structure
> - Project attribute estimates
> - Risk impacts and probability of occurrence

GG 4 *Institutionalize a Quantitatively Managed Process*

The process is institutionalized as a quantitatively managed process.

GP 4.1 *Establish Quantitative Objectives for the Process*

Establish and maintain quantitative objectives for the project planning process, which address quality and process performance, based on customer needs and business objectives.

CONTINUOUS ONLY

GP 4.2 STABILIZE SUBPROCESS PERFORMANCE

Stabilize the performance of one or more subprocesses to determine the ability of the project planning process to achieve the established quantitative quality and process-performance objectives.

GG 5 INSTITUTIONALIZE AN OPTIMIZING PROCESS

The process is institutionalized as an optimizing process.

GP 5.1 ENSURE CONTINUOUS PROCESS IMPROVEMENT

Ensure continuous improvement of the project planning process in fulfilling the relevant business objectives of the organization.

GP 5.2 CORRECT ROOT CAUSES OF PROBLEMS

Identify and correct the root causes of defects and other problems in the project planning process.

CONTINUOUS ONLY

PP

PROCESS AND PRODUCT QUALITY ASSURANCE
A Support Process Area at Maturity Level 2

Purpose

The purpose of Process and Product Quality Assurance (PPQA) is to provide staff and management with objective insight into processes and associated work products.

TIP

PPQA is often referred to as the "eyes and ears" of the organization. It ensures that the organization's policies, practices, and processes are followed.

Introductory Notes

The Process and Product Quality Assurance process area involves the following:

- Objectively evaluating performed processes, work products, and services against the applicable process descriptions, standards, and procedures
- Identifying and documenting noncompliance issues
- Providing feedback to project staff and managers on the results of quality assurance activities
- Ensuring that noncompliance issues are addressed

The Process and Product Quality Assurance process area supports the delivery of high-quality products and services by providing the project staff and managers at all levels with appropriate visibility into, and feedback on, processes and associated work products throughout the life of the project.

The practices in the Process and Product Quality Assurance process area ensure that planned processes are implemented, while the practices in the Verification process area ensure that the specified requirements are satisfied. These two process areas may on occasion address the same work product but from different perspectives. Projects should take advantage of the overlap in order to minimize duplication of effort while taking care to maintain the separate perspectives.

TIP

The phrase "process descriptions, standards, and procedures" is used in PPQA (and GP 2.9) to represent management's expectations as to how project work will be performed. The applicable process descriptions, standards, and procedures are typically identified during project planning.

TIP

Objectivity is required. Independence is not required but is often the means used to assure objectivity.

Objectivity in process and product quality assurance evaluations is critical to the success of the project. (See the definition of "objectively evaluate" in the glossary.) Objectivity is achieved by both independence and the use of criteria. A combination of methods providing evaluations against criteria by those not producing the work product is often used. Less formal methods can be used to provide broad day-to-day coverage. More formal methods can be used periodically to assure objectivity.

TIP

For less mature organizations, formal audits conducted by a separate QA group may be best. Implementing peer reviews as an objective evaluation method (second bullet) requires care; see upcoming notes and example box.

> Examples of ways to perform objective evaluations include the following:
> • Formal audits by organizationally separate quality assurance organizations
> • Peer reviews which may be performed at various levels of formality
> • In-depth review of work at the place it is performed (i.e., desk audits)
> • Distributed review and comment of work products

Traditionally, a quality assurance group that is independent of the project provides this objectivity. It may be appropriate in some organizations, however, to implement the process and product quality assurance role without that kind of independence. For example, in an organization with an open, quality-oriented culture, the process and product quality assurance role may be performed, partially or completely, by peers; and the quality assurance function may be embedded in the process. For small organizations, this might be the most feasible approach.

TIP

When an independent approach is not used, it is important to be able to demonstrate how the objectivity was achieved.

If quality assurance is embedded in the process, several issues must be addressed to ensure objectivity. Everyone performing quality assurance activities should be trained in quality assurance. Those performing quality assurance activities for a work product should be separate from those directly involved in developing or maintaining the work product. An independent reporting channel to the appropriate level of organizational management must be available so that noncompliance issues can be escalated as necessary.

> For example, in implementing peer reviews as an objective evaluation method:
> • Members are trained and roles are assigned for people attending the peer reviews.
> • A member of the peer review who did not produce this work product is assigned to perform the role of QA.
> • Checklists are available to support the QA activity.
> • Defects are recorded as part of the peer review report and are tracked and escalated outside the project when necessary.

Quality assurance should begin in the early phases of a project to establish plans, processes, standards, and procedures that will add value to the project and satisfy the requirements of the project and the organizational policies. Those performing quality assurance participate in establishing the plans, processes, standards, and procedures to ensure that they fit the project's needs and that they will be useable for performing quality assurance evaluations. In addition, the specific processes and associated work products that will be evaluated during the project are designated. This designation may be based on sampling or on objective criteria that are consistent with organizational policies and project requirements and needs.

When noncompliance issues are identified, they are first addressed within the project and resolved there if possible. Any noncompliance issues that cannot be resolved within the project are escalated to an appropriate level of management for resolution.

This process area applies primarily to evaluations of the activities and work products of a project, but it also applies to evaluations of nonproject activities and work products such as training activities. For these activities and work products, the term "project" should be appropriately interpreted.

> **HINT**
>
> Start QA early in your project.

> **TIP**
>
> For organizations just beginning to establish QA, sampling is usually 100%. However, as an organization becomes more experienced in QA, it becomes possible to select a smaller sample of the processes and work products to evaluate without compromising QA effectiveness.

PPQA

Related Process Areas

Refer to the Project Planning process area for more information about identifying processes and associated work products that will be objectively evaluated.

Refer to the Verification process area for more information about satisfying specified requirements.

Specific Goal and Practice Summary

SG 1 Objectively Evaluate Processes and Work Products
    SP 1.1   Objectively Evaluate Processes
    SP 1.2   Objectively Evaluate Work Products and Services
SG 2 Provide Objective Insight
    SP 2.1   Communicate and Ensure Resolution of Noncompliance Issues
    SP 2.2   Establish Records

Specific Practices by Goal

SG 1 OBJECTIVELY EVALUATE PROCESSES AND WORK PRODUCTS

HINT

You should evaluate processes and work products objectively.

Adherence of the performed process and associated work products and services to applicable process descriptions, standards, and procedures is objectively evaluated.

SP 1.1 OBJECTIVELY EVALUATE PROCESSES

Objectively evaluate the designated performed processes against the applicable process descriptions, standards, and procedures.

Objectivity in quality assurance evaluations is critical to the success of the project. A description of the quality assurance reporting chain and how it ensures objectivity should be defined.

Typical Work Products

1. Evaluation reports
2. Noncompliance reports
3. Corrective actions

Subpractices

TIP

Quality is everyone's job. It is important that everyone in the organization be comfortable identifying and openly discussing quality concerns.

1. Promote an environment (created as part of project management) that encourages employee participation in identifying and reporting quality issues.
2. Establish and maintain clearly stated criteria for the evaluations.

   The intent of this subpractice is to provide criteria, based on business needs, such as the following:
   • What will be evaluated
   • When or how often a process will be evaluated
   • How the evaluation will be conducted
   • Who must be involved in the evaluation

HINT

QA can often share best practices and processes with others in your organization. If you are using a traditional QA approach that involves a QA group, assign that group the responsibility to work with projects during project planning to identify what new practices and processes they might benefit from.

3. Use the stated criteria to evaluate performed processes for adherence to process descriptions, standards, and procedures.
4. Identify each noncompliance found during the evaluation.
5. Identify lessons learned that could improve processes for future products and services.

SP 1.2 OBJECTIVELY EVALUATE WORK PRODUCTS AND SERVICES

Objectively evaluate the designated work products and services against the applicable process descriptions, standards, and procedures.

Typical Work Products

1. Evaluation reports
2. Noncompliance reports
3. Corrective actions

Subpractices

1. Select work products to be evaluated, based on documented sampling criteria if sampling is used.

2. Establish and maintain clearly stated criteria for the evaluation of work products.

    The intent of this subpractice is to provide criteria, based on business needs, such as the following:

    • What will be evaluated during the evaluation of a work product
    • When or how often a work product will be evaluated
    • How the evaluation will be conducted
    • Who must be involved in the evaluation

3. Use the stated criteria during the evaluations of work products.
4. Evaluate work products before they are delivered to the customer.
5. Evaluate work products at selected milestones in their development.
6. Perform in-progress or incremental evaluations of work products and services against process descriptions, standards, and procedures.
7. Identify each case of noncompliance found during the evaluations.
8. Identify lessons learned that could improve processes for future products and services.

SG 2 PROVIDE OBJECTIVE INSIGHT

Noncompliance issues are objectively tracked and communicated, and resolution is ensured.

SP 2.1 COMMUNICATE AND ENSURE RESOLUTION OF NONCOMPLIANCE ISSUES

Communicate quality issues and ensure resolution of noncompliance issues with the staff and managers.

Noncompliance issues are problems identified in evaluations that reflect a lack of adherence to applicable standards, process descriptions, or procedures. The status of noncompliance issues provides an indication of quality trends. Quality issues include noncompliance issues and results of trend analysis.

When local resolution of noncompliance issues cannot be obtained, use established escalation mechanisms to ensure that the

---

HINT

You can embed objective evaluations of work products within some of the verification activities—particularly peer reviews—though doing so requires care. (See the Introductory Notes for more information.)

HINT

Subpractices 4 through 6 recommend evaluation of work products at different times and from different perspectives. The important point is that you think broadly about what will best give you the objective insight you need during your project.

TIP

QA reports and feedback help the organization identify what is and is not working.

HINT

Noncompliance issues may be common in low-maturity organizations and should be addressed at the lowest possible level. Don't "criminalize" those responsible for noncompliance.

PPQA

appropriate level of management can resolve the issue. Track non-compliance issues to resolution.

Typical Work Products

1. Corrective action reports
2. Evaluation reports
3. Quality trends

Subpractices

1. Resolve each noncompliance with the appropriate members of the staff where possible.
2. Document noncompliance issues when they cannot be resolved within the project.

Examples of ways to resolve noncompliance within the project include the following:
- Fixing the noncompliance
- Changing the process descriptions, standards, or procedures that were violated
- Obtaining a waiver to cover the noncompliance issue

3. Escalate noncompliance issues that cannot be resolved within the project to the appropriate level of management designated to receive and act on noncompliance issues.
4. Analyze the noncompliance issues to see if there are any quality trends that can be identified and addressed.
5. Ensure that relevant stakeholders are aware of the results of evaluations and the quality trends in a timely manner.
6. Periodically review open noncompliance issues and trends with the manager designated to receive and act on noncompliance issues.
7. Track noncompliance issues to resolution.

SP 2.2 ESTABLISH RECORDS

Establish and maintain records of the quality assurance activities.

Typical Work Products

1. Evaluation logs
2. Quality assurance reports
3. Status reports of corrective actions
4. Reports of quality trends

TIP

Also, in some cases, organizational requirements and project requirements are contradictory. Such a situation can require noncompliance issues to be escalated to a level that includes the project as well as QA.

HINT

QA activities are often seen as non-value added. The status and results of QA activities should be reported regularly. Also, consider reporting a "compliance percentage" rather than the number of noncompliance issues. This may encourage friendly competition across projects and increase appreciation for the QA role.

Subpractices

1. Record process and product quality assurance activities in sufficient detail such that status and results are known.
2. Revise the status and history of the quality assurance activities as necessary.

Generic Practices by Goal

GG 1 *ACHIEVE SPECIFIC GOALS*

The process supports and enables achievement of the specific goals of the process area by transforming identifiable input work products to produce identifiable output work products.

GP 1.1 *PERFORM SPECIFIC PRACTICES*

Perform the specific practices of the process and product quality assurance process to develop work products and provide services to achieve the specific goals of the process area.

CONTINUOUS ONLY

GG 2 *INSTITUTIONALIZE A MANAGED PROCESS*

The process is institutionalized as a managed process.

GP 2.1 *ESTABLISH AN ORGANIZATIONAL POLICY*

Establish and maintain an organizational policy for planning and performing the process and product quality assurance process.

Elaboration:

This policy establishes organizational expectations for objectively evaluating whether processes and associated work products adhere to the applicable process descriptions, standards, and procedures; and ensuring that noncompliance is addressed.

This policy also establishes organizational expectations for process and product quality assurance being in place for all projects. Process and product quality assurance must possess sufficient independence from project management to provide objectivity in identifying and reporting noncompliance issues.

GP 2.2 *PLAN THE PROCESS*

Establish and maintain the plan for performing the process and product quality assurance process.

> **TIP**
>
> Records provide a way to identify trends in QA activities (including noncompliance issues) that allow the organization to identify where additional guidance or process changes are needed.

PPQA

Elaboration:

This plan for performing the process and product quality assurance process can be included in (or referenced by) the project plan, which is described in the Project Planning process area.

GP 2.3 *Provide Resources*

Provide adequate resources for performing the process and product quality assurance process, developing the work products, and providing the services of the process.

Elaboration:

> Examples of resources provided include the following tools:
> • Evaluation tools
> • Noncompliance tracking tool

GP 2.4 *Assign Responsibility*

Assign responsibility and authority for performing the process, developing the work products, and providing the services of the process and product quality assurance process.

Elaboration:

To guard against subjectivity or bias, ensure that those people assigned responsibility and authority for process and product quality assurance can perform their evaluations with sufficient independence and objectivity.

GP 2.5 *Train People*

Train the people performing or supporting the process and product quality assurance process as needed.

Elaboration:

> Examples of training topics include the following:
> • Application domain
> • Customer relations
> • Process descriptions, standards, procedures, and methods for the project
> • Quality assurance objectives, process descriptions, standards, procedures, methods, and tools

GP 2.6 MANAGE CONFIGURATIONS

Place designated work products of the process and product quality assurance process under appropriate levels of control.

Elaboration:

> Examples of work products placed under control include the following:
> • Noncompliance reports
> • Evaluation logs and reports

GP 2.7 IDENTIFY AND INVOLVE RELEVANT STAKEHOLDERS

Identify and involve the relevant stakeholders of the process and product quality assurance process as planned.

Elaboration:

> Examples of activities for stakeholder involvement include the following:
> • Establishing criteria for the objective evaluations of processes and work products
> • Evaluating processes and work products
> • Resolving noncompliance issues
> • Tracking noncompliance issues to closure

GP 2.8 MONITOR AND CONTROL THE PROCESS

Monitor and control the process and product quality assurance process against the plan for performing the process and take appropriate corrective action.

Elaboration:

> Examples of measures and work products used in monitoring and controlling include the following:
> • Variance of objective process evaluations planned and performed
> • Variance of objective work product evaluations planned and performed
> • Schedule for objective evaluations

PPQA

GP 2.9 *OBJECTIVELY EVALUATE ADHERENCE*

Objectively evaluate adherence of the process and product quality assurance process against its process description, standards, and procedures, and address noncompliance.

Elaboration:

Refer to Table 7.2 on page 172 in Generic Goals and Generic Practices for more information about the relationship between generic practice 2.9 and the Process and Product Quality Assurance process area.

Examples of activities reviewed include the following:
- Objectively evaluating processes and work products
- Tracking and communicating noncompliance issues

Examples of work products reviewed include the following:
- Noncompliance reports
- Evaluation logs and reports

GP 2.10 *REVIEW STATUS WITH HIGHER LEVEL MANAGEMENT*

Review the activities, status, and results of the process and product quality assurance process with higher level management and resolve issues.

GG3 and its practices do not apply for a maturity level 2 rating, but do apply for a maturity level 3 rating and above.

S ONLY

GG 3 *INSTITUTIONALIZE A DEFINED PROCESS*

The process is institutionalized as a defined process.

GP 3.1 *ESTABLISH A DEFINED PROCESS*

Establish and maintain the description of a defined process and product quality assurance process.

GP 3.2 *COLLECT IMPROVEMENT INFORMATION*

Collect work products, measures, measurement results, and improvement information derived from planning and performing the process and product quality assurance process to support the future use and improvement of the organization's processes and process assets.

CONTINUOUS/MATURITY LEVELS 3 – 5 ONLY   *S ONLY*

Elaboration:

C/M LEVELS 3 - 5 ONLY

Examples of work products, measures, measurement results, and improvement information include the following:
- Evaluation logs
- Quality trends
- Noncompliance report
- Status reports of corrective action
- Cost of quality reports for the project

GG 4 INSTITUTIONALIZE A QUANTITATIVELY MANAGED PROCESS

The process is institutionalized as a quantitatively managed process.

GP 4.1 ESTABLISH QUANTITATIVE OBJECTIVES FOR THE PROCESS

Establish and maintain quantitative objectives for the process and product quality assurance process, which address quality and process performance, based on customer needs and business objectives.

GP 4.2 STABILIZE SUBPROCESS PERFORMANCE

Stabilize the performance of one or more subprocesses to determine the ability of the process and product quality assurance process to achieve the established quantitative quality and process-performance objectives.

GG 5 INSTITUTIONALIZE AN OPTIMIZING PROCESS

The process is institutionalized as an optimizing process.

GP 5.1 ENSURE CONTINUOUS PROCESS IMPROVEMENT

Ensure continuous improvement of the process and product quality assurance process in fulfilling the relevant business objectives of the organization.

GP 5.2 CORRECT ROOT CAUSES OF PROBLEMS

Identify and correct the root causes of defects and other problems in the process and product quality assurance process.

CONTINUOUS ONLY

QUANTITATIVE PROJECT MANAGEMENT
A Project Management Process Area at Maturity Level 4

Purpose

The purpose of Quantitative Project Management (QPM) is to quantitatively manage the project's defined process to achieve the project's established quality and process-performance objectives.

TIP

When asked to state why QPM is important, one friend replied, "The enterprise needs data for the next generation!"

Introductory Notes

The Quantitative Project Management process area involves the following:

TIP

The specific practices of QPM are best implemented by those who actually execute the project's defined process—not by management or consulting statisticians only.

- Establishing and maintaining the project's quality and process-performance objectives
- Identifying suitable subprocesses that compose the project's defined process based on historical stability and capability data found in process-performance baselines or models
- Selecting the subprocesses of the project's defined process to be statistically managed
- Monitoring the project to determine whether the project's objectives for quality and process performance are being satisfied, and identifying appropriate corrective action
- Selecting the measures and analytic techniques to be used in statistically managing the selected subprocesses
- Establishing and maintaining an understanding of the variation of the selected subprocesses using the selected measures and analytic techniques
- Monitoring the performance of the selected subprocesses to determine whether they are capable of satisfying their quality and process-performance objectives, and identifying corrective action
- Recording statistical and quality management data in the organization's measurement repository

TIP

When effectively implemented, QPM empowers individuals and teams by enabling them to accurately estimate (make predictions) and make commitments to these estimates (predictions) with confidence. This is a key indicator of a truly mature ML4-5 organization.

QPM

TIP

QPM and OPP are tightly coupled process areas. Each produces work products used by the other. An organization seeking to implement one of these should seek to implement both. Likewise, the CL4 GPs should not be addressed for any process area except in the context of implementing OPP and QPM.

TIP

QPM uses the organizational process assets established in OPD.

The quality and process-performance objectives, measures, and baselines identified here are developed as described in the Organizational Process Performance process area. Subsequently, the results of performing the processes associated with the Quantitative Project Management process area (e.g., measurement definitions and measurement data) become part of the organizational process assets referred to in the Organizational Process Performance process area.

To effectively address the specific practices in this process area, the organization should have already established a set of standard processes and related organizational process assets, such as the organization's measurement repository and the organization's process asset library for use by each project in establishing its defined process. The project's defined process is a set of subprocesses that form an integrated and coherent lifecycle for the project. It is established, in part, through selecting and tailoring processes from the organization's set of standard processes. (See the definition of "defined process" in the glossary.)

The project should also ensure that the measurements and progress of the supplier's efforts are made available. Establishment of effective relationships with suppliers is necessary for the successful implementation of this process area's specific practices.

Process performance is a measure of the actual process results achieved. Process performance is characterized by both process measures (e.g., effort, cycle time, and defect removal efficiency) and product measures (e.g., reliability, defect density, and response time).

Subprocesses are defined components of a larger defined process. For example, a typical organization's development process may be defined in terms of subprocesses such as requirements development, design, build, test, and peer review. The subprocesses themselves may be further decomposed as necessary into other subprocesses and process elements.

One essential element of quantitative management is having confidence in estimates (i.e., being able to predict the extent to which the project can fulfill its quality and process-performance objectives). The subprocesses that will be statistically managed are chosen based on identified needs for predictable performance. (See the definitions of "statistically managed process," "quality and process-performance objective," and "quantitatively managed process" in the glossary.)

Another essential element of quantitative management is understanding the nature and extent of the variation experienced in process performance, and recognizing when the project's actual performance may not be adequate to achieve the project's quality and process-performance objectives.

Statistical management involves statistical thinking and the correct use of a variety of statistical techniques, such as run charts, control charts, confidence intervals, prediction intervals, and tests of hypotheses. Quantitative management uses data from statistical management to help the project predict whether it will be able to achieve its quality and process-performance objectives and identify what corrective action should be taken.

This process area applies to managing a project, but the concepts found here also apply to managing other groups and functions. Applying these concepts to managing other groups and functions may not necessarily contribute to achieving the organization's business objectives, but may help these groups and functions control their own processes.

TIP

By "statistical thinking," we mean using statistical analysis techniques as tools in appropriate ways to estimate the variation in the performance of a process, to investigate its causes, and to recognize from the data when the process is not performing as it should.

Examples of other groups and functions include the following:
- Quality assurance
- Process definition and improvement
- Effort reporting
- Customer complaint handling
- Problem tracking and reporting

Related Process Areas

Refer to the Project Monitoring and Control process area for more information about monitoring and controlling the project and taking corrective action.

Refer to the Measurement and Analysis process area for more information about establishing measurable objectives, specifying the measures and analyses to be performed, obtaining and analyzing measures, and providing results.

Refer to the Organizational Process Performance process area for more information about the organization's quality and process-performance objectives, process-performance analyses, process-performance baselines, and process-performance models.

Refer to the Organizational Process Definition process area for more information about the organizational process assets, including the organization's measurement repository.

Refer to the Integrated Project Management process area for more information about establishing and maintaining the project's defined process.

Refer to the Causal Analysis and Resolution process area for more information about how to identify the causes of defects and other problems, and taking action to prevent them from occurring in the future.

QPM

X-REF

Florac, William A., and Anita D. Carleton. *Measuring the Software Process, Statistical Process Control for Software Process Improvement.* Addison-Wesley Professional, 1999.
Wheeler, Donald J., and David S. Chambers. *Understanding Statistical Process Control (2nd Edition).* SPC Press, Inc., 1992.
Wheeler, Donald J. *Understanding Variation: The Key to Managing Chaos (2nd Edition).* SPC Press, Inc., 1999.

Refer to the Organizational Innovation and Deployment process area for more information about selecting and deploying improvements that support the organization's quality and process-performance objectives.

Specific Goal and Practice Summary

SG 1 Quantitatively Manage the Project
    SP 1.1   Establish the Project's Objectives
    SP 1.2   Compose the Defined Process
    SP 1.3   Select the Subprocesses that Will Be Statistically Managed
    SP 1.4   Manage Project Performance
SG 2 Statistically Manage Subprocess Performance
    SP 2.1   Select Measures and Analytic Techniques
    SP 2.2   Apply Statistical Methods to Understand Variation
    SP 2.3   Monitor Performance of the Selected Subprocesses
    SP 2.4   Record Statistical Management Data

Specific Practices by Goal

SG 1   QUANTITATIVELY MANAGE THE PROJECT

The project is quantitatively managed using quality and process-performance objectives.

SP 1.1   ESTABLISH THE PROJECT'S OBJECTIVES

TIP

Generally, these objectives are established early during project planning, as customer requirements relating to product quality, service quality, and process performance are being established and analyzed.

Establish and maintain the project's quality and process-performance objectives.

When establishing the project's quality and process-performance objectives, it is often useful to think ahead about which processes from the organization's set of standard processes will be included in the project's defined process, and what the historical data indicates regarding their process performance. These considerations will help in establishing realistic objectives for the project. Later, as the project's actual performance becomes known and more predictable, the objectives may need to be revised.

HINT

The project's quality and process-performance objectives can be challenging but must be achievable. In other words, balance senior management's desire for improvement with what projects are realistically capable of achieving.

Typical Work Products

1. The project's quality and process-performance objectives

Subpractices

1. Review the organization's objectives for quality and process performance.

The intent of this review is to ensure that the project understands the broader business context in which the project will need to operate. The project's objectives for quality and process performance are developed in the context of these overarching organizational objectives.

Refer to the Organizational Process Performance process area for more information about the organization's quality and process-performance objectives.

2. Identify the quality and process performance needs and priorities of the customer, suppliers, end users, and other relevant stakeholders.

TIP

The project's objectives for quality and process performance are based, in part, on those of the organization (OPP SP 1.3). This approach helps ensure that the project's objectives for quality and process performance are aligned with those of the organization.

> **Examples of quality and process-performance attributes for which needs and priorities might be identified include the following:**
> - Functionality
> - Reliability
> - Maintainability
> - Usability
> - Duration
> - Predictability
> - Timeliness
> - Accuracy

3. Identify how process performance is to be measured.

    Consider whether the measures established by the organization are adequate for assessing progress in fulfilling customer, end-user, and other stakeholder needs and priorities. It may be necessary to supplement these with additional measures.

    Refer to the Measurement and Analysis process area for more information about defining measures.

4. Define and document measurable quality and process-performance objectives for the project.

    Defining and documenting objectives for the project involve the following:
    - Incorporating the organization's quality and process-performance objectives
    - Writing objectives that reflect the quality and process-performance needs and priorities of the customer, end users, and other stakeholders, and the way these objectives should be measured

---

Examples of quality attributes for which objectives might be written include the following:

• Mean time between failures

• Critical resource utilization

• Number and severity of defects in the released product

• Number and severity of customer complaints concerning the provided service

---

Examples of process-performance attributes for which objectives might be written include the following:

• Percentage of defects removed by product verification activities (perhaps by type of verification, such as peer reviews and testing)

• Defect escape rates

• Number and density of defects (by severity) found during the first year following product delivery (or start of service)

• Cycle time

• Percentage of rework time

HINT

Apply the organization's process-performance models to determine which interim objectives lead to the desired project outcomes. Review interim objectives later as part of monitoring the project's progress toward achieving its (overarching) objectives for quality and process performance. (See SP 1.4, Subpractice 2.)

5. Derive interim objectives for each lifecycle phase, as appropriate, to monitor progress toward achieving the project's objectives.

An example of a method to predict future results of a process is the use of process-performance models to predict the latent defects in the delivered product using interim measures of defects identified during product verification activities (e.g., peer reviews and testing).

---

6. Resolve conflicts among the project's quality and process-performance objectives (e.g., if one objective cannot be achieved without compromising another objective).

Resolving conflicts involves the following:

• Setting relative priorities for the objectives

• Considering alternative objectives in light of long-term business strategies as well as short-term needs

• Involving the customer, end users, senior management, project management, and other relevant stakeholders in the tradeoff decisions

• Revising the objectives as necessary to reflect the results of the conflict resolution

7. Establish traceability to the project's quality and process-performance objectives from their sources.

> Examples of sources for objectives include the following:
> • Requirements
> • Organization's quality and process-performance objectives
> • Customer's quality and process-performance objectives
> • Business objectives
> • Discussions with customers and potential customers
> • Market surveys

> An example of a method to identify and trace these needs and priorities is Quality Function Deployment (QFD).

8. Define and negotiate quality and process-performance objectives for suppliers.

 Refer to the Supplier Agreement Management process area for more information about establishing and maintaining agreements with suppliers.

9. Revise the project's quality and process-performance objectives as necessary.

SP 1.2 COMPOSE THE DEFINED PROCESS

Select the subprocesses that compose the project's defined process based on historical stability and capability data.

Refer to the Integrated Project Management process area for more information about establishing and maintaining the project's defined process.

Refer to the Organizational Process Definition process area for more information about the organization's process asset library, which might include a process element of known and needed capability.

Refer to the Organizational Process Performance process area for more information about the organization's process-performance baselines and process-performance models.

Subprocesses are identified from the process elements in the organization's set of standard processes and the process artifacts in the organization's process asset library.

Typical Work Products

1. Criteria used in identifying which subprocesses are valid candidates for inclusion in the project's defined process
2. Candidate subprocesses for inclusion in the project's defined process
3. Subprocesses to be included in the project's defined process
4. Identified risks when selected subprocesses lack a process-performance history

> **TIP**
>
> Some organizations may have only one standard process (e.g., because the projects are sufficiently similar to one another). In such cases, there are still some choices to explore (e.g., which verification subprocesses should be used with which work products).

> **TIP**
>
> Sources of historical stability and capability data include the organization's process-performance baselines and models (OPP SP 1.4 and 1.5). These organizational assets can help the project determine whether a defined process capable of achieving the project's objectives can be established from the organization's set of standard processes.

QPM

Subpractices

1. Establish the criteria to use in identifying which subprocesses are valid candidates for use.

   Identification may be based on the following:
   - Quality and process-performance objectives
   - Existence of process-performance data
   - Product line standards
   - Project lifecycle models
   - Customer requirements
   - Laws and regulations

2. Determine whether the subprocesses that are to be statistically managed, and that were obtained from the organizational process assets, are suitable for statistical management.

   A subprocess may be more suitable for statistical management if it has a history of the following:
   - Stable performance in previous comparable instances
   - Process-performance data that satisfies the project's quality and process-performance objectives

   Historical data are primarily obtained from the organization's process-performance baselines. However, these data may not be available for all subprocesses.

3. Analyze the interaction of subprocesses to understand the relationships among the subprocesses and the measured attributes of the subprocesses.

HINT

Analyze subprocess interactions (e.g., with process-performance models and system dynamic models) to determine whether they behave and interact as desired.

> Examples of analysis techniques include system dynamics models and simulations.

4. Identify the risk when no subprocess is available that is known to be capable of satisfying the quality and process-performance objectives (i.e., no capable subprocess is available or the capability of the subprocess is not known).

   Even when a subprocess has not been selected to be statistically managed, historical data and process-performance models may indicate that the subprocess is not capable of satisfying the quality and process-performance objectives.

   Refer to the Risk Management process area for more information about risk identification and analysis.

SP 1.3 SELECT THE SUBPROCESSES THAT WILL BE STATISTICALLY MANAGED

Select the subprocesses of the project's defined process that will be statistically managed.

Selecting the subprocesses to be statistically managed is often a concurrent and iterative process of identifying applicable project and organization quality and process-performance objectives, selecting the subprocesses, and identifying the process and product attributes to measure and control. Often the selection of a process, quality and process-performance objective, or measurable attribute will constrain the selection of the other two. For example, if a particular process is selected, the measurable attributes and quality and process-performance objectives may be constrained by that process.

Typical Work Products

1. Quality and process-performance objectives that will be addressed by statistical management
2. Criteria used in selecting which subprocesses will be statistically managed
3. Subprocesses that will be statistically managed
4. Identified process and product attributes of the selected subprocesses that should be measured and controlled

Subpractices

1. Identify which of the quality and process-performance objectives of the project will be statistically managed.
2. Identify the criteria to be used in selecting the subprocesses that are the main contributors to achieving the identified quality and process-performance objectives and for which predictable performance is important.

> Examples of sources for criteria used in selecting subprocesses include the following:
> - Customer requirements related to quality and process performance
> - Quality and process-performance objectives established by the customer
> - Quality and process-performance objectives established by the organization
> - Organization's performance baselines and models
> - Stable performance of the subprocess on other projects
> - Laws and regulations

HINT

Which subprocesses to statistically manage? There is no one answer, but answering the following questions might help. Which subprocesses: Provide visibility into what is happening by lifecycle phase? Contribute most to outcomes of interest? Account for the most variation in those outcomes? Provide data used in calibrating process performance models to predict ranges for future outcomes?

HINT

You can perform SP 1.1 through 1.3 concurrently and iteratively.

TIP

This specific practice focuses on more than just selecting subprocesses. It also focuses on identifying the attributes of each subprocess by which it will be statistically managed.

QPM

HINT

Identify which objectives will be addressed through statistically managing attributes of one or more subprocesses.

TIP

The project's selection of subprocesses to statistically manage is based, in part, on those selected by the organization (OPP SP 1.1).

3. Select the subprocesses that will be statistically managed using the selection criteria.

> It may not be possible to statistically manage some subprocesses (e.g., where new subprocesses and technologies are being piloted). In other cases, it may not be economically justifiable to apply statistical techniques to certain subprocesses.

4. Identify the product and process attributes of the selected subprocesses that will be measured and controlled.

TIP

The selection of subprocess attributes is not mentioned in OPP, or in any SP statement in QPM, and is thus easily overlooked.

Examples of product and process attributes include the following:
- Defect density
- Cycle time
- Test coverage

SP 1.4 MANAGE PROJECT PERFORMANCE

Monitor the project to determine whether the project's objectives for quality and process performance will be satisfied, and identify corrective action as appropriate.

Refer to the Measurement and Analysis process area for more information about analyzing and using measures.

A prerequisite for such a comparison is that the selected subprocesses of the project's defined process are being statistically managed and their process capability is understood. The specific practices of specific goal 2 provide detail on statistically managing the selected subprocesses.

Typical Work Products

1. Estimates (predictions) of the achievement of the project's quality and process-performance objectives
2. Documentation of the risks in achieving the project's quality and process-performance objectives
3. Documentation of actions needed to address the deficiencies in achieving the project's objectives

HINT

In the case of statistically managed attributes, review the process capability (i.e., natural process bounds compared to derived objectives).

Subpractices

1. Periodically review the performance of each subprocess and the capability of each subprocess selected to be statistically managed to appraise progress toward achieving the project's quality and process-performance objectives.

The process capability of each selected subprocess is determined with respect to that subprocess' established quality and process-performance objectives. These objectives are derived from the project's quality and process-performance objectives, which are for the project as a whole.

2. Periodically review the actual results achieved against established interim objectives for each phase of the project lifecycle to appraise progress toward achieving the project's quality and process-performance objectives.

3. Track suppliers' results for achieving their quality and process-performance objectives.

4. Use process-performance models calibrated with obtained measures of critical attributes to estimate progress toward achieving the project's quality and process-performance objectives.

X-REF

The organization's process-performance models (OPP SP 1.5) can help the project determine whether it will be able to achieve the project's objectives.

Process-performance models are used to estimate progress toward achieving objectives that cannot be measured until a future phase in the project lifecycle. An example is the use of process-performance models to predict the latent defects in the delivered product using interim measures of defects identified during peer reviews.

Refer to the Organizational Process Performance process area for more information about process-performance models.

The calibration is based on the results obtained from performing the previous subpractices.

5. Identify and manage the risks associated with achieving the project's quality and process-performance objectives.

Refer to the Risk Management process area for more information about identifying and managing risks.

Example sources of the risks include the following:
- Inadequate stability and capability data in the organization's measurement repository
- Subprocesses having inadequate performance or capability
- Suppliers not achieving their quality and process-performance objectives
- Lack of visibility into supplier capability
- Inaccuracies in the organization's process-performance models for predicting future performance
- Deficiencies in predicted process performance (estimated progress)
- Other identified risks associated with identified deficiencies

---

6. Determine and document actions needed to address the deficiencies in achieving the project's quality and process-performance objectives.

QPM

The intent of these actions is to plan and deploy the right set of activities, resources, and schedule to place the project back on track as much as possible to meet its objectives.

Examples of actions that can be taken to address deficiencies in achieving the project's objectives include the following:

- Changing quality or process-performance objectives so that they are within the expected range of the project's defined process
- Improving the implementation of the project's defined process so as to reduce its normal variability (reducing variability may bring the project's performance within the objectives without having to move the mean)
- Adopting new subprocesses and technologies that have the potential for satisfying the objectives and managing the associated risks
- Identifying the risk and risk mitigation strategies for the deficiencies
- Terminating the project

Refer to the Project Monitoring and Control process area for more information about taking corrective action.

SG 2   STATISTICALLY MANAGE SUBPROCESS PERFORMANCE

The performance of selected subprocesses within the project's defined process is statistically managed.

> **TIP**
>
> A "statistically managed process" does not require or expect control charts per se, but techniques that help determine the natural bounds in process variation and detect anomalous events. To date, control charts are the most widely used statistical analysis technique. When the circumstances warrant (e.g., when dealing with time-ordered event data from statistically independent events), control charts are a very practical technique for accomplishing these things.

This specific goal describes an activity critical to achieving the Quantitatively Manage the Project specific goal of this process area. The specific practices under this specific goal describe how to statistically manage the subprocesses whose selection was described in the specific practices under the first specific goal. When the selected subprocesses are statistically managed, their capability to achieve their objectives can be determined. By these means, it will be possible to predict whether the project will be able to achieve its objectives, which is key to quantitatively managing the project.

SP 2.1   SELECT MEASURES AND ANALYTIC TECHNIQUES

Select the measures and analytic techniques to be used in statistically managing the selected subprocesses.

Refer to the Measurement and Analysis process area for more information about establishing measurable objectives; on defining, collecting, and analyzing measures; and on revising measures and statistical analysis techniques.

Typical Work Products

1. Definitions of the measures and analytic techniques to be used in (or proposed for) statistically managing the subprocesses
2. Operational definitions of the measures, their collection points in the subprocesses, and how the integrity of the measures will be determined
3. Traceability of measures back to the project's quality and process-performance objectives
4. Instrumented organizational support environment to support automatic data collection

Subpractices

1. Identify common measures from the organizational process assets that support statistical management.

   Refer to the Organizational Process Definition process area for more information about common measures.

   Product lines or other stratification criteria may categorize common measures.

2. Identify additional measures that may be needed for this instance to cover critical product and process attributes of the selected subprocesses.

   In some cases, measures may be research oriented. Such measures should be explicitly identified.

3. Identify the measures that are appropriate for statistical management.

   Critical criteria for selecting statistical management measures include the following:

   - Controllable (e.g., can a measure's values be changed by changing how the subprocess is implemented?)
   - Adequate performance indicator (e.g., is the measure a good indicator of how well the subprocess is performing relative to the objectives of interest?)

TIP

The project's identification of common measures to support statistical management is based, in part, on measures established by the organization to be included in its process-performance analyses (OPP SP 1.2).

TIP

Additional measures may be needed, for example, to address unique customer requirements.

TIP

Much of the material found in the remaining subpractices (3 through 8) is a direct application of MA SG 1, Align Measurement and Analysis Activities, to statistically managing the selected subprocesses.

QPM

> Examples of subprocess measures include the following:
> • Requirements volatility
> • Ratios of estimated to measured values of the planning parameters (e.g., size, cost, and schedule)
> • Coverage and efficiency of peer reviews
> • Test coverage and efficiency
> • Effectiveness of training (e.g., percent of planned training completed and test scores)
> • Reliability
> • Percentage of the total defects inserted or found in the different phases of the project lifecycle
> • Percentage of the total effort expended in the different phases of the project lifecycle

4. Specify the operational definitions of the measures, their collection points in the subprocesses, and how the integrity of the measures will be determined.

   Operational definitions are stated in precise and unambiguous terms. They address two important criteria as follows:

   • Communication: What has been measured, how it was measured, what the units of measure are, and what has been included or excluded
   • Repeatability: Whether the measurement can be repeated, given the same definition, to get the same results

5. Analyze the relationship of the identified measures to the organization's and project's objectives, and derive objectives that state specific target measures or ranges to be met for each measured attribute of each selected subprocess.

6. Instrument the organizational support environment to support collection, derivation, and analysis of statistical measures.

   The instrumentation is based on the following:

   • Description of the organization's set of standard processes
   • Description of the project's defined process
   • Capabilities of the organizational support environment

7. Identify the appropriate statistical analysis techniques that are expected to be useful in statistically managing the selected subprocesses.

   The concept of "one size does not fit all" applies to statistical analysis techniques. What makes a particular technique appropriate is not just the type of measures, but more important, how the measures will be used and whether the situation warrants applying that technique. The appropriateness of the selection may need to be investigated from time to time.

TIP

Control charts and other statistical techniques (ANOVA and regression analyses, their non-parametric equivalents, and other Six Sigma analysis techniques) provide value in examining relationships among processes, their inputs, and sources that can assist in understanding process variation.

Examples of statistical analysis techniques are given in the next specific practice.

8. Revise the measures and statistical analysis techniques as necessary.

SP 2.2 APPLY STATISTICAL METHODS TO UNDERSTAND VARIATION

Establish and maintain an understanding of the variation of the selected subprocesses using the selected measures and analytic techniques.

Refer to the Measurement and Analysis process area for more information about collecting, analyzing, and using measurement results.

Understanding variation is achieved, in part, by collecting and analyzing process and product measures so that special causes of variation can be identified and addressed to achieve predictable performance.

A special cause of process variation is characterized by an unexpected change in process performance. Special causes are also known as "assignable causes" because they can be identified, analyzed, and addressed to prevent recurrence.

The identification of special causes of variation is based on departures from the system of common causes of variation. These departures can be identified by the presence of extreme values, or other identifiable patterns in the data collected from the subprocess or associated work products. Knowledge of variation and insight about potential sources of anomalous patterns are typically needed to detect special causes of variation.

> Sources of anomalous patterns of variation may include the following:
> - Lack of process compliance
> - Undistinguished influences of multiple underlying subprocesses on the data
> - Ordering or timing of activities within the subprocess
> - Uncontrolled inputs to the subprocess
> - Environmental changes during subprocess execution
> - Schedule pressure
> - Inappropriate sampling or grouping of data

TIP

Achieving a stable subprocess (in which special causes of variation are detected and removed) is not enough. A subprocess that otherwise appears to be stable may demonstrate unacceptably wide variation which should arouse suspicion. In any case, such a subprocess is not very predictable.

HINT

To address unacceptably wide variation, investigate the sources of that variation. How does the subprocess behave on certain data? How is its performance affected by upstream and lower-level subprocesses? The answers are opportunities to reduce variation in subprocess performance and more accurately predict future performance.

QPM

Typical Work Products

1. Collected measures
2. Natural bounds of process performance for each measured attribute of each selected subprocess
3. Process performance compared to the natural bounds of process performance for each measured attribute of each selected subprocess

Subpractices

1. Establish trial natural bounds for subprocesses having suitable historical performance data.

   Refer to the Organizational Process Performance process area for more information about organizational process-performance baselines.

   Natural bounds of an attribute are the range within which variation normally occurs. All processes will show some variation in process and product measures each time they are executed. The issue is whether this variation is due to common causes of variation in the normal performance of the process or to some special cause that can and should be identified and removed.

   When a subprocess is initially executed, suitable data for establishing trial natural bounds are sometimes available from prior instances of the subprocess or comparable subprocesses, process-performance baselines, or process-performance models. These data are typically contained in the organization's measurement repository. As the subprocess is executed, data specific to that instance are collected and used to update and replace the trial natural bounds. However, if the subprocess in question has been materially tailored, or if the conditions are materially different from those in previous instantiations, the data in the repository may not be relevant and should not be used.

   In some cases, there may be no historical comparable data (e.g., when introducing a new subprocess, when entering a new application domain, or when significant changes have been made to the subprocess). In such cases, trial natural bounds will have to be made from early process data of this subprocess. These trial natural bounds must then be refined and updated as subprocess execution continues.

TIP

If the circumstances of subprocess execution are similar to those on which a process-performance baseline is based, such a baseline may be used to help establish trial natural bounds.

HINT

If all other means of establishing trial natural bounds fail, use the first measurements obtained from performing the subprocess. Estimate natural bounds (a.k.a. trial control limits) when there are only three or four data points, but take care not to overinterpret "assignable cause signals" until natural bounds become substantiated with further data.

> Examples of criteria for determining whether data are comparable include the following:
> • Product lines
> • Application domain
> • Work product and task attributes (e.g., size of product)
> • Size of project

2. Collect data, as defined by the selected measures, on the subprocesses as they execute.

3. Calculate the natural bounds of process performance for each measured attribute.

Examples of where the natural bounds are calculated include the following:
- Control charts
- Confidence intervals (for parameters of distributions)
- Prediction intervals (for future outcomes)

4. Identify special causes of variation.

An example of a criterion for detecting a special cause of process variation in a control chart is a data point that falls outside of the 3-sigma control limits.

The criteria for detecting special causes of variation are based on statistical theory and experience and depend on economic justification. As criteria are added, special causes are more likely to be identified if present, but the likelihood of false alarms also increases.

5. Analyze the special cause of process variation to determine the reasons the anomaly occurred.

Examples of techniques for analyzing the reasons for special causes of variation include the following:
- Cause-and-effect (fishbone) diagrams
- Designed experiments
- Control charts (applied to subprocess inputs or to lower level subprocesses)
- Subgrouping (analyzing the same data segregated into smaller groups based on an understanding of how the subprocess was implemented facilitates isolation of special causes)

Some anomalies may simply be extremes of the underlying distribution rather than problems. The people implementing a subprocess are usually the ones best able to analyze and understand special causes of variation.

6. Determine what corrective action should be taken when special causes of variation are identified.

Removing a special cause of process variation does not change the underlying subprocess. It addresses an error in the way the subprocess is being executed.

Refer to the Project Monitoring and Control process area for more information about taking corrective action.

TIP

Control charts (in particular, XmR and XbarR charts) are a widely used statistical analysis technique for calculating natural bounds—especially in the case of software development.

TIP

Special causes of variation need to be identified and addressed to maintain predictable performance of the subprocess.

X-REF

For more information, see the references in "Related PAs" and the entry for "Control Charts" in Wikipedia, www.wikipedia.org.

HINT

To understand subprocess variation better, investigate at a lower level of granularity. Restratify the data (grouped to match input types or teams that will execute the subprocess), and testing data subsequences for stability to obtain tighter control. See example 7.1 in Florac, William A., and Anita D. Carleton, "Measuring the Software Process—Statistical Process Control for Software Process Improvement," Addison-Wesley, 1999.

QPM

7. Recalculate the natural bounds for each measured attribute of the selected subprocesses as necessary.

> Recalculating the (statistically estimated) natural bounds is based on measured values that signify that the subprocess has changed, not on expectations or arbitrary decisions.

Examples of when the natural bounds may need to be recalculated include the following:
- There are incremental improvements to the subprocess
- New tools are deployed for the subprocess
- A new subprocess is deployed
- The collected measures suggest that the subprocess mean has permanently shifted or the subprocess variation has permanently changed

---

SP 2.3 MONITOR PERFORMANCE OF THE SELECTED SUBPROCESSES

Monitor the performance of the selected subprocesses to determine their capability to satisfy their quality and process-performance objectives, and identify corrective action as necessary.

The intent of this specific practice is to do the following:

- Determine statistically the process behavior expected from the subprocess
- Appraise the probability that the process will meet its quality and process-performance objectives
- Identify the corrective action to be taken, based on a statistical analysis of the process-performance data

Corrective action may include renegotiating the affected project objectives, identifying and implementing alternative subprocesses, or identifying and measuring lower level subprocesses to achieve greater detail in the performance data. Any or all of these actions are intended to help the project use a more capable process. (See the definition of "capable process" in the glossary.)

A prerequisite for comparing the capability of a selected subprocess against its quality and process-performance objectives is that the performance of the subprocess is stable and predictable with respect to its measured attributes.

Process capability is analyzed for those subprocesses and those measured attributes for which (derived) objectives have been

---

TIP

The focus of the corrective action is on correcting subprocess execution, not subprocess definition. However, special causes of process variation may bring to light new promising candidate practices to be considered for future incorporation into the subprocess definition.

TIP

When corrective action is taken to address a special cause of variation, the affected data point (or data points) needs to be removed.

HINT

For each stable subprocess (i.e., stable relative to a particular attribute to be controlled), compare its natural bounds against its associated objectives for quality and process performance and take corrective action as necessary.

TIP

This comparison of the natural bounds against derived objectives is called "determining the process capability" and "comparing the Voice of the Process against the Voice of the Customer."

TIP

To determine whether a subprocess is capable relative to a particular attribute you must first know whether it is stable relative to that attribute.

established. Not all subprocesses or measured attributes that are statistically managed are analyzed regarding process capability.

The historical data may be inadequate for initially determining whether the subprocess is capable. It also is possible that the estimated natural bounds for subprocess performance may shift away from the quality and process-performance objectives. In either case, statistical control implies monitoring capability as well as stability.

Typical Work Products

1. Natural bounds of process performance for each selected subprocess compared to its established (derived) objectives
2. For each subprocess, its process capability
3. For each subprocess, the actions needed to address deficiencies in its process capability

Subpractices

1. Compare the quality and process-performance objectives to the natural bounds of the measured attribute.

   This comparison provides an appraisal of the process capability for each measured attribute of a subprocess. These comparisons can be displayed graphically, in ways that relate the estimated natural bounds to the objectives or as process capability indices, which summarize the relationship of the objectives to the natural bounds.

2. Monitor changes in quality and process-performance objectives and selected subprocess' process capability.
3. Identify and document subprocess capability deficiencies.
4. Determine and document actions needed to address subprocess capability deficiencies.

> **HINT**
>
> Display the comparison graphically instead of computing capability indices because the latter are more confusing when communicating to non-SPC experts.

QPM

Examples of actions that can be taken when a selected subprocess's performance does not satisfy its objectives include the following:

- Changing quality and process-performance objectives so that they are within the subprocess' process capability
- Improving the implementation of the existing subprocess so as to reduce its normal variability (reducing variability may bring the natural bounds within the objectives without having to move the mean)
- Adopting new process elements and subprocesses and technologies that have the potential for satisfying the objectives and managing the associated risks
- Identifying risks and risk mitigation strategies for each subprocess's process capability deficiency

> **HINT**
>
> Sometimes you can change the objectives derived for a particular attribute so that the subprocess's capability meets them by investigating whether some other subprocesses can give up some needed slack.

Refer to the Project Monitoring and Control process area for more information about taking corrective action.

SP 2.4 RECORD STATISTICAL MANAGEMENT DATA

Record statistical and quality management data in the organization's measurement repository.

Refer to the Measurement and Analysis process area for more information about managing and storing data, measurement definitions, and results.

Refer to the Organizational Process Definition process area for more information about the organization's measurement repository.

TIP

Statistical and quality management data may contribute to a future revision of the organization's process-performance baselines and models (OPP SP 1.4 and 1.5).

Typical Work Products

1. Statistical and quality management data recorded in the organization's measurement repository

Generic Practices by Goal

GG 1 ACHIEVE SPECIFIC GOALS

The process supports and enables achievement of the specific goals of the process area by transforming identifiable input work products to produce identifiable output work products.

GP 1.1 PERFORM SPECIFIC PRACTICES

Perform the specific practices of the quantitative project management process to develop work products and provide services to achieve the specific goals of the process area.

GG 2 INSTITUTIONALIZE A MANAGED PROCESS

The process is institutionalized as a managed process.

GG 3 INSTITUTIONALIZE A DEFINED PROCESS

The process is institutionalized as a defined process.

> *This generic goal's appearance here reflects its location in the staged representation.*

GP 2.1 ESTABLISH AN ORGANIZATIONAL POLICY

Establish and maintain an organizational policy for planning and performing the quantitative project management process.

CONTINUOUS ONLY

STAGED ONLY

Elaboration:

This policy establishes organizational expectations for quantitatively managing the project using quality and process-performance objectives, and statistically managing selected subprocesses within the project's defined process.

GP 2.2 PLAN THE PROCESS

Establish and maintain the plan for performing the quantitative project management process.

Elaboration:

This plan for performing the quantitative project management process can be included in (or referenced by) the project plan, which is described in the Project Planning process area.

GP 2.3 PROVIDE RESOURCES

Provide adequate resources for performing the quantitative project management process, developing the work products, and providing the services of the process.

Elaboration:

Special expertise in statistics and statistical process control may be needed to define the techniques for statistical management of selected subprocesses, but staff will use the tools and techniques to perform the statistical management. Special expertise in statistics may also be needed for analyzing and interpreting the measures resulting from statistical management.

Examples of other resources provided include the following tools:
- System dynamics models
- Automated test-coverage analyzers
- Statistical process and quality control packages
- Statistical analysis packages

GP 2.4 ASSIGN RESPONSIBILITY

Assign responsibility and authority for performing the process, developing the work products, and providing the services of the quantitative project management process.

GP 2.5 TRAIN PEOPLE

Train the people performing or supporting the quantitative project management process as needed.

Elaboration:

Examples of training topics include the following:
- Process modeling and analysis
- Process measurement data selection, definition, and collection

GP 2.6 MANAGE CONFIGURATIONS

Place designated work products of the quantitative project management process under appropriate levels of control.

Elaboration:

Examples of work products placed under control include the following:
- Subprocesses to be included in the project's defined process
- Operational definitions of the measures, their collection points in the subprocesses, and how the integrity of the measures will be determined
- Collected measures

GP 2.7 IDENTIFY AND INVOLVE RELEVANT STAKEHOLDERS

Identify and involve the relevant stakeholders of the quantitative project management process as planned.

Elaboration:

Examples of activities for stakeholder involvement include the following:
- Establishing project objectives
- Resolving issues among the project's quality and process-performance objectives
- Appraising performance of the selected subprocesses
- Identifying and managing the risks in achieving the project's quality and process-performance objectives
- Identifying what corrective action should be taken

GP 2.8 *MONITOR AND CONTROL THE PROCESS*

Monitor and control the quantitative project management process against the plan for performing the process and take appropriate corrective action.

Elaboration:

Examples of measures and work products used in monitoring and controlling include the following:
- Profile of subprocesses under statistical management (e.g., number planned to be under statistical management, number currently being statistically managed, and number that are statistically stable)
- Number of special causes of variation identified
- Schedule of data collection, analysis, and reporting activities in a measurement and analysis cycle as it relates to quantitative management activities

GP 2.9 *OBJECTIVELY EVALUATE ADHERENCE*

Objectively evaluate adherence of the quantitative project management process against its process description, standards, and procedures, and address noncompliance.

Elaboration:

Examples of activities reviewed include the following:
- Quantitatively managing the project using quality and process-performance objectives
- Statistically managing selected subprocesses within the project's defined process

Examples of work products reviewed include the following:
- Subprocesses to be included in the project's defined process
- Operational definitions of the measures
- Collected measures

GP 2.10 *REVIEW STATUS WITH HIGHER LEVEL MANAGEMENT*

Review the activities, status, and results of the quantitative project management process with higher level management and resolve issues.

GG 3 *INSTITUTIONALIZE A DEFINED PROCESS*

The process is institutionalized as a defined process.

> *This generic goal's appearance here reflects its location in the continuous representation.*

GP 3.1 *ESTABLISH A DEFINED PROCESS*

Establish and maintain the description of a defined quantitative project management process.

GP 3.2 *COLLECT IMPROVEMENT INFORMATION*

Collect work products, measures, measurement results, and improvement information derived from planning and performing the quantitative project management process to support the future use and improvement of the organization's processes and process assets.

Elaboration:

> Examples of work products, measures, measurement results, and improvement information include the following:
> - Records of statistical and quality management data from the project, including results from the periodic review of the actual performance of the statistically managed subprocesses against established interim objectives of the project
> - Process and product quality assurance report that identifies inconsistent but compliant implementations of subprocesses being considered for statistical management

GG 4 *INSTITUTIONALIZE A QUANTITATIVELY MANAGED PROCESS*

The process is institutionalized as a quantitatively managed process.

GP 4.1 *ESTABLISH QUANTITATIVE OBJECTIVES FOR THE PROCESS*

Establish and maintain quantitative objectives for the quantitative project management process, which address quality and process performance, based on customer needs and business objectives.

GP 4.2 *STABILIZE SUBPROCESS PERFORMANCE*

Stabilize the performance of one or more subprocesses to determine the ability of the quantitative project management process to achieve the established quantitative quality and process-performance objectives.

GG 5   INSTITUTIONALIZE AN OPTIMIZING PROCESS

The process is institutionalized as an optimizing process.

GP 5.1 ENSURE CONTINUOUS PROCESS IMPROVEMENT

Ensure continuous improvement of the quantitative project management process in fulfilling the relevant business objectives of the organization.

GP 5.2 CORRECT ROOT CAUSES OF PROBLEMS

Identify and correct the root causes of defects and other problems in the quantitative project management process.

CONTINUOUS ONLY

QPM

REQUIREMENTS DEVELOPMENT
An Engineering Process Area at Maturity Level 3

Purpose

The purpose of Requirements Development (RD) is to produce and analyze customer, product, and product component requirements.

TIP

REQM addresses managing requirements once they have been developed .

Introductory Notes

This process area describes three types of requirements: customer requirements, product requirements, and product component requirements. Taken together, these requirements address the needs of relevant stakeholders, including those pertinent to various product lifecycle phases (e.g., acceptance testing criteria) and product attributes (e.g., safety, reliability, and maintainability). Requirements also address constraints caused by the selection of design solutions (e.g., integration of commercial off-the-shelf products).

TIP

All requirements for the project fall into one of these three categories: customer, product, or product component requirements. Customer requirements address the customer's needs and those of other relevant stakeholders (including the organization). Since the product and product components are the result of transforming customer requirements into operational concepts and solutions, RD really addresses all requirements.

All development projects have requirements. In the case of a project that is focused on maintenance activities, the changes to the product or product components are based on changes to the existing requirements, design, or implementation. The requirements changes, if any, might be documented in change requests from the customer or users, or they might take the form of new requirements received from the requirements development process. Regardless of their source or form, the maintenance activities that are driven by changes to requirements are managed accordingly.

Requirements are the basis for design. The development of requirements includes the following activities:

- Elicitation, analysis, validation, and communication of customer needs, expectations, and constraints to obtain customer requirements that constitute an understanding of what will satisfy stakeholders
- Collection and coordination of stakeholder needs
- Development of the lifecycle requirements of the product

RD

465

- Establishment of the customer requirements
- Establishment of initial product and product component requirements consistent with customer requirements

TIP

Customer needs can prescribe particular solutions (e.g., a client-server application) in addition to describing the problem to be solved.

TIP

Product and product component requirements are usually written to provide insight into project development and engineering.

TIP

As long as they continue to be maintained, requirements provide value to those supporting the product throughout its life.

TIP

Requirements validation is addressed in RD because it is critical to align project and customer expectations. However, the practices in VAL may provide additional insight into how the RD validation activities can be performed.

This process area addresses all customer requirements rather than only product-level requirements because the customer may also provide specific design requirements.

Customer requirements are further refined into product and product component requirements. In addition to customer requirements, product and product component requirements are derived from the selected design solutions. Throughout the process areas, where we use the terms product and product component, their intended meanings also encompass services and their components.

Requirements are identified and refined throughout the phases of the product lifecycle. Design decisions, subsequent corrective actions, and feedback during each phase of the product's lifecycle are analyzed for impact on derived and allocated requirements.

The Requirements Development process area includes three specific goals. The Develop Customer Requirements specific goal addresses defining a set of customer requirements to use in the development of product requirements. The Develop Product Requirements specific goal addresses defining a set of product or product component requirements to use in the design of products and product components. The Analyze and Validate Requirements specific goal addresses the necessary analysis of customer, product, and product component requirements to define, derive, and understand the requirements. The specific practices of the third specific goal are intended to assist the specific practices in the first two specific goals. The processes associated with the Requirements Development process area and those associated with the Technical Solution process area may interact recursively with one another.

Analyses are used to understand, define, and select the requirements at all levels from competing alternatives. These analyses include the following:

- Analysis of needs and requirements for each product lifecycle phase, including needs of relevant stakeholders, the operational environment, and factors that reflect overall customer and end-user expectations and satisfaction, such as safety, security, and affordability
- Development of an operational concept
- Definition of the required functionality

The definition of functionality, also referred to as "functional analysis," is not the same as structured analysis in software development and does not presume a functionally oriented software design. In object-oriented software design, it relates to defining what are called "services" or "methods." The definition of functions, their logical groupings, and their association with requirements is referred to as a "functional architecture."

Analyses occur recursively at successively more detailed layers of a product's architecture until sufficient detail is available to enable detailed design, acquisition, and testing of the product to proceed. As a result of the analysis of requirements and the operational concept (including functionality, support, maintenance, and disposal), the manufacturing or production concept produces more derived requirements, including consideration of the following:

- Constraints of various types
- Technological limitations
- Cost and cost drivers
- Time constraints and schedule drivers
- Risks
- Consideration of issues implied but not explicitly stated by the customer or end user
- Factors introduced by the developer's unique business considerations, regulations, and laws

A hierarchy of logical entities (functions and subfunctions, object classes and subclasses) is established through iteration with the evolving operational concept. Requirements are refined, derived, and allocated to these logical entities. Requirements and logical entities are allocated to products, product components, people, or associated processes.

Involvement of relevant stakeholders in both requirements development and analysis gives them visibility into the evolution of requirements. This activity continually assures them that the requirements are being properly defined.

Related Process Areas

Refer to the Requirements Management process area for more information about managing customer and product requirements, obtaining agreement with the requirements provider, obtaining commitments with those implementing the requirements, and maintaining traceability.

Refer to the Technical Solution process area for more information about how the outputs of the requirements development processes are used, and the development of alternative solutions and designs used in refining and deriving requirements.

Refer to the Product Integration process area for more information about interface requirements and interface management.

Refer to the Verification process area for more information about verifying that the resulting product meets the requirements.

Refer to the Validation process area for more information about how the product built will be validated against the customer needs.

Refer to the Risk Management process area for more information about identifying and managing risks that are related to requirements.

Refer to the Configuration Management process area for information about ensuring that key work products are controlled and managed.

Specific Goal and Practice Summary

SG 1 Develop Customer Requirements
    SP 1.1   Elicit Needs
    SP 1.2   Develop the Customer Requirements
SG 2 Develop Product Requirements
    SP 2.1   Establish Product and Product Component Requirements
    SP 2.2   Allocate Product Component Requirements
    SP 2.3   Identify Interface Requirements
SG 3 Analyze and Validate Requirements
    SP 3.1   Establish Operational Concepts and Scenarios
    SP 3.2   Establish a Definition of Required Functionality
    SP 3.3   Analyze Requirements
    SP 3.4   Analyze Requirements to Achieve Balance
    SP 3.5   Validate Requirements

Specific Practices by Goal

SG 1 DEVELOP CUSTOMER REQUIREMENTS

> **TIP**
>
> In situations where project work is authorized through a contract, project requirements are documented in the supplier agreement (see SAM SP 1.3). Other requirements may be added to establish a larger set of customer requirements.

Stakeholder needs, expectations, constraints, and interfaces are collected and translated into customer requirements.

The needs of stakeholders (e.g., customers, end users, suppliers, builders, testers, manufacturers, and logistics support personnel) are the basis for determining customer requirements. The stakeholder needs, expectations, constraints, interfaces, operational concepts, and product concepts are analyzed, harmonized, refined, and elaborated for translation into a set of customer requirements.

Frequently, stakeholder needs, expectations, constraints, and interfaces are poorly identified or conflicting. Since stakeholder needs, expectations, constraints, and limitations should be clearly identified and understood, an iterative process is used throughout the life of the project to accomplish this objective. To facilitate the required interaction, a surrogate for the end user or customer is frequently involved to represent their needs and help resolve conflicts. The customer relations or marketing part of the organization as well as members of the development team from disciplines such as human engineering or support can be used as surrogates. Environmental, legal, and other constraints should be considered when creating and resolving the set of customer requirements.

SP 1.1 *Elicit Needs*

Elicit stakeholder needs, expectations, constraints, and interfaces for all phases of the product lifecycle.

Eliciting goes beyond collecting requirements by proactively identifying additional requirements not explicitly provided by customers. Additional requirements should address the various product lifecycle activities and their impact on the product.

Examples of techniques to elicit needs include the following:
- Technology demonstrations
- Interface control working groups
- Technical control working groups
- Interim project reviews
- Questionnaires, interviews, and operational scenarios obtained from end users
- Operational walkthroughs and end-user task analysis
- Prototypes and models
- Brainstorming
- Quality Function Deployment
- Market surveys
- Beta testing
- Extraction from sources such as documents, standards, or specifications
- Observation of existing products, environments, and workflow patterns
- Use cases
- Business case analysis
- Reverse engineering (for legacy products)
- Customer satisfaction surveys

TIP

Stakeholder needs are rarely communicated in an official document. They are communicated in documentation, conversations, meetings, demonstrations, and so on. Therefore, this information must be translated into requirements that the project and the customer can agree to.

HINT

Rarely does a customer know exactly what he wants. Plan for an iterative process so that you can learn the requirements for the product.

TIP

In the case of product lines or product families, SP 1.1 is sometimes implemented across the product line or product family. A special infrastructure project establishes common assets used in developing each product in the family. In such an organization, many requirements come from the organization and many components are acquired (i.e., SAM applies) from the infrastructure project.

HINT

Ask what the product must do and how it will behave. Also determine what is required to produce it (if it is a physical product), license it, install it, train end users, maintain it, migrate to new versions, support its use, retire it, and dispose of it.

RD

Examples of sources of requirements that might not be identified by the customer include the following:

- Business policies
- Standards
- Business environmental requirements (e.g., laboratories, testing and other facilities, and information technology infrastructure)
- Technology
- Legacy products or product components (reuse product components)

Subpractices

1. Engage relevant stakeholders using methods for eliciting needs, expectations, constraints, and external interfaces.

SP 1.2 DEVELOP THE CUSTOMER REQUIREMENTS

Transform stakeholder needs, expectations, constraints, and interfaces into customer requirements.

TIP

Neither the acquirer nor the project should abrogate or diminish project responsibility to implement appropriate verifications and validations.

The various inputs from the relevant stakeholders must be consolidated, missing information must be obtained, and conflicts must be resolved in documenting the recognized set of customer requirements. The customer requirements may include needs, expectations, and constraints with regard to verification and validation.

In some situations, the customer provides a set of requirements to the project, or the requirements exist as an output of a previous project's activities. In these situations, the customer requirements could conflict with the relevant stakeholders' needs, expectations, constraints, and interfaces and will need to be transformed into the recognized set of customer requirements after appropriate resolution of conflicts.

Relevant stakeholders representing all phases of the product's lifecycle should include business as well as technical functions. In this way, concepts for all product-related lifecycle processes are considered concurrently with the concepts for the products. Customer requirements result from informed decisions on the business as well as technical effects of their requirements.

Typical Work Products

1. Customer requirements
2. Customer constraints on the conduct of verification
3. Customer constraints on the conduct of validation

Subpractices

1. Translate the stakeholder needs, expectations, constraints, and interfaces into documented customer requirements.

2. Define constraints for verification and validation.

SG 2 DEVELOP PRODUCT REQUIREMENTS

Customer requirements are refined and elaborated to develop product and product component requirements.

Customer requirements are analyzed in conjunction with the development of the operational concept to derive more detailed and precise sets of requirements called "product and product component requirements." Product and product component requirements address the needs associated with each product lifecycle phase. Derived requirements arise from constraints, consideration of issues implied but not explicitly stated in the customer requirements baseline, and factors introduced by the selected architecture, the design, and the developer's unique business considerations. The requirements are reexamined with each successive, lower level set of requirements and functional architecture, and the preferred product concept is refined.

The requirements are allocated to product functions and product components including objects, people, and processes. The traceability of requirements to functions, objects, tests, issues, or other entities is documented. The allocated requirements and functions are the basis for the synthesis of the technical solution. As internal components are developed, additional interfaces are defined and interface requirements are established.

Refer to the Maintain Bidirectional Traceability of Requirements specific practice of the Requirements Management process area for more information about maintaining bidirectional traceability.

SP 2.1 ESTABLISH PRODUCT AND PRODUCT COMPONENT REQUIREMENTS

Establish and maintain product and product component requirements, which are based on the customer requirements.

The customer requirements may be expressed in the customer's terms and may be nontechnical descriptions. The product requirements are the expression of these requirements in technical terms that can be used for design decisions. An example of this translation is found in the first House of Quality Function Deployment, which

TIP

Recursion is built into SP 2.1. Product requirements are associated with the top level of the product hierarchy. Product component requirements are recursively developed for each lower level in parallel with the recursive development of a TS.

RD

X-REF

There are many sources of information on QFD, including the iSixSigma Web site (www.isixsigma.com) and the Quality Function Deployment Institute Website (www.qfdi.org).

TIP

The wording in SP 2.1, "… maintain product and product component requirements," should be interpreted to cover the modification of requirements, not the administration of such changes (REQM SP 1.3).

TIP

Architecture requirements express the qualities and performance points that are critical to product success (TS SP 2.1).

maps customer desires into technical parameters. For instance, "solid sounding door" might be mapped to size, weight, fit, dampening, and resonant frequencies.

Product and product component requirements address the satisfaction of customer, business, and project objectives and associated attributes, such as effectiveness and affordability.

Derived requirements also address the cost and performance of other lifecycle phases (e.g., production, operations, and disposal) to the extent compatible with business objectives.

The modification of requirements due to approved requirement changes is covered by the "maintain" function of this specific practice; whereas, the administration of requirement changes is covered by the Requirements Management process area.

Refer to the Requirements Management process area for more information about managing changes to requirements.

Typical Work Products

1. Derived requirements
2. Product requirements
3. Product component requirements

Subpractices

1. Develop requirements in technical terms necessary for product and product component design.

   Develop architecture requirements addressing critical product qualities and performance necessary for product architecture design.

2. Derive requirements that result from design decisions.

   Refer to the Technical Solution process area for more information about developing the solutions that generate additional derived requirements.

   Selection of a technology brings with it additional requirements. For instance, use of electronics requires additional technology-specific requirements such as electromagnetic interference limits.

3. Establish and maintain relationships between requirements for consideration during change management and requirements allocation.

   Refer to the Requirements Management process area for more information about maintaining requirements traceability.

   Relationships between requirements can aid in evaluating the impact of changes.

SP 2.2 *ALLOCATE PRODUCT COMPONENT REQUIREMENTS*

Allocate the requirements for each product component.

Refer to the Technical Solution process area for more information about alloca-tion of requirements to products and product components. This specific practice provides information for defining the allocation of requirements but must inter-act with the specific practices in the Technical Solution process area to establish solutions to which the requirements are allocated.

The requirements for product components of the defined solution include allocation of product performance; design constraints; and fit, form, and function to meet requirements and facilitate produc-tion. In cases where a higher level requirement specifies performance that will be the responsibility of two or more product components, the performance must be partitioned for unique allocation to each product component as a derived requirement.

Typical Work Products

1. Requirement allocation sheets
2. Provisional requirement allocations
3. Design constraints
4. Derived requirements
5. Relationships among derived requirements

Subpractices

1. Allocate requirements to functions.
2. Allocate requirements to product components.
3. Allocate design constraints to product components.
4. Document relationships among allocated requirements.

    Relationships include dependencies in which a change in one require-ment may affect other requirements.

SP 2.3 *IDENTIFY INTERFACE REQUIREMENTS*

Identify interface requirements.

Interfaces between functions (or between objects) are identified. Functional interfaces may drive the development of alternative solu-tions described in the Technical Solution process area.

Refer to the Product Integration process area for more information about the management of interfaces and the integration of products and product compo-nents.

TIP

Sometimes a higher-level requirement specifies perform-ance that is satisfied by multi-ple product components. Examples include a timing requirement on a transaction implemented by multiple prod-uct components, a constraint on memory that is met by a col-lection of components, and a safety requirement that is achieved by the components of a product.

TIP

The allocation of a higher-level requirement to product compo-nents is not necessarily fixed. Often a provisional allocation of a higher-level requirement to product components is made, but is later revised to account for the unique or emerging capabilities of individual sup-pliers, teams, or new COTS products.

TIP

Because of the importance of interfaces to effective product development, interfaces are addressed in multiple places: Identifying interface require-ments is covered in RD SP 2.3, design interfaces is covered in TS SP 2.3, and ensuring interface compatibility in product inte-gration is covered in PI SP 2.1.

RD

Interface requirements between products or product components identified in the product architecture are defined. They are controlled as part of product and product component integration and are an integral part of the architecture definition.

Typical Work Products

1. Interface requirements

Subpractices

1. Identify interfaces both external to the product and internal to the product (i.e., between functional partitions or objects).

   As the design progresses, the product architecture will be altered by technical solution processes, creating new interfaces between product components and components external to the product.

   Interfaces with product-related lifecycle processes should also be identified.

TIP

Identifying the interfaces for which requirements will be developed is not a one-time event, but continues for as long as new interfaces are established.

> Examples of these interfaces include interfaces with test equipment, transportation systems, support systems, and manufacturing facilities.

2. Develop the requirements for the identified interfaces.

   Refer to the Technical Solution process area for more information about generating new interfaces during the design process.

   Requirements for interfaces are defined in terms such as origination, destination, stimulus, data characteristics for software, and electrical and mechanical characteristics for hardware.

SG 3 ANALYZE AND VALIDATE REQUIREMENTS

The requirements are analyzed and validated, and a definition of required functionality is developed.

TIP

The purpose of requirements validation is to make sure you have a clear understanding of what the customer wants and needs. Often this understanding evolves over time and requires a series of requirements validation activities.

The specific practices of the Analyze and Validate Requirements specific goal support the development of the requirements in both the Develop Customer Requirements specific goal and the Develop Product Requirements specific goal. The specific practices associated with this specific goal cover analyzing and validating the requirements with respect to the user's intended environment.

Analyses are performed to determine what impact the intended operational environment will have on the ability to satisfy the stakeholders' needs, expectations, constraints, and interfaces. Considerations, such as feasibility, mission needs, cost constraints, potential market size, and acquisition strategy, must all be taken into account, depending on the product context. A definition of required functionality is also established. All specified usage modes for the product are considered, and a timeline analysis is generated for time-critical sequencing of functions.

The objectives of the analyses are to determine candidate requirements for product concepts that will satisfy stakeholder needs, expectations, and constraints; and then to translate these concepts into requirements. In parallel with this activity, the parameters that will be used to evaluate the effectiveness of the product are determined based on customer input and the preliminary product concept.

Requirements are validated to increase the probability that the resulting product will perform as intended in the use environment.

SP 3.1 ESTABLISH OPERATIONAL CONCEPTS AND SCENARIOS

Establish and maintain operational concepts and associated scenarios.

A scenario is typically a sequence of events that might occur in the use of the product, which is used to make explicit some of the needs of the stakeholders. In contrast, an operational concept for a product usually depends on both the design solution and the scenario. For example, the operational concept for a satellite-based communications product is quite different from one based on landlines. Since the alternative solutions have not usually been defined when preparing the initial operational concepts, conceptual solutions are developed for use when analyzing the requirements. The operational concepts are refined as solution decisions are made and lower level detailed requirements are developed.

Just as a design decision for a product may become a requirement for product components, the operational concept may become the scenarios (requirements) for product components. Operational concepts and scenarios are evolved to facilitate the selection of product component solutions that, when implemented, will satisfy the intended use of the product. Operational concepts and scenarios document the interaction of the product components with the environment, users, and other product components, regardless of engineering discipline. They should be documented for all modes and states within operations, product deployment, delivery, support (including maintenance and sustainment), training, and disposal.

TIP

Requirements analyses examine requirements from different perspectives (e.g., feasibility, cost, and risk) and using different abstractions (e.g., functional, data flow, entity-relationship, state diagrams, and temporal).

HINT

Identify technical performance parameters and measures that help in assessing or predicting performance, usability, cost, schedule, risk, etc. Use them to state product requirements, establish quality objectives, evaluate progress, manage risk, and conduct trade studies. They provide a data-driven approach to engineering the product.

X-REF

For more information about technical performance parameters, see "Using CMMI to Improve Earned Value Management" (www.sei.cmu.edu/publications/documents/02.reports/02tn016.html).

HINT

Think of an operational concept as a *picture* that portrays the product, end user, and other entities in the intended environment. Think of an operational scenario as a *story* describing a sequence of events and end-user and product interactions. An operational concept provides a context for developing or evaluating a set of scenarios.

RD

TIP

Operational concepts and scenarios are a way to demonstrate or bring to life what the requirements are trying to capture.

The scenarios may include operational sequences, provided those sequences are an expression of customer requirements rather than operational concepts.

Typical Work Products

1. Operational concept
2. Product or product component installation, operational, maintenance, and support concepts
3. Disposal concepts
4. Use cases
5. Timeline scenarios
6. New requirements

Subpractices

1. Develop operational concepts and scenarios that include functionality, performance, maintenance, support, and disposal as appropriate.

   Identify and develop scenarios, consistent with the level of detail in the stakeholder needs, expectations, and constraints in which the proposed product or product component is expected to operate.

2. Define the environment in which the product or product component will operate, including boundaries and constraints.

3. Review operational concepts and scenarios to refine and discover requirements.

   Operational concept and scenario development is an iterative process. The reviews should be held periodically to ensure that they agree with the requirements. The review may be in the form of a walk-through.

X-REF

Component selection is further described in TS.

4. Develop a detailed operational concept, as products and product components are selected, that defines the interaction of the product, the end user, and the environment, and that satisfies the operational, maintenance, support, and disposal needs.

SP 3.2 ESTABLISH A DEFINITION OF REQUIRED FUNCTIONALITY

Establish and maintain a definition of required functionality.

TIP

Functionality is typically documented using diagrams and descriptions. The diagrams provide a high-level picture of the overall functionality, whereas the descriptions provide the details.

The definition of functionality, also referred to as "functional analysis," is the description of what the product is intended to do. The definition of functionality can include actions, sequence, inputs, outputs, or other information that communicates the manner in which the product will be used.

Functional analysis is not the same as structured analysis in software development and does not presume a functionally oriented software design. In object-oriented software design, it relates to defining what are called "services" or "methods." The definition of functions, their logical groupings, and their association with requirements is referred to as a functional architecture. (See the definition of "functional architecture" in the glossary.)

Typical Work Products

1. Functional architecture
2. Activity diagrams and use cases
3. Object-oriented analysis with services or methods identified

Subpractices

1. Analyze and quantify functionality required by end users.
2. Analyze requirements to identify logical or functional partitions (e.g., subfunctions).
3. Partition requirements into groups, based on established criteria (e.g., similar functionality, performance, or coupling), to facilitate and focus the requirements analysis.
4. Consider the sequencing of time-critical functions both initially and subsequently during product component development.
5. Allocate customer requirements to functional partitions, objects, people, or support elements to support the synthesis of solutions.
6. Allocate functional and performance requirements to functions and subfunctions.

SP 3.3 ANALYZE REQUIREMENTS

Analyze requirements to ensure that they are necessary and sufficient.

In light of the operational concept and scenarios, the requirements for one level of the product hierarchy are analyzed to determine whether they are necessary and sufficient to meet the objectives of higher levels of the product hierarchy. The analyzed requirements then provide the basis for more detailed and precise requirements for lower levels of the product hierarchy.

As requirements are defined, their relationship to higher level requirements and the higher level defined functionality must be understood. One of the other actions is the determination of which key requirements will be used to track progress. For instance, the weight of a product or size of a software product may be monitored through development based on its risk.

TIP

The functional architecture is an abstraction of the product that describes the functions the product must perform. The architecture organizes these functions according to criteria to make them manageable and to assist in requirements identification, allocation, and analysis as well as evaluating and selecting a technical solution.

TIP

As the activities described in RD and TS progress, the functional architecture is refined to reflect decisions made.

TIP

Developing the functional architecture and allocating requirements to it helps enable the selection of product components and allocating requirements to them.

TIP

Requirements analyses help answer questions such as whether all requirements are necessary, whether are any missing, whether they are consistent with one other, and whether they can be implemented and verified.

X-REF

When analyzing requirements, look at some of the characteristics described in REQM SP 1.1 Subpractice 2 to understand the many factors that can be considered.

RD

TIP

The relationships among requirements up and down the product hierarchy are investigated and recorded (see REQM SP 1.4).

Refer to the Verification process area for more information about verification methods that could be used to support this analysis.

Typical Work Products

1. Requirements defects reports
2. Proposed requirements changes to resolve defects
3. Key requirements
4. Technical performance measures

HINT

As conflicts are removed, inform the relevant stakeholders of changes that affect the requirements they provided.

Subpractices

1. Analyze stakeholder needs, expectations, constraints, and external interfaces to remove conflicts and to organize into related subjects.
2. Analyze requirements to determine whether they satisfy the objectives of higher level requirements.
3. Analyze requirements to ensure that they are complete, feasible, realizable, and verifiable.

    While design determines the feasibility of a particular solution, this subpractice addresses knowing which requirements affect feasibility.

TIP

In these subpractices, you determine whether the requirements serve as an adequate basis for product development and how to track progress in achieving key requirements.

4. Identify key requirements that have a strong influence on cost, schedule, functionality, risk, or performance.
5. Identify technical performance measures that will be tracked during the development effort.

    Refer to the Measurement and Analysis process area for more information about the use of measurements.

6. Analyze operational concepts and scenarios to refine the customer needs, constraints, and interfaces and to discover new requirements.

    This analysis may result in more detailed operational concepts and scenarios as well as supporting the derivation of new requirements.

SP 3.4 ANALYZE REQUIREMENTS TO ACHIEVE BALANCE

Analyze requirements to balance stakeholder needs and constraints.

TIP

Often the wish list is too large. It is necessary to understand the tradeoffs and what is truly important.

Stakeholder needs and constraints can address cost, schedule, performance, functionality, reusable components, maintainability, or risk.

Typical Work Products

1. Assessment of risks related to requirements

Subpractices

1. Use proven models, simulations, and prototyping to analyze the balance of stakeholder needs and constraints.

   Results of the analyses can be used to reduce the cost of the product and the risk in developing the product.

2. Perform a risk assessment on the requirements and functional architecture.

   Refer to the Risk Management process area for information about performing a risk assessment on customer and product requirements and the functional architecture.

3. Examine product lifecycle concepts for impacts of requirements on risks.

SP 3.5 VALIDATE REQUIREMENTS

Validate requirements to ensure the resulting product will perform as intended in the user's environment.

Requirements validation is performed early in the development effort with end users to gain confidence that the requirements are capable of guiding a development that results in successful final validation. This activity should be integrated with risk management activities. Mature organizations will typically perform requirements validation in a more sophisticated way using multiple techniques and will broaden the basis of the validation to include other stakeholder needs and expectations.

> **TIP**
> Requirements validation should happen early and should be repeated to limit the risk of having inadequate requirements.

> Examples of techniques used for requirements validation include the following:
> • Analysis
> • Simulations
> • Prototyping
> • Demonstrations

Typical Work Products

1. Record of analysis methods and results

Subpractices

1. Analyze the requirements to determine the risk that the resulting product will not perform appropriately in its intended-use environment.

TIP

Requirements validation in this SP and product validation in VAL have the same goal, though different perspectives. Requirements validation focuses on the adequacy and completeness of the requirements. VAL focuses on predicting at multiple points in product development how well the product will satisfy user needs.

2. Explore the adequacy and completeness of requirements by developing product representations (e.g., prototypes, simulations, models, scenarios, and storyboards) and by obtaining feedback about them from relevant stakeholders.

> *Refer to the Validation process area for information about preparing for and performing validation on products and product components.*

3. Assess the design as it matures in the context of the requirements validation environment to identify validation issues and expose unstated needs and customer requirements.

Generic Practices by Goal

GG 1 ACHIEVE SPECIFIC GOALS

The process supports and enables achievement of the specific goals of the process area by transforming identifiable input work products to produce identifiable output work products.

GP 1.1 PERFORM SPECIFIC PRACTICES

Perform the specific practices of the requirements development process to develop work products and provide services to achieve the specific goals of the process area.

GG 2 INSTITUTIONALIZE A MANAGED PROCESS

The process is institutionalized as a managed process.

CONTINUOUS ONLY

GG 3 INSTITUTIONALIZE A DEFINED PROCESS

The process is institutionalized as a defined process.

> *This generic goal's appearance here reflects its location in the staged representation.*

STAGED ONLY

GP 2.1 ESTABLISH AN ORGANIZATIONAL POLICY

Establish and maintain an organizational policy for planning and performing the requirements development process.

Elaboration:

This policy establishes organizational expectations for collecting stakeholder needs, formulating product and product component requirements, and analyzing and validating those requirements.

GP 2.2 *PLAN THE PROCESS*

Establish and maintain the plan for performing the requirements development process.

Elaboration:

This plan for performing the requirements development process can be part of (or referenced by) the project plan as described in the Project Planning process area.

GP 2.3 *PROVIDE RESOURCES*

Provide adequate resources for performing the requirements development process, developing the work products, and providing the services of the process.

Elaboration:

Special expertise in the application domain, methods for eliciting stakeholder needs, and methods and tools for specifying and analyzing customer, product, and product component requirements may be required.

> Examples of other resources provided include the following tools:
> • Requirements specification tools
> • Simulators and modeling tools
> • Prototyping tools
> • Scenario definition and management tools
> • Requirements tracking tools

GP 2.4 *ASSIGN RESPONSIBILITY*

Assign responsibility and authority for performing the process, developing the work products, and providing the services of the requirements development process.

GP 2.5 *TRAIN PEOPLE*

Train the people performing or supporting the requirements development process as needed.

RD

Elaboration:

Examples of training topics include the following:
- Application domain
- Requirements definition and analysis
- Requirements elicitation
- Requirements specification and modeling
- Requirements tracking

GP 2.6 MANAGE CONFIGURATIONS

Place designated work products of the requirements development process under appropriate levels of control.

Elaboration:

Examples of work products placed under control include the following:
- Customer requirements
- Functional architecture
- Product and product component requirements
- Interface requirements

GP 2.7 IDENTIFY AND INVOLVE RELEVANT STAKEHOLDERS

Identify and involve the relevant stakeholders of the requirements development process as planned.

Elaboration:

Select relevant stakeholders from customers, end users, developers, producers, testers, suppliers, marketers, maintainers, disposal personnel, and others who may be affected by, or may affect, the product as well as the process.

Examples of activities for stakeholder involvement include the following:
- Reviewing the adequacy of requirements in meeting needs, expectations, constraints, and interfaces
- Establishing operational concepts and scenarios
- Assessing the adequacy of requirements
- Establishing product and product component requirements
- Assessing product cost, schedule, and risk

GP 2.8 MONITOR AND CONTROL THE PROCESS

Monitor and control the requirements development process against the plan for performing the process and take appropriate corrective action.

Elaboration:

> Examples of measures and work products used in monitoring and controlling include the following:
> - Cost, schedule, and effort expended for rework
> - Defect density of requirements specifications
> - Schedule for activities to develop a set of requirements

GP 2.9 OBJECTIVELY EVALUATE ADHERENCE

Objectively evaluate adherence of the requirements development process against its process description, standards, and procedures, and address noncompliance.

Elaboration:

> Examples of activities reviewed include the following:
> - Collecting stakeholder needs
> - Formulating product and product component requirements
> - Analyzing and validating product and product component requirements

> Examples of work products reviewed include the following:
> - Product requirements
> - Product component requirements
> - Interface requirements
> - Functional architecture

GP 2.10 REVIEW STATUS WITH HIGHER LEVEL MANAGEMENT

Review the activities, status, and results of the requirements development process with higher level management and resolve issues.

GG 3 INSTITUTIONALIZE A DEFINED PROCESS

The process is institutionalized as a defined process.

> *This generic goal's appearance here reflects its location in the continuous representation.*

CONT. ONLY

RD

GP 3.1 ESTABLISH A DEFINED PROCESS

Establish and maintain the description of a defined requirements development process.

GP 3.2 COLLECT IMPROVEMENT INFORMATION

Collect work products, measures, measurement results, and improvement information derived from planning and performing the requirements development process to support the future use and improvement of the organization's processes and process assets.

Elaboration:

> Examples of work products, measures, measurement results, and improvement information include the following:
> • List of the requirements for a product that are found to be ambiguous
> • Number of requirements introduced at each phase of the project lifecycle
> • Lessons learned from the requirements allocation process

GG 4 INSTITUTIONALIZE A QUANTITATIVELY MANAGED PROCESS

The process is institutionalized as a quantitatively managed process.

GP 4.1 ESTABLISH QUANTITATIVE OBJECTIVES FOR THE PROCESS

Establish and maintain quantitative objectives for the requirements development process, which address quality and process performance, based on customer needs and business objectives.

GP 4.2 STABILIZE SUBPROCESS PERFORMANCE

Stabilize the performance of one or more subprocesses to determine the ability of the requirements development process to achieve the established quantitative quality and process-performance objectives.

GG 5 INSTITUTIONALIZE AN OPTIMIZING PROCESS

The process is institutionalized as an optimizing process.

GP 5.1 ENSURE CONTINUOUS PROCESS IMPROVEMENT

Ensure continuous improvement of the requirements development process in fulfilling the relevant business objectives of the organization.

CONTINUOUS ONLY

GP 5.2 CORRECT ROOT CAUSES OF PROBLEMS

Identify and correct the root causes of defects and other problems in the requirements development process.

REQUIREMENTS MANAGEMENT
An Engineering Process Area at Maturity Level 2

Purpose

The purpose of Requirements Management (REQM) is to manage the requirements of the project's products and product components and to identify inconsistencies between those requirements and the project's plans and work products.

X-REF

REQM does not address eliciting or developing requirements. For more information on these topics, refer to the RD process area.

Introductory Notes

Requirements management processes manage all requirements received or generated by the project, including both technical and nontechnical requirements as well as those requirements levied on the project by the organization. In particular, if the Requirements Development process area is implemented, its processes will generate product and product component requirements that will also be managed by the requirements management processes. Throughout the process areas, where we use the terms product and product component, their intended meanings also encompass services and their components. When the Requirements Management, Requirements Development, and Technical Solution process areas are all implemented, their associated processes may be closely tied and be performed concurrently.

The project takes appropriate steps to ensure that the agreed-on set of requirements is managed to support the planning and execution needs of the project. When a project receives requirements from an approved requirements provider, the requirements are reviewed with the requirements provider to resolve issues and prevent misunderstanding before the requirements are incorporated into the project's plans. Once the requirements provider and the requirements receiver reach an agreement, commitment to the requirements is obtained from the project participants. The project manages changes to the requirements as they evolve and identifies any inconsistencies that occur among the plans, work products, and requirements.

TIP

REQM addresses *all requirements* handled by the project, thus providing a stable foundation for project planning, development, testing, and delivery.

TIP

Nontechnical requirements include requirements that address cost and schedule.

TIP

RD develops requirements, TS implements them, and REQM manages them from development through implementation.

TIP

Requirements providers can include customers, end users, suppliers, management, regulatory agencies, or standards bodies.

REQM

TIP

Managing changes to requirements ensures that all parts of the project are working on the most current set of requirements.

TIP

Bidirectional traceability, explained in SP 1.4, is a concept that is critical to implementing RD and TS.

TIP

In maintenance projects, requirements changes still need to be managed, regardless of their source.

TIP

The practices and principles in a process area are often more broadly applicable than first imagined. REQM is often valuable to an organization's training department, quality assurance group, marketing group, and so on.

Part of the management of requirements is to document requirements changes and rationale and to maintain bidirectional traceability between source requirements and all product and product component requirements. (See the definition of "bidirectional traceability" in the glossary.)

All development projects have requirements. In the case of a project that is focused on maintenance activities, the changes to the product or product components are based on changes to the existing requirements, design, or implementation. The requirements changes, if any, might be documented in change requests from the customer or users, or they might take the form of new requirements received from the requirements development process. Regardless of their source or form, the maintenance activities that are driven by changes to requirements are managed accordingly.

Related Process Areas

Refer to the Requirements Development process area for more information about transforming stakeholder needs into product requirements and deciding how to allocate or distribute requirements among the product components.

Refer to the Technical Solution process area for more information about transforming requirements into technical solutions.

Refer to the Project Planning process area for more information about how project plans reflect requirements and need to be revised as requirements change.

Refer to the Configuration Management process area for more information about baselines and controlling changes to configuration documentation for requirements.

Refer to the Project Monitoring and Control process area for more information about tracking and controlling the activities and work products that are based on the requirements and taking appropriate corrective action.

Refer to the Risk Management process area for more information about identifying and handling risks associated with requirements.

Specific Goal and Practice Summary

SG 1 Manage Requirements
  SP 1.1 Obtain an Understanding of Requirements
  SP 1.2 Obtain Commitment to Requirements
  SP 1.3 Manage Requirements Changes
  SP 1.4 Maintain Bidirectional Traceability of Requirements
  SP 1.5 Identify Inconsistencies Between Project Work and Requirements

Specific Practices by Goal

SG 1 MANAGE REQUIREMENTS

Requirements are managed and inconsistencies with project plans and work products are identified.

The project maintains a current and approved set of requirements over the life of the project by doing the following:

- Managing all changes to the requirements
- Maintaining the relationships among the requirements, the project plans, and the work products
- Identifying inconsistencies among the requirements, the project plans, and the work products
- Taking corrective action

Refer to the Technical Solution process area for more information about determining the feasibility of the requirements.

Refer to the Requirements Development process area for more information about ensuring that the requirements reflect the needs and expectations of the customer.

Refer to the Project Monitoring and Control process area for more information about taking corrective action.

SP 1.1 OBTAIN AN UNDERSTANDING OF REQUIREMENTS

Develop an understanding with the requirements providers on the meaning of the requirements.

As the project matures and requirements are derived, all activities or disciplines will receive requirements. To avoid requirements creep, criteria are established to designate appropriate channels, or official sources, from which to receive requirements. The receiving activities conduct analyses of the requirements with the requirements provider to ensure that a compatible, shared understanding is reached on the meaning of the requirements. The result of this analysis and dialog is an agreed-to set of requirements.

Typical Work Products

1. Lists of criteria for distinguishing appropriate requirements providers
2. Criteria for evaluation and acceptance of requirements

> **TIP**
>
> Requirements communicate expectations for the final product. These expectations evolve as the project progresses.

> **TIP**
>
> "Requirements creep" is the tendency for requirements to continually flow into a project (often from multiple sources) and expand the project's scope beyond what was planned.

> **TIP**
>
> Official sources of requirements are the people you select to get requirements from. Unofficial discussions that result in additional requirements can cause trouble.

REQM

3. Results of analyses against criteria
4. An agreed-to set of requirements

Subpractices

1. Establish criteria for distinguishing appropriate requirements providers.

2. Establish objective criteria for the evaluation and acceptance of requirements.

> Lack of evaluation and acceptance criteria often results in inadequate verification, costly rework, or customer rejection.

> Examples of evaluation and acceptance criteria include the following:
> - Clearly and properly stated
> - Complete
> - Consistent with each other
> - Uniquely identified
> - Appropriate to implement
> - Verifiable (testable)
> - Traceable

3. Analyze requirements to ensure that the established criteria are met.

4. Reach an understanding of the requirements with the requirements provider so that the project participants can commit to them.

SP 1.2 OBTAIN COMMITMENT TO REQUIREMENTS

Obtain commitment to the requirements from the project participants.

Refer to the Project Monitoring and Control process area for more information about monitoring the commitments made.

> When integrated teams are formed, the project participants are the integrated teams and their members. Commitment to the requirement for interacting with other integrated teams is as important for each integrated team as its commitments to product and other project requirements.
>
> IPPD ADD

Whereas the previous specific practice dealt with reaching an understanding with the requirements providers, this specific practice deals with agreements and commitments among those who have to carry out the activities necessary to implement the requirements. Requirements evolve throughout the project, especially as described by the specific practices of the Requirements Development process area and

---

TIP

An example of an agreed-to set of requirements is a requirements specification with appropriate sign-offs.

X-REF

Refer to GP 2.7 for examples of requirements providers (and other relevant stakeholders) that may be involved with the REQM process.

TIP

Two-way communication is critical to ensuring that a shared understanding of requirements exists between the project and the requirements providers.

TIP

Typically, at the beginning of a project, only about 50% of the requirements are known.

TIP

Project members who make commitments must continually evaluate whether they can meet their commitments, communicate immediately when they realize they cannot meet a commitment, and mitigate the impacts of not being able to meet a commitment.

the Technical Solution process area. As the requirements evolve, this specific practice ensures that project participants commit to the current, approved requirements and the resulting changes in project plans, activities, and work products.

Typical Work Products

1. Requirements impact assessments
2. Documented commitments to requirements and requirements changes

Subpractices

1. Assess the impact of requirements on existing commitments.

   The impact on the project participants should be evaluated when the requirements change or at the start of a new requirement.
2. Negotiate and record commitments.

   Changes to existing commitments should be negotiated before project participants commit to the requirement or requirement change.

SP 1.3 MANAGE REQUIREMENTS CHANGES

Manage changes to the requirements as they evolve during the project.

Refer to the Configuration Management process area for more information about maintaining and controlling the requirements baseline and on making the requirements and change data available to the project.

During the project, requirements change for a variety of reasons. As needs change and as work proceeds, additional requirements are derived and changes may have to be made to the existing requirements. It is essential to manage these additions and changes efficiently and effectively. To effectively analyze the impact of the changes, it is necessary that the source of each requirement is known and the rationale for any change is documented. The project manager may, however, want to track appropriate measures of requirements volatility to judge whether new or revised controls are necessary.

Typical Work Products

1. Requirements status
2. Requirements database
3. Requirements decision database

Subpractices

1. Document all requirements and requirements changes that are given to or generated by the project.

TIP

Commitments are a recurring theme in CMMI. They are also documented and reconciled in PP, monitored in PMC, and addressed more thoroughly in IPM.

TIP

Documented commitments can be in the form of meeting minutes, signed-off documents, or email.

TIP

Commitments comprise both the resources involved and the schedule for completion.

TIP

Controlling changes ensures that project members and customers have a clear and shared understanding of the requirements.

TIP

"Requirements volatility" is the rate at which requirements change once implementation begins. When requirements volatility is high, the project cannot progress as it continually adjusts to requirements changes. It is important to identify when high requirements volatility occurs, so appropriate action can be taken.

TIP

A database is an example of a tool used to manage the change history of the requirements.

REQM

TIP

Documentation of requirements can take many forms, including databases, electronic files, and prototypes.

TIP

The source of requirements changes can be either internal or external to the project.

TIP

A change history allows project members to review why decisions were made when they are questioned later.

TIP

In earlier versions of CMMI, this was one of the most confusing practices. The updated wording is designed to clearly state what is expected and yet provide flexibility in implementing bidirectional traceability to address a project's particular situation.

TIP

Tracing source requirements to lower-level requirements and then to the product component demonstrates where and how each requirement is met through product decomposition, and identifies which requirements are to be evaluated in work product verification (VER).

TIP

Maintaining traceability across horizontal relationships can greatly reduce problems encountered in product integration.

2. Maintain the requirements change history with the rationale for the changes.

   Maintaining the change history helps track requirements volatility.

3. Evaluate the impact of requirement changes from the standpoint of relevant stakeholders.

4. Make the requirements and change data available to the project.

SP 1.4 MAINTAIN BIDIRECTIONAL TRACEABILITY OF REQUIREMENTS

Maintain bidirectional traceability among the requirements and work products.

The intent of this specific practice is to maintain the bidirectional traceability of requirements for each level of product decomposition. (See the definition of "bidirectional traceability" in the glossary.) When the requirements are managed well, traceability can be established from the source requirement to its lower level requirements and from the lower level requirements back to their source. Such bidirectional traceability helps determine that all source requirements have been completely addressed and that all lower level requirements can be traced to a valid source.

Requirements traceability can also cover the relationships to other entities such as intermediate and final work products, changes in design documentation, and test plans. The traceability can cover horizontal relationships, such as across interfaces, as well as vertical relationships. Traceability is particularly needed in conducting the impact assessment of requirements changes on the project's activities and work products.

Typical Work Products

1. Requirements traceability matrix
2. Requirements tracking system

Subpractices

1. Maintain requirements traceability to ensure that the source of lower level (derived) requirements is documented.

2. Maintain requirements traceability from a requirement to its derived requirements and allocation to functions, interfaces, objects, people, processes, and work products.

3. Generate the requirements traceability matrix.

SP 1.5 IDENTIFY INCONSISTENCIES BETWEEN PROJECT WORK AND REQUIREMENTS

Identify inconsistencies between the project plans and work products and the requirements.

Refer to the Project Monitoring and Control process area for more information about monitoring and controlling the project plans and work products for consistency with requirements and taking corrective actions when necessary.

This specific practice finds the inconsistencies between the requirements and the project plans and work products and initiates the corrective action to fix them.

Typical Work Products

1. Documentation of inconsistencies including sources, conditions, and rationale
2. Corrective actions

Subpractices

1. Review the project's plans, activities, and work products for consistency with the requirements and the changes made to them.
2. Identify the source of the inconsistency and the rationale.
3. Identify changes that need to be made to the plans and work products resulting from changes to the requirements baseline.
4. Initiate corrective actions.

> **TIP**
>
> A traceability matrix can take many forms: a spreadsheet, a database, and so on.

> **HINT**
>
> When a requirement changes, update the traceability matrix to retain insight into the requirements-to-work product relationships mentioned earlier.

> **TIP**
>
> Especially for larger projects, product components are developed in parallel and it is challenging to keep all work products fully consistent with changes to the requirements.

> **TIP**
>
> A traceability matrix can help with this review of project plans, activities, and work products.

Generic Practices by Goal

GG 1 ACHIEVE SPECIFIC GOALS

The process supports and enables achievement of the specific goals of the process area by transforming identifiable input work products to produce identifiable output work products.

GP 1.1 PERFORM SPECIFIC PRACTICES

Perform the specific practices of the requirements management process to develop work products and provide services to achieve the specific goals of the process area.

CONTINUOUS ONLY

GG 2 INSTITUTIONALIZE A MANAGED PROCESS

The process is institutionalized as a managed process.

GP 2.1 *ESTABLISH AN ORGANIZATIONAL POLICY*

Establish and maintain an organizational policy for planning and performing the requirements management process.

Elaboration:

This policy establishes organizational expectations for managing requirements and identifying inconsistencies between the requirements and the project plans and work products.

GP 2.2 *PLAN THE PROCESS*

Establish and maintain the plan for performing the requirements management process.

Elaboration:

This plan for performing the requirements management process can be part of (or referenced by) the project plan as described in the Project Planning process area.

GP 2.3 *PROVIDE RESOURCES*

Provide adequate resources for performing the requirements management process, developing the work products, and providing the services of the process.

Elaboration:

> Examples of resources provided include the following tools:
> • Requirements tracking tools
> • Traceability tools

GP 2.4 *ASSIGN RESPONSIBILITY*

Assign responsibility and authority for performing the process, developing the work products, and providing the services of the requirements management process.

GP 2.5 *TRAIN PEOPLE*

Train the people performing or supporting the requirements management process as needed.

Elaboration:

> Examples of training topics include the following:
> • Application domain
> • Requirements definition, analysis, review, and management
> • Requirements management tools
> • Configuration management
> • Negotiation and conflict resolution

GP 2.6 MANAGE CONFIGURATIONS

Place designated work products of the requirements management process under appropriate levels of control.

Elaboration:

> Examples of work products placed under control include the following:
> • Requirements
> • Requirements traceability matrix

GP 2.7 IDENTIFY AND INVOLVE RELEVANT STAKEHOLDERS

Identify and involve the relevant stakeholders of the requirements management process as planned.

Elaboration:

Select relevant stakeholders from customers, end users, developers, producers, testers, suppliers, marketers, maintainers, disposal personnel, and others who may be affected by, or may affect, the product as well as the process.

> Examples of activities for stakeholder involvement include the following:
> • Resolving issues on the understanding of the requirements
> • Assessing the impact of requirements changes
> • Communicating the bidirectional traceability
> • Identifying inconsistencies among project plans, work products, and requirements

REQM

GP 2.8 MONITOR AND CONTROL THE PROCESS

Monitor and control the requirements management process against the plan for performing the process and take appropriate corrective action.

Elaboration:

> Examples of measures and work products used in monitoring and controlling include the following:
> • Requirements volatility (percentage of requirements changed)
> • Schedule for coordination of requirements
> • Schedule for analysis of a proposed requirements change

GP 2.9 OBJECTIVELY EVALUATE ADHERENCE

Objectively evaluate adherence of the requirements management process against its process description, standards, and procedures, and address non-compliance.

Elaboration:

> Examples of activities reviewed include the following:
> • Managing requirements
> • Identifying inconsistencies among project plans, work products, and requirements

> Examples of work products reviewed include the following:
> • Requirements
> • Requirements traceability matrix

GP 2.10 REVIEW STATUS WITH HIGHER LEVEL MANAGEMENT

Review the activities, status, and results of the requirements management process with higher level management and resolve issues.

Elaboration:

Proposed changes to commitments to be made external to the organization are reviewed with higher level management to ensure that all commitments can be accomplished.

GG3 and its practices do not apply for a maturity level 2 rating, but do apply for a maturity level 3 rating and above.

S Only

GG 3 INSTITUTIONALIZE A DEFINED PROCESS

The process is institutionalized as a defined process.

GP 3.1 ESTABLISH A DEFINED PROCESS

Establish and maintain the description of a defined requirements management process.

GP 3.2 COLLECT IMPROVEMENT INFORMATION

Collect work products, measures, measurement results, and improvement information derived from planning and performing the requirements management process to support the future use and improvement of the organization's processes and process assets.

Elaboration:

Examples of work products, measures, measurement results, and improvement information include the following:
• Requirements traceability matrix
• Number of unfunded requirements changes after baselining
• Lessons learned in resolving ambiguous requirements

CONTINUOUS/MATURITY LEVELS 3 – 5 ONLY

GG 4 INSTITUTIONALIZE A QUANTITATIVELY MANAGED PROCESS

The process is institutionalized as a quantitatively managed process.

GP 4.1 ESTABLISH QUANTITATIVE OBJECTIVES FOR THE PROCESS

Establish and maintain quantitative objectives for the requirements management process, which address quality and process performance, based on customer needs and business objectives.

GP 4.2 STABILIZE SUBPROCESS PERFORMANCE

Stabilize the performance of one or more subprocesses to determine the ability of the requirements management process to achieve the established quantitative quality and process-performance objectives.

CONTINUOUS ONLY

REQM

GG 5 *INSTITUTIONALIZE AN OPTIMIZING PROCESS*

The process is institutionalized as an optimizing process.

GP 5.1 *ENSURE CONTINUOUS PROCESS IMPROVEMENT*

Ensure continuous improvement of the requirements management process in fulfilling the relevant business objectives of the organization.

GP 5.2 *CORRECT ROOT CAUSES OF PROBLEMS*

Identify and correct the root causes of defects and other problems in the requirements management process.

CONTINUOUS ONLY

RISK MANAGEMENT
A Project Management Process Area at Maturity Level 3

Purpose

The purpose of Risk Management (RSKM) is to identify potential problems before they occur so that risk-handling activities can be planned and invoked as needed across the life of the product or project to mitigate adverse impacts on achieving objectives.

Introductory Notes

Risk management is a continuous, forward-looking process that is an important part of management. Risk management should address issues that could endanger achievement of critical objectives. A continuous risk management approach is applied to effectively anticipate and mitigate the risks that may have a critical impact on the project.

Effective risk management includes early and aggressive risk identification through the collaboration and involvement of relevant stakeholders, as described in the stakeholder involvement plan addressed in the Project Planning process area. Strong leadership across all relevant stakeholders is needed to establish an environment for the free and open disclosure and discussion of risk.

Risk management must consider both internal and external sources for cost, schedule, and performance risk as well as other risks. Early and aggressive detection of risk is important because it is typically easier, less costly, and less disruptive to make changes and correct work efforts during the earlier, rather than the later, phases of the project.

Risk management can be divided into three parts: defining a risk management strategy; identifying and analyzing risks; and handling identified risks, including the implementation of risk mitigation plans when needed.

As represented in the Project Planning and Project Monitoring and Control process areas, organizations may initially focus simply

> **TIP**
>
> RSKM also can apply to identifying, evaluating, and maximizing (or realizing) *opportunities*.

> **TIP**
>
> In a dynamic environment, risk management must be a continuous process of identifying, analyzing, and monitoring risks.

> **TIP**
>
> Without a free and open environment, many risks remain undisclosed until they surface as problems, when it is often too late to address them.

> **X-REF**
>
> PP and PMC have risk-management-related practices: See PP, SP 2.2 Identify Project Risks, and in PMC, SP 1.3 Monitor Project Risks.

HINT

Relevant stakeholders external to the project bring perspectives and insight into identifying and evaluating risks. They also may control the resources needed by the project, so it is important to maintain a dialog on related risks.

TIP

Sources of risks are not just technical, but can be programmatic (e.g., cost, schedule, supplier risks) or business related (e.g., competitor getting to market first).

TIP

A precondition to efficient risk management is having shared and consistent project objectives. Project objectives provide focus to risk management and help guide its activities.

X-REF

For more information, see Boehm, B., "Software Risk Management: Principles and Practices," IEEE Software, 1990; Project Management Institute, *A Guide to the Project Management Body of Knowledge (PMBOK® Guide) Third Edition*, 2004 (Chapter 11 deals with risk management); and www.sei.cmu.edu/risk/main.html.

on risk identification for awareness, and react to the realization of these risks as they occur. The Risk Management process area describes an evolution of these specific practices to systematically plan, anticipate, and mitigate risks to proactively minimize their impact on the project.

Although the primary emphasis of the Risk Management process area is on the project, the concepts can also be applied to manage organizational risks.

Related Process Areas

Refer to the Project Planning process area for more information about identification of project risks and planning for involvement of relevant stakeholders.

Refer to the Project Monitoring and Control process area for more information about monitoring project risks.

Refer to the Decision Analysis and Resolution process area for more information about using a formal evaluation process to evaluate alternatives for selection and mitigation of identified risks.

Specific Goal and Practice Summary

SG 1 Prepare for Risk Management
    SP 1.1   Determine Risk Sources and Categories
    SP 1.2   Define Risk Parameters
    SP 1.3   Establish a Risk Management Strategy
SG 2 Identify and Analyze Risks
    SP 2.1   Identify Risks
    SP 2.2   Evaluate, Categorize, and Prioritize Risks
SG 3 Mitigate Risks
    SP 3.1   Develop Risk Mitigation Plans
    SP 3.2   Implement Risk Mitigation Plans

Specific Practices by Goal

SG 1   PREPARE FOR RISK MANAGEMENT

Preparation for risk management is conducted.

Preparation is conducted by establishing and maintaining a strategy for identifying, analyzing, and mitigating risks. This is typically documented in a risk management plan. The risk management strategy addresses the specific actions and management approach used to apply and control the risk management program. This includes identifying the sources of risk; the scheme used to categorize risks; and the parameters used to evaluate, bound, and control risks for effective handling.

SP 1.1 DETERMINE RISK SOURCES AND CATEGORIES

Determine risk sources and categories.

Identification of risk sources provides a basis for systematically examining changing situations over time to uncover circumstances that impact the ability of the project to meet its objectives. Risk sources are both internal and external to the project. As the project progresses, additional sources of risk may be identified. Establishing categories for risks provides a mechanism for collecting and organizing risks as well as ensuring appropriate scrutiny and management attention for those risks that can have more serious consequences on meeting project objectives.

Typical Work Products

1. Risk source lists (external and internal)
2. Risk categories list

Subpractices

1. Determine risk sources.

   Risk sources are the fundamental drivers that cause risks within a project or organization. There are many sources of risks, both internal and external, to a project. Risk sources identify common areas where risks may originate. Typical internal and external risk sources include the following:

   - Uncertain requirements
   - Unprecedented efforts—estimates unavailable
   - Infeasible design
   - Unavailable technology
   - Unrealistic schedule estimates or allocation
   - Inadequate staffing and skills
   - Cost or funding issues
   - Uncertain or inadequate subcontractor capability
   - Uncertain or inadequate vendor capability
   - Inadequate communication with actual or potential customers or with their representatives
   - Disruptions to continuity of operations

   Many of these sources of risk are often accepted without adequate planning. Early identification of both internal and external sources of risk can lead to early identification of risks. Risk mitigation plans can

---

RSKM

HINT

If a project uses safety and security analysis methods, you should incorporate these methods as part of the risk management strategy.

TIP

Under stress, people lose perspective when it comes to risks. Some risks (e.g., those external to the team) may be given too much emphasis and others too little. Having a list of risk sources, both internal and external, helps bring objectivity to the identification of risks.

TIP

In a typical project, risks and their status change. A standard list of risk sources enables a project to be thorough in its identification of risks at each point in the project.

TIP

Disruptions to the continuity of operations is an external source (generally) that, if neglected, may have huge consequences, and yet for which cost-effective mitigation is often possible.

TIP

Categories are used to group related risks that can often be addressed by the same mitigation activities, thereby increasing risk management efficiency.

TIP

Risks are often grouped by lifecycle phase.

TIP

The risk taxonomies developed at the SEI and mentioned in Barry Boehm and Vic Basili's "Top 10" Software Risks (www.cebase.org/www /AboutCebase/News/top-10-defects.html) are useful even after a decade.

then be implemented early in the project to preclude occurrence of the risks or reduce the consequences of their occurrence.

2. Determine risk categories.

Risk categories reflect the "bins" for collecting and organizing risks. A reason for identifying risk categories is to help in the future consolidation of the activities in the risk mitigation plans.

The following factors may be considered when determining risk categories:
- The phases of the project's lifecycle model (e.g., requirements, design, manufacturing, test and evaluation, delivery, and disposal)
- The types of processes used
- The types of products used
- Program management risks (e.g., contract risks, budget/cost risks, schedule risks, resources risks, performance risks, and supportability risks)

A risk taxonomy can be used to provide a framework for determining risk sources and categories.

SP 1.2 DEFINE RISK PARAMETERS

Define the parameters used to analyze and categorize risks, and the parameters used to control the risk management effort.

Parameters for evaluating, categorizing, and prioritizing risks include the following:

- Risk likelihood (i.e., probability of risk occurrence)
- Risk consequence (i.e., impact and severity of risk occurrence)
- Thresholds to trigger management activities

HINT

Failure Mode and Effects Analysis (FMEA) is a method for identifying failure modes in designs (or processes), their causes, and their consequences. When you use FMEA to identify product engineering risks, make it part of your risk management strategy, as it helps define the risk sources, categories, and parameters to be considered when evaluating and prioritizing risks.

Risk parameters are used to provide common and consistent criteria for comparing the various risks to be managed. Without these parameters, it would be very difficult to gauge the severity of the unwanted change caused by the risk and to prioritize the necessary actions required for risk mitigation planning.

Typical Work Products

1. Risk evaluation, categorization, and prioritization criteria
2. Risk management requirements (e.g., control and approval levels, and reassessment intervals)

Subpractices

1. Define consistent criteria for evaluating and quantifying risk likelihood and severity levels.

   Consistently used criteria (e.g., the bounds on the likelihood and severity levels) allow the impacts of different risks to be commonly understood, to receive the appropriate level of scrutiny, and to obtain the management attention warranted. In managing dissimilar risks (e.g., personnel safety versus environmental pollution), it is important to ensure consistency in end result (e.g., a high risk of environmental pollution is as important as a high risk to personnel safety).

2. Define thresholds for each risk category.

   For each risk category, thresholds can be established to determine acceptability or unacceptability of risks, prioritization of risks, or triggers for management action.

   Examples of thresholds include the following:
   - Project-wide thresholds could be established to involve senior management when product costs exceed 10 percent of the target cost or when Cost Performance Indexes (CPIs) fall below 0.95.
   - Schedule thresholds could be established to involve senior management when Schedule Performance Indexes (SPIs) fall below 0.95.
   - Performance thresholds could be set to involve senior management when specified key items (e.g., processor utilization or average response times) exceed 125 percent of the intended design.

   These may be refined later, for each identified risk, to establish points at which more aggressive risk monitoring is employed or to signal the implementation of risk mitigation plans.

3. Define bounds on the extent to which thresholds are applied against or within a category.

   There are few limits to which risks can be assessed in either a quantitative or qualitative fashion. Definition of bounds (or boundary conditions) can be used to help scope the extent of the risk management effort and avoid excessive resource expenditures. Bounds may include exclusion of a risk source from a category. These bounds can also exclude any condition that occurs less than a given frequency.

RSKM

TIP

To be effective, risk management must be objective and quantitative. Therefore, you must treat risks consistently with respect to key parameters. Defining criteria for evaluating risks helps to ensure consistency (e.g., helping to decide which risks get escalated, mitigated, and so on, based only on the values of their parameters).

TIP

In the middle of a project, you often lose perspective. Defining thresholds in advance enables a more objective treatment of risks.

TIP

These thresholds may need to be refined later as part of risk mitigation planning.

TIP

Bounds are intended to scope the risk management effort in sensible ways that help conserve project resources.

TIP

The risk management strategy includes the results of the first two specific practices.

TIP

An important part of the strategy is to determine the frequency of monitoring activities and of reassessing risks for changes in status.

TIP

Some organizations develop a standard risk management strategy template that is tailored to meet the needs of individual projects.

TIP

The risk management strategy is often documented as part of a risk management plan, or as a section in the project plan.

TIP

All relevant stakeholders must understand fully the risk management strategy.

SP 1.3 ESTABLISH A RISK MANAGEMENT STRATEGY

Establish and maintain the strategy to be used for risk management.

A comprehensive risk management strategy addresses items such as the following:

- The scope of the risk management effort
- Methods and tools to be used for risk identification, risk analysis, risk mitigation, risk monitoring, and communication
- Project-specific sources of risks
- How these risks are to be organized, categorized, compared, and consolidated
- Parameters, including likelihood, consequence, and thresholds, for taking action on identified risks
- Risk mitigation techniques to be used, such as prototyping, piloting, simulation, alternative designs, or evolutionary development
- Definition of risk measures to monitor the status of the risks
- Time intervals for risk monitoring or reassessment

The risk management strategy should be guided by a common vision of success that describes the desired future project outcomes in terms of the product that is delivered, its cost, and its fitness for the task. The risk management strategy is often documented in an organizational or a project risk management plan. The risk management strategy is reviewed with relevant stakeholders to promote commitment and understanding.

Typical Work Products

1. Project risk management strategy

SG 2   IDENTIFY AND ANALYZE RISKS

TIP

Risk identification and analysis is a continuing activity for the duration of the project.

Risks are identified and analyzed to determine their relative importance.

The degree of risk impacts the resources assigned to handle an identified risk and the determination of when appropriate management attention is required.

Analyzing risks entails identifying risks from the internal and external sources identified and then evaluating each identified risk to determine its likelihood and consequences. Categorization of the risk, based on an evaluation against the established risk categories and criteria developed for the risk management strategy, provides the information needed for risk handling. Related risks may be grouped for efficient handling and effective use of risk management resources.

SP 2.1 IDENTIFY RISKS

Identify and document the risks.

> The particular risks associated with conducting the project using integrated teams should be considered, such as risks associated with loss of inter-team or intra-team coordination.

IPPD ADD

The identification of potential issues, hazards, threats, and vulnerabilities that could negatively affect work efforts or plans is the basis for sound and successful risk management. Risks must be identified and described in an understandable way before they can be analyzed and managed properly. Risks are documented in a concise statement that includes the context, conditions, and consequences of risk occurrence.

Risk identification should be an organized, thorough approach to seek out probable or realistic risks in achieving objectives. To be effective, risk identification should not be an attempt to address every possible event regardless of how highly improbable it may be. Use of the categories and parameters developed in the risk management strategy, along with the identified sources of risk, can provide the discipline and streamlining appropriate to risk identification. The identified risks form a baseline to initiate risk management activities. The list of risks should be reviewed periodically to reexamine possible sources of risk and changing conditions to uncover sources and risks previously overlooked or nonexistent when the risk management strategy was last updated.

Risk identification activities focus on the identification of risks, not placement of blame. The results of risk identification activities are not used by management to evaluate the performance of individuals.

There are many methods for identifying risks. Typical identification methods include the following:

- Examine each element of the project work breakdown structure to uncover risks.
- Conduct a risk assessment using a risk taxonomy.
- Interview subject matter experts.
- Review risk management efforts from similar products.

TIP

"Can a project have no risks?" "Can multiple projects have the same risk lists?" If these questions are asked, someone does not understand risks. Some risks may be product specific, contract specific, or staff specific.

TIP

Context, conditions, and consequences of a risk statement provide much of the information that is needed later to understand and evaluate the risk.

HINT

Establish an environment in which risks can be disclosed and discussed openly, without fear of repercussions. (Don't shoot the messenger!)

TIP

Many of the methods used for identifying risks use organizational process assets such as a risk taxonomy, risk repository, and lessons learned from past projects. Subject-matter experts may also be utilized. Other methods involve reviewing project artifacts such as the project shared vision, WBS, designs, project interfaces, and contractual requirements.

- Examine lessons-learned documents or databases.
- Examine design specifications and agreement requirements.

Typical Work Products

1. List of identified risks, including the context, conditions, and consequences of risk occurrence

Subpractices

1. Identify the risks associated with cost, schedule, and performance.

TIP

One approach to identifying risks is to consider the cost, schedule, and performance issues associated with each lifecycle phase. As each phase typically has a clear set of objectives and a completion milestone, a phase is a suitable context for identifying the risks associated with that phase.

HINT

Sometimes customers are short-sighted about their requirements. Explain to customers the implications of their requirements and associated risks. However, the result may be a decision to not mitigate the associated risks (unless required or desired for other reasons).

TIP

Performance risks may be associated with lifecycle phases, new technology, or desired attributes of the product.

Cost, schedule, and performance risks should be examined to the extent that they impact project objectives. There may be potential risks discovered that are outside the scope of the project's objectives but vital to customer interests. For example, the risks in development costs, product acquisition costs, cost of spare (or replacement) products, and product disposition (or disposal) costs have design implications. The customer may not have considered the full cost of supporting a fielded product or using a delivered service. The customer should be informed of such risks, but actively managing those risks may not be necessary. The mechanisms for making such decisions should be examined at project and organization levels and put in place if deemed appropriate, especially for risks that impact the ability to verify and validate the product.

In addition to the cost risks identified above, other cost risks may include those associated with funding levels, funding estimates, and distributed budgets.

Schedule risks may include risks associated with planned activities, key events, and milestones.

Performance risks may include risks associated with the following:
- Requirements
- Analysis and design
- Application of new technology
- Physical size
- Shape
- Weight
- Manufacturing and fabrication
- Functional performance and operation
- Verification
- Validation
- Performance maintenance attributes

Performance maintenance attributes are those characteristics that enable an in-use product or service to provide originally required performance, such as maintaining safety and security performance.

RSKM

There are other risks that do not fall into cost, schedule, or performance categories.

> Examples of these other risks include the following:
> • Risks associated with strikes
> • Diminishing sources of supply
> • Technology cycle time
> • Competition

2. Review environmental elements that may impact the project.

   Risks to a project that frequently are missed include those supposedly outside the scope of the project (i.e., the project does not control whether they occur but can mitigate their impact), such as weather, natural or manmade disasters that affect continuity of operations, political changes, and telecommunications failures.

3. Review all elements of the work breakdown structure as part of identifying risks to help ensure that all aspects of the work effort have been considered.

4. Review all elements of the project plan as part of identifying risks to help ensure that all aspects of the project have been considered.

   Refer to the Project Planning process area for more information about identifying project risks.

5. Document the context, conditions, and potential consequences of the risk.

   Risks statements are typically documented in a standard format that contains the risk context, conditions, and consequences of occurrence. The risk context provides additional information such that the intent of the risk can be easily understood. In documenting the context of the risk, consider the relative time frame of the risk, the circumstances or conditions surrounding the risk that has brought about the concern, and any doubt or uncertainty.

6. Identify the relevant stakeholders associated with each risk.

SP 2.2 EVALUATE, CATEGORIZE, AND PRIORITIZE RISKS

Evaluate and categorize each identified risk using the defined risk categories and parameters, and determine its relative priority.

The evaluation of risks is needed to assign relative importance to each identified risk, and is used in determining when appropriate management attention is required. Often it is useful to aggregate risks based on their interrelationships, and develop options at an

TIP

Environmental risks are often ignored, even though some cost-effective mitigation activities are possible.

TIP

A good risk statement is fact based, actionable, and brief.

TIP

A standard format for documenting risks makes it easier to train staff on what is needed in risk statements. Also, senior managers have a quicker understanding of risk statements across different projects if they are all in the same format.

HINT

It is important to identify who is affected by each risk.

HINT

You can simplify risk management when you can treat a number of risks as one group from evaluation and mitigation perspectives.

aggregate level. When an aggregate risk is formed by a roll up of lower level risks, care must be taken to ensure that important lower level risks are not ignored.

Collectively, the activities of risk evaluation, categorization, and prioritization are sometimes called "risk assessment" or "risk analysis."

Typical Work Products

1. List of risks, with a priority assigned to each risk

Subpractices

1. Evaluate the identified risks using the defined risk parameters.

TIP

Risk exposure is the result of the combination of the likelihood and the consequence of a risk (expressed quantitatively).

Each risk is evaluated and assigned values in accordance with the defined risk parameters, which may include likelihood, consequence (severity, or impact), and thresholds. The assigned risk parameter values can be integrated to produce additional measures, such as risk exposure, which can be used to prioritize risks for handling.

Often, a scale with three to five values is used to evaluate both likelihood and consequence. Likelihood, for example, can be categorized as remote, unlikely, likely, highly likely, or a near certainty.

> Examples for consequences include the following:
> - Low
> - Medium
> - High
> - Negligible
> - Marginal
> - Significant
> - Critical
> - Catastrophic

TIP

Determining values for risk likelihood and consequence is easier and more repeatable if there are clear statements of objectives, criteria exist for assigning values, there is appropriate representation of relevant stakeholders, and staff have been trained.

Probability values are frequently used to quantify likelihood. Consequences are generally related to cost, schedule, environmental impact, or human measures (e.g., labor hours lost and severity of injury).

This evaluation is often a difficult and time-consuming task. Specific expertise or group techniques may be needed to assess the risks and gain confidence in the prioritization. In addition, priorities may require reevaluation as time progresses.

2. Categorize and group risks according to the defined risk categories.

Risks are categorized into the defined risk categories, providing a means to look at risks according to their source, taxonomy, or project component. Related or equivalent risks may be grouped for efficient handling. The cause-and-effect relationships between related risks are documented.

3. Prioritize risks for mitigation.

    A relative priority is determined for each risk based on the assigned risk parameters. Clear criteria should be used to determine the risk priority. The intent of prioritization is to determine the most effective areas to which resources for mitigation of risks can be applied with the greatest positive impact to the project.

TIP

Priority assignment can likewise be a repeatable process.

SG 3 MITIGATE RISKS

Risks are handled and mitigated, where appropriate, to reduce adverse impacts on achieving objectives.

The steps in handling risks include developing risk-handling options, monitoring risks, and performing risk-handling activities when defined thresholds are exceeded. Risk mitigation plans are developed and implemented for selected risks to proactively reduce the potential impact of risk occurrence. This can also include contingency plans to deal with the impact of selected risks that may occur despite attempts to mitigate them. The risk parameters used to trigger risk-handling activities are defined by the risk management strategy.

X-REF

RSKM heavily influences both engineering (to adjust requirements, design, implementation, verification, and validation in light of risks and risk mitigation) and project management (to plan for these activities and monitor thresholds that trigger the deployment of mitigation plans).

SP 3.1 DEVELOP RISK MITIGATION PLANS

Develop a risk mitigation plan for the most important risks to the project as defined by the risk management strategy.

A critical component of a risk mitigation plan is to develop alternative courses of action, workarounds, and fallback positions, with a recommended course of action for each critical risk. The risk mitigation plan for a given risk includes techniques and methods used to avoid, reduce, and control the probability of occurrence of the risk, the extent of damage incurred should the risk occur (sometimes called a "contingency plan"), or both. Risks are monitored and when they exceed the established thresholds, the risk mitigation plans are deployed to return the impacted effort to an acceptable risk level. If the risk cannot be mitigated, a contingency plan can be invoked. Both risk mitigation and contingency plans are often generated only for selected risks where the consequences of the risks are determined to be high or unacceptable; other risks may be accepted and simply monitored.

TIP

The risk management literature uses the term *contingency plans* in various ways. In CMMI, a risk contingency plan is the part of a risk mitigation plan that addresses what actions to take *after* a risk is realized.

HINT

Reward staff members who prevent crises, as opposed to those who allow a crisis to happen and then heroically resolve it.

HINT

One way to identify actions to avoid, reduce, or control a risk, is to perform a causal analysis on the sources of the risk. Actions that eliminate or reduce causes may be suitable candidates for inclusion in a risk mitigation plan.

TIP

A risk mitigation plan should, when its associated threshold is exceeded, return the project to an acceptable risk level.

HINT

Generate more than one approach or option for high-priority risks.

Options for handling risks typically include alternatives such as the following:

- Risk avoidance: Changing or lowering requirements while still meeting the user's needs
- Risk control: Taking active steps to minimize risks
- Risk transfer: Reallocating requirements to lower the risks
- Risk monitoring: Watching and periodically reevaluating the risk for changes to the assigned risk parameters
- Risk acceptance: Acknowledgment of risk but not taking any action

Often, especially for high risks, more than one approach to handling a risk should be generated.

For example, in the case of an event that disrupts continuity of operations, approaches to risk management can include the following:
- Resource reserves to respond to disruptive events
- Lists of appropriate back-up equipment to be available
- Back-up personnel for key personnel
- Plans and results of/for testing emergency response systems
- Posted procedures for emergencies
- Disseminated lists of key contacts and information resources for emergencies

---

In many cases, risks will be accepted or watched. Risk acceptance is usually done when the risk is judged too low for formal mitigation, or when there appears to be no viable way to reduce the risk. If a risk is accepted, the rationale for this decision should be documented. Risks are watched when there is an objectively defined, verifiable, and documented threshold of performance, time, or risk exposure (the combination of likelihood and consequence) that will trigger risk mitigation planning or invoke a contingency plan if it is needed.

Adequate consideration should be given early to technology demonstrations, models, simulations, pilots, and prototypes as part of risk mitigation planning.

HINT

You can establish thresholds for different attributes (cost, schedule, and performance) and trigger different activities (contingency plan deployment, risk mitigation planning).

Typical Work Products

1. Documented handling options for each identified risk
2. Risk mitigation plans
3. Contingency plans
4. List of those responsible for tracking and addressing each risk

Subpractices

1. Determine the levels and thresholds that define when a risk becomes unacceptable and triggers the execution of a risk mitigation plan or a contingency plan.

   Risk level (derived using a risk model) is a measure combining the uncertainty of reaching an objective with the consequences of failing to reach the objective.

   Risk levels and thresholds that bound planned or acceptable performance must be clearly understood and defined to provide a means with which risk can be understood. Proper categorization of risk is essential for ensuring appropriate priority based on severity and the associated management response. There may be multiple thresholds employed to initiate varying levels of management response. Typically, thresholds for the execution of risk mitigation plans are set to engage before the execution of contingency plans.

2. Identify the person or group responsible for addressing each risk.

3. Determine the cost-to-benefit ratio of implementing the risk mitigation plan for each risk.

   Risk mitigation activities should be examined for the benefits they provide versus the resources they will expend. Just like any other design activity, alternative plans may need to be developed and the costs and benefits of each alternative assessed. The most appropriate plan is then selected for implementation. At times the risk may be significant and the benefits small, but the risk must be mitigated to reduce the probability of incurring unacceptable consequences.

4. Develop an overall risk mitigation plan for the project to orchestrate the implementation of the individual risk mitigation and contingency plans.

   The complete set of risk mitigation plans may not be affordable. A tradeoff analysis should be performed to prioritize the risk mitigation plans for implementation.

5. Develop contingency plans for selected critical risks in the event their impacts are realized.

   Risk mitigation plans are developed and implemented as needed to proactively reduce risks before they become problems. Despite best efforts, some risks may be unavoidable and will become problems that impact the project. Contingency plans can be developed for critical risks to describe the actions a project may take to deal with the occurrence of this impact. The intent is to define a proactive plan for handling the risk, either to reduce the risk (mitigation) or respond to the risk (contingency), but in either event to manage the risk.

TIP

Thresholds trigger actions that may impact the work of staff and relevant stakeholders. Thus, it is important that the motivation for particular thresholds and the actions they invoke are well understood by all who will be affected.

TIP

Assigning responsibility for risk mitigation is easier to do if mitigation activities and responsibilities are documented in a plan, such as the project plan.

TIP

Alternative risk mitigation plans may be formally evaluated (using DAR) to choose the best one. Relevant stakeholders may play an important role in such an evaluation (particularly for risks that impact them).

HINT

If you integrate all the risk mitigation plans together and find
that the result is not affordable,
trim the list using the priorities
assigned in SP 2.2 or repriori-
tize them using a group-consen-
sus approach (e.g., multivoting
within risk categories).

Some risk management literature may consider contingency plans a synonym or subset of risk mitigation plans. These plans also may be addressed together as risk-handling or risk action plans.

SP 3.2 IMPLEMENT RISK MITIGATION PLANS

Monitor the status of each risk periodically and implement the risk mitigation plan as appropriate.

To effectively control and manage risks during the work effort, follow a proactive program to regularly monitor risks and the status and results of risk-handling actions. The risk management strategy defines the intervals at which the risk status should be revisited. This activity may result in the discovery of new risks or new risk-handling options that can require replanning and reassessment. In either event, the acceptability thresholds associated with the risk should be compared against the status to determine the need for implementing a risk mitigation plan.

Typical Work Products

1. Updated lists of risk status
2. Updated assessments of risk likelihood, consequence, and thresholds
3. Updated lists of risk-handling options
4. Updated list of actions taken to handle risks
5. Risk mitigation plans

HINT

Weekly or monthly updates to
risk status are typical.

TIP

Incorporating risk mitigation
plans into the project plan
enables their status to be
reviewed as part of the project's regular progress reviews.

HINT

Ensure that risk management
activities are consolidated from
the top, all the way down, of
the project hierarchy. Also
ensure that risks are escalated
to the level relevant to the
exposure they create. Their mitigation is then delegated to the
appropriate project or team.

Subpractices

1. Monitor risk status.

   After a risk mitigation plan is initiated, the risk is still monitored. Thresholds are assessed to check for the potential execution of a contingency plan.

   A periodic mechanism for monitoring should be employed.

2. Provide a method for tracking open risk-handling action items to closure.

   Refer to the Project Monitoring and Control process area for more information about tracking action items.

3. Invoke selected risk-handling options when monitored risks exceed the defined thresholds.

   Quite often, risk handling is only performed for those risks judged to be "high" and "medium." The risk-handling strategy for a given risk may include techniques and methods to avoid, reduce, and control the likelihood of the risk or the extent of damage incurred should the risk (anticipated event or situation) occur or both. In this context, risk handling includes both risk mitigation plans and contingency plans.

Risk-handling techniques are developed to avoid, reduce, and control adverse impact to project objectives and to bring about acceptable outcomes in light of probable impacts. Actions generated to handle a risk require proper resource loading and scheduling within plans and baseline schedules. This replanning effort needs to closely consider the effects on adjacent or dependent work initiatives or activities.

> **TIP**
> To be sure risk mitigation activities are performed properly they must be planned, scheduled, and resourced, just as any other project activity.

Refer to the Project Monitoring and Control process area for more information about revising the project plan.

4. Establish a schedule or period of performance for each risk-handling activity that includes the start date and anticipated completion date.
5. Provide continued commitment of resources for each plan to allow successful execution of the risk-handling activities.
6. Collect performance measures on the risk-handling activities.

Generic Practices by Goal

GG 1 ACHIEVE SPECIFIC GOALS

The process supports and enables achievement of the specific goals of the process area by transforming identifiable input work products to produce identifiable output work products.

GP 1.1 PERFORM SPECIFIC PRACTICES

Perform the specific practices of the risk management process to develop work products and provide services to achieve the specific goals of the process area.

CONTINUOUS ONLY

GG 2 INSTITUTIONALIZE A MANAGED PROCESS

The process is institutionalized as a managed process.

GG 3 INSTITUTIONALIZE A DEFINED PROCESS

The process is institutionalized as a defined process.

> *This generic goal's appearance here reflects its location in the staged representation.*

STAGED ONLY

GP 2.1 ESTABLISH AN ORGANIZATIONAL POLICY

Establish and maintain an organizational policy for planning and performing the risk management process.

Elaboration:

This policy establishes organizational expectations for defining a risk management strategy and identifying, analyzing, and mitigating risks.

GP 2.2 PLAN THE PROCESS

Establish and maintain the plan for performing the risk management process.

Elaboration:

This plan for performing the risk management process can be included in (or referenced by) the project plan, which is described in the Project Planning process area. The plan called for in this generic practice would address the comprehensive planning for all of the specific practices in this process area. In particular, this plan provides the overall approach for risk mitigation, but is distinct from mitigation plans (including contingency plans) for specific risks. In contrast, the risk mitigation plans called for in the specific practices would address more focused items such as the levels that trigger risk-handling activities.

GP 2.3 PROVIDE RESOURCES

Provide adequate resources for performing the risk management process, developing the work products, and providing the services of the process.

Elaboration:

Examples of resources provided include the following tools:
• Risk management databases
• Risk mitigation tools
• Prototyping tools
• Modeling and simulation

GP 2.4 ASSIGN RESPONSIBILITY

Assign responsibility and authority for performing the process, developing the work products, and providing the services of the risk management process.

GP 2.5 TRAIN PEOPLE

Train the people performing or supporting the risk management process as needed.

Elaboration:

> Examples of training topics include the following:
> - Risk management concepts and activities (e.g., risk identification, evalua-tion, monitoring, and mitigation)
> - Measure selection for risk mitigation

GP 2.6 MANAGE CONFIGURATIONS

Place designated work products of the risk management process under appro-priate levels of control.

Elaboration:

> Examples of work products placed under control include the following:
> - Risk management strategy
> - Identified risk items
> - Risk mitigation plans

GP 2.7 IDENTIFY AND INVOLVE RELEVANT STAKEHOLDERS

Identify and involve the relevant stakeholders of the risk management process as planned.

Elaboration:

> Examples of activities for stakeholder involvement include the following:
> - Establishing a collaborative environment for free and open discussion of risk
> - Reviewing the risk management strategy and risk mitigation plans
> - Participating in risk identification, analysis, and mitigation activities
> - Communicating and reporting risk management status

GP 2.8 MONITOR AND CONTROL THE PROCESS

Monitor and control the risk management process against the plan for per-forming the process and take appropriate corrective action.

Elaboration:

Examples of measures and work products used in monitoring and controlling include the following:
- Number of risks identified, managed, tracked, and controlled
- Risk exposure and changes to the risk exposure for each assessed risk, and as a summary percentage of management reserve
- Change activity for the risk mitigation plans (e.g., processes, schedule, and funding)
- Occurrence of unanticipated risks
- Risk categorization volatility
- Comparison of estimated versus actual risk mitigation effort and impact
- Schedule for risk analysis activities
- Schedule of actions for a specific mitigation

GP 2.9 OBJECTIVELY EVALUATE ADHERENCE

Objectively evaluate adherence of the risk management process against its process description, standards, and procedures, and address noncompliance.

Elaboration:

Examples of activities reviewed include the following:
- Establishing and maintaining a risk management strategy
- Identifying and analyzing risks
- Mitigating risks

Examples of work products reviewed include the following:
- Risk management strategy
- Risk mitigation plans

GP 2.10 REVIEW STATUS WITH HIGHER LEVEL MANAGEMENT

Review the activities, status, and results of the risk management process with higher level management and resolve issues.

Elaboration:

Reviews of the project risk status are held on a periodic and event-driven basis, with appropriate levels of management, to provide visibility into the potential for project risk exposure and appropriate corrective action.

Typically, these reviews include a summary of the most critical risks, key risk parameters (such as likelihood and consequence of the risks), and the status of risk mitigation efforts.

GG 3 INSTITUTIONALIZE A DEFINED PROCESS

The process is institutionalized as a defined process.

> *This generic goal's appearance here reflects its location in the continuous representation.*

CONT. ONLY

GP 3.1 ESTABLISH A DEFINED PROCESS

Establish and maintain the description of a defined risk management process.

GP 3.2 COLLECT IMPROVEMENT INFORMATION

Collect work products, measures, measurement results, and improvement information derived from planning and performing the risk management process to support the future use and improvement of the organization's processes and process assets.

Elaboration:

> Examples of work products, measures, measurement results, and improvement information include the following:
> - Risk parameters
> - Risk categories
> - Risk status reports

GG 4 INSTITUTIONALIZE A QUANTITATIVELY MANAGED PROCESS

The process is institutionalized as a quantitatively managed process.

GP 4.1 ESTABLISH QUANTITATIVE OBJECTIVES FOR THE PROCESS

Establish and maintain quantitative objectives for the risk management process, which address quality and process performance, based on customer needs and business objectives.

CONTINUOUS ONLY

GP 4.2 STABILIZE SUBPROCESS PERFORMANCE

Stabilize the performance of one or more subprocesses to determine the ability of the risk management process to achieve the established quantitative quality and process-performance objectives.

GG 5 *INSTITUTIONALIZE AN OPTIMIZING PROCESS*

The process is institutionalized as an optimizing process.

GP 5.1 *ENSURE CONTINUOUS PROCESS IMPROVEMENT*

Ensure continuous improvement of the risk management process in fulfilling the relevant business objectives of the organization.

GP 5.2 *CORRECT ROOT CAUSES OF PROBLEMS*

Identify and correct the root causes of defects and other problems in the risk management process.

SUPPLIER AGREEMENT MANAGEMENT
A Project Management Process Area at Maturity Level 2

Purpose

The purpose of Supplier Agreement Management (SAM) is to manage the acquisition of products from suppliers.

Introductory Notes

The Supplier Agreement Management process area involves the following:

- Determining the type of acquisition that will be used for the products to be acquired
- Selecting suppliers
- Establishing and maintaining agreements with suppliers
- Executing the supplier agreement
- Monitoring selected supplier processes
- Evaluating selected supplier work products
- Accepting delivery of acquired products
- Transitioning acquired products to the project

> **TIP**
>
> SAM helps prevent problems such as suppliers who can't meet requirements, supplier agreements that prevent a proactive approach to supplier management, poor visibility into supplier activities, and failing to address risks associated with the use of in-house vendors and COTS.

This process area primarily addresses the acquisition of products and product components that are delivered to the project's customer. Throughout the process areas, where we use the terms product and product component, their intended meanings also encompass services and their components.

> **TIP**
>
> Although SAM primarily addresses the acquisition of products and product components that are delivered to your customer, SAM can apply to other acquisitions critical to the success of the business.

HINT

Take a broad view when applying SAM to reduce business-critical risks in obtaining products from suppliers. However, also be aware that not all practices apply equally to all situations. (See notes in SP 2.2 and 2.3.)

TIP

"Products" and "product components" in SAM practices include services and service components.

HINT

If you need to acquire a product, the *earlier* you prepare, the more likely you are to provide the right product of the right quality at the right time for project success.

HINT

When a supplier is integrated into the project team, pick the best process for the situation and then determine whether it maps to SAM, IPPD-related practices (in IPM), or both.

TIP

Acquisitions from in-house vendors often proceed without well-defined requirements, a formal agreement, and agreed-to acceptance tests. Is it any wonder that relationships with in-house vendors can be problematic?

TIP

The terms *formal agreement* and *supplier agreement* mean the same thing and can be used interchangeably.

> Examples of products and product components that may be acquired by the project include the following:
> - Subsystems (e.g., navigational system on an airplane)
> - Software
> - Hardware
> - Documentation (e.g., installation, operator's, and user's manuals)
> - Parts and materials (e.g., gauges, switches, wheels, steel, and raw materials)

To minimize risks to the project, this process area can also address the acquisition of significant products and product components not delivered to the project's customer but used to develop and maintain the product or service (for example, development tools and test environments).

Typically, the products to be acquired by the project are determined during the early stages of the planning and development of the product. The Technical Solution process area provides practices for determining the products and product components that may be acquired from suppliers.

This process area does not directly address arrangements in which the supplier is integrated into the project team and uses the same processes and reports to the same management as the product developers (for example, integrated teams). Typically, these situations are handled by other processes or functions, possibly external to the project, though some of the specific practices of this process area may be useful in managing the formal agreement with such a supplier.

Suppliers may take many forms depending on business needs, including in-house vendors (i.e., vendors that are in the same organization but are external to the project), fabrication capabilities and laboratories, and commercial vendors. (See the definition of "supplier" in the glossary.)

A formal agreement is established to manage the relationship between the organization and the supplier. A formal agreement is any legal agreement between the organization (representing the project) and the supplier. This agreement may be a contract, license, service level agreement, or memorandum of agreement. The acquired product is delivered to the project from the supplier according to this formal agreement (also known as the "supplier agreement").

Related Process Areas

Refer to the Project Monitoring and Control process area for more information about monitoring projects and taking corrective action.

Refer to the Requirements Development process area for more information about defining requirements.

Refer to the Requirements Management process area for more information about managing requirements, including the traceability of requirements for products acquired from suppliers.

Refer to the Technical Solution process area for more information about determining the products and product components that may be acquired from suppliers.

Specific Goal and Practice Summary

SG 1 Establish Supplier Agreements
    SP 1.1   Determine Acquisition Type
    SP 1.2   Select Suppliers
    SP 1.3   Establish Supplier Agreements
SG 2 Satisfy Supplier Agreements
    SP 2.1   Execute the Supplier Agreement
    SP 2.2   Monitor Selected Supplier Processes
    SP 2.3   Evaluate Selected Supplier Work Products
    SP 2.4   Accept the Acquired Product
    SP 2.5   Transition Products

Specific Practices by Goal

SG 1   ESTABLISH SUPPLIER AGREEMENTS

Agreements with the suppliers are established and maintained.

SP 1.1   DETERMINE ACQUISITION TYPE

Determine the type of acquisition for each product or product component to be acquired.

Refer to the Technical Solution process area for more information about identifying the products and product components to be acquired.

There are many different types of acquisition that can be used to acquire products and product components that will be used by the project.

> **TIP**
>
> The entry point for SAM is normally TS SP 2.4, when the decision is made to buy rather than build a product component.

> **TIP**
>
> The type of acquisition varies according to the nature of products that are available to satisfy the project's needs and requirements (including COTS).

> Examples of types of acquisition include the following:
> • Purchasing commercial off-the-shelf (COTS) products
> • Obtaining products through a contractual agreement
> • Obtaining products from an in-house vendor
> • Obtaining products from the customer
> • Combining some of the above (e.g., contracting for a modification to a COTS product or having another part of the business enterprise code-velop products with an external supplier)

In the event that COTS products are desired, care in evaluating and selecting these products and the vendor may be critical to the project. Things to consider in the selection decision include proprietary issues and the availability of the products.

Typical Work Products

1. List of the acquisition types that will be used for all products and product components to be acquired

X-REF

The use of COTS involves additional considerations. See TS, SAM SP 1.2 Subpractice 5, and SAM SP 1.3 Subpractice 3. Also, see www.sei.cmu.edu/cbs/index.html.

SP 1.2 *SELECT SUPPLIERS*

Select suppliers based on an evaluation of their ability to meet the specified requirements and established criteria.

Refer to the Decision Analysis and Resolution process area for more information about formal evaluation approaches that can be used to select suppliers.

Refer to the Requirements Management process area for more information about specified requirements.

Criteria should be established to address factors that are important to the project.

HINT

Select a capable supplier that can meet your requirements with a quality product on time and within costs.

TIP

The criteria used to select a supplier depend on the project, its requirements, and other factors. If you enter "supplier selection criteria" into your favorite search engine, you will be amazed by both the commonality and the variety of supplier selection criteria used in different industries.

> Examples of factors include the following:
> • Geographical location of the supplier
> • Supplier's performance records on similar work
> • Engineering capabilities
> • Staff and facilities available to perform the work
> • Prior experience in similar applications

Typical Work Products

1. Market studies
2. List of candidate suppliers
3. Preferred supplier list

4. Trade study or other record of evaluation criteria, advantages and disadvantages of candidate suppliers, and rationale for selection of suppliers
5. Solicitation materials and requirements

Subpractices

1. Establish and document criteria for evaluating potential suppliers.
2. Identify potential suppliers and distribute solicitation material and requirements to them.

   A proactive manner of performing this activity is to conduct market research to identify potential sources of candidate products to be acquired, including candidates from suppliers of custom-made products and vendors of COTS products.

   Refer to the Organizational Innovation and Deployment process area for examples of sources of process and technology improvements and how to pilot and evaluate such improvements.

3. Evaluate proposals according to evaluation criteria.
4. Evaluate risks associated with each proposed supplier.

   Refer to the Risk Management process area for more information about evaluating project risks.

5. Evaluate proposed suppliers' ability to perform the work.

Examples of methods to evaluate the proposed supplier's ability to perform the work include the following:

- Evaluation of prior experience in similar applications
- Evaluation of prior performance on similar work
- Evaluation of management capabilities
- Capability evaluations
- Evaluation of staff available to perform the work
- Evaluation of available facilities and resources
- Evaluation of the project's ability to work with the proposed supplier
- Evaluation of the impact of candidate COTS products on the project's plan and commitments

---

When COTS products are being evaluated consider the following:

- Cost of the COTS products
- Cost and effort to incorporate the COTS products into the project
- Security requirements
- Benefits and impacts that may result from future product releases

---

SAM

HINT

Consider using DAR when evaluating potential suppliers. These subpractices describe some of what is involved in such an evaluation.

TIP

A proactive approach provides benefits such as addressing a capability gap of the organization uniformly, reducing time that projects take to select suppliers, establishing a more efficient umbrella agreement with a preferred supplier, and protecting core competencies.

TIP

Risks are typically included as criteria in a formal evaluation.

X-REF

Capability evaluation methods associated with CMMI include the SCAMPI A and B appraisal methods. See www.sei.cmu.edu/appraisal-program.

Future releases of the COTS product may provide additional features that support planned or anticipated enhancements for the project, but may result in the supplier discontinuing support of its current release.

6. Select the supplier.

SP 1.3 ESTABLISH SUPPLIER AGREEMENTS

Establish and maintain formal agreements with the supplier.

When integrated teams are formed, team membership should be negotiated with suppliers and incorporated into the agreement. The agreement should identify any integrated decision making, reporting requirements (business and technical), and trade studies requiring supplier involvement. The supplier efforts should be orchestrated to support the IPPD efforts undertaken by the acquirer.

IPPD ADD

A formal agreement is any legal agreement between the organization (representing the project) and the supplier. This agreement may be a contract, license, service level agreement, or memorandum of agreement.

The content of the agreement should specify the reviews, monitoring, evaluations, and acceptance tests to be performed, if such activities are appropriate to the acquisition or product being acquired.

Typical Work Products

1. Statements of work
2. Contracts
3. Memoranda of agreement
4. Licensing agreement

Subpractices

1. Revise the requirements (e.g., product requirements and service level requirements) to be fulfilled by the supplier to reflect negotiations with the supplier when necessary.

    Refer to the Requirements Development process area for more information about revising requirements.

    Refer to the Requirements Management process area for more information about managing changes to requirements.

2. Document what the project will provide to the supplier.

    Include the following:
    - Project-furnished facilities
    - Documentation
    - Services

3. Document the supplier agreement.

HINT

If it's not documented in the supplier agreement, don't count on it happening! Renegotiating an agreement can be expensive, so make sure it covers everything that is important to you for managing the supplier and receiving the product that you are expecting.

HINT

Create a formal agreement in the form suitable to the nature of the business transaction.

TIP

The project must engage the supplier in reviews, monitoring, and evaluations to a depth and breadth appropriate to the circumstances and risks. The supplier agreement must cover details of these reviews.

X-REF

Establishing (and revising) an agreement often requires *negotiation skills*. See Ury, William, Roger Fisher, and Bruce Patton. *Getting to Yes: Negotiating Agreement Without Giving in*, Revised 2nd Edition. Penguin USA, 1991.

The supplier agreement should include a statement of work, a specification, terms and conditions, a list of deliverables, a schedule, a budget, and a defined acceptance process.

This subpractice typically includes the following:

- Establishing the statement of work, specification, terms and conditions, list of deliverables, schedule, budget, and acceptance process
- Identifying who from the project and supplier are responsible and authorized to make changes to the supplier agreement
- Identifying how requirements changes and changes to the supplier agreement are to be determined, communicated, and addressed
- Identifying standards and procedures that will be followed
- Identifying critical dependencies between the project and the supplier
- Identifying the type and depth of project oversight of the supplier, procedures, and evaluation criteria to be used in monitoring supplier performance including selection of processes to be monitored and work products to be evaluated
- Identifying the types of reviews that will be conducted with the supplier
- Identifying the supplier's responsibilities for ongoing maintenance and support of the acquired products
- Identifying warranty, ownership, and usage rights for the acquired products
- Identifying acceptance criteria

In some cases, selection of COTS products may require a supplier agreement in addition to the agreements in the product's license.

Examples of what could be covered in an agreement with a COTS supplier include the following:

- Discounts for large quantity purchases
- Coverage of relevant stakeholders under the licensing agreement, including project suppliers, team members, and the project's customer
- Plans for future enhancements
- On-site support, such as responses to queries and problem reports
- Additional capabilities that are not in the product
- Maintenance support, including support after the product is withdrawn from general availability

---

4. Periodically review the supplier agreement to ensure it accurately reflects the project's relationship with the supplier and current risks and market conditions.
5. Ensure that all parties to the agreement understand and agree to all requirements before implementing the agreement or any changes.

HINT

The supplier agreement is the basis for monitoring your supplier and accepting the product. Make sure it covers all critical information.

SAM

TIP

Often projects overlook a supplier's responsibilities for ongoing maintenance and support. Some companies have tied staff compensation, in part, to maintenance and support costs incurred following product delivery, thus motivating the staff to consider longer-term support needs when establishing an agreement with a supplier.

TIP

Especially with long-term agreements (more than one year), technical and nontechnical requirements may change. It is necessary to document these changes in the supplier agreement because this is often the legal document that will make these significant changes binding.

6. Revise the supplier agreement as necessary to reflect changes to the supplier's processes or work products.

7. Revise the project's plans and commitments, including changes to the project's processes or work products, as necessary to reflect the supplier agreement.

   Refer to the Project Monitoring and Control process area for more information about revising the project plan.

SG 2 SATISFY SUPPLIER AGREEMENTS

Agreements with the suppliers are satisfied by both the project and the supplier.

SP 2.1 EXECUTE THE SUPPLIER AGREEMENT

Perform activities with the supplier as specified in the supplier agreement.

Refer to the Project Monitoring and Control process area for more information about monitoring projects and taking corrective action.

Typical Work Products

1. Supplier progress reports and performance measures
2. Supplier review materials and reports
3. Action items tracked to closure
4. Documentation of product and document deliveries

Subpractices

1. Monitor supplier progress and performance (schedule, effort, cost, and technical performance) as defined in the supplier agreement.

2. Conduct reviews with the supplier as specified in the supplier agreement.

   Refer to the Project Monitoring and Control process area for more information about conducting reviews.

X-REF

Including suppliers in the project's progress and milestone reviews is covered in PMC SP 1.6 and 1.7.

   Reviews cover both formal and informal reviews and include the following steps:
   • Preparing for the review
   • Ensuring that relevant stakeholders participate
   • Conducting the review
   • Identifying, documenting, and tracking all action items to closure
   • Preparing and distributing to the relevant stakeholders a summary report of the review

3. Conduct technical reviews with the supplier as defined in the supplier agreement.

    Technical reviews typically include the following:

    - Providing the supplier with visibility into the needs and desires of the project's customers and end users, as appropriate
    - Reviewing the supplier's technical activities and verifying that the supplier's interpretation and implementation of the requirements are consistent with the project's interpretation
    - Ensuring that technical commitments are being met and that technical issues are communicated and resolved in a timely manner
    - Obtaining technical information about the supplier's products
    - Providing appropriate technical information and support to the supplier

4. Conduct management reviews with the supplier as defined in the supplier agreement.

    Management reviews typically include the following:

    - Reviewing critical dependencies
    - Reviewing project risks involving the supplier
    - Reviewing schedule and budget

    Technical and management reviews may be coordinated and held jointly.

5. Use the results of reviews to improve the supplier's performance and to establish and nurture long-term relationships with preferred suppliers.

6. Monitor risks involving the supplier and take corrective action as necessary.

    Refer to the Project Monitoring and Control process area for more information about monitoring project risks.

SP 2.2 MONITOR SELECTED SUPPLIER PROCESSES

Select, monitor, and analyze processes used by the supplier.

In situations where there must be tight alignment between some of the processes implemented by the supplier and those of the project, monitoring these processes will help prevent interface problems.

The selection must consider the impact of the supplier's processes on the project. On larger projects with significant subcontracts for development of critical components, monitoring of key processes is expected. For most vendor agreements where a product is not being developed or for smaller, less critical components, the selection process may determine that monitoring is not appropriate. Between

> **TIP**
>
> The purpose of a *technical review* is to review the supplier's technical progress and identify and resolve issues.

> **TIP**
>
> The purpose of a *management review* is to review the supplier's progress against the plan and identify and resolve issues (usually risks).

> **TIP**
>
> Just as peer reviews provide secondary benefits, so do reviews conducted with the supplier.

> **HINT**
>
> Select appropriate processes for monitoring and evaluating work products to obtain visibility into supplier progress and performance and to identify and mitigate risks.

SAM

TIP

Monitoring is a cost to both parties, so which processes to select for monitoring depends on which ones provide the most insight into supplier activities, pose the most risk, and provide an early indication of problems.

these extremes, the overall risk should be considered in selecting processes to be monitored.

The processes selected for monitoring should include engineering, project management (including contracting), and support processes critical to successful project performance.

Monitoring, if not performed with adequate care, can at one extreme be invasive and burdensome, or at the other extreme be uninformative and ineffective. There should be sufficient monitoring to detect issues, as early as possible, that may affect the supplier's ability to satisfy the requirements of the supplier agreement.

Analyzing selected processes involves taking the data obtained from monitoring selected supplier processes and analyzing it to determine whether there are serious issues.

Typical Work Products

1. List of processes selected for monitoring or rationale for non-selection
2. Activity reports
3. Performance reports
4. Performance curves
5. Discrepancy reports

Subpractices

TIP

In cases of low risk, no processes are monitored.

1. Identify the supplier processes that are critical to the success of the project.
2. Monitor the selected supplier's processes for compliance with requirements of the agreement.
3. Analyze the results of monitoring the selected processes to detect issues as early as possible that may affect the supplier's ability to satisfy the requirements of the agreement.

    Trend analysis can rely on internal and external data.

    Refer to the Verification process area for more information about recording the results of verification and analyses.

    Refer to the Project Monitoring and Control process area for more information about taking corrective action.

SP 2.3 EVALUATE SELECTED SUPPLIER WORK PRODUCTS

Select and evaluate work products from the supplier of custom-made products.

The scope of this specific practice is limited to suppliers providing the project with custom-made products, particularly those that present some risk to the program due to complexity or criticality. The intent of this specific practice is to evaluate selected work products produced by the supplier to help detect issues as early as possible that may affect the supplier's ability to satisfy the requirements of the agreement. The work products selected for evaluation should include critical products, product components, and work products that provide insight into quality issues as early as possible.

HINT

There is often more risk with a custom-made product. The requirements may not be defined fully or the supplier may not address all the requirements fully. Evaluate selected work products to uncover issues early in the lifecycle.

SAM

Typical Work Products

1. List of work products selected for monitoring or rationale for non-selection
2. Activity reports
3. Discrepancy reports

Subpractices

1. Identify those work products that are critical to the success of the project and that should be evaluated to help detect issues early.

TIP

In cases of low risk, no work products are evaluated.

> Examples of work products that may be critical to the success of the project include the following:
> • Requirements
> • Analyses
> • Architecture
> • Documentation

2. Evaluate the selected work products.

    Work products are evaluated to ensure the following:
    • Derived requirements are traceable to higher level requirements.
    • The architecture is feasible and will satisfy future product growth and reuse needs.
    • Documentation that will be used to operate and to support the product is adequate.
    • Work products are consistent with one another.
    • Products and product components (e.g., custom-made, off-the-shelf, and customer-supplied products) can be integrated.

3. Determine and document actions needed to address deficiencies identified in the evaluations.

    Refer to the Project Monitoring and Control process area for more information about taking corrective action.

SP 2.4 *Accept the Acquired Product*

Ensure that the supplier agreement is satisfied before accepting the acquired product.

HINT

Before accepting the product, be sure you are getting what you wanted (which should be documented in the supplier agreement).

Acceptance reviews and tests and configuration audits should be completed before accepting the product as defined in the supplier agreement.

Typical Work Products

1. Acceptance test procedures
2. Acceptance test results
3. Discrepancy reports or corrective action plans

Subpractices

X-REF

Acceptance procedures, reviews, and tests are also covered in VER and VAL, so consult their practices for more information about establishing the appropriate environment, procedures, and criteria for verification and validation (and thus for accepting the acquired product).

1. Define the acceptance procedures.
2. Review and obtain agreement with relevant stakeholders on the acceptance procedures before the acceptance review or test.
3. Verify that the acquired products satisfy their requirements.

   Refer to the Verification process area for more information about verifying products.

4. Confirm that the nontechnical commitments associated with the acquired work product are satisfied.

   This may include confirming that the appropriate license, warranty, ownership, usage, and support or maintenance agreements are in place and that all supporting materials are received.

HINT

Share pertinent parts of the schedule and criteria for assembly with suppliers of work products to reduce the occurrence of delays and component failure (PI SP 3.1).

5. Document the results of the acceptance review or test.
6. Establish and obtain supplier agreement on an action plan for any acquired work products that do not pass their acceptance review or test.
7. Identify, document, and track action items to closure.

   Refer to the Project Monitoring and Control process area for more information about tracking action items.

HINT

Be sure to address proprietary issues related to the acquired product before the supplier accepts the product.

SP 2.5 *Transition Products*

Transition the acquired products from the supplier to the project.

TIP

A successful transition involves planning for the appropriate facilities, training, use, maintenance, and support.

Before the acquired product is transferred to the project for integration, appropriate planning and evaluation should occur to ensure a smooth transition.

Refer to the Product Integration process area for more information about integrating the acquired products.

Typical Work Products

1. Transition plans
2. Training reports
3. Support and maintenance reports

Subpractices

1. Ensure that there are appropriate facilities to receive, store, use, and maintain the acquired products.
2. Ensure that appropriate training is provided for those involved in receiving, storing, using, and maintaining the acquired products.
3. Ensure that storing, distributing, and using the acquired products are performed according to the terms and conditions specified in the supplier agreement or license.

Generic Practices by Goal

GG 1   ACHIEVE SPECIFIC GOALS

The process supports and enables achievement of the specific goals of the process area by transforming identifiable input work products to produce identifiable output work products.

GP 1.1 PERFORM SPECIFIC PRACTICES

Perform the specific practices of the supplier agreement management process to develop work products and provide services to achieve the specific goals of the process area.

GG 2   INSTITUTIONALIZE A MANAGED PROCESS

The process is institutionalized as a managed process.

GP 2.1 ESTABLISH AN ORGANIZATIONAL POLICY

Establish and maintain an organizational policy for planning and performing the supplier agreement management process.

Elaboration:

This policy establishes organizational expectations for establishing, maintaining, and satisfying supplier agreements.

GP 2.2 PLAN THE PROCESS

Establish and maintain the plan for performing the supplier agreement management process.

Elaboration:

Portions of this plan for performing the supplier agreement management process can be part of (or referenced by) the project plan as described in the Project Planning process area. Often, however, some portions of the plan reside outside of the project with an independent group, such as contract management.

GP 2.3 PROVIDE RESOURCES

Provide adequate resources for performing the supplier agreement management process, developing the work products, and providing the services of the process.

Elaboration:

Examples of resources provided include the following tools:
- Preferred supplier lists
- Requirements tracking programs
- Project management and scheduling programs

GP 2.4 ASSIGN RESPONSIBILITY

Assign responsibility and authority for performing the process, developing the work products, and providing the services of the supplier agreement management process.

GP 2.5 TRAIN PEOPLE

Train the people performing or supporting the supplier agreement management process as needed.

Elaboration:

> Examples of training topics include the following:
> - Regulations and business practices related to negotiating and working with suppliers
> - Acquisition planning and preparation
> - COTS products acquisition
> - Supplier evaluation and selection
> - Negotiation and conflict resolution
> - Supplier management
> - Testing and transitioning of acquired products
> - Receiving, storing, using, and maintaining acquired products

GP 2.6 MANAGE CONFIGURATIONS

Place designated work products of the supplier agreement management process under appropriate levels of control.

Elaboration:

> Examples of work products placed under control include the following:
> - Statements of work
> - Supplier agreements
> - Memoranda of agreement
> - Subcontracts
> - Preferred supplier lists

GP 2.7 IDENTIFY AND INVOLVE RELEVANT STAKEHOLDERS

Identify and involve the relevant stakeholders of the supplier agreement management process as planned.

Elaboration:

> Examples of activities for stakeholder involvement include the following:
> - Establishing criteria for evaluation of potential suppliers
> - Reviewing potential suppliers
> - Establishing supplier agreements
> - Resolving issues with suppliers
> - Reviewing supplier performance

GP 2.8 MONITOR AND CONTROL THE PROCESS

Monitor and control the supplier agreement management process against the plan for performing the process and take appropriate corrective action.

Elaboration:

> Examples of measures and work products used in monitoring and controlling include the following:
> • Number of changes made to the requirements for the supplier
> • Cost and schedule variance per supplier agreement
> • Number of supplier work product evaluations completed (planned versus actuals)
> • Number of supplier process evaluations completed (planned versus actuals)
> • Schedule for selecting a supplier and establishing an agreement

GP 2.9 OBJECTIVELY EVALUATE ADHERENCE

Objectively evaluate adherence of the supplier agreement management process against its process description, standards, and procedures, and address noncompliance.

Elaboration:

> Examples of activities reviewed include the following:
> • Establishing and maintaining supplier agreements
> • Satisfying supplier agreements

> Examples of work products reviewed include the following:
> • Plan for Supplier Agreement Management
> • Supplier agreements

GP 2.10 REVIEW STATUS WITH HIGHER LEVEL MANAGEMENT

Review the activities, status, and results of the supplier agreement management process with higher level management and resolve issues.

> GG3 and its practices do not apply for a maturity level 2 rating, but do apply for a maturity level 3 rating and above. **S ONLY**

GG 3 INSTITUTIONALIZE A DEFINED PROCESS

The process is institutionalized as a defined process.

GP 3.1 ESTABLISH A DEFINED PROCESS

Establish and maintain the description of a defined supplier agreement management process.

GP 3.2 COLLECT IMPROVEMENT INFORMATION

Collect work products, measures, measurement results, and improvement information derived from planning and performing the supplier agreement management process to support the future use and improvement of the organization's processes and process assets.

Elaboration:

> Examples of work products, measures, measurement results, and improvement information include the following:
> • Results of supplier reviews
> • Trade studies used to select suppliers
> • Revision history of supplier agreements
> • Supplier performance reports
> • Results of supplier work product and process evaluations

GG 4 INSTITUTIONALIZE A QUANTITATIVELY MANAGED PROCESS

The process is institutionalized as a quantitatively managed process.

GP 4.1 ESTABLISH QUANTITATIVE OBJECTIVES FOR THE PROCESS

Establish and maintain quantitative objectives for the supplier agreement management process, which address quality and process performance, based on customer needs and business objectives.

GP 4.2 STABILIZE SUBPROCESS PERFORMANCE

Stabilize the performance of one or more subprocesses to determine the ability of the supplier agreement management process to achieve the established quantitative quality and process-performance objectives.

GG 5 INSTITUTIONALIZE AN OPTIMIZING PROCESS

The process is institutionalized as an optimizing process.

GP 5.1 ENSURE CONTINUOUS PROCESS IMPROVEMENT

Ensure continuous improvement of the supplier agreement management process in fulfilling the relevant business objectives of the organization.

GP 5.2 CORRECT ROOT CAUSES OF PROBLEMS

Identify and correct the root causes of defects and other problems in the supplier agreement management process.

CONTINUOUS ONLY

TECHNICAL SOLUTION
An Engineering Process Area at Maturity Level 3

Purpose

The purpose of Technical Solution (TS) is to design, develop, and implement solutions to requirements. Solutions, designs, and implementations encompass products, product components, and product-related lifecycle processes either singly or in combination as appropriate.

Introductory Notes

The Technical Solution process area is applicable at any level of the product architecture and to every product, product component, and product-related lifecycle process. Throughout the process areas, where we use the terms product and product component, their intended meanings also encompass services and their components.

The process area focuses on the following:

- Evaluating and selecting solutions (sometimes referred to as "design approaches," "design concepts," or "preliminary designs") that potentially satisfy an appropriate set of allocated requirements
- Developing detailed designs for the selected solutions (detailed in the context of containing all the information needed to manufacture, code, or otherwise implement the design as a product or product component)
- Implementing the designs as a product or product component

Typically, these activities interactively support each other. Some level of design, at times fairly detailed, may be needed to select solutions. Prototypes or pilots may be used as a means of gaining sufficient knowledge to develop a technical data package or a complete set of requirements.

> **HINT**
>
> You may apply these bullets recursively at each level of the product hierarchy.

HINT

It is not enough to consider product functionality and behavior in the intended operational environment when developing a solution. Also ask questions about other phases in the life of the product, including whether the solution can be manufactured; whether it is easy to test, install, repair, migrate to new versions or platforms, and support; and what the costs and legal implications will be.

X-REF

TS is driven by the requirements established by RD which are managed by REQM. The processes associated with these PAs interact significantly to accomplish their purposes.

TIP

TS applies not only to developing a product, but also to maintaining a product (i.e., corrective, adaptive, and perfective maintenance).

Technical Solution specific practices apply not only to the product and product components but also to product-related lifecycle processes. The product-related lifecycle processes are developed in concert with the product or product component. Such development may include selecting and adapting existing processes (including standard processes) for use as well as developing new processes.

Processes associated with the Technical Solution process area receive the product and product component requirements from the requirements management processes. The requirements management processes place the requirements, which originate in requirements development processes, under appropriate configuration management and maintain their traceability to previous requirements.

For a maintenance or sustainment project, the requirements in need of maintenance actions or redesign may be driven by user needs or latent defects in the product components. New requirements may arise from changes in the operating environment. Such requirements can be uncovered during verification of the product(s) where actual performance can be compared against the specified performance and unacceptable degradation can be identified. Processes associated with the Technical Solution process area should be used to perform the maintenance or sustainment design efforts.

Related Process Areas

Refer to the Requirements Development process area for more information about requirements allocations, establishing an operational concept, and interface requirements definition.

Refer to the Verification process area for more information about conducting peer reviews and verifying that the product and product components meet requirements.

Refer to the Decision Analysis and Resolution process area for more information about formal evaluation.

Refer to the Requirements Management process area for more information about managing requirements. The specific practices in the Requirements Management process area are performed interactively with those in the Technical Solution process area.

Refer to the Organizational Innovation and Deployment process area for more information about improving the organization's technology.

Specific Goal and Practice Summary

SG 1 Select Product Component Solutions
    SP 1.1   Develop Alternative Solutions and Selection Criteria
    SP 1.2   Select Product Component Solutions

SG 2 Develop the Design
    SP 2.1   Design the Product or Product Component
    SP 2.2   Establish a Technical Data Package
    SP 2.3   Design Interfaces Using Criteria
    SP 2.4   Perform Make, Buy, or Reuse Analyses

SG 3 Implement the Product Design
    SP 3.1   Implement the Design
    SP 3.2   Develop Product Support Documentation

Specific Practices by Goal

SG 1 *Select Product Component Solutions*

Product or product component solutions are selected from alternative solutions.

Alternative solutions and their relative merits are considered in advance of selecting a solution. Key requirements, design issues, and constraints are established for use in alternative solution analysis. Architectural features that provide a foundation for product improvement and evolution are considered. Use of commercial off-the-shelf (COTS) product components are considered relative to cost, schedule, performance, and risk. COTS alternatives may be used with or without modification. Sometimes such items may require modifications to aspects such as interfaces or a customization of some of the features to better achieve product requirements.

One indicator of a good design process is that the design was chosen after comparing and evaluating it against alternative solutions. Decisions on architecture, custom development versus off the shelf, and product component modularization are typical of the design choices that are addressed. Some of these decisions may require the use of a formal evaluation process.

Refer to the Decision Analysis and Resolution process area for more information about the use of a formal evaluation process.

Sometimes the search for solutions examines alternative instances of the same requirements with no allocations needed for lower level product components. Such is the case at the bottom of the product architecture. There are also cases where one or more of the solutions are fixed (e.g., a specific solution is directed or available product components, such as COTS, are investigated for use).

> **HINT**
>
> When you consider the successful products or services you use, ask what makes them successful. Is it features, usability, cost, customer support, response time, reliability, etc.? These characteristics were achieved through careful identification and evaluation of alternative design approaches.

> **TIP**
>
> Sometimes an insignificant requirements change can greatly improve the merits of a COTS-based solution, especially with regard to cost and schedule risks. However, the use of COTS may constrain the overall solution's performance and the support that can be offered later in the product's life. A relationship with a vendor may need to be maintained.

> **X-REF**
>
> See www.sei.cmu.edu/cbs/index.html for more information about using COTS.

TIP

The iteration in these practices eventually results in a product component solution and design that are either implemented (TS SG 3), acquired (SAM), or reused (TS SP 2.4).

HINT

Whether you are defining or evaluating an alternative solution, treat its components together, not individually. For example, do not rush to select a promising COTS component or new technology without considering the impacts and risks.

X-REF

RD SP 2.2 describes allocating requirements after a solution has been selected. However, it can also be applied prior to selection (a "provisional allocation") to gain insight into the relative merits of an alternative solution.

TIP

The importance of involving relevant stakeholders in selecting a solution is generally true; not just for IPPD.

TIP

Selection criteria typically include cost, schedule, performance, and risk. How these criteria are defined in detail, however, depends on the requirements.

In the general case, solutions are defined as a set. That is, when defining the next layer of product components, the solution for each of the product components in the set is established. The alternative solutions are not only different ways of addressing the same requirements, but they also reflect a different allocation of requirements among the product components comprising the solution set. The objective is to optimize the set as a whole and not the individual pieces. There will be significant interaction with processes associated with the Requirements Development process area to support the provisional allocations to product components until a solution set is selected and final allocations are established.

Product-related lifecycle processes are among the product component solutions that are selected from alternative solutions. Examples of these product-related lifecycle processes are the manufacturing, delivery, and support processes.

SP 1.1 DEVELOP ALTERNATIVE SOLUTIONS AND SELECTION CRITERIA

Develop alternative solutions and selection criteria.

Refer to the Allocate Product Component Requirements specific practice in the Requirements Development process area for more information about obtaining allocations of requirements to solution alternatives for the product components.

Refer to the Decision Analysis and Resolution process area for more information about establishing criteria used in making decisions.

The activity of selecting alternative solutions and issues to be subject to decision analyses and trade studies is accomplished by the involvement of relevant stakeholders. These stakeholders represent both business and technical functions and the concurrent development of the product and the product-related lifecycle processes (e.g., manufacturing, support, training, verification, and disposal). In this way, important issues surface earlier in product development than with traditional serial development and can be addressed before they become costly mistakes.

IPPD ADDITION

Alternative solutions need to be identified and analyzed to enable the selection of a balanced solution across the life of the product in terms of cost, schedule, and performance. These solutions are based on proposed product architectures that address critical product qualities and span a design space of feasible solutions. Specific practices associated with the Develop the Design specific goal provide more information on developing potential product architectures that can be incorporated into alternative solutions for the product.

Alternative solutions frequently encompass alternative requirement allocations to different product components. These alternative solutions can also include the use of COTS solutions in the product architecture. Processes associated with the Requirements Development process area would then be employed to provide a more complete and robust provisional allocation of requirements to the alternative solutions.

Alternative solutions span the acceptable range of cost, schedule, and performance. The product component requirements are received and used along with design issues, constraints, and criteria to develop the alternative solutions. Selection criteria would typically address costs (e.g., time, people, and money), benefits (e.g., performance, capability, and effectiveness), and risks (e.g., technical, cost, and schedule). Considerations for alternative solutions and selection criteria include the following:

- Cost of development, manufacturing, procurement, maintenance, and support, etc.
- Performance
- Complexity of the product component and product-related lifecycle processes
- Robustness to product operating and use conditions, operating modes, environments, and variations in product-related lifecycle processes
- Product expansion and growth
- Technology limitations
- Sensitivity to construction methods and materials
- Risk
- Evolution of requirements and technology
- Disposal
- Capabilities and limitations of end users and operators
- Characteristics of COTS products

The considerations listed here are a basic set; organizations should develop screening criteria to narrow down the list of alternatives that are consistent with their business objectives. Product lifecycle cost, while being a desirable parameter to minimize, may be outside the control of development organizations. A customer may not be willing to pay for features that cost more in the short term but ultimately decrease cost over the life of the product. In such cases, customers should at least be advised of any potential for reducing

HINT

Consider the entire life of the product when selecting, designing, and implementing a solution to ensure that it will have the desired versatility and market endurance.

HINT

Consider a range of alternative solutions. Input from stakeholders with diverse skills and backgrounds can help teams identify and address assumptions, constraints, and biases. Brainstorming sessions may stimulate innovative alternatives. Also, consider the "ilities" addressed in the requirements (e.g., usability, reliability, maintainability, interoperability, and security).

TIP

Complexity is a "double-edged sword." Sometimes today's high-performance solution becomes tomorrow's high-maintenance solution.

HINT

Explore the use of COTS (or open source or new technology) early in product development because to use COTS effectively, you may need to consider changes to requirements. Fully understand such requirements-and-design tradeoffs early, before committing to (and putting under contract) a particular development approach.

TIP

Screening criteria may involve setting thresholds for selected quality attributes (e.g., response time) that must be met by alternative solutions.

TIP

It may be possible to exploit a technology not available to competitors.

TIP

Since a solution has yet to be selected, this requirements allocation is referred to as a "provisional allocation of requirements." Such allocation provides better insight into the solutions' pros and cons.

lifecycle costs. The criteria used in selections of final solutions should provide a balanced approach to costs, benefits, and risks.

Typical Work Products

1. Alternative solution screening criteria
2. Evaluation reports of new technologies
3. Alternative solutions
4. Selection criteria for final selection
5. Evaluation reports of COTS products

Subpractices

1. Identify screening criteria to select a set of alternative solutions for consideration.
2. Identify technologies currently in use and new product technologies for competitive advantage.

    Refer to the Organizational Innovation and Deployment process area for more information about improving the organization's technology.

    The project should identify technologies applied to current products and processes and monitor the progress of currently used technologies throughout the life of the project. The project should identify, select, evaluate, and invest in new technologies to achieve competitive advantage. Alternative solutions could include newly developed technologies, but could also include applying mature technologies in different applications or to maintain current methods.

3. Identify candidate COTS products that satisfy the requirements.

    Refer to the Supplier Agreement Management process area for more information about evaluating suppliers.

    These requirements include the following:
    • Functionality, performance, quality, and reliability
    • Terms and conditions of warranties for the products
    • Risk
    • Suppliers' responsibilities for ongoing maintenance and support of the products

4. Generate alternative solutions.
5. Obtain a complete requirements allocation for each alternative.
6. Develop the criteria for selecting the best alternative solution.

    Criteria should be included that address design issues for the life of the product, such as provisions for more easily inserting new technologies or the ability to better exploit commercial products. Examples include criteria related to open design or open architecture concepts for the alternatives being evaluated.

SP 1.2 SELECT PRODUCT COMPONENT SOLUTIONS

Select the product component solutions that best satisfy the criteria established.

Refer to the Allocate Product Component Requirements and Identify Interface Requirements specific practices of the Requirements Development process area for information on establishing the allocated requirements for product components and interface requirements among product components.

Selecting product components that best satisfy the criteria establishes the requirement allocations to product components. Lower level requirements are generated from the selected alternative and used to develop the product component design. Interface requirements among product components are described, primarily functionally. Physical interface descriptions are included in the documentation for interfaces to items and activities external to the product.

The description of the solutions and the rationale for selection are documented. The documentation evolves throughout development as solutions and detailed designs are developed and those designs are implemented. Maintaining a record of rationale is critical to downstream decision making. Such records keep downstream stakeholders from redoing work and provide insights to apply technology as it becomes available in applicable circumstances.

Typical Work Products

1. Product component selection decisions and rationale
2. Documented relationships between requirements and product components
3. Documented solutions, evaluations, and rationale

Subpractices

1. Evaluate each alternative solution/set of solutions against the selection criteria established in the context of the operational concepts and scenarios.

   Develop timeline scenarios for product operation and user interaction for each alternative solution.

2. Based on the evaluation of alternatives, assess the adequacy of the selection criteria and update these criteria as necessary.
3. Identify and resolve issues with the alternative solutions and requirements.
4. Select the best set of alternative solutions that satisfy the established selection criteria.
5. Establish the requirements associated with the selected set of alternatives as the set of allocated requirements to those product components.

TIP

DAR supports the selection of product component solutions from among alternative solutions, especially in novel situations.

TIP

Selecting product component solutions from alternative solutions positions us for further requirements development and design.

HINT

You may want to examine the rationale for a particular selection when you later learn that a promising technology or COTS component is now available. It will save effort and time if the implications were already explored and records were maintained.

HINT

To gain the insight needed to fully evaluate alternative solutions, you may need to refine operational concepts and scenarios to understand the implications of each alternative solution. Also, you may need to develop scenarios for other phases of the product lifecycle.

X-REF

You may also consider different user roles and types. See RD SP 3.1 for more information.

HINT

No solution will rank best for every criterion used. Instead, select a solution that provides a balanced approach to cost, schedule, performance, and risks across the product lifecycle.

HINT

Following the evaluation, you may conclude that the selection criteria were not complete or detailed enough to adequately differentiate alternative solutions. If so, you may need to iterate through SP 1.1 and 1.2.

X-REF

The provisional allocation of requirements now becomes the allocation. See RD SP 2.2 for more information.

TIP

Documentation assists product maintenance and support later in the life of the product.

6. Identify the product component solutions that will be reused or acquired.

Refer to the Supplier Agreement Management process area for more information about acquiring products and product components.

7. Establish and maintain the documentation of the solutions, evaluations, and rationale.

SG 2 DEVELOP THE DESIGN

Product or product component designs are developed.

Product or product component designs must provide the appropriate content not only for implementation, but also for other phases of the product lifecycle such as modification, reprocurement, maintenance, sustainment, and installation. The design documentation provides a reference to support mutual understanding of the design by relevant stakeholders and supports future changes to the design both during development and in subsequent phases of the product lifecycle. A complete design description is documented in a technical data package that includes a full range of features and parameters including form, fit, function, interface, manufacturing process characteristics, and other parameters. Established organizational or project design standards (e.g., checklists, templates, and object frameworks) form the basis for achieving a high degree of definition and completeness in design documentation.

> The integrated teams develop the designs of the appropriate product-related life-cycle processes concurrently with the design of the product. These processes may be selected without modification from the organization's set of standard processes, if appropriate.
>
> *IPPD ADD*

SP 2.1 DESIGN THE PRODUCT OR PRODUCT COMPONENT

Develop a design for the product or product component.

TIP

A design describes a product's components and their interconnections. It guides the activities of a broad range of stakeholders, including implementers, testers, installers, and maintainers. Thus, stakeholders will use a design over the life of the product.

Product design consists of two broad phases that may overlap in execution: preliminary and detailed design. Preliminary design establishes product capabilities and the product architecture, including product partitions, product component identifications, system states and modes, major intercomponent interfaces, and external product interfaces. Detailed design fully defines the structure and capabilities of the product components.

Refer to the Requirements Development process area for more information about developing architecture requirements.

Architecture definition is driven from a set of architectural requirements developed during the requirements development processes. These requirements express the qualities and performance points that are critical to the success of the product. The architecture defines structural elements and coordination mechanisms that either directly satisfy requirements or support the achievement of the requirements as the details of the product design are established. Architectures may include standards and design rules governing development of product components and their interfaces as well as guidance to aid product developers. Specific practices in the Select Product Component Solutions specific goal contain more information about using product architectures as a basis for alternative solutions.

Architects postulate and develop a model of the product, making judgments about allocation of requirements to product components including hardware and software. Multiple architectures, supporting alternative solutions, may be developed and analyzed to determine the advantages and disadvantages in the context of the architectural requirements.

Operational concepts and scenarios are used to generate use cases and quality scenarios that are used to refine the architecture. They are also used as a means to evaluate the suitability of the architecture for its intended purpose during architecture evaluations, which are conducted periodically throughout product design.

Refer to the Establish Operational Concepts and Scenarios specific practice of the Requirements Development process area for information about developing operational concepts and scenarios used in architecture evaluation.

> **TIP**
> Organizational standards can help achieve consistency and completeness in design.

> **TIP**
> A good design does more than identify functionality. "Design is not just what it looks like and feels like. Design is how it works. ... Design is the fundamental soul of a human-made creation that ends up expressing itself in successive outer layers of the product or service." – Steve Jobs

Examples of architecture definition tasks include the following:
- Establishing the structural relations of partitions and rules regarding interfaces between elements within partitions, and between partitions
- Identifying major internal interfaces and all external interfaces
- Identifying product components and interfaces between them
- Defining coordination mechanisms (e.g., for software and hardware)
- Establishing infrastructure capabilities and services
- Developing product component templates or classes and frameworks
- Establishing design rules and authority for making decisions
- Defining a process/thread model
- Defining physical deployment of software to hardware
- Identifying major reuse approaches and sources

> **TIP**
> Architecture requirements express the qualities and performance points (i.e., thresholds) critical to the success of the product. They are developed in RD SP 2.1.

TIP

An architecture includes structural elements (e.g., product partitions and components), coordination mechanisms (e.g., interfaces), design rules and principles, standards, and guidance.

HINT

Use scenarios to help refine the architecture and evaluate it against the architecture requirements.

TIP

In detailed design, we fully define the structure and capabilities of the product components. Product component designs may be optimized relative to particular quality and performance characteristics (e.g., response time).

HINT

A design is a document used by stakeholders over the life of the product, and thus must communicate clearly and accommodate change. Consider this when selecting criteria to be used in evaluating the value of a design.

During detailed design, the product architecture details are finalized, product components are completely defined, and interfaces are fully characterized. Product component designs may be optimized for certain qualities or performance characteristics. Designers may evaluate the use of legacy or COTS products for the product components. As the design matures, the requirements assigned to lower level product components are tracked to ensure that those requirements are satisfied.

Refer to the Requirements Management process area for more information about tracking requirements for product components.

FOR SOFTWARE ENGINEERING
Detailed design is focused on software product component development. The internal structure of product components is defined, data schemas are generated, algorithms are developed, and heuristics are established to provide product component capabilities that satisfy allocated requirements.

FOR HARDWARE ENGINEERING
Detailed design is focused on product development of electronic, mechanical, electro-optical, and other hardware products and their components. Electrical schematics and interconnection diagrams are developed, mechanical and optical assembly models are generated, and fabrication and assembly processes are developed.

Typical Work Products

1. Product architecture
2. Product component designs

Subpractices

1. Establish and maintain criteria against which the design can be evaluated.

Examples of attributes, in addition to expected performance, for which design criteria can be established, include the following:

- Modular
- Clear
- Simple
- Maintainable
- Verifiable
- Portable
- Reliable
- Accurate
- Secure
- Scalable
- Usable

2. Identify, develop, or acquire the design methods appropriate for the product.

Effective design methods can embody a wide range of activities, tools, and descriptive techniques. Whether a given method is effective or not depends on the situation. Two companies may have very effective design methods for products in which they specialize, but these methods may not be effective in cooperative ventures. Highly sophisticated methods are not necessarily effective in the hands of designers who have not been trained in the use of the methods.

Whether a method is effective also depends on how much assistance it provides the designer, and the cost effectiveness of that assistance. For example, a multiyear prototyping effort may not be appropriate for a simple product component but might be the right thing to do for an unprecedented, expensive, and complex product development. Rapid prototyping techniques, however, can be highly effective for many product components. Methods that use tools to ensure that a design will encompass all the necessary attributes needed to implement the product component design can be very effective. For example, a design tool that "knows" the capabilities of the manufacturing processes can allow the variability of the manufacturing process to be accounted for in the design tolerances.

TS

TIP

An effective design method (and design language and tool) enables a designer to describe the entities that comprise a design and its connections, analyze attributes of interest (e.g., design cohesiveness, presence of race conditions), test the design against use cases or scenarios, and revise the design to reflect decisions made.

TIP

Prototyping is an important technique that can help you discover design deficiencies early, before fully committing to implementing a particular design.

X-REF

For more information about design approaches, see "Architecture Description Language," "Unified Modeling Language," "Prototyping," and "Design Patterns" on the Wikipedia site, www.wikipedia.org.

> Examples of techniques and methods that facilitate effective design include the following:
> • Prototypes
> • Structural models
> • Object-oriented design
> • Essential systems analysis
> • Entity relationship models
> • Design reuse
> • Design patterns

TIP

Verification methods that help ensure that a design adheres to applicable standards and criteria include peer reviews, design simulations, and prototyping. (See VER for more information.)

3. Ensure that the design adheres to applicable design standards and criteria.

> Examples of design standards include the following (some or all of these standards may be design criteria, particularly in circumstances where the standards have not been established):
> • Operator interface standards
> • Test scenarios
> • Safety standards
> • Design constraints (e.g., electromagnetic compatibility, signal integrity, and environmental)
> • Production constraints
> • Design tolerances
> • Parts standards (e.g., production scrap and waste)

TIP

Verification methods that help ensure that a design adheres to allocated requirements include holding design reviews with the customer (for functional requirements) and simulation (for performance requirements). (See VER for more information.)

4. Ensure that the design adheres to allocated requirements.
   Identified COTS product components must be taken into account. For example, putting existing product components into the product architecture might modify the requirements and the requirements allocation.
5. Document the design.

TIP

A technical data package is the complete design documentation for a product or product component and the additional information needed to support its effective use.

SP 2.2 ESTABLISH A TECHNICAL DATA PACKAGE

Establish and maintain a technical data package.

A technical data package provides the developer with a comprehensive description of the product or product component as it is developed. Such a package also provides procurement flexibility in a variety of circumstances such as performance-based contracting or build to print.

The design is recorded in a technical data package that is created during preliminary design to document the architecture definition. This technical data package is maintained throughout the life of the product to record essential details of the product design. The technical data package provides the description of a product or product component (including product-related lifecycle processes if not handled as separate product components) that supports an acquisition strategy, or the implementation, production, engineering, and logistics support phases of the product lifecycle. The description includes the definition of the required design configuration and procedures to ensure adequacy of product or product component performance. It includes all applicable technical data such as drawings, associated lists, specifications, design descriptions, design databases, standards, performance requirements, quality assurance provisions, and packaging details. The technical data package includes a description of the selected alternative solution that was chosen for implementation.

A technical data package should include the following if such information is appropriate for the type of product and product component (for example, material and manufacturing requirements may not be useful for product components associated with software services or processes):

- Product architecture description
- Allocated requirements
- Product component descriptions
- Product-related lifecycle process descriptions, if not described as separate product components
- Key product characteristics
- Required physical characteristics and constraints
- Interface requirements
- Materials requirements (bills of material and material characteristics)
- Fabrication and manufacturing requirements (for both the original equipment manufacturer and field support)
- The verification criteria used to ensure that requirements have been achieved
- Conditions of use (environments) and operating/usage scenarios, modes and states for operations, support, training, manufacturing, disposal, and verifications throughout the life of the product
- Rationale for decisions and characteristics (requirements, requirement allocations, and design choices)

TIP

A technical data package is maintained throughout the life of the product. It is an essential input to the acquisition of the product (if it is to be "bought") as well as to implementation, production, maintenance, and support (if it is to be "built").

TS

HINT

Technical data packages contain a lot of data. To increase usability and usefulness, use criteria to define what to include, organize data according to the product architecture, and provide relevant views.

Because design descriptions can involve a very large amount of data and can be crucial to successful product component development, it is advisable to establish criteria for organizing the data and for selecting the data content. It is particularly useful to use the product architecture as a means of organizing this data and abstracting views that are clear and relevant to an issue or feature of interest. These views include the following:

- Customers
- Requirements
- The environment
- Functional
- Logical
- Security
- Data
- States/modes
- Construction
- Management

These views are documented in the technical data package.

Typical Work Products

1. Technical data package

Subpractices

HINT

Determine early in the project how much documentation is needed for each level of design. Perhaps use cases are sufficient for designs to be fully implemented in software or human operations.

1. Determine the number of levels of design and the appropriate level of documentation for each design level.

    Determining the number of levels of product components (e.g., subsystem, hardware configuration item, circuit board, computer software configuration item [CSCI], computer software product component, and computer software unit) that require documentation and requirements traceability is important to manage documentation costs and to support integration and verification plans.

2. Base detailed design descriptions on the allocated product component requirements, architecture, and higher level designs.

3. Document the design in the technical data package.

4. Document the rationale for key (i.e., significant effect on cost, schedule, or technical performance) decisions made or defined.

5. Revise the technical data package as necessary.

SP 2.3 DESIGN INTERFACES USING CRITERIA

Design product component interfaces using established criteria.

Interface designs include the following:

- Origination
- Destination
- Stimulus and data characteristics for software
- Electrical, mechanical, and functional characteristics for hardware
- Services lines of communication

The criteria for interfaces frequently reflect critical parameters that must be defined, or at least investigated, to ascertain their applicability. These parameters are often peculiar to a given type of product (e.g., software, mechanical, electrical, and service) and are often associated with safety, security, durability, and mission-critical characteristics.

Refer to the Identify Interface Requirements specific practice in the Requirements Development process area for more information about identifying product and product component interface requirements.

Typical Work Products

1. Interface design specifications
2. Interface control documents
3. Interface specification criteria
4. Rationale for selected interface design

Subpractices

1. Define interface criteria.

    These criteria can be a part of the organizational process assets.

    Refer to the Organizational Process Definition process area for more information about establishing and maintaining organizational process assets.

2. Identify interfaces associated with other product components.
3. Identify interfaces associated with external items.
4. Identify interfaces between product components and the product-related lifecycle processes.

    For example, such interfaces could include those between a product component to be fabricated and the jigs and fixtures used to enable that fabrication during the manufacturing process.

HINT

Where possible, reach early agreement on interface design. Lack of agreement leads to wasted time, as assumptions made by the teams on each side of an interface need to be validated. Project costs increase and the schedule may slip.

TIP

Interface design may sometimes follow a formal evaluation (DAR) process: Establish criteria for correctness of an interface (based in part on interface requirements), identify design alternatives, and so on.

TIP

Interface control documents define interfaces in terms of data items passed, protocols used for interaction, and so on. These documents are particularly useful in controlling product components being built by different teams.

X-REF

For examples of interfaces, see PI SP 2.1.

5. Apply the criteria to the interface design alternatives.

   Refer to the Decision Analysis and Resolution process area for more information about identifying criteria and selecting alternatives based on those criteria.

6. Document the selected interface designs and the rationale for the selection.

SP 2.4 PERFORM MAKE, BUY, OR REUSE ANALYSES

Evaluate whether the product components should be developed, purchased, or reused based on established criteria.

HINT

Interface designs should be documented in the technical data package.

TIP

This is also known as make-or-buy analysis.

TIP

Organizations in all kinds of industries (including public institutions such as school systems) increasingly engage in such analyses to reduce costs or improve time-to-market of their products and services.

The determination of what products or product components will be acquired is frequently referred to as a "make-or-buy analysis." It is based on an analysis of the needs of the project. This make-or-buy analysis begins early in the project during the first iteration of design; continues during the design process; and is completed with the decision to develop, acquire, or reuse the product.

Refer to the Requirements Development process area for more information about determining the product and product component requirements.

Refer to the Requirements Management process area for more information about managing requirements.

Factors affecting the make-or-buy decision include the following:

- Functions the products will provide and how these functions will fit into the project
- Available project resources and skills
- Costs of acquiring versus developing internally
- Critical delivery and integration dates
- Strategic business alliances, including high-level business requirements
- Market research of available products, including COTS products
- Functionality and quality of available products
- Skills and capabilities of potential suppliers
- Impact on core competencies
- Licenses, warranties, responsibilities, and limitations associated with products being acquired
- Product availability
- Proprietary issues
- Risk reduction

The make-or-buy decision can be conducted using a formal evaluation approach.

Refer to the Decision Analysis and Resolution process area for more information about defining criteria and alternatives and performing formal evaluations.

As technology evolves, so does the rationale for choosing to develop or purchase a product component. While complex development efforts may favor purchasing an off-the-shelf product component, advances in productivity and tools may provide an opposing rationale. Off-the-shelf products may have incomplete or inaccurate documentation and may or may not be supported in the future.

> **TIP**
>
> As technology evolves, a make-or-buy analysis might lead to a different decision.

Once the decision is made to purchase an off-the-shelf product component, the requirements are used to establish a supplier agreement. There are times when "off the shelf" refers to an existing item that may not be readily available in the marketplace. For example, some types of aircraft and engines are not truly "off the shelf" but can be readily procured. In some cases the use of such nondeveloped items is because the specifics of the performance and other product characteristics expected need to be within the limits specified. In these cases, the requirements and acceptance criteria may need to be included in the supplier agreement and managed. In other cases, the off-the-shelf product is literally off the shelf (word processing software, for example) and there is no agreement with the supplier that needs to be managed.

> **TIP**
>
> If an off-the-shelf product component cannot be readily purchased but must be procured from a supplier, a supplier agreement may be used to manage the procurement.

Refer to the Supplier Agreement Management process area for more information about how to address the acquisition of the product components that will be purchased.

Typical Work Products

1. Criteria for design and product component reuse
2. Make-or-buy analyses
3. Guidelines for choosing COTS product components

Subpractices

1. Develop criteria for the reuse of product component designs.
2. Analyze designs to determine if product components should be developed, reused, or purchased.
3. Analyze implications for maintenance when considering purchased or nondevelopmental (e.g., COTS, government off the shelf, and reuse) items.

> **TIP**
>
> If the organization has already been using design methods as part of a larger systematic reuse effort, it has already established the reuse criteria. Otherwise, reuse is unlikely to significantly improve the economics of design.

HINT

When using off-the-shelf and other nondevelopmental items, plan how they will be maintained.

> Examples of implications for maintenance include the following:
> - Compatibility with future releases of COTS products
> - Configuration management of vendor changes
> - Defects in the nondevelopment item and their resolution
> - Unplanned obsolescence

SG 3   IMPLEMENT THE PRODUCT DESIGN

Product components, and associated support documentation, are implemented from their designs.

Product components are implemented from the designs established by the specific practices in the Develop the Design specific goal. The implementation usually includes unit testing of the product components before sending them to product integration and development of end-user documentation.

SP 3.1 IMPLEMENT THE DESIGN

Implement the designs of the product components.

Once the design has been completed, it is implemented as a product component. The characteristics of that implementation depend on the type of product component.

TIP

At an upper level of the product hierarchy, implementing the design implies recursion (i.e., repeating RD SG 2-3 and TS SG 1-2) to establish the next level of product components. At the lowest level of the product hierarchy, there is no more decomposition or recursion; the design is directly implemented.

Design implementation at the top level of the product hierarchy involves the specification of each of the product components at the next level of the product hierarchy. This activity includes the allocation, refinement, and verification of each product component. It also involves the coordination between the various product component development efforts.

Refer to the Requirements Development process area for more information about the allocation and refinement of requirements.

Refer to the Product Integration process area for more information about the management of interfaces and the integration of products and product components.

Example characteristics of this implementation are as follows:

- Software is coded.
- Data is documented.
- Services are documented.
- Electrical and mechanical parts are fabricated.
- Product-unique manufacturing processes are put into operation.
- Processes are documented.
- Facilities are constructed.
- Materials are produced (e.g., a product-unique material could be petroleum, oil, a lubricant, or a new alloy).

Typical Work Products

1. Implemented design

Subpractices

1. Use effective methods to implement the product components.

> **FOR SOFTWARE ENGINEERING**
> Examples of software coding methods include the following:
> - Structured programming
> - Object-oriented programming
> - Automatic code generation
> - Software code reuse
> - Use of applicable design patterns

> **FOR HARDWARE ENGINEERING**
> Examples of hardware implementation methods include the following:
> - Gate level synthesis
> - Circuit board layout (place and route)
> - Computer Aided Design drawing
> - Post layout simulation
> - Fabrication methods

2. Adhere to applicable standards and criteria.

TIP

Which implementation method to use depends on the type of product component being implemented. An organization may establish its own implementation methods.

TIP

The implementation standards and criteria used depend on the type of product component being implemented. An organization may establish its own implementation standards and criteria.

Examples of implementation standards include the following:
- Language standards (e.g., standards for software programming languages and hardware description languages)
- Drawing requirements
- Standard parts lists
- Manufactured parts
- Structure and hierarchy of software product components
- Process and quality standards

Examples of criteria include the following:
- Modularity
- Clarity
- Simplicity
- Reliability
- Safety
- Maintainability

X-REF

In VER SP 1.1, you select work products to be verified and the verification method to use for each. In particular, you select which product components to be verified through peer review (e.g., software code).

TIP

The product component should now be ready for product integration (see PI).

3. Conduct peer reviews of the selected product components.

Refer to the Verification process area for more information about conducting peer reviews.

4. Perform unit testing of the product component as appropriate.

Note that unit testing is not limited to software. Unit testing involves the testing of individual hardware or software units or groups of related items prior to integration of those items.

Refer to the Verification process area for more information about verification methods and procedures and about verifying work products against their specified requirements.

FOR SOFTWARE ENGINEERING

Examples of unit testing methods include the following:
- Statement coverage testing
- Branch coverage testing
- Predicate coverage testing
- Path coverage testing
- Boundary value testing
- Special value testing

FOR HARDWARE ENGINEERING

Examples of unit testing methods include the following:

- Functional testing
- Radiation inspection testing
- Environmental testing

5. Revise the product component as necessary.

> An example of when the product component may need to be revised is when problems surface during implementation that could not be foreseen during design.

TIP

Another reason to revise the product component is to remove defects discovered through peer reviews or unit testing.

SP 3.2 *DEVELOP PRODUCT SUPPORT DOCUMENTATION*

Develop and maintain the end-use documentation.

This specific practice develops and maintains the documentation that will be used to install, operate, and maintain the product.

Typical Work Products

1. End-user training materials
2. User's manual
3. Operator's manual
4. Maintenance manual
5. Online help

Subpractices

1. Review the requirements, design, product, and test results to ensure that issues affecting the installation, operation, and maintenance documentation are identified and resolved.
2. Use effective methods to develop the installation, operation, and maintenance documentation.
3. Adhere to the applicable documentation standards.

Examples of documentation standards include the following:
- Compatibility with designated word processors
- Acceptable fonts
- Numbering of pages, sections, and paragraphs
- Consistency with a designated style manual
- Use of abbreviations
- Security classification markings
- Internationalization requirements

TIP

Documentation can be treated as a type of product component for which a solution may be selected, designed, and implemented. There are design and implementation methods and standards for documentation.

TIP

Installers, operators, end users, and maintainers may have different documentation needs that may be addressed in different documents.

TIP

Relevant stakeholders (engineers, technical writers, QA personnel, and so on) can reduce the number of serious issues that must be resolved through documentation by participating in reviews of intermediate work products. In these reviews, issues impacting installation, operation, and so on, are identified and resolved.

TS

TIP

A preliminary version of a document produced for review by relevant stakeholders can be considered a prototype of the final document.

HINT

Use peer reviews to evaluate end-user documentation.

4. Develop preliminary versions of the installation, operation, and maintenance documentation in early phases of the project lifecycle for review by the relevant stakeholders.

5. Conduct peer reviews of the installation, operation, and maintenance documentation.

> *Refer to the Verification process area for more information about conducting peer reviews.*

6. Revise the installation, operation, and maintenance documentation as necessary.

Examples of when documentation may need to be revised include when the following events occur:
- Requirements change
- Design changes are made
- Product changes are made
- Documentation errors are identified
- Workaround fixes are identified

Generic Practices by Goal

GG 1 ACHIEVE SPECIFIC GOALS

The process supports and enables achievement of the specific goals of the process area by transforming identifiable input work products to produce identifiable output work products.

GP 1.1 PERFORM SPECIFIC PRACTICES

Perform the specific practices of the technical solution process to develop work products and provide services to achieve the specific goals of the process area.

GG 2 INSTITUTIONALIZE A MANAGED PROCESS

The process is institutionalized as a managed process.

GG 3 INSTITUTIONALIZE A DEFINED PROCESS

The process is institutionalized as a defined process.

> *This generic goal's appearance here reflects its location in the staged representation.*

CONTINUOUS ONLY

STAGED ONLY

GP 2.1 Establish an Organizational Policy

Establish and maintain an organizational policy for planning and performing the technical solution process.

Elaboration:

This policy establishes organizational expectations for addressing the iterative cycle in which product component solutions are selected, product and product component designs are developed, and the product component designs are implemented.

GP 2.2 Plan the Process

Establish and maintain the plan for performing the technical solution process.

Elaboration:

This plan for performing the technical solution process can be part of (or referenced by) the project plan as described in the Project Planning process area.

GP 2.3 Provide Resources

Provide adequate resources for performing the technical solution process, developing the work products, and providing the services of the process.

Elaboration:

Special facilities may be required for developing, designing, and implementing solutions to requirements. When necessary, the facilities required for the activities in the Technical Solution process area are developed or purchased.

Examples of other resources provided include the following tools:
- Design specification tools
- Simulators and modeling tools
- Prototyping tools
- Scenario definition and management tools
- Requirements tracking tools
- Interactive documentation tools

GP 2.4 Assign Responsibility

Assign responsibility and authority for performing the process, developing the work products, and providing the services of the technical solution process.

GP 2.5 *TRAIN PEOPLE*

Train the people performing or supporting the technical solution process as needed.

Elaboration:

Examples of training topics include the following:
- Application domain of the product and product components
- Design methods
- Interface design
- Unit testing techniques
- Standards (e.g., product, safety, human factors, and environmental)

GP 2.6 *MANAGE CONFIGURATIONS*

Place designated work products of the technical solution process under appropriate levels of control.

Elaboration:

Examples of work products placed under control include the following:
- Product, product component and interface designs
- Technical data packages
- Interface design documents
- Criteria for design and product component reuse
- Implemented designs (e.g., software code and fabricated product components)
- User, installation, operation, and maintenance documentation

GP 2.7 *IDENTIFY AND INVOLVE RELEVANT STAKEHOLDERS*

Identify and involve the relevant stakeholders of the technical solution process as planned.

Elaboration:

Select relevant stakeholders from customers, end users, developers, producers, testers, suppliers, marketers, maintainers, disposal personnel, and others who may be affected by, or may affect, the product as well as the process.

Examples of activities for stakeholder involvement include the following:
- Developing alternative solutions and selection criteria
- Obtaining approval on external interface specifications and design descriptions
- Developing the technical data package
- Assessing the make, buy, or reuse alternatives for product components
- Implementing the design

GP 2.8 *MONITOR AND CONTROL THE PROCESS*

Monitor and control the technical solution process against the plan for performing the process and take appropriate corrective action.

Elaboration:

Examples of measures and work products used in monitoring and controlling include the following:
- Cost, schedule, and effort expended for rework
- Percentage of requirements addressed in the product or product component design
- Size and complexity of the product, product components, interfaces, and documentation
- Defect density of technical solutions work products
- Schedule for design activities

GP 2.9 *OBJECTIVELY EVALUATE ADHERENCE*

Objectively evaluate adherence of the technical solution process against its process description, standards, and procedures, and address noncompliance.

Elaboration:

Examples of activities reviewed include the following:
- Selecting product component solutions
- Developing product and product component designs
- Implementing product component designs

Examples of work products reviewed include the following:
- Technical data packages
- Product, product component, and interface designs
- Implemented designs (e.g., software code and fabricated product components)
- User, installation, operation, and maintenance documentation

GP 2.10 *REVIEW STATUS WITH HIGHER LEVEL MANAGEMENT*

Review the activities, status, and results of the technical solution process with higher level management and resolve issues.

GG 3 **INSTITUTIONALIZE A DEFINED PROCESS**

The process is institutionalized as a defined process.

> *This generic goal's appearance here reflects its location in the continuous representation.*

CONT. ONLY

GP 3.1 *ESTABLISH A DEFINED PROCESS*

Establish and maintain the description of a defined technical solution process.

GP 3.2 *COLLECT IMPROVEMENT INFORMATION*

Collect work products, measures, measurement results, and improvement information derived from planning and performing the technical solution process to support the future use and improvement of the organization's processes and process assets.

Elaboration:

Examples of work products, measures, measurement results, and improvement information include the following:
- Results of the make, buy, or reuse analysis
- Design defect density
- Results of applying new methods and tools

GG 4 **INSTITUTIONALIZE A QUANTITATIVELY MANAGED PROCESS**

The process is institutionalized as a quantitatively managed process.

GP 4.1 *ESTABLISH QUANTITATIVE OBJECTIVES FOR THE PROCESS*

Establish and maintain quantitative objectives for the technical solution process, which address quality and process performance, based on customer needs and business objectives.

GP 4.2 *STABILIZE SUBPROCESS PERFORMANCE*

Stabilize the performance of one or more subprocesses to determine the ability of the technical solution process to achieve the established quantitative quality and process-performance objectives.

CONTINUOUS ONLY

GG 5 INSTITUTIONALIZE AN OPTIMIZING PROCESS

The process is institutionalized as an optimizing process.

GP 5.1 ENSURE CONTINUOUS PROCESS IMPROVEMENT

Ensure continuous improvement of the technical solution process in fulfilling the relevant business objectives of the organization.

GP 5.2 CORRECT ROOT CAUSES OF PROBLEMS

Identify and correct the root causes of defects and other problems in the technical solution process.

VALIDATION
An Engineering Process Area at Maturity Level 3

Purpose

The purpose of Validation (VAL) is to demonstrate that a product or product component fulfills its intended use when placed in its intended environment.

TIP

Validation is a series of evaluations in which end users, the product (or prototype), and other stakeholders or systems in the *intended environment* (real or simulated) interact with each other in various typical and not-so-typical ways to determine whether the product will fulfill its *intended use.* The results may increase confidence in the product or identify issues to be resolved.

VAL

HINT

If you wait until the acceptance test to find issues, you may be in big trouble.

Introductory Notes

Validation activities can be applied to all aspects of the product in any of its intended environments, such as operation, training, manufacturing, maintenance, and support services. The methods employed to accomplish validation can be applied to work products as well as to the product and product components. (Throughout the process areas, where we use the terms product and product component, their intended meanings also encompass services and their components.) The work products (e.g., requirements, designs, and prototypes) should be selected on the basis of which are the best predictors of how well the product and product component will satisfy user needs and thus validation is performed early and incrementally throughout the product lifecycle.

The validation environment should represent the intended environment for the product and product components as well as represent the intended environment suitable for validation activities with work products.

Validation demonstrates that the product, as provided, will fulfill its intended use; whereas, verification addresses whether the work product properly reflects the specified requirements. In other words, verification ensures that "you built it right"; whereas, validation ensures that "you built the right thing." Validation activities use approaches similar to verification (e.g., test, analysis, inspection, demonstration, or simulation). Often, the end users and other relevant stakeholders are involved in the validation activities. Both validation

HINT

Consider VER first. Only a well-verified work product should be used in validation; otherwise, you may lose valuable time with disruptions or rediscovering requirements you already knew. Conversely, validation helps you to uncover missing needs that you can incorporate into requirements.

TIP

RD addresses requirements validation. Requirements validation determines the adequacy and completeness of the requirements.

and verification activities often run concurrently and may use portions of the same environment.

Refer to the Verification process area for more information about verification activities.

Whenever possible, validation should be accomplished using the product or product component operating in its intended environment. The entire environment can be used or only part of it. However, validation issues can be discovered early in the life of the project using work products by involving relevant stakeholders. Validation activities for services can be applied to work products such as proposals, service catalogs, statements of work, and service records.

When validation issues are identified, they are referred to the processes associated with the Requirements Development, Technical Solution, or Project Monitoring and Control process areas for resolution.

The specific practices of this process area build on each other in the following way:

- The Select Products for Validation specific practice enables the identification of the product or product component to be validated and the methods to be used to perform the validation.
- The Establish the Validation Environment specific practice enables the determination of the environment that will be used to carry out the validation.
- The Establish Validation Procedures and Criteria specific practice enables the development of validation procedures and criteria that are aligned with the characteristics of selected products, customer constraints on validation, methods, and the validation environment.
- The Perform Validation specific practice enables the performance of validation according to the methods, procedures, and criteria.

Related Process Areas

Refer to the Requirements Development process area for more information about requirements validation.

Refer to the Technical Solution process area for more information about transforming requirements into product specifications and for corrective action when validation issues are identified that affect the product or product component design.

Refer to the Verification process area for more information about verifying that the product or product component meets its requirements.

Specific Goal and Practice Summary

SG 1 Prepare for Validation
SP 1.1   Select Products for Validation
SP 1.2   Establish the Validation Environment
SP 1.3   Establish Validation Procedures and Criteria
SG 2 Validate Product or Product Components
SP 2.1   Perform Validation
SP 2.2   Analyze Validation Results

Specific Practices by Goal

SG 1   PREPARE FOR VALIDATION

Preparation for validation is conducted.

Preparation activities include selecting products and product components for validation and establishing and maintaining the validation environment, procedures, and criteria. The items selected for validation may include only the product or it may include appropriate levels of the product components that are used to build the product. Any product or product component may be subject to validation, including replacement, maintenance, and training products, to name a few.

The environment required to validate the product or product component is prepared. The environment may be purchased or may be specified, designed, and built. The environments used for product integration and verification may be considered in collaboration with the validation environment to reduce cost and improve efficiency or productivity.

SP 1.1 SELECT PRODUCTS FOR VALIDATION

Select products and product components to be validated and the validation methods that will be used for each.

Products and product components are selected for validation on the basis of their relationship to user needs. For each product component, the scope of the validation (e.g., operational behavior, maintenance, training, and user interface) should be determined.

HINT

Any product or product component can benefit from validation. What you select to validate should depend on the issues relating to user needs that pose the highest risk to project success and available resources.

TIP

Integration tests can address validation-type activities (with an end user present to evaluate the integrated product under different scenarios). Thus, for some product components, product integration, verification, and validation activities may be addressed together.

TIP

Validation can be an expensive activity. It takes good judgment to select (and limit) what needs to be validated.

VAL

HINT

When you seek to validate a product component that has not yet been built, consider developing a prototype based on the component's requirements and design. The timely end-user feedback you obtain may more than compensate for the expense of the validation exercise.

X-REF

Customer constraints are briefly mentioned as part of the development of customer requirements in RD SP 1.2.

HINT

The product (or prototype) may need special interfaces and functionality to properly interact with elements of the validation environment (e.g., data recording equipment). You can develop their requirements and incorporate them with other product requirements.

TIP

Because validation generally involves stakeholders external to the project, it is important early in the project to identify and communicate with them about validation methods so that appropriate preparations can begin.

Examples of products and product components that can be validated include the following:
- Product and product component requirements and designs
- Product and product components (e.g., system, hardware units, software, and service documentation)
- User interfaces
- User manuals
- Training materials
- Process documentation

The requirements and constraints for performing validation are collected. Then, validation methods are selected based on their ability to demonstrate that user needs are satisfied. The validation methods not only define the approach to product validation, but also drive the needs for the facilities, equipment, and environments. This may result in the generation of lower level product component requirements that are handled by the requirements development processes. Derived requirements, such as interface requirements to test sets and test equipment, can be generated. These requirements are also passed to the requirements development processes to ensure that the product or product components can be validated in an environment that supports the methods.

Validation methods should be selected early in the life of the project so that they are clearly understood and agreed to by the relevant stakeholders.

The validation methods address the development, maintenance, support, and training for the product or product component as appropriate.

Examples of validation methods include the following:
- Discussions with the users, perhaps in the context of a formal review
- Prototype demonstrations
- Functional demonstrations (e.g., system, hardware units, software, service documentation, and user interfaces)
- Pilots of training materials
- Test of products and product components by end users and other relevant stakeholders
- Analyses of product and product components (e.g., simulations, modeling, and user analyses)

FOR HARDWARE ENGINEERING

Hardware validation activities include modeling to validate form, fit, and function of mechanical designs; thermal modeling; maintainability and reliability analysis; timeline demonstrations; and electrical design simulations of electronic or mechanical product components.

Typical Work Products

1. Lists of products and product components selected for validation
2. Validation methods for each product or product component
3. Requirements for performing validation for each product or product component
4. Validation constraints for each product or product component

Subpractices

1. Identify the key principles, features, and phases for product or product component validation throughout the life of the project.
2. Determine which categories of user needs (operational, maintenance, training, or support) are to be validated.

   The product or product component must be maintainable and supportable in its intended operational environment. This specific practice also addresses the actual maintenance, training, and support services that may be delivered along with the product.

> An example of evaluation of maintenance concepts in the operational environment is a demonstration that maintenance tools are operating with the actual product.

3. Select the product and product components to be validated.
4. Select the evaluation methods for product or product component validation.
5. Review the validation selection, constraints, and methods with relevant stakeholders.

SP 1.2 *ESTABLISH THE VALIDATION ENVIRONMENT*

Establish and maintain the environment needed to support validation.

The requirements for the validation environment are driven by the product or product components selected, by the type of the work products (e.g., design, prototype, and final version), and by the

HINT

Items selected for validation might be shown as a *table* with columns identifying items to be validated, issue to be investigated, related requirements and constraints, and validation methods. The table might also list the work products to be verified and the verification methods to be used. Using one table to address both may lead you to discover opportunities to combine verification and validation.

TIP

Validation is not applied only to discover missing functionality and is not limited only to the end-user operational environment. Other features, environments, and categories of user needs should be considered.

HINT

How might a "shrink-wrapped" product be validated? Observe users with a prototype in their operational environment; bring users to a special testing laboratory; or release a beta version for end-user testing and feedback.

HINT

Preparing for and conducting validation requires coordination with many external groups. Obtain commitment from these groups to support the planned validation efforts.

VAL

methods of validation. These may yield requirements for the purchase or development of equipment, software, or other resources. These requirements are provided to the requirements development processes for development. The validation environment may include the reuse of existing resources. In this case, arrangements for the use of these resources must be made. Examples of the type of elements in a validation environment include the following:

- Test tools interfaced with the product being validated (e.g., scope, electronic devices, and probes)
- Temporary embedded test software
- Recording tools for dump or further analysis and replay
- Simulated subsystems or components (by software, electronics, or mechanics)
- Simulated interfaced systems (e.g., a dummy warship for testing a naval radar)
- Real interfaced systems (e.g., aircraft for testing a radar with trajectory tracking facilities)
- Facilities and customer-supplied products
- The skilled people to operate or use all the preceding elements
- Dedicated computing or network test environment (e.g., pseudo-operational telecommunications-network testbed or facility with actual trunks, switches, and systems established for realistic integration and validation trials)

TIP

Validation, verification, and product integration environments can sometimes be one and the same, or at a minimum, can share some of the same resources.

Early selection of the products or product components to be validated, the work products to be used in the validation, and the validation methods is needed to ensure that the validation environment will be available when necessary.

The validation environment should be carefully controlled to provide for replication, analysis of results, and revalidation of problem areas.

Typical Work Products

1. Validation environment

Subpractices

1. Identify validation environment requirements.
2. Identify customer-supplied products.
3. Identify reuse items.
4. Identify test equipment and tools.

5. Identify validation resources that are available for reuse and modification.

6. Plan the availability of resources in detail.

SP 1.3 ESTABLISH VALIDATION PROCEDURES AND CRITERIA

Establish and maintain procedures and criteria for validation.

Validation procedures and criteria are defined to ensure that the product or product component will fulfill its intended use when placed in its intended environment. Acceptance test cases and procedures may meet the need for validation procedures.

The validation procedures and criteria include test and evaluation of maintenance, training, and support services.

> Examples of sources for validation criteria include the following:
> • Product and product component requirements
> • Standards
> • Customer acceptance criteria
> • Environmental performance
> • Thresholds of performance deviation

Typical Work Products

1. Validation procedures
2. Validation criteria
3. Test and evaluation procedures for maintenance, training, and support

Subpractices

1. Review the product requirements to ensure that issues affecting validation of the product or product component are identified and resolved.

2. Document the environment, operational scenario, procedures, inputs, outputs, and criteria for the validation of the selected product or product component.

3. Assess the design as it matures in the context of the validation environment to identify validation issues.

SG 2 VALIDATE PRODUCT OR PRODUCT COMPONENTS

The product or product components are validated to ensure that they are suitable for use in their intended operating environment.

TIP

Because validation resembles a controlled experiment and because of the need for fidelity with the operational environment, many tools, simulations, computers, networks, and skilled people may need to be involved. Thus, validation planning may itself be challenging.

TIP

This practice helps answer questions such as how you will exercise the product prototype to better understand a particular issue (validation procedures) and how you will know whether the performance is acceptable (validation criteria).

TIP

Validation procedures and criteria should address operations, maintenance, and services.

VAL

The validation methods, procedures, and criteria are used to validate the selected products and product components and any associated maintenance, training, and support services using the appropriate validation environment. Validation activities are performed throughout the product lifecycle.

SP 2.1 PERFORM VALIDATION

Perform validation on the selected products and product components.

HINT

The bottom line is to determine whether the product will perform as expected.

TIP

The validation environment may support the automatic collection of much of the data.

To be acceptable to users, a product or product component must perform as expected in its intended operational environment.

Validation activities are performed and the resulting data are collected according to the established methods, procedures, and criteria.

The as-run validation procedures should be documented and the deviations occurring during the execution should be noted, as appropriate.

Typical Work Products

1. Validation reports
2. Validation results
3. Validation cross-reference matrix
4. As-run procedures log
5. Operational demonstrations

SP 2.2 ANALYZE VALIDATION RESULTS

Analyze the results of the validation activities.

HINT

Validation activities are expensive and it is important to maximize learning. Therefore, analyzing the results of the validation activities may help you to discover missing requirements, features in the product that delight the customer, lingering issues, and risks.

The data resulting from validation tests, inspections, demonstrations, or evaluations are analyzed against the defined validation criteria. Analysis reports indicate whether the needs were met; in the case of deficiencies, these reports document the degree of success or failure and categorize probable cause of failure. The collected test, inspection, or review results are compared with established evaluation criteria to determine whether to proceed or to address requirements or design issues in the requirements development or technical solution processes.

Analysis reports or as-run validation documentation may also indicate that bad test results are due to a validation procedure problem or a validation environment problem.

Typical Work Products

1. Validation deficiency reports
2. Validation issues
3. Procedure change request

Subpractices

1. Compare actual results to expected results.
2. Based on the established validation criteria, identify products and product components that do not perform suitably in their intended operating environments, or identify problems with the methods, criteria, and/or environment.
3. Analyze the validation data for defects.
4. Record the results of the analysis and identify issues.
5. Use validation results to compare actual measurements and performance to intended use or operational need.

> **HINT**
>
> If requirements are missing, you need to revisit your engineering processes. If there are problems with the validation methods, environment, procedures, or criteria, you need to revisit project activities that correspond to the specific practices of SG 1.

Generic Practices by Goal

GG 1 ACHIEVE SPECIFIC GOALS

The process supports and enables achievement of the specific goals of the process area by transforming identifiable input work products to produce identifiable output work products.

CONTINUOUS ONLY

GP 1.1 PERFORM SPECIFIC PRACTICES

Perform the specific practices of the validation process to develop work products and provide services to achieve the specific goals of the process area.

GG 2 INSTITUTIONALIZE A MANAGED PROCESS

The process is institutionalized as a managed process.

GG 3 INSTITUTIONALIZE A DEFINED PROCESS

The process is institutionalized as a defined process.

> *This generic goal's appearance here reflects its location in the staged representation.*

STAGED ONLY

GP 2.1 ESTABLISH AN ORGANIZATIONAL POLICY

Establish and maintain an organizational policy for planning and performing the validation process.

VAL

Elaboration:

This policy establishes organizational expectations for selecting products and product components for validation; for selecting validation methods; and for establishing and maintaining validation procedures, criteria, and environments that ensure the products and product components satisfy user needs in their intended operating environment.

GP 2.2 PLAN THE PROCESS

Establish and maintain the plan for performing the validation process.

Elaboration:

This plan for performing the validation process can be included in (or referenced by) the project plan, which is described in the Project Planning process area.

GP 2.3 PROVIDE RESOURCES

Provide adequate resources for performing the validation process, developing the work products, and providing the services of the process.

Elaboration:

Special facilities may be required for validating the product or product components. When necessary, the facilities required for validation are developed or purchased.

Examples of other resources provided include the following tools:
- Test-management tools
- Test-case generators
- Test-coverage analyzers
- Simulators
- Load, stress, and performance tools

GP 2.4 ASSIGN RESPONSIBILITY

Assign responsibility and authority for performing the process, developing the work products, and providing the services of the validation process.

GP 2.5 TRAIN PEOPLE

Train the people performing or supporting the validation process as needed.

Elaboration:

Examples of training topics include the following:
- Application domain
- Validation principles, standards, and methods
- Intended-use environment

GP 2.6 MANAGE CONFIGURATIONS

Place designated work products of the validation process under appropriate levels of control.

Elaboration:

Examples of work products placed under control include the following:
- Lists of products and product components selected for validation
- Validation methods, procedures, and criteria
- Validation reports

GP 2.7 IDENTIFY AND INVOLVE RELEVANT STAKEHOLDERS

Identify and involve the relevant stakeholders of the validation process as planned.

Elaboration:

Select relevant stakeholders from customers, end users, developers, producers, testers, suppliers, marketers, maintainers, disposal personnel, and others who may be affected by, or may affect, the product as well as the process.

Examples of activities for stakeholder involvement include the following:
- Selecting the products and product components to be validated
- Establishing the validation methods, procedures, and criteria
- Reviewing results of product and product component validation and resolving issues
- Resolving issues with the customers or end users

Issues with the customers or end users are resolved particularly when there are significant deviations from their baseline needs for the following:

VAL

- Waivers on the contract or agreement (what, when, and for which products)
- Additional in-depth studies, trials, tests, or evaluations
- Possible changes in the contracts or agreements

GP 2.8 MONITOR AND CONTROL THE PROCESS

Monitor and control the validation process against the plan for performing the process and take appropriate corrective action.

Elaboration:

Examples of measures and work products used in monitoring and controlling include the following:
- Number of validation activities completed (planned versus actual)
- Validation problem report trends (e.g., number written and number closed)
- Validation problem report aging (i.e., how long each problem report has been open)
- Schedule for a specific validation activity

GP 2.9 OBJECTIVELY EVALUATE ADHERENCE

Objectively evaluate adherence of the validation process against its process description, standards, and procedures, and address noncompliance.

Elaboration:

Examples of activities reviewed include the following:
- Selecting the products and product components to be validated
- Establishing and maintaining validation methods, procedures, and criteria
- Validating products or product components

Examples of work products reviewed include the following:
- Validation methods, procedures, and criteria

GP 2.10 REVIEW STATUS WITH HIGHER LEVEL MANAGEMENT

Review the activities, status, and results of the validation process with higher level management and resolve issues.

GG 3 *INSTITUTIONALIZE A **DEFINED** PROCESS*

The process is institutionalized as a defined process.

> *This generic goal's appearance here reflects its location in the continuous representation.*

GP 3.1 *ESTABLISH A DEFINED PROCESS*

Establish and maintain the description of a defined validation process.

GP 3.2 *COLLECT IMPROVEMENT INFORMATION*

Collect work products, measures, measurement results, and improvement information derived from planning and performing the validation process to support the future use and improvement of the organization's processes and process assets.

Elaboration:

Examples of work products, measures, measurement results, and improvement information include the following:
- Product component prototype
- Percent of time the validation environment is available
- Number of product defects found through validation per development phase
- Validation analysis report

GG 4 *INSTITUTIONALIZE A **QUANTITATIVELY MANAGED** PROCESS*

The process is institutionalized as a quantitatively managed process.

GP 4.1 *ESTABLISH QUANTITATIVE OBJECTIVES FOR THE PROCESS*

Establish and maintain quantitative objectives for the validation process, which address quality and process performance, based on customer needs and business objectives.

GP 4.2 *STABILIZE SUBPROCESS PERFORMANCE*

Stabilize the performance of one or more subprocesses to determine the ability of the validation process to achieve the established quantitative quality and process-performance objectives.

GG 5   INSTITUTIONALIZE AN OPTIMIZING PROCESS

The process is institutionalized as an optimizing process.

GP 5.1   ENSURE CONTINUOUS PROCESS IMPROVEMENT

Ensure continuous improvement of the validation process in fulfilling the relevant business objectives of the organization.

GP 5.2   CORRECT ROOT CAUSES OF PROBLEMS

Identify and correct the root causes of defects and other problems in the validation process.

VERIFICATION
An Engineering Process Area at Maturity Level 3

Purpose

The purpose of Verification (VER) is to ensure that selected work products meet their specified requirements.

TIP

Testing and peer reviews are verification methods covered in this process area.

Introductory Notes

The Verification process area involves the following: verification preparation, verification performance, and identification of corrective action.

X-REF

Managing corrective action to closure is addressed in PMC SG 2.

Verification includes verification of the product and intermediate work products against all selected requirements, including customer, product, and product component requirements. Throughout the process areas, where we use the terms product and product component, their intended meanings also encompass services and their components.

Verification is inherently an incremental process because it occurs throughout the development of the product and work products, beginning with verification of the requirements, progressing through the verification of the evolving work products, and culminating in the verification of the completed product.

The specific practices of this process area build on each other in the following way:

- The Select Work Products for Verification specific practice enables the identification of the work products to be verified, the methods to be used to perform the verification, and the requirements to be satisfied by each selected work product.
- The Establish the Verification Environment specific practice enables the determination of the environment that will be used to carry out the verification.
- The Establish Verification Procedures and Criteria specific practice then enables the development of verification procedures and criteria

VER

that are aligned with the selected work products, requirements, methods, and characteristics of the verification environment.

• The Perform Verification specific practice conducts the verification according to the available methods, procedures, and criteria.

Verification of work products substantially increases the likelihood that the product will meet the customer, product, and product component requirements.

The Verification and Validation process areas are similar, but they address different issues. Validation demonstrates that the product, as provided (or as it will be provided), will fulfill its intended use, whereas verification addresses whether the work product properly reflects the specified requirements. In other words, verification ensures that "you built it right"; whereas, validation ensures that "you built the right thing."

Peer reviews are an important part of verification and are a proven mechanism for effective defect removal. An important corollary is to develop a better understanding of the work products and the processes that produced them so that defects can be prevented and process improvement opportunities can be identified.

Peer reviews involve a methodical examination of work products by the producers' peers to identify defects and other changes that are needed.

> Examples of peer review methods include the following:
> • Inspections
> • Structured walkthroughs

Related Process Areas

Refer to the Validation process area for more information about confirming that a product or product component fulfills its intended use when placed in its intended environment.

Refer to the Requirements Development process area for more information about the generation and development of customer, product, and product component requirements.

Refer to the Requirements Management process area for more information about managing requirements.

TIP

Peer reviews also focus on getting the product "right" and on obtaining the data necessary to prevent defects and improve the process.

X-REF

Many books and other sources describe testing and peer reviews (sometimes known as inspections). For a summary of software testing principles and terminology, see the entry for "Software Testing" on the Wikipedia site, www.wikipedia.org.

Specific Goal and Practice Summary

Specific Practices by Goal

SG 1   PREPARE FOR VERIFICATION

Preparation for verification is conducted.

Up-front preparation is necessary to ensure that verification provisions are embedded in product and product component requirements, designs, developmental plans, and schedules. Verification includes selection, inspection, testing, analysis, and demonstration of work products.

Methods of verification include, but are not limited to, inspections, peer reviews, audits, walkthroughs, analyses, simulations, testing, and demonstrations. Practices related to peer reviews as a specific verification method are included in specific goal 2.

Preparation also entails the definition of support tools, test equipment and software, simulations, prototypes, and facilities.

SP 1.1 SELECT WORK PRODUCTS FOR VERIFICATION

Select the work products to be verified and the verification methods that will be used for each.

Work products are selected based on their contribution to meeting project objectives and requirements, and to addressing project risks.

The work products to be verified may include those associated with maintenance, training, and support services. The work product requirements for verification are included with the verification methods. The verification methods address the approach to work product verification and the specific approaches that will be used to verify that specific work products meet their requirements.

HINT

Identify which work products put the project (or product) at the highest risk.

VER

HINT

Don't forget to verify work products important to other phases of the product lifecycle, such as maintenance documentation, installation services, and operator training.

TIP

When a work product cannot be executed (e.g., designs), testing is not an option. It may be possible to develop prototypes and models, and "execute" these to gain insight into product characteristics. Peer reviews may be another option.

TIP

Reverification is not called out separately in this process area, since reverification is actually an iteration of the verification process. However, reverification should be considered when planning verification activities.

HINT

Work products that have been "reworked" need to be reverified.

TIP

Methods used for each work product may be shown in a *table* with columns identifying the work product to be verified, requirements to be satisfied, and verification methods to be used.

FOR SOFTWARE ENGINEERING

Examples of verification methods include the following:
- Path coverage testing
- Load, stress, and performance testing
- Decision-table-based testing
- Functional decomposition-based testing
- Test-case reuse
- Acceptance tests

FOR SYSTEMS ENGINEERING

Verification for systems engineering typically includes prototyping, modeling, and simulation to verify adequacy of system design (and allocation).

FOR HARDWARE ENGINEERING

Verification for hardware engineering typically requires a parametric approach that considers various environmental conditions (e.g., pressure, temperature, vibration, and humidity), various input ranges (e.g., input power could be rated at 20V to 32V for a planned nominal of 28V), variations induced from part to part tolerance issues, and many other variables. Hardware verification normally tests most variables separately except when problematic interactions are suspected.

Selection of the verification methods typically begins with involvement in the definition of product and product component requirements to ensure that these requirements are verifiable. Reverification should be addressed by the verification methods to ensure that rework performed on work products does not cause unintended defects. Suppliers should be involved in this selection to ensure that the project's methods are appropriate for the supplier's environment.

The verification methods should be developed concurrently and iteratively with the product and product component designs.

IPPD ADD

Typical Work Products

1. Lists of work products selected for verification
2. Verification methods for each selected work product

Subpractices

1. Identify work products for verification.
2. Identify the requirements to be satisfied by each selected work product.

   Refer to the Maintain Bidirectional Traceability of Requirements specific practice in the Requirements Management process area to help identify the requirements for each work product.

3. Identify the verification methods that are available for use.
4. Define the verification methods to be used for each selected work product.
5. Submit for integration with the project plan the identification of work products to be verified, the requirements to be satisfied, and the methods to be used.

   Refer to the Project Planning process area for information about coordinating with project planning.

TIP

By incorporating such a table into the project plan (perhaps by reference), resources can be provided and commitments made to perform the appropriate verification activities.

SP 1.2 ESTABLISH THE VERIFICATION ENVIRONMENT

Establish and maintain the environment needed to support verification.

An environment must be established to enable verification to take place. The verification environment can be acquired, developed, reused, modified, or a combination of these, depending on the needs of the project.

The type of environment required will depend on the work products selected for verification and the verification methods used. A peer review may require little more than a package of materials, reviewers, and a room. A product test may require simulators, emulators, scenario generators, data reduction tools, environmental controls, and interfaces with other systems.

TIP

Some work products and verification methods may require special facilities and tools. These should be identified and obtained in advance.

TIP

In the case of peer reviews, a co-located team might meet in a room where the document being peer reviewed can be displayed. Remote team members might participate through teleconferencing and use of a Web-based collaboration tool that allows them to see the document while hearing the discussion.

Typical Work Products

1. Verification environment

Subpractices

1. Identify verification environment requirements.
2. Identify verification resources that are available for reuse and modification.
3. Identify verification equipment and tools.
4. Acquire verification support equipment and an environment, such as test equipment and software.

TIP

The organization's IT or Facilities Group, or perhaps other projects, might have some of the verification resources that a project might need. In some cases, environmental labs or antenna ranges are common resources used by multiple projects and must be reserved for use.

VER

SP 1.3 *Establish Verification Procedures and Criteria*

Establish and maintain verification procedures and criteria for the selected work products.

IPPD Add

The verification procedures and criteria should be developed concurrently and iteratively with the product and product component designs.

Verification criteria are defined to ensure that the work products meet their requirements.

> Examples of sources for verification criteria include the following:
> • Product and product component requirements
> • Standards
> • Organizational policies
> • Test type
> • Test parameters
> • Parameters for tradeoff between quality and cost of testing
> • Type of work products
> • Suppliers
> • Proposals and agreements

Typical Work Products

1. Verification procedures
2. Verification criteria

Subpractices

1. Generate the set of comprehensive, integrated verification procedures for work products and any commercial off-the-shelf products, as necessary.
2. Develop and refine the verification criteria when necessary.
3. Identify the expected results, any tolerances allowed in observation, and other criteria for satisfying the requirements.
4. Identify any equipment and environmental components needed to support verification.

SG 2 *Perform Peer Reviews*

Peer reviews are performed on selected work products.

HINT

The bottom line is to determine verification methods, environments, and procedures as early in the project as practical.

TIP

In the case of engineering artifacts (e.g., architectures, designs, and implementations), the primary source for verification criteria is likely to be the requirements assigned to the work product being verified.

HINT

Remember to establish comprehensive verification procedures and criteria for nondevelopmental items (such as off-the-shelf products) that subject the project to moderate or high risk.

HINT

Often there isn't a single right result, but a range of results that might be acceptable. In such instances, specify how much variability from the expected answer is still acceptable.

Peer reviews involve a methodical examination of work products by the producers' peers to identify defects for removal and to recommend other changes that are needed.

The peer review is an important and effective verification method implemented via inspections, structured walkthroughs, or a number of other collegial review methods.

Peer reviews are primarily applied to work products developed by the projects, but they can also be applied to other work products such as documentation and training work products that are typically developed by support groups.

SP 2.1 PREPARE FOR PEER REVIEWS

Prepare for peer reviews of selected work products.

Preparation activities for peer reviews typically include identifying the staff who will be invited to participate in the peer review of each work product; identifying the key reviewers who must participate in the peer review; preparing and updating any materials that will be used during the peer reviews, such as checklists and review criteria, and scheduling peer reviews.

Typical Work Products

1. Peer review schedule
2. Peer review checklist
3. Entry and exit criteria for work products
4. Criteria for requiring another peer review
5. Peer review training material
6. Selected work products to be reviewed

Subpractices

1. Determine what type of peer review will be conducted.

> Examples of types of peer reviews include the following:
> • Inspections
> • Structured walkthroughs
> • Active reviews

2. Define requirements for collecting data during the peer review.

> *Refer to the Measurement and Analysis process area for information about identifying and collecting data.*

TIP

Peers are generally co-workers from your project that have interest in the item under peer review. Peer review participants should generally not include your management because that could restrain open and beneficial dialog.

TIP

Peer reviews provide opportunities to learn and share information across the team.

HINT

Use peer reviews not just for development artifacts, but also for project management artifacts (e.g., plans), process management artifacts (e.g., process descriptions), and support artifacts (e.g., measure definitions).

TIP

Easily overlooked, training improves the effectiveness of peer reviews.

TIP

While many different types of reviews might be considered "peer reviews" (e.g., informal walkthroughs), these specific practices focus on those having some formality and discipline in their performance.

X-REF

For a summary of peer review principles and terminology, see the entry for "Software Inspections" on the Wikipedia site, www.wikipedia.org.

VER

HINT

A checklist identifies the classes of defects that commonly occur for a type of work product. By using the checklist, you're less likely to overlook certain classes of defects. Also, some classes of defects might be assigned to different peer review participants, helping to ensure adequate coverage of the checklist.

3. Establish and maintain entry and exit criteria for the peer review.
4. Establish and maintain criteria for requiring another peer review.
5. Establish and maintain checklists to ensure that the work products are reviewed consistently.

Examples of items addressed by the checklists include the following:
• Rules of construction
• Design guidelines
• Completeness
• Correctness
• Maintainability
• Common defect types

The checklists are modified as necessary to address the specific type of work product and peer review. The peers of the checklist developers and potential users review the checklists.

6. Develop a detailed peer review schedule, including the dates for peer review training and for when materials for peer reviews will be available.
7. Ensure that the work product satisfies the peer review entry criteria prior to distribution.
8. Distribute the work product to be reviewed and its related information to the participants early enough to enable participants to adequately prepare for the peer review.
9. Assign roles for the peer review as appropriate.

TIP

A classic problem that arises in low-maturity organizations is that participants skip preparation when under schedule pressure. One way to address this is to incorporate the peer review schedule into the development plans and schedule to help ensure adequate allocation of time. Another way is to postpone the peer review if participants have not prepared.

Examples of roles include the following:
• Leader
• Reader
• Recorder
• Author

HINT

To maximize the effectiveness of the peer review, participants need to prepare prior to the meeting.

10. Prepare for the peer review by reviewing the work product prior to conducting the peer review.

SP 2.2 CONDUCT PEER REVIEWS

Conduct peer reviews on selected work products and identify issues resulting from the peer review.

One of the purposes of conducting a peer review is to find and remove defects early. Peer reviews are performed incrementally as work products are being developed. These reviews are structured and are not management reviews.

Peer reviews may be performed on key work products of specification, design, test, and implementation activities and specific planning work products.

The focus of the peer review should be on the work product in review, not on the person who produced it.

When issues arise during the peer review, they should be communicated to the primary developer of the work product for correction.

Refer to the Project Monitoring and Control process area for information about tracking issues that arise during a peer review.

Peer reviews should address the following guidelines: there must be sufficient preparation, the conduct must be managed and controlled, consistent and sufficient data must be recorded (an example is conducting a formal inspection), and action items must be recorded.

Typical Work Products

1. Peer review results
2. Peer review issues
3. Peer review data

Subpractices

1. Perform the assigned roles in the peer review.
2. Identify and document defects and other issues in the work product.
3. Record the results of the peer review, including the action items.
4. Collect peer review data.

    Refer to the Measurement and Analysis process area for more information about data collection.

5. Identify action items and communicate the issues to relevant stakeholders.
6. Conduct an additional peer review if the defined criteria indicate the need.
7. Ensure that the exit criteria for the peer review are satisfied.

SP 2.3 *Analyze Peer Review Data*

Analyze data about preparation, conduct, and results of the peer reviews.

TIP

The ratio often reported that compares the cost to find a defect late in the project to the cost to find a defect early in the project is 100:1.

HINT

Provide a nonthreatening environment so that open discussions can occur.

HINT

During peer review training, train the staff in all of the roles necessary to conduct the peer reviews. These roles can vary from one peer review to the next.

TIP

Defects and issues are often recorded in a *table* with columns for such things as location of defect, defect description (including type and origin), discussion, and action items.

VER

TIP

The analysis can help us answer questions such as what types of defects we are encountering, their severity, in which phases they are being injected and detected, the peer review "yield" (percent of defects detected), the review rate (pages per hour), and the cost (or hours expended) per defect found.

Refer to the Measurement and Analysis process area for more information about obtaining and analyzing data.

Typical Work Products

1. Peer review data
2. Peer review action items

Subpractices

1. Record data related to the preparation, conduct, and results of the peer reviews.

   Typical data are product name, product size, composition of the peer review team, type of peer review, preparation time per reviewer, length of the review meeting, number of defects found, type and origin of defect, and so on. Additional information on the work product being peer reviewed may be collected, such as size, development stage, operating modes examined, and requirements being evaluated.

2. Store the data for future reference and analysis.
3. Protect the data to ensure that peer review data are not used inappropriately.

> Examples of inappropriate use of peer review data include using data to evaluate the performance of people and using data for attribution.

4. Analyze the peer review data.

> Examples of peer review data that can be analyzed include the following:
> • Phase defect was injected
> • Preparation time or rate versus expected time or rate
> • Number of defects versus number expected
> • Types of defects detected
> • Causes of defects
> • Defect resolution impact

SG 3 VERIFY SELECTED WORK PRODUCTS

HINT

Think of verification as a "tool" used throughout the project to help ensure that the project delivers a quality product to the customer.

Selected work products are verified against their specified requirements.

The verification methods, procedures, and criteria are used to verify the selected work products and any associated maintenance, training, and support services using the appropriate verification environment. Verification activities should be performed throughout the product lifecycle. Practices related to peer reviews as a specific verification method are included in specific goal 2.

SP 3.1 PERFORM VERIFICATION

Perform verification on the selected work products.

Verifying products and work products incrementally promotes early detection of problems and can result in the early removal of defects. The results of verification save considerable cost of fault isolation and rework associated with troubleshooting problems.

Typical Work Products

1. Verification results
2. Verification reports
3. Demonstrations
4. As-run procedures log

Subpractices

1. Perform verification of selected work products against their requirements.
2. Record the results of verification activities.
3. Identify action items resulting from verification of work products.
4. Document the "as-run" verification method and the deviations from the available methods and procedures discovered during its performance.

SP 3.2 ANALYZE VERIFICATION RESULTS

Analyze the results of all verification activities.

Actual results must be compared to established verification criteria to determine acceptability.

The results of the analysis are recorded as evidence that verification was conducted.

For each work product, all available verification results are incrementally analyzed to ensure that the requirements have been met. Since a peer review is one of several verification methods, peer review data should be included in this analysis activity to ensure that

---

TIP

This goal should follow the planning and preparation activities that were addressed in SG 1.

TIP

Performing peer reviews is addressed in SG 2; this specific practice addresses all other forms of verification.

TIP

Verification often means "testing"; however, verification methods may also include analyses, simulations, demonstrations, and formal methods.

X-REF

For more information, see the entries for "Software Testing," "Simulation," and "Formal Methods" on the Wikipedia site, www.wikipedia.org.

TIP

When requirements change, it is necessary to determine the work products affected (REQM), rework them (RD, TS, and PI), and reverify them against the changed requirements. Thus, requirements volatility can significantly increase the cost of verification activities and can lead to schedule slips.

HINT

Sometimes the verification procedure cannot be run as defined (e.g., incorrect assumptions were made as to the nature of the work product or verification environment). If so, record any deviations.

VER

TIP

Analysis helps to identify areas (or risks) on which to focus limited resources.

HINT

When piloting a new verification tool, analyze results to help identify ways to adjust the process or tool to increase the effectiveness of verification activities.

TIP

The verification criteria established in SP 1.3 play an important role in determining where problems lie.

TIP

Technical performance parameters help to monitor key characteristics of the emerging product.

the verification results are analyzed sufficiently. Analysis reports or "as-run" method documentation may also indicate that bad verification results are due to method problems, criteria problems, or a verification environment problem.

Typical Work Products

1. Analysis report (e.g., statistics on performances, causal analysis of nonconformances, comparison of the behavior between the real product and models, and trends)
2. Trouble reports
3. Change requests for the verification methods, criteria, and environment

Subpractices

1. Compare actual results to expected results.
2. Based on the established verification criteria, identify products that have not met their requirements or identify problems with the methods, procedures, criteria, and verification environment
3. Analyze the verification data on defects.
4. Record all results of the analysis in a report.
5. Use verification results to compare actual measurements and performance to technical performance parameters.
6. Provide information on how defects can be resolved (including verification methods, criteria, and verification environment) and initiate corrective action.

Refer to the corrective action practices of Project Monitoring and Control process area for more information about implementing corrective action.

Generic Practices by Goal

GG 1 ACHIEVE SPECIFIC GOALS

The process supports and enables achievement of the specific goals of the process area by transforming identifiable input work products to produce identifiable output work products.

GP 1.1 PERFORM SPECIFIC PRACTICES

Perform the specific practices of the verification process to develop work products and provide services to achieve the specific goals of the process area.

GG 2 INSTITUTIONALIZE A MANAGED PROCESS

The process is institutionalized as a managed process.

CONTINUOUS ONLY

GG 3 INSTITUTIONALIZE A DEFINED PROCESS

The process is institutionalized as a defined process.

> *This generic goal's appearance here reflects its location in the staged representation.*

GP 2.1 ESTABLISH AN ORGANIZATIONAL POLICY

Establish and maintain an organizational policy for planning and performing the verification process.

Elaboration:

This policy establishes organizational expectations for establishing and maintaining verification methods, procedures, criteria, and the verification environment, as well as for performing peer reviews and verifying selected work products.

GP 2.2 PLAN THE PROCESS

Establish and maintain the plan for performing the verification process.

Elaboration:

This plan for performing the verification process can be included in (or referenced by) the project plan, which is described in the Project Planning process area.

GP 2.3 PROVIDE RESOURCES

Provide adequate resources for performing the verification process, developing the work products, and providing the services of the process.

Elaboration:

Special facilities may be required for verifying selected work products. When necessary, the facilities required for the activities in the Verification process area are developed or purchased.

Certain verification methods may require special tools, equipment, facilities, and training (e.g., peer reviews may require meeting rooms and trained moderators; and certain verification tests may require special test equipment and people skilled in the use of the equipment).

VER

Examples of other resources provided include the following tools:
- Test management tools
- Test-case generators
- Test-coverage analyzers
- Simulators

***GP 2.4** ASSIGN RESPONSIBILITY*

Assign responsibility and authority for performing the process, developing the work products, and providing the services of the verification process.

***GP 2.5** TRAIN PEOPLE*

Train the people performing or supporting the verification process as needed.

Elaboration:

> Examples of training topics include the following:
> • Application or service domain
> • Verification principles, standards, and methods (e.g., analysis, demonstration, inspection, and test)
> • Verification tools and facilities
> • Peer review preparation and procedures
> • Meeting facilitation

***GP 2.6** MANAGE CONFIGURATIONS*

Place designated work products of the verification process under appropriate levels of control.

Elaboration:

> Examples of work products placed under control include the following:
> • Verification procedures and criteria
> • Peer review training material
> • Peer review data
> • Verification reports

***GP 2.7** IDENTIFY AND INVOLVE RELEVANT STAKEHOLDERS*

Identify and involve the relevant stakeholders of the verification process as planned.

Elaboration:

Select relevant stakeholders from customers, end users, developers, producers, testers, suppliers, marketers, maintainers, disposal personnel, and others who may be affected by, or may affect, the product as well as the process.

Examples of activities for stakeholder involvement include the following:
• Selecting work products and methods for verification
• Establishing verification procedures and criteria
• Conducting peer reviews
• Assessing verification results and identifying corrective action

GP 2.8 MONITOR AND CONTROL THE PROCESS

Monitor and control the verification process against the plan for performing the process and take appropriate corrective action.

Elaboration:

Examples of measures and work products used in monitoring and controlling include the following:
• Verification profile (e.g., the number of verifications planned and performed, and the defects found; or perhaps categorized by verification method or type)
• Number of defects detected by defect category
• Verification problem report trends (e.g., number written and number closed)
• Verification problem report status (i.e., how long each problem report has been open)
• Schedule for a specific verification activity

GP 2.9 OBJECTIVELY EVALUATE ADHERENCE

Objectively evaluate adherence of the verification process against its process description, standards, and procedures, and address noncompliance.

Elaboration:

Examples of activities reviewed include the following:
• Selecting work products for verification
• Establishing and maintaining verification procedures and criteria
• Performing peer reviews
• Verifying selected work products

Examples of work products reviewed include the following:
• Verification procedures and criteria
• Peer review checklists
• Verification reports

VER

GP 2.10 *Review Status with Higher Level Management*

Review the activities, status, and results of the verification process with higher level management and resolve issues.

CONT. ONLY

GG 3 *Institutionalize a Defined Process*

The process is institutionalized as a defined process.

This generic goal's appearance here reflects its location in the continuous representation.

GP 3.1 *Establish a Defined Process*

Establish and maintain the description of a defined verification process.

GP 3.2 *Collect Improvement Information*

Collect work products, measures, measurement results, and improvement information derived from planning and performing the verification process to support the future use and improvement of the organization's processes and process assets.

Elaboration:

Examples of work products, measures, measurement results, and improvement information include the following:
- Peer review records that include conduct time and average preparation time
- Number of product defects found through verification per development phase
- Verification and analysis report

GG 4 *Institutionalize a Quantitatively Managed Process*

The process is institutionalized as a quantitatively managed process.

GP 4.1 *Establish Quantitative Objectives for the Process*

Establish and maintain quantitative objectives for the verification process, which address quality and process performance, based on customer needs and business objectives.

CONTINUOUS ONLY

GP 4.2 STABILIZE SUBPROCESS PERFORMANCE

Stabilize the performance of one or more subprocesses to determine the ability of the verification process to achieve the established quantitative quality and process-performance objectives.

GG 5 INSTITUTIONALIZE AN OPTIMIZING PROCESS

The process is institutionalized as an optimizing process.

GP 5.1 ENSURE CONTINUOUS PROCESS IMPROVEMENT

Ensure continuous improvement of the verification process in fulfilling the relevant business objectives of the organization.

GP 5.2 CORRECT ROOT CAUSES OF PROBLEMS

Identify and correct the root causes of defects and other problems in the verification process.

CONTINUOUS ONLY

VER

PART THREE

The Appendices and Glossary

REFERENCES

Publicly Available Sources

Ahern 2003   Ahern, Dennis M.; Clouse, Aaron; & Turner, Richard. *CMMI Distilled: A Practical Introduction to Integrated Process Improvement*, Second Edition. Boston: Addison-Wesley, 2003.

Ahern 2005   Ahern, Dennis M.; Armstrong, Jim; Clouse, Aaron; Ferguson, Jack R.; Hayes, Will; & Nidiffer, Kenneth E. *CMMI SCAMPI Distilled: Appraisals for Process Improvement*. Boston: Addison-Wesley, 2005.

Chrissis 2003   Chrissis, Mary Beth; Konrad, Mike; & Shrum, Sandy. *CMMI: Guidelines for Process Integration and Product Improvement*. Boston: Addison-Wesley, 2003.

Crosby 1979   Crosby, Philip B. *Quality Is Free The Art of Making Quality Certain*. New York: McGraw-Hill, 1979.

Curtis 2002   Curtis, Bill; Hefley, William E.; & Miller, Sally A. *The People Capability Maturity Model Guidelines for Improving the Workforce*. Boston: Addison-Wesley, 2002.

Deming 1986   Deming, W. Edwards. *Out of the Crisis*. Cambridge, MA: MIT Center for Advanced Engineering, 1986.

DoD 1996   Department of Defense. *DoD Guide to Integrated Product and Process Development (Version 1.0)*. Washington, DC: Office of the Under Secretary of Defense (Acquisition and Technology), February 5, 1996.
http://www.abm.rda.hq.navy.mil/navyaos/content/download/1000/4448/file/ippdhdbk.pdf.

Dymond 2004   Dymond, Kenneth M. *A Guide to the CMMI: Interpreting the Capability Maturity Model Integration*. Annapolis, MD: Process Transition International Inc., 2004.

EIA 1994 Electronic Industries Alliance. *EIA Interim Standard: Systems Engineering (EIA/IS-632)*. Washington, DC, 1994.

EIA 1998 Electronic Industries Alliance. *Systems Engineering Capability Model (EIA/IS-731)*. Washington, DC, 1998.
(Note: This model has been retired by EIA.)

GEIA 2004 Government Electronic Industries Alliance. *Data Management (GEIA-859)*. Washington, DC, 2004.
http://webstore.ansi.org/ansidocstore/product.asp?sku=GEIA-859-2004.

Gibson 2006 Gibson, Diane L.; Goldenson, Dennis R.; & Kost, Keith. *Performance Results of CMMI-Based Process Improvement. (CMU/SEI-2006-TR-004, ESC-TR-2006-004)*. Pittsburgh, PA: Software Engineering Institute, Carnegie Mellon University, August 2006. http://www.sei.cmu.edu/publications/documents/06.reports/06tr004.html.

Humphrey 1989 Humphrey, Watts S. *Managing the Software Process*. Reading, MA: Addison-Wesley, 1989.

IEEE 1990 Institute of Electrical and Electronics Engineers. *IEEE Standard Computer Dictionary: A Compilation of IEEE Standard Computer Glossaries*. New York: IEEE, 1990.

ISO 1987 International Organization for Standardization. *ISO 9000: International Standard*. 1987.
http://www.iso.ch/.

ISO 1995 International Organization for Standardization and International Electrotechnical Commission. *ISO/IEC TR 12207 Information Technology—Software Life Cycle Processes, 1995*.
http://www.jtc1-sc7.org.

ISO 1998 International Organization for Standardization and International Electrotechnical Commission. *ISO/IEC TR 15504 Information Technology—Software Process Assessment, 1998*.
http://www.iso.ch/.

ISO 2000 International Organization for Standardization. *ISO 9001, Quality Management Systems—Requirements, 2000*.
http://www.iso.ch/.

ISO 2002a International Organization for Standardization and International Electrotechnical Commission. *ISO/IEC 15939 Software Engineering—Software Measurement Process, 2002*.
http://www.iso.ch/.

ISO 2002b International Organization for Standardization and International Electrotechnical Commission. *ISO/IEC 15288 Systems Engineering—System Life Cycle Processes, 2002*.
http://www.jtc1-sc7.org/.

ISO 2006 International Organization for Standardization and International Electrotechnical Commission. *ISO/IEC TR 15504 Information*

Technology—Software Process Assessment Part 1: Concepts and Vocabulary, Part 2: Performing an Assessment, Part 3: Guidance on Performing an Assessment, Part 4: Guidance on Use for Process Improvement and Process Capability Determination, Part 5: An Exemplar Process Assessment Model, 2003-2006.
http://www.jtc1-sc7.org/.

Juran 1988   Juran, Joseph M. *Juran on Planning for Quality.* New York: Macmillan, 1988.

McGarry 2000   McGarry, John; Card, David; Jones, Cheryl; Layman, Beth; Clark, Elizabeth; Dean, Joseph; & Hall, Fred. *Practical Software Measurement: Objective Information for Decision Makers.* Boston: Addison-Wesley, 2002.

SEI 1995   Software Engineering Institute. *The Capability Maturity Model: Guidelines for Improving the Software Process.* Reading, MA: Addison-Wesley, 1995.

SEI 1997a   *Integrated Product Development Capability Maturity Model, Draft Version 0.98.* Pittsburgh, PA: Enterprise Process Improvement Collaboration and Software Engineering Institute, Carnegie Mellon University, July 1997.

(Note: This model was never officially released and is no longer publicly available.)

SEI 1997b   Software Engineering Institute. *Software CMM, Version 2.0 (Draft C)*, October 22, 1997.

(Note: This model was never officially released and is no longer publicly available.)

SEI 2001   Paulk, Mark C. & Chrissis, Mary Beth. *The 2001 High Maturity Workshop (CMU/SEI-2001-SR-014).* Pittsburgh, PA: Software Engineering Institute, Carnegie Mellon University, January 2002. http://www.sei.cmu.edu/publications/documents/01.reports/ 01sr014.html.

SEI 2002a   CMMI Product Development Team. *CMMI for Systems Engineering/Software Engineering/Integrated Product and Process Development/Supplier Sourcing, Version 1.1 Staged Representation (CMU/SEI-2002-TR-012, ESC-TR-2002-012).* Pittsburgh, PA: Software Engineering Institute, Carnegie Mellon University, March 2002. http://www.sei.cmu.edu/publications/documents/02.reports/ 02tr012.html.

SEI 2002b   CMMI Product Development Team. *CMMI for Systems Engineering/Software Engineering/Integrated Product and Process Development/Supplier Sourcing, Version 1.1 Continuous Representation (CMU/SEI-2002-TR-011, ESC-TR-2002-011).* Pittsburgh, PA: Software Engineering Institute, Carnegie Mellon University, March 2002. http://www.sei.cmu.edu/publications/documents/02.reports/ 02tr011.html.

SEI 2002c   Software Engineering Institute. *Software Acquisition Capability Maturity Model (SA-CMM) Version 1.03 (CMU/SEI-2002-TR-010, ESC-TR-2002-010).* Pittsburgh, PA: Software Engineering Institute, Carnegie Mellon University, March 2002.
http://www.sei.cmu.edu/publications/documents/02.reports/02tr010.html.

SEI 2004   Software Engineering Institute. *CMMI A-Specification, Version 1.6.*
http://www.sei.cmu.edu/cmmi/background/aspec.html (February 2004).

SEI 2005   Software Engineering Institute. *CMMI Acquisition Module (CMMI-AM) Version 1.1 (CMU/SEI-2005-TR-011).* Pittsburgh, PA: Software Engineering Institute, Carnegie Mellon University, May 2005.
http://www.sei.cmu.edu/publications/documents/05.reports/05tr011/05tr011.html.

SEI 2006a   CMMI Product Development Team. *ARC v1.2, Appraisal Requirements for CMMI, Version 1.2 (CMU/SEI-2006-TR-011).* Pittsburgh, PA: Software Engineering Institute, Carnegie Mellon University, July 2006.
http://www.sei.cmu.edu/publications/documents/01.reports/06tr011.html.

SEI 2006b   CMMI Product Development Team. *SCAMPI v1.2, Standard CMMI Appraisal Method for Process Improvement, Version 1.2: Method Definition Document (CMU/SEI-2006-HB-002).* Pittsburgh, PA: Software Engineering Institute, Carnegie Mellon University, July 2006.
http://www.sei.cmu.edu/publications/documents/06.reports/06hb002.html.

Shewhart 1931   Shewhart, Walter A. *Economic Control of Quality of Manufactured Product.* New York: Van Nostrand, 1931.

Regularly Updated Sources

SEI 1   Software Engineering Institute. *The IDEAL Model.*
http://www.sei.cmu.edu/ideal/ideal.html.

SEI 2   Software Engineering Institute. *CMMI Frequently Asked Questions (FAQs).*
http://www.sei.cmu.edu/cmmi/adoption/cmmi-faq.html.

SEI 3   Software Engineering Institute. *CMMI Performance Results.*
http://www.sei.cmu.edu/cmmi/results.html.

APPENDIX B

ACRONYMS

API   application program interface

ARC   Appraisal Requirements for CMMI

CAD   computer-aided design

CAR   Causal Analysis and Resolution (process area)

CCB   configuration control board

CL   capability level

CM   Configuration Management (process area)

CMM   Capability Maturity Model

CMMI   Capability Maturity Model Integration

CMMI-DEV   CMMI for Development

CMMI-DEV+IPPD   CMMI for Development +IPPD

COTS   commercial off the shelf

CPI   cost performance index

CPM   critical path method

CSCI   computer software configuration item

DAR   Decision Analysis and Resolution (process area)

DoD   Department of Defense

EIA   Electronic Industries Alliance

EIA/IS   Electronic Industries Alliance/Interim Standard

EPG   engineering process group

FCA   functional configuration audit

GG   generic goal

GP   generic practice

IBM   International Business Machines

IDEAL   Initiating, Diagnosing, Establishing, Acting, Learning

IEEE   Institute of Electrical and Electronics Engineers

INCOSE International Council on Systems Engineering

IPD-CMM Integrated Product Development Capability Maturity Model

IPM Integrated Project Management (process area)

IPM+IPPD Integrated Project Management +IPPD (process area)

IPPD integrated product and process development

ISO International Organization for Standardization

ISO/IEC International Organization for Standardization and International Electrotechnical Commission

MA Measurement and Analysis (process area)

MDD Method Definition Document

ML maturity level

NDI nondevelopmental item

NDIA National Defense Industrial Association

OID Organizational Innovation and Deployment (process area)

OPD Organizational Process Definition (process area)

OPD+IPPD Organizational Process Definition +IPPD (process area)

OPF Organizational Process Focus (process area)

OPP Organizational Process Performance (process area)

OT Organizational Training (process area)

OUSD (AT&L) Office of the Under Secretary of Defense (Acquisition, Technology, and Logistics)

P-CMM People Capability Maturity Model

PA process area

PCA physical configuration audit

PERT Program Evaluation and Review Technique

PI Product Integration (process area)

PMC Project Monitoring and Control (process area)

PP Project Planning (process area)

PPQA Process and Product Quality Assurance (process area)

QA quality assurance

QFD Quality Function Deployment

QPM Quantitative Project Management (process area)

RD Requirements Development (process area)

REQM Requirements Management (process area)

ROI return on investment

RSKM Risk Management (process area)

SA-CMM Software Acquisition Capability Maturity Model

SAM Supplier Agreement Management (process area)

SCAMPI Standard CMMI Appraisal Method for Process Improvement

SECM Systems Engineering Capability Model

SEI Software Engineering Institute

SG specific goal

SP specific practice

SPI schedule performance index

SW-CMM Capability Maturity Model for Software or Software Capability Maturity Model

TS Technical Solution (process area)

URL uniform resource locator

VAL Validation (process area)

VER Verification (process area)

WBS work breakdown structure

CMMI FOR DEVELOPMENT PROJECT PARTICIPANTS

Many talented people have been part of the product team that has created and maintained the CMMI Product Suite since its inception. This appendix recognizes the people involved in the update of CMMI for the version 1.2 release. The four primary groups involved in this development were the Product Team, Sponsors, Steering Group, and Configuration Control Board. Current members of these groups are listed. If you wish to see a more complete listing of participants from previous years, see Appendix C of the version 1.1 models.

Product Team

The Product Team reviewed change requests submitted by CMMI users to change the CMMI Product Suite, including the framework, models, training, and appraisal materials. Development activities were based on change requests, version 1.2 guidelines provided by the Steering Group, and input from Configuration Control Board members.

The program manager for the version 1.2 release was Mike Phillips. He coordinated the efforts of the following teams.

Model Team Members

Armstrong, Jim (Systems and Software Consortium)
Bate, Roger (Software Engineering Institute)
Cepeda, Sandra (RD&E Command, Software Engineering Directorate)
Chrissis, Mary Beth (Software Engineering Institute)
Clouse, Aaron (Raytheon)
D'Ambrosa, Mike (BAE Systems)
Hollenbach, Craig (Northrop Grumman)

Konrad, Mike (Software Engineering Institute)*
Norimatsu, So (Norimatsu Process Engineering Laboratory, Inc.)
Richter, Karen (Institute for Defense Analyses)
Shrum, Sandy (Software Engineering Institute)

SCAMPI Upgrade Team Members

Busby, Mary (Lockheed Martin)**
Cepeda, Sandra (RD&E Command, Software Engineering Directorate)
Ferguson, Jack (Software Engineering Institute)**
Hayes, Will (Software Engineering Institute)
Heil, James (U.S. Army) in memoriam
Kirkham, Denise (Boeing)
Masters, Steve (Software Engineering Institute)
Ming, Lisa (BAE Systems)
Ryan, Charlie (Software Engineering Institute)
Sumpter, Beth (National Security Agency)
Ulrich, Ron (Northrop Grumman)
Wickless, Joe (Software Engineering Institute)

Training Team Members

Chrissis, Mary Beth (Software Engineering Institute)
Gibson, Diane (Software Engineering Institute)
Knorr, Georgeann (Software Engineering Institute)
Kost, Keith (Software Engineering Institute)
Matthews, Jeanne (Software Engineering Institute)
Shrum, Sandy (Software Engineering Institute)
Svolou, Agapi (Software Engineering Institute)
Tyson, Barbara (Software Engineering Institute)*
Wickless, Joe (Software Engineering Institute)
Wolf, Gary (Raytheon)

Architecture Team Members

Bate, Roger (Software Engineering Institute)
Chrissis, Mary Beth (Software Engineering Institute)
Hoffman, Hubert (General Motors)
Hollenbach, Craig (Northrop Grumman)

---

* Team Leader
** Co-Team Leaders

Ming, Lisa (BAE Systems)
Phillips, Mike (Software Engineering Institute)*
Scibilia, John (U.S. Army)
Wilson, Hal (Northrop Grumman)
Wolf, Gary (Raytheon)

Hardware Team Members

Armstrong, Jim (Systems and Software Consortium)
Bishop, Jamie (Lockheed Martin)
Cattan, Denise (Spirula)
Clouse, Aaron (Raytheon)
Connell, Clifford (Raytheon)
Fisher, Jerry (Aerospace Corporation)
Hertneck, Christian (Siemens)
Phillips, Mike (Software Engineering Institute)*
Russwurm, Winfried (Siemens)
Zion, Christian (THALES)

Piloting Team Members

Brown, Rhonda (Software Engineering Institute)**
Chrissis, Mary Beth (Software Engineering Institute)
Ferguson, Jack (Software Engineering Institute)
Konrad, Mike (Software Engineering Institute)
Phillips, Marilyn (Q-Labs, Inc.)
Phillips, Mike (Software Engineering Institute)**
Tyson, Barbara (Software Engineering Institute)

Quality Team Members

Brown, Rhonda (Software Engineering Institute)*
Kost, Keith (Software Engineering Institute)
McSteen, Bill (Software Engineering Institute)
Shrum, Sandy (Software Engineering Institute)

Sponsors

The CMMI version 1.2 project was sponsored by both government and industry. Government sponsorship was provided by the U.S.

---

* Team Leader
** Co-Team Leaders

Department of Defense (DoD), specifically the Office of the Under Secretary of Defense (Acquisition, Technology, and Logistics) (OUSD [AT&L]). Industry sponsorship was provided by the Systems Engineering Committee of the National Defense Industrial Association (NDIA).

Rassa, Bob (NDIA Systems Engineering Division)
Schaeffer, Mark (OUSD [AT&L])

Steering Group

The Steering Group has guided and approved the plans of the version 1.2 Product Team, provided consultation on significant CMMI project issues, and ensured involvement from a variety of interested communities.

Steering Group Members

Baldwin, Kristen (OUSD [AT&L] DS/SE)
Chittister, Clyde (Software Engineering Institute)
D'Agosto, Tony (U.S. Army RDECOM-ARDEC)
Gill, Jim (Boeing Integrated Defense Systems)
Kelly, John (NASA HQ)
Lundeen, Kathy (Defense Contract Management Agency)
McCarthy, Larry (Motorola, Inc.)
Nicol, Mike (U.S. Air Force ASC/EN)[†]
Peterson, Bill (Software Engineering Institute)
Rassa, Bob (Raytheon Space & Airborne Systems)[††]
Weszka, Joan (Lockheed Martin)
Wilson, Hal (Northrop Grumman Mission Systems)
Zettervall, Brenda (U.S. Navy, ASN/RDA CHENG)

Ex-Officio Steering Group Members

Anderson, Lloyd (Department of Homeland Security)
Bate, Roger; chief architect (Software Engineering Institute)
Drake, Thomas (National Security Agency)
Phillips, Mike; CMMI program manager (Software Engineering Institute)
Sumpter, Beth (National Security Agency)
Yedlin, Debbie (General Motors)

[†] Government Co-Chair
[††] Industry Co-Chair

Steering Group Support: Acquisition

Gallagher, Brian (Software Engineering Institute)

Steering Group Support: CCB

Konrad, Mike (Software Engineering Institute)

Configuration Control Board

The Configuration Control Board has been the official mechanism for controlling changes to the version 1.2 CMMI for Development models. This group was responsible for product integrity by reviewing all changes to the baselines and approving only changes that met the criteria for version 1.2.

CCB Members

Atkinson, Shane (Borland/TeraQuest)
Bate, Roger (Software Engineering Institute)
Bernard, Tom (U.S. Air Force)
Chrissis, Mary Beth (Software Engineering Institute)
Croll, Paul (Computer Sciences Corporation)
Gristock, Stephen (JPMorganChase)
Hefner, Rick (Northrop Grumman Corporation)
Jacobsen, Nils (Motorola)
Konrad, Mike (Software Engineering Institute)[§]
Osiecki, Lawrence (U.S. Army)
Peterson, Bill (Software Engineering Institute)
Phillips, Mike (Software Engineering Institute)
Rassa, Bob (Raytheon)
Richter, Karen (Institute for Defense Analyses)
Sapp, Millee (U.S. Air Force)
Schoening, Bill (Boeing and INCOSE)
Schwomeyer, Warren (Lockheed Martin)
Smith, Katie (U.S. Navy)
Wolf, Gary (Raytheon)

[§] Configuration Control Board Chair

Non-Voting CCB Members

Brown, Rhonda (Software Engineering Institute)

Shrum, Sandy (Software Engineering Institute)

APPENDIX D

GLOSSARY

The CMMI glossary defines the basic terms used in the CMMI models. Glossary entries are typically multiple-word terms consisting of a noun and one or more restrictive modifiers. (There are some exceptions to this rule that account for one-word terms in the glossary.)

To formulate definitions appropriate for CMMI, we consult multiple sources. We first consult the *Merriam-Webster's OnLine* dictionary (www.m-w.com) and the source models (i.e., EIA 731, SW-CMM v2, draft C, and IPD-CMM v0.98). We also consult other standards as needed, including the following:

- ISO 9000 [ISO 1987]
- ISO/IEC 12207 [ISO 1995]
- ISO/IEC 15504 [ISO 2006]
- ISO/IEC 15288 [ISO 2002b]
- IEEE [IEEE 1990]
- SW-CMM v1.1
- EIA 632 [EIA 1994]
- SA-CMM [SEI 2002c]
- P-CMM [Curtis 2002]

We developed the glossary recognizing the importance of using terminology that all model users can understand. We also recognized that words and terms can have different meanings in different contexts and environments. The glossary in CMMI models is designed to document the meanings of words and terms that should have the widest use and understanding by users of CMMI products.

acceptance criteria The criteria that a product or product component must satisfy to be accepted by a user, customer, or other authorized entity.

acceptance testing Formal testing conducted to enable a user, customer, or other authorized entity to determine whether to accept a product or product component. (See also "unit testing.")

achievement profile In the continuous representation, a list of process areas and their corresponding capability levels that represent the organization's progress for each process area while advancing through the capability levels. (See also "capability level profile," "target profile," and "target staging.")

acquisition The process of obtaining products (goods and services) through contract.

acquisition strategy The specific approach to acquiring products and services that is based on considerations of supply sources, acquisition methods, requirements specification types, contract or agreement types, and the related acquisition risk.

addition In the CMMI Product Suite, a clearly marked model component that contains information of interest to particular users. In a CMMI model, all additions bearing the same name (e.g., IPPD addition) may be optionally selected as a group for use.

adequate This word is used so that you can interpret goals and practices in light of your organization's business objectives. When using any CMMI model, you must interpret the practices so that they work for your organization. This term is used in goals and practices where certain activities may not be done all of the time. (See also "appropriate" and "as needed.")

allocated requirement Requirement that levies all or part of the performance and functionality of a higher level requirement on a lower level architectural element or design component.

alternative practice A practice that is a substitute for one or more generic or specific practices contained in CMMI models that achieves an equivalent effect toward satisfying the generic or specific goal associated with model practices. Alternative practices are not necessarily one-for-one replacements for the generic or specific practices.

amplification Amplifications are informative model components that contain information relevant to a particular discipline. For example, to find an amplification for software engineering, you would look in the model for items labeled "For Software Engineering." The same is true for other disciplines.

appraisal   In the CMMI Product Suite, an examination of one or more processes by a trained team of professionals using an appraisal reference model as the basis for determining, at a minimum, strengths and weaknesses. (See also "assessment" and "capability evaluation.")

appraisal findings   The results of an appraisal that identify the most important issues, problems, or opportunities for process improvement within the appraisal scope. Appraisal findings are inferences drawn from corroborated objective evidence.

appraisal participants   Members of the organizational unit who participate in providing information during the appraisal.

appraisal rating   As used in CMMI appraisal materials, the value assigned by an appraisal team to (a) a CMMI goal or process area, (b) the capability level of a process area, or (c) the maturity level of an organizational unit. The rating is determined by enacting the defined rating process for the appraisal method being employed.

appraisal reference model   As used in CMMI appraisal materials, the CMMI model to which an appraisal team correlates implemented process activities.

appraisal scope   The definition of the boundaries of the appraisal encompassing the organizational limits and the CMMI model limits within which the processes to be investigated operate.

appropriate   This word is used so that you can interpret goals and practices in light of your organization's business objectives. When using any CMMI model, you must interpret the practices so that they work for your organization. This term is used in goals and practices where certain activities may not be done all of the time. (See also "adequate" and "as needed.")

as needed   This phrase is used so that you can interpret goals and practices in light of your organization's business objectives. When using any CMMI model, you must interpret the practices so that they work for your organization. This term is used in goals and practices where certain activities may not be done all the time. (See also "adequate" and "appropriate.")

assessment   In the CMMI Product Suite, an appraisal that an organization does internally for the purposes of process improvement. The word *assessment* is also used in the CMMI Product Suite in an everyday English sense (e.g., risk assessment). (See also "appraisal" and "capability evaluation.")

assignable cause of process variation   In CMMI, the term *special cause of process variation* is used in place of *assignable cause of process variation* to ensure consistency. The two terms are defined identically. (See "special cause of process variation.")

audit In CMMI process improvement work, an objective examination of a work product or set of work products against specific criteria (e.g., requirements).

base measure A distinct property or characteristic of an entity and the method for quantifying it. (See also "derived measures.")

baseline A set of specifications or work products that has been formally reviewed and agreed on, which thereafter serves as the basis for further development, and which can be changed only through change control procedures. (See also "configuration baseline" and "product baseline.")

bidirectional traceability An association among two or more logical entities that is discernable in either direction (i.e., to and from an entity). (See also "requirements traceability" and "traceability.")

business objectives (See "organization's business objectives.")

capability evaluation An appraisal by a trained team of professionals used as a discriminator to select suppliers, to monitor suppliers against the contract, or to determine and enforce incentives. Evaluations are used to gain insight into the process capability of a supplier organization and are intended to help decision makers make better acquisition decisions, improve subcontractor performance, and provide insight to a purchasing organization. (See also "appraisal" and "assessment.")

capability level Achievement of process improvement within an individual process area. A capability level is defined by the appropriate specific and generic practices for a process area. (See also "generic goal," "generic practice," "maturity level," and "process area.")

capability level profile In the continuous representation, a list of process areas and their corresponding capability levels. (See also "achievement profile," "target profile," and "target staging.")

The profile may be an achievement profile when it represents the organization's progress for each process area while advancing through the capability levels. Or, the profile may be a target profile when it represents an objective for process improvement.

capability maturity model A model that contains the essential elements of effective processes for one or more disciplines and describes an evolutionary improvement path from ad hoc, immature processes to disciplined, mature processes with improved quality and effectiveness.

capable process A process that can satisfy its specified product quality, service quality, and process-performance objectives. (See also "stable process," "standard process," and "statistically managed process.")

causal analysis The analysis of defects to determine their cause.

change management   Judicious use of means to effect a change, or a proposed change, on a product or service. (See also "configuration management.")

CMMI Framework   The basic structure that organizes CMMI components, including common elements of the current CMMI models as well as rules and methods for generating models, appraisal methods (including associated artifacts), and training materials. The framework enables new disciplines to be added to CMMI so that the new disciplines will integrate with the existing ones. (See also "CMMI model" and "CMMI Product Suite.")

CMMI model   One from the entire collection of possible models that can be generated from the CMMI Framework. Since the CMMI Framework can generate different models based on the needs of the organization using it, there are multiple CMMI models. (See also "CMMI Framework" and "CMMI Product Suite.")

CMMI model component   Any of the main architectural elements that compose a CMMI model. Some of the main elements of a CMMI model include specific practices, generic practices, specific goals, generic goals, process areas, capability levels, and maturity levels.

CMMI Product Suite   The complete set of products developed around the CMMI concept. These products include the framework itself, models, appraisal methods, appraisal materials, and various types of training. (See also "CMMI Framework" and "CMMI model.")

common cause of process variation   The variation of a process that exists because of normal and expected interactions among the components of a process. (See also "special cause of process variation.")

concept of operations   (See "operational concept.")

configuration audit   An audit conducted to verify that a configuration item, or a collection of configuration items that make up a baseline, conforms to a specified standard or requirement. (See also "audit," "configuration item," "functional configuration audit," and "physical configuration audit.")

configuration baseline   The configuration information formally designated at a specific time during a product's or product component's life. Configuration baselines, plus approved changes from those baselines, constitute the current configuration information. (See also "product lifecycle.")

configuration control   An element of configuration management consisting of the evaluation, coordination, approval or disapproval, and implementation of changes to configuration items after formal establishment of their configuration identification. (See also "configuration identification," "configuration item," and "configuration management.")

configuration control board   A group of people responsible for evaluating and approving or disapproving proposed changes to configuration items, and for ensuring implementation of approved changes. (See also "configuration item.")

Configuration control boards are also known as change control boards.

configuration identification   An element of configuration management consisting of selecting the configuration items for a product, assigning unique identifiers to them, and recording their functional and physical characteristics in technical documentation. (See also "configuration item," "configuration management," and "product.")

configuration item   An aggregation of work products that is designated for configuration management and treated as a single entity in the configuration management process. (See also "configuration management.")

configuration management   A discipline applying technical and administrative direction and surveillance to (1) identify and document the functional and physical characteristics of a configuration item, (2) control changes to those characteristics, (3) record and report change processing and implementation status, and (4) verify compliance with specified requirements. (See also "configuration audit," "configuration control," "configuration identification," and "configuration status accounting.")

configuration status accounting   An element of configuration management consisting of the recording and reporting of information needed to manage a configuration effectively. This information includes a listing of the approved configuration identification, the status of proposed changes to the configuration, and the implementation status of approved changes. (See also "configuration identification" and "configuration management.")

continuous representation   A capability maturity model structure wherein capability levels provide a recommended order for approaching process improvement within each specified process area. (See also "capability level," "process area," and "staged representation.")

contractor   (See "supplier.")

corrective action   Acts or deeds used to remedy a situation, remove an error, or adjust a condition.

COTS   Items that can be purchased from a commercial vendor. (COTS stands for "commercial off the shelf.")

customer   The party (individual, project, or organization) responsible for accepting the product or for authorizing payment. The customer is external to the project (except possibly when integrated teams are used, as in IPPD), but not necessarily external to the organization. The customer may be a higher level project. Customers are a subset of stakeholders. (See also "stakeholder.")

In most cases where this term is used, the preceding definition is intended; however, in some contexts, the term "customer" is intended to include other relevant stakeholders. (See also "customer requirement.")

customer requirement   The result of eliciting, consolidating, and resolving conflicts among the needs, expectations, constraints, and interfaces of the product's relevant stakeholders in a way that is acceptable to the customer. (See also "customer.")

data   Recorded information, regardless of the form or method of recording, including technical data, computer software documents, financial information, management information, representation of facts, numbers, or datum of any nature that can be communicated, stored, and processed.

data management   The disciplined processes and systems that plan for, acquire, and provide stewardship for business and technical data, consistent with data requirements, throughout the data lifecycle.

defect density   Number of defects per unit of product size (e.g., problem reports per thousand lines of code).

defined process   A managed process that is tailored from the organization's set of standard processes according to the organization's tailoring guidelines; has a maintained process description; and contributes work products, measures, and other process improvement information to the organizational process assets. (See also "managed process.")

derived measures   Data resulting from the mathematical function of two or more base measures. (See also "base measure.")

derived requirements   Requirements that are not explicitly stated in the customer requirements, but are inferred (1) from contextual requirements (e.g., applicable standards, laws, policies, common practices, and management decisions), or (2) from requirements needed to specify a product component. Derived requirements can also arise during analysis and design of components of the product or system. (See also "product requirements.")

design review   A formal, documented, comprehensive, and systematic examination of a design to evaluate the design requirements and the capability of the design to meet these requirements, and to identify problems and propose solutions.

development   In the CMMI Product Suite, not only development activities but also maintenance activities may be included. Projects that benefit from the best practices of CMMI can focus on development, maintenance, or both.

developmental plan   A plan for guiding, implementing, and controlling the design and development of one or more products. (See also "product lifecycle" and "project plan.")

discipline   In the CMMI Product Suite, the bodies of knowledge available to you when selecting a CMMI model (e.g., systems engineering). The CMMI Product Team envisions that other bodies of knowledge will be integrated into the CMMI Framework in the future.

document   A collection of data, regardless of the medium on which it is recorded, that generally has permanence and can be read by humans or machines. So, documents include both paper and electronic documents.

enterprise   The full composition of companies. Companies may consist of many organizations in many locations with different customers. (See also "organization.")

entry criteria   States of being that must be present before an effort can begin successfully.

equivalent staging   A target staging, created using the continuous representation, which is defined so that the results of using the target staging can be compared to the maturity levels of the staged representation. (See also "capability level profile," "maturity level," "target profile," and "target staging.")

Such staging permits benchmarking of progress among organizations, enterprises, and projects, regardless of the CMMI representation used. The organization may implement components of CMMI models beyond those reported as part of equivalent staging. Equivalent staging is only a measure to relate how the organization is compared to other organizations in terms of maturity levels.

establish and maintain   In the CMMI Product Suite, you will encounter goals and practices that include the phrase "establish and maintain." This phrase means more than a combination of its component terms; it includes documentation and usage. For example, "Establish and maintain an organizational policy for planning and performing the organizational process focus process" means that not only must a policy be formulated, but it also must be documented and it must be used throughout the organization.

evidence   (See "objective evidence.")

executive   (See "senior manager.")

exit criteria   States of being that must be present before an effort can end successfully.

expected CMMI components   CMMI components that explain what may be done to satisfy a required CMMI component. Model users can implement the expected components explicitly or implement equivalent alternative practices to these components. Specific and generic practices are expected model components.

finding   (See "appraisal findings.")

formal evaluation process   A structured approach to evaluating alternative solutions against established criteria to determine a recommended solution to address an issue.

framework   (See "CMMI Framework.")

functional analysis   Examination of a defined function to identify all the subfunctions necessary to the accomplishment of that function; identification of functional relationships and interfaces (internal and external) and capturing these in a functional architecture; and flow down of upper level performance requirements and assignment of these requirements to lower level subfunctions. (See also "functional architecture.")

functional architecture   The hierarchical arrangement of functions, their internal and external (external to the aggregation itself) functional interfaces and external physical interfaces, their respective functional and performance requirements, and their design constraints.

functional configuration audit   An audit conducted to verify that the development of a configuration item has been completed satisfactorily, that the item has achieved the performance and functional characteristics specified in the functional or allocated configuration identification, and that its operational and support documents are complete and satisfactory. (See also "configuration audit," "configuration management," and "physical configuration audit.")

generic goal   A required model component that describes the characteristics that must be present to institutionalize the processes that implement a process area. (See also "institutionalization.")

generic practice   An expected model component that is considered important in achieving the associated generic goal. The generic practices associated with a generic goal describe the activities that are expected to result in achievement of the generic goal and contribute to the institutionalization of the processes associated with a process area.

generic practice elaboration   An informative model component that appears after a generic practice to provide guidance on how the generic practice should be applied to the process area.

goal   A required CMMI component that can be either a generic goal or a specific goal. When you see the word *goal* in a CMMI model, it always refers to a model component (e.g., generic goal and specific goal). (See also "generic goal," "objective," and "specific goal.")

hardware engineering   The application of a systematic, disciplined, and quantifiable approach to transform a set of requirements representing the collection of stakeholder needs, expectations, and constraints using documented techniques and technology to design, implement, and maintain a tangible product. (See also "software engineering" and "systems engineering.")

In CMMI, hardware engineering represents all technical fields (e.g., electrical or mechanical) that transform requirements and ideas into tangible and producible products.

higher level management   The person or persons who provide the policy and overall guidance for the process, but do not provide the direct day-to-day monitoring and controlling of the process. Such persons belong to a level of management in the organization above the immediate level responsible for the process and can be (but are not necessarily) senior managers. (See also "senior manager.")

incomplete process   A process that is not performed or is performed only partially (also known as capability level 0). One or more of the specific goals of the process area are not satisfied.

informative CMMI components   CMMI components that help model users understand the required and expected components of a model. These components can contain examples, detailed explanations, or other helpful information. Subpractices, notes, references, goal titles, practice titles, sources, typical work products, amplifications, and generic practice elaborations are informative model components.

institutionalization   The ingrained way of doing business that an organization follows routinely as part of its corporate culture.

integrated product and process development   A systematic approach to product development that achieves a timely collaboration of relevant stakeholders throughout the product lifecycle to better satisfy customer needs.

integrated team   A group of people with complementary skills and expertise who are committed to delivering specified work products in timely collaboration. Integrated team members provide skills and advocacy appropriate to all phases of the work products' life and are collectively responsible for delivering the work products as specified. An integrated team should include empowered representatives from organizations, disciplines, and functions that have a stake in the success of the work products.

interface control   In configuration management, the process of (1) identifying all functional and physical characteristics relevant to the interfacing of two or more configuration items provided by one or more organizations, and (2) ensuring that the proposed changes to these characteristics are evaluated and approved prior to implementation. (See also "configuration item" and "configuration management.")

lifecycle model   A partitioning of the life of a product or project into phases.

managed process   A performed process that is planned and executed in accordance with policy; employs skilled people having adequate resources to produce controlled outputs; involves relevant stakeholders; is monitored, controlled, and reviewed; and is evaluated for adherence to its process description. (See also "performed process.")

manager   In the CMMI Product Suite, a person who provides technical and administrative direction and control to those performing tasks or activities within the manager's area of responsibility. The traditional functions of a manager include planning, organizing, directing, and controlling work within an area of responsibility.

maturity level   Degree of process improvement across a predefined set of process areas in which all goals in the set are attained. (See also "capability level" and "process area.")

memorandum of agreement   Binding documents of understanding or agreements between two or more parties. Also known as a "memorandum of understanding."

natural bounds   The inherent process reflected by measures of process performance, sometimes referred to as "voice of the process." Techniques such as control charts, confidence intervals, and prediction intervals are used to determine whether the variation is due to common causes (i.e., the process is predictable or "stable") or is due to some special cause that can and should be identified and removed.

nondevelopmental item (NDI)   An item of supply that was developed prior to its current use in an acquisition or development process. Such an item may require minor modifications to meet the requirements of its current intended use.

nontechnical requirements   Contractual provisions, commitments, conditions, and terms that affect how products or services are to be acquired. Examples include products to be delivered, data rights for delivered commercial off-the-shelf (COTS) nondevelopmental items (NDIs), delivery dates, and milestones with exit criteria. Other nontechnical requirements include training requirements, site requirements, and deployment schedules.

objective   When used as a noun in the CMMI Product Suite, the term *objective* replaces the word *goal* as used in its common everyday sense, since the word *goal* is reserved for use when referring to the CMMI model components called specific goals and generic goals. (See also "goal.")

objective evidence   As used in CMMI appraisal materials, documents or interview results used as indicators of the implementation or institutionalization of model practices. Sources of objective evidence can include instruments, presentations, documents, and interviews.

objectively evaluate   To review activities and work products against criteria which minimize subjectivity and bias by the reviewer. An example of an objective evaluation is an audit against requirements, standards, or procedures by an independent quality assurance function. (See also "audit.")

observation   As used in CMMI appraisal materials, a written record that represents the appraisal team members' understanding of information either seen or heard during the appraisal data collection activities. The written record may take the form of a statement or may take alternative forms as long as the information content is preserved.

operational concept   A general description of the way in which an entity is used or operates. (Also known as "concept of operations.")

operational scenario   A description of an imagined sequence of events that includes the interaction of the product with its environment and users, as well as interaction among its product components. Operational scenarios are used to evaluate the requirements and design of the system and to verify and validate the system.

optimizing process   A quantitatively managed process that is improved based on an understanding of the common causes of variation inherent in the process. The focus of an optimizing process is on continually improving the range of process performance through both incremental and innovative improvements. (See also "common cause of process variation," "defined process," and "quantitatively managed process.")

organization   An administrative structure in which people collectively manage one or more projects as a whole, and whose projects share a senior manager and operate under the same policies. However, the word *organization* as used throughout CMMI models can also apply to one person who performs a function in a small organization that might be performed by a group of people in a large organization. (See also "enterprise" and "organizational unit.")

organizational maturity   The extent to which an organization has explicitly and consistently deployed processes that are documented, managed, measured, controlled, and continually improved. Organizational maturity may be measured via appraisals.

organizational policy   A guiding principle typically established by senior management that is adopted by an organization to influence and determine decisions.

organizational process assets   Artifacts that relate to describing, implementing, and improving processes (e.g., policies, measurements, process descriptions, and process implementation support tools). The term *process assets* is used to indicate that these artifacts are developed or acquired to meet the business objectives of the organization, and they represent investments by the organization that are expected to provide current and future business value. (See also "process asset library.")

organizational unit   The part of an organization that is the subject of an appraisal. An organizational unit deploys one or more processes that have a coherent process context and operates within a coherent set of business objectives. An organizational unit is typically part of a larger organization, although in a small organization, the organizational unit may be the whole organization.

organization's business objectives   Senior management developed strategies designed to ensure an organization's continued existence and enhance its profitability, market share, and other factors influencing the organization's success. (See also "quality and process-performance objectives" and "quantitative objective.")

Such objectives may include reducing the number of change requests during a system's integration phase, reducing development cycle time, increasing the number of errors found in a product's first or second phase of development, and reducing the number of customer-reported defects, when applied to systems engineering activities.

organization's measurement repository   A repository used to collect and make available measurement data on processes and work products, particularly as they relate to the organization's set of standard processes. This repository contains or references actual measurement data and related information needed to understand and analyze the measurement data.

organization's process asset library   A library of information used to store and make available process assets that are useful to those who are defining, implementing, and managing processes in the organization. This library contains process assets that include process-related documentation such as policies, defined processes, checklists, lessons-learned documents, templates, standards, procedures, plans, and training materials.

organization's set of standard processes   A collection of definitions of the processes that guide activities in an organization. These process descriptions cover the fundamental process elements (and their relationships to each other, such as ordering and interfaces) that must be incorporated into the defined processes that are implemented in projects across the organization. A standard process enables consistent development and maintenance activities across the organization and is essential for long-term stability and improvement. (See also "defined process" and "process element.")

outsourcing   (See "acquisition.")

peer review   The review of work products performed by peers during development of the work products to identify defects for removal. The term *peer review* is used in the CMMI Product Suite instead of the term *work product inspection*. (See also "work product.")

performance parameters   The measures of effectiveness and other key measures used to guide and control progressive development.

performed process   A process that accomplishes the needed work to produce work products. The specific goals of the process area are satisfied.

physical configuration audit   An audit conducted to verify that a configuration item, as built, conforms to the technical documentation that defines and describes it. (See also "configuration audit," "configuration management," and "functional configuration audit.")

planned process   A process that is documented by both a description and a plan. The description and plan should be coordinated, and the plan should include standards, requirements, objectives, resources, assignments, and so on.

policy   (See "organizational policy.")

process In the CMMI Product Suite, activities that can be recognized as implementations of practices in a CMMI model. These activities can be mapped to one or more practices in CMMI process areas to allow a model to be useful for process improvement and process appraisal. (See also "process area," "subprocess," and "process element.")

There is a special use of the phrase "the process" in the statements and descriptions of the generic goals and generic practices. "The process," as used in Part Two, is the process or processes that implement the process area.

process action plan A plan, usually resulting from appraisals, that documents how specific improvements targeting the weaknesses uncovered by an appraisal will be implemented.

process action team A team that has the responsibility to develop and implement process improvement activities for an organization as documented in a process action plan.

process and technology improvements Incremental and innovative improvements to processes and to process or product technologies.

process architecture The ordering, interfaces, interdependencies, and other relationships among the process elements in a standard process. Process architecture also describes the interfaces, interdependencies, and other relationships between process elements and external processes (e.g., contract management).

process area A cluster of related practices in an area that, when implemented collectively, satisfy a set of goals considered important for making improvement in that area. All CMMI process areas are common to both continuous and staged representations.

process asset Anything that the organization considers useful in attaining the goals of a process area. (See also "organizational process assets.")

process asset library A collection of process asset holdings that can be used by an organization or project. (See also "organization's process asset library.")

process attribute A measurable characteristic of process capability applicable to any process.

process capability The range of expected results that can be achieved by following a process.

process definition The act of defining and describing a process. The result of a process definition is a process description. (See also "process description.")

process description   A documented expression of a set of activities performed to achieve a given purpose.

A process description provides an operational definition of the major components of a process. The description specifies, in a complete, precise, and verifiable manner, the requirements, design, behavior, or other characteristics of a process. It also may include procedures for determining whether these provisions have been satisfied. Process descriptions can be found at the activity, project, or organizational level.

process element   The fundamental unit of a process. A process can be defined in terms of subprocesses or process elements. A subprocess can be further decomposed into subprocesses or process elements; a process element cannot. (See also "process" and "subprocess.")

Each process element covers a closely related set of activities (e.g., estimating element and peer review element). Process elements can be portrayed using templates to be completed, abstractions to be refined, or descriptions to be modified or used. A process element can be an activity or task.

process group   A collection of specialists who facilitate the definition, maintenance, and improvement of the processes used by the organization.

process improvement   A program of activities designed to improve the performance and maturity of the organization's processes and the results of such a program.

process improvement objectives   A set of target characteristics established to guide the effort to improve an existing process in a specific, measurable way either in terms of resultant product characteristics (e.g., quality, performance, and conformance to standards) or in the way in which the process is executed (e.g., elimination of redundant process steps, combination of process steps, and improvement of cycle time). (See also "organization's business objectives" and "quantitative objective.")

process improvement plan   A plan for achieving organizational process improvement objectives based on a thorough understanding of the current strengths and weaknesses of the organization's processes and process assets.

process measurement   The set of definitions, methods, and activities used to take measurements of a process and its resulting products for the purpose of characterizing and understanding the process.

process owner   The person (or team) responsible for defining and maintaining a process. At the organizational level, the process owner is the person (or team) responsible for the description of a standard process; at the project level, the process owner is the person (or team) responsible for the description of the defined process. A process may therefore have multiple owners at different levels of responsibility. (See also "defined process" and "standard process.")

process performance   A measure of actual results achieved by following a process. It is characterized by both process measures (e.g., effort, cycle time, and defect removal efficiency) and product measures (e.g., reliability, defect density, and response time).

process-performance baseline   A documented characterization of the actual results achieved by following a process, which is used as a benchmark for comparing actual process performance against expected process performance. (See also "process performance.")

process-performance model   A description of the relationships among attributes of a process and its work products that is developed from historical process-performance data and calibrated using collected process and product measures from the project and that is used to predict results to be achieved by following a process.

process tailoring   Making, altering, or adapting a process description for a particular end. For example, a project tailors its defined process from the organization's set of standard processes to meet the objectives, constraints, and environment of the project. (See also "defined process," "organization's set of standard processes," and "process description.")

product   In the CMMI Product Suite, a work product that is intended for delivery to a customer or end user. The form of a product can vary in different contexts. (See also "customer," "product component," "service," and "work product.")

product baseline   In configuration management, the initial approved technical data package (including, for software, the source code listing) defining a configuration item during the production, operation, maintenance, and logistic support of its lifecycle. (See also "configuration item" and "configuration management.")

product component   In the CMMI Product Suite, a work product that is a lower level component of the product. Product components are integrated to produce the product. There may be multiple levels of product components. (See also "product" and "work product.")

product component requirements   A complete specification of a product component, including fit, form, function, performance, and any other requirement.

product lifecycle   The period of time, consisting of phases, which begins when a product is conceived and ends when the product is no longer available for use. Since an organization may be producing multiple products for multiple customers, one description of a product lifecycle may not be adequate. Therefore, the organization may define a set of approved product lifecycle models. These models are typically found in published literature and are likely to be tailored for use in an organization.

A product lifecycle could consist of the following phases: (1) concept/vision, (2) feasibility, (3) design/development, (4) production, and (5) phase out.

product line   A group of products sharing a common, managed set of features that satisfy specific needs of a selected market or mission.

product-related lifecycle processes   Processes associated with a product throughout one or more phases of its life (e.g., from conception through disposal), such as the manufacturing and support processes.

product requirements   A refinement of the customer requirements into the developers' language, making implicit requirements into explicit derived requirements. (See also "derived requirements" and "product component requirements.")

The developer uses the product requirements to guide the design and building of the product.

product suite   (See "CMMI Product Suite.")

profile   (See "achievement profile" and "target profile.")

program   (1) A project. (2) A collection of related projects and the infrastructure that supports them, including objectives, methods, activities, plans, and success measures. (See also "project.")

project   In the CMMI Product Suite, a managed set of interrelated resources which delivers one or more products to a customer or end user. A project has a definite beginning (i.e., project startup) and typically operates according to a plan. Such a plan is frequently documented and specifies what is to be delivered or implemented, the resources and funds to be used, the work to be done, and a schedule for doing the work. A project can be composed of projects. (See also "project startup.")

project manager   In the CMMI Product Suite, the person responsible for planning, directing, controlling, structuring, and motivating the project. The project manager is responsible for satisfying the customer.

project plan   A plan that provides the basis for performing and controlling the project's activities, which addresses the commitments to the project's customer.

Project planning includes estimating the attributes of the work products and tasks, determining the resources needed, negotiating commitments, producing a schedule, and identifying and analyzing project risks. Iterating through these activities may be necessary to establish the project plan.

project progress and performance   What a project achieves with respect to implementing project plans, including effort, cost, schedule, and technical performance.

project startup   When a set of interrelated resources are directed to develop or deliver one or more products for a customer or end user. (See also "project.")

project's defined process   The integrated and defined process that is tailored from the organization's set of standard processes. (See also "defined process.")

prototype   A preliminary type, form, or instance of a product or product component that serves as a model for later stages or for the final, complete version of the product. This model (e.g., physical, electronic, digital, and analytical) can be used for the following (and other) purposes:
- Assessing the feasibility of a new or unfamiliar technology
- Assessing or mitigating technical risk
- Validating requirements
- Demonstrating critical features
- Qualifying a product
- Qualifying a process
- Characterizing performance or product features
- Elucidating physical principles

quality   The ability of a set of inherent characteristics of a product, product component, or process to fulfill requirements of customers.

quality and process-performance objectives   Objectives and requirements for product quality, service quality, and process performance. Process-performance objectives include quality; however, to emphasize the importance of quality in the CMMI Product Suite, the phrase *quality and process-performance objectives* is used rather than just *process-performance objectives*.

quality assurance   A planned and systematic means for assuring management that the defined standards, practices, procedures, and methods of the process are applied.

quality control The operational techniques and activities that are used to fulfill requirements for quality. (See also "quality assurance.")

quantitative objective Desired target value expressed as quantitative measures. (See also "process improvement objectives" and "quality and process-performance objectives.")

quantitatively managed process A defined process that is controlled using statistical and other quantitative techniques. The product quality, service quality, and process-performance attributes are measurable and controlled throughout the project. (See also "defined process," "optimizing process," and "statistically managed process.")

rating (See "appraisal rating.")

reference An informative model component that points to additional or more detailed information in related process areas.

reference model A model that is used as a benchmark for measuring some attribute.

relevant stakeholder A stakeholder that is identified for involvement in specified activities and is included in a plan. (See also "stakeholder.")

representation The organization, use, and presentation of a CMM's components. Overall, two types of approaches to presenting best practices are evident: the staged representation and the continuous representation.

required CMMI components CMMI components that are essential to achieving process improvement in a given process area. These components are used in appraisals to determine process capability. Specific goals and generic goals are required model components.

requirement (1) A condition or capability needed by a user to solve a problem or achieve an objective. (2) A condition or capability that must be met or possessed by a product or product component to satisfy a contract, standard, specification, or other formally imposed documents. (3) A documented representation of a condition or capability as in (1) or (2).

requirements analysis The determination of product-specific performance and functional characteristics based on analyses of customer needs, expectations, and constraints; operational concept; projected utilization environments for people, products, and processes; and measures of effectiveness.

requirements elicitation Using systematic techniques, such as prototypes and structured surveys, to proactively identify and document customer and end-user needs.

requirements management   The management of all requirements received by or generated by the project, including both technical and nontechnical requirements as well as those requirements levied on the project by the organization.

requirements traceability   A discernable association between requirements and related requirements, implementations, and verifications. (See also "bidirectional traceability" and "traceability.")

return on investment   The ratio of revenue from output (product) to production costs, which determines whether an organization benefits from performing an action to produce something.

risk analysis   The evaluation, classification, and prioritization of risks.

risk identification   An organized, thorough approach to seek out probable or realistic risks in achieving objectives.

risk management   An organized, analytic process to identify what might cause harm or loss (identify risks); to assess and quantify the identified risks; and to develop and, if needed, implement an appropriate approach to prevent or handle causes of risk that could result in significant harm or loss.

risk management strategy   An organized, technical approach to identify what might cause harm or loss (identify risks); to assess and quantify the identified risks; and to develop and, if needed, implement an appropriate approach to prevent or handle causes of risk that could result in significant harm or loss. Typically, risk management is performed for project, organization, or product developing organizational units.

root cause   A source of a defect such that if it is removed, the defect is decreased or removed.

senior manager   In the CMMI Product Suite, a management role at a high enough level in an organization that the primary focus of the person filling the role is the long-term vitality of the organization rather than short-term project and contractual concerns and pressures. A senior manager has authority to direct the allocation or reallocation of resources in support of organizational process improvement effectiveness. (See also "higher level management.")

A senior manager can be any manager who satisfies this description, including the head of the organization. Synonyms for "senior manager" include "executive" and "top-level manager." However, to ensure consistency and usability, these synonyms are not used in CMMI models.

service   In the CMMI Product Suite, a service is a product that is intangible and non-storable. (See also "product," "customer," and "work product.")

shared vision   A common understanding of guiding principles including mission, objectives, expected behavior, values, and final outcomes, which are developed and used by a project.

software engineering   (1) The application of a systematic, disciplined, quantifiable approach to the development, operation, and maintenance of software. (2) The study of approaches as in (1). (See also "hardware engineering" and "systems engineering.")

solicitation   The process of preparing a package to be used in selecting a supplier (contractor).

special cause of process variation   A cause of a defect that is specific to some transient circumstance and not an inherent part of a process. (See also "common cause of process variation.")

specific goal   A required model component that describes the unique characteristics that must be present to satisfy the process area. (See also "capability level," "generic goal," "organization's business objectives," and "process area.")

specific practice   An expected model component that is considered important in achieving the associated specific goal. The specific practices describe the activities expected to result in achievement of the specific goals of a process area. (See also "process area" and "specific goal.")

stable process   The state in which all special causes of process variation have been removed and prevented from recurring so that only the common causes of process variation of the process remain. (See also "capable process," "common cause of process variation," "special cause of process variation," "standard process," and "statistically managed process.")

staged representation   A model structure wherein attaining the goals of a set of process areas establishes a maturity level; each level builds a foundation for subsequent levels. (See also "maturity level" and "process area.")

stakeholder   In the CMMI Product Suite, a group or individual that is affected by or is in some way accountable for the outcome of an undertaking. Stakeholders may include project members, suppliers, customers, end users, and others. (See also "customer" and "relevant stakeholder.")

standard   When you see the word *standard* used as a noun in a CMMI model, it refers to the formal mandatory requirements developed and used to prescribe consistent approaches to development (e.g., ISO/IEC standards, IEEE standards, and organizational standards). Instead of using standard in its common everyday sense, we use another term that means the same thing (e.g., typical, traditional, usual, or customary).

standard process   An operational definition of the basic process that guides the establishment of a common process in an organization.

A standard process describes the fundamental process elements that are expected to be incorporated into any defined process. It also describes the relationships (e.g., ordering and interfaces) among these process elements. (See also "defined process.")

statement of work   A description of contracted work required to complete a project.

statistical predictability   The performance of a quantitative process that is controlled using statistical and other quantitative techniques.

statistical process control   Statistically based analysis of a process and measurements of process performance, which will identify common and special causes of variation in the process performance and maintain process performance within limits. (See also "common cause of process variation," "special cause of process variation," and "statistically managed process.")

statistical techniques   An analytic technique that employs statistical methods (e.g., statistical process control, confidence intervals, and prediction intervals).

statistically managed process   A process that is managed by a statistically based technique in which processes are analyzed, special causes of process variation are identified, and performance is contained within well-defined limits. (See also "capable process," "special cause of process variation," "stable process," "standard process," and "statistical process control.")

subpractice   An informative model component that provides guidance for interpreting and implementing a specific or generic practice. Subpractices may be worded as if prescriptive, but are actually meant only to provide ideas that may be useful for process improvement.

subprocess   A process that is part of a larger process. A subprocess can be decomposed into subprocesses and/or process elements. (See also "process," "process description," and "process element.")

supplier   (1) An entity delivering products or performing services being acquired. (2) An individual, partnership, company, corporation, association, or other service having an agreement (contract) with an acquirer for the design, development, manufacture, maintenance, modification, or supply of items under the terms of an agreement (contract).

sustainment   The processes used to ensure that a product can be utilized operationally by its end users or customers. Sustainment ensures that maintenance is done such that the product is in an operable condition whether or not the product is in use by customers or end users.

systems engineering   The interdisciplinary approach governing the total technical and managerial effort required to transform a set of customer needs, expectations, and constraints into a product solution and to support that solution throughout the product's life. (See also "hardware engineering" and "software engineering.")

This includes the definition of technical performance measures, the integration of engineering specialties toward the establishment of a product architecture, and the definition of supporting lifecycle processes that balance cost, performance, and schedule objectives.

tailoring   Tailoring a process makes, alters, or adapts the process description for a particular end. For example, a project establishes its defined process by tailoring from the organization's set of standard processes to meet the objectives, constraints, and environment of the project.

tailoring guidelines   Organizational guidelines that enable projects, groups, and organizational functions to appropriately adapt standard processes for their use. The organization's set of standard processes is described at a general level that may not be directly usable to perform a process.

Tailoring guidelines aid those who establish the defined processes for projects. Tailoring guidelines cover (1) selecting a standard process, (2) selecting an approved lifecycle model, and (3) tailoring the selected standard process and lifecycle model to fit project needs. Tailoring guidelines describe what can and cannot be modified and identify process components that are candidates for modification.

target profile   In the continuous representation, a list of process areas and their corresponding capability levels that represent an objective for process improvement. (See also "achievement profile" and "capability level profile.")

target staging   In the continuous representation, a sequence of target profiles that describes the path of process improvement to be followed by the organization. (See also "achievement profile," "capability level profile," and "target profile.")

technical data package   A collection of items that can include the following if such information is appropriate to the type of product and product component (e.g., material and manufacturing requirements may not be useful for product components associated with software services or processes):

- Product architecture description
- Allocated requirements
- Product component descriptions
- Product-related lifecycle process descriptions if not described as separate product components
- Key product characteristics
- Required physical characteristics and constraints
- Interface requirements
- Materials requirements (bills of material and material characteristics)
- Fabrication and manufacturing requirements (for both the original equipment manufacturer and field support)
- Verification criteria used to ensure requirements have been achieved
- Conditions of use (environments) and operating/usage scenarios, modes and states for operations, support, training, manufacturing, disposal, and verifications throughout the life of the product
- Rationale for decisions and characteristics (e.g., requirements, requirement allocations, and design choices)

technical requirements   Properties (attributes) of products or services to be acquired or developed.

test procedure   Detailed instructions for the setup, execution, and evaluation of results for a given test.

traceability   A discernable association among two or more logical entities such as requirements, system elements, verifications, or tasks. (See also "bidirectional traceability" and "requirements traceability.")

trade study   An evaluation of alternatives, based on criteria and systematic analysis, to select the best alternative for attaining determined objectives.

training   Formal and informal learning options, which may include in-class training, informal mentoring, Web-based training, guided self-study, and formalized on-the-job training programs. The learning options selected for each situation are based on an assessment of the need for training and the performance gap to be addressed.

typical work product   An informative model component that provides sample outputs from a specific practice. These examples are called typical work products because there are often other work products that are just as effective, but are not listed.

unit testing   Testing of individual hardware or software units or groups of related units. (See also "acceptance testing.")

validation   Confirmation that the product, as provided (or as it will be provided), will fulfill its intended use. In other words, validation ensures that "you built the right thing." (See also "verification.")

verification   Confirmation that work products properly reflect the requirements specified for them. In other words, verification ensures that "you built it right." (See also "validation.")

version control   The establishment and maintenance of baselines and the identification of changes to baselines that make it possible to return to the previous baseline.

work breakdown structure (WBS)   An arrangement of work elements and their relationship to each other and to the end product.

work product   In the CMMI Product Suite, a useful result of a process. This can include files, documents, products, parts of a product, services, process descriptions, specifications, and invoices. A key distinction between a work product and a product component is that a work product is not necessarily part of the product. (See also "product" and "product component.")

In CMMI models, you will see the phrase *work products and services*. Even though the definition of work product includes services, this phrase is used to emphasize the inclusion of services in the discussion.

work product and task attributes   Characteristics of products, services, and project tasks used to help in estimating project work. These characteristics include items such as size, complexity, weight, form, fit, and function. They are typically used as one input to deriving other project and resource estimates (e.g., effort, cost, and schedule).

Book Contributors

BOOK AUTHORS

Sandy Shrum, Mary Beth Chrissis, Mike Konrad (l. to r.)

Mary Beth Chrissis

Mary Beth Chrissis is a senior member of the technical staff at the Software Engineering Institute (SEI). Since joining the SEI in 1988, Mary Beth has been involved in all releases of CMMI models and the Capability Maturity Model for Software (SW-CMM). She is one of the primary contributors to *The Capability Maturity Model: Guidelines for Improving the Software Process*. Mary Beth is a member of the CMMI Architecture Team and CMMI Model Team. She is the manager of the SEI's CMMI Training Team, which is responsible for the development and deployment of the SEI's process improvement courses. Previously, she managed the CMMI Interpretive Guidance Project, which focused on understanding and addressing CMMI adoption issues and perceived barriers to CMMI adoption in the software community with a special focus on information technology, information systems (IS), and commercial software. Mary Beth is a member of the CMMI Configuration Control Board and is an instructor of various SW-CMM and CMMI model-related courses at the SEI. Prior to joining the SEI, Mary Beth worked at GTE Government Systems in Rockville, Maryland, developing a voice processing system. Mary Beth has a B.S. from Carnegie Mellon and is a member of the IEEE Software and Systems Engineering Standards Committee (S2ESC) Executive Committee.

Mike Konrad

Mike Konrad has been with the Software Engineering Institute since 1988. Currently, Mike is manager of the CMMI Models Team and chairs the CMMI Configuration Control Board, the approving body for changes to CMMI models and the Introduction to CMMI course. From 1988 through 1997, Mike contributed to the development of the Capability Maturity Model for Software (SW-CMM) and the ISO/IEC 15504 standard. Since the inception of the CMMI project in 1998, Mike has been leader or co-leader of every CMMI model development effort. Mike is also a member of the International Process Research Consortium (www.sei.cmu.edu/iprc). Prior to joining the SEI, Mike worked with International Software Systems, Inc. (ISSI) of Austin, Texas, where he contributed to the development of a rapid prototyping system. He has also worked with SAIC, George Mason University, University of Maryland, and Honeywell Information Systems. Mike obtained his Ph.D. in mathematics from Ohio University, Athens, Ohio, in 1978.

Sandy Shrum

Sandy Shrum is a senior writer/editor at the Software Engineering Institute. She has been a member of the CMMI Development Team since the CMMI project's inception in 1998. Her roles on the project have included Model Team member, Glossary Team leader, reviewer, editor, model development process administrator, and quality assurance coordinator. Sandy is also a member of the SEI Configuration Control Board, and is the CMMI communications coordinator. Before joining the SEI, Sandy spent eight years working for Legent Corporation, a Virginia-based software company. Her experience as a technical writer dates back to 1988, when she earned her M.A. in professional writing from Carnegie Mellon University. Her undergraduate degree, a B.S. in business administration, was earned at Gannon University.

Victor R. Basili, Kathleen C. Dangle, and Michele A. Shaw

Victor R. Basili is professor of computer science at the University of Maryland, College Park, and chief scientist at the Fraunhofer Center for Experimental Software Engineering, Maryland. He was a founder and principal in the Software Engineering Laboratory (SEL). Focusing on the measurement, evaluation, and improvement of the software development process and product through empirical research, his influential work includes the Goal/Question/Metric Approach, the Quality Improvement Paradigm, and the Experience Factory. Kathleen C. Dangle and Michele A. Shaw are scientists at the Fraunhofer Center and collaborate with Dr. Basili on the application of empirical thinking in real-world software contexts.

Pointers: Basili, V.; and Caldiera, G. "Improve Software Quality by Reusing Knowledge and Experience." Sloan Management Review, MIT Press, 37, no. 1, pp. 55-64 (Fall 1995).

Boehm, B.; Rombach, H. D.; and Zelkowitz, M. V. (eds.). *Foundations of Empirical Software Engineering: The Legacy of Victor R. Basili* (Springer, 2005).

Roger Bate

Roger Bate, a visiting scientist at the Software Engineering Institute (SEI) at Carnegie Mellon University, is the chief architect of the CMMI Framework. Dr. Bate previously was chief computer scientist for Texas Instruments, and a TI fellow, chief of the Reactor Theory Branch of the Oak Ridge National Laboratory, and professor at the U.S. Air Force Academy. He is a fellow of the ACM, a fellow of the Society for Design and Process Science, and a recipient of the SEI Leadership Award.

David N. Card

David N. Card is a fellow of Q-Labs. He is the author of *Measuring Software Design Quality* (Prentice Hall, 1990), coauthor of *Practical Software Measurement* (Addison-Wesley, 2002), coeditor of *ISO/IEC Standard 15939: Software Measurement Process* (International Organization for Standardization, 2002), and editor-in-chief of the *Journal of Systems and Software.*

Pointer: Card, D. "Defect Analysis: Basic Techniques for Management and Learning." Advances in Computers, 65 (2005).

Bill Curtis

Bill Curtis is the chief process officer of Borland Software Corporation. Prior to his company's acquisition by Borland, he was cofounder and chief scientist of TeraQuest Metrics, Inc., in Austin, Texas. A former director of the Software Process Program in the Software Engineering Institute (SEI) at Carnegie Mellon University, Dr. Curtis is both a coauthor of the Capability Maturity Model for Software and the principal architect of the People Capability Maturity Model.

Pointer: Curtis, Bill, et al. *The People Capability Maturity Model: Guidelines for Improving the Workforce* (Addison-Wesley, 2001).

Khaled El Emam

Khaled El Emam is associate professor, Faculty of Medicine, and Canada Research Chair in Electronic Health Information at the University of Ottawa. He also is chief scientist at TrialStat Corporation. Previously, Dr. Khaled was a senior research officer at the National Research Council of Canada, where he served as the technical lead of the Software Quality Laboratory, and head of the Quantitative Methods Group at the Fraunhofer Institute for Experimental Software Engineering in Kaiserslautern, Germany.

Pointer: El Emam, K.; and Goldenson, D. "An Empirical Review of Software Process Assessments." Advances in Computers, Academic Press, 53, pp. 319–423 (2000).

Watts S. Humphrey

Watts S. Humphrey, a fellow of the Software Engineering Institute (SEI), founded the SEI's Software Process Program, led the initial development of the Capability Maturity Model (CMM), and created both the Personal Software Process (PSP) and Team Software Process

(TSP). He previously was director of programming and vice president of technical development at IBM. Among Mr. Humphrey's numerous publications are eleven books, including *Winning with Software* (Addison-Wesley, 2002) and several works detailing *PSP*^{SM} (Addison-Wesley, 2005), and *TSP*^{SM}—*Coaching Development Teams* (Addison-Wesley, 2006). The Watts Humphrey Software Quality Institute in Chennai, India, was named in his honor, and in 2005, the President of the United States awarded him the National Medal of Technology.

Pointer: Humphrey, Watts S. *Winning with Software: an Executive Strategy* (Addison-Wesley, 2001).

Gargi Keeni

Gargi Keeni is vice president of quality consulting at Tata Consultancy Services, India. She also serves on the advisory board of *IEEE Software* and the advisory panel of the NASSCOM Quality Forum. An SEI-authorized lead appraiser for CMMI and People CMM, Dr. Keeni's research interests include process improvement, quality management systems, and business excellence.

Pointer: Keeni, Gargi. "The Evolution of Quality Processes at Tata Consultancy Services." *IEEE Software* (July/August 2000).

Hans Jürgen Kugler

Hans-Jürgen Kugler is adjunct professor at the University of Limerick, where he is industrial director of Lero, the Irish Software Engineering Research Centre. In addition, he is principal and chief scientist of Kugler Maag Cie. Mr. Kugler previously was a lecturer at Trinity College, Dublin; a director of software product and services companies; and technical director of the European Software Institute.

Pointer: Kotter, John P. *Leading Change* (Harvard Business School Press, 1996).

Tomoo Matsubara

Tomoo Matsubara is an independent consultant on software technology, management, and business. He currently serves on the editorial board of the *Cutter IT Journal* and on the advisory board of *IEEE Software,* for which he previously edited the "Soapbox" forum on everyday issues in software development. Prior to the start of his consulting business, Dr. Matsubara was chief

engineer and project manager for Hitachi Software Engineering in Japan.

Pointers: Matsubara, Tomoo. "Japan: A Huge IT Consumption Market." IEEE Software, 18 (no. 5), Sept./Oct. 2001.

Matsubara, Tomoo. "Process Certification: A Double-Edged Sword." IEEE Software, 17, (no. 6), Nov./Dec. 2000.

Matsubara, Tomoo; and Ebert, Christof. "Benefits and Applications of Cross-Pollination." IEEE Software, 17 (no. 1), Jan./Feb. 2000.

Matsubara, Tomoo. "Does ISO 9000 Really Help Improve Software Quality?" American Programmer, 7 (no. 2), Feb. 1994, pp. 38–45.

James W. Moore

James W. Moore is a thirty-five-year veteran of software engineering, first at IBM and now at the MITRE Corporation. He is an executive editor of the IEEE Computer Society's *Guide to the Software Engineering Body of Knowledge* and the author of *The Road Map to Software Engineering: A Standards-Based Guide* (IEEE Press-Wiley, 2006). An IEEE fellow and a charter member of the IEEE Computer Society's Golden Core, Mr. Moore is the Society's liaison for international standards on software and systems engineering.

Pointers: Moore, James W. *The Road Map to Software Engineering: A Standards-Based Guide* (IEEE Press-Wiley, 2006).

IEEE Computer Society. *The Guide to the Software Engineering Body of Knowledge* (IEEE Computer Society, 2004).

Lynn Penn

Lynn Penn is director of quality systems and process manager with Lockheed Martin Integrated Systems & Solutions. She oversees policies and process compliance and improvement across the organization and recently coordinated and managed their CMMI adoption and appraisal. Lynn has been an SEI affiliate, a CMMI instructor, a candidate lead appraiser, a certified ISO 9000 internal auditor, and a Black Belt certified in Six Sigma and Lean Techniques.

Pointer: Siviy, Jeannine; Penn, M. Lynn; and Harper, Erin. *Relationships Between CMMI and Six Sigma (CMU/SEI-2005-TN-005)* (Software Engineering Institute, Carnegie Mellon University, 2005).

Bill Peterson

Bill Peterson is director of the SEI's Software Engineering Process Management Program. Beyond his broad management role in the development and transition of the CMMI, his current thrust is to integrate the CMMI with other SEI process improvement and measurement initiatives, such as TSP, into a cross-discipline framework. Prior to joining the SEI, Mr. Peterson managed software development projects at IBM, orchestrated process improvement activities there, and taught software engineering.

Pointer: The CMMI Web site, www.sei.cmu.edu/cmmi.

Mike Phillips

Mike Phillips is the program manager for CMMI v1.2 at the SEI, a position created to lead the SEI's CMMI expansion. He previously was responsible for the SEI's transition-enabling activities. He has authored Technical Reports, Technical Notes, CMMI Columns, and various articles, in addition to presenting CMMI material at conferences around the world. Prior to his retirement from the Air Force, Colonel Phillips managed the $36 billion development program for the B-2 in the B-2 SPO and commanded the 4950th Test Wing at Wright-Patterson AFB, Ohio.

Pointers: Moore, Geoffrey A. *Crossing the Chasm* (Collins, 2002).

CMMI Transition Aids Web site, https://bscw.sei.cmu.edu/pub/bscw.cgi/0/79783.

Bob Rassa

Bob Rassa is director of system supportability at Raytheon Space and Airborne Systems, El Segundo, California. Prior to joining Raytheon, he served as group vice-president at ManTech International Corporation and in a variety of management positions at Westinghouse Electric Corporation. Dr. Rassa, an IEEE fellow, is founder and chairman of the National Defense Industry Association Systems Engineering Division. He is the industry sponsor and steering group chair of the Capability Maturity Model Integration (CMMI) Project for systems, software, and hardware design "best practices."

Hal Wilson

Hal Wilson is senior director for Systems Engineering and chief engineer within the Northrop Grumman Mission Systems Sector's Defense Mission Systems Division. He currently leads a group of senior engineers who help bring effective systems engineering to start-up programs. Mr. Wilson is the vice chairman of the NDIA Systems Engineering Division, a charter member of the Capability Maturity Model Integration (CMMI) steering group, and a member of the CMMI-AM author team, the CMMI-architecture team, and the author team for *CMMI for Use in Acquisition: A Guidebook*.

Pointer: West, Michael. *Real Process Improvement Using CMMI* (Auerbach, 2004).

CASE STUDY AUTHORS

Juan Ceva

Juan Ceva is the department manager of the Navigation and GPS Applications Department of Raytheon Pasadena Operations in Pasadena, California. He is also the EPG Manager and Raytheon Six Sigma Expert of the operation. He joined Raytheon in 1995.

Mark Pumar

Mark Pumar is a principal software engineer and activity lead for software for the Navigation and GPS Applications Department at Raytheon. He has more than twenty-four years of expertise in software and systems engineering. Mark is also Certified Raytheon Six Sigma specialist.

John Ryskowski

John Ryskowski is president of JFR Consulting and an SEI Partner. He has been appraising process capabilities since 1989 for clients in the United States, Asia, and Europe. John creates process improvement solutions for systems, software, hardware, and services organizations.

Gordon Ward

Gordon Ward is the director of Quality and Raytheon Six Sigma for Raytheon Information Solutions. Gordon joined Raytheon in 1998 and brings twenty years' experience in quality management and process improvement. He is an American Society for Quality Certified Quality Manager (CQMgr) and Certified Quality Auditor (CQA), as well as a Certified Raytheon Six Sigma Expert.

INDEX

Team Software Process (TSP):
The SEI-Recommended Approach
to Implementing CMMI

The Software Engineering Institute (SEI) Team Software
Process[SM] (TSP[SM]) methodology applies integrated team
concepts to the development of software-intensive systems.
TSP builds high-performance teams that
  • produce quality software products
  • create secure software products
  • improve the performance of an organization

TSP can be used to accelerate CMMI success. TSP provides
the solution to get to high maturity and high performance.
TSP implements more than 60% of the CMMI practices and
has been shown to cut CMMI implementation cost
and schedule by a factor of two. (*Mapping TSP to CMMI,*
CMU/SEI-2004-TR014, *www.sei.cmu.edu/publications*)

To learn more about TSP, read
Winning With Software
by Watts S. Humphrey
www.sei.cmu.edu/publications/books
or go to
www.sei.cmu.edu/tsp

Software Engineering Institute
Carnegie Mellon

ESSENTIAL GUIDES TO CMMI

CMMI®, Second Edition: Guidelines for Process Integration and Product Improvement

Mary Beth Chrissis, Mike Konrad, and Sandy Shrum

0-321-27967-0

The definitive guide to CMMI—now updated for CMMI v1.2! Whether you are new to CMMI or already familiar with some version of it, this book is the essential resource for managers, practitioners, and process improvement team members who to need to understand, evaluate, and/or implement a CMMI model.

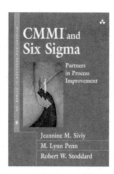

CMMI® and Six Sigma: Partners in Process Improvement

Jeannine M. Siviy, M. Lynn Penn, and Robert W. Stoddard

0-321-51608-7

Focuses on the synergistic, rather than competitive, implementation of CMMI and Six Sigma—with synergy translating to "faster, better, cheaper" achievement of mission success.

CMMI® Survival Guide: Just Enough Process Improvement

Suzanne Garcia and Richard Turner

0-321-42277-5

Practical guidance for any organization, large or small, considering or undertaking process improvement, with particular advice for implementing CMMI successfully in resource-strapped environments.

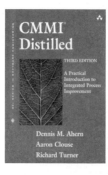

CMMI® Distilled, Third Edition: A Practical Introduction to Integrated Process Improvement

Dennis M. Ahern, Aaron Clouse, and Richard Turner

0-321-46108-8

Updated for CMMI version 1.2, this third edition again provides a concise and readable introduction to the model, as well as straightforward, no-nonsense information on integrated, continuous process improvement.

CMMI® for Outsourcing: Guidelines for Software, Systems, and IT Acquisition

Hubert F. Hofmann, Deborah K. Yedlin, Joseph Elm, John W. Mishler, and Susan Kushner

0-321-47717-0

Best practices for outsourcing and acquiring technology within the CMMI framework, reflecting initial results from a joint General Motors-Software Engineering Institute project, and written for both vendors and suppliers needing to improve their processes.

Also Available

CMMI® Assessments: Motivating Positive Change

Marilyn Bush and Donna Dunaway

0-321-17935-8

CMMI® SCAMPI Distilled: Appraisals for Process Improvement

Dennis M. Ahern, Jim Armstrong, Aaron Clouse, Jack R. Ferguson, Will Hayes, and Kenneth E. Nidiffer

0-321-22876-6

For more information on these and other books in The SEI Series in Software Engineering, please visit www.informit.com/seiseries

Process Areas Presented in the Staged Representation

Maturity Level 2

REQM Requirements Management

PP Project Planning

PMC Project Monitoring and Control

SAM Supplier Agreement Management

MA Measurement and Analysis

PPQA Process and Product Quality Assurance

CM Configuration Management

Maturity Level 3

RD Requirements Development

TS Technical Solution

PI Product Integration

VER Verification

VAL Validation

OPF Organizational Process Focus

OPD Organizational Process Definition +IPPD

OT Organizational Training

IPM Integrated Project Management +IPPD

RSKM Risk Management

DAR Decision Analysis and Resolution

Maturity Level 4

OPP Organizational Process Performance

QPM Quantitative Project Management

Maturity Level 5

OID Organizational Innovation and Deployment

CAR Causal Analysis and Resolution

Addison
Wesley

REGISTER

THIS PRODUCT

informit.com/register

Register the Addison-Wesley, Exam Cram, Prentice Hall, Que, and Sams products you own to unlock great benefits.

To begin the registration process, simply go to **informit.com/register** to sign in or create an account. You will then be prompted to enter the 10- or 13-digit ISBN that appears on the back cover of your product.

Registering your products can unlock the following benefits:

- Access to supplemental content, including bonus chapters, source code, or project files.
- A coupon to be used on your next purchase.

Registration benefits vary by product. Benefits will be listed on your Account page under Registered Products.

About InformIT — **THE TRUSTED TECHNOLOGY LEARNING SOURCE**

INFORMIT IS HOME TO THE LEADING TECHNOLOGY PUBLISHING IMPRINTS Addison-Wesley Professional, Cisco Press, Exam Cram, IBM Press, Prentice Hall Professional, Que, and Sams. Here you will gain access to quality and trusted content and resources from the authors, creators, innovators, and leaders of technology. Whether you're looking for a book on a new technology, a helpful article, timely newsletters, or access to the Safari Books Online digital library, InformIT has a solution for you.

informIT.com

THE TRUSTED TECHNOLOGY LEARNING SOURCE

Addison-Wesley | Cisco Press | Exam Cram
IBM Press | Que | Prentice Hall | Sams

SAFARI BOOKS ONLINE

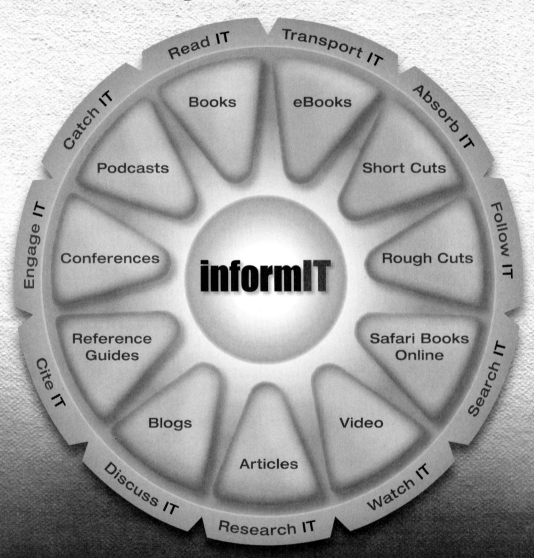

LearnIT at InformIT

Go Beyond the Book

Read IT

Transport IT

Catch IT

Absorb IT

Books

eBooks

Podcasts

Short Cuts

Engage IT

Follow IT

Conferences

informIT

Rough Cuts

Reference
Guides

Safari Books
Online

Cite IT

Search IT

Blogs

Video

Discuss IT

Watch IT

Articles

Research IT

11 WAYS TO LEARN IT at **www.informIT.com/learn**

The online portal of the information technology
publishing imprints of Pearson Education

Addison
Wesley

Cisco Press

EXAM/**CRAM**

IBM
Press

que

PRENTICE
HALL